Lecture Notes in Computer Science 13785

The series Lecture Notes in Computer Science (LNCS), including its subseries Lecture Notes in Artificial Intelligence (LNAI) and Lecture Notes in Bioinformatics (LNBI), has established itself as a medium for the publication of new developments in computer science and information technology research, teaching, and education.

LNCS enjoys close cooperation with the computer science R & D community, the series counts many renowned academics among its volume editors and paper authors, and collaborates with prestigious societies. Its mission is to serve this international community by providing an invaluable service, mainly focused on the publication of conference and workshop proceedings and postproceedings. LNCS commenced publication in 1973.

Sokratis Katsikas · Frédéric Cuppens ·
Christos Kalloniatis · John Mylopoulos ·
Frank Pallas · Jörg Pohle · M. Angela Sasse ·
Habtamu Abie · Silvio Ranise · Luca Verderame ·
Enrico Cambiaso · Jorge Maestre Vidal ·
Marco Antonio Sotelo Monge ·
Massimiliano Albanese · Basel Katt ·
Sandeep Pirbhulal · Ankur Shukla
Editors

Computer Security

ESORICS 2022 International Workshops

CyberICPS 2022, SECPRE 2022, SPOSE 2022, CPS4CIP 2022,
CDT&SECOMANE 2022, EIS 2022, and SecAssure 2022
Copenhagen, Denmark, September 26–30, 2022
Revised Selected Papers

 Springer

Editors

Sokratis Katsikas (ID)
Norwegian University of Science and Technology
Gjøvik, Norway

Christos Kalloniatis (ID)
University of the Aegean
Mytilene, Greece

Frank Pallas (ID)
Technical University of Berlin
Berlin, Germany

M. Angela Sasse (ID)
Ruhr University Bochum
Bochum, Germany

Silvio Ranise (ID)
University of Trento
Trento, Italy

Enrico Cambiaso (ID)
Consiglio Nazionale delle Ricerche (CNR)
Genoa, Italy

Marco Antonio Sotelo Monge (ID)
Indra
Alcobendas, Spain

Basel Katt (ID)
Norwegian University of Science and Technology
Gjøvik, Norway

Ankur Shukla (ID)
Institute for Energy Technology
Halden, Norway

Frédéric Cuppens (ID)
Polytechnique Montréal
Montreal, Canada

John Mylopoulos
University of Toronto
Toronto, ON, Canada

Jörg Pohle (ID)
Alexander von Humboldt Institute for Internet
and Society
Berlin, Germany

Habtamu Abie (ID)
Norwegian Computing Center
Oslo, Norway

Luca Verderame (ID)
University of Genoa
Genoa, Italy

Jorge Maestre Vidal (ID)
Indra
Alcobendas, Spain

Massimiliano Albanese (ID)
George Mason University
Fairfax, VA, USA

Sandeep Pirbhulal (ID)
Norwegian Computing Center
Oslo, Norway

ISSN 0302-9743 ISSN 1611-3349 (electronic)
Lecture Notes in Computer Science
ISBN 978-3-031-25459-8 ISBN 978-3-031-25460-4 (eBook)
https://doi.org/10.1007/978-3-031-25460-4

This Springer imprint is published by the registered company Springer Nature Switzerland AG
The registered company address is: Gewerbestrasse 11, 6330 Cham, Switzerland

Preface

The 27th edition of the European Symposium on Research in Computer Security (ESORICS) was held as a hybrid event in Copenhagen, Denmark, September 26–30, 2022. In addition to the main conference, 13 workshops were organized and held in the same time period.

This volume includes the accepted contributions to 7 of these workshops, as follows:

- the 8th Workshop on the Security of Industrial Control Systems and of Cyber-Physical Systems (CyberICPS 2022);
- the 6th International Workshop on Security and Privacy Requirements Engineering (SECPRE 2022);
- the 4th Workshop on Security, Privacy, Organizations, and Systems Engineering (SPOSE 2022);
- the 3rd Cyber-Physical Security for Critical Infrastructures Protection (CPS4CIP 2022);
- the 2nd International Workshop on Cyber Defence Technologies and Secure Communications at the Network Edge (CDT & SECOMANE 2022).
- the 1st International Workshop on Election Infrastructure Security (EIS 2022); and
- the 1st International Workshop on System Security Assurance (SecAssure 2022).

While each of the workshops had a high-quality program of its own, the organizers opted for publishing jointly the proceedings; these are included in this volume, which contains 39 full papers. The authors improved and extended these papers based on the reviewers' feedback as well as the discussions at the workshops.

We would like to thank each and every one who was involved in the organization of the ESORICS 2022 workshops. Special thanks go to the ESORICS 2022 Workshop Chairs and to all the workshop organizers and their respective Program Committees who contributed to making the ESORICS 2022 workshops a real success. We would also like to thank the ESORICS 2022 Organizing Committee for supporting the day-to-day operation and execution of the workshops.

October 2022

Sokratis Katsikas
Frédéric Cuppens
John Mylopoulos
Christos Kalloniatis
Frank Pallas
Jörg Pohle
Angela Sasse
Habtamu Abie
Silvio Ranise
Luca Verderame
Enrico Cambiaso
Jorge Maestre Vidal
Marco Antonio Sotelo Monge
Massimiliano Albanese
Jack Davidson
Basel Katt
Sandeep Pirbhulal
Ankur Shukla

Contents

6th International Workshop on Security and Privacy Requirements Engineering (SECPRE 2022)

4th Workshop on Security, Privacy, Organizations, and Systems Engineering (SPOSE 2022)

3rd Cyber-Physical Security for Critical Infrastructures Protection (CPS4CIP 2022)

1st International Workshop on System Security Assurance (SecAssure 2022)

8th Workshop on Security of Industrial Control Systems and of Cyber-Physical Systems (CyberICPS 2022)

Preface

This book contains revised versions of the papers presented at the 8th Workshop on Security of Industrial Control Systems and Cyber-Physical Systems (CyberICPS 2022). The workshop was co-located with the 27th European Symposium on Research in Computer Security (ESORICS 2022) and was held in Copenhagen, Denmark, on September 29th, 2022.

Cyber-physical systems (CPS) are physical and engineered systems that interact with the physical environment, whose operations are monitored, coordinated, controlled, and integrated using information and communication technologies. These systems exist everywhere around us, and range in size, complexity, and criticality, from embedded systems used in smart vehicles, to SCADA systems in smart grids, to control systems in water distribution systems, to smart transportation systems, to plant control systems, engineering workstations, substation equipment, programmable logic controllers (PLCs), and other Industrial Control Systems (ICS). These systems also include the emerging trend of Industrial Internet of Things (IIoT) that will be the central part of the fourth industrial revolution. As ICS and CPS proliferate, and increasingly interact with us and affect our lives, their security becomes of paramount importance.

CyberICPS 2022 brought together researchers, engineers, and governmental actors with an interest in the security of ICS and CPS in the context of their increasing exposure to cyberspace, by offering a forum for discussion on all issues related to their cyber security. CyberICPS 2022 attracted 15 high-quality submissions, each of which was assigned to 3 referees for review; the review process resulted in 8 papers being accepted to be presented and included in the proceedings i.e., the acceptance rate was 53%. The chairs and members of the Program Committee had no involvement with or visibility of the reviewing process of submissions authored or co-authored by them. The accepted papers cover topics related to many aspects of cyber security in cyber-physical and industrial control systems, ranging from threats, to risks that such systems face, to cyber-attacks that may be launched against such systems, to ways of detecting and responding to such attacks.

We would like to express our thanks to all those who assisted us in organizing the event and putting together the program. We are very grateful to the members of the Program Committee for their timely and rigorous reviews. Thanks are also due to the ESORICS Workshop Chairs and to the ESORICS Organizers. Last, but by no means least, we would like to thank all the authors who submitted their work to the workshop and contributed to an interesting set of proceedings.

October 2022

Sokratis Katsikas
Frédéric Cuppens
Nora Cuppens
Costas Lambrinoudakis

Organization

General Chairs

Costas Lambrinoudakis   University of Piraeus, Greece
Nora Cuppens   Polytechnique Montréal, Canada

Program Chairs

Sokratis Katsikas   Norwegian University of Science and Technology, Norway
Frédéric Cuppens   Polytechnique Montréal, Canada

Publicity Chair

Vasileios Gkioulos   Norwegian University of Science and Technology, Norway

Program Committee

Cristina Alcaraz   University of Malaga, Spain
Marios Anagnostopoulos   Aalborg University, Denmark
Mauro Conti   University of Padua, Italy
David Espes   University of Brest, France
Joaquin Garcia-Alfaro   Institut Polytechnique de Paris, France
Vasileios Gkioulos   Norwegian University of Science and Technology, Norway
Dieter Gollmann   Hamburg University of Technology, Germany
Georgios Kavallieratos   Norwegian University of Science and Technology, Norway
Youssef Laarouchi   EDF R&D, France
Stefano Longari   Politecnico di Milano, Italy
Weizhi Meng   Technical University of Denmark, Denmark
Pankaj Pandey   Norwegian University of Science and Technology, Norway
Nikolaos Pitropakis   Edinburgh Napier University, UK
Rodrigo Roman   University of Malaga, Spain
Andrea Saracino   Consiglio Nazionale delle Ricerche, Italy
Georgios Spathoulas   University of Thessaly, Greece

Nils Ole Tippenhauer   CISPA, Germany
Khan Ferdous Wahid   Airbus Group, France
Jianying Zhou   Singapore University of Technology and
                             Design, Singapore

External Reviewers

Amrita Ghosal   University of Limerick, Ireland
Subir Halder   University of Limerick, Ireland
Gulshan Kumar   University of Padua, Italy

Towards Comprehensive Modeling of CPSs to Discover and Study Interdependencies

Aida Akbarzadeh$^{(\boxtimes)}$ ⓘ and Sokratis Katsikas ⓘ

Norwegian University of Science and Technology, Gjøvik, Norway
{aida.akbarzadeh,sokratis.katsikas}@ntnu.no

Abstract. To a large extent, modeling Cyber-Physical systems (CPSs) and interdependency analysis collaborate in the security enhancement of CPSs and form the basis of various research domains such as risk propagation, attack path analysis, reliability analysis, robustness evaluation, and fault identification. Interdependency analysis as well as modeling of interdependent systems such as CPSs rely on the understanding of system dynamics and flows. Despite the major efforts, previously developed methods could not provide the required knowledge as they have either followed data-driven or physics-based modeling approaches. To fill this gap, we propose a new modeling approach called BG2 based on Graph theory and Bond graph. Our proposed method is able to portray the physical process of CPSs from different domains and capture both information and commodity flows. Based on the fundamental characteristics of the Graph theory and Bond graph in the BG2 model, we discover higher order of dependencies in CPSs and analyze causal relationships within the system components. We illustrate the workings of the proposed method by applying it to a realistic case study of a CPS in the energy domain. The results provide valuable insight into the dependencies among the system components and substantiate the applicability of the proposed method in modeling and analyzing interdependent systems.

Keywords: Interdependency analysis · CPS Modeling · Cyber-physical systems · Bond graph · Graph theory · Security

1 Introduction

Cyber-Physical Systems (CPSs) integrate computation, communication, and control capabilities of Information and Communication Technology (ICT) into physical objects and traditional infrastructures to facilitate the monitoring and controlling of objects in the physical world. Based on the NIST framework for

This work was supported by the Research Council of Norway under project 280617 (Cyber-Physical Security in Energy Infrastructure of Smart Cities - CPSEC) and under project 310105 (Norwegian Centre for Cybersecurity in Critical Sectors - NORCICS).

cyber-physical systems, a CPS can be seen as an individual block or as a system of systems (SoS) that encompasses multiple subsystems with several heterogeneous parameters [17]. It is worth mentioning that CPSs are the building blocks of Critical Infrastructures (CIs) which are essential for the maintenance of vital societal functions, such as manufacturing, healthcare, transportation, and the energy sector [8,38].

In a CPS, as a system of systems, individual parts work collectively to accomplish the main objective of the system, and the service provided by the system is actually formed based on the behavior of all constitutive parts and interactions among them. That also implies that the functionality and security of a CPS depend on each constitutive part and the relationship among them. Indeed, each part has its own characteristic and may react differently in case of an unexpected situation like a cyber attack. Any failure or malfunction in an individual part not only can affect the functionality of the part itself but also may influence the dependent parts and the entire system. The electric power disruption in California [35], the attack on Florida water treatment plant [2] and the Maroochy attack [1] are examples of failures and cyber attacks which initiated at an individual part but significantly affected the entire system. Therefore, researchers in many domains attempt to develop appropriate methods to model Cyber Physical systems with an eye to studying underlying relations and dependencies between the components of a CPS. Identification of these dependencies in a CPS provides an insightful view of cause and effect relationships, failure types, response behavior, state of operation, and risks to the system [23,29]. For this reason, dependency analysis is an underlying basis for various research domains such as reliability analysis [27], robustness evaluation [14] and failure propagation [46] to name a few.

Significant efforts have been dedicated to modeling and analysis of CPSs and their interactions, particularly in recent years. These proposed methods were mainly developed based on Graph theory [47], Input-Output Models [39], Bayesian networks, Petri nets [26], Agent-Based Models, and Multi-Agent Modelling [43] and differ broadly according to the granularity, details, and level of abstraction applied. Jensen et al. explained that a comprehensive model of a CPS should portray the coupling of physical processes and computations in the system by considering the environment in which the system resides [21]. Nevertheless, the main focus of previously developed methods dedicated to model CPSs as disjoint services/layers, and the interactions within a CPS and heterogeneity of these interactions gained fewer attention [11]. Considering these modeling requirements for CPSs as well as the heterogeneous components and their interactions in a system, Khaitan argued that the current modeling approaches and frameworks are inadequate [22].

The concurrency of different physical and computational processes as well as the heterogeneous nature of CPSs turn the CPS modeling into a complex task. Zhang et al. [46] mentioned that current literature is lacking approaches that can capture the engineering aspects of interdependent networks. The authors in [27] also pointed to the differences between the physical and cyber facets in a CPS and highlighted the lack of interdependent system modeling in literature to portray these fundamental differences. That becomes more critical when system modeling aims to study the security of CPSs. We have recently witnessed sophisticated cyber-physical attacks such as Stuxnet [13] and the Florida water plant attack [2] that revealed the necessity of dependency analysis in CPSs more than ever. Considering the concept of "kill chain" which describes an attack as a step-by-step approach [45], the authors in [5] stated that each attack (or attack path) refers to a "chain of dependency" in a system that has been successfully materialized by attackers. Krotofil et al. showed that the physical process layer should be included in system modeling in the security scope as the physical process can be utilized as a communication medium to deliver malicious payloads between system components [24]. Furthermore, the multidisciplinary nature of CPSs is another factor that an ideal system modeling should be capable of addressing to provide a deeper understanding of interdependencies and their implications for system security [34]. Among different modeling methods, our research showed that Bond graph (BG) has the capability of providing the aforementioned requirements. Bond graph is a description formalism that can portray the physical process of a system based on the flows of system commodities from different energy domains such as the electrical, mechanical, mechatronics, chemical, hydraulic, and thermal as well as multidisciplinary dynamic engineering systems [10]. Additionally, the BG diagram can represent the causality between system elements that contributes to the formulation of system equations and investigation of the system behavior in terms of controllability, observability, and fault diagnosis [9]. These characteristics of Bond graph turn it into an ideal method for modeling the physical processes of CPSs and analyzing dependencies between the system components. Moreover, reviewing recent interdependency studies showed us that Graph theory, as the most common underlying method applied for dependency analysis in complex systems, has significant features for modeling and analyzing the cyber part of CPSs which performs the controlling and monitoring tasks [7,37,41]. Therefore, in order to fill the gap found in the literature for modeling CPSs and interdependency study as a basis of various research domains, in particular, for the cybersecurity domain, we attempt to develop a new method based on merging Bond graph and Graph theory. Based on the proposed method, we will not only be able of extracting dependencies in CPSs, but also we can study the cause and effect relationship between the system components. Our main contribution is twofold:

- We develop a novel method, called BG2 model, based on Graph theory and Bond graph for modeling cyber-physical systems considering the multidisciplinary nature of such systems, and
- we apply the proposed BG2 model to discover and analyze dependencies and causal relationships within the system components in a CPS.

The remaining of the paper is structured as follows: Sect. 2 reviews the related work on modeling CPSs and dependency analysis. Section 3 provides the necessary knowledge background of Graph theory and Bond graph. We describe the proposed method in Sect. 4, and a case study to expound on the application of the proposed method is presented in Sect. 5. Finally, Sect. 6 summarizes our findings and indicates possible future work.

2   Related Work

A survey conducted by Hehenberger et al. on methods and applications of modeling CPSs revealed the necessity of developing transdisciplinary models and conceptual frameworks to encompass attributes of CPSs stem from different domains such as electronics, mechanics, engineering, and control [18]. Rinaldi et al. also reviewed pertinent approaches for modeling and simulating CIs and their interdependencies and concluded that the multidisciplinary science of interdependent systems such as CPSs which consists of multiple disciplines is relatively immature [34]. To address this challenge, recently Akbarzadeh et al. proposed a unified IT&OT modeling approach based on Bond graph to model CPSs, facilitate collaboration between IT and OT experts, and discover the attack surface of system components with the goal of improving cybersecurity of CPSs. Their work showed Bond graph as a promising basis for modeling CPSs and analyzing their dependencies, particularly for the physical process of the systems. Bond graph is an explicit graphical model for capturing and representing the common energy structure of systems. Besides, one can apply the causal and structural properties of BGs to study systems' behavior. Kumar et al. utilized Bond graph to model a system of systems (SoS) [25], while other researchers applied BG as a homogeneous and multi-domain modeling approach to study fault detection and isolation, observability, and controllability in complex systems [9,44].

Interdependency analysis in CPSs contributes to assessing the consequences of failures occurrence and failures propagations in a system. Moreover, this helps to understand how failures can disturb the functionality of a CPS and consequently affect the reliability of the system. As a result, modeling CPSs with the aim of interdependency analysis provides an insightful view of inter-system and intra-system causal relationships, response behaviors, failure types, state of operations, and risks the systems might encounter [23,29]. Besides, interdependency modeling and studying the systems' behaviors in the presence of failures is a common approach to evaluating the security and reliability of CPSs, as these failures may be caused by adversaries [15,33].

Rinaldi et al. proposed six dimensions of infrastructure interdependencies namely, type of failure, coupling and response behavior, infrastructure characteristics, environment, types of interdependencies, and state of operation to study dependencies in CIs [34]. In the follow-up paper [34], the same authors highlighted the necessity of developing interdependency analysis capabilities and improving information integration in modeling and simulation methods to protect CIs. The authors mentioned that these objectives are also aligned with the homeland security programs and can provide insights into rare events like complex cyber-physical attacks [20].

Satumtira et al. [37] surveyed 162 papers on interdependency modeling and discovered that Graph theory is the most common method to study interdependencies in CIs. later on, Torres [41] compared different methods applied for modeling CIs including Agent-based Models, Petri Nets, Bayesian Networks, and Graph theory based on six different objectives namely *Scalability, CPU time, Usability, Tools accessibility, Dynamic simulation* and *Large systems modeling.* Their evaluation confirmed the capacity of Graph theory as the most suitable method found in the literature to study CPSs, as Graph theory gained the highest value in four out of six different objectives in the comparison. Recently, the authors in [4] proposed the Modified Dependency Structure Matrix (MDSM) based on Graph theory to identify, illustrate and evaluate the quantitative characteristics of connections, including multi-order dependencies, in large-scale CPSs. Nevertheless, the Graph theory-based approaches mainly provide a high-level perspective of CPSs with an emphasis on the topological characteristics of the systems. In our previous paper, we reviewed and compared recent graph-based interdependency analysis methods in the power domain based on different features including the *communication direction, applied control parameters, system functionality, system security, complexity* and *scalability,* and the results showed us there are still remarkable open challenges require to address [7]. Graja et al. also conducted a critical review of different modeling and analysis techniques found in 62 papers and stated that despite significant efforts, current research is still at the beginning stage [16]. In a nutshell, dependency analysis as a basis for various research fields requires a paradigm shift from a disjoint modeling approach to transdisciplinary models that enables to capture of the physical processes in lower levels, the monitoring and controlling of the cyber part as well as the communication between cyber and physical parts and their corresponding functionalities in a CPS to portray the behavior of a CPS as a collection of functionalities from different domains. This paves the way towards causality analysis in complex systems and contributes highly to improving the security of such systems [11,16,28,44].

3 Background

In this section, a brief overview of Graph theory and Bond graph is given.

3.1 Graph Theory

A graph is a mathematical representation of a network. A network can be modeled as a graph $G(V, E)$ where V is a set of vertices and E is a set of links [31]. A vertex (node) V is an intersection point of a graph and can denote a component of a system, while an edge (link) E is a link between two nodes. $V(G)$ and $E(G)$ are referred to as the *vertex (node) set* and the *edge (link) set* of graph G, respectively. Graphs can be *Directed* or *Undirected*. If the direction of each edge is defined in a graph, that is a directed graph. Otherwise, it is known as an undirected graph. In Graph theory, a directed graph D is a pair (V, E) where E is a subset of $V \times V \equiv \{(x, x) | x \in V\}$ and $(u, v) \in E$ implies that there is an edge e which joins the initial node (tail) u to its terminal node (head) v [40].

In graph G, the *Indegree Centrality* shows the number of links that enter each node, while the *Outdegree Centrality* refers to the total number of outgoing links from each node. Graph theory is the study of the relationship between edges and vertices and can be applied to any scenarios that aim to examine the structure of a network of connected objects.

3.2   Bond Graph

A Bond graph is a graphical representation of a physical dynamic system based on the energy exchange phenomenon between the system components. Due to the fact that in each energy domain, the amount of power transferred equals the product of two physical quantities, i.e., Power = Effort × Flow, Bond graph provides a uniform notation for modeling dynamic systems from different domains such as electrical, hydraulic and mechanical as well as multi-domain dynamic systems [12]. For instance in electrical domain power exchange is computed based on the *Voltage* (V) and *Current* (I) while in the hydraulic domain the two physical quantities utilized to compute power are *Pressure* (ρ) and *Volume Flow Rate* (Q). Bond graph is composed of *bonds (edges)* and *port elements*. Bonds connect port elements and portray the direction of power flow by half arrows while the two power conjugated variables named *effort (e)* and *flow (f)* are assigned to each bond. Port elements indicate how energy exchanges across bonds based on the underlying physics principles in which energy can convert into another energy form, transform in the same energy domain, transfer from one power port to another, be distributed, or be stored [10]. Figure 1 shows port elements and their corresponding causality in the Bond graph.

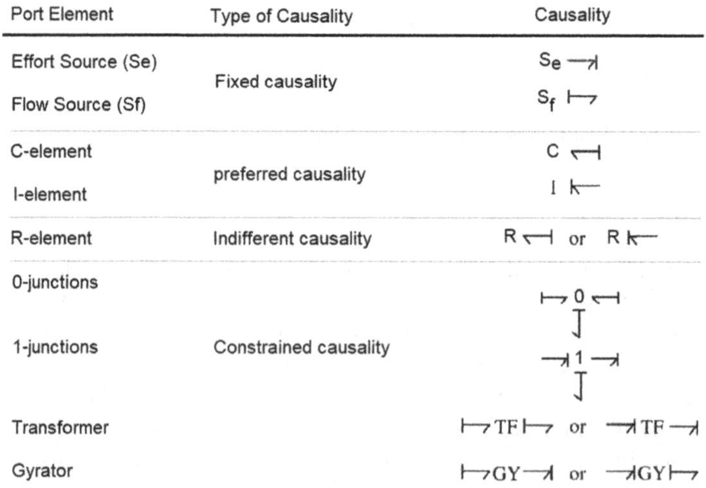

Port Element	Type of Causality	Causality
Effort Source (Se)	Fixed causality	S_e ⟶⫮
Flow Source (Sf)		S_f ⊢⟶
C-element	preferred causality	C ⇀⊣
I-element		I ⊢←
R-element	Indifferent causality	R ⇀⊣ or R ←⊢
0-junctions	Constrained causality	⊢⟶ 0 ⇀⊣
1-junctions		⟶⫮ 1 ⟶⫮
Transformer		⊢⟶ TF ⊢⟶ or ⟶⫮ TF ⟶⫮
Gyrator		⊢⟶ GY ⟶⫮ or ⟶⫮ GY ⊢⟶

Fig. 1. Bond graph port elements and their corresponding causality [6].

One of the main advantages of BG modeling is its capability to study the characteristics of causality in a system. This facilitates the analysis of interactions and cause-effect relationships between the system components, as well as the structural analysis of systems such as controllability and observability.

Causal stroke: In BG diagrams, a *causal stroke* shows the direction of imposing effort (e) and represents by a short line perpendicular to the bond at one of its ends, either the tip or tail of the half arrow. Notice that the causal stroke is independent of the power transfer direction shown by the half arrow. In Bond graph when one side causes effort, the other side causes flow and the causal stroke is placed near the element for which the effort is known [30]. For instance, in Fig. 2-(a), X imposes the effort (e) to Y, i.e. effort (e) is known for Y, whose effect sets the flow (f) towards X. Figure 2-(b) shows the opposite situation in which effort (e) is known for X.

Causality assignment: As explained earlier, the causal stroke is only assigned to one end of a power bond. This assignment of causal strokes known as *causality assignment* follows the systematic procedure called Sequential Causal Assignment Procedure (SCAP). The SCAP algorithm begins with the elements having the strongest causality constraints and continues until all elements get their causality assigned in the following order: (1) effort and flow sources, (2) I- and C-elements, (3) transformers and gyrators, (4) junctions and (5) R-elements. After that, if a port element has still remained without the causal stroke, it has flexibility in the causality placement, and its causality will be determined at the end [36].

Causal paths: A path between two ports connected via 0-junction, 1-junction, or Transformer (TY) is called a *causal path* if bonds have similar causal stroke directions and the sequence of the causal strokes follows the same pattern. Notice that when a Gyrator (GY) connects two ports the causal stroke direction is altered. Figure 3 shows two different types of causal paths, simple and indirect causal paths, in which direction of causal paths are denoted by green dashed lines.

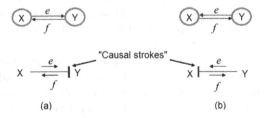

Fig. 2. Causality strokes in bond graphs. (a) Effort is known for Y. (b) Effort is known for X.

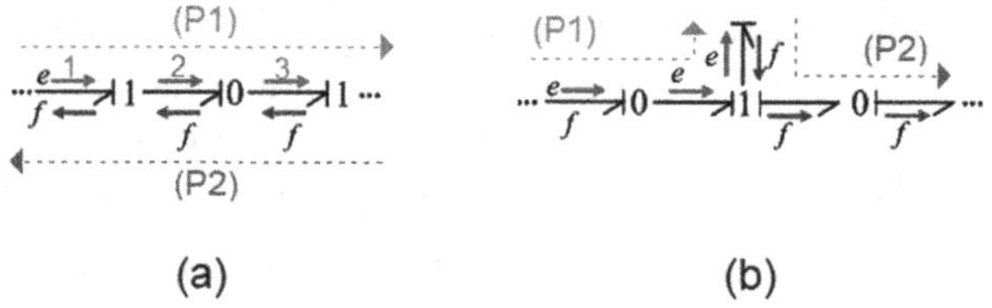

Fig. 3. Causal paths in bond graphs. (a) Simple causal paths and (b) indirect causal paths.

4 Method

In this section, the process of modeling a CPS based on the BG2 model is described. Then the relationships within the cyber and physical layers of a CPS is extracted and relevant metrics of Bond graph and Graph theory are applied to analyze the different characteristics of dependencies within the system.

4.1 BG2 Model

As mentioned earlier in Sect. 2, Graph theory has been widely applied to model CPSs in recent years. In these research works, system components are modeled as nodes and the interactions among the nodes are represented by edges. This modeling approach can clearly represent the topology of a system and facilitate analysis of different characteristics of a system based on Graph-based metrics. For instance, the authors in [3] proposed a method to rank the importance of nodes and links in a CPS based on the Closeness Centrality and two novel graph-based metrics, namely the Tacit Input Centrality (TIC) and the Tacit Output Centrality (TOC).

Graph theory provides a high-level and asset-oriented representation of a system which makes it an appropriate choice for modeling the cyber part of CPSs, which relies on information flow to monitor and control the systems, and analyzing the dependency among the IT components. However, studying the dependency in the physical part of a CPS as well as the interactions between the cyber and physical parts requires considering the physics of the system which Graph theory cannot cover. To fill this gap, we can apply Bond graph to model the physical processes of CPSs based on their commodity flows as explained earlier in Sect. 1. Therefore, to study different types of dependencies within a CPS we propose the BG2 model which utilizes Graph theory and Bond graph to model the cyber and physical parts of a CPS respectively and represents the two different types of flow passing through each part, namely commodity flow and information flow. However, unlike the Graph theory, Bond graph demonstrates a system based on the power transfer principle between the system components. Therefore, to be able to apply both Graph theory and Bond graph to model a CPS we leverage the cyber-physical components that exist in CPSs as the interfaces between the cyber and physical parts of the system. Consequently, these interfaces perform as merging points between the Graph and Bond graph diagrams.

A Physical-to-Cyber interface is a component that converts the commodity flow of a CPS into information flow, while a Cyber-to-Physical interface acts the opposite (Fig. 4). A sensor and an actuator can be seen as the Physical-to-Cyber (P2C) and the Cyber-to-Physical (C2P) interfaces, respectively. As a result, considering the characteristics of cyber and physical parts of a CPS, in our proposed model, the cyber part in which the information flow plays the main role is modeled based on the Graph theory, and the physical part of the system which operates based on the commodity flow is modeled based on the Bond graph, while the P2C and C2P interfaces merge these two parts together. We will explain the BG2 modeling based on a case study represented in Sect. 5 in more detail. Figure 4 illustrates the proposed BG2 modeling for CPSs.

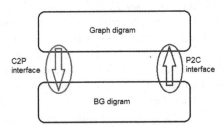

Fig. 4. Conceptual representation of the BG2 model.

4.2   Dependency Identification Based on the BG2 Model

Here, we aim to track dependencies within the system components to study how the behavior of an entity in a CPS depends on the other entities and subsystems. The result of this step provides insight into improving the security of CPSs and to a high extent collaborates in various research domains such as analyzing cascading failures, attack path analysis, and risk management to name a few. For this purpose, after modeling a CPS based on the BG2 model, we utilize the properties of Graph theory and Bond graph to discover dependencies. It is worth mentioning that, *Dependency* is a linkage between two entities in a system, through which the state of one entity influences the state of the other. Besides, the term *Interdependency* defines a bidirectional dependency between two entities in a system in which the state of the first entity affects the state of the second one and vice versa

As explained in Subsect. 4.1, the cyber part of a CPS is modeled following Graph theory in the BG2 model. Accordingly, the cyber part can also be portrayed in form of an Adjacency Matrix (A). In Graph theory, an adjacency matrix A is a square matrix used to represent whether the vertex v_i is adjacent to the vertex v_j in a network or not, which shows with one or zero, respectively. Based on the same definition, we define the **Dependency Matrix (D)** which represents the value of information flow (I_{ij}) moves from vertex v_i to vertex v_j in the corresponding cell of the matrix D. Besides, the C2P and P2C interfaces in the BG2 model have interactions with the physical part through the output/input commodity flow. Therefore, to capture the entire interactions for interfaces, an extra column and row labeled as (M) are assigned in the Dependency matrix (D). The pair (M, M) will be further utilized to derive dependencies between the two parts of CPSs as jumping points. Notice that the information flow can be divided into **Sensed data** (I_d) and **Control command** (I_c). This facilitates distinguishing between faults/attacks on monitoring and controlling parts in further steps. The *sensed data* (I_d) is collected from the physical layer by means of P2C interfaces and moves towards the specific components in the cyber layer for monitoring reasons, while the *control command* (I_c) is issued by components like controllers in the cyber layer and moves towards the C2P interfaces to apply the desired changes in the physical process of the system.

Given that the physical part of a CPS is modeled based on Bond graph in the BG2 model, we can extract the dependencies in this part by following the commodity flow and tracking *"Causal Paths"*. Causal Paths are one of the significant characteristics of Bond graphs which are derived based on the causality in a system. Indeed, *Causality* indicates the dependencies between the dual variables effort and flow in a system, and specifies the independent variable(s). For all the P2C and C2P interfaces in a BG2 model, we extract pertinent causal paths. These causal paths reveal the dependencies between each interface and system assets in the physical part. Therefore, one can use Dependency matrix D to derive dependencies in the cyber part until reaching an interface (jumping point) and then extract dependencies in the physical part based on the causal paths corresponding to that interface. This enables us to extract higher order of dependencies between those system components that are placed in different parts or subsystems yet affect each other.

For each component in a BG2 model, particularly for the interfaces, we can write a functional dependency relation. Assume that the elements of X, $X = \{x_1, x_2, ..., x_i\}$, are inputs and the elements of Y, $Y = \{y_1, y_2, ..., y_j\}$, are outputs of the component S, so that g expresses a functional input-output relationship $(g : X \rightarrow Y)$ as shown in Eq. 1, which is defined to represent both cyber and physical aspects of this function.

$$Y = g(S|X) \tag{1}$$

Equation 1 represents inputs, outputs, and the device S with the corresponding inner functionality. Consequently, this mathematical representation of the functional properties of a CPS component allows us to analyze both cyber and physical aspects of a relation between inputs and outputs at the same time. This can be further used to identify attack vectors in cyber-physical systems.

5   Case Study

In this section, we apply the proposed BG2 model into a realistic cyber physical system shown in Fig. 5 and extract dependencies within this system based on the method described in Subsect. 4.2.

5.1 BG2 Model of the System

Our case study is developed based on the realistic network infrastructures proposed by Homer et al. [19] and Pan et al. [32], and encompasses four network zones namely Corporate network, Demilitarized zone (DMZ), Field network, and Control network. As shown in Fig. 5, the physical process of the system occurs in the field network, while the other three networks collaborate in monitoring and controlling. Therefore, the field network in this CPS is considered as the *physical part* and the rest of the network zones form the *cyber part*. To model the cyber part of the case study as a BG2 diagram, the first step is to discover the direction of the interactions within the system components. Homer et al. [19] explained that the web server (A7) and the VPN server (A8) are accessible from the Internet (A6), and the VPN server (A8) has access to the File server (A9), Workstations (A10) and Citrix server (A11). The web server (A7) has only access to the file server (A9). The Citrix server (A11) has access to the Data historian (A3) and Communication servers (A1). Operators can monitor the field network and send commands to the field devices (if necessary) from the Human Machine Interface (HMI). The Communication servers (A1) provide central monitoring and control and additionally interfaced with the data historian (A3) so historical data could be collected and preserved and studied outside of real-time operations. Given this information, we model the cyber part of the system as a graph diagram shown in Fig. 6, in which system components are depicted as nodes (V) and connections among components are represented by links (E). Here, the Graph diagram of the entire system is displayed to help readers compare the graphical representation of a system based on Graph theory and the new proposed BG2 model. In Fig. 6, devices belonging to the cyber part

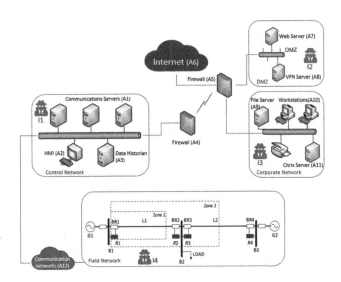

Fig. 5. Graphical representation of the case study

are depicted in red color, blue circles denoted to those components are placed in the physical part which will be modeled later based on Bond graph, and the P2C/C2P interfaces are depicted in half blue and red.

Following the BG2 model procedures, the second step is to model the *physical part* of the system, i.e. the filed network, based on the Bond graph. In Fig. 5, the field network is a three-bus two-line transmission system which is a modified version of the IEEE nine-bus three-generator system [32]. This physical part illustrates the process of generating and transmitting power to the consumer (Load). G1 and G2 refer to the power generators, BR1 through BR4 denotes the circuit breakers, and R1 through R4 are relays. Each relay is able to trip and open the related circuit breaker when a fault occurs on a transmission line. Operators are also able to issue commands via HMI to each relay to open and close the corresponding circuit breaker. Based on the port elements of Bond graph represented in Fig. 1, we model the physical part of the system as shown in the lower part of Fig. 7. The generators G1 and G2 are modeled as effort sources (Se) and Load L_3 as an R-element. Besides, the dissipation phenomena on the transmission lines L1 and L2 are modeled by impedance R:L1 and R:L2, respectively. Following the approach proposed by Umarikar et al. for modeling switches [42], we modeled circuit breakers BR1 through BR4 as 1s-junctions. A circuit breaker switches between two states (on and off) to protect an electrical circuit from damage caused by an over-current or short circuit. Likewise, 1s-junction switches between two states that are determined by Boolean variables U and $\overline{U}$. The role of the Relays in the system is to measure the current that

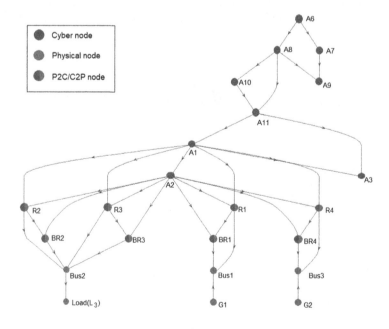

Fig. 6. Digraph of the system

passes through transmission lines and send the trip command to the associated circuit breakers in case of overcurrent. Therefore, as explained in [6], a relay in the BG diagram can be modeled as one sensor which measures the current and one actuator that triggers the corresponding circuit breaker. Considering the roles and input-output of the circuit breakers and relays in the system clears that these components are connecting the cyber and physical parts of the system and are the C2P/P2C Interfaces. In the BG2 model of the system shown in Fig. 7, cyber components are depicted as solid red nodes while the C2P/P2C Interfaces can be distinguished easily by the red border drawn around port elements.

5.2   Dependency Analysis

According to the proposed method explained in Sect. 4.2, dependencies among the components placed in the cyber part of a CPS are represented via the dependency matrix D, while dependencies in the physical part derive based on the causal paths. Therefore, considering the BG2 model of the system displayed in figure 7, here, we write the dependency matrix D of the system (see table 1). The next step is to write the causal paths for interfaces. In this regard, we should label the bonds and assign the causal strokes as explained in Sect. 3. Causal strokes display the direction of the effort variable (e) in a BG diagram and are necessary for writing the system equations and causal paths correctly.

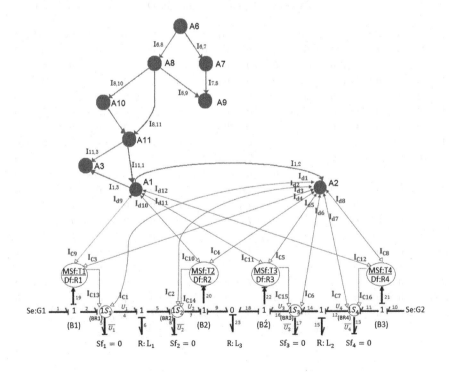

Fig. 7. BG2 representation of the system

Therefore, we assign the causal strokes of effort/flow sources in the first place, then the I- and C-elements, afterward the transformers and gyrators, and finally junctions and R-elements. Following that, as shown in Fig. 7, all bonds were labeled and the causality assignment was accomplished. After that, we are able to write the causal paths for interfaces that have non-zero values on row M in matrix D. For instance, consider the commodity flow (f_{19}) in table 1 which is an input from the physical part of the system to relay R_1. Based on Fig. 7, the causal paths terminating at relay R_1 are as follows:

(R1- Path1) $Sf_1 : 0 \xrightarrow{f_3} 1S_1 \xrightarrow{f_2} 1 \xrightarrow{f_{19}} Df : R1$

(R1- Path2) $Sf_2 : 0 \xrightarrow{f_8} 1S_2 \xrightarrow{f_5} 1 \xrightarrow{f_4} 1S_1 \xrightarrow{f_2} 1 \xrightarrow{f_{19}} Df : R1$

(R1- Path3) $Df : R2 \xrightarrow{f_{20}} 1 \xrightarrow{f_7} 1S_2 \xrightarrow{f_5} 1 \xrightarrow{f_4} 1S_1 \xrightarrow{f_2} 1 \xrightarrow{f_{19}} Df : R1$

Notice that for writing the causal paths, we start from Relay R1 and track the sequence of port elements with analogous causality as R1. As an example, in Fig. 7, relay R1 is connected to effort source $G1$ and $1S_1$-junction. Here, only the direction of casual stroke belonging to the $1S_1$-junction is similar to R1, which means that for extracting the casual path, we have to take a step towards the $1S_1$-junction, not $G1$. Moreover, to write the causal paths for R1 we follow the flow variable (f) as we aim to derive the commodity flow (f_{19}). Following the same approach, one can extract the causal paths for other interfaces.

Table 1. Dependency matrix D

	A_6	A_7	A_8	A_9	A_{10}	A_{11}	A_3	A_1	A_2	R_1	R_2	R_3	R_4	BR_1	BR_2	BR_3	BR_4	M
A_6	0	$I_{6,7}$	$I_{6,8}$	0	0	0	0	0	0	0	0	0	0	0	0	0	0	0
A_7	0	0	0	$I_{7,9}$	0	0	0	0	0	0	0	0	0	0	0	0	0	0
A_8	0	0	0	$I_{8,9}$	$I_{8,10}$	$I_{8,11}$	0	0	0	0	0	0	0	0	0	0	0	0
A_9	0	0	0	0	0	0	0	0	0	0	0	0	0	0	0	0	0	0
A_{10}	0	0	0	0	0	$I_{10,11}$	0	0	0	0	0	0	0	0	0	0	0	0
A_{11}	0	0	0	0	0	$I_{11,3}$	$I_{11,1}$	0	0	0	0	0	0	0	0	0	0	0
A_3	0	0	0	0	0	0	0	0	0	0	0	0	0	0	0	0	0	0
A_1	0	0	0	0	0	$I_{1,3}$	0	$I_{1,2}$	I_{C9}	I_{C10}	I_{C11}	I_{C12}	0	0	0	0	0	
A_2	0	0	0	0	0	0	0	0	I_{C3}	I_{C4}	I_{C5}	I_{C8}	I_{C1}	I_{C2}	I_{C6}	I_{C7}	0	
R_1	0	0	0	0	0	0	I_{d9}	I_{d3}	0	0	0	0	I_{C13}	0	0	0	0	
R_2	0	0	0	0	0	0	I_{d10}	I_{d4}	0	0	0	0	0	I_{C14}	0	0	0	
R_3	0	0	0	0	0	0	I_{d11}	I_{d5}	0	0	0	0	0	0	I_{C15}	0	0	
R_4	0	0	0	0	0	0	I_{d12}	I_{d8}	0	0	0	0	0	0	0	I_{C16}	0	
BR_1	0	0	0	0	0	0	0	I_{d1}	0	0	0	0	0	0	0	0	0	
BR_2	0	0	0	0	0	0	0	I_{d2}	0	0	0	0	0	0	0	0	0	
BR_3	0	0	0	0	0	0	0	I_{d6}	0	0	0	0	0	0	0	0	0	
BR_4	0	0	0	0	0	0	0	I_{d7}	0	0	0	0	0	0	0	0	0	
M	0	0	0	0	0	0	0	0	f_{19}	f_{20}	f_{22}	f_{21}	f_2	f_5	f_{14}	f_{11}	0	

Based on the above causal paths we have:

$$R1, f_{19} \not\perp \{BR1, BR2, R2\} \tag{2}$$

which implies that R1 and value f_{19} depends on the functionality of BR1, BR2, and R2. As explained in Sect. 4, we can also extract the functional dependency of each system component. Therefore, we can write the functional dependency of components BR1, BR2, and R2 based on Eq. 1 and considering the pertinent variables shown in dependency matrix D, as follows:

$$U_1 f_4 + \overline{U_1} f_3 = g(BR1|Ic_1, Ic_{13}, f_2) \tag{3}$$

$$U_2 f_7 + \overline{U_2} f_8 = g(BR2|Ic_2, Ic_{14}, f_5) \tag{4}$$

$$U_1 f_4 + \overline{U_1} f_3 = g(BR1|Ic_1, Ic_{13}, f_2) \tag{5}$$

By substituting Eqs. (3–5) into Eq. 2 we have:

$$R1, f_{19} \not\perp \{Ic_1, Ic_{13}, f_2, Ic_2, Ic_{14}, f_5, Ic_1, Ic_{13}, f_2\}, g(BR1), g(BR2), g(R2) \tag{6}$$

Equation 6 clears that R1 and the value of f_{19} depends on operation of BR1, BR2, and R2 and their inputs $\{Ic_1, Ic_{13}, f_2, Ic_2, Ic_{14}, f_5, Ic_1, Ic_{13}, f_2\}$. Also, based on the matrix D we extract those chains of dependencies in the cyber part that terminates at $R1$ in the following:

$A6 \rightarrow A8 \rightarrow A11 \rightarrow A1 \rightarrow R1$,

$A6 \rightarrow A8 \rightarrow A11 \rightarrow A1 \rightarrow A2 \rightarrow R1$,

$A6 \rightarrow A8 \rightarrow A10 \rightarrow A11 \rightarrow A1 \rightarrow R1$, and

$A6 \rightarrow A8 \rightarrow A10 \rightarrow A11 \rightarrow A1 \rightarrow A2 \rightarrow R1$.

Therefore, by considering the above dependency chains and Eq. 6 which are derived based on the causal paths for R1, one can analyze how different components in the case study may affect R1 in case of any accidental failure or cyber-attack. Following this approach not only helps to identify dependencies in a cyber-physical system, but more precisely, it reveals the cause and effect relations between the system components and shed light on studying the behaviors of complex CPSs in different scenarios such as security assessment, failure propagation, or reliability analysis. For instance, the causal path (R1- Path1) reveals the causality between f_{19} and the state of BR1 which is modeled as $1S_1$-junction. Indeed, if $\overline{U_1}$ equals to 1, then this causal path exist and Sf_1 passes through bond 3, i.e. $f_3 = Sf_1$. Besides, the causal path (R1- Path1) also shows that the value of f_{19} depends on f_2 and f_3. So, we can see that if $\overline{U_1}$ equals 1, f_{19} will be zero and R1 will sense and send this value to the cyber part. Considering the function of circuit breakers, this $f_{19} = 0$ happens when a fault has occurred on transmission line L1 and BR1 has tripped upon receiving a trip command from R1 or HMI to protect line L1. In the same way, the causal path (R1- Path2) reveals that f_{19} depends on the functionality and states of $1S_1$-junction (BR1) and $1S_2$-junction (BR2). Here, Sf_2 passes through bond 8 when $\overline{U_2}$ equals to 1. One can write the structural equations for all junctions that exist in the casual path to find the value of f_{19}. Starting from $1S_2$-junction, we have $f_5 = f_8$ if $\overline{U_2}$ is 1 and we know $f_8 = Sf_2$. Notice that in a BG diagram, the same flow passes through all bonds connected to a 1-junction, while a 0-junction implies connected bonds have the same effort. Therefore, when $\overline{U_1}$ equals to 1, because of the 1-junction placed between bonds 4 and 5, we know that $f_5 = f_4$. For the same reason, f_2 is equal to f_{19} and we can conclude that $f_{19} = Sf_2 = 0$. This implies that BR1 is working in a normal situation while BR2 has been tripped because of a fault occurrence on transmission line L1 and the fault was closer to BR2 than BR1. Finally, the last causal path (R1- Path3) reveals the relation between the two relays R1 and R2 as well as commodity flows f_{19} and f_{20}. In this case, if $\overline{U_1} = \overline{U_2} = 1$, then system is in the normal situation and the same flow is passing through transmission line L1, i.e. $f_{19} = f_{20}$ and relays R1 and R2 measure the same value. Therefore, based on the above causal paths, we could discover components and states that influence the value of f_{19}. Besides, we showed that these causal paths can reveal different scenarios regarding fault occurrence in a system. Indeed, one of the advantages of Bond graph is its ability to study controllability and observability in a system. Therefore, merging the information gained from the causal paths with the chain of dependencies that can be extracted from the dependency matrix D will assist us to study complex scenarios in which both cyber attacks and faults may occur. For instance, consider the causal path (R1- Path2) as a simple example in which the value of f_{19} depends on the functionality of $1S_1$-junction. Therefore, in the bottom-up direction which relates to the monitoring, any fault, failure, or cyber-attack on $BR1$ can change the value of f_{19} and affect interdependent components in the cyber layer, i.e. $\{A1, A2, A11, A10\}$. And from the top-down direction which relates to the controlling feature, any malfunction or cyber attack on $\{A1, A2, A11, A10, R1(Msf : T1)\}$ may change the state of $BR1$ and consequently influence the value of f_{19}.

Based on the matrix D, one can extract dependency chains $A6 \rightarrow A8 \rightarrow A10 \rightarrow A11 \rightarrow A1 \rightarrow A2$ and $A6 \rightarrow A8 \rightarrow A11 \rightarrow A1 \rightarrow A2$ and leverage interfaces BR1-BR4 and R1-R4 to merge dependency chains with pertinent causal paths to evaluate all possible scenarios.

Besides, as explained in Sect. 4, the BG2 model supports all the conventional graph-based metrics. To clear that, we compute the Indegree/Outdegree centrality of the system components based on the Graph diagram depicted in Fig. 6 and the BG2 model represented in Fig. 7 as shown in Table 2. Comparing the values in Table 2 shows a slight difference between the measured values for components placed in the physical part of the system. That is because the BG2 model can provide a realistic abstraction of the physical process of the system and consequently, the Indegree/Outdegree centrality measured based on the BG2 model is more precise than the Graph diagram.

Table 2. Comparing Indegree/Outdegree centrality derive from the BG2 model and Graph diagram.

Nodes:	A_6	A_7	A_8	A_9	A_{10}	A_{11}	A_3	A_1	A_2	$G1$	$G2$	$B1$	$R1$	$BR1$	$BR2$	$B2$	$R3$	$B3$	$BR4$	$BR3$	$R2$	$R4$
Out (BG2)	2	1	3	0	1	2	0	6	8	1	1	2	3	2	2	3	3	2	2	2	3	3
In (BG2)	0	1	1	2	1	2	2	5	9	0	0	1	3	3	3	2	3	1	3	3	3	3
Out (Graph)	2	1	3	0	1	2	0	6	8	1	1	0	2	1	1	2	0	1	1		2	2
In (Graph)	0	1	1	2	1	2	2	5	9	0	0	3	2	2	2	4	2	3	2	2	2	2

6 Conclusion

In this paper, we proposed the BG2 model to capture and demonstrate the topological and functional characteristics of Cyber Physical Systems as an underlying basis for interdependency analysis. The BG2 model is developed based on Graph theory and Bond Graph to characterize the cyber and physical facets of a CPS and the relationship between them. Interdependency analysis as well as modeling of interdependent systems such as CPSs rely on the understanding of system dynamics and flows. In the BG2 model, the information flow that passes through the cyber components for monitoring and controlling purposes is modeled based on Graph theory, while the Bond graph is applied to model the physical process of the system whose in charge of generating and delivering commodity flow(s). We utilized physical-to-cyber and cyber-to-physical interfaces in the BG2 model to bridge the gap between the data-driven and physics-based driven nature of Graph theory and Bond graph and merge these two underlying methods. In the BG2 model, the relationships between the system components belonging to the cyber part are recorded in a dependency matrix D, causal paths are applied to track the cause and effect relationships between those system components placed in the physical part of a CPS, and the interfaces act as jumping points between these two parts. The interfaces enable us to identify the chains of dependencies for each component, regardless of which part its dependent components belong to or geographical distance. In other words, we can extract the higher order of dependencies for every component in a BG2 model. This facilitates studying cascading failures in CPSs.

In reality, CPSs encounter failures and cyber-attacks. A cyber attack may happen in different parts, and in a worst-case scenario, several attacks may happen together. As explained in Sect. 5, based on the proposed BG2 model, one can distinguish between accidental failures and cyber-attacks in a CPS by analyzing the behavior of the system and dependent components, particularly by noticing the physical process of the system and causal paths. Unlike previous works, BG2 model is not only able to discover the dependencies between the system components but also the cause and effect relationships. Studying the causality in a system can address the "what-if" questions that relate to analyzing changes, that might occur due to a cyber attack or failure, to the system under study. The proposed method also satisfies Graph theory-based metrics that have been applied and developed in previous works. We measured the Indegree/Outdegree centrality based on the Graph diagram and the BG2 model and the comparison showed that the BG2 model can provide a more realistic result for the physical part of the system.

Interdependency analysis substantially collaborates in improving the security of CPSs and is the foundation of various research domains such as risk propagation, attack path analysis, fault identification and isolation, reliability analysis, and robustness evaluation. Modeling CPSs based on the BG2 model and analyzing dependencies can help us to identify cyber-attacks and predict corresponding consequences and enable us to protect CPSs against them. Furthermore, based on the significant features of Bond Graphs, such as the causal paths, we can derive fault indicator algebraic equations for the physical process of the systems and enhance system controlling and fault isolation. As a result, we aim to apply the BG2 model to develop a new method to discover and analyze cyber-physical attack paths in CPS. It can also help us to investigate the possibility of parallel attack path analysis in cyber-physical systems to identify complex attacks. Designing a unified safety and security risk management method based on the BG2 model is also among our future research plans.

References

1. Abrams, M., Weiss, J.: Malicious control system cyber security attack case study-Maroochy water services, Australia. Technical report, MITRE CORP MCLEAN VA MCLEAN (2008)
2. Addeen, H.H., Xiao, Y., Li, J., Guizani, M.: A survey of cyber-physical attacks and detection methods in smart water distribution systems. IEEE Access **9**, 99905–99921 (2021)
3. Akbarzadeh, A., Katsikas, S.: Identifying critical components in large scale cyber physical systems. In: Proceedings of the IEEE/ACM 42nd International Conference on Software Engineering Workshops, pp. 230–236 (2020)
4. Akbarzadeh, A., Katsikas, S.: Identifying and analyzing dependencies in and among complex cyber physical systems. Sensors **21**(5), 1685 (2021)
5. Akbarzadeh, A., Katsikas, S.: Dependency-based security risk assessment for cyber-physical systems. Int. J. Inf. Secur. (2022)
6. Akbarzadeh, A., Katsikas, S.: Unified it&ot modeling for cybersecurity analysis of cyber-physical systems. IEEE Open J. Industr. Electron. Soc. (2022)
7. Akbarzadeh, A., Pandey, P., Katsikas, S.: Cyber-physical interdependencies in power plant systems: a review of cyber security risks. In: 2019 IEEE Conference on Information and Communication Technology, pp. 1–6. IEEE (2019)
8. Ashibani, Y., Mahmoud, Q.H.: Cyber physical systems security: analysis, challenges and solutions. Comput. Secur. **68**, 81–97 (2017)
9. Benmoussa, S., Bouamama, B.O., Merzouki, R.: Bond graph approach for plant fault detection and isolation: application to intelligent autonomous vehicle. IEEE Trans. Autom. Sci. Eng. **11**(2), 585–593 (2013)
10. Borutzky, W.: Bond Graph Methodology: Development and Analysis of Multidisciplinary Dynamic System Models. Springer, London (2009). https://doi.org/10.1007/978-1-84882-882-7

11. Carhart, N., Rosenberg, G.: A framework for characterising infrastructure interdependencies. Int. J. Complex. Appl. Sci. Technol. **1**(1), 35–60 (2016)
12. Carreira, P., Amaral, V., Vangheluwe, H.: Foundations of Multi-paradigm Modelling for Cyber-Physical Systems. Springer, Cham (2020). https://doi.org/10.1007/978-3-030-43946-0
13. Chen, T.M., Abu-Nimeh, S.: Lessons from stuxnet. Computer **44**(4), 91–93 (2011)
14. Chen, Y., et al.: Cascading failure analysis of cyber physical power system with multiple interdependency and control threshold. IEEE Access **6**, 39353–39362 (2018)
15. Falahati, B., Fu, Y.: Reliability assessment of smart grids considering indirect cyber-power interdependencies. IEEE Trans. Smart Grid **5**(4), 1677–1685 (2014)
16. Graja, I., Kallel, S., Guermouche, N., Cheikhrouhou, S., Hadj Kacem, A.: A comprehensive survey on modeling of cyber-physical systems. Concurr. Comput. Pract. Exp. **32**(15), e4850 (2020)
17. Griffor, E.R., Greer, C., Wollman, D.A., Burns, M.J.: Framework for cyber-physical systems: Volume 1, overview. Technical report (2017)
18. Hehenberger, P., Vogel-Heuser, B., Bradley, D., Eynard, B., Tomiyama, T., Achiche, S.: Design, modelling, simulation and integration of cyber physical systems: methods and applications. Comput. Ind. **82**, 273–289 (2016)
19. Homer, J., Varikuti, A., Ou, X., McQueen, M.A.: Improving attack graph visualization through data reduction and attack grouping. In: Goodall, J.R., Conti, G., Ma, K.-L. (eds.) VizSec 2008. LNCS, vol. 5210, pp. 68–79. Springer, Heidelberg (2008). https://doi.org/10.1007/978-3-540-85933-8_7
20. House, W.: The national strategy for the physical protection of critical infrastructures and key assets (2003). http://www.whitehouse.gov/pcipb/physical_strategy.pdf
21. Jensen, J.C., Chang, D.H., Lee, E.A.: A model-based design methodology for cyber-physical systems. In: 2011 7th International Wireless Communications and Mobile Computing Conference, pp. 1666–1671. IEEE (2011)
22. Khaitan, S.K., McCalley, J.D.: Design techniques and applications of cyberphysical systems: A survey. IEEE Syst. J. **9**(2), 350–365 (2014)
23. Kotzanikolaou, P., Theoharidou, M., Gritzalis, D.: Assessing n-order dependencies between critical infrastructures. Int. J. Crit. Infrastruct. 6 **9**(1–2), 93–110 (2013)
24. Krotofil, M., Kursawe, K., Gollmann, D.: Securing industrial control systems. In: Alcaraz, C. (ed.) Security and Privacy Trends in the Industrial Internet of Things. ASTSA, pp. 3–27. Springer, Cham (2019). https://doi.org/10.1007/978-3-030-12330-7_1
25. Kumar, P., Merzouki, R., Bouamama, B.O., Koubeissi, A.: Bond graph modeling of a class of system of systems. In: 2015 10th System of Systems Engineering Conference (SoSE), pp. 280–285. IEEE (2015)
26. Li, X., Yu, W.: A hybrid fuzzy petri nets and neural networks framework for modeling critical infrastructure systems. In: 2018 IEEE International Conference on Fuzzy Systems (FUZZ-IEEE), pp. 1–6. IEEE (2018)
27. Marashi, K., Sarvestani, S.S.: Towards comprehensive modeling of reliability for smart grids: requirements and challenges. In: 2014 IEEE 15th International Symposium on High-Assurance Systems Engineering, pp. 105–112. IEEE (2014)
28. Marashi, K., Sarvestani, S.S., Hurson, A.R.: Identification of interdependencies and prediction of fault propagation for cyber-physical systems. Reliab. Eng. Syst. Saf. **215**, 107787 (2021)

29. Mathew, J., Ma, L., Tan, A., Weijnen, M., Lee, J.: Engineering Asset Management and Infrastructure Sustainability. Proceedings of the 5th World Congress on Engineering Asset Management (WCEAM 2010). Springer, London (2011). https://doi.org/10.1007/978-0-85729-493-7
30. Merzouki, R., Samantaray, A.K., Pathak, P.M., Bouamama, B.O.: Intelligent Mechatronic Systems: Modeling, Control and Diagnosis. Springer, London (2013). https://doi.org/10.1007/978-1-4471-4628-5
31. Newman, M.: Networks. Oxford University Press, Oxford (2018)
32. Pan, S., Morris, T., Adhikari, U.: Classification of disturbances and cyber-attacks in power systems using heterogeneous time-synchronized data. IEEE Trans. Industr. Inf. **11**(3), 650–662 (2015)
33. Rausand, M.: Risk Assessment: Theory, Methods, and Applications, vol. 115. Wiley, Hoboken (2013)
34. Rinaldi, S.M.: Modeling and simulating critical infrastructures and their interdependencies. In: Proceedings of the 37th Annual Hawaii International Conference on System Sciences, 8-p. IEEE (2004)
35. Rinaldi, S.M., Peerenboom, J.P., Kelly, T.K.: Identifying, understanding, and analyzing critical infrastructure interdependencies. IEEE Control Syst. Mag. **21**(6), 11–25 (2001)
36. Roychoudhury, I., Daigle, M.J., Biswas, G., Koutsoukos, X.: Efficient simulation of hybrid systems: a hybrid bond graph approach. Simulation **87**(6), 467–498 (2011)
37. Satumtira, G., Dueñas-Osorio, L.: Synthesis of modeling and simulation methods on critical infrastructure interdependencies research. In: Gopalakrishnan, K., Peeta, S. (eds.) Sustainable and Resilient Critical Infrastructure Systems, pp. 1–51. Springer, Heidelberg (2010). https://doi.org/10.1007/978-3-642-11405-2_1
38. Tagarev, T., Stoianov, N., Sharkov, G.: Integrative approach to understand vulnerabilities and enhance the security of cyber-bio-cognitive-physical systems. In: European Conference on Cyber Warfare and Security, pp. 492-XIX. Academic Conferences International Limited (2019)
39. Tan, R.R., Aviso, K.B., Promentilla, M.A.B., Yu, K.D.S., Santos, J.R.: Input–output models of infrastructure systems. In: Input-Output Models for Sustainable Industrial Systems. LNMIE, pp. 63–74. Springer, Singapore (2019). https://doi.org/10.1007/978-981-13-1873-3_5
40. Thulasiraman, K., Arumugam, S., Nishizeki, T., Brandstädt, A., et al.: Handbook of Graph Theory, Combinatorial Optimization, and Algorithms. Taylor & Francis, Boca Raton (2016)
41. Torres, J.L.S.: Vulnerability, interdependencies and risk analysis of coupled infrastructures: power distribution network and ICT. Ph.D. thesis (2013)
42. Umarikar, A.C., Umanand, L.: Modelling of switching systems in bond graphs using the concept of switched power junctions. J. Franklin Inst. **342**(2), 131–147 (2005)
43. Wei, J., Kundur, D.: Biologically inspired hierarchical cyber-physical multi-agent distributed control framework for sustainable smart grids. In: Khaitan, S.K., McCalley, J.D., Liu, C.C. (eds.) Cyber Physical Systems Approach to Smart Electric Power Grid. PS, pp. 219–259. Springer, Heidelberg (2015). https://doi.org/10.1007/978-3-662-45928-7_9
44. White, M.J.: Bond graph modeling of critical infrastructures for cyber-physical security implementation. Master's thesis, Department of Electrical and Computer Engineering, Missouri University of Science and Technology (2021)

45. Wolf, M., Serpanos, D.N.: Safe and Secure Cyber-Physical Systems and Internet-of-Things Systems. Springer, Cham (2020). https://doi.org/10.1007/978-3-030-25808-5
46. Zhang, Y., Yağan, O.: Modeling and analysis of cascading failures in interdependent cyber-physical systems. In: 2018 IEEE Conference on Decision and Control (CDC), pp. 4731–4738. IEEE (2018)
47. Zhu, W., Milanović, J.V.: Interdepedency modeling of cyber-physical systems using a weighted complex network approach. In: 2017 IEEE Manchester PowerTech, pp. 1–6. IEEE (2017)

Coordinated Network Attacks on Microgrid Dispatch Function: An EPIC Case Study

Muhammad Ramadan Saifuddin[1], Lin Wei[1(✉)], Heng Chuan Tan[2(✉)], and Binbin Chen[1(✉)]

[1] Singapore University of Technology and Design, Singapore, Singapore
{muhammad_ramadan,binbin_chen}@sutd.edu.sg, wei_lin@mymail.sutd.edu.sg
[2] Advanced Digital Sciences Center, Illinois at Singapore, Singapore, Singapore
hc.tan@adsc-create.edu.sg

Abstract. Communication network dependencies for microgrid's operations increases cybersecurity risks, where vulnerabilities found in communication protocols can be exploited for malicious intent. In this paper, we enumerate important attack techniques on multiple communication protocols and investigate their impacts on the microgrid dispatch function. We also show that an attacker can leverage multiple protocols to launch coordinated attacks that offers longer-term, stealthier, and larger adversarial impact, an advanced persistent threat. Our main contribution in this work is a detailed case study carried out on Electrical Power and Intelligent Control (EPIC) testbed located in Singapore. Through a series of experiments, we demonstrated individual protocols' vulnerability, verified their negative impacts on several microgrid's dispatch functions, and also illustrated the practicality of coordinated attacks through the manipulation of multiple protocols.

Keywords: Microgrid · Cyber-physical power system · Cybersecurity

1 Introduction

The general term "Smart Grid" implies the convergence of communications network and power system technologies to form a cyber-physical power system (CPPS). Particularly in the presence of widespread penetration of distributed energy resources (DER), e.g., solar panels, small-scaled generators, and energy storage systems, CPPS offers solutions in coordinating various DERs for operational needs, especially in the domain of improving operational efficiency, reliability, and sustainability. Over the years, smart grid deployment has shifted towards nano-structured ecosystem as a transactive hub that aggregates multiple stand-alone microgrid systems. Thus, a set of coordinated control action involving DER control and command, assets dispatch control, protection, etc., are imperative to steer a microgrid community that is sustainable and reliable;

S. Katsikas et al. (Eds.): ESORICS 2022 Workshops, LNCS 13785, pp. 26–45, 2023.
https://doi.org/10.1007/978-3-031-25460-4_2

(a) it hides complexity and paves DER interoperability at the edge of the power grid, (b) it allows efficient coordination of local energy generation and usage, and (c) it can benefit power quality and resiliency at the global transmission level, by aggregating local DERs through a dispatch control system. Hence, several microgrid research projects (e.g., the Illinois Institute of Technology campus grid [1] and the PUSPIPTEK project [2]) are developing and demonstrating new and advanced dispatch functions for microgrids. Ultimately, these microgrids must be prepared to function in a stand-alone mode (i.e., intentional islanded mode) that is cost efficient and resilient in black-start operations.

Realization in microgrid dispatch functions for islanding operation require digitization of control systems and instrument devices with network capabilities— an interconnected network architecture that interacts with the physical power system environment by utilizing communication, control, and computing resources [13]. In industrial practices, mixture of communication network standards and protocols are common because: (a) transitions are done in phases thus their CPPS implementations could be heterogeneous; (b) devices that serve different roles usually inherit and adopt different protocols; and (c) different vendors could favor different protocols. Regardless of the diversified practice for network communication standards, e.g., IEEE 1815-DNP3, IEC 61850, IEC 60870-5-104, HTTP/S, and Modbus standards, efforts are driven towards promoting system interoperability and scalability across multi-vendor devices during microgrid-forming enterprise [15]. Each of these standards provides tradeoffs between the IT/OT characteristics that involves data transportation (distance), information transfer time & latency, synchronicity & scalability, and information reliability & security.

While digitization is essential for microgrids, it also expands the attacking surface. Adversaries exploit vulnerabilities in the communication protocols or coupling layers of CPPS to corrupt industrial control and protection systems. Hence, users must take necessary steps to mitigate such vulnerabilities, e.g., IEC 62351 standard was developed to secure series of power grid protocols including IEC 60870-5 series, IEC 60870-6 series, and IEC 61850 series [16]. DNP3 can use an authentication mechanism to protect the established communication, thus countering threats such as spoofing, modification, and replay attacks [17]. IEC 60870-5-104 protocol adds an additional TLS encryption layer [18]. Despite various security controls have been proposed for these communication protocols, the real-world adoption is far from ideal. Many deployment still operates in insecure mode and many implementations have weakness [8], [9]. The Ukraine power grid attack is an example of how attackers can penetrate into a power system to cause massive disruptions [10].

In this paper, we present a case study of coordinated network attacks against islanded microgrid operations and demonstrate them on a high-fidelity power grid testbed, the Electrical Power and Intelligent Control (EPIC) testbed located in Singapore. As summarized in Table 1, we demonstrate capability in performing long-term reconnaissance operations to learn about the dispatch functions' characteristics and execute a highly synchronized, multistage attack that is stealthy

Table 1. Summary of cyberattacks on dispatch function requirements for Islanded operation targeting different communication protocols.

Comm. protocol	Attack techniques	Data flow	Adversarial impact
IEC 61850 GOOSE	DoS	IED status & sensor readings	No implication on the dispatch function requirements for Islanded operation while obvious attack traces visible on HMI
	HSN	IED status & sensor readings	A persistent 1 s transmission delay between HSN-infected GOOSE packet and the next legitimate packet. No implication on cyber network and physical systems
	Data manipulation	IED status & circuit breaker position	Significant impact on physical system forcing genset to stop spinning and cause CB to trip (alarm). Can be rectified by manually resetting the breaker and toggle to manual mode. But, such malicious tripping can propagates to other gensets due to overloading
IEC 61850 MMS	MITM, FDI	IED status to PLC	Significant impact on the dispatch control functions as physical system becomes unresponsive or haywire due to falsified state environment provided by IED. But, attack traces are visible on SCADA-HMI
		Sensor readings from PLC to HMI	Stealthier approach as it deceives operators monitoring SCADA-HMI with malicious alteration on the true operational status of physical system, but, no operational consequences
Modbus	MITM, FDI	Command actuators	Significant impact on the dispatch control function as actuator deviate from it intended operations. However, the attack traces are reflected on HMI providing information/traces
Multiple Protocol: GOOSE, MMS, Modbus	Data Manipulation, MITM, FDI	IED trip & circuit breaker status	Malicious circuit breaker tripping at PCC causes unintentional switching from grid-tied to Island and vice versa causing potential outage. But, can be easily rectified by toggling circuit breaker to manual mode
		sensor readings, command actuator	Stealthier approach that creates long-term impact (i.e., monetary, equipment lifespan). Mask all measurement readings on SCADA-HMI and tamper the dispatch control functions (i.e., AGC)

in comparison to attacking a single protocol. The attack objective of our coordinated attack is no longer focused on direct power supply interruptions but rather driven towards long-term adversarial impact (i.e., monetary, equipment lifespan) that goes undetected for months of operations. We plan to open source our collected attack traces to help promote the awareness of potential attack techniques and tactics, and also to help evaluate different cyber defense solutions [12,21].

Table 2. Microgrid dispatch function overview (simplified for islanded operation only).

Elements of the function	Function characterization	Parameters & metrics
DER control & command	Single dispatch	P,V,Q,f meets operating requirements
	Coordinated dispatch	
Load management	Demand response, load prioritization & shedding, load scheduling (BESS)	Balance supply-demand, freq. deviation within threshold
Dispatch control	Look-up table	Dynamic response, quantify performance
	Optimization problem	
Voltage regulation & power quality	Inverter-based volt/var control, constant freq. control	V,f, deviate within operating limit, inverter quality (THD), %flicker, rapid voltage change (RVC)
Switching device	Control commands	Device status
Data acquisition	Sensor request/response	Signal availability, measurement accuracy

2 Dispatch Function for Islanded Microgrid Operation

Consider a microgrid that consists of rooftop solar PV systems, battery energy storage systems (BESS), and two backup diesel engine-driven synchronous gensets, which is interacting with the external grid at one point, t, but, intentionally islanded at $(t+1)$. Such automation can be well directed by a centralized microgrid controller, programmed with operating costs minimization dispatch function while considering power quality management. Before the microgrid decouples itself from the external grid (i.e., opening of circuit breaker at point of common coupling (PCC)), under steady-state condition for islanded operation, the dispatch function specifications must include [19]:

- full access to DER asset control & command, individually or collectively.
- load control management; critical, non-critical, and adjustable loads.
- optimal dispatch to satisfy operational requirements (i.e., grid-forming— gensets running in isochronous mode to maintain system inertia while inverter-based DERs operate in droop mode).
- Switching control of circuit breaker, and other switching devices.
- System reliability and power quality (i.e., voltage regulation) using inverter-based Volt/Var control.
- V/f control in grid-forming operation and synchronization for load sharing (i.e., isochronous generator & BESS).

The list of dispatch control requirements in Table 2 are interdependent of each other as they ensure operational stability during Islanded, and if any of these establishments were to fail, it can lead to a cascading tripping effect or worst, connected equipment or appliances getting severely damaged. The dispatch function generates and executes control orders (i.e., sets of commands) to appropriate assets based on the received state information. Although the dispatch function for a Microgrid control does cover a wider range of operations that includes black start, grid-connected, re-connection from Island to grid-connected and vice versa, however, we limit our discussions to only steady-state dispatch function for Islanded Microgrid as we want to relate our attack strategies on these functional requirements (see Sect. 4 and 4.4).

3   Communication Protocols and Standards for Microgrid

Modern power grid communication technology has evolved from a serial communication architecture to an Ethernet-based network as seen in Fig. 1. Such advancement is required to support the increasing integration of diverse monitoring devices (i.e., IED, smart meters) and data-driven intelligent systems (i.e., PLC, RTU). The transition from analog to digital channels enables reliable synchronicity and scalability, allowing for data transfer over long distances. In the following, we review several communication protocols and discuss their applications in modern power grid system. Table 3 summaries the communication data flow (i.e., protocols) against different applications.

IEEE 1815 – The IEEE 1815 standard, also known as DNP3, is an open standard protocol that defines communication between process control systems. It provides a lightweight method of transferring simple data for control and data acquisition purposes. It is a polling protocol in which the master can poll the slaves for data. The slaves (i.e., outstation) can also transmit data to the master without being polled. This can occurs if there have been changes since the last poll or if certain parameters are met. Regarding security, the DNP3 protocol uses TLS encryption to protect TCP/IP channels and supports an optional secure authentication mechanism to authenticate specific requests.

IEC 61850 – The IEC 61850 standard defines the functional requirements for grid communications. The result of this standardization is the definition of data models and services that can be used to enhance process automation and device interoperability. This standardization enables devices to map power system functions to MMS, GOOSE, or SV protocols for communications.

 – **MMS** is a client/server communication protocol. It utilizes the TCP/IP protocol stack to ensure reliable message delivery. It is used for time-insensitive applications such as file transfers, data management, remote control of plant operations, and remote monitoring of devices. The standard defines ≈ 87 MMS services to support read, write, modify, create, and delete data operations. The MMS client sends a service request to the MMS server and the server responds back with the requested data.

- **GOOSE** is a layer 2 protocol that operates over the Ethernet. It is used for fast data transfer between IEDs—mainly to provide protection relay operations. It detects faults in the system and initiates fault responses, such as tripping the circuit breakers. Other functionalities include transmitting up-to-date information about the state of the power system, e.g., status and fault messages. Each GOOSE message contains a status number (stNum) and a sequence number (sqNum) to monitor any event change in the system. When a new event (e.g., a breaker trip signal) occurs, the stNum value will increment by 1 and sqNum will reset to 0. This is followed by a burst of transmissions to ensure that all subscribed IEDs receive the state change. If there is no event change, only sqNum is incremented.
- **SV** is an Ethernet-based protocol for sending voltage and current samples between MUs and IEDs. Each SV packet is indexed by a sample count (smpCnt) value that increments each time the MU sends a new message. Each packet contains a dataset comprising eight digitized values; 3-phase voltage with neutral and 3-phase current with neutral. Unlike GOOSE protocol, there are no re-transmissions in SV. The sending interval for SV messages depends on the sampling rate (smpRate), which according to the standard, is defined as 80 samples per cycle for basic protection and 256 samples per cycle for measurement applications. For 50 Hz power system, the sending rate is 250 μs for protection and 78.12 μs for measurement.

Modbus is a legacy communication standard used by many power grid operators. It is well supported by many device manufacturers due to its simple message structure. The protocol is based on a master/slave architecture where one master device can poll one or more slaves to request data. The slaves cannot initiate communication with the master devices. Modbus protocols include Modbus ASCII and Modbus RTU for serial communications, and Modbus TCP/IP for Ethernet communications. The difference between Modbus ASCII and Modbus RTU lies in the way the data is encoded. Modbus ASCII encodes data using ASCII characters while Modbus RTU uses binary encoding. Thus, Modbus ASCII requires more bytes to transmit than Modbus RTU. On the other hand, Modbus TCP is a Modbus RTU packet encapsulated in TCP/IP headers to facilitate data transfer over the Ethernet networks. Despite the different encoding formats, each Modbus payload begins with a function code followed by the data value. The function code determines the types of operation (read/write) and register types. For example, function code 16 represents a write operation to multiple holding registers. A function code of value 5 represents a write single coil operation.

IEC 60870 – The IEC 60870 standard defines the functional requirements for systems used for telecontrol which are supervisory control and data acquisition. The result of this standardization is to fulfill the special requirements of communication and co-ordination between control centers which are not defined in DNP3 and IEC 61850. For instance, both IEC 60870-5-101 and IEC 60870-5-104 are used to transmit SCADA data. The difference is that IEC 60870-5-101

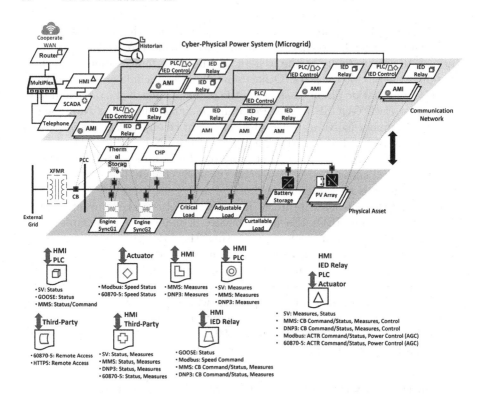

Fig. 1. The cyber-physical infrastructure of microgrid, interacting with physical devices using different communication network protocols and standards.

is based on serial communication (such as RS-232, FSK based modems) while IEC 60870-5-104 is the network access for IEC 60870-5-101 using standard transport profiles. IEC 60870-5-101 supports partyline (polling, multipoint, multidrop, unbalanced) and point-to-point operation mode. IEC 60870-5-104 only supports point-to-point operation mode.

As an example, we will look into the dispatch function requirements of DER Control and Command (listed in Table 2) for islanded operation, e.g., generator synchronization and automatic generation control (AGC) involving two diesel engine-driven synchronous generators as seen in Fig. 1. We assume that the microgrid is initially operating in grid-tied mode and we want to transition its operations into islanded (stand-alone) by opening circuit breaker at PCC. The control logic is as follows:

– Ensure the the circuit breaker at PCC is at close position and monitor the exchanged power flow to determine the total demand load consumed by Microgrid.
– Calculate the total available power generation locally (i.e., generators, CHP, solar PV, BESS). If $P_{Ld} \leq P_{gen}^{max}$ then, perform Islanding. If no, proceed with load curtailment first until the criterion meets.

Table 3. Network protocols for different applications.

Applications	Secure / Unsecure	IEC 61850			IEEE 1815		IEC 60870	
		GOOSE	MMS	SV	DNP3	Mod bus	IEC 60870 -5-104	HTTPS / HTTP
Supervisory control & data acquisition (SCADA)				X	X	X	X	
Distributed Energy Resources Management System (DERMS)				X		X		
Advance Distribution Management Systems (ADMS)				X	X			
Isochronous generator control						X	X	
Distribution automation systems (DA), integrated with substation, ADMS, or communications				X	X			
Protection communications within the substation		X		X				
Protection communications outside the substation (to another substation)		X					X	
Equipment monitoring (transformer, breaker, battery, etc.)			X		X	X		
Power quality monitoring			X	X	X	X	X	
Metering (i.e., AMI, IED)			X	X	X	X	X	
Planning & design								X
Cyber access control and monitoring								X
Third party access (remote vendors)			X					X
LAN/WAN management, monitoring and control							X	X
TCP Port		NILL	102	NILL	20000	501	2404	80 443

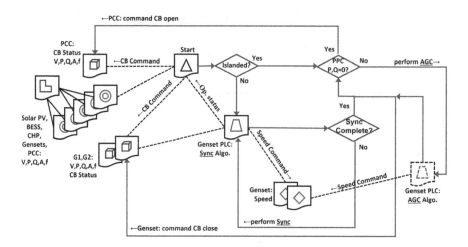

Fig. 2. Process flow of communication protocols to perform gensets synchronization and AGC based on DER control and command dispatch function, transitioning from grid-tied to islanded operation (symbols refer to Fig. 1).

- Command to run the synchronous generators offline until the operating frequency is leveled with the grid (i.e., 50/60Hz).
- We perform generator synchronization with the grid by adjusting the rotating speed in real-time to align the phase angle. Once align, close the circuit breaker of the affiliated genset. Do the same process for the subsequent gensets.
- Once these gensets have successfully coupled to the grid, we launch AGC algorithm to attune the gensets' generation output (speed control) until P, Q at PCC is zero.
- Once the Microgrid assets have took full control over the demand loading and secure the power quality, open circuit breaker at PCC.

Referencing from Fig. 1, Fig. 2 illustrates the data flow process in relations to the control logic listed above.

4   Case Study: Attacks on Microgrid Dispatch Functions

Using the dispatch function provided in Table 2, e.g. DER control and command for generator synchronization and AGC (see Fig. 2), we aim to evaluate the feasibility and adversarial impacts on microgrid dispatch function. We target our attacks on several communication protocols and verify them on the Electrical Power and Intelligent Control (EPIC) testbed. EPIC [20] is a power grid testbed located in Singapore, designed for cybersecurity researchers to conduct experiments and assess effectiveness of cyber attack and defense mechanisms.

4.1   EPIC System Overview

In our experiment setup, we configured EPIC to operate similar to our dispatch function for Islanded microgrid employing; 2 Variable Speed Driver (VSD) driven generator sets, each rated at 15 kVA, equipped with protection relay and remote controlled circuit breaker, a 21 kVA Loadbank, and a 34 kW MPPT-based PV. Both the generators operate in isochronous mode and uses synchrophasor to establish synchronization during parallel operations. Moreover, with in-built automatic generation control (AGC) capability, users can control the amount of output power generation of each gensets from SCADA.

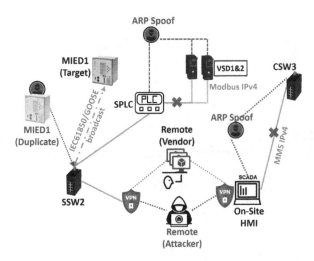

Fig. 3. Attacks on different communication protocols in IEC 61850 and Modbus. Masquerade as MIED1 to inject malicious GOOSE packets into the network, and perform MITM attack to intercept MMS and Modbus packets between user and an application and ultimately modify the packets' payload on the EPIC.

EPIC uses the IEC 61850 MMS protocol that operates over the TCP/IP model and IEC 61850 GOOSE protocol, which is capable of obtaining responses from different parts of the system within 4 ms. It includes standard features such as standardization of data names, fast transfer of events and data storage, and device interoperability. GOOSE and MMS are used in the ring network for data transfer between IEDs and the SCADA workstation. The field bus communication among physical processes to PLCs, master PLC, and SCADA is realized through wired channels. The PLC uses Modbus TCP/IP protocol to send commands to actuators.

4.2   Attacks on IEC 61850-Based Communication Protocols

Assuming that we have gained visibility on EPIC's network, we launch the attack on either GOOSE or MMS packets as seen in Fig. 3. Although the attack objectives on these protocols deemed successful, some do not imply any adversarial impact on Islanded microgrid operation and attack traces were easily identified on HMI.

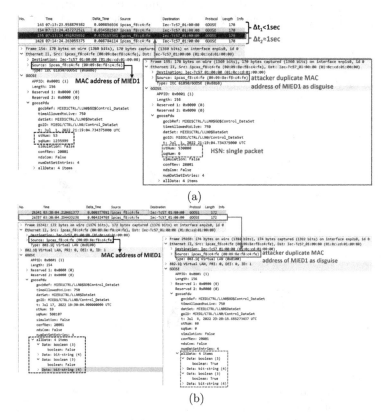

Fig. 4. Masquerade as MIED1 and inject malicious GOOSE packet into the network. (a) HSN attack introduces a delay in broadcasting GOOSE packets by injecting a single packet. (b) Modifies the GOOSE packets' payload (Boolean values) for malicious circuit breaker tripping.

GOOSE Packets. The GOOSE packets in EPIC works through a publisher-subscriber mechanism on a broadcast service, thus, from SSW2, we are able to gain visibility on all connected IEDs of different network rings. We duplicate the MAC address and masquerade as legitimate IED (i.e., MIED1) and begin injecting malicious GOOSE packets into the traffic using Denial-of-Service (DoS), High Status Number (HSN), and False Data Injection (FDI) attack approach.

- **Denial-of-Service:** In DoS attack, we flood the network with malicious GOOSE packets to prevent legitimate IEDs from receiving critical messages or updates. We inject 1000 dummy GOOSE packets posing as MIED1 with *stnum* in running number sequence (but larger than the legitimate MIED1's GOOSE packet) while *sqNum* set to zero. When DoS attack was underway, we observed that all alarms associated with the protection relay coupled to MIED1 were triggered maliciously, and real-time sensor measurements of MIED1 reflected on SCADA (MMS packets) were replaced with "question mark" icon. This verifies that attack objective is successful, leaving the network lost in the flooded transmission while awaiting for a legitimate GOOSE packet from MIED1. This poses an issue when operator wants to perform a manual synchronization between the incoming and running generators due to ambiguity in the phase angle differences ($\Delta\theta°$) shown at SCADA (synchrophasor). Likewise, in the dispatch function for Islanded operation, synchronization serves as the core requirement to bring these gensets online before microgrid can decouple itself from the grid. Operating in isochronous, they provide inertia to IES and inverter-based DERs online; thus, without them, microgrid must remain grid-tied. Even if the DoS attack is launched during Islanded, where only a single genset is running and the operator intend to bring the incoming genset online to meet the high demand capacity during the next period, operator is forced to revert back into grid-tied mode and, if left unattended, the microgrid will collapse as frequency will dip and genset being overloaded.

Contrarily, in practice, the DoS attack has no implication on the microgrid's operation, e.g., successfully establishing synchronization, because; (a) the synchronization is done automatically by the PLC, (b) the PLC is able to take reference from MIED2, $\Delta\theta°$. If EPIC is already operating in parallel mode, then, it has no impact on the system's stability and operation of AGC. In view of the attack traces, operator can identify the problem had surfaced from MIED1 as shown in SCADA. Hence, the attack objective is met but had no negative impact on grid operations.

- **High Status Number:** Instead of flooding the network with malicious GOOSE packets, we inject a single malicious GOOSE packet with HSN (*stNum*=5000) into the network posing as MIED1. The HSN takes precedence over any legitimate GOOSE packets coming from MIED1. In theory, the network drops any MIED1's GOOSE packet with smaller *stNum* and holds on to HSN-infected GOOSE packet the network. Hence, some researchers have reported that HSN attack offers a stealthier attack approach as compared to DoS attack and yet gained similar outcome, e.g., flooding of GOOSE packet can be easily detected visually but not for single packet injection. Contrarily, in practice, neither the network nor physical systems suffered any implication as to what we have seen in DoS attack. Legitimate GOOSE packets with lower *stNum* from MIED1 were still picked up in the network after the HSN-infected packet as shown in Fig. 4(a). There was a persistent 1sec transmission delay between the HSN-infected GOOSE packet and the next legitimate packet whenever HSN is launched compared to a normal GOOSE packet transmission. Regardless, the HSN-infected GOOSE packet failed to achieve its attack objective and worst, had no negative impact on both the network and physical operations.

– **Data Manipulation:** In data manipulation attack, we aim to modify MIED1
GOOSE packets' payload. The payload contains two pairs of data item representing the status of circuit breaker Q2B affiliated to MIED1; trip status
and mode open status. By modifying the payloads' values from False to True
and injecting the packets into the network as shown in Fig. 4(b), we aim to
broadcast malicious status of Q2B being tripped and in open position. We
specify $stNum$ in running sequence, $sqNum$ to zero, update the timestamp
to conform a legitimate GOOSE packet, and modify both the Boolean values
to True. The attack generates a significant impact on the physical system
as seen from Fig. 5 where Generator 2 was forced to stop spinning and an
alarm "trip" is flagged. The alarm is broadcast to the speed drive controller
of Generator 2 causing it to intentionally break as mandated by the protection
control logic. We can expect similar adversarial impact on microgrid under
the data manipulation attack on gensets' IED. Despite an eventful attack
sequence, i.e., forcing Generator 2 to decoupled from the grid and leaving
Generator 1 serving the demand load alone, operator can easily pinpoint the
problem caused and trace the attacker's footprint. Meaning, operator can
manually reset the breaker and switch to manual operation. If the alarm persist, then the problem is isolated to the circuit breaker command running
in the background. However, in times where demand load capacity is high
(i.e., $P_L > P_{G1}^{max}$) and data manipulation attack is underway, an intentional
tripping can propagates towards Generator 1 as it is now overloaded.

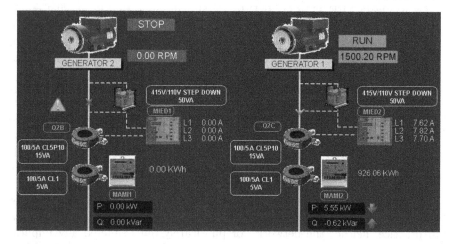

Fig. 5. Impact on EPIC under data manipulation attack, attacker posing as MIED1
and broadcast into the network indicating that Q2B is tripped and in open position.

MMS Packets. We direct our attacks to modify gensets' IED MMS packets'
payload to make synchronization process unresponsive on the incoming genset
as shown in Fig. 3. The objective is to launch man-in-the-middle (MITM) attack
and intercepts MMS packets from IEDs to PLC and modify its payload (i.e.,

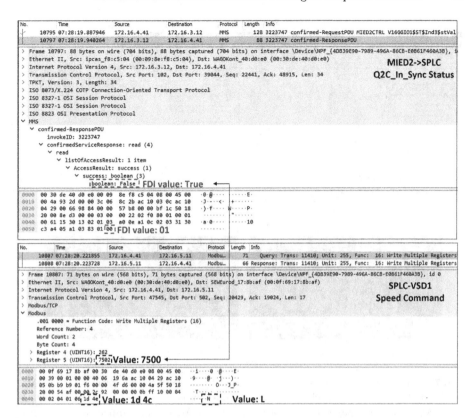

Fig. 6. Malicious insider MITM attack on MMS packet between PLC and IED1/2 and tamper MIED2 MMS's payload with false declaration on the synchronization status. TRUE at all times even before initiating synchronization.

synchronization status) as seen in Fig. 6. Based on the control logic defined in generators' PLC, if the in-synchronization status is TRUE, it signifies that both gensets have established synchronization and there will no command change on the speed values leaving the associated circuit breaker in the open position. While, if it is False, PLC will initiate the synchronization algorithm and closes the circuit breaker once its phase angles converges with the running genset (by attuning the incoming genset's speed). This attack approach is feasible to an untrained attacker who has no prior knowledge on generator synchronization process as it exploit operational status instead of implementing physical changes to influence the status, e.g., tampering the synchronous speed during synchronization to ensure the status remains False). Moreover, pinpointing attacks on IED would be an intelligent guess for an attacker as it holds vital information on equipment status and measurements which are gold for data-driven industrial control.

Contrarily, we target our attacks on MMS packets coming from PLC to HMI as seen in Fig. 3. These packets' payload contains real-time sensor measurements

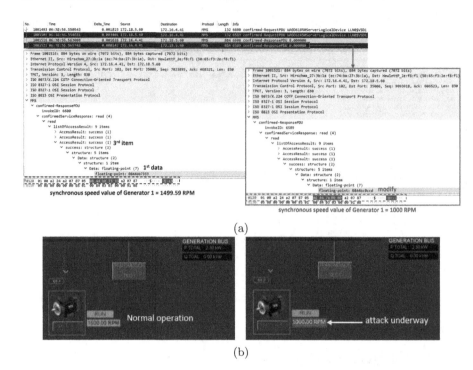

Fig. 7. Performing MITM attack on MMS packets' payload coming from PLC to HMI, modifying Generator 1's synchronous speed values away from its true values. (a) Modifying MMS packets' payload, generator speed. (b) Adversarial impact on HMI with the modified values.

of the physical systems' performances and also some remote control functionalities for microgrid operations (i.e., switching of circuit breakers and load capacity selections). Likewise, we will perform MITM attack to redirect the packets' payload for tampering, e.g., modify the SCADA's real-time synchronous generator's speed value to 1000rpm using MITM attack and mask its true values as seen in Fig. 7(a). In consequence, the modified synchronous speed value is updated on the SCADA workstation, deceiving grid operators its true operating behavior as seen in Fig. 7(b).

4.3   EPIC Modbus Communication Network

In this section, we direct our attacks on the Modbus communication coming from PLC to actuators as seen from Fig. 3. The objective is to launch MITM attack to redirect those Modbus packets containing gensets' synchronous speed values commanding individual VSDs and perform FDI attack to modify their payloads.

To a trained attacker who has knowledge on generator synchronization process, tampering of these synchronous speed values not only hinders the synchronization process but also derail the AGC performances causing negative economic standpoint and destabilizes the grid's operating frequency beyond the threshold limits. In this attack sequence, we aim to create a non-responsive synchronization process between the running and incoming genset.

Synchronization of gensets is governed by a closed-loop speed controller that commands incoming genset's VSD to ramp-up or -down until the phase angle differences between both gensets is less than $\pm 1°$, e.g., PLC commands VSD1 (Generator 1) to spin at 1500.4rpm (or 7502 sent via a Modbus) until the phase angle aligns with Generator 2. Once achieved, immediately, Generator 1's circuit breaker (Q2C) will close and the user-defined AGC algorithm takes over the speed controller. Moreover, ordering of these gensets' synchronous speed values must not deviate by more than 1rpm to avoid introducing unintentional frequency swelling or dipping ($\pm 1\%Hz$). Figure 8(c) illustrates the synchronization control sequences during normal operation followed by a balanced AGC (i.e., 50%–50%).

However, when FDI attack is underway, e.g., assigning Generator 1 speed command constant at 1500rpm (Modbus command 7500) as seen in Fig. 8(a), $|\Delta\theta°|$ failed to converge thus leaving Q2C to remain open. This forces Generator 2 to serve the total load capacity alone, raising the concern that it could overload as demand capacity reaches its peak at $(t + 1.)$ Alternatively, we can alternate high/low speed values to render unstable $|\Delta\theta°|$ profile (oscillating), but, exploiting these values can easily trigger bad data detection in state estimation.

Although FDI attack has little impact on the microgrid's stability (i.e., healthy frequency/voltage levels), from economical viewpoint, it hampers the ability to achieve optimal unit-commitment for economic dispatch. Even so, the implications can get serious when the attack is strategically launched during peak demand periods where incoming gensets are needed online to share the load capacities and maintain frequency levels at nominal. Seen from Fig. 8(b), at tail end of the graph, it shows that an overloading alarm is flagged ($>9.5\,kVA$) on Generator 2 when the load capacity increases to $10\,kW$ as compared to a successful synchronization where gensets are operating at 50% loading.

4.4   Coordinated Attacks Targeting Multiple Protocols

From the case studies learned in Sects. 4.2–4.3, we aim to formulate a stealthier attacks on EPIC by targeting different combination of communication protocols, coordinated attacks. We define stealthy as the act of deceiving the grid operators comprehending from what is shown on the HMI versus the true operations of the physical systems. The attack objective is driven towards long-term adversarial impact during Islanded operation, e.g., to incur high operating costs and depreciate equipment lifespan exponentially. We point the attack vectors on the communication protocols of several dispatch control functions and synchronize the attack on; DER control and command (synchronization of isochronous generators), dispatch control (AGC), and switching device (circuit breaker at PCC).

Procedure 1 guides attackers in gaining the initial state operation of the microgrid, e.g., grid-tied, islanded. Once appreciated, attacker can program to raise an alert whenever the microgrid is transitioning between grid-connected

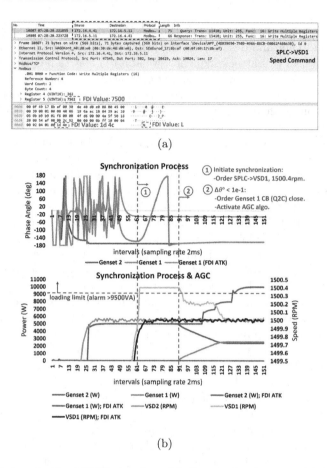

(a)

(b)

Fig. 8. Malicious insider MITM attack on Modbus packet between PLC and VSDs. (a) Tampering the Modbus packets' payload (i.e., synchronous speed) of incoming genset to cease the synchronization process. (b) Comparative profiles of gensets' power generation capacities, phase angles differences, and speed command, under attacking and non-attacking scenarios during the synchronization process.

mode and islanded mode. Assuming the microgrid is transitioning from grid-tied to islanded mode and gensets are in the process of synchronizing (isochronous generators), attacker proceeds to execute stealthy attack on DER control and command. We aim to cease the synchronization process forcing microgrid to remain grid-tied. We tamper the speed command from PLC to gensets' VSDs (actuator) with large values which then forces synchrophasor unable to converge. However, we need to strategically attune the tampered speed values within the operating frequency threshold ($\pm$0.5Hz) as not to render obvious anomaly that could potentially trip the genset due to overspeed.

Procedure 1. *Stealthy attack on DER control and command.*

Step 1: *Perform reconnaissance on the following packets:*

– *Modbus packets: speed command and status.*
– *MMS packets: synchronization status.*
– *circuit breaker located at PCC.*

Step 2: *modify speed command values to actuators by increasing it speed within the operating frequency limit.*

Step 3: *Update speed measurements on HMI with dummy values by displaying nominal operating synchronous speed value.*

Procedure 2 guides attackers in executing stealthy attack on dispatch control (AGC). Upon establishing synchronization and Microgrid is operating in Islanded mode, we intent to force one of the two gensets to operate near its rated operating power limit without intentionally tripping it. To achieve this, we tamper the AGC settings of a single genset, i.e., assigning to its maximum loading without causing reverse power on other generators, constantly stressing the targeted genset to cover high percentage of demand loading. Such operation also causes negative implication on the economic dispatch (minimization of operating costs). However, on HMI, the sensor measurement are in accordance to the user-defined AGC.

Procedure 2. *Stealthy attack on dispatch control during Islanded.*

Step 1: *Perform reconnaissance on the following packets:*

– *Modbus packets: speed command and status.*
– *MMS packets: speed value measurement, generator output power and maximum loading threshold, load capacity.*
– *GOOSE packet: CB status;*

Step 2: *Update sensor measurements on HMI with dummy values:*

– *compute the total active and reactive power of gensets.*
– *compute the desired output power of each gensets based on user-specified AGC settings.*
– *Inject computed power generation measurements into HMI.*

Step 3: *modify the AGC in the background, ramping up the synchronous speed without causing reverse power on the other genset. Disable the generator's maximum loading threshold*

Procedure 3 guides attackers in executing stealthy attack on circuit breaker at PCC. We aim to deny transitional operation from Islanded to grid-tied mode by tampering the IED status of PCC. In consequence, option to initiate grid-tied transition is unabled on HMI unless switching it to manual operation and may imply to operator that the circuit breaker is faulty in automation mode and will need replacement.

Procedure 3. *Stealthy attack on circuit breaker switching event*

Step 1: *Perform reconnaissance on GOOSE packet, CB status.*
Step 2: *Update CB status at PCC to trip and always in open position.*

---

5   Conclusion

In this paper, we provided detailed case study on applying attack techniques to target the individual and multiple communication protocols used on the EPIC testbed. We studied the impacts of these attacks on the microgrid dispatch function. We show that the EPIC testbed has security vulnerabilities that attackers can leverage to disrupt operations or even cause physical damage.

Acknowledgment. This research is supported in part by the National Research Foundation, Singapore, under its National Satellite of Excellence Programme "Design Science and Technology for Secure Critical Infrastructure" (Award Number: NSoE_DeST-SCI2019-0008 and NSoE_DeST-SCI2021TG-0003), and in part by the National Research Foundation, Prime Minister's Office, Singapore under its Campus for Research Excellence and Technological Enterprise (CREATE) programme, and in part by the SUTD Start-up Research Grant (SRG Award No: SRG ISTD 2020 157). Any opinions, findings and conclusions or recommendations expressed in this material are those of the author(s) and do not reflect the views of National Research Foundation, Singapore.

References

1. Shahidehpour, M., et al.: Transforming a national historic landmark into a green nanogrid: the case of crown hall. IEEE Electrification Mag. **8**(4), 20–35 (2020)
2. Nurdiana, E., Riza, R., Ifanda, I., Basharah, A.A.: Performance of 10 kWp PV rooftop system based on smart grid in energy building PUSPIPTEK. In: International Conference on Sustainable Energy Engineering and Application (ICSEEA) 2019, pp. 193–200 (2019)
3. Song, Q., et al.: Smart substation integration technology and its application in distribution power grid. CSEE J. Power Energy Syst. **2**(4), 31–36 (2016)
4. Yu, X., Xue, Y.: Smart grids: a cyber-physical systems perspective. Proc. IEEE **104**(5), 1058–1070 (2016)
5. IEEE approved draft recommended practice for implementing an IEC 61850 based substation communications, protection, monitoring and control system. In: IEEE P2030.100/D12, March 2017, pp. 1–70, 1 January 2017

6. Brand, K.P., Ostertag, M., Wimmer, W.: Safety related, distributed functions in substations and the standard IEC 61850. In: 2003 IEEE Bologna Power Tech Conference Proceedings, vol. 2, 5 p. (2003)
7. IEEE standard for the specification of microgrid controllers. In: IEEE Std 2030.7-2017, pp. 1–43, 23 April 2018
8. Biswas, P.P., Li, Y., Tan, H.C., Mashima, D., Chen, B.: An attack-trace generating toolchain for cybersecurity study of iec61850 based substations. In: 2020 IEEE International Conference on Communications, Control, and Computing Technologies for Smart Grids (SmartGridComm), pp. 1–7 (2020)
9. Khodabakhsh, A., Yayilgan, S.Y., Houmb, S.H., Hurzuk, N., Foros, J., Istad, M.: Cyber-security gaps in a digital substation: from sensors to SCADA. In: 2020 9th Mediterranean Conference on Embedded Computing (MECO), pp. 1–4 (2020)
10. Case, Defense Use: Analysis of the cyber attack on the Ukrainian power grid. Electricity Information Sharing and Analysis Center (E-ISAC), pp. 1–29 (2016)
11. Slowik, J.: Crashoverride: reassessing the 2016 Ukraine electric power event as a protection-focused attack. Dragos Inc. (2019)
12. Tan, H.C., Cheh, C., Chen, B., Mashima, D.: Tabulating cybersecurity solutions for substations: towards pragmatic design and planning. IEEE Innov. Smart Grid Technol. Asia (ISGT Asia) **2019**, 1018–1023 (2019)
13. Vu, T.V., Nguyen, B.L.H., Cheng, Z., Chow, M.-Y., Zhang, B.: Cyber-physical microgrids: toward future resilient communities. IEEE Ind. Electron. Mag. **14**(3), 4–17 (2020)
14. Anderson, D., Zhao, C., Hauser, C., Venkatasubramanian, V., Bakken, D., Bose, A.: "Intelligent design" real-time simulation for smart grid control and communications design. IEEE Power Energy Mag. **10**(1), 49–57 (2012)
15. IEEE recommended practice for network communication in electric power substations. In: IEEE Std 1615-2019 (Revision of IEEE Std 1615-2007, pp. 1–140, 8 November 2019
16. Ustun, T.S., Hussain, S.M.S.: IEC 62351-4 security implementations for IEC 61850 MMS messages. IEEE Access **8**, 123979–123985 (2020)
17. Amoah, R., Camtepe, S., Foo, E.: Securing DNP3 broadcast communications in SCADA systems. IEEE Trans. Industr. Inf. **12**(4), 1474–1485 (2016)
18. Todeschini, M.G., Dondossola, G.: Securing IEC 60870-5-104 communications following IEC 62351 standard: lab tests and results. In: AEIT International Annual Conference (AEIT) 2020, pp. 1–6 (2020)
19. IEEE standard for the specification of microgrid controllers. In: IEEE Std 2030.7-2017, pp. 1–43, 23 April 2018. https://doi.org/10.1109/IEEESTD.2018.8340204
20. Siaterlis, C., Genge, B., Hohenadel, M.: EPIC: a testbed for scientifically rigorous cyber-physical security experimentation. IEEE Trans. Emerg. Top. Comput. **1**(2), 319–330 (2013). https://doi.org/10.1109/TETC.2013.2287188
21. Tan, H.C., Cheh, C., Chen, B.: CoToRu: automatic generation of network intrusion detection rules from code. In: IEEE INFOCOM 2022 - IEEE Conference on Computer Communications, pp. 720–729 (2022). https://doi.org/10.1109/INFOCOM48880.2022.9796697

Adversarial Attacks and Mitigations on Scene Segmentation of Autonomous Vehicles

Yuqing Zhu[1], Sridhar Adepu[1,2]([✉]), Kushagra Dixit[1,2], Ying Yang[3], and Xin Lou[3,4]

[1] University of Bristol, Bristol, UK
sridhar.adepu@bristol.ac.uk
[2] Reperion, Singapore, Singapore
kd@reperion.io
[3] Advanced Digital Sciences Center, Singapore, Singapore
[4] Singapore Institute of Technology, Singapore, Singapore
https://reperion.io

Abstract. In this study, we focus on the effectiveness of adversarial attacks on the scene segmentation function of autonomous driving systems (ADS). We explore both offensive as well as defensive aspects of the attacks in order to gain a comprehensive understanding of the effectiveness of adversarial attacks with respect to semantic segmentation. More specifically, in the offensive aspect, we improved the existing adversarial attack methodology with the idea of momentum. The adversarial examples generated by the improved method show higher transferability in both targeted as well as untargeted attacks. In the defensive aspect, we implemented and analyzed five different mitigation techniques proven to be effective in defending against adversarial attacks in image classification tasks. The image transformation methods such as JPEG compression and low pass filtering showed good performance when used against adversarial attacks in a white box setting.

Keywords: Security · Autonomous vehicles · Deep learning · Adversarial attacks · Semantic segmentation

1 Introduction

With the rapid development of deep learning, fully autonomous driving is gradually becoming a reality. Deep Neural Networks (DNNs) show incredible performance in solving computer vision tasks such as classification, detection, and segmentation, and provide efficient solutions to Autonomous Driving Systems (ADS) for the same. ADS use a wide range of sensors including cameras, RADAR's and LIDAR's to monitor the environment around them and collect visual, positioning and mapping data. This data is then used by the ADS to

---

Sridhar Adepu: Primary affiliation is University of Bristol.

S. Katsikas et al. (Eds.): ESORICS 2022 Workshops, LNCS 13785, pp. 46–66, 2023.
https://doi.org/10.1007/978-3-031-25460-4_3

have a comprehensive understanding of the surrounding environment with the help of DNNs where the techniques which are used for sensor fusion and scene segmentation are fairly mature. However, ADS is extremely security critical, and any safety and reliability issues can lead to severe and irreversible consequences. In [14], authors divided the attacks on autonomous driving vehicles into three categories. These are attacks on the physical sensors, control systems and connection mechanisms. In this work, we focus on a specific attack technique called the adversarial attack which is a technique that utilizes the vulnerabilities of the DNN to mislead control systems into making wrong decisions.

In [8], authors demonstrated that DNNs are vulnerable to adversarial attacks. These adversarial attacks can cause machine learning models to give an incorrect output with a high level of confidence by adding subtle perturbations to the input samples. Therefore, adversarial attacks become a potential security threat to autonomous vehicles that use DNN. In [11], authors mitigated the adversarial attack by utilizing JPEG compression. However, most of these studies about adversarial attacks and defence against them focus on image classification tasks, which require less computational complexity compared to semantic segmentation. Semantic segmentation plays a key role in autonomous vehicles since it helps the ADS to differentiate between various important regions in visual data. In [1], authors evaluated the robustness of semantic segmentation models to adversarial attacks. In [20], authors created a dense attack generation approach to generate adversarial instances that challenge DNN-based scene segmentation and object detection models at the same time. However, the required computational intensity demands harder optimization for training segmentation models and thus adversarial attacks require much more effort.

In this paper, we propose a momentum based adversarial attack that specifically addresses the semantic segmentation tasks in autonomous vehicles. The proposed method utilizes momentum which is a technique used in deep learning to achieve an efficient black-box attack, i.e., the attack can work well against various segmentation models. Moreover, our methodology can launch effective attacks in either targeted or untargeted scenarios, which gives flexibility for the attacker's objectives. We also implemented and analyzed five mitigation methods based on image transformation. In summary, following are our contributions:

- We analyze the robustness of DNN based semantic segmentation models against adversarial attacks in an autonomous vehicles scenario. To address the computationally demanding nature of semantic segmentation models, we propose to leverage the idea of momentum to the Iterative Fast Gradient Sign Method (I-FGSM) adversarial attack algorithm which can reduce the required computational effort and significantly increase the transferability.
- We validate adversarial attack methodology by attacking state-of-the-art semantic segmentation models on a common real-world segmentation dataset i.e. "Cityscapes". Our experiments show that momentum based I-FGSM performs significantly better than the original I-FGSM in a targeted setting.
- We verified the viability of using image transformations as a mitigation technique against adversarial attack in the context of semantic segmentation models. We add another preprocessing layer before sending data into the semantic

segmentation model that can remove the effect of the adversarial perturbation in the input image without modify the architecture of the model or the training process. The results show that image transformation functions such as low pass filtering and JPEG compression can mitigate adversarial attacks in a white box setting against semantic scene segmentation models.

The remaining article organisation: Sect. 2 reviews prior work in adversarial attack. Section 3 elaborates on the momentum based I-FGSM attack. Section 4 shows the experimental settings together with the results including both attack and defence scenarios. Section 5 concludes the article.

2 Background

This section aims to provide an introduction to semantic segmentation (Sect. 2.1) and adversarial attacks (Sect. 2.2).

2.1 Semantic Segmentation

Semantic segmentation is a pixel-level classification task. The semantic segmentation model needs to assign each pixel of the input image to a class. It is an important task in autonomous vehicles that is used to help the ADS understand the input image and solve vision tasks such as discovering drivable/undrivable areas. DNN-based semantic segmentation models have been widely employed by ADS to help autonomous vehicles when it comes to performing tasks such as scene perception. However, the safety of DNN when it comes to such tasks is questionable at best, for example, DNN shows low reliability while facing malicious attacks that use adversarial attack methodologies [8,18].

2.2 Adversarial Attack

The adversarial attack is a technique that can cause a malfunction in a DNN. It can cause the DNN to give an incorrect output with a high level of confidence by adding subtle disturbances to the input samples. In [18], authors showed that adversarial examples have strange transferability. That is, the neural network is statistically vulnerable to the adversarial examples generated by another neural network. There are two types of adversarial attacks - white box attacks and black box attacks. For white box attacks, the attacker has information about the architecture of the target neural network. For a black box attack, the architecture of the target neural network is not available to the attacker. There are various ways of generating adversarial examples. The Fast Gradient Sign Method (FGSM) [8] utilizes the gradient of the loss function to generate adversarial examples. Carlini & Wagner's attack [4] utilizes optimization-based methods to launch an adversarial attack. Jacobian-based Saliency Map attack [13] exploits saliency maps and increases high-saliency pixels to lead to a misclassification by the deep neural network. In the following sub-section, we briefly introduce FGSM and its variants.

Fast Gradient Sign Method (FGSM). FGSM was one of the first effective adversarial attacks introduced in [8]. FGSM generates adversarial perturbations by maximizing the gradient of the loss for the input. Equation (1) shows the detail of untargeted FGSM:

$$x_{adv} = x + \varepsilon \cdot \text{sign}\left(\nabla_x L\left(x, y\right)\right), \tag{1}$$

where x_{adv} is the adversarial example, x is the input without perturbation, y is the label of the input, L is the loss function of the model, ∇_x is the gradient function and $\text{sign}\left(\nabla_x L\left(x, y\right)\right)$ is the direction that will maximise the loss. The constant value ε is the magnitude of the perturbation. The attack calculates $\left(\nabla_x L\left(x, y\right)\right)$ by back-propagating the gradient. Then it adjusts the input in the direction of $\text{sign}\left(\nabla_x L\left(x, y\right)\right)$.

Iterative Fast Gradient Sign Method (I - FGSM). In [12], the author raised an iterative version of FGSM (I-FGSM) that applied FGSM in a recurring fashion with a smaller step size to increase the efficiency of the attack. Equation (2) shows the detail of untargeted I-FGSM:

$$x_{adv}^{t+1} = x_{adv}^t + \varepsilon \cdot \alpha \cdot \text{sign}\left(\nabla_x L\left(x_{adv}^t, y\right)\right), \tag{2}$$

where Eq. (2) is inherited from Eq. (1), α is the step size of I-FGSM and set to ε/T to restrict the adversarial example in a bounded L2 norm where T is the number of iterations. For a targeted attack, the aim is to minimize the loss between the adversarial example and the target label $y*$ such that the adversarial example will be predicted as target label $y*$. Equation (3) shows the detail of targeted I-FGSM:

$$x_{adv}^{t+1} = x_{adv}^t + \varepsilon \cdot \alpha \cdot \text{sign}\left(\nabla_x L\left(x_{adv}^t, y^*\right)\right). \tag{3}$$

The I-FGSM can generate finer adversarial examples that do not spoil the visual content even with a greater attack magnitude [12].

3   Work Execution

Section 3.1 list the two main drawbacks of the original I-FGSM. Section 3.2 elaborates our Momentum-based I-FGSM attack method. Section 3.3 shows the structure of mitigation methodologies.

3.1   Drawbacks of I-FGSM

As introduced in Sect. 2, I-FGSM can successfully cause an incorrect prediction during image classification tasks. However, this method shows two drawbacks when attacking semantic segmentation models. The first drawback being that adversarial examples generated by I-FGSM show poor transferability, which leads to deficient performance in a black box setting. The transferability of adversarial examples occur because multiple machine learning models learn comparable decision boundaries around a data point [7], making adversarial examples designed for one model effective against others. However, the I-FGSM is prone to falling into a suboptimal local optimum which greatly reduces the transferability of the adversarial examples. The second drawback is that it is hard to achieve convergence with I-FGSM. This disadvantage becomes more apparent in the case of segmentation networks as they are more complex in nature than classification models, with higher computational complexity, rendering the process of searching for minute perturbations difficult. To improve I-FGSM and to overcome these drawbacks, we integrate the idea of momentum into the original I-FGSM algorithm.

3.2 Momentum-Based I-FGSM

The momentum based I-FGSM attack is inspired by the momentum technique which is used to optimize the Stochastic Gradient Descent (SGD) algorithm in DNN [15]. Figure 1 shows the details of the progression of our momentum based adversarial attack algorithm.

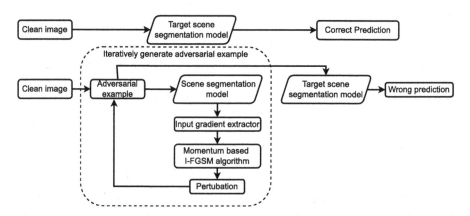

Fig. 1. Workflow of momentum based I-FGSM adversarial attack. The segmentation model used to generate adversarial examples is same with the target scene segmentation model in white box settings and is different in black box settings

In DNN, SGD is widely used to modify the network parameters in minimizing the difference between the prediction by the network and the real data. For each iteration, the weights are updated, and the weight vector is moved towards the direction of the negative gradient at the current position. However, there is a certain probability that SGD is stuck in a local minimum or saddle instead of the global minimum. Momentum is used to mitigate and optimize the SGD algorithm in this aspect. In Gradient Descent with Momentum, the change in the weight vector depends on both the current gradient and the previous sequence of gradients. The Eqs. (4) and (5) show the Gradient Descent with Momentum:

$$V_t = \beta V_{t-1} + \alpha \nabla_w L(W, X, y), \tag{4}$$

where:
$$W = W - V_t, \tag{5}$$

Here, L is the loss function, α is the learning rate, β is a hyperparameter that is used to adjust the influence of the earlier gradients. V_t stands for the "current descent velocity" which is based on the metaphor of velocity from physics. V_t is updated depending on the current gradient and the previous velocity.

The idea of momentum can level out the variations and lead to faster convergence when the direction of the gradient keeps changing. When in a ravine, it is difficult to find the global minimum utilising pure SGD because the direction of the gradient is almost perpendicular to the direction of the global minimum hence the algorithm will oscillate in the ravine and make small actual progress in the direction towards the global minimum. Momentum can be used to mitigate this oscillatory behavior and accelerate the SGD. This is because the optimization direction depends on both the current as well as the previous gradient directions which leads to the oscillations being counteracted between them. The technical background of the I-FGSM is introduced in Sect. 2.2. Here we try to integrate momentum into the I-FGSM. In following section, the I-FGSM with momentum for both targeted attack and untargeted attack will be introduced.

Reviewing the equations for I-FGSM:

$$x_{adv}^{t+1} = x_{adv}^{t} + \varepsilon \cdot \alpha \cdot \text{sign}\left(\nabla_x L\left(x_{adv}^{t}, y\right)\right). \tag{6}$$

In I-FGSM for each iteration the adversarial example is updated along the direction of the current gradient. In I-FGSM with momentum, for each iteration the adversarial example is updated along the direction of momentum where the momentum accumulates the direction vector for gradients in previous steps. Equations (7) and (8) are the equations for I-FGSM with momentum:

$$x_{adv}^{t+1} = x_{adv}^{t} + \alpha \cdot \text{sign}\left(g_{t+1}\right), \tag{7}$$

where:

$$g_{t+1} = \mu \cdot g_t + \frac{\nabla_x L\left(x_{adv'}^{t}, y\right)}{||\nabla_x L\left(x_{adv'}^{t}, y\right)||_p}, \tag{8}$$

where μ is a hyperparameter called decay factor that is used to adjust the influence of the earlier gradients, α is the learning rate, p denotes the order of the norm which is normally set as 1 or 2 to represent L1 norm and L2 norm. Algorithm 1 shows the algorithm for momentum based I-FGSM untargeted attack bounded by L2 norm.

Algorithm 1: Momentum based I-FGSM

   Input :
        A semantic segmentation network f with loss function L;
        Input image x;
        Ground-truth label y;
        The size of perturbation ϵ;
        Iteration number T;
        Decay factor μ;
   Output:
        An adversarial example x^* with $\|x^* - x\|_2 < \varepsilon$

1   $\alpha = \epsilon/T$;
2   $g_0 = 0$;
3   $x_0^* = x$;
4   **for** $t = 0$ *to* $T - 1$ **do**
5   Input x_t^* to f and calculate the gradient $\nabla_x J(x_t^*, y)$;
6   Update g_{t+1} by accumulating the velocity vector in the gradient direction as:
7      $g_{t+1} = \mu \cdot g_t + \dfrac{\nabla_x J(x_t^*, y)}{\left\|\nabla_x J(x_t^*, y)\right\|_2}$;
8   Update x_{t+1}^* by applying the sign gradient as
9      $x_{t+1}^* = x_t^* + \alpha \cdot \text{sign}(g_{t+1})$;
10 **end**
11 **return** $x^* = x_T^*$;

In a targeted attack, the goal is to make the model misclassify with a specific target in mind, i.e., the predicted class of input x to be a targeted class y^* in y. This kind of attack is a source target misclassification. When it comes to the result, the predicted class of the input x will be changed from the original class label to y^*.

Equations (9) and (10) are the details to targeted I-FGSM with momentum:

$$x_{adv}^{t+1} = x_{adv}^t - \alpha \cdot \text{sign}\left(g_{t+1}^*\right), \tag{9}$$

where:

$$g_{t+1}^* = \mu \cdot g_t - \frac{\nabla_x L\left(x_{adv}^t, y^*\right)}{||\nabla_x L\left(x_{adv}^t, y^*\right)||_p}, \tag{10}$$

Here Y^* is the target label. Unlike a nontargeted attack, a targeted attack tries to drive the output towards a target classification. Hence it needs to minimize the loss function. Algorithm 2 shows the algorithm for targeted I-FGSM with momentum. Compared with algorithm 1, the ground truth label y is replaced by the target label Y^* so that the adversarial example x will lead the DNN to make the prediction as target label Y^*.

Algorithm 2: Momentum based I-FGSM for targeted attack

    Input :

        A semantic segmentation network f with loss function L;

        Input image x;

        Target label y^*;

        The size of perturbation ϵ;

        Iteration number T;

        Decay factor μ;

    Output:

        An adversarial example x^* with $\|x^* - x\|_2 < \varepsilon$

1   $\alpha = \epsilon/T$;

2   $g_0 = 0$;

3   $x_0^* = x$;

4   **for** $t = 0$ *to* $T - 1$ **do**

5   Input x_t^* to f and calculate the gradient $\nabla_x J\left(x_t^*, y^*\right)$;

6   Update g_{t+1} by accumulating the velocity vector in the gradient direction as:

7      $g_{t+1}^* = \mu \cdot g_t - \dfrac{\nabla_x L\left(x_{adv}^t, y^*\right)}{\left|\nabla_x L\left(x_{adv}^t, y^*\right)\right|_2}$;

8   Update x_{t+1}^* by applying the sign gradient as

9      $x_{adv}^{t+1} = x_{adv}^t - \alpha \cdot \mathrm{sign}\left(g_{t+1}^*\right)$;

10 **end**

11 **return** $x^* = x_T^*$;

3.3 Mitigation

We studied five different image pre-processing mitigation techniques In this experiment, we added another preprocessing layer before sending the data into the semantic segmentation model. Using this layer, we evaluated five different image transformation functions, these are: JPEG compression [6,11], bit-depth reduction [21], total variance minimization [9], low pass filtering [16] and PCA denoising [3]. Figure 2 shows the workflow of the mitigation methodology.

Fig. 2. Workflow of the preprocessing defence. We tested 5 different image transformation functions in the preprocessing layer including JPEG Compression, Bit-depth Reduction, Total Variance Minimization, Low Pass Filter and PCA Denoising.

4 Experiments and Results

This section presents the setting and results for the experiments that demonstrate the performance of I-FGSM with momentum.

4.1   Experiment Settings

Dataset. In this study, we evaluate the proposed adversarial attack methodology using the Cityscapes segmentation dataset. Cityscapes [5] is a widely used segmentation dataset and entire dataset consists of street scenes from 50 different cities. In this study, we generate adversarial examples against and evaluate the performance of this validation data set.

Target Models. Dual Graph Convolutional Network (Dual-GCN) [22] uses a graph neural network to capture object correlation and improve semantic linkages. On Cityscapes, Dual-GCN achieves SOTA performance of 76% mIoU. In this exercise, Dual-GCN is used to generate adversarial examples against the target model to evaluate the performance of the adversarial attacks in white box setting. Image Cascade Network (ICNet) [23] is a real-time lightweight semantic segmentation model that guarantees speed and accuracy. It uses a cascade of image inputs to employ a cascade of feature fusion units and uses cascade label guidance during training, which can refine semantic predictions with relatively low computational cost. On Cityscapes, ICNet achieves 74% mIoU. In this study, ICNet is used as the target model in a black box setting to test the transferability of adversarial examples.

Experimental Setups. This work has been implemented using Pytorch on Python 3.7. The experiments were run using Google Colab and The Bristol Blue Crystal 4 supercomputer. Both platforms provided a single Nvidia Tesla P100 GPU with 16GB of memory as the main AI accelerator. In the experiments mean Intersection over Union per class (mIoU) is utilised as a metric to assess the performance of untargeted attacks while the class wise Intersection over Union (IoU) utilized for the assessment of targeted attacks. The adversarial examples in the experiments are generated by attacking the Dual-GCN. In a white box attack setting the adversarial examples are tested against the same model that they are generated from i.e. the Dual-GCN. In a black box attack setting the adversarial examples are evaluated against ICNet.

Hyperparameter Configuration. We evaluate the relationship between decay factor and the effects of momentum based I-FGSM. The decay factor controls the size of impact of the earlier gradients as mentioned in Sect. 3.2. With a larger decay factor the past gradients have a greater impact on the direction of change of the weight vector. When the decay factor is equal to 0 the past gradients have no impact on the update direction and the momentum based I-FGSM reverts to a normal I-FGSM. In this experiment the attack strength is set to 40 and the iteration number is set to 10. The decay factor is evaluated from 0 to 2 with an interval of 0.2. Both white box as well as black box attack scenarios are evaluated.

Number of Iterations. We compare the effect of the number of iterations between I-FGSM and momentum based I-FGSM. In this experiment the attack strength is set to 40 for both I-FGSM and momentum based I-FGSM. The decay factor for momentum based I-FGSM is set to 1.0, based on the results detailed in Sect. 4.2. Iterations ranging from 1 to 10 times are tested for both attack methodologies. White box as well as black box attack testing is done for both I-FGSM and momentum based I-FGSM to check the relationship between the number of iterations and the transferability of adversarial examples.

Attack Strength. We evaluate the effectiveness of adversarial attacks with differing attack strengths for I-FGSM as well as momentum based I-FGSM. The number of iterations for both the attacks are set to 10. Same as the previous experiment, the decay factor of the momentum based I-FGSM is set to 1.0. The attack strength is evaluated from 5 to 40 in increments of 5. Both white box as well as black box attacks are evaluated.

Target Attack. The study of targeted attacks is important for autonomous vehicles since the detection accuracy of certain classes such as "person" and "car" largely affects the safety of such ADS. Therefore, in this experiment we evaluate the performance of a targeted attack using I-FGSM and momentum based I-FGSM with varying attack strengths. Configurations for the target labels are inspired by [10]. Two sets of targeted labels are generated by modifying the original labels from the Cityscapes dataset. The details of the targeted sets are as follows:

- Set 1: The labels of classes "person", "rider", "motorcycle" and "bicycle" are replaced by the label "vegetation".
- Set 2: The labels of classes "car", "truck", "bus" and "train" are changed to "road".

Defence. We also implement and evaluate five mitigation methodologies based on different image transformation functions. All of the five mitigation methodologies are introduced in Sect. 3.3. Specifically, JPEG compression is performed with a 75% quality ratio. For bit-depth reduction input image bit depth is reduced to 5 bits. The scikit-image package [19] is used to implement the total variance minimization and low pass filter. For total variance minimization the strength is set to 2.5 and we have applied the low pass filter to each color channel with a 20% frequency cut of ratio. PCA was performed on each input image by selecting the 150 largest principal components. All the defence methods are tested against both I-FGSM based as well as momentum based I-FGSM adversarial attacks with different attack strengths in the range of 5 to 40. Testing is done in both a white box as well as a black box setting for a comprehensive analysis.

4.2 Impact of Parameters

This sub-section shows the results of the experiments detailed in Sect. 4.1.

Decay Factor. As mentioned in Sect. 3.2, the decay factor is an important hyperparameter for momentum based I-FGSM. Figure 3 shows the mIoU of the ICNet and Dual-GCN with the momentum based I-FGSM adversarial examples generated from Dual-GCN. The Y axis shows the mIoU of the model. In this experiment, smaller mIoU means better performance of the adversarial attack. X axis shows the size of the decay factor. Larger the decay factor greater the effect the previous gradients have on the updated direction of the adversarial example. For a white box attack, the performance of the attack decreases with an increase of the decay factor starting from 0.2.

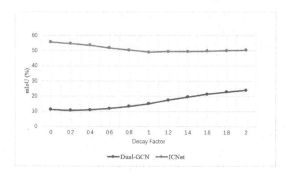

Fig. 3. The mIoU (%) of the adversarial examples generated for Dual-GCN against Dual-GCN (whitebox) and ICNet (blackbox), with a decay factor ranging from 0 to 2

These results show that the momentum based I-FGSM has the best performance when the decay factor is equal to 0.2 for a white box attack setting. However, for a black box attack, the performance of momentum based I-FGSM increases with an increase of the decay factor and archives best performance when the decay factor is equal to 1.0. Subsequently the performance slowly decreases with an increase in the decay factor. When the decay factor is equal to 1.0, the weight update for each iteration is simply represented by the sum of all prior gradients.

Number of Iteration. The number of iterations influences the performance of iterative adversarial attacks. Here are the results of the experiments that study the effect of the number of iterations against momentum based I-FGSM and I-FGSM. Figure 4(a) shows the result for a white box attack while Fig. 4(b) shows the result for a black box attack. In these two figures the Y axis shows the mIoU of the model and X axis shows the number of iterations.

Momentum based I-FGSM converged at around 4 iterations while I-FGSM shows no evidence of convergence even at 10 iterations. When the number of iterations is 10, the I-FGSM has a 4% reduction in the mIoU when compared with the momentum based I-FGSM. The I-FGSM has a constant learning rate. The reason I-FGSM has difficulty converging may be due to the direction of the update being completely dependent on the current gradient, but the gradient

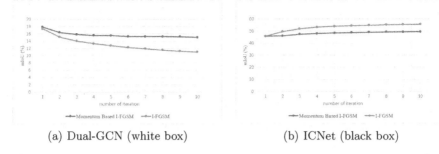

(a) Dual-GCN (white box)   (b) ICNet (black box)

Fig. 4. The mIoU (%) of the adversarial examples generated for Dual-GCN with momentum based I-FGSM and I-FGSM against (a): Dual-GCN (white box) (b): ICNet (black box), with the number of iterations ranging from 1 to 10.

will become exceedingly small when approaching the optimal value and because of the constant learning rate, the I-FGSM will slow down, and might even fall into a local optimum. From the result it is obvious that I-FGSM shows better performance in a white box attack setting which proves that I-FGSM can very easily overfit a specific model. Figure 4(b) shows that the momentum based I-FGSM outperformed the I-FGSM in a black box attack setting. The momentum based I-FGSM reduces the mIoU of the model by 5% compared to the I-FGSM when the number of iterations equals 10. This also proves that the adversarial examples generated from I-FGSM can easily overfit with the white box model and have poor transferability.

Attack Strength. We then study the relationship between the attack strength of adversarial examples and the accuracy of the semantic segmentation models. Figure 5(a) shows the results of attacking Dual-GCN by Momentum based I-FGSM and I-FGSM. Here the Y axis is the mIoU of the model and the X axis is the attack strength. The lines for momentum based I-FGSM and I-FGSM almost overlap when the attack strength is small in a white box setting and the I-FGSM is shown to have an exceedingly small advantage when the attack strength is larger than 35. Both the momentum based I-FGSM and I-FGSM show good performance in a black box setting and the mIoU of the semantic segmentation model decreases linearly with the strength of the attack.

Figure 5(b) shows the results for a black box setting. With an increase in the attack strength, the momentum based I-FGSM leads to a faster decrease of the mIoU of the semantic segmentation model compared with I-FGSM. When the attack strength is 40 the momentum based I-FGSM leads to a 6% greater decrease in mIoU compared with the original I-FGSM. In a black box attack, the momentum based I-FGSM can reach the required effect with a smaller attack strength which means it would be more difficult to detect such an attack manually.

Targeted Attack. In this section, we demonstrate the results of the targeted adversarial attack. As introduced in Sect. 4.1. We designed two sets of target labels. Figure 6 shows two examples of momentum based I-FGSM targeted

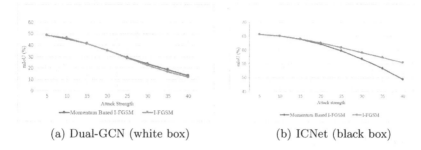

(a) Dual-GCN (white box)   (b) ICNet (black box)

Fig. 5. The mIoU (%) of the adversarial examples generated for Dual-GCN with momentum based I-FGSM and I-FGSM against (a): Dual-GCN (white box) (b): ICNet (black box), with the attack strength ranging from 5 to 40.

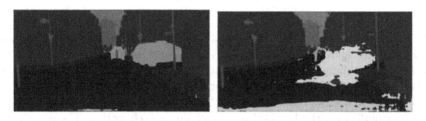

Fig. 6. Two examples for targeted momentum based I-FGSM: The left image shows an example from target label set 1 and where right image is from target label set 2.

attack. the left image shows an example from target label set 1 and the right image shows an example from target label set 2. In the image on the left the model cannot classify the pixels belonging to the class "person" correctly and in the right image the network cannot correctly classify the pixels in proximity to the car.

I: Targeted Attack with White-Box Setting. Table 1 shows the results of a targeted adversarial attack with label set 1 and Table 2 shows the results of label set 2. The details of the label set 1 and 2 are shown in Sect. 4.1. The results shows that both momentum based I-FGSM and I-FGSM show good performance in a white box attack. Both adversarial attack methods can reduce the targeted categories IoU to 0 with a small attack magnitude. It is worth noting that the mIoU increases as the attack magnitude increases. A similar observation is made with the untargeted attack, I-FGSM shows better performance with the same attack magnitude. Adversarial examples generated from I-FGSM lead to a higher mIoU while keeping the IoU of targeted classes at 0. In other words, the adversarial examples generated by I-FGSM cause less damage to the other classes while maintaining 100% attack success rate for targeted classes.

Table 1. Black box targeted attacks set 1: misclassified person, rider, motorcycle, and bicycle into the label of vegetation

Attack method	Attack strength	mIoU	Categories IoU			
			Person	Rider	Motorcycle	Bicycle
Momentum based I-FGSM	40	70.770	0	0	0	0
Momentum based I-FGSM	5	62.677	0	0	0	0
I-FGSM	40	74.028	0	0	0	0
I-FGSM	5	62.864	0	0	0	0
No attack	0	76.113	80.952	60.235	62.777	76.125

Table 2. White box targeted attacks set 2: misclassified car, truck, bus, and train into the label of road

Attack method	Attack strength	mIoU	Categories IoU			
			Car	Truck	Bus	Train
Momentum based I-FGSM	40	73.600	0	0	0	0
Momentum based I-FGSM	5	49.882	0	0	0	0
I-FGSM	40	71.520	0	0	0	0
I-FGSM	5	59.203	0	0	0	0
No attack	0	76.113	94.178	74.254	83.002	67.480

II: Targeted Attack with Black-box Setting. Table 3 shows the results of a targeted adversarial attack with label set 1 and Table 4 shows the results of label set 2 in a black box setting. The momentum based I-FGSM performs better than I-FGSM in a black box attack. The momentum based I-FGSM significantly reduces the IoU for all the targeted classes with the same attack strength when compared with I-FGSM. This proves that the addition of momentum helps to increase the transferability of adversarial examples. From Table 3, it can be observed that the effect of the attack varies for the various categories. The experimental results do not clearly show a reason for such a difference.

Table 3. Black box targeted attacks set 1: misclassified person, rider, motorcycle, and bicycle into the label of vegetation

Attack method	Attack strength	mIoU	Categories IoU			
			Person	Rider	Motorcycle	Bicycle
Momentum based I-FGSM	40	73.520	69.369	41.148	36.341	65.658
Momentum based I-FGSM	5	65.966	74.501	53.059	47.163	71.101
I-FGSM	40	68.970	73.332	49.496	43.461	70.015
I-FGSM	5	65.959	74.500	53.061	47.165	71.010
No attack	0	74.068	78.707	57.704	58.407	74.274

Table 4. Black box targeted attacks set 2: misclassified car, truck, bus, and train into the label of road

Attack method	Attack strength	mIoU	Categories IoU			
			Car	Truck	Bus	Train
Momentum based I-FGSM	40	67.916	88.322	36.989	53.580	49.906
Momentum based I-FGSM	5	65.934	93.037	49.303	62.108	56.909
I-FGSM	40	68.537	92.095	43.962	58.154	51.463
I-FGSM	5	65.924	93.037	49.260	62.064	56.909
No attack	0	74.068	94.159	76.607	81.329	60.075

4.3 Defence

This sub-section details the results for the various mitigation techniques when used against adversarial attacks. The results are separated into white box and black box scenarios. For both white box and black box setting the effect of the five defence methodologies against the momentum based I-FGSM and I-FGSM are tested at attack strengths ranging from 5 to 40. The impact of the defence methodologies on the model with a clean input are shown in Table 5.

Table 5. mIoU of defence methods on Dual-GCN model with clean input

Defence	No Defence	JPEG	Low Pass Filter	Bit-depth Reduction	TVM	PCA
mIoU (%)	76.113	65.911	70.990	50.095	59.487	65.989

It is important to note that all of the defensive methodologies have a negative impact on the accuracy of the model. As it can be observed, the Bit-depth Reduction and PCA Denoising yield the smallest decrease in the mIoU on clean inputs, followed by JPEG. Low-pass filtering and Total Variance Minimization lead to a more significant decrease in the performance of the semantic segmentation model. The negative impact of these defensive methodologies may have a worse effect on the network accuracy compared to adversarial attacks of a smaller intensity.

I: Defence against White-box Attack Fig. 7 shows the performance of the various defence methodologies performance in a white box setting. Figure 7(a) shows the effectiveness of the 5 defence methodologies against an I-FGSM attack and fig.7(b) shows the results of the defence methodologies against a momentum based I-FGSM attack. Here the Y axis is the mIoU of the model and the X axis is the attack strength.

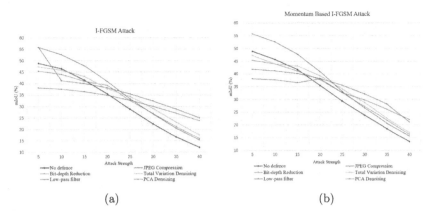

Fig. 7. The mIoU (%) of Dual-GCN with defence methods against (a): I-FGSM attack and (b): momentum based I-FGSM attack (white box setting).

In a white box setting the five defence methodologies show a similar effect when utilised against momentum based I-FGSM and I-FGSM. The low pass filter is effective at all attack magnitudes and increases the accuracy of the model in both the adversarial attack scenarios. The remaining four defence methodologies do not perform very well when the intensity of the attack is low. However, JPEG compression and PCA denoising show better performance compared to the other three defence methods as the strength of the attack increases.

As mentioned above, JPEG compression shows the best defensive performance under high intensity adversarial attacks and low pass filtering shows the best performance among the five defences against adversarial attacks of a low intensity. Both the JPEG compression and the low pass filtering remove the high frequency information from the input image. Therefore, it is reasonable to believe that the perturbation produced by the adversarial attack contain high frequency components.

In [16] and [9], the results show that these basis transformation functions are more effective when used against adversarial attacks in a classification task. This may be due to the classification networks being more sensitive to adversarial attacks and having a larger tolerance for image transformations. For the dataset used in [16] and [9], each image contains only one object so the image transformation functions such as blurring have a lesser effect on the accuracy of the classification models compared to this experiment.

II: Defence Against Black-Box Attack. Figure 8 shows the performance of the various defence methodologies in a black box setting. Figure 8(a) is the results of five defence methods against I-FGSM attack and Fig. 8(b) shows the results of defence methodologies against a momentum based I-FGSM attack.

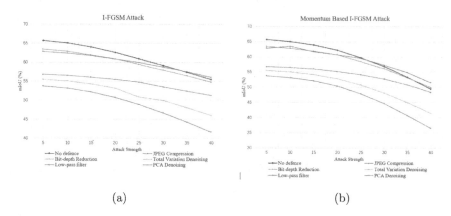

Fig. 8. The mIoU (%) of ICNet with defence methods against (a): I-FGSM attack and (b): momentum based I-FGSM attack (black box setting).

Among the five defence methodologies, JPEG compression becomes effective only when the attack strength is greater than 35 for I-FGSM and greater than 30 for momentum based I-FGSM. The bit depth reduction is effective for momentum based I-FGSM when the attack strength reaches 40. PCA denoising, total variation denoising and PCA denoising do not perform well against any of the attacks at any given strength.

None of the tested defence methodologies are effective when used against small perturbations in this setting. This is consistent with the result of basis transformation defences when used against classification in [16]. Since the adversarial examples with a small attack strength have a limited impact on the performance of the network in a black box setting, the various image pre-processing methodologies lead to negative impacts on the accuracy of the network which are comparable to adversarial perturbations. Table 6 Shows the impact of the 5 image pre-processing methodologies on the ICNet network with a clean input. The lowpass filter denoising and total variance denoising lead to a significant reduction in the accuracy of the network. This largely impacts the effectiveness of these two defensive methodologies to eliminate the adversarial perturbation and mitigate the adversarial attack.

Table 6. mIoU of defence methods on ICNet model with clean input

Defence	No defence	JPEG	Low pass filter	Bit-depth reduction	TVM	PCA
mIoU (%)	74.068	69.499	71.232	54.318	54.879	67.170

4.4 Discussions

The Effectiveness of Adversarial Attacks on Scene Segmentation. The experiment results show that adversarial attacks can significantly decrease the performance of semantic segmentation models based on DNN. In a white box setting, the mIoU of SOTA semantic segmentation models can easily drop from around 75% to about 12% with the adversarial examples generated from early adversarial attack methods. The result from a targeted attack is also not optimistic. Adversarial attacks can greatly decrease the models' accuracy for certain classes while maintaining a high mIoU. This means such targeted attacks are more difficult to detect since the model can still make a correct prediction for the rest of the classes and function normally. In autonomous vehicles, this deserves more attention since the accuracy for certain classes such as pedestrians and traffic lights are naturally more important than the accuracy for some other classes and hence average accuracy is not a good indicator of reliability. In a black box setting, although the semantic segmentation model shows better resistance to adversarial attacks, the adversarial examples still lead to about 25% decrease in the mIoU. This shows that the adversarial examples are effective against different models.

Momentum Based I-FGSM Shows Better Transferability. The results show that the idea of momentum improves the transferability of I-FGSM in both targeted as well as untargeted attacks which compensates for the drawbacks of I-FGSM. The momentum based I-FGSM outperforms the original I-FGSM in a black box setting and has similar performance in a white-box settings. The transferability of adversarial examples is based on the fact that different DNNs learn through similar decision boundaries [7]. The original I-FGSM adjusts the adversarial examples by relying solely on the current gradient of the iteration which has a high probability of falling into suboptimal local maximas. As a result, the adversarial noise only interferes with a local decision boundary and the adversarial examples have extremely poor transferability. The momentum based I-FGSM solves this problem by changing the direction of adversarial examples utilizing past gradients as well as the current gradient into a single gradient which can level out the variations in the weight change direction and hence help the adversarial examples in finding the global maxima. Therefore, the adversarial examples generated by momentum based I-FGSM have better transferability.

The Performance of Defence Methods. In a black box setting all of these image transformation methods show relatively poor effectiveness when used against adversarial attacks with a small attack strength in semantic segmentation tasks. This is in comparison to their performance in image classification tasks detailed in prior research. Transformations such as low pass filter denoising and total variance denoising lead to a large decrease in the accuracy of the semantic segmentation model itself. The image transformation functions tested in this study all have negative impacts on the quality of the images to some extent. For example, the JPEG compression is a lossy compression that discards some of the high frequency components of the image. This quality loss caused by the transformation function leads to a greater impact on the model accuracy compared to the impact of adversarial examples in the context of black box testing.

Related Works: In [25], the authors evaluated the adversarial attack against semantic segmentation models. Unlike this work that uses the visual data collected from camera, [25] the focus was on the data from LiDAR (Light Detection and Ranging) sensors. They showed that the LiDAR semantic segmentation models used in ADS are also vulnerable to adversarial attacks. Combined with this work, the adversarial attack could still be a security threat to ADS that utilise different sensors since semantic segmentation models utilising various types of data are vulnerable to adversarial attacks. In [24] authors designed a pre-processing model that exploits the invariant features. The pre-processing model can disentangle the invariant features that represent sematic classification informations from adversarial noise and then restore the examples without adversarial perturbation by utilizing these invariant features. The authors declared that this defence methodology presents superior effectiveness when used against previously unseen adversarial attacks so it is effective when used against a black box attack. However, like most of the prior studies, this study focused on the image classification models so the effectiveness of this mitigating method in semantic segmentation scenario is uncertain.

Recently many researches are also focusing on using model-specific strategies to mitigate adversarial attacks. These strategies usually change the architecture or the training procedures of the DNN and utilise the learning algorithms or regularization method to enforce features such as invariance and smoothness [17]. [2] focused on utilizing adversarial training and defensive distillation to increase the robustness of traffic sign classification models. The results showed that the combination of these two defence techniques can achieve higher accuracy when used against different kinds of adversarial attacks in traffic sign classification tasks.

5   Conclusion

In this study, we focused on the adversarial attack and its mitigations in semantic segmentation tasks. We first applied the I-FGSM adversarial attack methodology to the task of semantic segmentation. Next, in order to enhance the transferability of the adversarial examples, we integrated the idea of momentum into the original I-FGSM algorithm. Extensive experiments were conducted to verify the efficacy of this momentum based I-FGSM technique. The results showed that momentum based I-FGSM has similar performance when compared to the original I-FGSM in both targeted as well as untargeted attack in a white box settings and outperformed the same in black box settings. From a mitigation standpoint, we focused on image pre-processing, and applied and tested five different image transformation functions. The results of the experiments showed that Low pass filtering and JPEG compression have superior performance when used against adversarial attacks in a white box setting. However, all five transformation methods showed limited performance when used against adversarial attacks in a black box setting. In future work, we want to investigate the feasibility of combining pre-processing defence methodologies with adversarial training to improve the robustness of AV systems.

Acknowledgment. This project is supported by the National Research Foundation, Singapore and National University of Singapore through its National Satellite of Excellence in Trustworthy Software Systems (NSOE-TSS) office under the Trustworthy Computing for Secure Smart Nation Grant (TCSSNG) award no. NSOE-TSS2020-01. This research was supported by grants from NVIDIA and utilised NVIDIA Quadro RTX 6000 GPUs.

References

1. Arnab, A., Miksik, O., Torr, P.H.: On the robustness of semantic segmentation models to adversarial attacks. In: Proceedings of the IEEE Conference on Computer Vision and Pattern Recognition, pp. 888–897 (2018)
2. Aung, A.M., Fadila, Y., Gondokaryono, R., Gonzalez, L.: Building robust deep neural networks for road sign detection. arXiv preprint arXiv:1712.09327 (2017)
3. Bhagoji, A.N., Cullina, D., Sitawarin, C., Mittal, P.: Enhancing robustness of machine learning systems via data transformations. In: 2018 52nd Annual Conference on Information Sciences and Systems (CISS). pp. 1–5. IEEE (2018)
4. Carlini, N., Wagner, D.: Towards evaluating the robustness of neural networks. In: 2017 IEEE Symposium on Security and Privacy (SP), pp. 39–57. IEEE (2017)
5. Cordts, M., et al.: The cityscapes dataset for semantic urban scene understanding. In: Proceedings of the IEEE Conference on Computer Vision and Pattern Recognition, pp. 3213–3223 (2016)
6. Das, N., et al.: Keeping the bad guys out: protecting and vaccinating deep learning with jpeg compression. arXiv preprint arXiv:1705.02900 (2017)
7. Dong, Y., et al.: Boosting adversarial attacks with momentum. In: Proceedings of the IEEE Conference on Computer Vision and Pattern Recognition, pp. 9185–9193 (2018)
8. Goodfellow, I.J., Shlens, J., Szegedy, C.: Explaining and harnessing adversarial examples. arXiv preprint arXiv:1412.6572 (2014)
9. Guo, C., Rana, M., Cisse, M., Van Der Maaten, L.: Countering adversarial images using input transformations. arXiv preprint arXiv:1711.00117 (2017)
10. Kang, X., Song, B., Du, X., Guizani, M.: Adversarial attacks for image segmentation on multiple lightweight models. IEEE Access **8**, 31359–31370 (2020)
11. Kurakin, A., Goodfellow, I., Bengio, S.: Adversarial machine learning at scale. arXiv preprint arXiv:1611.01236 (2016)
12. Kurakin, A., Goodfellow, I., Bengio, S., et al.: Adversarial examples in the physical world (2016)
13. Papernot, N., McDaniel, P., Jha, S., Fredrikson, M., Celik, Z.B., Swami, A.: The limitations of deep learning in adversarial settings. In: 2016 IEEE European symposium on security and privacy (EuroS&P), pp. 372–387. IEEE (2016)
14. Pham, M., Xiong, K.: A survey on security attacks and defense techniques for connected and autonomous vehicles. Comput. Secur. **109**, 102269 (2021)
15. Qian, N.: On the momentum term in gradient descent learning algorithms. Neural Netw. **12**(1), 145–151 (1999)
16. Shaham, U., et al.: Defending against adversarial images using basis functions transformations. arXiv preprint arXiv:1803.10840 (2018)
17. Shaham, U., Yamada, Y., Negahban, S.: Understanding adversarial training: Increasing local stability of neural nets through robust optimization. arXiv (2015)
18. Szegedy, C., et al.: Intriguing properties of neural networks. arXiv (2013)

19. Van der Walt, S., et al.: scikit-image: image processing in python. PeerJ **2**, e453 (2014)
20. Xie, C., Wang, J., Zhang, Z., Zhou, Y., Xie, L., Yuille, A.: Adversarial examples for semantic segmentation and object detection. In: Proceedings of the IEEE international conference on computer vision. pp. 1369–1378 (2017)
21. Xu, W., Evans, D., Qi, Y.: Feature squeezing: Detecting adversarial examples in deep neural networks. arXiv preprint arXiv:1704.01155 (2017)
22. Zhang, L., Li, X., Arnab, A., Yang, K., Tong, Y., Torr, P.H.: Dual graph convolutional network for semantic segmentation. arXiv preprint arXiv:1909.06121 (2019)
23. Zhao, H., Qi, X., Shen, X., Shi, J., Jia, J.: ICNet for real-time semantic segmentation on high-resolution images. In: Ferrari, V., Hebert, M., Sminchisescu, C., Weiss, Y. (eds.) ECCV 2018. LNCS, vol. 11207, pp. 418–434. Springer, Cham (2018). https://doi.org/10.1007/978-3-030-01219-9_25
24. Zhou, D., Liu, T., Han, B., Wang, N., Peng, C., Gao, X.: Towards defending against adversarial examples via attack-invariant features. In: International Conference on Machine Learning, pp. 12835–12845. PMLR (2021)
25. Zhu, Y., Miao, C., Hajiaghajani, F., Huai, M., Su, L., Qiao, C.: Adversarial attacks against lidar semantic segmentation in autonomous driving. In: Proceedings of the 19th ACM Conference on Embedded Networked Sensor Systems, pp. 329–342 (2021)

Threat Sensitive Networking: On the Security of IEEE 802.1CB and (un)Effectiveness of Existing Security Solutions

Adriaan de Vos[1]([⊠])[iD], Alessandro Brighente[2][iD], and Mauro Conti[1,2][iD]

[1] Delft University of Technology, Delft, The Netherlands
info@adriaandevos.nl, m.conti@tudelft.nl
[2] University of Padua, Padua, Italy
{alessandro.brighente,mauro.conti}@unipd.it

Abstract. IEEE 802.1CB provides a standard for reliable packet delivery within Time-Sensitive Networking (TSN). As this standard is envisioned to be used in mission-critical networks in the near future, it has to be protected against security threats. The integrity of the network communication should be the biggest focus as guaranteed delivery is essential. However, IEEE 802.1CB does not come with security guarantees. Indeed, as we show in this paper, an attacker may be able to exploit different threat vectors to impair the correctness of communication, impacting on the safety of users. Due to TSN strict delay and reliability requirements, classical security solutions can not be easily applied without significant efforts. Therefore, researchers proposed multiple solutions to guarantee secure communication. However, the current state-of-the-art is not able to guarantee both security and timing guarantees.

In this paper, we provide a detailed analysis of the security of IEEE 802.1CB exploiting the STRIDE methodology. Compared to the existing state-of-the art on the subject, we provide a deeper analysis of the possible threats and their effect. We then analyze available solutions for security in IEEE 802.1CB, and compare their performance in terms of time, reliability, and security guarantees. Based on our analysis, we show that, although there exist promising solutions trying to provide security to 802.1CB, there is still a gap to be filled both in terms of security and latency guarantees.

Keywords: IEEE 802.1CB · Time-Sensitive Networking (TSN) · Replication and Elimination for Reliability (FRER) · Ethernet · Security

1 Introduction

Traditional networking solutions can not be used for mission-critical applications such as automotive, avionics, and industrial networks. Indeed, traditional

S. Katsikas et al. (Eds.): ESORICS 2022 Workshops, LNCS 13785, pp. 67–80, 2023.
https://doi.org/10.1007/978-3-031-25460-4_4

networks were not designed to deliver real-time and ultra-reliable communication. In addition, many existing network solutions are incompatible with each other, a factor that complicates the development and deployment of real-time networks. As a response to these problems, the IEEE has published the specification of a new networking standard called Time-Sensitive Networking (TSN) [1]. This standard extends the Ethernet data link layer to ensure that time- and safety-critical traffic achieves an extremely low packet loss rate and a finite, low, and stable end-to-end latency. Due to this, TSN is the prominent standard to be implemented in modern Cyber-Physical Systems (CPS). These systems cover the edge between the digital and the real world and include industrial applications such as flood defence, smart grids, transportation networks, automotive vehicles, etc. With these systems, insufficient security could cause serious adverse effects as people trust their lives to the correct working of these systems. In recent years CPS are becoming more connected to the internet [2] and are increasingly often the target of malicious actors [3–6], so they need to be secured.

One specific standard within TSN is IEEE 802.1CB [7]. This standard focuses on providing increased redundancy to network communications. This standard is also called Frame Replication and Elimination for Reliability (FRER), and it is often combined with IEEE 802.1Qca to configure multiple disjoint paths within a network. This technique increases frame delivery reliability by using sequence numbering and sending duplicate frames over disjoint paths within IEEE 802.1CB compatible switches and endpoints. These replicated frames protect against hard and soft errors of the underlying links and nodes. Finally, these duplicate frames need to be detected and eliminated at their destination as the standard defines that only the first arrived frame should propagate further. This functionality, however, introduces a security issue which we explore further throughout the paper, as an attacker could modify or delay frames to spoof the sequence numbers, tamper with the payload, or execute Denial of Service (DoS) attacks. These attacks impact the integrity and availability of the network communications and could therefore result in acting upon incorrect data, or involve serious consequences to the performance of critical infrastructure.

In this paper, we first provide an in-depth analysis of the security of IEEE 802.1CB. Although other researchers analyzed TSN security at a high level, there are no contributions providing a detailed analysis of the security of IEEE 802.1CB. To this aim, we exploit the widely accepted STRIDE methodology [15] to identify all the possible threats and their effect on IEEE 802.1CB. We then analyze and compare existing state-of-the-art security solutions for IEEE 802.1CB. We compare these solutions in terms of their capability in mitigating the attacks identified via our analysis and in terms of their time requirements and delay guarantees. Via our analysis, we show that, although some solutions propose promising approaches, there is no available solution able to guarantee full security to IEEE 802.1CB, nor is there a solution able to provide jitter guarantees (which is among the requirements of IEEE 802.1CB).

The rest of the paper is organized as follows. Section 2 provides a summary of the Time-Sensitive Networking standard and short descriptions of the available features, Sect. 3 dives into the specifics of IEEE 802.1CB, Sect. 4 describes the possible security risks and their effects, Sect. 5 summarizes existing solutions that try solving these security risks, Sect. 6 gives an overview of these solutions, and Sect. 7 discusses the related work. Finally, the conclusions are presented in Sect. 8.

2   Time-Sensitive Networking

The IEEE 802.1 Time-Sensitive Networking (TSN) standard extends the IEEE 802.1 Audio Video Bridging (AVB) standards released in 2011. These AVB standards provide some extended features for IEEE 802.1 networks in regards to low-latency traffic flows, bandwidth reservation, and synchronization [8]. While these features improved the feasibility of using it for mission-critical applications, it was not extensive enough to support a wide variety of applications as it only focused on audio and video streams. While modern automotive, avionics, and industrial networks might transfer these kinds of streams, they also require other types of streams. Moreover, these applications require a wide variety of sensors and actuators that need reliable real-time communication to ensure good operation. For this, there has been quite some development in the last decade by different companies to create their proprietary network solutions [9]. However, these solutions are not compatible with each other. Therefore, IEEE released the TSN standard to ensure that all components of different networks can efficiently work together while achieving the requirements for such mission-critical applications.

For this section, we take IEEE 802.1Q-2018 [10] as the central reference implementation and describe the TSN related features released within. This central reference document bundles the latest features and updates once every 3 to 6 years. The standard focuses on providing a deterministic service with the following Key Performance Indicators (KPI) [11], namely guaranteed delivery with bounded latency, low delay variation (jitter), and low packet loss.

For guaranteed delivery with bounded latency, the protocol makes sure that some capacity is reserved for specific data streams to prevent congestion throughout the network. The bounded latency provides a guarantee about the worst-case delay for packet delivery. The low delay variation reduces the likelihood that delivered packets arrive in an incorrect order. Furthermore, the low packet loss reduces the likelihood that no message is received at all. Combining these KPIs provides a very reliable and deterministic network that would fit well for mission-critical systems.

The IEEE 802.1Q-2018 standard focuses on delivering wired network communication in a network of switches/bridges and some end devices that are each connected to this network through separate cables. These end devices could be workstations, sensors, actuators, or other devices requiring network communication. The basic functionality of this standard is to provide Quality of Service (QoS) and virtual Local Area Networks (LANs) to an Ethernet network. In addition, this standard contains many optional features, of which only a subset has to be implemented based on the application's requirements for network communication. As each feature focuses on a different improvement, we can divide them into the following categories according to [11].

Timing and Synchronization ensures that all components within the network (both the bridge and end-devices) have synchronized clocks. This synchronization is necessary for mission-critical systems such as fully automatic driving as they require a common notion of time for sensor fusion.

Bounded Low latency ensures configuration within the network to reserve capacity for certain types of messages or allow time-critical messages to interrupt non-time-critical messages. This traffic shaping ensures minimal delay for critical messages within the network, which is needed for mission-critical systems to quickly act upon their received sensors.

Resource Management provides algorithms and configuration options to divide the available network bandwidth into reserved streams by establishing and enforcing bandwidth contracts between network components. These reservations ensure a deterministic network where no packet loss due to congestion occurs as each application has a maximum throughput they need to adhere to.

High-Reliability provides methods to improve the reliability of packet delivery within the network by using Quality Of Service (QoS), non-shortest network paths, or redundant packet transmission. As mission-critical systems often have real-time applications, they cannot tolerate delays due to re-transmissions of lost frames.

3   IEEE 802.1CB

In this section, we delve deeper into the High-Reliability category of the TSN standards and specifically into 802.1CB-2017 Frame Replication and Elimination for Reliability (FRER). This standard specifies procedures and protocols for network components that provide identification and replication of packets for redundant transmission and identification/elimination of duplicate packets. However, it does not describe how these disjoint paths should be created and configured. This feature provides an increased probability that a given packet will be delivered. However, it is highly suggested to use it in cooperation with other means to increase the probability of correct delivery further. Research has shown that while this standard does a great job in improving the reliability, there are still some difficult challenges that have to be resolved to increase the reliability of this feature even further [7,12]. We give a short description of the various functions and explain the inner workings below.

Frame Replication provides the generation of packet sequence numbers for a given stream and encoding it in each packet. This sequence generation function adds an IEEE 802.1CB specific header to provide packet identification. This header allows other network components to detect duplicate packets. After adding the sequence number to a packet, the packet propagates through multiple network paths and, if configured, multiple streams on the same path.

Frame Elimination provides the elimination of duplicate packets. It keeps track of the received sequence numbers and only relays the first packet for each received sequence number. This functionality ensures that no loops or exact duplicates will be relayed and delivered to the next component along the path.

After elimination, each network component can replicate the packet again on separate paths if configured.

Latent Error Detection provides a detection mechanism for an unexpected number of packets either due to network failure, invalid network configuration, or an attacker. This detection assumes that the number of discarded packets per sequence number should always stay the same if everything works well. A configurable threshold ensures that there is some leeway for naturally occurring packet loss, which is very rare [13], but should not cause an alarm when this event occurs. However, if it detects that a significantly lower number of packets is received suddenly, it raises an alarm to indicate that a network link has gone down. In contrast, if it detects a significantly higher number of packets, there is a possibility that an attacker is spoofing packets.

Implementation of this IEEE 802.1CB standard can be gradually rolled out within a network as it is backwards compatible with non-supporting systems. Different network configurations provide different guarantees and loss rates depending on their support for this standard and the actual topology [14]. For example, an existing ring topology network with the end devices connected to a ring of switches can already upgrade reliability by only updating the switches. This partial upgrade will ensure that the message will go both clockwise and counterclockwise, resulting in a higher resilience against link failure (hard error). Another example is if we only update the end devices in this topology. This upgrade will cause the packets to be sent twice through the same route and eliminated at the end device. While this does not protect against link failure, it does protect against soft errors such as a CRC mismatch. Partially upgrading a combination of switches and devices will already result in a much more reliable delivery, even if not all devices support this feature. See Fig. 1 for a graphical overview of the variations.

4 Possible Security Risks

In this section, we use the threat modelling framework STRIDE [15] to analyse the possible security attacks and effects on IEEE 802.1CB. This framework covers Spoofing, Tampering, Repudiation, Information disclosure, Denial of service, and Elevation of privilege threats against system components. As IEEE 802.1CB has no built-in security, the protection against possible threats is non-existent. For example, there is no mitigation against the misuse of the elimination function and the latent error detection function. Therefore, an adversary can target the network communication to disrupt it. In addition, an incorrect network configuration could also prevent it from delivering its service. We describe these threats in the following sections.

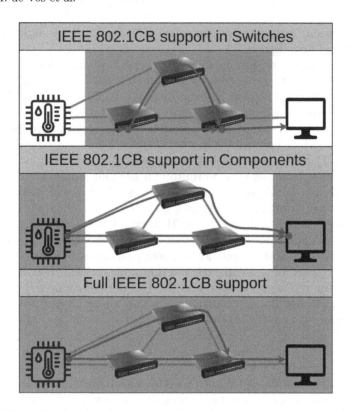

Fig. 1. Different implementation configurations showing support for seamless redundancy by enabling 802.1CB

4.1 Sequence Numbering

As the elimination of packets is done based on the sequence number, changes to this value could have adverse effects on the reliability. For the above mentioned attacks, we focus on the sequence number part of the FRER header as shown in Fig. 2.

If an attacker can intercept packets to modify them, or if the attacker can create new packets within the network, the following attacks are feasible.

- The attacker uses **spoofing** to create new packets within the network with existing sequence numbers that arrive earlier than the correct packets. This attack causes the elimination function to drop the original packets resulting in a **denial of service**.
- The attacker uses **spoofing** to create new packets within the network with existing sequence numbers that arrive later than the correct packets. This attack causes the Latent Error Detection function to trigger a warning signal as too many packets are delivered, resulting in the mission-critical system taking unnecessary precaution measures. In addition, if the network has a

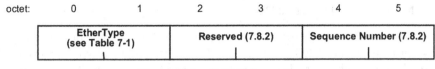

Fig. 2. IEEE 802.1CB header format (from [17])

failure, the attacker can spoof enough packets so that the latent error detection function does not notice this, and it generates no warning signal, creating the illusion that the system is reliable.

- The attacker uses **tampering** by modifying existing packets to have random sequence numbers. This attack causes unexpected packets to drop and delivery of out-of-order packets. This effect will result in a **denial of service**.
- The attacker uses **tampering** by modifying the sequence number of replicate packets. This attack causes the same packet to arrive multiple times at the end destination without a way of detecting it. An adversary can use this to perform a replay attack.

4.2 Path Configuration

As some parts of the network are configurable during run-time, specific protocols enable the configuration of redundant paths and streams that could be abused. While this is not caused by IEEE 802.1CB as it does not provide this configuration, it affects the performance and reliability. These attack threats are described as follows.

- The attacker changes the network configuration to add multiple paths of redundant streams on the same link or multiple redundant streams on different links. This attack causes extra bandwidth usage and possibly higher latency due to this increased computing and throughput that is now required. Additionally, this attack will cause degradation in QoS and could lead to a **denial of service**.
- The attacker changes the network configuration to add intersecting paths. All packets will now go through switches that have received packets with the same sequence number earlier. These packets will be dropped and never delivered to the destination. This attack will result in a **denial of service**.

5 Existing Solutions

All the above mentioned attacks are widely known in the general networking community, and therefore there exist solutions to mitigate them. While not all of these solutions are designed explicitly for TSN, as this is a very recent technology, they are all designed for automotive networks and other related applications. In this section, we describe how these solutions work and analyze their effects on the KPIs required for TSN.

5.1   MACsec - 802.1AE-2018

MACsec is an IEEE standard that works at the medium access control layer. It works just below the IEEE 802.1CB standard as they both provide functionality to the data link layer. There has been research on the specific application of this standard to automotive Ethernet backbones and their performance and reliability [18]. Although this solution does not explicitly describe the security improvements of IEEE 802.1CB, it does ensure the confidentiality, integrity and authenticity of data within Ethernet frames resulting in mitigation of most attack threats described above. It replaces the existing Ethernet frames and encapsulates them into MACsec-compliant ones. The content is then encrypted and decrypted with symmetric keys by using AES-GCM. This solution depends on IEEE 802.1X for discovering network nodes and configuring and distributing the encryption keys and cryptographic parameters.

Ethernet frames consist of the destination address, source address and user data. MACsec makes the three following modifications to Ethernet frames.

- It adds a **SECTag** between the source address and the user data, which provides recognition of the MACsec frame and contains security information such as packet numbering, key length, and replay protection data. This section is 8 to 16 bytes long.
- If the packet requires confidentiality, the user data is optionally encrypted. The length of this section will be equally long as the original section.
- After the user data, it adds a 16 bytes long section for the Integrity Check Value. The **ICV** cover the integrity of the destination and source addresses and the integrity of the user data.

In [18], the authors provide a detailed descriptions of the actual hardware implementations and some design choices they have made regarding the automotive network environment. They also include performance tests of their implementation and conclude that their latency is smaller than 350 nanoseconds. This added latency is due to the increased packet size and the required calculations. Finally, they conclude that for a car driving 100 km/h, the physical delay will be less than a millimetre. Therefore this can even be used in safety-related systems such as a braking system.

5.2   MACsec - TSN-MIC

Another take at implementing MACsec for time-sensitive networking is called TSN-MIC [19]. This solution differs from other MAC-layer security schemes, such as the 802.1AE solution described in the previous section, as it only adds checking of the message integrity and no encryption of the payload data. Authors of [19] have first researched the performance of various lightweight cryptography solutions available. They decided on using Chaskey-12 as this is among the fastest algorithms available and is 7 to 15 times faster than AES-CMAC. In addition, this lightweight cryptography is provably secure, patent-free, and provides better key agility than using a key schedule. For the configuration of encryption keys, they have decided on using a modified version of IEC 11770 over IEEE 802.1X. They conclude that their method is more efficient than IEEE 802.1X and more secure than IEC 11770.

This solution works just below the data link layer, and it would require no changes to the IEEE 801.1CB layer. They have implemented their solution and simulated the network to gain insight into the performance. The absolute added delay would be between 200 and 800 microseconds depending on the Ethernet frame size. This increase would cause a 35% delay to short frames and just a 1% delay to long frames. They conclude that their proposed security schema has a less significant impact on the delay than the frame payload size. Therefore, this will be a feasible solution to time- and mission-critical applications.

5.3   Chaos Cipher

The authors of [20] propose their Chaotic Cipher solution that ciphers the network traffic to hide the complete Ethernet traffic pattern without introducing overhead and throughput loss. For this, they use a stream cipher in combination with symmetric keys that are known to both end devices of a single network link. This solution provides a different approach as it implements a physical layer encryption method instead of a medium access control layer. One big gap in this paper is that they have no recommendation as to how keys should be shared and exchanged.

Their implementation works on the Physical Coding Sublayer (PCS) by directly encrypting the 8b10b symbol flow. This method provides physical layer encryption and obfuscates the traffic pattern as the control symbols such as start/end are also obfuscated. This layer consists of 256 data symbols and 12 control symbols, containing 268 possible symbols. It uses a symmetric key to generate a mapping of the original symbols to the ciphered symbols. This mapping can easily be reversed if the symmetric key is known. The keystream generation is based on the chaotic map method called Skew Tent Map (STM), which provides chaoticity and no periodic windows.

Finally, they conclude with a performance comparison related to other physical layer solutions. They show that their solution has the highest encryption throughput compared to other algorithms. Moreover, this is sufficient to support a Gigabit Ethernet connection without introducing additional delays.

5.4   KD and SC

The following solution proposes an application layer Key Distribution and Secure Communications module in [21]. This solution cannot prevent the security issues of IEEE 802.1CB as it works on a higher layer. However, it can detect possible attacks and encrypt the data so that attackers can not eavesdrop.

The Key Distribution Module works as a gateway during the start-up phase of the system by distributing the asymmetric keys to all legitimate end devices. The gateway has a database of identities and keys for each end device used to exchange keys securely. Each end device has a hard-coded asymmetric key used only for this key exchange. This method ensures that an eavesdropping attacker cannot gain information about the encryption keys used for the subsequent communications.

Each supported end device should implement the Secure Communication Module, and it should provide the ability to encrypt, decrypt, and authenticate messages. For this, it uses DES and HMAC-MD5. In addition, it uses a sequence number to prevent replay attacks.

Finally, the authors provide a real-time performance evaluation of their proposed solution for both the key distribution and the impact on secure communication. This start-up delay is negligible because the key distribution is only done once on boot. However, the communication response time increases by 2 to 6 milliseconds depending on the CPU clock rate.

6   Evaluation of Attacks and Solutions

Table 1 shows a comparison of the different existing solutions in regards to the TSN KPIs and the discussed attack threats. Each attack scenario from Sect. 4 is shown with an indication if it can be prevented, detected, or if it is unaffected by the proposed solutions. This comparison is purely theoretical based on the description and details of the corresponding research paper.

Prevent means that the reviewed solution, in theory, has the ability to prevent these kinds of attacks from happening. Unaffected means that the reviewed solution has no effect on the attack feasibility. Detect means that the solution is able to notice that the network's communication has been tampered with, but is unable to prevent it from happening. Improve means that the reviewed solution has a positive effect on the amount of packet loss as it is able to filter out some malicious packets, therefore improving the number of legitimate packets that will arrive.

Table 1. Comparison of effectiveness for all reviewed solutions.

	802.1AE-2018 [18]	TSN-MIC [19]	Chaos Cipher [20]	KD & SC [21]
Latency	<350 ns	<800 μs	0	<6 ms
Jitter	–	–	–	–
Packet Loss	improve	improve	improve	–
Spoof DoS	prevent	prevent	prevent	unaffected
Spoof Error	prevent	prevent	prevent	unaffected
Tamper RND	prevent	prevent	prevent	detect
Tamper Replay	prevent	prevent	prevent	detect
Duplicate Paths	unaffected	unaffected	unaffected	unaffected
Intersect Paths	unaffected	unaffected	unaffected	unaffected

It is interesting to see significant differences in the introduced latency by the various solutions. The Chaos Cipher does not introduce any latency as it does not require any processing overhead because it merely shuffles the physical layer symbols according to a keystream generator. The KD & SC solution, on the other hand, introduces a significant latency of several milliseconds. It is expected from a higher-level solution to be slower, but this performance impact is several orders of scale slower than the other available mitigation solutions. Finally, the 802.1AE-2018 and TSN-MIC have only a slight latency impact. The main difference is that the TSN-MIC paper focuses explicitly on time optimization by picking the most performant encryption methods.

Jitter is one of the KPIs in Time-Sensitive Networking, but none of the reviewed solutions provides any information about the delay variation. We think including these measurements is essential to ensure the correct order of packet delivery within mission-critical systems. We assume the papers did not provide this information as they primarily provide theoretical solutions. The jitter should be measured by performing experiments on a hardware test-bed as many external variables could impact it.

Regarding packet loss, most papers can prevent some attacks and are therefore more resilient to accidental packet corruption or malicious actors trying to abuse the system. Unfortunately, they do not provide additional functionality to recover from link failures such as flipped bits. However, as the solutions provide detection of such failures, they can ensure to drop this incorrect packet to ensure that the correct packet travelling on a different path will continue. Therefore, by filtering bad packets, they can improve the number of correct packets arriving at the destination. For the KD & SC solution, they do not have an impact on the packet loss as it is an application layer solution.

Finally, as Table 1 shows, multiple solutions can prevent most attacks from happening. The physical and data link layer solutions can effectively prevent tampering with the packet and sequence number. However, they do not have an impact on malicious path configurations. If these solutions' limitations are resolved and implemented in a practical use case, they might provide proper mitigation.

7   Related Work

As TSN and especially IEEE 802.1CB are recent developments, there have not been widespread contributions to the research field. Especially concerning the security of these network standards, the current knowledge is limited. However, redundancy within industrial Ethernet networks has been an area of interest for quite some time. An excellent overview of available solutions has been provided by the authors of [22]. This paper describes the requirements of industrial networks and how they can be partially solved by using the Spanning Tree Protocol (STP) or the more recent Rapid Spanning Tree Protocol (RSTP). These protocols are currently implemented in many industrial networks. In addition, they provide an overview of 15 Ethernet redundancy solutions, and all of them have a fail-over time ranging from 30ms to 30s. On the other hand, IEEE802.1CB has an instant fail-over time meaning that no packet loss will occur when one of the paths fails.

The authors of [11] provide an extensive overview of the recently published IEEE 802.1 TSN standards. It describes relevant applications for each standard, which aspects it focuses on, and how these standards can best be combined for optimal effect. The standards provide solutions related to Timing and Synchronization, Bounded Low Latency, Reliability, and Resource Management. A summary is given for all the introduced TSN standards, and finally, they conclude with some use cases to show their usefulness. It describes an industrial automation scenario and an automotive in-vehicle networking scenario. For both these scenarios, they recommend using IEEE 802.1CB to improve the reliability of the network communications.

However, security should be of the utmost importance for industrial networks, and therefore the authors of [16] provide an analysis of the security of IEEE 802.1 Time-Sensitive Networking. Just as in the previously mentioned paper, it categorizes the standards and provides a summary of each standard. The main contribution of this paper is its insights into the possible TSN threats. They theorize about threats such as Time Synchronization Threats, Scheduling Threats, Control and Orchestration Threats, and Policing and Redundancy Threats. This paper provided the starting point of our research into the Policing and Redundancy threats introduced by the IEEE 802.1CB standard. The paper concludes with the observation that security has not been one of the main design concerns for TSN as it prioritizes practicality and ease of use.

Finally, the authors of [7] provide a deep dive into the challenges and the limitations of IEEE 802.1CB. It identifies and theorizes possible challenges of this networking standard, such as Insufficient Buffer Dimensioning, Transmission Error Feedback, and Out-of-Order Delivery. In addition, when implementing this standard, there are certain limitations as each switch has to be configured individually. Furthermore, introducing redundant packets could create network inference, and this standard is still dependent on physical redundancy measures to provide disjoint paths. While this paper does not detail any security challenges or limitations, it provides interesting insights into the standard's limitations and suggests making a formal worst-case analysis framework to determine the possible impact.

8   Conclusion

As shown by the overview table in Sect. 6, there is significant overlap in the capabilities of most proposed solutions, and some interesting distinctions become apparent. One substantial similarity is that all these proposed solutions cannot prevent attacks based on the network configuration. This limitation is expected as the IEEE 802.1CB standard is not responsible for the routing and network configuration. Therefore, further research should be done to identify security measures to mitigate these threats.

The most significant difference between these algorithms is the latency impact they have. As the Chaos Cipher and TSN-MIC have a latency impact lower than 1ns, they can most likely be used for all mission-critical applications. On the other hand, the 802.1AE-2018 solution has a higher impact on the latency and is therefore limited in its applications. However, the paper ensured that it is sufficient for automotive networks. Finally, the KD & SC solution has a very high latency mainly due to its implementation in the application layer instead. In addition, this solution cannot prevent any attacks and only provides detection for a subset of the threats.

As these solutions provide no information about their effects on the jitter, we suggest that further research should be done to identify the impact.

This paper provides a threat overview by using the STRIDE model and we recommend further research to focus on a corresponding risk assessment to analyze the exact impact of these identified threats.

Finally, looking at the latency impact and the prevention of security threats, we can conclude that both the TSN-MIC solution and the Chaos Cipher would be feasible. While both solutions have certain drawbacks, further research can improve upon these proposed mitigations. Alternatively, combining them might provide a complete solution.

References

1. Finn, N.: Introduction to time-sensitive networking. IEEE Commun. Stand. Mag. **2**(2), 22–28 (2018)
2. Alcaraz, C., Roman, R., Najera, P., Lopez, J.: Security of industrial sensor network-based remote substations in the context of the internet of things. Ad Hoc Netw. **11**(3), 1091–1104 (2013)
3. Case, D.U.: Analysis of the cyber attack on the Ukrainian power grid. Electricity Inf. Sharing Anal. Center (E-ISAC) **388**, 1–29 (2016)
4. Lee, R.M., Assante, M.J., Conway, T., SANS Industrial Control Systems: ICS CP/PE (Cyber-to-Physical or Process Effects) Case Study Paper-Media report of the Baku-Tbilisi-Ceyhan (BTC) pipeline Cyber Attack (2014)
5. Slay, J., Miller, M.: Lessons learned from the maroochy water breach. In: International Conference on Critical Infrastructure Protection, pp. 73–82, March 2007
6. Farwell, J.P., Rohozinski, R.: Stuxnet and the future of cyber war. Survival **53**(1), 23–40 (2011)
7. Hofmann, R., Nikolić, B., Ernst, R.: Challenges and Limitations of IEEE 802.1 CB-2017. IEEE Embedded Syst. Lett. **12**(4), 105–108 (2019)
8. Teener, M.D.J., et al.: Heterogeneous networks for audio and video: Using IEEE 802.1 audio video bridging. Proc. IEEE **101**(11), 2339–2354 (2013)
9. Nasrallah, A., Thyagaturu, A.S., Alharbi, Z., Wang, C., Shao, X., Reisslein, M., ElBakoury, H.: Ultra-low latency (ULL) networks: the IEEE TSN and IETF DetNet standards and related 5G ULL research. IEEE Commun. Surv. Tutorials **21**(1), 88–145 (2018)
10. IEEE Standards Association. (2018). IEEE Standard for Local and Metropolitan Area Network-Bridges and Bridged Networks. IEEE Std 802.1 Q-2018 (Revision of IEEE Std 802.1 Q-2014): 1–1993 (2018)

11. Bello, L.L., Steiner, W.: A perspective on IEEE time-sensitive networking for industrial communication and automation systems. Proc. IEEE **107**(6), 1094–1120 (2019)
12. Ergenç, D., Fischer, M.: On the Reliability of IEEE 802.1 CB FRER. In IEEE INFOCOM 2021-IEEE Conference on Computer Communications, pp. 1–10. May 2021
13. Prinz, F., Schoeffler, M., Lechler, A., Verl, A.: End-to-end redundancy between real-time I4. 0 Components based on Time-Sensitive Networking. In: 2018 IEEE 23rd International Conference on Emerging Technologies and Factory Automation (ETFA), vol. 1, pp. 1083–1086, September 2018
14. Pannell, D., Navet, N.: Practical Use Cases for Ethernet Redundancy. In: 2020 IEEE Standards Association (IEEE-SA) (2020)
15. Shostack, A., Hernan, S., Lambert, S., Ostwald, T.: Uncover Security Design Flaws Using The STRIDE Approach. MSDN Magazine 2006.11, November 2006
16. Ergenç, D., Brülhart, C., Neumann, J., Krüger, L., Fischer, M.: On the security of IEEE 802.1 time-sensitive networking. In: 2021 IEEE International Conference on Communications Workshops (ICC Workshops), pp. 1–6, June 2021
17. Frame Replication and Elimination for Reliability, IEEE standard P802.1CB, 2017
18. Carnevale, B., Fanucci, L., Bisase, S., Hunjan, H.: Macsec-based security for automotive ethernet backbones. J. Circuits Syst. Comput. **27**(05), 1850082 (2018)
19. Watson, V., Ruland, C., Waedt, K.: 2021. MAC-layer Security for Time-Sensitive Switched Ethernet Networks, INFORMATIK (2020)
20. Pérez-Resa, A., Garcia-Bosque, M., Sánchez-Azqueta, C., Celma, S.: Using a chaotic cipher to encrypt Ethernet traffic. In: 2018 IEEE International Symposium on Circuits and Systems (ISCAS), pp. 1–5, May 2018
21. Wang, C.T., Qin, G. H., Zhao, R., Song, S.M.: An information security protocol for automotive ethernet. J. Comput. **32**(1), 39–52 (2021). International Symposium on Circuits and Systems (ISCAS), pp. 1–5
22. Prytz, G.: Redundancy in industrial Ethernet networks. In: 2006 IEEE International Workshop on Factory Communication Systems, pp. 380–385, June 2006

The Effects of the Russo-Ukrainian War on Network Infrastructures Through the Lens of BGP

Zisis Tsiatsikas[1,2] , Georgios Karopoulos[3(✉)] , and Georgios Kambourakis[3]

[1] University of the Aegean, 83200 Karlovasi, Greece
tzisis@aegean.gr
[2] Atos, 14122 Athens, Greece
zisis.tsiatsikas@atos.net
[3] European Commission, Joint Research Centre (JRC), 21027 Ispra, Italy
{georgios.karopoulos,georgios.kampourakis}@ec.europa.eu, gkamb@aegean.gr

Abstract. One of the most critical building blocks of the reliable operation of the Internet is the Border Gateway Protocol (BGP) that is used to exchange routing messages, signaling active and defective routing paths. During large-scale catastrophic incidents, such as conventional military operations or cyberwarfare, the stability of the Internet is affected, causing the announcements of defective routing paths to increase substantially. This work studies the relation between major incidents, such as armed conflicts in a country scale, and the corresponding network outages observed in the core of the Internet infrastructure as announced by BGP. We focus on the Russo-Ukrainian war as a timely and prominent use case and examine geolocalized BGP data for a 2-month period. Our methodology allows us to cherry-pick long-term network outages among temporary interruptions of service in this specific time window, and pinpoint them to the areas of the operations. Our results indicate that there is a high correlation between the start of military operations and network outages in a city and country level. Furthermore, we show that the last few days before the start of the operations network outages rise as well, indicating that preparatory cyberattack activities take place. No less important, network outages remain at much higher than usual levels during the operations, something that can be attributed to infrastructure destruction possibly backed by cyberattacks.

Keywords: BGP · Internet measurement · Russo-Ukrainian war · Internet resilience · Security

1 Introduction

The physical infrastructure of the Internet comprises the backbone of current and future information and communication systems. These systems provide a plethora of diverse services over the Internet, ranging from entertainment and

The original version of this chapter was previously published without open access. A correction to this chapter is available at https://doi.org/10.1007/978-3-031-25460-4_41

S. Katsikas et al. (Eds.): ESORICS 2022 Workshops, LNCS 13785, pp. 81–96, 2023.
https://doi.org/10.1007/978-3-031-25460-4_5

social media to emergency calls over non-traditional voice communications, Voice over Long-Term Evolution (VoLTE), Voice over New Radio (VoNR), Voice over 5G (Vo5G), and Voice over WiFi (VoWiFi). This fact underlines the importance of round-the-clock Internet availability not only for routine activities, but also for public safety and security.

The Internet is considered tolerant to errors due to its mesh architecture and the humongous number of interconnected networks. However, even though the existence of multiple different communication paths between endpoints offers redundancy and robustness, Internet availability can be affected by two major categories of large-scale events. The first consists of natural disasters, such as hurricanes, floods, earthquakes, and so on [1]. The second is related to man-made actions which, in a large-scale level, can impact Internet stability, such as Distributed Denial of Service (DDoS) attacks [2]. To the best of our knowledge, our study is the first one that shows that armed conflicts could also be included in the man-made actions that affect the stability of the Internet. In both cases, an Internet disruption is perceived as a difficulty to access specific Internet Protocol (IP) ranges due to external factors.

The protocol that forms the cornerstone of Internet routing is Border Gateway Protocol (BGP) [3], which is used to communicate routing information between Autonomous Systems (ASs). Each AS has external routers to exchange BGP routing information with neighboring ASs, and each such router keeps the relevant paths in a routing table. When a new routing path is available, the router broadcasts it to its neighbours who further advertise this new path to their neighbors. When a catastrophic incident renders an IP prefix unreachable, the existing path is withdrawn with a similar BGP-based broadcast procedure, resulting in the update of the relevant routing tables. And even though it is always possible to have short-term, temporary outages lasting a few minutes, more extended periods of network unreachability can be associated with external factors, such as infrastructure destruction.

Intuitively, military operations target critical infrastructures, such as nuclear plants and communication networks [4,5], with disastrous consequences in their stability and everyday operation, as demonstrated in, at the time of writing, ongoing Russo-Ukrainian war. Besides that, the scenario of parallel cyberattacks, like DDoS, that target the enemy's infrastructure, is considered a common tactic [6]. The work at hand is the first to our knowledge to examine the impact of military operations in network infrastructures using the Russo-Ukrainian war as a representative use case. More specifically, by analyzing BGP data for a two-month period, we identify the extend and severity of catastrophic incidents from the beginning of Russia's war against Ukraine. The main contributions of this paper can be summarized as follows: (a) we analyze the effect of military operations in network infrastructures, (b) we geolocalize network outages in the level of cities and countries close to the theatre of operations, and (c) we discuss potential associations behind the observed network outages and publicly known events.

The remainder of the paper is structured as follows. The next section offers an introduction around the BGP protocol and how it is used for tracking routing incidents and abnormalities. Section 3 presents our methodology and collection of results, as well as discusses our observations. Section 4 offers a comparison between our proposal and the prior state-of-the-art. Finally, the last section draws the conclusions and gives pointers for future work.

2 Preliminaries

The Internet backbone is comprised of connections between large strategical ASs. These are the structural networking elements of the Internet. Each AS corresponds to a network or group of IP networks which share the same unified routing policy. This policy is used by an AS to exchange routing information with the corresponding peer networks, which are administered by a different Internet Service Provider (ISP). It is also the basic characteristic that differentiates each AS from the rest. Every AS is assigned a unique number, namely the Autonomous System Number (ASN). Each ASN is used to track a network in a distinctive way. The Internet Assigned Names Authority (IANA) is responsible to manage and provide an ASN to the corresponding AS.

As has already been discussed, BGP is employed to exchange information between ASs. The major piece of information conveyed over BGP are the IP ranges which are controlled by a specific AS. This is done by announcing the range of IP addresses, which are reachable to the closest AS. Each AS spreads the information to the closest neighbours, and this is how the different ASs are informed for the routing options they have. Each time an AS wishes to route information to a different AS, it consults the routing information to deduce which is the shortest path. The basic messages used in BGP are the following: OPEN, UPDATE, NOTIFICATION, and KEEPALIVE. In the rest of this paper, we consider UPDATE messages only; for more information regarding the rest of these messages, the interested reader can refer to [3]. Figure 1 offers an overview of the interconnections between different AS elements.

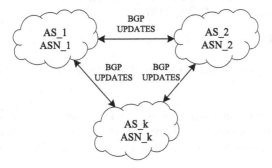

Fig. 1. AS connections

2.1 BGP UPDATE

The main purpose of BGP UPDATE messages is to spread routing information among peers. Specifically, an UPDATE message can be used either to announce a new route or withdraw an existing one. As the name indicates, the announcement of a route is used to announce a route towards the AS that hosts the network prefix under consideration and let the other peers be aware for alternative communication paths. It contains information such as: (a) the identity of the monitoring router, that is, the AS number and IP address of the BGP router that received the update message, (b) timestamp of the message's reception, (c) the network prefix under consideration, and (d) the path (sequence of ASNs) that has to be traversed for the prefix's origin AS to be reached. On the other hand, a withdrawal is used for revoking an existing routing path. A withdrawal contains information such as: (a) the identity of the monitoring router, (b) timestamp of the message's reception, and (c) the prefix under consideration.

Figure 2 shows two BGP UPDATE messages; an announcement at the top of the figure and a withdrawal at the bottom. The fields of the announcement are: BGP protocol, unix time in seconds, type of update ("A" for announcement), IP address of the announcing router, AS number of the announcing AS, announced prefix, AS path, source of the update ("IGP" for Internal Gateway Protocol or "EGP" for External Gateway Protocol), next hop, local preference, preferred path, grouped routes with similar policies, atomic aggregator, and aggregator. The atomic aggregator is a flag showing that some information was lost when an AS aggregated prefixes. The aggregator field identifies the AS and router that aggregated prefixes received from different peers into a single prefix. The fields of the withdrawal are: BGP protocol, unix time in seconds, type of update ("W" for withdrawal), IP address of the announcing router, AS number of the announcing AS, withdrawn prefix.

```
BGP4MP|1064963009|A|129.250.0.11|2914|202.128.64.0/19|
        2914 701 18864 9548|IGP|129.250.0.11|0|58|2914:420
        2914:2000 2914:3000|NAG| |

BGP4MP|1064963016|W|64.200.199.3|7911|200.49.32.0/22
```

Fig. 2. Example of BGP Update messages (top: announcement, bottom: withdrawal)

As BGP UPDATE messages are received by routers, the reachability information of the network prefixes contained therein changes. With the reception of every new BGP update message for a given prefix, the following priority scheme is followed [3]:

- the reception of a withdrawal obsoletes any previous announcement, and
- an announcement is made obsolete by a newer announcement which contains a shorter path.

It is expected that, after a large scale catastrophic incident, the update messages should contain useful information regarding network outages.

2.2 Outages

A network outage can be considered the difficulty to access a network location. This can be experienced as a delay in the network or even as a ferocious Denial of Service (DoS). Usually, the recovery of network paths allows a client to access a service even if the service quality is not considered satisfactory. For example, in [7] an outage is considered a continuous period with Mean Opinion Score (MOS) < 2, something that affects voice quality.

In the context of this paper, we consider as outage an extended period during which a broadcast BGP withdrawal is not followed by an announcement for a given IP prefix; in practice, this means that the prefix is unreachable during this period. In our analysis, we only take into account outages that last more than 5 min. Outages that last less than this time threshold are considered temporary, fortuitous disruptions and are ignored.

3 Measurements

3.1 Collecting and Analyzing BGP Data

In order to collect and analyze the BGP traffic data, we developed two separate scripts whose source code is made publicly available[1]; the procedure we followed for collecting our results is depicted in the flow diagram in Fig. 3. The first one is a Linux bash script that downloads raw BGP data from the University of Oregon Route views project[2], for a date range between February and March 2022. Since these files are in binary format, we processed them with `bgpdump` [8] in order to be converted to ASCII. The second script, developed in Perl, analyzes BGP UPDATE messages. The script processes each UPDATE message from the raw files downloaded before, and calculates the outages for each affected IP prefix. That is, while parsing the UPDATE messages, the script marks the IP prefixes for which a path was withdrawn and keeps this information in a special structure called Patricia Trie. A Patricia Trie is a data structure based on a radix tree with a radix of two, and it is used to quickly perform IP address prefix matching during IP subnet, network or routing table lookups. In the next step, the script checks if a new path for the same prefix was not announced in less than 5 min; essentially, these are considered outages and are stored in a database.

For each prefix that is entered in the database, we retrieve its actual geographic location using geolocation databases from [9]. Keep in mind that these databases come in two different flavours: the first one maps an IP prefix to a country, while the other one to a city. In the context of our experiments, both database types were used. It should be noted, however, that country-level geolocalization is more reliable than city-level, as stated in the relevant bibliography [10].

---

[1] https://github.com/gkarop/bgp_outages.
[2] http://archive.routeviews.org/bgpdata.

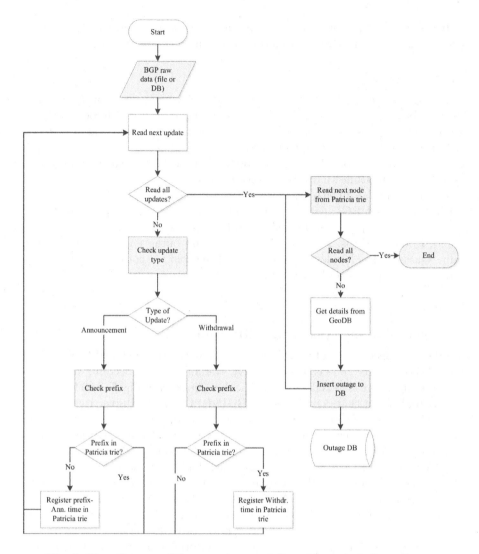

Fig. 3. Flow diagram of the procedure we followed for calculating outages

3.2   Results and Discussion

As far as it concerns our measurements, we concentrated in two different scenarios. In the first one, we draw a relation between the war activities and the outages in the level of a city. In the second one, we delve into the outages in four major countries during February and March 2022.

Regarding the first case, we attempt to draw a connection between conventional military operations, say, shelling, and the rise in the number of outages. According to [11], the Russian army attacked the city of Kharkiv on the 24th of February. Figure 4a shows the number of outages in that city for the second half of February. It is easily observable that during this period the number of outages remained below 500, except the 24th of the same month. Based on the measurement results we obtained, the outages on this day reached almost 9,000, i.e., an increase exceeding 1700%. Moreover, already from the 21st of February, the observed number of outages was slightly higher than the previous days, something that indicates that tactical cyberattacks preceded the actual assault. Additionally, the number of outages remained considerably higher after the first day of the invasion and this fact can be mostly attributed to physical destruction of networking infrastructure.

Focusing more on the first day of the invasion, that is the 24th of February, and breaking down the outages in the level of hour, we found out that two major peaks appeared between 2–3 AM, and 4–5 PM. The maximum values in these cases were almost 650. Overall, a very high number of outages was observed throughout the day. These results are depicted in Fig. 4b.

In the second case, we compared the outages in four important countries, the two involved in the war, that is Russia and Ukraine, and two neighboring countries, one supporting Russia, namely Belarus, and one supporting Ukraine, namely Poland. Tables 1 and 2 offer an analytical view of the results we obtained for these countries for the entire February and March respectively, whereas Fig. 5 depicts the outages observed in the second half of February 2022 and the whole of March 2022.

In Ukraine, it is clear that the number of outages steeply rose on the day of the invasion (>10,000) compared to the previous days (<2,000) and it remained at the same high levels (between 4,000 and 40,000, most of the days above 10,000) for the rest of February and March. The big difference in the median value for February (739) and March (12,403) further supports this key observation.

In Russia, on the other hand, the peak in February 2022 was observed some days later, on the 27th with 61,490 outages; later, it was announced that this day a DoS campaign was launched against Russia from compromised Information Technology (IT) infrastructure [12]. Then, a similar trend was observed: the number of outages was between 600 and 8,000 until the 27th, and then rose to between 6,000 and 40,000 in the majority of March. Indeed in March, Russian companies, government entities and state-owned companies have confronted an increased number of DDoS attacks [13,14]. The median values for February and March 2022 were 2,582 and 13,467, respectively. It is worth mentioning that Russia presents more outages than Ukraine, especially on the 8th of March. We assume that this result is perceived due to the fact that on this day two major ISPs stopped offering their services in Russia [15]. Obviously, this fact resulted in a major Internet outage.

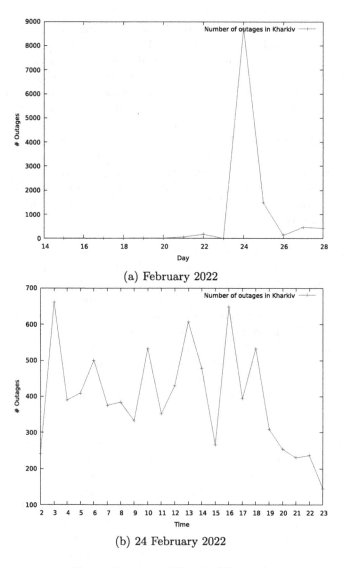

(a) February 2022

(b) 24 February 2022

Fig. 4. Outages in Kharkiv (Ukraine)

Table 1. Number of outages per day and country for February 2022 (red font: the day of the invasion, bold font: max value for the country in February)

Day	Russia	Ukraine	Belarus	Poland
1	4998	1253	–	855
2	2132	1175	2	424
3	4191	360	2	426
4	1379	471	–	434
5	671	87	–	531
6	817	78	–	108
7	1853	297	10	341
8	2670	522	–	2225
9	2032	732	–	951
10	2630	1036	9	692
11	1178	585	2	209
12	930	137	–	142
13	873	874	–	165
14	8062	1697	186	848
15	2972	1170	23	395
16	1066	8	–	121
17	623	86	15	48
18	4606	996	**547**	407
19	5573	452	45	841
20	2262	746	71	645
21	2534	669	4	309
22	2212	1582	7	490
23	3232	624	–	568
24	4110	**10913**	1	244
25	2958	2900	1	132
26	2715	8694	–	402
27	**61490**	4431	22	662
28	4405	7055	2	**3386**
Median:	2582	739	9	425

Table 2. Number of outages per day and country for March 2022 (bold font: max value for the country in March)

Day	Russia	Ukraine	Belarus	Poland
1	32849	38519	955	3662
2	28494	21496	845	3267
3	18448	11284	489	1156
4	23993	24750	724	2501
5	18717	28669	140	1770
6	7985	29017	492	589
7	6330	12403	14	2484
8	**39350**	14257	993	**7805**
9	9330	25355	60	3209
10	9834	21360	27	1002
11	10463	9286	151	1895
12	10841	12391	394	1135
13	9679	13487	75	1939
14	6789	12059	109	1272
15	13467	11444	279	2848
16	8046	10148	88	1169
17	17918	**39391**	90	2242
18	13942	10930	68	2054
19	32855	7258	312	1376
20	9601	7850	14	572
21	15977	4475	300	1047
22	15809	6252	112	3855
23	16813	20588	395	3544
24	13778	23196	284	1601
25	10967	13057	416	2618
26	7434	5959	82	754
27	5812	10247	147	4006
28	12934	32592	**1359**	920
29	26587	19576	618	3941
30	16268	10051	397	1604
31	3379	8126	208	757
Median:	13467	12403	279	1895

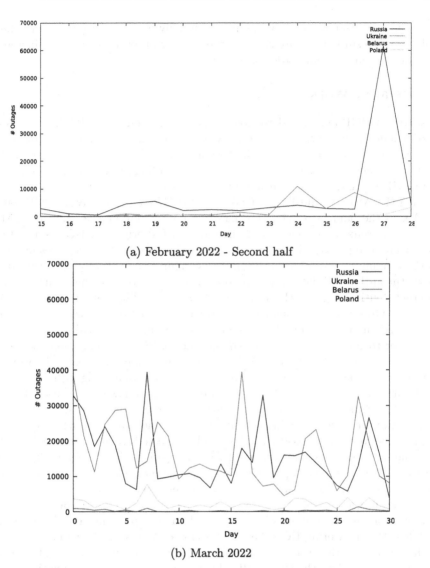

(a) February 2022 - Second half

(b) March 2022

Fig. 5. Outages in four major countries

The differences in the median values for the other two countries (from 9 to 279 for Belarus and from 425 to 1,895 for Poland) clearly suggest that countries that are not directly involved in the war operations are not immune to network outages either.

As far as it concerns the median values per 15 d for February, the results indicate a triple increase in the number of outages for Russia. That is, from 2,492 outages perceived in the first half, the second reached 7,522. In the case of Ukraine the values were almost quadrupled. From 698 outages in the first 15 d, it reached 3,012 at the end of the month. Finally, with respect to Belarus and Poland, the results designate a rise in the number of outages, but the difference remains low, in the same order of magnitude.

4   Related Work

A survey of BGP anomaly detection methods is presented in [16]. The authors also include an evaluation methodology for comparing these methods and propose new detection algorithms. The first method is Nemecis [17], which checks for inconsistencies between policy information residing in Internet Routing Registries (IRRs) and actual routing. The next two methods, Prefix Hijack Alert System (PHAS) [18] and Pretty Good BGP (PGBGP) [19], rely on BGP data. PHAS, as the name suggests, is a real-time notification system that alerts the owner of a prefix when there is a change to the BGP origin. PGBGP is a system that delays the propagation of new routes, and uses known alternatives instead, so that human operators have the time to examine routes that seem suspicious. Next, the authors of the survey propose their own algorithm that is using both Internet Routing Registry (IRR) and BGP trace data. The aforementioned methods look into detecting anomalies and attacks on BGP routes, whereas our aim is to detect anomalies caused by disruptive events in a large scale.

Closer to our work is [20], which proposes a BGP anomaly detection system. It is focused on detecting different types of abnormal events like worms, power outages, and submarine cable cuts, using data mining algorithms; similar works are [21,22]. Li et al. [21] propose a detection framework that uses rules of abnormal events and data mining techniques to detect new events. The authors present two use cases, one of a blackout event and one of a worm, where the rules of previous events were used and successfully detected the new events. The second one, [22], is about understanding what happens to BGP during large-scale power outages, and investigates the USA/Canada incident [23] as a use case. All these works are similar to what we aim to achieve; one of our requirements that is not met in these works, however, is the geolocation of network outages.

The work in [1] examines the impact of catastrophic incidents in Internet stability. By monitoring BGP data for specific events, such as earthquakes, the authors conclude that the routing table size is limited during the events. Additionally, they analyze the BGP UPDATE messages with respect to withdrawals and announcements. Based on these findings, they come up with the result that natural-based emergency incidents affect Internet stability.

In the same direction, [24,25] examine the potential of measuring natural disasters by exploiting Internet data. The authors rely on BGP data to identify the routing paths that are affected by earthquakes. According to their results, the *I-seismograph* tool can identify which ASs are related to abnormalities in the routing paths. The basic idea is to define a "normal" state for the Internet and then at any time compare it with the current state in order to conclude whether an "abnormal" state is observed or not. These works consider the Internet address space as a whole and try to quantify its anomalies; our focus is on identifying disruptions in specific geographic locations.

The authors in [26] present an analysis regarding the stability of Internet routes to popular web destinations. Based on their study, the authors state that a small number of destinations which is visited by the biggest portion of traffic, is considered to have stable routes. Finally, BGP analysis proved that the vast amount of UPDATE messages concerns the least visited domains.

The recovery from large-scale incidents for emergency communications is discussed in [27]. This study is focused on improving the existing routing mechanisms by offering a new architecture that tackles the issues of communication overhead and tracking the location of overlay nodes. According to their results, the authors claim that their approach can significantly improve the exchange of routing information up to 9 times.

A work that takes a direction towards near real-time anomaly detection in BGP is [28]. They combine visual-, statistical-, and signature-based methods for detecting anomalies more accurately. In order to perform near real-time detection experiments they use historical BGP data which are replayed in a testbed. In this case, the authors limit their input data to specific BGP UPDATE messages from selected prefixes.

Other approaches include learning-based ones like [29] and [30], which propose two methods: one for signature-based and one for statistics-based detection. In these papers the authors concentrate on anomalous routing behavior for single prefixes and select BGP updates for the selected prefixes only. A slightly different approach is [31], which is a system that detects malicious BGP UPDATE messages by observing the network topology; the consistency check relies upon a model of AS connectivity.

Another group of research analyzes the impact of certain incidents on BGP UPDATE messages. A report [23] from Renesys Corp. analyses two blackouts in 2003: the first one was in USA/Canada on 14–16 August 2003 and the other in Italy on 28 September 2003. In this report, a list of networks around the blackout area is used to create statistics about network outages around the time of the event. There are a few works investigating the effects of worm propagation on BGP. The work in [32] look into the effects on BGP during the propagation of Code Red II and Nimda worms in July and September 2001, respectively. Another work [33] examines the Slammer worm for the period of January 2003. Dainotti et al. [34] analyze the impact of Internet outages caused deliberately for censorship, in Egypt and Libya. These works only analyze historical data and do not perform any kind of incident detection.

5   Conclusions

This work aspires to delve into the relation between the impact of tactical military missions, potentially backed up by cyberwarfare operations, and Internet's routing stability from a BGP viewpoint. Taking the Russo-Ukrainian war as an eminent and timely use-case, and exploiting publicly available geolocalized BGP data over a two-month period, i.e., between February and March 2022, we analyze major network outages in both a city and country level. Specifically, our experiments highlight two cases: (a) the attack against the city of Kharkiv on the 24th of February, the D-Day of the Russian further military operations in Ukraine, and (b) the overall BGP outages in four directly involved or affected by the war countries, namely Belarus, Russia, Ukraine, and Poland. Our findings clearly showcase that there is a tight link between conventional military, and potentially supporting or preparatory cyber offensive operations, with the number of BGP outages. As a strongly indicative example, the first day of the invasion, the difference in the perceived number of outages in the city of Kharkiv surpassed 1,700%. As a general observation, it can be argued that BGP UPDATE data can be used to not only examine how and to which extent a physical or man-made major event or action affected the Internet infrastructure, but also to opportunely expose significant major events that certain parties may wish to keep out of the spotlight.

Two significant directions for future work are identified. First, given that at the time of writing, we are already at the fifth month of the war, the analysis can consider the time period starting from the first of April onward. Second, additional datasets of BGP data, say, from different route collectors like RIPE RIS[3] can be considered; in this way meaningful comparisons between results stemming from diverse vantage points can be drawn.

References

1. Palmieri, F., Fiore, U., Castiglione, A., Leu, F.-Y., De Santis, A.: Analyzing the internet stability in presence of disasters. In: Cuzzocrea, A., Kittl, C., Simos, D.E., Weippl, E., Xu, L. (eds.) CD-ARES 2013. LNCS, vol. 8128, pp. 253–268. Springer, Heidelberg (2013). https://doi.org/10.1007/978-3-642-40588-4_18

2. Smith, J.M., Schuchard, M.: Routing around congestion: Defeating DDOS attacks and adverse network conditions via reactive BGP routing. IEEE Symp. Secur. Privacy **2018**, 599–617 (2018)

3. Rekhter, Y., Li, T., Hares, S.: A Border Gateway Protocol 4 (BGP-4). RFC 4271 (Draft Standard), Internet Engineering Task Force, Jan. 2006, updated by RFCs 6286, 6608, 6793. http://www.ietf.org/rfc/rfc4271.txt

4. Energy Monitor. Russia's war on Ukraine spotlights critical energy infrastructure. Accessed 24 June 2022. https://www.energymonitor.ai/tech/networks-grids/russias-war-on-ukraine-spotlights-critical-energy-infrastructure

5. Endpoint. Russia's Cyberwar Targets Western Critical Infrastructure. Accessed 24 June 2022. https://www.tanium.com/blog/russias-cyberwar-targets-western-critical-infrastructure/

6. Schulze, M.: Cyber in war: Assessing the strategic, tactical, and operational utility of military cyber operations. In: 2020 12th International Conference on Cyber Conflict (CyCon), vol. 1300, pp. 183–197 (2020)

7. Kushman, N., Kandula, S., Katabi, D.: Can you hear me now?! it must be BGP. SIGCOMM Comput. Commun. Rev. **37**(2), 75–84 (2007). https://doi.org/10.1145/1232919.1232927

8. Ardelean, D.: BGPDUMP. https://manpages.debian.org/

---

[3] https://ris.ripe.net/docs/10_routecollectors.html#bgp-timer-settings.

9. MaxMind Inc. GeoLite country database. http://dev.maxmind.com/geoip/legacy/geolite
10. Poese, I., Uhlig, S., Kaafar, M.A., Donnet, B., Gueye, B.: Ip geolocation databases: Unreliable? SIGCOMM Comput. Commun. Rev. **41**(2), 53–56 (2011). https://doi.org/10.1145/1971162.1971171
11. Fedorenko, V., Fedorenko, M.V.: Russia's military invasion of Ukraine in 2022: Aim, reasons, and implications. Krytyka Prawa. Niezależne Studia nad Prawem **14**(1), 7–42 (2022). https://doi.org/10.7206/kp.2080-1084.506
12. ComputerWeekly, IT infrastructure used to launch DDoS attack on Russian targets. https://www.computerweekly.com/news/252516773/IT-infrastructure-used-to-launch-DDoS-attack-on-Russian-targets. Accessed 20 June 2022
13. Reuters. Russian company websites hit by increased hacking in March, says cyber firm. https://www.reuters.com/technology/russian-company-websites-hit-by-increased-hacking-march-says-cyber-firm-2022-03-11/
14. CYBERSCOOP. Putin's government lists IPs and domains allegedly aiming DDoS traffic at Russia. https://www.cyberscoop.com/russian-internet-ddos-incidents-ip-domain-list/
15. Emerging cyber threats in the ongoing russia-ukraine conflict. https://www.cyfirma.com/outofband/emerging-cyber-threats-in-the-ongoing-russia-ukraine-conflict/. Accessed 04 June 2022
16. Sriram, K., Borchert, O., Kim, O., Gleichmann, P., Montgomery, D.: A comparative analysis of BGP anomaly detection and robustness algorithms. In: Conference for Homeland Security: CATCH '09. Cybersecurity Applications Technology, vol. **2009**, pp. 25–38 (2009)
17. Siganos, G., Faloutsos, M.: Analyzing BGP Policies: Methodology and Tool. In: Proceedings of IEEE INFOCOM, pp. 1640–1651 (2004)
18. Lad, M., Massey, D., Pei, D., Wu, Y., Zhang, B., Zhang, L.: PHAS: A prefix hijack alert system. In: Proceedings of the 15th Conference on USENIX Security Symposium - Volume 15, Ser. USENIX-SS'06. USENIX Association, Berkeley (2006). http://dl.acm.org/citation.cfm?id=1267336.1267347
19. Karlin, J.: Pretty Good BGP: Improving BGP by cautiously adopting routes. In: Proceedings of International Conference on Network Protocols (2006)
20. de Urbina Cazenave, I., Kosluk, E., Ganiz, M.: An anomaly detection framework for BGP. In: Innovations in Intelligent Systems and Applications (INISTA), 2011 International Symposium on, pp. 107–111 (2011)
21. Li, J., Dou, D., Wu, Z., Kim, S., Agarwal, V.: An internet routing forensics framework for discovering rules of abnormal BGP events. SIGCOMM Comput. Commun. Rev. **35**(5), 55–66 (2005). https://doi.org/10.1145/1096536.1096542
22. Li, J., Wu, Z., Purpus, E.: CAM04-5: Toward understanding the behavior of BGP during large-scale power outages. In: Global Telecommunications Conference: GLOBECOM '06, vol. 2006, pp. 1–5. IEEE (2006)
23. Cowie, J.H., Ogielski, A.T., Premore, B., Smith, E.A., Underwood, T., Corporation, R.: Impact of the 2003 Blackouts on Internet Communications. Tech. Rep. (2003). http://www.renesys.com/news
24. Li, J., Brooks, S.: I-seismograph: Observing and measuring internet earthquakes in INFOCOM. Proc. IEEE **2011**, 2624–2632 (2011)
25. Zhang, M., Li, J., Brooks, S.: I-seismograph: Observing, measuring, and analyzing internet earthquakes. IEEE/ACM Trans. Netw. **25**(6), 3411–3426 (2017)

26. Rexford, J., Wang, J., Xiao, Z., Zhang, Y.: BGP routing stability of popular destinations. In: Proceedings of the 2nd ACM SIGCOMM Workshop on Internet Measurement, ser. IMW '02. Association for Computing Machinery, New York (2002),
pp. 197–202. https://doi.org/10.1145/637201.637232
27. Hasegawa, G., Kamei, S., Murata, M.: Emergency communication services based
on overlay networking technologies. In: Fourth International Conference on Networking and Services (ICNS 2008), pp. 159–164 (2008)
28. Teoh, S.T., Zhang, K., Tseng, S.-M., Ma, K.-L., Wu, S.F.: Combining visual and
automated data mining for near-real-time anomaly detection and analysis in BGP.
In: Proceedings of the 2004 ACM Workshop on Visualization and Data Mining for
Computer Security, ser. VizSEC/DMSEC '04. ACM, New York (2004), pp. 35–44.
https://doi.org/10.1145/1029208.1029215
29. Zhang, J., Rexford, J., Feigenbaum, J.: Learning-based anomaly detection in BGP
updates. In: Proceedings of the 2005 ACM SIGCOMM Workshop on Mining Network Data, ser. MineNet '05, pp. 219–220. ACM, New York (2005). https://doi.
org/10.1145/1080173.1080189
30. Zhang, K., Yen, A., Zhao, X., Massey, D., Wu, S.F., Zhang, L.: On detection of
anomalous routing dynamics in BGP. In: Mitrou, N., Kontovasilis, K., Rouskas,
G.N., Iliadis, I., Merakos, L. (eds.) NETWORKING 2004. LNCS, vol. 3042, pp.
259–270. Springer, Heidelberg (2004). https://doi.org/10.1007/978-3-540-24693-
0_22
31. Kruegel, C., Mutz, D., Robertson, W., Valeur, F.: Topology-based detection of
anomalous BGP messages. In: Proceedings of the 6th Symposium on Recent
Advances in Intrusion Detection (RAID), pp. 17–35 (2003)
32. Cowie, B.P.J., Ogielski, A., Yuan, Y.: Global Routing Instabilities During Code
Red II and Nimda Worm Propagation. Tech. Rep, Renesys (2001)
33. Lad, M., Zhao, X., Zhang, B., Massey, D., Zhang, L.: Analysis of BGP update
surge during slammer worm attack. In: Das, S.R., Das, S.K. (eds.) IWDC 2003.
LNCS, vol. 2918, pp. 66–79. Springer, Heidelberg (2003). https://doi.org/10.1007/
978-3-540-24604-6_7
34. Dainotti, A., Squarcella, C., Aben, E., Claffy, K.C., Chiesa, M., Russo, M., Pescapé,
A.: Analysis of country-wide internet outages caused by censorship. In: Proceedings
of the 2011 ACM SIGCOMM Conference on Internet Measurement Conference,
ser. IMC '11, pp. 1–18. ACM, New York (2011). https://doi.org/10.1145/2068816.
2068818

Cybersecurity Awareness for Small and Medium-Sized Enterprises (SMEs): Availability and Scope of Free and Inexpensive Awareness Resources

Sunil Chaudhary[1]([✉]), Vasileios Gkioulos[1], and David Goodman[2]

[1] Department of Information Security and Communication Technology, Norwegian University of Science and Technology, Gjøvik, Norway
sunil.chaudhary@ntnu.no
[2] Trust in Digital Life, Brussels, Belgium

Abstract. Small and medium-sized enterprises (SMEs) are considered the backbone of Europe's economy. However, SMEs are often bounded by resource constraints that also limit their cybersecurity posture. In such circumstances, SMEs could potentially benefit from the *free and inexpensive* cybersecurity awareness (CSA) resources produced and distributed by various public and private entities. SMEs can utilize these affordable resources to elevate the knowledge and skills of employees and transform their cybersecurity attitudes and behavior. The security-conscious employees can serve as the organization's first line of defense against cyber-attacks and -crimes. However, prior to employing such awareness resources, it would require answering the question *"how abundance and well-suited are the (affordable) awareness resources for SMEs?"* To address this concern, we used an exploratory approach and examined the awareness resources from 71 sources chosen after the review of 938 potential sources. Since the primary audience of the study was European SMEs, most of the sources analyzed come from European organizations. Based on our findings, while these affordable awareness resources could benefit SMEs, they do *require some adjustment* to better meet the requirements and situations of SMEs. Furthermore, the awareness resources exclusively targeting SMEs and the diverse business areas SMEs serve, are insufficient. As a result, all involved entities, at the national and European levels, are encouraged to *produce and distribute more localized awareness resources* that are affordable and best match the demands and business areas of SMEs. Finally, the awareness resources should also include *appropriate features* for interested users to submit their feedback.

Keywords: Cybersecurity awareness · Small and medium sized enterprise · Free and affordable awareness resources · European Union · Exploratory approach

1 Introduction

According to the European Union (EU) recommendation 2003/361, small and medium-sized enterprises (SMEs) are defined as *"individual firms that have staff headcount less*

S. Katsikas et al. (Eds.): ESORICS 2022 Workshops, LNCS 13785, pp. 97–115, 2023.
https://doi.org/10.1007/978-3-031-25460-4_6

than 250 and have either an annual turnover of less than or equal to €50 million or an annual balance sheet total of less than equal to €43 million" [1]. SMEs account for the majority of businesses in the EU; to be specific, around 99% of enterprises in the EU are SMEs that provide two-thirds of private-sector employment in the region [2].

SMEs possess a very different profile than their large counterparts in terms of work environment and organizational structure, management, and culture. Most micro-SMEs are plagued by financial and resource constraints [3–5], practice informal management with centralized decision making, and have multi-tasking employees with low adherence to established procedures and standards [6]. Moreover, due to their limited size and growth needs, SMEs are obliged to modify plans and strategies considerably faster than large enterprises. Furthermore, SMEs are constantly under pressure to innovate and improve quality [3], so they must take advantage of new technology and economic prospects. However, a major concern due to this dynamic nature is that SMEs incorporate emerging technologies and work practices into their operations without performing a thorough cybersecurity assessment [7], particularly, without comprehending the risks they will introduce, and how they would affect the organization's overall cybersecurity hygiene. Such adaptability or quickness to change aids SMEs in positioning themselves on the *productivity frontier* [8] and allows them to establish themselves among the leading innovative enterprises; nevertheless, it also leaves them more exposed to cyber-attacks and crimes.

To further exacerbate the problem, many SMEs underestimate the severity of cyber-security and do not consider them a strategic component of the company plans, despite the fact that cybersecurity is a genuine and rising phenomenon. There is a common misconception among the owners (or decision-makers) of SMEs that cybercriminals prefer large organizations over SMEs, thus, cybersecurity is less critical for SMEs and worth ignoring [7, 9, 10]. This fallacious mentality becomes scarier considering Fire-Eye's finding that over 77% of all cybercrimes target SMEs [11]. Cybercriminals are attracted to SMEs mainly because of two reasons, firstly, it is relatively more lucrative to target SMEs that require a minimal effort to attack but results in a substantial cumulative payoff [11], and secondly, many SMEs do business with large enterprises so they can be a steppingstone to reach and attack the large enterprises [5].

The stakes of SMEs in terms of security are tremendous, particularly for small and micro enterprises, for which sustaining a major cyberattack can be extremely difficult; reputational damage, commercial losses, and penalties levied after a cyberattack or data breach might force them out of business. This is further worsened by their budgetary and resource constraints that impede them from implementing up-to-date security defenses (e.g., security technology, established standards and practices, and cybersecurity training and awareness) and hiring people with relevant knowledge and expertise [7], required to maintain a standard cybersecurity posture and to keep up with the pace of ever-evolving cybersecurity challenges. Even among SMEs with sufficient financial resources, many of them commit insufficient budgets and resources to CSA. One of the main reasons for underbudgeting for CSA is businesses' overemphasis on technology security solutions (which are typically expensive) [12–15]. They often view employees as a part of the cybersecurity problem and not its solutions, thus, downplaying the role of human factors in cybersecurity. It is quite unfortunate for them to distrust their employees and not realize that even technical measures produce the desired results only if they are implemented and used correctly. Indeed, employees are susceptible to manipulation (e.g., social engineering tricks), and prone to errors and there is no silver bullet to completely alleviate these innate weaknesses, however, they can be controlled and minimized by raising the employees' cybersecurity awareness (CSA) and empowering them with necessary cybersecurity knowledge and skills.

The purpose of CSA activities is to persuade employees to engage in safe and secure behavior [16]. This is accomplished by communicating security principles and procedures to personnel so that they develop a healthy level of skepticism when encountering unusual situations and make well-informed or rational decisions to keep themselves and their firm safe and secure. This preventive measure can be cost-effective and the first line of security for SMEs providing a reasonable level of protection for them.

2   Rationale and Research Objectives

A variety of public and private entities generate and distribute free and inexpensive CSA programs and materials. Some of them produce and distribute SME-specific awareness programs and materials. Given the restrictions of budget and resources, it would be beneficial for SMEs to make use of free and inexpensive awareness programs and materials [4]. Furthermore, according to a survey conducted by the SANS Institute [17], most enterprises employ part-time CSA professionals with awareness mounted on their other obligations. Using the readily available CSA programs and materials without constraining the budget might assist these part-time professionals to manage time efficiently and execute responsibilities in a better way.

However, the question "*how abundant and well-suited is the freely available and inexpensive awareness resources to SMEs?*" remains unanswered. By well-suited, we refer to the aspects that are imperative to use the awareness programs and materials easily and effectively, more specifically,

a) What types of SME-specific awareness programs and materials are available?
b) What are the cybersecurity issues addressed by the available awareness programs and materials?
c) In which phase of CSA (pre-implementation, implementation, and post-implementation [18]) can the available awareness materials be used?
d) How accessible are the awareness programs and materials to SMEs?
e) Do the publishers have the capabilities to track how many individuals have accessed the awareness programs and materials and receive feedback on the quality of awareness programs and materials if users intend to submit them?
f) What challenges might SMEs encounter in implementing the available awareness programs and materials?
g) What other things can publishers do to increase the quality and effectiveness of the awareness programs and materials?

These questions provide answers to what SMEs can expect from the awareness programs and materials and at the same time recommend what these sources can do to improve the accessibility and quality of the awareness programs and materials at the very least. The recommendations are entirely based on a review of the awareness programs and materials posted on the website and how they were presented. We believe that realizing this information will facilitate and encourage SMEs to adopt and benefit from these awareness resources, thus, enhancing their CSA postures and situations presumably in a cost-effective way.

3 Analysis and Findings

To get answers to these questions, we used an exploratory approach. We reviewed CSA programs and materials from a range of sources. However, because European SMEs were the primary audience of this study, priority was given to the sources from Europe. The five types of sources explored for the purpose are:

- European Agencies and Organizations—16 European institutions and bodies, and 51 European agencies listed on the EU website [19],
- EU Funded and National Projects—246 EU-funded and national projects that are listed in the cyberwatching.eu "R & I Project Hub" [20],
- National Organizations from the European Economic Area (EEA) and the United Kingdom (UK)—around 310 national bodies responsible for cybersecurity in 30 EEA countries and the UK from the national strategies mentioned in the CyberWISER.eu's cartography [21],
- European Trade and Associations and Federations—296 organizations mentioned in the two lists, i.e., Top industry associations in the EU [22] and Top 200 EU trade associations [23] of the Association of Accredited Public Policy Advocates to the European Union (AALEP),
- Private Organizations—around 20 private organizations that have either operation in the EU or collaboration with EU organizations.

As shown in Fig. 1, after reviewing around 938 potential sources, we found 71 of them (listed in the Appendix) that offer free awareness programs and materials. Among the relevant sources, the majority of them do not produce and distribute CSA programs and materials exclusively to SMEs, but to all organizations. Nonetheless, these sources were included because SMEs are organizations, and the awareness programs and materials are free, allowing even SMEs with limited resources to benefit from them.

3.1 European Agencies and Organizations

Out of 66 organizations (comprising 15 European institutions and bodies and 51 European agencies) [19], only 5 were found to provide CSA resources. The types of awareness resources, security threats and risks covered, and CSA phases targeted by them are listed in Table 1. The European Union Agency for Cybersecurity (ENISA) and European Union Agency for Law Enforcement Cooperation (EUROPOL) are particularly active, publishing awareness resources on a regular basis on various existential cybersecurity risks and

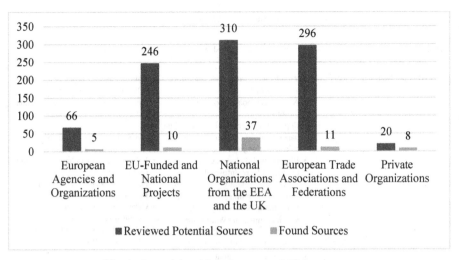

Fig. 1. Potential and found sources of CSA resource.

Table 1. Summary of the resource types offered, threats and risks covered, and CSA phases targeted.

Organization Types	Targeted CSA phases and available resource types	Topics covered
European Agencies and Organizations	***Pre-implementation phase (planning and designing)*** • Assessment tools, quizzes, and questionnaires • Position papers, and reports (e.g., threat landscape, technical reports, and guidebooks) ***Implementation phase*** • Brochures, Comics, Illustrations, Infographics, Posters, Presentations, Screensavers, Videos (e.g., clips, lecture videos), Websites • Competitions and events (e.g., Cybersecurity month, Cybersecurity challenge) • Training, workshops, and webinars ***Post-implementation phase (evaluation and adjustment)*** • Assessment tools, quizzes, and questionnaires	• Cyber threats and risks including new emerging, evolving, and advanced ones, as well as data protection issues relevant and prevalent to organizations (including SMEs), and sector-specific organizations, e.g., maritime, finance, etc. • Cybersecurity best practices and cyber hygiene for organizations • Information on the existing and proposed EU and international acts, regulations, and standards on ICT, cybersecurity, and data protection for organizations • Information on cybersecurity certifications • CSA frameworks, key performance indicators (KPIs), and measuring methods

(*continued*)

Table 1. (*continued*)

Organization Types	Targeted CSA phases and available resource types	Topics covered
EU-Funded and National Projects	***Pre-implementation phase (planning and designing)*** • Assessment tools, quizzes, and questionnaires • Reports (e.g., technical reports, white papers), guidebooks, and booklets ***Implementation phase*** • Blog posts, Brochures, Courses & tutorials, Flyers, Infographics, Newsletters, Literary graphics (e.g., comics, storytelling), Presentations, User stories, Videos (e.g., video lectures, clips), and Word games • Competitions and contests (e.g., hackathons, innovation contests) • Workshops and training ***Post-implementation phase (evaluation and adjustment)*** • Assessment tools, quizzes, and questionnaires	• Data and privacy protection, and cyber threats and risks including emerging and evolving ones relevant to SMEs, supply chain, and healthcare • Cybersecurity best practices and cyber hygiene for SMEs • EU cybersecurity policies, laws, and regulations • National cybersecurity strategies and legislation • Cybersecurity standards and certifications for SMEs • Cybersecurity skills and technologies relevant to SMEs

(*continued*)

Table 1. (*continued*)

Organization Types	Targeted CSA phases and available resource types	Topics covered
National Organizations from the EEA and the UK	***Pre-implementation phase (planning and designing)*** • Assessment tools (e.g., guides for assessment, assessment questionnaire, assessment tests) • Cybersecurity exercises and guides to design them • Reports and documents (informing about security issues, security best practices, security tips, security assessment, national security guidelines, security advice, and recommendations), translation of third-party reports • Malicious content (threat-wise) instructions ***Implementation phase*** • Animated gifs, Awareness kits and tools, Blog posts, Brochures, Infographics, Leaflets, Guidebooks, Posters, Paper toys, News (news section on website), Newsletters, Simulations, Social media posts (e.g., Twitter, Facebook), Video, Web docs, Websites • Alert and notification messages about cyber threats and incidents • Awareness campaigns, On-hand (e.g., banners, posters, leaflets, videos), and on-request (e.g., presentation for awareness program, awareness message texts, human resource) campaign materials • Awareness workshops, webinars, lectures, training, seminars, education, and tutoring • Events (e.g., National security month, Awareness conferences & colloquia, Cyber exercises) • Security tips and instructions (remedial tips, online tests, preventive tips) • Suggests games, books, movies, and other fun ways to use for awareness-raising • Useful link to third-party portals with ***Post-implementation phase (evaluation and adjustment)*** • Assessment tools (e.g., guides for assessment, assessment questionnaire, assessment tests)	• Cyber threats and risks relevant to organizations including SMEs • Cybersecurity best practices and cyber hygiene • National and EU cybersecurity, data protection, and privacy guidelines, policies, laws, and regulations for organizations • Cybersecurity standards and certifications for organizations • Response actions for cybersecurity incidents

(*continued*)

Table 1. (*continued*)

Organization Types	Targeted CSA phases and available resource types	Topics covered
European Trade Associations and Federations	***Pre-implementation phase (planning and designing)*** • Assessment guidelines • Threat landscape • Guidelines and frameworks ***Implementation phase*** • Events, Interviews, Podcasts, Reports, Third-party materials (from ENISA and EUROPOL), Website, Videos ***Post-implementation phase (evaluation and adjustment)*** • Assessment guidelines	• Cyber risks and threats relevant to their particular sector or industry • Cybersecurity best practices and cyber hygiene • Cybersecurity mechanisms, assessment guidelines, and frameworks for their sector or industry • International and regional regulations and standardizations • Cybersecurity incident reporting • Cybersecurity requirements specific to their sector or industry • Cybersecurity tools and references of third-party resources useful to their sector or industry
Private Organizations	***Pre-implementation phase (planning and designing)*** • Assessment questionnaires, tools, and quizzes • Reports (threat reports, analyst reports, white papers), Research fact sheets ***Implementation phase*** • Ask security experts, Blog posts, Campaigns, E-books, Hear from your peers (case studies), Leaflets, Magazines, Memes and graphics, Newsletters, Simulation playbooks, Posters, Tips and advice sheets, Videos (YouTube blogs, podcasts, video clips, and training course videos), Webinars ***Post-implementation phase (evaluation and adjustment)*** • Assessment questionnaires, tools, and quizzes	• Cyber threats and risks including the existing and emerging ones • Cybersecurity best practices and hygiene • Cybersecurity assessment tools and guidelines • Refer to third-party cybersecurity awareness resources

threats, as well as reflecting the current state of cybersecurity knowledge primarily covering security issues. The European Digital SME Alliance then covers and disseminates awareness resources on numerous cybersecurity issues that are relevant to SMEs, while the European Maritime Safety Agency (EMSA) provides awareness training exclusively in maritime cybersecurity.

Most of the awareness resources provided by European agencies and organizations are designed to be used during the implementation phase of a CSA program. Additionally, they organize various cybersecurity events and challenges to promote cybersecurity among EU citizens and organizations, and to provide up-to-date security information through awareness-raising and sharing of best practices, such as European Cybersecurity Month (ECSM) [24] and International Cybersecurity Challenge [25] are coordinated by ENISA and other European organizations, Symposium on Global Cybersecurity [26] is organized by EUROPOL in collaboration with the Anti-Phishing Working Group, and European Conference on Transport Cybersecurity [27] is organized by EMSA in cooperation with other European agencies and organizations. However, the reports and position papers from ENISA, European Cyber Security Organization (ECSO), and European Digital SME Alliance can be beneficial for planning and designing a CSA program. Similarly, ENISA and European Digital SME Alliance disseminate resources, such as cybersecurity assessment tools (e.g., Cybersecurity Self-assessment tool, Cyber risk temperature tool, GDPR Temperature Tool, Information Notice Tool, and Awareness quiz templates) that can be used to determine an organization's level of CSA before and after implementing a CSA program.

The awareness resources are largely available for free or after a simple registration. The resources from EMSA require authentication and are only available to its beneficiaries. Downloading and using the resources is simple and hassle-free. It requires basic computer and Internet skills (e.g., browsing websites, downloading files, playing movies, installing screensavers, and registering to a website) to use the resources.

The awareness resources developed and disseminated by these organizations are mostly focused on learning how to *'identify'*, *'detect'*, and *'protect'* against cyberattacks. Some of EUROPOL's awareness resources discuss how to *'respond'* and *'recover'* when an organization has suffered a cyberattack or data breach. For example, it provides instructions and resources for recovering from ransomware attacks, as well as advice on how to respond in the event of a cyberattack or data breach.

However, some major aspects that could potentially play role in improving the awareness resources but are found lacking in many of them are as follows:

- Several awareness materials did not provide the complete information that the audience needs to know, and preferably to act. By completeness, we refer to the needful information that could motivate people to change their attitude, and preferably to act. Complete information should contain, for instance, what is the threat, why the audience should know about it (benefits of knowing about it or consequences of not knowing about it), how to identify or detect it, and how to behave (to do and not to do) if it is detected.
- Except for feedback on some workshops, webinars, and training, we did not find any feedback functionality (e.g., a hyperlink for feedback) integrated into other awareness materials. Indeed, webpage visits, materials download logs, and registrations can give an idea of the popularity of the awareness materials, but it is not sufficient to know how useful the provided materials were to the end-users or companies. This information can be obtained only if the end-users have the means and opportunity to provide their feedback.
- We found materials only from EUROPOL that provided a feature or plugin to share the awareness materials on social media platforms and send them through email. This feature to ease the dissemination is important to encourage the end-users to share the awareness materials and thus improve their visibility and adoption.
- Most of the awareness materials were in English and used neutral colors. A few materials from ENISA had translations in different European languages. Certainly, awareness materials in English can be used by many, however, translating them into the native language of the audience and preferably also incorporating localization

strategies (e.g., colors, images, examples, and other cultural aspects) would help to improve the materials' acceptance and usability.

3.2 EU Funded and National Projects

Of the 246 EU-funded and national projects [20], we mainly concentrated on the projects that are still active (or running) and have working groups for CSA. After this first level of screening, we browsed and reviewed the website contents of all the active projects and a few finished projects whose websites were still live and presumably could be useful for SMEs. Based on the two-level screenings to find if they offer awareness resources, we found 10 projects that produce and/or distribute such resources mostly to SMEs. Except for these three projects, the DOGANA project (end date was 31 August 2018), SMESEC project (end date was 01 May 2020), and FORTIKA project (end date was 31 May 2020), others were ongoing projects when the study was conducted in April 2021. These completed projects have several awareness resources that cover the existential cyber risks and threats and so can be relevant to SMEs.

These projects produce and distribute various types of awareness resources covering different cybersecurity issues relevant to SMEs and the supply chain and are beneficial in all three phases of CSA. Table 1 lists the different types of awareness resources, as well as the threats and risks they cover, and the CSA phases they target. Along with the implementation phase of a CSA program, these projects seem to equally emphasize awareness resources that can be used to assess the CSA level of an organization. Tools and services (e.g. Cyber risk temperature tool, Cybersecurity self-assessment tool for SMEs, Definition and recommendation tool, GDPR temperature tool, Information notice tool, Lessons from testing & validation, Threat protection & response tool, Vulnerability discovery & resolution tool, Wizard tool) produced or distributed by cyberwatching.eu, SMESEC project, GEIGER project, and SecureHospitals project can be useful for the CSA assessment of organizations before and after a CSA program to realize its outcome. Moreover, their deliverables with different frameworks and models can be helpful in planning and designing a CSA program. Additionally, some projects have utilized more intuitive and engaging techniques like literary graphic and gaming competitions (DOGANA project), quizzes (SMESEC project), and simulation (Cyberwiser.eu), which are found to improve the effectiveness of CSA initiatives. All the projects organize CSA events (e.g., webinars, seminars, workshops, hackathons, training, Massive open online course, literary graphics and gaming competitions, and others) to raise the awareness in community and organizations.

Most of the awareness resources are free of cost or require registration to download and use. Some resources from the SMESEC project are made available privately to users contacting the project. Similarly, the Cyber-MAR project offers reports and training only to authorized users, i.e., requiring authentication. While Cyberwiser.eu also offers awareness training courses but for a fee. Some of the awareness materials by Cyberwatching.eu are accessible only to registered users.

In general, it requires basic computer and Internet skills to access the awareness materials. Taking awareness quizzes and using assessment tools (again available in the form of a questionnaire) can be accessed in a browser and are simple to use.

In addition to *'identification'*, *'detection'*, and *'protection'* actions, their deliverable reports and other materials also discuss *'response'* and *'recovery'* actions that need to be taken if a cyberattack or data breach has occurred.

Some important factors which will potentially improve the overall usability of these awareness materials are:

- Only the DOGANA project and FORTIKA project have produced awareness materials in multiple European languages. Once again, the awareness materials have relied mostly on translation rather than localization.
- The awareness materials produced by these projects do not ask for feedback from the end-users. Indeed, determined end-users can contact and write an email of feedback to the project email address but how many will attempt that is questionable. Integrating a feedback section or functionality, for example, a feedback weblink in posters and leaflets and a comment section in blogs and articles can be a practical way to get feedback from the end-users.
- Except for cyberwatching.eu, other projects have a feature (or plugin) in their event webpage to share it on social media platforms (e.g., Facebook, Twitter, LinkedIn, and others) and send it through email. This feature will help the audience to contribute to the diffusion of the information.

3.3 National Organizations from the EEA Countries and the United Kingdom

To begin, we compiled a list of 310 national bodies responsible for cybersecurity in 30 EEA countries and the UK from the *national strategies* [21]. Each country has multiple organizations, although not all of them are responsible for CSA. This was followed by visiting and examining each national body's website to see if the entity is responsible for or has a part in the CSA of organizations and SMEs. We identified 37 national organizations responsible for CSA in 31 countries.

Interestingly, these organizations depend on diversified forms of awareness resources listed in Table 1. The table also contains the cyber threats and risks covered as well as the CSA phases the resources are aimed at. Most of the awareness resources are useful for the implementation phase of a CSA program. Only a few of the organizations appear to distribute cybersecurity assessment tools and services that can be used to realize the awareness level in the organization, i.e., appropriate for the pre-and post-implementation phases of a CSA program. Additionally, the majority of the resources targeted organizations in general rather than SMEs in particular. However, the UK's National Cyber Security Centre, Belgium's Cyber Security Coalition and Centre for Cyber Security, France's National Cybersecurity Agency, and Greece's Hellenic Computer Security Incident Response Team are exceptions that also distribute awareness resources exclusive to SMEs.

We also observed that some nations have national organizations or centers dedicated to cyber and information security (namely, Austria, Belgium, Cyprus, Czech Republic, Denmark, Estonia, Finland, France, Germany, Ireland, Lithuania, Malta, Netherlands, Norway, Portugal, Romania, UK), whereas in the majority of nations the Computer Emergency Response Team (CERT) is in charge of CSA for citizens and organizations. Further, the Center for Cyber Security Belgium offers an initiative called 'Safeonweb' that is dedicated to increasing CSA in the nation. Likewise, CERT Iceland and CERT Poland collaborate with the SANS Institute to provide CSA resources.

We also noticed that the websites of CERT Bulgaria and Cyprus Cybercrime Center of Excellence are no longer active. Based on the website's activities, we observed that the remaining organizations are active and continue to update their awareness materials to comprehend evolving cyber threat landscape and advancements in technology. This means that SMEs and other types of organizations are more likely to find relevant awareness resources on their websites.

To access the awareness resources from these organizations, the users typically need a working knowledge of computers and the Internet.

It could be because most countries are dependent on CERT, in addition to *'identification'*, *'detection'*, and *'protection'* actions, their awareness materials also discuss *'response'* and *'recovery'* actions that need to be taken if a cyberattack or data breach has occurred.

Since each national body has produced awareness materials for a specific country, the materials can be considered to be localized to that nation.

Finally, many of these organizations are dependent mostly on log data (e.g., download and view counts) to realize the popularity of the distributed awareness resources. Some organizations have integrated a feature to share the awareness content on social media platforms, e.g., Facebook, Twitter, and LinkedIn. The Cyber Security Coalition from Belgium has asked for feedback on its awareness tools from the end-users. Similarly, the Republic of Estonia Information System Authority has asked for feedback on its awareness content. For the purpose of future planning, updating, and improving awareness materials, it is crucial to continuously get feedback from end-users in order to identify the shortcomings in the quality of awareness content and delivery channels.

3.4 European Trade Associations and Federations

Amidst the vast number of trade associations and federations in Europe, we have considered only 296 of them for this study. They are from the two lists maintained by the Association of Accredited Public Policy Advocates to the European Union (AALEP), which are the Top industry associations in the EU [22], and the Top 200 EU trade associations [23].

We identified only 11 trade associations and federations that offer very limited types of CSA resources but only to members, and for membership they charge a fee. Moreover, each organization belongs to a particular sector and provides awareness resources suitable to a particular sector and industry. Organizations like Trust in Digital Life, the Federation of Small Business UK, and the Confederation of British Industry also publish awareness resources for SMEs. Then, the Luxembourg Banker's Association refers to awareness resources from third parties like ENISA and EUROPOL relevant to the banking sector. Interestingly, the focus of most trade associations and federations is on compliance with the General Data Protection Regulation (GDPR). Table 1 lists the several categories of awareness resources, the security topics they cover, and the CSA program phases they are targeted for.

The websites of these trade associations and federations are active and found to regularly update the contents with discussions on existential cyber risks and threats including emerging and evolving ones. However, these organizations rely mostly on a small number of very specific sorts of materials, like events, reports, and articles, to increase the CSA of their members. Further, most awareness resources required user authentication to access them. Some articles and reports that are open for everyone include a feature to share on social media or send through email.

In addition to *'identification'*, *'detection'*, and *'protection'* actions, the awareness resources also discuss *'response'* and *'recovery'* actions that need to be taken if a cyberattack or data breach has occurred.

Almost all European organizations currently use or depend, in varying degrees, on digital infrastructures, and this need will only grow in the future. This suggests that they are all vulnerable to online crimes and attacks. Moreover, these groups (organizations) are often closer to their trade associations and federations. Therefore, we think that the trade associations and federations might play a significant role in advancing cybersecurity and distributing CSA information to their members. The irony, however, is that not many trade associations and federations offer CSA resources to their members.

3.5 Private Organizations

Because there are so many private organizations that provide CSA resources, we reviewed only 20 of them and discovered 8 that provide at least some awareness resources for free. Furthermore, these private organizations or sources either collaborate with European organizations or have operations in Europe, providing awareness products and services to European companies including SMEs. For example,

- Computer Emergency Response Team (CERT) Poland and CERT Iceland collaborate with the SANS Institute,
- CERT Latvia collaborates with STOP.THINK. CONNECT.
- Proofpoint partners with companies such as Atos, Capgemini, Deloitte, Orange, Telefonica, and Cognizant, in Europe,
- KnowBe4 and Global Knowledge have operations in European countries, and
- CyberReady and InfoSec Institute offer awareness resources in different European languages.

The reviewed private organizations offer awareness resources in diversified forms but most of the awareness training courses and services are for a fee. Some basic CSA materials are offered for free, but often after registration. The awareness resource types offered for free by the private organizations, cyber risks and threats covered by them and CSA phases where they can be appropriate are listed in Table 1.

Almost all the awareness resources are in English (with exceptions from CyberReady and InfoSec Institute which offer awareness materials in other European languages).

Among the freely available awareness materials, most of them do not include an immediate feedback feature, for example, InfoSec's YouTube channel for cybersecurity awareness has a feedback section just underneath where it has received a large number of feedbacks from the end-users. Most of the awareness materials have a feature that allows end-users to share them on social media and send them through email.

The awareness resources also contain '*detection*' and '*protection*' actions that must be taken if a cyberattack or data breach has occurred in addition to '*identification*', '*detection*', and '*protection*' actions.

4 Discussions and Conclusions

SMEs are the backbone of Europe's economy. At the same time, they are also highly vulnerable and targeted by cyber-attacks and -crimes. Thus, the budget and resource constraints SMEs can benefit from the free and inexpensive CSA resources produced and distributed by various public and private entities.

In order to realize "*how abundance and well-suited are the (free and inexpensive) awareness resources for SMEs?*", this study explored and reviewed five types of sources, namely

- European agencies and organizations,
- EU-funded and national projects,
- National organizations of EEA countries and the UK,
- European trade associations and federations, and
- Private companies offering information security and cybersecurity training and awareness resources.

Most of the listed sources are from Europe, which has prepared awareness materials and programs to meet the needs of European citizens, industry, and enterprises. Overall, these sources produce and distribute a large variety of awareness resources that target all three phases of a CSA program, and cover mainly these issues:

- cybersecurity threats and risks including new emerging and evolving ones,
- good practices and cyber hygiene,
- national and EU cybersecurity and data protection regulations and laws,
- security mechanisms and assessment guidelines and frameworks,
- information and communication technology (ICT) and security requirements,
- cybersecurity tools and resources from third parties, and
- cybersecurity standardization and certifications.

However, when considering a large number of SMEs in Europe and the wide range of business sectors they serve, the amount of localized and sector-specific awareness resources produced and disseminated by these sources for SMEs is insufficient. Less than 8% of the potential sources we investigated for this study actually produce or distribute awareness resources. The situation is further worsened if consider the awareness resources produce exclusively for SMEs, which are scarcer.

Among the five source categories, the first three mostly produce and distribute awareness resources that can be used during the implementation phase of a CSA program. Only a few of them disseminate CSA assessment tools that can be used during both the pre- and post-implementation phases of a CSA program. Moreover, they largely depend on log data (e.g., download and visit logs) to monitor the popularity of their awareness resources. They do not have any integrated functionality to get direct feedback from the users of the awareness resources. More importantly, very few of them have awareness resources using communication channels like games and simulations, more engaging and intuitive media for CSA. Except for the awareness materials from the EEA national organizations, others have simply performed a translation and not localization of the awareness materials. The fourth category distributes awareness resources only to members, and there is a membership fee. The fifth category distributes only basic awareness resources. For more advanced awareness resources, SMEs have to pay for them. Further, the fifth category has utilized more diverse communication channels for CSA and has an abundance of awareness resources on more emerging and evolving cyber threats and risks including those that originated due to COVID-19.

In approaching these resources, many of the resources may not exactly fit the business needs, organizational culture, and IT infrastructure of a particular SME, which may require tailoring the materials to fit the needs and context of the business. Specific properties wise, the awareness resources should be accessible, suitable for the user's circumstance and situations or conditions, communication strategies and techniques that suit the preference of the users, interactive and innovative to engage the audiences, and be inclusive so that no subset of the audience feels left out. Moreover, they should include tracking capabilities like self-assessment and feedback that can help to verify whether people are actually learning, and also facilitate interested users to participate and contribute to the future improvement of the awareness program. It is suggested that SMEs should use multiple forms of awareness materials that can fulfill the needs of diversified users [4, 28]. Availability of awareness materials in different forms helps to cover a larger mass of audiences with different learning preferences [29], for example, someone with no interest in reading can utilize cybersecurity awareness materials available in the form of video, games, or simulation. Moreover, people can easily acclimate to the cybersecurity awareness materials, if always provided in the same form, thus reducing their effectiveness. Further, using multiple channels also ensures that personnel is exposed to the same information multiple times in different ways.

Last but not least, there is a critical need for the production and distribution of more *free or affordable*, and *high-quality* CSA resources *exclusively targeting SMEs*. For a better result, these resources should be *localized, business sector-specific, and use more engaging and intuitive communication channels*. Additionally, each awareness resource should *incorporate the applicable features to facilitate the user*, for example, to share the resources with others (which is necessary for its diffusion) and to comment on the resource's quality (which is necessary for the update and modification of resource).

Acknowledgement. The authors would like to thank Panayiotis Kotzanikolaou (UPRC, Greece), Jozef Vyskoc (VaF, Slovak Republic), and Christine Jamieson (TDL, Belgium) for reviewing and providing feedback on the deliverable report submitted to the CyberSec4Europe.

Funding. This work has financially been supported by the CyberSec4Europe project (Proposal No. 830929). This paper is a revised and shortened version of the deliverable report D9.11 [30] from CyberSec4Europe's WP9: Dissemination, Outreach, Spreading of Competence, Raising Awareness.

Appendix

S.N.	Sources
	European Agencies and Organizations (refer to [19] to get the list of European agencies and organizations)
1	European Union Agency for Cybersecurity (ENISA)
2	European Union Agency for Law Enforcement Cooperation (EUROPOL)
3	European Maritime Safety Agency (EMSA)
4	European Cybersecurity Organization (ECSO)
5	European Digital SME Alliance
	EU-Funded and National Projects (refer to [20] to get the list of EU-funded and national projects)
6	Cyberwatching.eu
7	Cyberwiser.eu
8	SMESEC Project
9	GEIGER Project
10	Cyber-MAR Project
11	SecureHospitals Project
12	DOGANA Project
13	FORTIKA Project
14	CyberSec4Europe Project
15	PUZZLE Project
	National Organizations (refer to [21] to get the list of national organizations working in cybersecurity)
16	Cyber Security Austria
17	Cyber Security Coalition - Belgium
18	Centre for Cyber security Belgium
19	Safeonweb - Belgium
20	Computer Emergency Response Team Bulgaria
21	CARNet's National Computer Emergency Response Team - Croatia
22	Cyprus Cybercrime Centre of Excellence
23	National Cyber and Information Security Agency - Czech Republic
24	The National Computer Security Incident Response Team of the Czech Republic
25	Danish Centre for Cyber Security
26	Republic of Estonia Information System Authority
27	Finnish Transport and Communication Agency National Cyber Security Centre
28	The National Cybersecurity Agency of France

(*continued*)

(*continued*)

S.N.	Sources
29	Federal Office for Information Security - Germany
30	Hellenic Computer Security Incident Response Team
31	Gov Computer Emergency Response Team Hungary
32	Computer Emergency Response Team-Iceland
33	Irish Reporting and Information Security Service
34	Computer Security Incident Response Team-Italia
35	Information Technology Security Incident Response Institution, Republic of Latvia
36	National Cyber Security Centre of Lithuania
37	Computer Emergency Response Team, Luxembourg
38	Cyber Security Malta
39	National Cyber Security Centrum - Netherlands
40	Norwegian National Security Authority
41	The Norwegian Centre for Information Security
42	Computer Emergency Response Team Polska
43	Centro Nacional de Cibersegurança - Portugal
44	Cyber Security Research Centre - Romania
45	Centrul Naţional de Răspuns la Incidente de Securitate Cibernetică - Romania
46	Computer Security Incident Response Team Slovakia
47	Slovenian Computer Emergency Response Team
48	The Spanish National Cybersecurity Institute - Computer Emergency Response Team
49	Centro Criptológico Nacional Computer Emergency Response Team - Spain
50	Computer Emergency Response Team Sweden
51	SWITCH's Computer Emergency Response Team
52	The National Cyber Security Centre - UK
	European Trade Associations and Federations (refer to [22] and [23] to get the list of European trade associations and federations)
53	Federation of Small Businesses - UK
54	The Software Alliance
55	The Association of the Swedish Engineering Industries
56	Investment Company Institute Global
57	Europe's Distribution System Operators
58	The Luxembourg Banker's Association
59	Association of Mutual Insurers and Insurance Cooperatives in Europe
60	GSMA Europe
61	Confederation of British Industry

(*continued*)

(continued)

S.N.	Sources
62	Insurance Europe
63	European Banking Federation
	Private Organizations
64	SANS Institute
65	InfoSec Institute
66	Cyber Safe Work
67	STOP.THINK. CONNECT
68	Proofpoint
69	CybeReady
70	KnowBe4
71	Global Knowledge

References

1. European Commission: What is an SME. https://ec.europa.eu/growth/smes/sme-definitio n_en. Accessed 22 June 2022
2. European Commission: Entrepreneurship and small and medium-sized enterprises (SMEs). https://ec.europa.eu/growth/smes_en. Accessed 22 June 2022
3. European Commission: Guide for training in SMEs. https://op.europa.eu/en/publication-det ail/-/publication/1020b85f-dcc4-4c80-8d6e-65f4617aa3cd. Accessed 22 June 2022
4. Bada, M., Nurse, J.R.C.: Developing cybersecurity education and awareness programmers for small and medium-sized enterprises (SMEs). Inf. Comput. Secur. **27**(3), 393–410 (2019)
5. U.S. Securities and Exchange Commission: The Need for Greater Focus on the Cybersecurity Challenges Facing Small and Midsize Businesses. https://www.sec.gov/news/statement/cyb ersecurity-challenges-for-small-midsize-businesses.html. Accessed 22 June 2022
6. Ponsard, C., Grandclaudon, J., Dallons, V.: Towards a cyber security label for SMEs: a European perspective. In: 4th International Conference on Information Systems Security and Privacy, Funchal, Madeira, Portugal, 24–26 January, pp. 426–431 (2018)
7. European Commission: Supporting specialized skills development: Big Data, Internet of Things and Cybersecurity for SMEs. https://op.europa.eu/en/publication-detail/-/publication/ 7bc063b9-5f5b-11ea-b735-01aa75ed71a1/language-en. Accessed 22 June 2022
8. OECD: Strengthening SMEs and Entrepreneurship for Productivity and Inclusive Growth: Key Issue Paper. https://www.oecd.org/cfe/smes/ministerial/documents/2018-SME-Minist erial-Conference-Key-Issues.pdf. Accessed 22 June 2022
9. Dojkovski, S., Lichtenstein, S., Warren, M.: Challenges in fostering an information security culture in Australian small and medium sized enterprises. In: European Conference on Information Warfare and Security, Helsinki, Finland (2006)
10. ZyXel, T.K.: The SME security challenge. Comput. Fraud Secur. **2015**(3), 5–7 (2015)
11. FireEye: Stopping Cyber Crime Against Small and Midsize Enterprises: Enterprise Security to Protect Budget-conscious Organizations from Disruptive Attacks. https://www.fireeye.com/ offers/stop-cyber-crime-against-small-medium-enterprises.html. Accessed 31 Jan 2021

12. Kaspersky: The Human Factor in IT security: How Employees are Making Businesses Vulnerable from Within. https://www.kaspersky.com/blog/the-human-factor-in-it-security/. Accessed 22 June 2022
13. KPMG: Cyber security: it's not just about technology. https://assets.kpmg/content/dam/kpmg/pdf/2014/05/cyber-security-not-just-technology.pdf. Accessed 22 June 2022
14. Harvard Business Review: Cybersecurity Is Not (Just) a Tech Problem. https://hbr.org/2021/01/cybersecurity-is-not-just-a-tech-problem. Accessed 22 June 2022
15. Siponen, M.: Five dimensions of information security awareness. Comput. Soc. **31**(2), 24–29 (2001)
16. Bada, M., Sasse, A., Nurse, J.R.C.: Cyber security awareness campaigns: why do they fail to change behaviour? In: International Conference on Cyber Security for Sustainable Society, Coventry, UK (2015)
17. SANS: 2019 Security Awareness Report: The Rising Era of Awareness Training. https://adcg.org/wp-content/uploads/2020/02/SANS-Security-Awareness-Report-2019.pdf. Accessed 22 June 2022
18. NIST: SP 800-50 Building an Information Technology Security Awareness and Training Program. https://nvlpubs.nist.gov/nistpubs/legacy/sp/nistspecialpublication800-50.pdf. Accessed 22 June 2022
19. European Union: Institutions, Bodies & Agencies – Contact & Visit Details. https://europa.eu/european-union/contact/institutions-bodies_en. Accessed 27 Aug 2021
20. Cyberwatching.eu: R&I Project Hub. https://www.cyberwatching.eu/projects. Accessed 27 Aug 2021
21. Cyberwiser.eu: Cartography - EU National Strategies. https://www.cyberwiser.eu/cartography. Accessed 27 Aug 2021
22. AALEP: Top industry associations in the EU. http://www.aalep.eu/top-industry-associations-eu. Accessed 27 Aug 2021
23. AALEP: Top 200 EU trade associations. http://www.aalep.eu/top-industry-associations-eu. Accessed 27 Aug 2021
24. ENISA: European Cybersecurity Month. https://www.enisa.europa.eu/topics/cybersecurity-education/european-cyber-security-month. Accessed 21 June 2022
25. ENISA: International Cybersecurity Challenge. https://www.enisa.europa.eu/topics/cybersecurity-education/international-cybersecurity-challenge-icc. Accessed 21 June 2022
26. APWG: Symposium on Global Cybersecurity Awareness. https://apwg.org/symposium-on-global-cybersecurity-awareness/. Accessed 21 June 2022
27. ENISA: 1st Transport Cybersecurity Conference. https://www.enisa.europa.eu/events/first-transport-cyber-security-conference. Accessed 21 June 2022
28. Gattiker, U.E.: Can an early warning system for home users and SMEs make a difference? A field study. In: Lopez, J. (ed.) CRITIS 2006. LNCS, vol. 4347, pp. 112–127. Springer, Heidelberg (2006). https://doi.org/10.1007/11962977_10
29. Pattinson, M., et al.: Adapting cyber security training to your employees. In: 12th International Symposium on Human Aspects of Information Security & Assurance, Dundee, Scotland, UK, 29–31 August (2018)
30. CyberSec4Europe: D9.11 SME cybersecurity awareness program 2. https://cybersec4europe.eu/wp-content/uploads/2021/05/D9.11-SME-cybersecurity-awareness-program-2-FINAL-submitted-1.pdf. Accessed 22 June 2022

A Framework for Developing Tabletop Cybersecurity Exercises

Nabin Chowdhury$^{(\boxtimes)}$ and Vasileios Gkioulos

Norwegian University of Science and Technology,
Teknologivegen 22, 2815 Gjøvik, Norway
{nabin.chowdhury,vasileios.gkioulos}@ntnu.no
https://www.ntnu.edu/

Abstract. As remote work increases in adoption, partly pushed by the 2020 COVID-19 pandemic, conducting and offering security training to employees is ever more challenging, due to physical constraints. Cyber-security training is ever more critical as both digitalization of controls and services increases, and remote working increases the risks of cyber-threats, due to vulnerable communication channels and lack of security practices from remote location working. As physical presence and coordination of large groups of employees becomes more challenging, it is necessary to offer more flexible, adaptable and lightweight training and exercise solutions for cyber-security training. For this reason, in this work we propose a lightweight tabletop framework for conducting cybersecurity exercises. The framework has been developed taking into consideration personalized learning theory concepts and feedback from academic and industrial stakeholders. Evaluation of the framework was conducted through a series of exercises with industrial personnel and university students. According to the results of the experiments, the framework is effective at developing a great range of table-top exercises for both students, security professionals and technical operators. By focusing on flexibility, ease of implementation, remote accessibility and other key attributes, the exercises developed with the framework have been reported to be successful in achieving the goals, and found engaging and motivating by participants.

Keywords: Cyber-security · Training · Awareness · Table-top · Exercise

1 Introduction

Physical presence in offices from personnel with CS responsibilities has been steadily decreasing over the last decade, thanks to access to tools and software for remote work [26]. This reality has been further exacerbated by the recent COVID-19 pandemic, which forced many industries to close access to their

---

Supported by the Norwegian University of Science and Technology.

physical location. As access to these location has been re-opening, many factors have pushed many workers to continue working remotely instead of returning to the offices. These factor include: increased internal flexibility, worker mobility, cost reduction for office maintenance and in-office demands among others [14]. While this has proven to be advantageous in many ways, remote working has brought several disadvantages as well. Among these, one of the most critical is the increased risk of cyber-attacks [12]. It has been shown that since the start of the COVID-19 pandemic, cyber attacks have increased by 81% [13], with data exfiltration and phishing email attacks having the highest increase in occurrence [19]. This data highlights the importance, now more than ever, of cyber-security (CS) training of employees.

Companies, internationally, have adopted many forms of CS training activities for their employees, both for basic CS concept training and for more advanced, role-focused training. As training activities and offerings continue to be developed, one factor to consider remains the physical availability of participants. In fact, due to the lessened physical presence of personnel, many forms of training have become more challenging to employ, such as physical classroom training. Conducting CS exercises has also been more challenging, due to limitations in resource and time availability. While many online solutions have been proposed and are continuously developed for individual training, additional factors that are often not considered during development and implementation of these training exercises is whether they are found to be engaging and correspond to participants' preferences for training. It has been shown in the literature that engagement and motivation can greatly affect the outcome of a training exercise, and as such should always be considered [29,31]. Additionally, when offering CS training, team-based exercises such as table-top exercises should be considered due to their ability to increase participants' engagement [3] and success in skill acquisition [3]. Furthermore, this type of training greatly aids in building critical skills such as communication skills and team skills [9].

For this, in this paper we design and develop a framework for developing tabletop CS exercises. The framework is developed to be adaptable to both physical and online use, team-based and discussion-based exercises. This has been done to permit high flexibility of use, based on the goals, requirements and resource constraints that may be put in place by the training organization. The framework takes into consideration a number of aspects of Personalize Learning Theory (PLT) such as creating learning paths and learning profiles for participants [33], as well as involvement of training participants in the design and development of the exercise, following the recommendations found in [10]. The framework has been tested by conducting a number of CS exercises with both university students and with industrial personnel.

The remainder of this work is organized as follows: in Sect. 2, we discuss related work focused in CS table-top exercises and training development. In Sect. 3, we discuss the methods utilized to design, develop and evaluate the framework. In Sect. 4, we discuss the resulting framework and analyze the results of the experimentation conducted using the proposed framework. In Sect. 5, a summary and analysis of the results from the experiment is conducted. Finally, in Sect. 6 we provide closing remarks on the work conducted, as well as discuss planned and possible future work to be conducted.

2   Related Work

In the literature, a number of table-top games for CS training has been proposed over the years. These proposals have been used both in academic and industrial settings. While the majority of the proposals that have been found in the literature do not take into account PLT consideration for exercise development, as far as the author knows, they have been consulted to aid in the development of this work. Following is a description of these works.

In [3], the authors conduct a literature review of table-top games for CS training. In particular, both table-top proposed in the literature and commercial products have been reviewed, which has shown that use of these type of games has been steadily increasing both in academia and in industry. Additionally, the authors discussed how these games can improve awareness, understanding, strategic-decision making, technical and non-technical skills. In a continuation of the previous work, in [2] the authors discuss the skills gap in current CS sphere and how table-top exercises can aid in filling these gaps. By enhancing the development of skills such as problem-solving, communication, teamwork and business processes understanding, these exercises are recommended by the authors for CS awareness and training. Moreover, their cost-effectiveness and adaptability is additionally valued in business environments. All the aspects mentioned by the authors in these two studies were taken into consideration during the development of our proposed framework.

[23] present a light-weight tabletop exercise for CS education. The exercise differs from other offerings as it requires a lower overhead for development and set-up, making it ideal for smaller educational environments. From initial evaluation conducted on master level students, the exercise was shown to be effective and engaging. The lightweight aspect of the exercise in this work was a key consideration which was adopted also in our proposed work.

[4] propose a model for web-based online table-top games. The model includes all stages of exercise development, including identification, planning, conduction and evaluation. Additional consideration for role assignment, scenario and event generation and trainee evaluation make the model proposed by the authors valid for training purposes, although further evaluation should be conducted.

[15] propose a more theoretically founded approach for the use of table-top exercises in CS education. In particular, the authors refer to elements of interdisciplinary integration of learning, human-computer interaction and management theories. Experiential learning and situated cognition are also cited as measures for learning outcome, via Bloom's revised taxonomy of educational objectives.

More recently, [21] developed a tabletop CS simulation, and conducted a large scale exercise specifically concerning the role of CEOs and C-suite-level executives during a CS emergency scenario. The exercise conducted lasted 3.5 h and was based on a 3-phase case study ransomware attack on an Academic Health Center (AHC). Participants were divided in teams with specific roles and discussed thorough the running of the scenarios which defensive strategies should be put in place and run. The authors noted that the live experiment conducted highlighted a lack of agreement on preferred strategies and actions in case of a cyber threat.

As it can bee seen, research and development of CS table-top exercises has advanced significantly. That being said, one commonality of the works discussed in this section is their lack of consideration of participants' preferences and collection of their feedback during the design and development of the exercises. Moreover, additional stakeholders should also be consulted during these phases, to conciliate the objectives of each party.

3 Methods

The framework proposed in this work is based on the CS development framework we developed in [10]. The framework presented in [10] is a generic framework that allows for the development of different types of CS training and exercises, using different training delivery methods and with different attributes. Due to the very broad nature of the framework proposed in [10], a more refined model specific for the development of Tabletop exercises was developed. An additional reason for the development of this framework was due to feedback collection from various different target groups which indicated table-top exercises both as preferred over other methods and easier to implement [7]. Additional input to refine and improve the framework was collected from the three following sources:

- Recommendations from Literature: through literature analysis and consultation of literature review works, standards, best practices and general recommendations for CS exercise development were collected.
- Recommendations from Academic Stakeholders: During previous research, feedback from a variety of stakeholders from the academia has been collected regarding preferences, needs and goals of CS training and training delivery methods. This information has been utilized and compared with remarks from stakeholders from the industry.
- Recommendations from Industrial Stakeholders: During previous research, feedback from a variety of stakeholders from the industry has been collected regarding preferences, needs and goals of CS training and training delivery methods. This information has been utilized and compared with remarks from stakeholders from academia.

3.1 Recommendations from Literature

The use and selection of tabletop exercises as a form of CS training comes from specific advantages of this type of training delivery method over others. These advantages have been widely studied and reported in the literature. In Table 1, the main advantages and disadvantages of table-top exercises over other type of training delivery methods are highlighted.

Table 1. Advantages and disadvantages of using table-top exercises for training, as indicated in the literature

Advantages	Disadvantages
Ease of participation [2]	Limitations in realism of scenario simulation [5]
Facilitate group discussion and team building skills [2]	Does not provide way of demonstrating a dysfunctional system in practice
Cost-effective and efficient [6]	Exercise may provide only superficial view of configurations and procedures [28]
Effective in scenario-based knowledge acquisition [22]	

Additionally to the advantages mentioned in Table 1, this type of exercises can also be useful for facilitating understanding of Industrial Relationships (IR) and Employee Relationships (ER) processes and procedures, as well as teach hands-on skills for CS Incident Response Teams (CSIRTs) and incident prevention skills [2] based on the design and content of the exercise.

To deal with some of the limitations indicated in Table 1, many newer table-top exercise tools offer simulated environment that try to give real-time input on different stages of a cyber-incident, based on the selected scenario. Cyber Incident Simulation (CIS) [27] is an example of such type of offering.

Selected proposals of tabletop exercises for CS training in the literature have also been consulted for more in-depth design considerations of our proposed framework.

[23] in particular describes a lightweight strategy for developing red team vs blue team table-top exercises. One of the main differences of their proposed format for table-top exercises is in it's distinctively low overhead of resources needed for design, development and implementation of exercises. This advantage has proven to be particularly practical in Small-to-Medium sized Enterprises (SMEs), where the size of teams participating to exercises is reduced and both time and resource constraints are strong limitations to training offerings.

3.2 Recommendations from Academic Stakeholders

During our previous research in [7,10], various stakeholders from the academia have been consulted to understand their preferences and requirements when it comes to CS training. These included students in Information Security, researchers and professors who had previously worked on CS training research and development.

In [10], both industrial personnel and academic personnel had been consulted for the purpose of understanding preferences when it comes to CS training development. Overall, both groups had expressed aligned views on the attributes that were to be prioritized when developing CS training, which are listed in the following:

- Suitability
- Real-life Experience
- Scalability & Adaptability
- Accessibility
- Frequency of Training and Periodical Updates
- Cost Efficiency
- Consideration for the human factor

When it comes to development methods for training, in [10] a revised ADDIE model was agreed upon among the stakeholders involved in the discussion. Detail regarding the model and its phases is shown in Fig. 1.

When it comes to training delivery methods, simulation-based and game-based solutions were suggested to be most effective in the literature [8] and have been also agreed to be preferable by stakeholders. These two methods were found to be more engaging and consequentially more motivating than other traditional training delivery methods [18,25]. The criticality of ensuring that training is engaging comes from studies showing how tedious training often fail to change employees' security behaviour and attitudes [17].

When it comes to training assessment and evaluation, feedback collection and comparison between pre and post-training performance were selected as preferred methods in [10]. With one approach being more qualitative in nature, while the latter being a quantitative approach that analyzes specific performance indicators (PI), the two approaches complement each others suitably.

According to [1], the following 5 attributes are fundamental in post-training feedback collection: effectiveness of training (overall result-oriented metrics to evaluate the success of the training), comprehension (ease of understanding and completion of training by the participants), attractiveness of training (overall appeal and interest from participants), engagement and finally suggestions from participants.

When developing PIs or evaluation metrics for CS training, [30] suggests that at least one indicator should measure one of the following attributes: Accuracy (correctness of the information), Timeliness (how up-to-date the training is to current standards), Completeness (comprehensiveness of topics and material of the training), Reliability (comparison of the training material information to other source) and Relevance (utility of the training compared to objectives). Additional measurements should be based on the specific objectives of the training exercise, a well as its overall design.

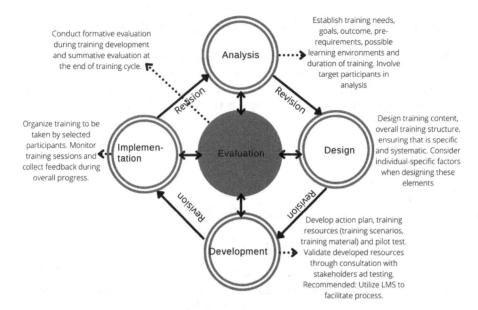

Fig. 1. ADDIE model, proposed and validated by academic and industrial stakeholders in [10]

Lastly, an important consideration often lacking in current training offerings is that of PLT concepts. Recent studies have shown that integrating PLT concepts in current training offerings has several benefits, such as increased and faster progress in learning [24] and higher participant engagement. Based on these considerations, two key elements of personalization have been suggested in [10]:

- **Involvement of participants in design and development process**: to ensure that the participants goals and preferences are aligned with the training offered, it is recommended to involve them during the design and development stages of the ADDIE model shown in Fig. 1. This can be done via continuous feedback collection, which can also occur outside of these two phases.
- **Development of Learning Paths or learner profiles**: based on initial objectives and pre-assessment of participants' knowledge and skills, learning paths and learner profiles can be developed. The first are useful to design tailored and modular learning paths based on progress, motivations, and goals of the individual or the target group. Learner's profiles instead consist in dedicated folders that provide information regarding an individual's strengths, needs, motivations, progress and goals.

3.3   Recommendations from Industry Stakeholders

Previous research in [10,11] and continuous research was also conducted to obtain feedback from industrial personnel and organizers of CS training for industry regarding their requirements and preferences in CS training. In [11], several industrial workers with key CS responsibilities in their respective companies had been consulted to obtain an overview of the current CS training solutions adopted at their respective companies. According to the interviewed participants, many of the adopted CS training offerings lacked development of team skills, communication skills and managerial skills and instead focused more on technical skills. Additionally, offerings were reportedly generalized for all roles in the company instead of focusing on specific target groups and roles. This in turn meant that role-specific knowledge and skills were often not developed effectively during training. In this respect, table-top exercises can be useful in both aspects, as they enable team-based discussion as well as targeted work on specific sub-groups and roles, based on the scenario implemented.

As mentioned in Sect. 3.2, in [10] we conducted a Delphi process with stakeholders from both industry and academia. Additionally, during the requirement analysis of the exercise described in Sect. 4.2, additional feedback from industrial personnel had been collected.

Overall, the main factors to prioritize when developing exercises for CS training mentioned by the industry stakeholders include: (1)ease of implementation, (2) time and resource constraints, (3)remote accessibility. The most noticeable difference between the attributes selected by industrial personnel and academic personnel involve a prioritization of efficiency over optimization of training. During the feedback collection of the experiment described in Sect. 4.2, it was noted that a lower degree of personalization would have been preferred, with a more focused and shorter in duration exercise being preferred. Additionally, participants expressed preferring the use of real-time data during scenarios as an initial input.

4   Results

After analysis the requirements and recommendations discussed in Sects. 3.1–3.3, based on overall prioritization and prevalence in selection among the different groups of stakeholders, the following attributes for a table-top exercise were selected for the final framework:

- Ease of Implementation;
- Engaging and Motivating;
- Tailored to target groups' objectives, requirements and preferences;
- Flexible and adaptable to changes (last minute changes may also be required during some exercises);
- Accessible both remotely and physically (hybridly-run exercises should also be possible).

Based on these attributes, an initial design of the final framework has been commenced. The design followed the recommendations of [10]. In particular, the specific components of the table-top exercise were still developed using the ADDIE model shown in Fig. 1. The basic framework instead has been developed to follow a stage-based scheme, following the Lockheed Martin Cyber Kill Chain (LMCKC). Cyber kill Chains (CKCs) are a model to describe cyber-attacks, and consequently develop incident response and analysis capabilities [34]. In brief, a CKC is an attack chain that describes the path that an intruder takes to penetrate information systems over time to execute an attack on the target [34]. The LMCKC is one of the more renowned CKCs and is comprised of 7 stages. Table 2 describes in detail the actions that an attacker may take during each stage of the LMCKC to achieve their goals.

Table 2. Stages of the LMCKC

Stage	Description
Reconnaissance	Select target. research and collect as much information information as possible about and attempt to identify vulnerabilities in the target network
Weaponization	Create remote access malware weapon (or payload). This could be a virus or worm or other type of payload, tailored to one or more vulnerabilities identified during reconnaissance
Delivery	Transmit weapon to target (via e-mail attachment, websites or USB drives or other method). This could consist in transmitting to a single target or a large number of targets
Exploitation	Malware weapon's program code launches itself on the targets, possibly also expanding to additional targets
Installation	Malware weapon installs and create stable access point (e.g., "backdoor") usable by intruder
Command and control (C&C)	After initiation a "connection" with the infected workstation, intruder has the ability of conducting further actions on it
Actions on Objective	Intruder tries to achieve their initial goals by completing the remaining actions required, such as data exfiltration and data destruction

While the LMCKC is considered one of the standards in regards to attack chain description, many critiques against it have been raised over the years [20] and alternative proposals have been developed [16,35]. For this reason, the framework is flexible enough to accommodate any other types of kill chains, as well as other types of adversary tactics and techniques descriptors, such as the MITRE att&ck framework [32]. Furthermore, the exercise can be designed to focus on just one or a specific subset of the stages of the kill chains instead of all of the stages, based on the necessities of the training.

For the purpose of designing exercises, two approaches have been selected: LMCKC discussion-based table-top exercise and LMCKC team-based table-top exercise. For the first approach, different sequential stages of an attack will be presented in each scenario. This may be done either via written scenario presentation or via simulated data information, by utilizing simulation tools or testbeds. After each stage description and presentation, a discussion will be commenced with the participants, with the goal of understanding whether they would be able to successfully perform the actions related to their roles in the exercise. For this purpose, we utilized exemplary data provided by CISA tabletop exercise packages and the online tool Exercise in a Box to develop scenario and questionnaire templates.

For the second approach, multiple teams will be formed with different roles, following the general guidelines for blue team vs red team table-top exercises. The two basic teams will consist of a red team and a blue team. The general goal of the red team is to break through the defense systems in place and defensive measures taken by the blue team to successfully compromise the system and achieve their malicious intents. The blue team instead has to protect the system and the network against the malicious attacks that may come forth during the exercise. Additional goals may be defined during the design and development of the scenario of the exercises, as well as other components, based on the objectives analysis conducted with the participants. Furthermore, additional teams may be present with either hybrid roles to the ones described or other different roles; notable example being a purple team (a mixture of red and blue teams focused on data analysis and implementation of the measures of the other two teams). After defining the goals and designing the scenario, the exercise will be run on a turn-based sequence, with the first turn started by the red team, who will decide the initial injects (or attack vectors) to be used during the exercise.

Figure 2 describes the sequence of actions to be conducted for each team during the turns of the exercise.

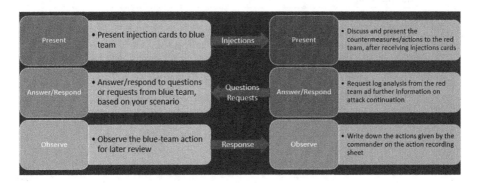

Fig. 2. Actions conducted by Red team and Blue team during each turn (Color figure online)

The sequence of actions shown in Fig. 2 will be conducted for each stage of the LMCKC.

After the conclusion of each scenario, this will be reviewed together with the participants to both analyse retrospectively the actions taken and the results based on the evaluation metrics established during the design and development of the exercise.

To allow for remote accessibility, a number of online tools have been selected and used during experimentation that allow for collaborative work. Namely, the sketch-sharing website WebWhiteBoard was used to share scenario description information, as well as the actions taken by each team. For communication with participants, the communication platform Microsoft Teams was used due to its many services facilitating both team-based communication and file sharing.

Additionally, two digital forms are shared with participants of each team to fill out at the beginning and during each turn of the exercise. In these forms, the respective team has to indicate the actions to be taken for each stage and turn of the exercise. Table 3 and 4 schematize these two forms, respectively.

Table 3. Table scheme of the template form for the Red Team

	Answer	Description
Inject		
Who (Target)		
When (Timing)		
How (Action Plan)		
Stages		
Stage	Description	Input for Blue Team
Reconnaissance		
Weaponization		
Delivery		
Exploitation		
Installation		
Command and control (C&C)		
Actions on Objective		

Table 4. Table scheme of the template form for the Blue Team

Stage	Red Team Input	Defensive Actions
Reconnaissance		
Weaponization		
Delivery		
Exploitation		
Installation		
Command and control (C&C)		
Actions on Objective		

As can be seen from Tables 3 and 4, the red team has to indicate precise information regarding each inject that they will be using during the exercises, including the target, the timeline of the attack (at each stage) and how this will be conducted. More detailed information and description about actions to be performed at each stage of the LMCKC has to be also indicated in the appropriate box. Additionally, the Red team will have to also write information to be shared with the blue team regarding how the attack will be viewed at the defender's side. In case of use of a I&C simulation tool to assist in the exercise, this information can be extracted from the tool. Multiple variations and extensions of both exercise models are possible and have been designed, based on participants' preferences.

The framework was evaluated by conducting several exercises with both students and industrial personnel. Each of the experiments and their results is presented in the sections below.

4.1 Experiment 1

The first experiment conducted using the framework involved a group of 12 students from the Norwegian Institute of Science and Technology (NTNU) Information Security master's degree program, as described in [7]. The experiment was divided into two parts, the second of which involved the running of a red

Table 5. Target group, objectives and general description of the first experiment run with the framework

Target Group	Objectives	Description
Information Security Master's Students	Assess & Improve knowledge in Cyber Incident Management Assess & Improve knowledge in Network Traffic Analysis Assess & Improve general CS knowledge	Exercise run physically. Two teams of 4 students. Focus on Network Traffic Analysis, which was assessed to be a knowledge gap of the target group. 3 runs, using a simplified LMCKC model

team vs blue team exercise. Table 5 summarizes the main details regarding the first experiment.

After a brief introduction regarding the general scenario, the exercise proceeded by allowing the teams to conduct initial internal consultation to determine the key requirements shown in Table 6.

Table 6. Initial requirements to be determined by both teams

Blue Team Requirements	Red Team Requirements
– Establish roles for each participant; – Determine security measures that company should have in place; – Determine possible vulnerabilities; – Generic cyber-incident response plan;	– Determine three different techniques to achieve your goals; – Use the MITRE ATT&CK Matrix or the Lockheed Martin Cyber Kill Chain to determine all tactics and steps of your attack; – Determine possible countermeasures to your attacks and ways to circumvent them;

When selecting and designing attack vectors, the red team was encouraged to take advantage of possible network security vulnerabilities over other exploits. This was done in order to ensure that participants focused on the knowledge gaps revealed from the pre-assessment exercise conducted during the first part of the experiment. Three different scenarios where completed during the exercise, with the blue team defending twice successfully. After completing the exercise, feedback was collected from participants. The students expressed overall positive sentiments regarding the design and implementation of the exercise. In particular, participation to the design and development of the exercise had increased overall engagement, as well as allowed for better targeting of goals and requirements from the students' side.

4.2 Experiment 2

The second exercise was conducted with a group of CS experts of a Norwegian energy-focused company. Specifically, the members belonged to the SOC team and the CSERT team of the company, also included the Chief Information Security Office (CISO). Table 7 summarizes the main details regarding the second experiment.

Table 7. Target group, objectives and general description of the second experiment run with the framework

Target Group	Objectives	Description
CS experts and personnel	Test & Assess & Improve knowledge in Cyber Incident Management Test Insider threat handling Test ransomware attack handling Test Reporting knowledge and practices	Two teams. 4 members per team. Hybrid exercise. Blue team was connected physically and red team digitally. Focus on ransomware and insider threats, based on participants' preferences and company's profile. 1 Run, using the LMCKC model

After introducing participants to the scenario, members of the blue team were assigned the following roles: 2 SOC team members, 1 CISO and communication coordinator with external parties and 1 technical operator. The red team instead represented an international cyber-crime group with the goal of conducting a successful ransomware campaign, with the help of an insider threat. The insider threat was selected randomly between the group of blue team members and collaborated both with the red team and with the blue team, until preventive action to restrict confidential data and access was taken.

After conclusion of the exercise, feedback from the participants was collected in three modalities: post-training discussion, internal consultation, and finally post-assessment survey. The feedback collected was later analyzed to address any further recommendation to improve the initial design of the exercise and the framework itself, which was later incorporated in the final framework. Table 8 summarizes the recommendations for improvements suggested by participants and the improvement strategy selected to incorporate the recommendations.

Table 8. Recommendations and improvement strategies collected after completion of the second experiment.

Feedback on Attribute	Recommendations	Improvement Strategy
Training Delivery Method	Lack of flexibility and ability to improvise in the scenario. Also, the initial scenario description was found complex. Recommended to simplify both components	Design simplified template scenarios, to later adapt based on the requirements of the exercise and the target group
Duration	Time to complete all stages of LMCKC too excessive. Shorten or focus on selected phases	Design exercise focused on selected stages of the LMCKC, based on objectives
Feedback Collection	The post-assessment feedback collection lacked structure, although allowing for open discussion is appreciated	Combine survey-based feedback collection with semi-structured

A follow-up experiment is currently being developed for the same target group, to target the recommendations and further objectives of the learning path defined for the participants.

4.3 Experiment 3

The final experiment conducted with the participants involved a group of nuclear power plant operators. The operators had mainly a technical background, with only minor CS knowledge and experience. Additionally, during initial data collection, they stated that they had received minimal CS training and had little experience in CS incident handling. For this reason, a pilot test was conducted to assess their ability to detect CS attack and distinguish them from hardware or network malfunctions, followed by a discussion-based exercise.

Table 7 summarizes the main details regarding the second experiment.

Table 9. Target group, objectives and general description of the third experiment run with the framework

Target Group	Objectives	Description
Nuclear Power Plant Operators	Assess & Improve general CS knowledge Assess ability to detect cyber attacks Assess & Improve CIR procedures	Three technical operators. Simulation-based exercise. Exercise run fully digitally and remotely. Focus on faulty and misleading instruction data

The exercise comprised a combination of simulation-based data input, which involved the use of a nuclear ICS simulator and human behaviour observing laboratory, known as HAMMLab. The software allowed for simulating real-time control data of a nuclear facility control room. The exercise consisted in multiple phases of routine activities for the operators, one of which introduced some malfunctions to the control system. After each phase of the exercise, we commenced a discussion with the participants, based on a semi-structured questionnaire focused on assessing their knowledge in detecting and handling the initial stages of a cyber-incident.

While the exercise was simplified, due to the lessened CS knowledge of participants, it demonstrated to be an effective generic CS training exercise for basic CS skills and competences. All participants stated that the exercise was useful both as a self-assessment tool for CS threat detection and CS incident handling.

5   Discussion

After completion of the experimentation, the suggestions from each target group were analyzed for the purpose of improving the proposed framework. Specifically, the following improvements were recommended:

– Simplified data and feedback collection: during the first experiment, it was suggested to simplify and shorten the data collection process. Specifically, participants expressed a preference on having less open ended questions and more multiple choice questions, The survey collection has later been adapted to this recommendation.
– Simplified scenario: When proposing a scenario, participants expressed preferring more flexibility over the type of offensive and preventive measures to be allowed. Overall, less scenario guidance was preferred during the introduction of a scenario. Finally, allowing to concentrate on a sub-section of the phases of the LMCKC chain was also recommended, to reduce fatigue and experiment duration and allow for more targeted training.
– Real-time data input: Supplement to real-time data or simulated data has also been recommended by participants. For this, the last experiment was designed with input from simulated data, and was positively received.

After redesigning the framework and experiments based on the mentioned recommendations, we obtained a more flexible, easy to implement general framework for running CS exercises. The exercises developed with the framework were all well received by the participants. In particular, the first two group of participants who had previous experience in CS training exercises found the exercises to be comparatively more engaging and in certain cases more effective than previous, more traditional formats. All three groups of participants expressed interest in continuing conducting exercises using the proposed framework, as well as using some of the components of the framework, such as continuous feedback collection, in their scheduled CS training and exercise offerings.

6   Conclusion

CS training is nowadays more critical than ever, both when it comes to academic education and industrial personnel training. Due to current trends increasing the use of remote work, traditional and physical training options are becoming less prevalent and usable. Additionally, In this work, we proposed a CS training framework that allows for the development of tailored and personalized tabletop exercises. The framework allows for the development of both team-based and discussion-based tabletop exercises. The exercises developed with the framework follow the stages of the LMCKC, and are tailored around different stages of a cyber-attack based on the requirements and goals of the training. The framework is flexible, easy to implement and lightweight, requiring both low time and software and hardware resources to be usable in most of its iterations. To allow for remote accessibility, the exercises developed with the framework can be run fully online, as well as physically and in a hybrid manner. Three experiments using the framework have been conducted. The first experiment was conducted with a group of masters' students at the information security faculty at NTNU. The second experiment was conducted with a group of CS experts and personnel at an energy company located in Norway and the last experiment involved a group of technical nuclear operators. According to the feedback collected from each group, the exercises developed with the framework were well received. They were found to be engaging, effective at developing knowledge and skills targeted, as well as easy to implement and run. When compared to other exercises conducted by the same target groups, they were also evaluated to be preferable, especially by the students.

Additional work is being conducted to refine the framework and develop additional reusable and adaptable scenarios for both the previous target group and other groups. Further experimentation is also planned with the goal of refining the framework and supporting supplementary tools for simulation. Future work on CS table-top exercises should also focus on specific KPIs and/or measurable criteria, reflecting the improvement of awareness of the tested subjects.

References

1. Andriotis, N.: 5 elements to include in any post training evaluation questionnaire. Efront Learning (2018)
2. Angafor, G.N., Yevseyeva, I., He, Y.: Bridging the cyber security skills gap: Using tabletop exercises to solve the CSSG crisis. In: Ma, M., Fletcher, B., Göbel, S., Baalsrud Hauge, J., Marsh, T. (eds.) JCSG 2020. LNCS, vol. 12434, pp. 117–131. Springer, Cham (2020). https://doi.org/10.1007/978-3-030-61814-8_10
3. Angafor, G.N., Yevseyeva, I., He, Y.: Game-based learning: A review of tabletop exercises for cybersecurity incident response training. Secur. Privacy **3**(6), e126 (2020)
4. Brilingaitė, A., et al.: Environment for Cybersecurity Tabletop Exercises. In: ECGBL 2017 11th European Conference on Game-Based Learning, pp. 47–55. Academic Conferences and Publishing Limited (2017)
5. Brown, M.L.: Use of tabletop exercises for disaster preparedness training. PhD thesis. The University of Texas School of Public Health (2010)
6. Chen, K.-C., Chen, C.-C., Wang, T.-L.: The role tabletop exercise using START in improving triage ability in disaster medical assistance team. Ann. Disast. Med. **1**(2) (2003)
7. Chowdhury, N.: A personalized learning theory-based cyber-security training exercise. Inf. Comput. Secur. (2022)
8. Chowdhury, N., Gkioulos, V.: Cyber security training for critical infrastructure protection: A literature review. Comput. Sci. Rev. **40**, 100361 (2021)
9. Chowdhury, N., Gkioulos, V.: Key competencies for critical infrastructure cybersecurity: A systematic literature review. Inf. Comput. Secur. (2021)
10. Chowdhury, N., Katsikas, S., Gkioulos, V.: Modeling effective cybersecurity training frameworks: A Delphi method-based study. Comput. Secur. **113**, 102551 (2022)
11. Chowdhury, N., et al.: Cybersecurity training in Norwegian critical infrastructure companies. Int. J. Saf. Secur. Eng. (2021)
12. Debusmann, B.: Why remote working leaves us vulnerable to cyber-attacks. In: BBC News (2021)
13. Dolezal, A.: Cyber threats have increased 81% since global pandemic. In: Business Wire (2021)
14. Ferreira, R., et al.: Decision factors for remote work adoption: Advantages, disadvantages, driving forces and challenges. J. Open Innov. Technol. Mark. Complex. **7**(1), 70 (2021)
15. Forero, C.A.M.: Tabletop exercise for cybersecurity educational training; theoretical grounding and development. In: MS thesis (2016)
16. Haga, K., Meland, P.H., Sindre, G.: Breaking the cyber kill chain by modelling resource costs. In: Eades III, H., Gadyatskaya, O. (eds.) GraMSec 2020. LNCS, vol. 12419, pp. 111–126. Springer, Cham (2020). https://doi.org/10.1007/978-3-030-62230-5_6
17. He, W., Zhang, Z.: Enterprise cybersecurity training and awareness programs: Recommendations for success. J. Organiz. Comput. Electron. Comm. **29**(4), 249–257 (2019)
18. Jin, G., Manghui, T., Kim, T.-H., Heffron, J., White, J.: Evaluation of game-based learning in cybersecurity education for high school students. J. Educ. Learn. (EduLearn) **12**(1), 150–158 (2018)
19. Johnson, J.: Where do it professionals see an increase in cyber attacks and attack attempts following the covid-19 pandemic? In: Statista (2021)

20. Klosek, T.: Limitations of the Lockheed Martin Cybersecurity Kill Chain Model. PhD thesis, Utica College (2020)
21. Maggio, L.A., et al.: Cybersecurity challenges and the academic health center: An interactive tabletop simulation for executives. Acad. Med. **96**(6), 850–853 (2021)
22. Mirzaei, S., Eftekhari, A., Mohammadinia, L., Tafti, A.A.D., Norouzinia, R., Nasiriani, K.: Comparison of the effect of lecturing and tabletop exercise methods on level of preparedness of nurses against natural disasters. J. Holist. Nurs. Midwif. **30**(1), 17–26 (2020)
23. Ottis, R.: Light weight tabletop exercise for cybersecurity education. J. Homeland Secur. Emerg. Manag. **11**(4), 579–592 (2014)
24. Pane, J.F., et al.: Continued progress: Promising evidence on personalized learning In: Rand Corporation (2015)
25. Pastor, V., Diaz, G., Castro, M.: State-of-the-art simulation systems for information security education, training and awareness. In: IEEE EDUCON 2010 Conference, pp. 1907–1916. IEEE (2010)
26. Popken, B.: Full return to office is 'dead', experts say — and remote is only growing. In: NBC News (2021)
27. Radvanovsky, R.: Cybersecurity simulation exercises: Is simply waiting for a security breach the right strategy? In: Ernest & Young Advisory Services (2017)
28. Radvanovsky, R.: Tabletop/red-blue exercises. In: Handbook of SCADA/Control Systems Security, pp. 368–377. Routledge (2016)
29. Reeves, A., Delfabbro, P., Calic, D.: Encouraging employee engagement with cybersecurity: How to tackle cyber fatigue. SAGE Open **11**(1), 21582440211000050 (2021)
30. Samuel, J.: Cyber security—key performance indicators. In: Infosec Write-ups (2019)
31. Sitzmann, T., Weinhardt, J.M.: Training engagement theory: A multilevel perspective on the effectiveness of work-related training. J. Manag. **44**(2), 732–756 (2018)
32. Strom, B.E., et al.: Mitre attack: Design and philosophy. In: Technical report (2018)
33. Walkington, C., Bernacki, M.L.: Appraising research on personalized learning: Definitions, theoretical alignment, advancements, and future directions (2020)
34. Yadav, T., Rao, A.M.: Technical aspects of cyber kill chain. In: Abawajy, J.H., Mukherjea, S., Thampi, S.M., Ruiz-Martínez, A. (eds.) SSCC 2015. CCIS, vol. 536, pp. 438–452. Springer, Cham (2015). https://doi.org/10.1007/978-3-319-22915-7_40
35. Zhou, X., et al.: Kill chain for industrial control system. In: MATEC Web of Conferences, vol. 173, p. 01013. EDP Sciences (2018)

A Hybrid Dynamic Risk Analysis Methodology for Cyber-Physical Systems

Christos Lyvas[1]([✉]) [ID], Konstantinos Maliatsos[2] [ID], Andreas Menegatos[1] [ID],
Thrasyvoulos Giannakopoulos[1] [ID], Costas Lambrinoudakis[1] [ID],
Christos Kalloniatis[3] [ID], and Athanasios Kanatas[1] [ID]

[1] Department of Digital Systems, University of Piraeus, Piraeus, Greece
{clyvas,amenegatos,tgian,clam,kanatas}@unipi.gr
[2] Department of Information and Communication Systems Engineering,
University of the Aegean, Samos, Greece
kmaliat@aegean.gr
[3] Department of Cultural Technology and Communication, University of the Aegean,
Mitilini, Greece
chkallon@aegean.gr

Abstract. Recent technological advances allow us to design and implement sophisticated infrastructures to assist users' everyday life; technological paradigms such as Intelligent Transportation Systems (ITS) and Multi-modal Transport are excellent instances of those cases. Therefore, a systematic risk evaluation process in conjunction with proper threat identification are essential for environments like those mentioned above as they involve human safety. Threat modelling is the process of identifying and understanding threats while risk analysis is the process of identifying and analyzing potential risks. This research initially focuses on the most widely-used threat modelling and risk analysis approaches and reviewing their characteristics. Then, it presents a service-oriented dynamic risk analysis approach that focuses on Cyber-Physical Systems (CPS) by adopting threat modelling characteristics and by blending other methods and well-established sources to achieve automation in several stages. Finally, it provides the qualitative features of the proposed method and other related threat modelling and risk analysis approaches with a discussion regarding their similarities, differences, advantages and drawbacks.

Keywords: Dynamic risk analysis · Threat analysis · Threat modelling · Security and asset management · Intelligent transportation systems security · Multimodal transport security · Cyber-physical systems security

1 Introduction

Over the past years, advances in information and communications technology (ICT) enabled the implementation of numerous technological paradigms where a global network of machines and devices can interact with each other for medical, industrial, transportation, decision-making or other purposes. In this context, both security and privacy aspects are considered crucial for those types of infrastructures. That is because, in

S. Katsikas et al. (Eds.): ESORICS 2022 Workshops, LNCS 13785, pp. 134–152, 2023.
https://doi.org/10.1007/978-3-031-25460-4_8

many cases, the effect of new emerging threats targeting those schemes ranges from cyber to physical impacts, resulting frequently in severe safety implications for their users.

There are several systematic approaches and methodologies in cybersecurity regarding the identification, mitigation, assessment and quantification of vulnerabilities, threats, risks and countermeasures. Generally, Risk Management (RM) [21] is the procedure of managing risk to an acceptable level mainly consisting of two main stages; the risk assessment and the risk treatment. Risk Assessment [25] allows analysts to identify vulnerabilities and threats on specific elements. In the risk analysis (RA) a score is assigned to each identified risk using one of two types of scoring system: quantitative or qualitative. These scores enable analysts to prioritize risks in order to determine the best ways to address them with controls and countermeasures known as Risk Treatment (RT). Moreover, Threat Modelling (TM) is an essential part of the risk analysis with its definition varying from a process that can be used to analyze potential attacks and threats to the thorough analysis of architectures for potential security threats identification and the appropriate selection of countermeasures and controls for their mitigation [52].

Many risk analysis and threat modelling methodologies exist from academic [17,22,37,39,42,44,46,50,53], corporate [7,38,49] and national organizations [3,15, 19,24,34] perspectives. Regarding the limitations of existing risk analysis and threat modelling approaches, several of them are too technical [49,53] and thus require deep knowledge in order to be applied, while others are too generic [7,34] and provide non-insightful but high-level results. Also, some of them are very well-documented [19,24,49], while others are mainly targeted to non-English speaking users [3,15]. Furthermore, some require manual intervention [49,50] by the analysts, while others are tool-assisted [15,19,24] and provide automation to some extent. The majority of them are generic approaches that support exclusively conventional information technology (IT) infrastructures [15,19,22,24,34,46] based upon the size [17] and scope of the system under review. In contrast, others require modifications and extensions [24,49] in order to support analysis in Cyber-Physical Systems and Industrial Internet of Things (IIoT) architectures. In addition, several approaches borrow characteristics [24] or require input [34,46] from other methodologies in order to provide a holistic analysis. Finally, some are privacy-oriented [50] whereas others are mostly security-oriented [24,34,46] and others supporting both security and privacy [15,19,24].

This research describes a dynamic Risk Analysis (RA) methodology with Threat Modeling (TM) characteristics dedicated to Cyber-Physical Systems, especially for Intelligent Transportation Systems and Multimodal transport. Its novelty relies on the detailed description of complicated assets constructed by elementary assets which allow the method to be applied to any non-conventional Information Technology (IT) infrastructure such as Industrial Internet of Things (IIoT) Multi-Modal Transportation, Intelligent Transportation etc. Moreover, it leverages well-established sources to perform automated threat valuations and risk assessments.

Summarizing, the contributions of this work are:

– The design of a prototype hybrid dynamic risk analysis framework with embedded automatic threat modeling capabilities.

- A thorough comparative analysis among the proposed framework and other related risk analysis and threat modeling approaches from literature.
- Access to the current proof-of-concept implementation[1] of the proposed framework.

The rest of this paper is structured as follows. Section 2 provides an overview of the related work. Section 3 presents the dynamic risk analysis framework design along with it's applicability in 4. Further discussion is elaborated in Sect. 5 by introducing a comparative analysis with other related works. Finally, Sect. 6 provides both the conclusions and pointers for future improvements.

2 Related Work

Risk analysis and threat modelling methodologies are undoubtedly vital procedures for Cyber-Physical Systems, from security and privacy by design to quantitative or qualitative assessment of the security level of such systems. The approaches mentioned above are further discussed in the following subsections, while a comparative analysis between these methods and the proposed one in this research is provided in Sect. 5.

2.1 Threat Modelling Methodologies

UcedaVélez and Morana [47] developed a risk-centric threat modeling framework named PASTA (Process for Attack Simulation and Threat Analysis) to process attack scenarios and vulnerabilities within either a proposed or existing information technology (IT) infrastructure in order to identify risks and impact levels. PASTA is composed of seven stages. At the initial stage, the objectives are defined, including business objectives, security and compliance requirements, along with business impact analysis. In the second stage, the technical scope is defined, and then the decomposition of the infrastructure takes place. The fourth stage appertains to the threat analysis with probabilistic attack scenarios and threat intelligence correlation. The fifth stage regards the vulnerability and weaknesses analysis, followed by the attack modelling. Finally, in the latter stage, the risk and impact analysis are conducted.

LINDDUN (Linkability, Identifiability, Non-Repudiation, Detectability, Disclosure of Information, Unawareness, Non-Compliance) [50,51] is another threat modelling methodology, which is dedicated to privacy and data protection for privacy impact assessment. It consists of six stages. In the first stage LINDDUN, with the aid of Data Flow Diagrams (DFDs), define the system's boundaries with data flows, data storages, processes, and external entities. Stage two refers to the mapping of privacy threats to the system model. Stage three entails scenarios in which these threats could apply. Stage four concerns the selection and prioritization of identified threats followed by the next stage in which the elicit mitigation strategies are defined. Finally, stage six concerns the selection of appropriate privacy-enhancing technologies.

STRIDE [38] is one of the most known threat modelling methods initially maintained by Microsoft. STRIDE consists of three phases. In the first phase, data flow diagrams (DFDs) model the scope and the under examination system. In the second

---

[1] https://rmt.ds.unipi.gr.

phase, STRIDE proceeds with the threat identification based on a predefined set of known threats. In the final phase, the identified threats and mitigation strategies are documented and prioritized.

Hamad et al. [37] proposed a threat modelling approach for classifying attacks in vehicular environments. It consists of three (3) layers: (i) target domains, in which all the vulnerabilities within an asset are considered to identify potential threats affecting it, (ii) requirements violation, in which any of the security requirements that have been violated by exploiting a specific vulnerability within an asset is defined, (iii) accessibility, referring to how the vehicle is accessed (remotely, directly) to take advantage of a specific vulnerability. Based upon the collected information, attack trees are then formed to compute the probability of a successful attack within each asset. The root of each tree represents the threat to be accomplished and the overall tree indicates the attack path to exploit an asset's certain vulnerability.

Petit et al. [42] created a threat modelling tool based on attack trees to represent the distinct attack steps of individual attack scenarios targeting the vehicular domain. During the attack tree construction phase, for high-level attacks, authors considered necessary to create reusable "general" attack trees to evade redundancy. However, as the attack trees become more detailed, these general attack sub-trees may become more specific as different applications are subject to different kinds of vulnerabilities.

Jbair et al. [39] proposed a threat modeling approach for Industrial Cyber-Physical Systems (ICPS) making use of a digital twin that was built with the VueOne tool. Their threat modelling process consists of five steps. In the first step, ICPS target assets are identified while in the second step feasible attack scenarios are built based on Tactics, Techniques, and Procedures (TTPs) from MITREs ATT&CK [18] for Industrial Control Systems (ICS). In the next step, both the Attack Vector (AV) and the Attack Likelihood (AL) are measured for each attack, with step four producing a risk matrix based on the measured values of the previous step by using both a quantitative and a qualitative method to measure the risks. Finally, countermeasures are proposed to reduce the calculated risk.

2.2 Risk Analysis Methodologies

IT-Grundschutz [2] is a risk management rather than a risk analysis method developed by the German Federal Office for Information Security (BSI). Part of the BSI Standards of Information Security, IT-Grundschutz provides a methodology for establishing and operating an Information Security Management System (ISMS), and a risk analysis methodology. BSI also publishes the IT-Grundschutz Compendium [8] that analyzes the most common threats and vulnerabilities and determines the risks involved. The risk analysis methodology based on IT-Grundschutz [4] consists of four steps regarding risk determination and risk treatment. In step one a threat overview is created from threats that may arise from different situations. Step two is the risk classification where the frequency of occurrence and the impact is estimated. Step three consists of various risk treatment techniques. Finally in step four the security concept is consolidated, with the integration of any additional safeguards.

OCTAVE Allegro (Operationally Critical Threat, Asset, and Vulnerability Evaluation) [22] is a variation of the apparently discontinued, OCTAVE [16] risk management methodology. OCTAVE Allegro is an asset-based methodology, focusing on how the assets are used and exposed to threats and vulnerabilities that can cause disruptions. It is composed of eight steps across four phases. Phase one focuses on risk measurement criteria. In phase two critical assets are identified and profiled, identifying boundaries and security requirements. Phase three identifies the threats, with the last phase focusing on risk identification, risk analysis and risk mitigation. OCTAVE-S [17] was developed to support small-sized organizations (with less than 100 employees). The difference with the other variants is that the assessment team has an extensive knowledge of the organisation, thus reducing the need for workshops to gather information. It is also more structured and contains security concepts in the provided worksheets and guidance. Finally, OCTAVE-S includes a limited selection of infrastructure risks in order to assist with adoption. OCTAVE FORTE (FOR The Enterprise) [46] method aims to help organizations evaluate their security risks and use Enterprise Risk Management (ERM) to bridge the gap between managerial and technical personnel. It consists of 10 iterative steps that, among other things, establish risk requirements, identify critical assets and estimate their resiliency, identify risks, threats and vulnerabilities for those assets and finally implement controls, before the process starts again.

Perhaps the most well known information security risk management framework is the ISO/IEC 27005 [7] which is part of the ISO/IEC 27000 [6] series. The methodology consists of several steps. The initial step is the context establishment step. The second step is the risk assessment which is comprised by the risk analysis that contains the risk identification and the risk estimation steps, followed by risk evaluation. The third step is the risk treatment, which may result in the entire process starting again if the remaining risk level is considered as not acceptable. Throughout the whole process the risk communication and the risk monitoring and review steps take place. ISO also publishes ISO/IEC 31000 [5], that follows a similar approach to ISO/IEC 27005 [7], with a more generic risk management methodology that isn't specific to information security.

EBIOS Risk Manager [19] is a risk management method developed by ANSSI. It adopts an iterative approach that can be used by any kind of organization and consists of five (5) phases defined as workshops: (i) scope and security baseline, in which both organizational and risk analysis aspects are considered (ii) risk origins along with their targets, which are identified and organized in pairs with the most relevant of them being chosen at the end of this phase (iii) strategic scenarios, which are high-level attack scenarios against the business assets that are followed by an assessment process to define the security measures for the studied ecosystem (iv) operational scenarios, which are technical scenarios with an approach similar to that of the previous workshop dedicated to support assets, and (v) risk treatment, during which security measures are applied to calculate the residual risks and set up the risk-monitoring framework.

The Methodology of Analysis and Management of Risks of Information Systems (MAGERIT) [15] is a qualitative risk management framework for public administration. Over the years, MAGERIT established itself as an asset-based method consisting of three books [13–15]. The main phases of MAGERIT are the following: (i) asset identification and evaluation, based on security requirements as well as on a scale ranging from 0 (negligible) to 10 (very high) to calculate both the impact on an asset and the likelihood of threat occurrence on a yearly basis. Also, the bidirectional relationships between the assets are represented in either tree or graph structures, indicating that the top-layer assets rely on the lower-layer assets and vice versa. (ii) In the second phase, certain safeguards are determined to mitigate the impact of the assets to the identified threats. In this context, potential safeguards per asset type are enlisted in [13]. Finally, (iii) a security plan for risk monitoring is formed where security projects are defined and the specification of the appropriate continuously-monitored risk treatment actions is finalized. MAGERIT provides a complete commercial [26] software solution named as EAR-PILAR[2]. The latter incorporates a standard library that contains a predefined list of assets, threats and safeguards [48].

MONARC (Optimised Risk Analysis Method) is a tool-assisted methodology [24] that was developed to provide a framework for organizations to conduct repeatable risk assessments regardless of their size. MONARC abides to several standards [36,40]. Furthermore, it makes use of a qualitative evaluation method, while for vulnerabilities, threats and impacts it uses quantitative criteria. MONARC consists of four (4) phases. (i) In the Context Establishment phase, all the information regarding the scope of the risk analysis is collected as well as the valuation, the acceptance and impact criteria. (ii) In the Risk Modelling phase, the threats, vulnerabilities, and the impacts are explicitly defined. (iii) In the Risk Assessment and Treatment phase, risk calculation is performed along with the development of a risk treatment plan to reduce the risk to acceptable levels in quantifying manner. (iv) In the Implementation and Monitoring phase, a management phase with continuous security monitoring and control of security measures is carried out.

ITSRM[2] [34] is a process-based risk framework developed by the European Commission that consists of seven (7) phases: (i) system security characterization, which entails a high-level representation of the system, roles and security requirements, (ii) primary assets' identification, where data, functions, and other assets are recognized with both their value and impact being quantified based on predetermined catalogues, (iii) supporting assets definition, that are being used/managed by the primary assets, (iv) system modelling, where the dependencies between the assets, the data paths and the system architecture is provided, (v) risk identification, where the system model of the previous phase is used to develop the risk scenarios against the primary assets, (vi) risk analysis and evaluation which, after enforcing security measures to mitigate each risk identified in the previous step, calculates the residual risk for each one, (vii) risk treatment, where the best applicable risk treatment option for each identified risk is specified.

Zeddini et al. [53] proposed a qualitative risk analysis of Intelligent Transport Systems based on the ETSI-TVRA [35] methodology. According to the ETSI Intelligent Transport Systems-Station (ITS-S) Communication Architecture, first the system is modelled focusing on its assets and then weaknesses are identified for each one. Afterwards, a table of attacks is produced which indicates the impact to authentication and availability, based on both the asset and its vulnerabilities. Then, considering the difficulty of carrying out an attack and the potential gain, the attack likelihood is calculated,

---

[2] https://www.pilar-tools.com/en/tools/buy.html.

with the impact taken into account on a scale of low to high. The result of their analysis is a comprehensive list of Intelligent Transport Systems vulnerabilities, with their respective severities followed by countermeasures for those identified attacks.

Semertzis *et al.* [44] proposed a quantitative risk assessment method for Cyber-Physical Power Systems (CPPS) which uses attack graphs by leveraging a combination of probabilistic and deterministic techniques. Their proposed methodology relies on attack graphs to calculate the probability of attack through Time-to-Compromise (TTC) and Mean-Time to Detect (MTTD) metrics and the impact calculation based on power system stability using metrics such as the loss of load and voltage deviation. In order to accomplish that, a digital twin on the cyber-physical system is proposed to run simulations and calculate cascading failures of the power system as a result of the cyber attacks. To calculate the TTC metric the attack steps are initially defined, based on MITRE ATT&CK [18] for Industrial Control Systems (ICS), for each asset in the attack graph and then use CVE [10] to identify the known vulnerabilities of each asset and categorise them based on the type of compromise. Then, to calculate the TTC, they use Monte-Carlo simulations taking as inputs the number of vulnerabilities, the attacker skill level and the number of simulation samples. Finally, to capture a wide gamut of attacker skill levels, probabilistic distributions are fed into the Monte-Carlo simulations.

3   System Model

An adaptable, dynamic, quantifying risk analysis method is presented in this section to overcome both the limitations and the adaptation overhead introduced by the already existing risk analysis methodologies to specific architectures (such as Industrial IoT and Cyber-Physical Systems). The main characteristics of the proposed dynamic risk analysis methodology revolve around the ability to automatically assign new vulnerabilities to the architecture's assets and automatically evaluate the impact of a successful exploitation of a vulnerability. As Fig. 1 depicts, it consists of several phases: the service-oriented scope establishment and valuation, the composition of basic assets or decomposition of composite assets, the correlation of threats and vulnerabilities and, finally, the risk estimation.

3.1   Service-Oriented Scope Establishment and Valuation

In the initial phase, the analyst is responsible for defining the boundaries of the under examination infrastructure. This process involves the identification of the architecture's purpose and services. Figure 2 illustrates such an example (derived from the use cases of CitySCAPE [1] project) where several devices interact with each other in order to provide Multi-Modal Transport services.

The design of the proposed methodology is fully aligned with the fact that most of Cyber-Physical Systems tend to become Service-Oriented Architectures (SOAs) [45]; for this purpose, the analysts, after the definition of the scope and the involved services, valuate their impact based on several factors, such as integrity, confidentiality, availability, reputation, financial consequences and safety. The impact scales range from zero (0)

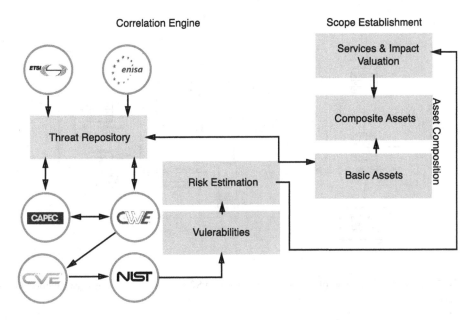

Fig. 1. Dynamic risk analysis high-level overview

to five (5). For instance, concerning confidentiality, the zero impact implies that no confidentiality requirements are needed for the reviewed service, whereas five indicates very strong confidentiality requirements for the service.

3.2   Manual Composition or Automatic Decomposition of Assets

The asset identification phase is one of the most critical and the last user-driven part of the proposed methodology. It consists of either the manual composition of assets by risk analysts for outlined architectures or the automatic decomposition of assets for already existing infrastructures. For the first case, a set of generic basic assets exists in a predefined list in the methodology's rule engine named as correlation engine. The main concept behind the definition of the basic asset is re-usability and the fact that all assets involved in a Cyber-Physical System can be decomposed into basic assets - thus, sharing a large number of standard features, threats and vulnerabilities.

More precisely, as Fig. 3 depicts, several basic assets such as an Operating System, a Mobile Application, a Central Process Unit *etc.* originating from different asset categories Application Software (blue), Storage (purple), System Software and Middleware (red), Hardware (green), Network (green) can be combined to formulate a composite asset such as a mobile device. For existing infrastructures, various network scanners, asset inventory, and vulnerability assessment tools are combined in order to decompose composite assets to basic assets and identify those that interact inside a service. In both cases, the methodology follows a top-down approach for the impact valuation of the basic assets in respect with the composite asset and the service they belong to. Thus,

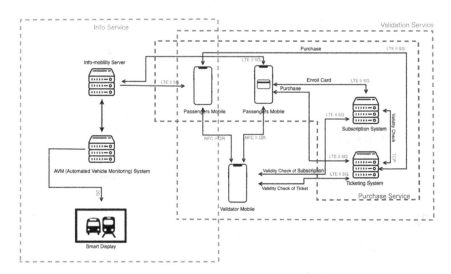

Fig. 2. High-level overview of the first indicative CitySCAPE [1] project use-case divided in services

a composite asset inherits the impact valuations based on the service it belongs to, as well as the basic assets that comprise it. Therefore,

- The composite asset retrieves the vulnerabilities and threats of the basic assets that compose it, enabling an automatic threat-vulnerability assignment process.
- The impact on a composite asset is defined by the service requirements.

3.3 Correlation of Threats and Vulnerabilities

The correlation of threats and vulnerabilities phase entails the proposed method's correlation engine. It provides all the automation from vulnerability identification to the estimation of the identified threats' probability on basic assets into a service.

Initially, the method contains a set of threats extracted from several ENISA reports referring to various fields including critical infrastructures. Also, threats correlated to new technologies (e.g. 5G) were appended and Cyber-Physical Systems with threats from ETSI-TVRA were reviewed. The following reports were included in the generation of the correlation engine's threat list: a) Baseline Security Recommendations for IoT [30], that focuses mainly on IoT on critical infrastructure, b) the ENISA Smartphones: Information security risks, opportunities and recommendations for users report [28], c) the Cloud Computing Security Risk Assessment [27] d) the ENISA Threat Landscape For 5G Networks [33], e) the Smart Grid Threat Landscape and Good Practice Guide [29], f) Port Cybersecurity - Good practices for cybersecurity in the maritime sector [32] g) the ENISA good practices for security of Smart Cars [31] and finally, technical specifications by ETSI-TVRA standard [35].

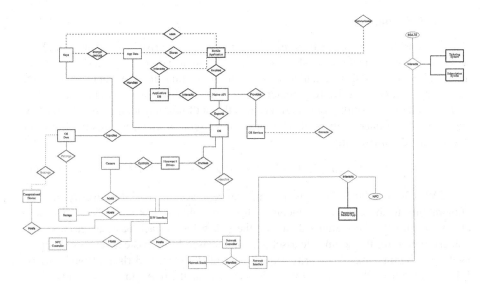

Fig. 3. Synthesis of basic assets that form the composite asset mobile device

Once the threats were identified, and after some merging towards a common threat taxonomy, correlations between Threats, Common Weakness Enumerations (CWEs) [11] and Common Attack Pattern Enumeration and Classifications (CAPECs) were created [9]. Because of the fact that Common Vulnerability Enumerations (CVEs) do not have a direct mapping to CAPECs, threats that are mapped to CAPECs are linked using the CWE-CAPEC relations. By using this approach the method is able to map threats to new vulnerabilities, as soon as they are analyzed by NIST's National Vulnerability Database (NVD), and assigned related weaknesses (CWE) as well as a Common Vulnerability Scoring System (CVSS) score [43]. Also, by using CVSS metrics the methodology is able to distinguish the impact that each new vulnerability will pose to the service in terms of confidentiality, integrity and availability independently, in order to provide a more accurate estimation of the impact across these requirements.

The aforementioned approach regarding the correlation among threats and CWEs allows the automatic estimation of the occurrence probability for the identified threats, which contrasts with other risk analysis methodologies where those values are user-driven estimations based on the experience of the analyst. More precisely, whenever an instance of a particular basic asset is generated with vendor-specific characteristics (type, vendor and version) during the process of risk assessment, the correlation engine calculates the probability of occurrence as the threat occurrence rate. This is calculated as the amount of CVEs concerning the specific threat and the instance of the basic asset (type, vendor and version), divided by the total amount of the CVEs regarding the threat and the product family.

3.4   Risk Estimation

This phase is the final step of the presented service-oriented risk analysis methodology focusing on the calculation of risks. First, for each instance of a basic asset (BA) during an assessment, the risk is calculated as the multiplication of its impact valuation (I) based on the three security requirements of confidentiality, integrity, and availability (C,I,A) with the probability of occurrence of a threat (T) for any identified vulnerability and the CVSS Vulnerability Scale (V) for the three security requirements (C, I, A) and any identified vulnerability.

$$R_{BA}[C, I, A] = I[C, I, A] \times T \times V[C, I, A] \tag{1}$$

The CVSS Vulnerability Scale is a numerical representation of the severity of each vulnerability to the CIA requirements with the possible values being None (0), Low (1) and High (2). Then, after calculating the risk value of each basic asset (BA), the risk estimation for the composite asset (CA) comprised by N basic assets is calculated as the maximum for each security requirement of the identified risks of basic assets. Likewise, the overall risk score for services (S) equals the maximum risk scores of the involved composite assets. Therefore:

$$\begin{aligned} R_{CA}[C, I, A] &= \{R_{BA}[C, I, A]_1^N\}_{\max} \\ R_S[C, I, A] &= \{R_{CA}[C, I, A]_1^N\}_{\max} \end{aligned} \tag{2}$$

4   Dynamic Risk Analysis and Threat Modelling

This section provides example of the risk assessment conducted with the proposed methodology in the first multi-modal transport use case of CitySCAPE's project (in Genoa city), as Fig. 2 depicts. For simplification and presentation purposes, only a small number of basic assets per composite asset are considered as parts of a service.

Initially, the risk analyst is responsible for defining the scope and the infrastructural functional services. In the current example, as Table 1 shows, the *SERV-GEN-02 - Ticket Validation* service is chosen. It is noted that in the context of the project, the following naming notation is used: Level of Abstraction (e.g. service, CA, BA, etc.), - use case (GEN refers to the city of Genoa), - the type of asset (applicable to CAs and BAs only), and - an index used to enumerate the different services, or assets in the use case. The valuation of the service impact entails several factors as explained in Sect. 3, resulting in high (4) confidentiality and very high (5) integrity and availability requirements due the financial and operational needs.

Then, the analysts define the high-level components known as composite assets (CA) along with their interactions; in this case these are the *COM-GEN-AS-01 - Validator's Mobile Device* which is used to validate passengers' digital tickets via either Near Field Communication (NFC) or Quick Response Codes (QR) and the *COM-GEN-AS-03 - Ticketing System* which is the server for issuing and validating the tickets. In the final stage, the analyst synthesizes basic assets (BA) and their interconnection to construct the service's composite assets. In this case, the analyst should synthesize *AS-OS-04 - Android 11* Operating System for the composite asset *COM-GEN-AS-01 - Validator's Mobile Device* and the *AS-OS-04 - Debian Linux 10* along with the *AS-SO-01*

Apache HTTP Server 2.4.18 for the composite asset *COM-GEN-AS-03 - Ticketing System*). In the specific example, the network is considered trusted and it is excluded by the analysis. Table 1 depicts the decomposition of the service to composite assets and subsequently to basic assets.

The user-defined catalogue of services, their impact valuation, the composite assets with their network connection, and the basic assets along with their interconnections are all provided to the correlation engine where the risk analysis is performed. The correlation engine first assigns impact valuations to composite and basic assets hierarchically and then searches and identifies threats for the given basic asset types (*AS-OS-04 - Operating System* and *AS-SO-01 - Web-Based Services*). Afterwards, upon identifying threats on basic assets and their instances (type, vendor, product, version *etc.*) the correlation engine identifies the applicable to them CVEs. For example, in the asset *COM-GEN-AS-01 - Validator's Mobile Device* for *TH-25 - Abuse of Authorisation/Privilege Escalation* among others, the CVEs that were identified were CVE-2021-39627[3] and CVE-2022-20114[4] with their CIA impact being (High, High, High) in both cases. For *AS-OS-04 - Debian Linux 10* and *TH-02 - Denial of Service* a couple of CVEs that were identified are CVE-2022-0908[5] and CVE-2019-9516[6] with both their CIA impacts being (None, None, High). For the asset *AS-SO-01 Apache HTTP Server 2.4.18* and *TH-11 - Software Exploitation/Malicious Code Injection* CVE-2016-8740[7] and CVE-2017-3169[8] were identified, among others, with their CIA impacts being (None, None, High) and (High, High, High) respectively. It should be emphasised that due to the basic asset decomposition, this process can be done automatically.

Finally, risk estimations take place using (2) as demonstrated in Table 1. The overall risk of the under examination service is calculated following the risk estimation of the involved composite assets and their basic assets. More precisely, for the composite asset *COM-GEN-AS-01 - Validator's Mobile Device*, the risk is estimated as the maximum risk of it's basic asset $\max([3.44, 4.3, 4.3]) = [3.44, 4.3, 4.3]$. Similarly, for the composite asset *COM-GEN-AS-03 - Ticketing System* the risk score is calculated as the maximum among its basic assets, *i.e.* $\max(([0, 0, 2.4], [0, 0, 2.4]), ([0, 0, 5.4], [4.32, 5.4, 5.4])) = [4.32, 5.4, 5.4]$. Finally, the overall risk for the service (*SERV-GEN-02 - Ticket Validation*) is calculated as the maximum risk of the composite assets that comprises it, *i.e.* $\max([3.44, 4.3, 4.3], [4.32, 5.4, 5.4]) = [4.32, 5.4, 5.4]$.

5   Comparative Analysis

As discussed in Sect. 2, several risk analysis, privacy impact assessment, and threat modelling methodologies have been proposed from corporate and academic perspectives in order to provide an insightful analysis regarding the nature and purpose of each

---

[3] https://nvd.nist.gov/vuln/detail/CVE-2021-39627.
[4] https://nvd.nist.gov/vuln/detail/CVE-2022-20114.
[5] https://nvd.nist.gov/vuln/detail/CVE-2022-0908.
[6] https://nvd.nist.gov/vuln/detail/CVE-2019-9516.
[7] https://nvd.nist.gov/vuln/detail/CVE-2016-8740.
[8] https://nvd.nist.gov/vuln/detail/CVE-2017-3169.

Table 1. Snapshot of CitySCAPE Genoa use case risk assessment

Service	Impact			Composite Asset	Basic Asset		Threat	Threat Probability	Vulnerability	Vulnerability Scale			Risk		
	C	I	A		Type	Instance				C	I	A	C	I	A
SERV-GEN-02	4	5	5	COM-GEN-AS-01	AS-OS-04	Android 11	TH-25	0,43	CVE-2021-39627	High (2)	High (2)	High (2)	3,44	4,3	4,3
									CVE-2022-20114	High (2)	High (2)	High (2)	3,44	4,3	4,3
				COM-GEN-AS-03	AS-OS-04	Debian Linux 10	TH-02	0,24	CVE-2022-0908	None (0)	None (0)	High (2)	0	0	2,4
									CVE-2019-9516	None (0)	None (0)	High (2)	0	0	2,4
					AS-SO-01	Apache Tomcat 10.0	TH-11	0,54	CVE-2016-8740	None (0)	None (0)	High (2)	0	0	5,4
									CVE-2017-3169	High (2)	High (2)	High (2)	4,32	5,4	5,4

method. Table 2 provides a list of *qualitative* properties with the main characteristics and the major limitations of each related to our proposed framework methodologies.

More precisely, regarding threat modelling methodologies, IT-Grundschutz [4] despite its wide applicability, frequently requires manual intervention by the analysts in order to perform a risk analysis. Additionally, in several cases, target objects may not be depicted correctly with the existing modules of IT-Grundschutz. Finally, even BSI acknowledges on their website [2] that the English version of the IT-Grundschutz Compendium may contain errors and omissions. OCTAVE [16,17,22,46] has plenty of variations that differ significantly. For example, OCTAVE-S and OCTAVE Allegro provide threat and vulnerability catalogues, while OCTAVE FORTE does not and recommends other sources for threats such as PASTA or STRIDE [34]. EBIOS Risk Manager's [19] most valuable solution is its large toolbox[9]. Many of those tools are provided as freemium [20]. Nonetheless, the fact that new threats can only be added manually to the provided threat repository along with the case that no vulnerability catalogues are provided as well as new vulnerabilities cannot be imported should be considered [34]. MAGERIT [13–15] contemplates all aspects of a risk management procedure providing either a qualitative or a quantitative approach. There is no clear distinction between threats and vulnerabilities in the respective catalogues. In addition, a large part of MAGERIT [13,14] is written solely in Spanish which hinders the study process for non-Spanish speakers. Finally, another limitation is that a commercial license is required to conduct risk analysis projects [48]. MONARC [23] simplifies risk management procedure by supplying a risk management solution that permits importing data from existing and customizable models during the risk analysis phase but it does not provide measures catalogues [34]. MOSP[10] platform provides new objects to the MONARC's knowledge base. Also, to conduct a risk analysis for cyber-physical systems or ITSs, the knowledge base of MONARC should be extended manually. ITSRM[2] [34] offers both a qualitative and a quantitative process-based approach. It borrows threats from MAGERIT/PILAR [34] and measures from NIST SP800-53r5 [41]. Finally, ITSRM[2] is too strict in the process of computing the residual risk, narrowing down its flexibility. The work proposed by Zeddini *et al.* [53] is noteworthy, producing an extensive list of attacks, the vulnerabilities that cause them, the threats they pose on each asset and proposed countermeasures, all within the scope of ITSs, based on the ETSI-TVRA methodology. However it appears to be a mostly manual process and a theoretical approach. The risk

---

[9] https://www.ssi.gouv.fr/entreprise/management-du-risque/la-methode-ebios-risk-manager/label-ebios-risk-manager-des-outils-pour-faciliter-le-management-du-risque-numerique.

[10] https://objects.monarc.lu.

assessment methodology of Semertzis *et al.* [44] offers a major advantage over other methodologies, given that it uses a digital twin of Cyber-Physical Systems, it is able to calculate the cascading effects on attacks to various components of the system. However, it appears that the CVE categorisation of the different types of compromise is manual and since the vulnerabilities affecting assets can be vast, that categorisation will require a lot of user intervention to get results.

Additionally, regarding threat modelling approaches, though the effectiveness and novelty of PASTA [47] methodology is beyond doubt, it seems that it requires manual intervention and technical skills in several stages by the analysts in order to perform a reliable audit. Due to its very technical nature, threat modelling can be a very time-consuming and complex process as it provides neither automation nor any supportive tool. Using the PASTA methodology in non-trivial environments such as IoT (Internet of Things) infrastructures requires several modifications and extensions in the method's core, especially for adding hardware support and extending threat categories [49]. STRIDE [38] is a well-documented method that can be applied. Still, it can be a time-consuming process with increasing complexity equivalent to the size and scope of the analysis, meaning that the number of threats can overgrow when it is applied to complicated systems. Additionally, even though Microsoft does not support STRIDE anymore, there is an open-source tool [12] which supports the methodology. LINDDUN [50] is a privacy-oriented threat modelling approach. Despite the fact that it contains an extensive privacy knowledge base including threats, thorough documentation and prioritization of mitigation mechanisms, the analysis is a very time-consuming process requiring deep knowledge in order to be applied with increasing complexity equivalent to the size and scope of the analysis. Additionally, it has been reported that LINDDUN can provide sets of not relevant, impossible, or insignificant threats during an analysis [51]. The three-layer threat modelling approach presented by Hamad *et al.* [37] is a comprehensive model that makes use of attack trees to assess the security risks of the system as well as calculate the probability of a potential attack. However, in the vehicular domain, the computation of the probability by assigning numeric values to each level of the factors that pertain to the specific possibility (e.g. time needed to conduct an attack, required attack tools) is no-longer sufficient. Also, no mitigation mechanisms for the identified risks are provided. In the threat modelling approach proposed by Petit *et al.* [42], general attack trees for the high-level attacks are used by the authors to evade redundancy, during the attack tree construction phase. Nevertheless, as the attack trees become more detailed, those general attack sub-trees tend to become specific leading to scalability and extendability issues. The threat modelling approach of Jbair *et al.* [39] provides threat modeling for the lifetime of the ICPS using threats derived from MITRE ATT&CK for ICS. However asset categorisation is based on the Purdue model and as such does not appear to provide a method for user based asset criticality.

The proposed methodology shares similarities with several approaches. It uses well-established sources [9, 11, 27–33, 35] for threats and vulnerability identification in the correlation engine similarly to what MONARC [24] and ITSRM^2 [34] do. Additionally, PASTA [47] and the proposed risk analysis approach use CWEs but for different means. PASTA primarily uses CWEs as vulnerabilities while our presented method

correlates CWEs with all the identified threats and assets to measure the threat probability of occurrences, assign actual vulnerabilities to them, and measure their risk at the
service level automatically. In contrast with the existing approaches, it is designed to
support and perform risk analysis on any information technology asset with the concept
of composition of basic assets to larger entities, the composite assets, in order to support non-conventional architectures such as IIoT, CPS, ITS and Multi-Modal Transport
environments.

Table 2. Comparative analysis among threat modelling (TM), risk analysis (RA) and privacy
impact assessment (PIA) methodologies.

Method	Type			Characteristics	Limitations
	RA	TM	PIA		
PASTA [47]	✓	✓	✗	A technical and holistic approach with thorough documentation that leverages well-established sources [9–11] to provide reliable threat models	It requires manual intervention and profound technical knowledge in order to be applied. For environments such as IIoT and CPS infrastructures it would require several modifications and extensions [49].
LINDDUN [50,51]	✗	✓	✓	Extensive privacy knowledge base, thorough documentation and prioritization of mitigation mechanisms	It requires manual evaluation of identified threats due to the reporting of not relevant, impossible, or insignificant threats.
STRIDE [38]	✗	✓	✗	An easy to apply and well documented tool-assisted methodology	A time-consuming process with overgrown risks that requires manual evaluation whenever it is applied in complex architectures.
IT-Grundschutz [3]	✓	✓	✗	It provides an extensive list of security recommendations for a variety of topics, including safeguards. It does not require risk analysis for some cases	It is mostly targeted to German speaking organisations and requires a manual risk analysis for several cases.
OCTAVE Allegro [22]	✓	✓	✗	It can be tailored for most organisations and provides guidance and worksheets	It does not provide extensive threat and vulnerability catalogues.
OCTAVE-S [17]	✓	✓	✗	It is tailored for small organisations and can be led by a small team	The team conducting the method requires knowledge of both business and security processes of the organization.
OCTAVE FORTE [46]	✓	✗	✗	Compared to OCTAVE Allegro, OCTAVE FORTE analyzes all types of risks, with cyber risks being part of the risk portfolio	It does not provide any threat and vulnerability catalogues and makes recommendations using other methodologies for threat modeling such as PASTA or STRIDE.
ISO/IEC 27005 [7]	✓	✗	✗	It is the de-facto risk management method and compatible with most other methods	Because of its general nature, it requires a lot of effort in context establishment, risk identification etc. As such the implementation cost will be substantial.
EBIOS Risk Manager [19]	✓	✗	✓	A configurable and agile approach providing quick results to the decision makers. Large set of tools available for free	New threats can be added only manually to the provided threat repository [34]. Also, no vulnerability catalogues are provided, and new vulnerabilities cannot be imported [34].
MAGERIT [15]	✓	✓	✓	Contemplates all aspects of a risk management procedure providing either a qualitative or a quantitative approach	Threat and vulnerabilites catalogues are not clearly distinguished. [34]. Requires a commercial license to conduct risk analysis projects [48]. Books 2 and 3 [13,14] are written solely in Spanish.
MONARC [24]	✓	✓	✓	It takes advantage of risk analyses already carried out. The provided tool promotes flexibility and expandability by permitting new elements to be added to its knowledge base.	It does not provide a countermeasures catalogue and requires manual extensions to conduct risk analysis in CPS or ITS.

(*continued*)

Table 2. (*continued*)

Method	Type			Characteristics	Limitations
	RA	TM	PIA		
ITSRM[2] [34]	✓	✗	✗	It offers both a qualitative and a quantitative process-based approach	It does not permit new asset categories to be appended and retrieves threats and countermeasures from other methodologies [34,41]. Vulnerabilities are not used in the overall risk analysis process. It is strict in the process of computing the residual risks.
Semertzis *et al.* [44]	✓	✗	✗	An approach that is able to calculate the cascading effects on attack of Cyber-Physical Systems, using digital twins	The CVE categorisation of the different types of compromises appears to be manual. Difficult to deploy
Zeddini *et al.* [53]	✓	✓	✗	It offers an extensive list of attacks, assets, vulnerabilities, and countermeasures	The approach appears to be theoretical and the list generation a manual process.
Hamad *et al.* [37]	✓	✓	✗	A threat modelling approach for vehicular environments that uses attack trees to represent attack paths to exploit an asset's certain vulnerability	It does not appear to be a scalable solution. It does not provide mitigation mechanisms for the identified risks.
Petit *et al.* [42]	✓	✓	✗	It provides a threat modelling tool based on attack trees that illustrate individual attack scenarios for the vehicular domain	As the attack trees become more detailed, the general attack sub-trees may become more specific which could lead to scalability issues.
Jbair *et al.* [39]	✓	✓	✗	It uses digital twins to perform threat modeling for the lifetime of the ICPS, based on MITREs ATT&CK for ICS	It does not appear to provide a method for user control over asset criticality.
Proposed Framework	✓	✓	✗	Dynamic Service-Oriented Risk Analysis Method focusing on Cyber-Physical Systems. Automated, hierarchical process covering a multitude of CPS domains	The current version does not provide measures nor controls regarding the identified vulnerabilities. This is currently under development. Future work includes integration of PIA

6   Conclusions

The current research introduces a hybrid dynamic risk analysis with threat modelling capabilities and characteristics of a proof-of-concept implementation. Our procedure allows automatic valuation of risks and impacts through a hierarchical model that decomposes services to composite assets and then to basic assets, as well as through the integration of new vulnerabilities automatically using well-established public sources (CVEs, CWEs, CAPECs). Since it currently does not support risk mitigation for suggesting measures or controls for the identified vulnerabilities, the development of a security control and countermeasure suggestion mechanism to the identified vulnerabilities is in progress. To do so, the use of a machine-learning based approach to automatically assign CVEs to high-level vulnerabilities, as well as assign threats to unlabeled CVEs with CWEs will be developed, using our existing mapping of CWEs - Threats. Finally, through the use of probabilistic models, we aim to be able to evaluate the impact of a threat on an asset as well as how it cascades into other threats for connected assets in order to enhance the threat modelling capabilities of the proposed risk analysis methodology.

Acknowledgment. This work is a part of the CitySCAPE project. CitySCAPE has received funding from the European Union's Horizon 2020 research & innovation programme under grant agreement no 883321. Content reflects only the authors' view and European Commission is not responsible for any use that may be made of the information it contains.

References

1. The H2020 CitySCAPE Project. https://www.cityscape-project.eu
2. BSI-Standard 200–1. Information Security Management Systems (ISMS) (2018).https:// www.bsi.bund.de/EN/Topics/ITGrundschutz/itgrundschutz_node.htm
3. BSI-Standard 200–2. IT-Grundschutz-Methodology (2018). https://www.bsi.bund.de/EN/ Topics/ITGrundschutz/itgrundschutz_node.htm
4. BSI-Standard 200–3. Risk Analysis based on IT-Grundschutz (2018). https://www.bsi.bund. de/EN/Topics/ITGrundschutz/itgrundschutz_node.htm
5. ISO 31000:2018 Risk Management - Guidelines (2018). https://www.iso.org/standard/ 65694.html
6. ISO/IEC 27000:2018 Information technology - Security techniques - Information security management systems - Overview and vocabulary (2018). https://www.iso.org/standard/ 73906.html
7. ISO/IEC 27005:2018 Information Technology - Security Techniques - Information Security Risk Management (2018). https://www.iso.org/standard/75281.html
8. IT-Grundschutz-Compendium (2021). https://www.bsi.bund.de/EN/Topics/ITGrundschutz/ itgrundschutz_node.htm
9. Common Attack Pattern Enumeration and Classification (2022). https://capec.mitre.org
10. Common Vulnerabilities and Exposures (2022). https://cve.mitre.org
11. Common Weakness Enumeration (2022). https://cwe.mitre.org
12. Threat Modeling (2022). https://www.microsoft.com/en-us/securityengineering/sdl/ threatmodeling
13. Spanish Ministry of Finance & Public Administration. MAGERIT - versión 3.0.Metodología de Análisis y Gestión de Riesgos de los Sistemas de Información. Libro II - Catálogo de Elementos (2012)
14. Spanish Ministry of Finance & Public Administration. MAGERIT - versión 3.0.Metodología de Análisis y Gestión de Riesgos de los Sistemas de Información. Libro III - Guía de Técnicas (2012)
15. Spanish Ministry of Finance & Public Administration. MAGERIT-version 3.0.Methodology for Information Systems Risk Analysis and Management. Book I - The Method (2014)
16. Alberts, C., Behrens, S., Pethia, R., Wilson, W.: Operationally Critical Threat, Asset, and Vulnerability Evaluation (OCTAVE) Framework, Version 1.0. Tech. Rep. CMU/SEI-99-TR-017, Software Engineering Institute, Carnegie Mellon University, Pittsburgh, PA (1999)
17. Alberts, C., Dorofee, A., Stevens, J., Woody, C.: Introduction to the OCTAVE Approach (2003)
18. Alexander, O., Belisle, M., Steele, J.: MITRE ATT&CK® for Industrial Control Systems: Design and Philosophy (2020)
19. ANNSI. EBIOS Risk Manager (2019). https://www.ssi.gouv.fr/uploads/2019/11/anssi-guide-ebios_risk_manager-en-v1.0.pdf
20. ANSSI. Label EBIOS Risk Manager: Solutions Logicielles Conformes Ebios Risk Manager (2018). https://www.ssi.gouv.fr/entreprise/management-du-risque/la-methode-ebios-risk-manager/label-ebios-risk-manager-des-outils-pour-faciliter-le-management-du-risque-numerique
21. Bojanc, R., Jerman-Blažič, B.: A quantitative model for information-security risk management. Eng. Manag. J. **25**(2), 25–37 (2013)
22. Caralli, R., Stevens, J., Young, L., Wilson, W.: Introducing OCTAVE Allegro: Improving the Information Security Risk Assessment Process. Tech. Rep. CMU/SEI-2007-TR-012, Software Engineering Institute, Carnegie Mellon University, Pittsburgh, PA (2007). http:// resources.sei.cmu.edu/library/asset-view.cfm?AssetID=8419

23. CASES. Optimised risk analysis method (2016). https://www.cases.lu/assets/docs/CASES_Monarc2016EN-web.pdf
24. CASES MONARC. Technical Guide (2021). https://www.monarc.lu/documentation/technical-guide/
25. Cherdantseva, Y., Burnap, P., Blyth, A., Eden, P., Jones, K., Soulsby, H., Stoddart, K.: A review of cyber security risk assessment methods for SCADA systems. Comput. Secur. **56**, 1–27 (2016)
26. ENISA. Magerit. https://www.enisa.europa.eu/topics/threat-risk-management/risk-management/current-risk/risk-management-inventory/rm-ra-methods/m_magerit.html
27. ENISA. Cloud Computing Risk Assessment (2009). https://www.enisa.europa.eu/publications/cloud-computing-risk-assessment
28. ENISA.. Smartphones: information security risks, opportunities and recommendations for users (2010). https://www.enisa.europa.eu/publications/smartphones-information-security-risks-opportunities-and-recommendations-for-users
29. ENISA. Smart Grid Threat Landscape and Good Practice Guide (2013). https://www.enisa.europa.eu/publications/smart-grid-threat-landscape-and-good-practice-guide
30. ENISA. Baseline Security Recommendations for IoT (2017). https://www.enisa.europa.eu/publications/baseline-security-recommendations-for-iot
31. ENISA. ENISA good practices for security of Smart Cars (2019). https://www.enisa.europa.eu/publications/smart-cars
32. ENISA. Port Cybersecurity - Good practices for cybersecurity in the maritime sector (2019). https://www.enisa.europa.eu/publications/port-cybersecurity-good-practices-for-cybersecurity-in-the-maritime-sector
33. ENISA. ENISA Threat Landscape for 5G Networks Report (2020). https://www.enisa.europa.eu/publications/enisa-threat-landscape-report-for-5g-networks
34. ENISA. Interoperable EU Risk Management Framework (2022). https://www.enisa.europa.eu/publications/interoperable-eu-risk-management-framework
35. ETSI. Telecommunications and internet converged services and protocols for advanced networking (tispan); methods and protocols; part 1: Method and proforma for threat, risk, vulnerability analysis (2011)
36. EUR-LEX. Regulation (EU) 2016/679 of the European Parliament and of the Council of 27 April 2016 on the protection of natural persons with regard to the processing of personal data and on the free movement of such data, and repealing Directive 95/46/EC (General Data Protection Regulation. https://eur-lex.europa.eu/legal-content/EN/TXT/?uri=CELEX
37. Hamad, M., Nolte, M., Prevelakis, V.: Towards comprehensive threat modeling for vehicles. In: The 1st Workshop on Security and Dependability of Critical Embedded Real-Time Systems, p. 31 (2016)
38. Hernan, S., Lambert, S., Ostwald, T., Shostack, A.: Uncover security design flaws using the STRIDE approach (2006). https://docs.microsoft.com/en-us/archive/msdn-magazine/2006/november/uncover-security-design-flaws-using-the-stride-approach
39. Jbair, M., Ahmad, B., Maple, C., Harrison, R.: Threat modelling for industrial cyber physical systems in the era of smart manufacturing. Comput. Indust. **137**, 103611 (2022)
40. Mataracioglu, T.: Comparison of PCI DSS and ISO/IEC 27001 Standards. ISACA **1** (2016). https://www.isaca.org/resources/isaca-journal/issues/2016/volume-1/comparison-of-pci-dss-and-isoiec-27001-standards#f1
41. NIST. Security and Privacy Controls for Information Systems and Organizations. Tech. rep. (2020). https://nvlpubs.nist.gov/nistpubs/SpecialPublications/NIST.SP.800-53r5.pdf
42. Petit, J., Shladover, S.E.: Potential cyberattacks on automated vehicles. IEEE Trans. Intell. Transp. Syst. **16**(2), 546–556 (2015)

43. Scarfone, K., Mell, P.: An analysis of CVSS version 2 vulnerability scoring. In: 2009 3rd International Symposium on Empirical Software Engineering and Measurement, pp. 516–525. IEEE (2009)
44. Semertzis, I., Rajkumar, V.S., Ştefanov, A., Fransen, F., Palensky, P.: Quantitative risk assessment of cyber attacks on cyber-physical systems using attack graphs, pp. 1–6 (2022)
45. Stefan Sacala, I., Pop, E., Alexandru Moisescu, M., Dumitrache, I., Iuliana Caramihai, S., Culita, J.: Enhancing cps architectures with SOA for industry 4.0 enterprise systems. In: 2021 29th Mediterranean Conference on Control and Automation (MED), pp. 71–76 (2021)
46. Tucker, B.: Advancing Risk Management Capability Using the OCTAVE FORTE Process. Tech. rep., Software Engineering Institute, Carnegie Mellon University, Pittsburgh, PA (2020). http://resources.sei.cmu.edu/library/asset-view.cfm?AssetID=644636
47. UcedaVélez, T., Morana, M.M.: Risk Centric Threat Modeling: Process for attack simulation and threat analysis. Wiley (2015). https://www.wiley.com/en-us/Risk+Centric+Threat+Modeling%3A+Process+for+Attack+Simulation+and+Threat+Analysis-p-9780470500965
48. Vega, R., Arroyo, R., Yoo, S.G.: Experience in applying the analysis and risk management methodology called Magerit to identify threats and vulnerabilities in an agro-industrial company. Int. J. Appl. Eng. Res. **12**, 6741–6750 (2017)
49. Wolf, A., Simopoulos, D., D'Avino, L., Schwaiger, P.: The PASTA threat model implementation in the IoT development life cycle. INFORMATIK **2020**, 1195–1204 (2021)
50. Wuyts, K., Joosen, W.: Linddun privacy threat modeling: A tutorial (2015). https://lirias.kuleuven.be/retrieve/331950
51. Wuyts, K., Van Landuyt, D., Hovsepyan, A., Joosen, W.: Effective and efficient privacy threat modeling through domain refinements. In: Proceedings of the 33rd Annual ACM Symposium on Applied Computing (SAC '18), pp. 1175–1178. Association for Computing Machinery, New York (2018)
52. Xiong, W., Lagerström, R.: Threat modeling - A systematic literature review. Comput. Secur. **84**, 53–69 (2019)
53. Zeddini, B., Maachaoui, M., Inedjaren, Y.: Security threats in intelligent transportation systems and their risk levels. Risks **10**(5) (2022)

6th International Workshop on Security and Privacy Requirements Engineering (SECPRE 2022)

Preface

This volume contains revised versions of the papers presented at the Sixth International Workshop on Security and Privacy Requirements Engineering (SECPRE 2022) which was co-located with the 27th European Symposium on Research in Computer Security (ESORICS 2021) virtually held in Copenhagen, Denmark on September 29th, 2022.

Data protection regulations, the complexity of modern environments (such as IoT, IoE, Cloud Computing, Big Data, Cyber-Physical Systems, etc.) and the increased level of users awareness in IT have forced software engineers to identify security and privacy as fundamental design aspects leading to the implementation of more trusted software systems and services. Researchers have addressed the necessity and importance of implementing design methods for security and privacy requirements elicitation, modeling, and implementation in recent decades in various innovative research domains. Today Security by Design (SbD) and Privacy by Design (PbD) are established research areas that focus on these directions. The new GDPR regulation sets even stricter requirements for organizations regarding its applicability. SbD and PbD play a very critical and important role in assisting stakeholders in understanding their needs, complying with the new legal, organizational, and technical requirements, and finally selecting the appropriate measures for fulfilling these requirements. SECPRE aimed to provide researchers and professionals with the opportunity to present novel and cutting-edge research on these topics.

SECPRE 2022 attracted 5 high-quality submissions, each of which was assigned to 4 referees for review; the review process resulted in 2 papers being selected for presentation and inclusion in these proceedings. The topics covered included theoretical and practical aspects of privacy and cybersecurity.

We would like to express our thanks to all those who assisted us in organizing the events and putting together the programs. We are very grateful to the members of the Program Committee for their timely and rigorous reviews. Thanks are also due to the Organizing Committee of the events. Last, but by no means least, we would like to thank all the authors who submitted their work to the workshop and contributed to an interesting set of proceedings.

September 2022

John Mylopoulos
Christos Kalloniatis
Annie Anton
Stefanos Gritzalis

Organization

General Chairs

Annie Anton — Georgia Institute of Technology, USA
Stefanos Gritzalis — University of Piraeus, Greece

Program Committee Chairs

John Mylopoulos — University of Ottawa, Canada
Christos Kalloniatis — University of the Aegean, Greece

Program Committee

Travis Breaux	Carnegie Mellon, USA
Frederic Cuppens	Telecom Bretange, France
Sabrina De Capitani di Vimercati	Università degli Studi di Milano, Italy
Vasiliki Diamantopoulou	University of the Aegean, Greece
Eduardo Fernandez-Medina	University of Castilla-La Mancha, Spain
Mohamad Gharib	University of Florence, Italy
Maritta Heisel	University of Duisburg-Essen, Germany
Jan Juerjens	University of Koblenz-Landau, Germany
Maria Karyda	University of the Aegean, Greece
Costas Lambrinoudakis	University of Piraeus, Greece
Tong Li	University of Technology, China
Javier Lopez	University of Malaga, Spain
Aaron Massey	University of Maryland, USA
Haralambos Mouratidis	University of Brighton, UK
Michalis Pavlidis	University of Brighton, UK
William Robinson	Georgia State University, USA
David Garcia Rosado	University of Castilla-La Mancha, Spain
Pierangela Samarati	Università degli Studi di Milano, Italy
Aggeliki Tsohou	Ionian University, Greece
Nicola Zannone	Eindhoven University of Technology, The Netherlands

OntoCyrene: Towards Ontology-Enhanced Asset Modelling for Supply Chains in the Context of Cyber Security

Mohammad Heydari[1]([✉]), Haralambos Mouratidis[2], and Vahid Heydari Fami Tafreshi[3]

[1] Cyber Security Researcher at Stockholm University, Stockholm, Sweden
heydari@dsv.su.se
[2] School of Computer Science and Electronic Engineering, University of Essex, Colchester, UK
h.mouratidis@essex.ac.uk
[3] Staffordshire University London, London, UK
v.heydari@staffs.ac.uk

Abstract. A Supply chain in the era of the Internet of Industrial Things faces new challenges in terms of modelling. The challenges stem from a number of characteristics like scalability, dependency and dynamism. In this paper, we introduce an ontology-enhanced method for modelling assets and their dependency in the context of supply chains. This method enables us to infer new insights from the domain. It also provides a dynamic knowledge representation and reasoning by capturing all aspects of supply chains from three different perspectives including business, asset, and sector. The results show that the proposed method can address the challenges by utilizing ontology and synching three relevant perspectives. Moreover, the developed ontology (OntoCyrene) is rich enough to bring light to the dark angles of the modelled scenarios. The theme chosen for this work is cyber security and we used real-world scenarios derived from the Cyrene (Cyrene EU H2020 Project is available at: https://www.cyrene.eu.) project to populate and evaluate the ontology.

Keywords: Asset modelling · Ontology · Supply chain service · Industrial internet of things · Business process model and notation

The work of this paper has been carried out within EU Project CYRENE, which has received funding from the European Union's Horizon 2020 research and innovation programme under grant agreement No 952690

1 Introduction

In the era of the Covid pandemic, the definition and the scope of the critical infrastructure have been changed. Many supply chain services (SCSs) related to producing masks, vaccines etc. were classified as "critical". Moreover, some cyber-attacks like the SolarWinds breach reminded us of the concerns about the security of the supply chain services. One of the very first steps in securing supply chains is to build an asset model. The model is used not only for managing assets but also can be used for the purpose of monitoring and cyber threat intelligence. Such a model should accurately represent enough details on the assets and the dependencies among them. Such a model can be used for various analyses like cyber security analysis.

This paper presents an ontology-based method to represent supply chain assets along with their dependencies among them. Since the definition of supply chains contains business processes as well as infrastructure, considering processes and people is inevitable in modelling. Thus, to capture all aspects of the supply chains, three views need to be considered for such modelling: i) Business view: The core component of this view is the business process. As such, in this view, details of organizational processes, business partners that contribute to such processes, and related business logic need to be considered. ii) Asset/Technical view: The asset perspective focuses on the concept of the asset in the field of SCS. Assets may vary from any ICT and network-connected machines to software stacks and human resources in the SCS. Iii) *Sector view*: Supply chain may consist of a number of partners which belong to different sectors. These partners need to analyse the domain from their own sector-specific view. Therefore, the model should be able to facilitate different sectors with their preferences. Moreover, identifying the internal and external supply chain linkage is another important view from the sector perspective.

Taking these views into consideration helps to build a comprehensive semantic model that can be utilized in cyber threat intelligence. The current efforts focus mainly on the asset perspective to employ a risk-aware analysis.

Therefore, integrating different perspectives under the same umbrella needs more attention in order to reach a more realistic and accurate model.

The organization of this document is as follows: Sect. 2 reviews the main frameworks that are used for building this ontology. Section 3 summarizes the surveyed papers in this field. The methodology for asset modelling is discussed in Sect. 4. Section 4 provides information in detail about the design and implementation of the ontology-based on the methodology. Ontology validation is discussed in Sect. 6. Section 7 concludes the paper.

2 Background

This section reviews the main concepts behind OntoCyrene. The rest of this chapter is dedicated to the concept of Business Process Model and Notation (BPMN) and Ontology. The main contributions in the literature are reviewed at the end of the chapter.

2.1 Business Process Model and Notation (BPMN)

One of the perspectives considered in asset modelling is the business-driven perspective. As discussed in Sect. 1, the business process is at the heart of this perspective. Therefore, finding a standard for modelling business processes is a crucial task. In order to model the business process, there is a number of techniques and languages. The most popular ones are UML, BPMN, EPC and CMMN. In the Cyrene project, BPMN was used as the basis for modelling the business process. This is due to the fact that BPMN is a de-facto standard for business process modelling. BPMN brings a uniform notation to visually model the steps of a business process from end to end. BPMN is proposed by the Object Management Group (OMG[1]). A process in BPMN describes a sequence or flow of activities in an organization with the objective of carrying out work. Therefore, such a process is modelled as a graph of elements, including Activities, Events, Gateways, and Sequence Flows that define finite execution semantics. Using these elements, any process can be formally modelled using BPMN.

2.2 Ontology

The semantic web stack consists of a number of building blocks including RDF, RDFS, SPARQL and Ontology Web Language (OWL). Ontology is placed at the heart of the structure and plays an important role to achieve interoperability and communication among software systems. Ontology relies on the other mentioned blocks. Therefore, utilizing these components to build an ontology is inevitable. Resource Description Framework (RDF) was developed to standardize the definition and use of metadata. RDF offers a graph data model to represent machine-understandable metadata for resources. It encodes the properties (relationships) among entities in the ontology. Graph data is a collection of triples, each consisting of a subject, a predicate and an object. RDF is constructed by a set of those triples. RDFS is constructed based on the RDF and enriched with features like the Object-Oriented paradigm (class, subclass, inheritance etc.). These changes make the relations in RDFS less dependent on concepts and make it a better choice for definition and classification. On top of RDFS, Ontology Web Language (OWL) was designed to fill the gap for expressing meaning and semantics in an effective way thus OWL goes beyond these languages in terms of the ability to represent machine interpretable content. In terms of rules and reasoning in the semantic web, there are several efforts aiming at building rule-based standards for ontology such as RuleML[2],SWRL[3] and SPARQL[4]. Since SPARQL as a rule-based language can be used to express queries across RDF and RDFS, OntoCyrene benefits from it to implement a number of queries against the ontology.

3 Related Works

In this sub section, a number of papers are surveyed. These papers have one thing in common, the authors benefited from *BPMN* and *ontology* in order to model the business process.

---

[1] https://www.omg.org/spec/BPMN/2.0.

[2] The Rule Mark-up Initiative can be accessible at: www.ruleml.org.

[3] Semantic web Rule Language accessible at: www.w3.org/Submission/SWRL.

[4] SPARQL is accessible at: https://www.w3.org/TR/rdf-sparql-query/.

Anane et al. [1] introduced an ontology named BBO based on pre-existing ontologies and BPMN 2.0 meta-model. The ontology was implemented using protege software in the context of industry v4.0. The building blocks of the ontology were chosen and implemented based on the BPMN 2.0 elements including flow elements, activities, gateways events etc. all these concepts were designed in the form of classes and subclasses in the ontology. The proposed ontology was populated using a real-world example and the results indicated that this ontology is able to represent the dynamic aspects of the example and returns correct results based on the designed queries. In order to evaluate the ontology, the authors used competency questions as an evaluation method. As a result, SPARQL queries derived from competency questions were designed to check the quality of answers. The results showed that the ontology has enough richness and quality.

In another contribution Anane et al., [2] compared the nine most cited business process ontologies in the literature. The motivation behind this work is to compare BPMN based ontologies with non-BPMN based ontologies in representing business process specification and execution. Studied ontologies were divided into two categories: Ontologies developed from scratch and ontologies implemented based on BPMN 2.0. The benchmark for this comparative study were process specification and process execution attributes. The result of the study indicates that BPMN based ontologies have better representation capabilities in comparison with the non-BPMN based ontologies.

Diego et al. [3] designed a quadrable multistage semantic representation of BPMN models in order to enhance the mechanization of business process management. The proposed method saved the response time of the queries against the ontology. The building blocks of the proposed model has three levels: metamodel, business process model and finally an assertional layer. The proposed representation model was evaluated using real-world case studies and the results indicated the ontology is able to return the result of the queries in an acceptable time frame.

Sanfilipo et al. [4] conducted an ontology-based analysis on two of BPMN main elements including event and activity. The results showed that activities are neither homomeric nor cumulative, neither atomic nor anti-atomic but events (throw and catch events) are atomic and anti-cumulative.

Adamo et al. [5] presented an ontology-based analysis of business processes modelling notations among four modelling languages/standards including BPMN, UML-AD, EPC and CMMN. The evaluation criteria are classified into 3 categories namely behavioural, data and the organisation. The findings of this study show that if BPMN is able to support this property that if two processes have had different participants, they must be separate processes. Likewise, if two or more activities had some shared participants, they may belong to the same process under some circumstances.

Doynikova et al. [6] proposed an ontology to represent a number of metrics for cyber security management. This ontology aggregates primary security metrics with security information. The ontology formed a set of hierarchically interconnected security metrics for assessment and decision making in the field of cyber security threats. The results showed that the proposed ontology has advantages over other methods in terms of representing the granularity of details, and applying an inference engine to check inconsistency in the domain.

All surveyed BPMN-oriented models suffered from two main problems: **First**, they only consider one perspective (asset-driven) for the sake of modelling, and this limits the final model in expressing all needed facts about the systems for which those models were developed. The **second** problem arises from the lack of proper evaluation methods which results in developing an invalid model.

4 Methodology

The methodology used to model the supply chain consists of two main building blocks namely BPMN and Ontology. This section explains them in detail.

As mentioned in Sect. 1, three perspectives were defined in order to be used in this task. For a business-driven perspective, BPMN version 2 was chosen for modelling the business process. It is because BPMN is a de-facto standard for modelling a business process. Moreover, according to the literature, consolidated findings show that BPMN has better usability for modelling business processes than other standards and schemes like UMA AD, EPC and CMMN.

Another part of the methodology is applying Ontology in order to model the asset and its dependencies. Ontology is a promising tool to advance BPMN. With a semantic annotation of the business process, creation, reuse, search, validation, and execution of process models can be widely extended. Furthermore, using ontology for modelling facilitates us with a number of features that are missing in other modelling paradigms/platforms:

- Ontology encompasses the concept of the Object-Oriented paradigm and all its features. It is also based on set and graph theories which are necessary for asset modelling.
- Applying ontology for modelling assets in supply chain networks with many collaborations/companies brings a machine inference engine to modelling. The ability of the inference engine to check the model for inconsistency, interoperability, and integrity in such a scalable domain is truly needed.
- Modelling assets using ontology reduces human intervention in the verification/validation of the generated model. Therefore, such modelling is less prone to human error.

According to the literature [7], at least five methodologies exist in order to develop an ontology including TOVE [8], enterprise ontology [9], methodology [10], simple knowledge-engineering methodology [11] and on-to-knowledge methodology [12].

Each of them defines a process to develop an ontology. The procedure of developing ontologies for these methodologies is like each other but they are different in labelling the steps. In this research, we employ the "simple knowledge engineering" methodology to develop OntoCyrene. We also extend the evaluation step of this methodology to encompass both quantitative and qualitative approaches. According to [11], the process of developing an ontology has the following steps:

Step 1: Determine the domain and the scope, *Step 2*: Consider reusing existing ontology, *Step 3*: Enumerate important terms in the ontology, *Step 4*: Define class hierarchy, *Step 5*: Define the properties of classes *Step 6*: Define facets of the slots and *Step 7* which includes creating instances. We extend the evaluation procedure of this methodology and add one more step (*Step 8*) to the methodology in this regard.

5 Design and Implementation

In this section, the process of developing OntoCyrene ontology will be discussed based on the methodology. The rest of this section is organized as follows: in 5.1 the implementation of the first three steps of the methodology will be presented. Subsection 5.2 shows the implementation of Step 4. Steps 5–6 of the methodology will be presented in 5.3. Finally, the results of populating the ontology will be shown in 5.4.

5.1 Architecture of OntoCyrene

OntoCyrene is composed of four main sub ontologies namely, Asset, Business, Sector and Certification. These components were selected based on the requirement analysis of the Cyrene project. All these components were implemented as superclass/subclass using the object-oriented concept.

The asset component deals with the asset/technical perspective of the ontology. The business part of the ontology deals with a business-driven perspective and contains the concept of the process. Sector sub ontology handles the sector view for asset modelling and the certification component deals with the certification and conformity assessment in the Cyrene project. Figure 1 demonstrates these components.

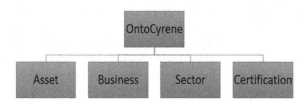

Fig. 1. Main sub ontologies in OntoCyrene

5.2 OntoCyrene Class Hierarchy

Designing class/subclass is a main step in the methodology to build the ontology. In order to implement the architecture depicted in Fig. 1, a number of super classes and subclasses need to be designed. Figure 2 shows all super classes which were designed in OntoCyrene.

For each of the three defined perspectives, there is a superclass designed in the ontology with corresponding names (Asset, Business and Sector). The hierarchy also includes the "Certification" superclass for the conformity assessment part of the Cyrene project. Moreover, all security-related concepts like weakness, vulnerability and attack were classified under the "Security" superclass. "Agent" superclass was designed for all active participants in the ontology including humans and software. "Role" superclass

Fig. 2. OntoCyrene super classes in class hierarchy

includes all subclasses related to various roles that can be taken by humans, machines and software. Part of these super classes contains subclasses. Figure 3 shows all sub classes designed for Business perspective.

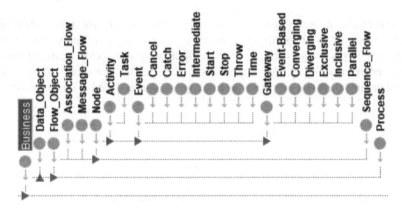

Fig. 3. Sub classes designed for modelling Business driven perspective

As can be seen in Fig. 2, main BPMN elements are modelled in ontology in the form of class/subclass. This includes data object, flow object, connecting object and the process itself. All these elements are discussed in 2.1.1. In order to model these BPMN elements, we have used a number of rules/restrictions in terms of OWL axioms which were defined and implemented by Amina Annane et al. [1] from natural language specifications.

The asset perspective has a number of subclasses including Hardware, Human (subclasses: individual and group) and Software. Asset in terms of hardware is considered as any machine which is assigned by an IP address and a role. As an example, a network-connected machine may be assigned a "client" role. Humans and software may also accept a role (or a number of roles) in different supply chain scenarios. Thus, the ontology has a superclass called "Role". Figure 4 shows the class hierarchy for superclass "Role". Defined roles in this ontology are just examples and need to be extended based on the SCS scenario.

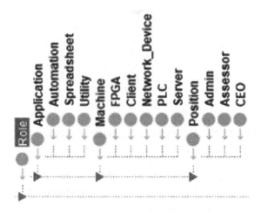

Fig. 4. Roles modelled in OntoCyrene

Another main sub ontology is related to Sector driven perspective (Fig. 5). According to the definition of this perspective mentioned in 1.3, in this view, a Supply Chain Service Provider (SCSP) is analysed/modelled from different aspects including its partners, its internal and external linkage and also by its sub-sectors. Thus, for each of these aspects, a corresponding class and properties were designed and modelled in OntoCyrene.

Fig. 5. Sector-driven perspective modelled in the Ontology

The last component discussed here is "Security". In OntoCyrene, assets are assigned by a number of security-related values like CVSS score, Criticality Score, CVE_ID, CWE_ID etc. These metrics are related to threat, vulnerability, weakness, attack and risk in the context of cyber security. Therefore, Security superclass and all its object and data properties (discussed in 4.3) reflect corresponding blocks of these metrics.

5.3 OntoCyrene Object and Data Properties (Relationships)

In this subsection, all defined relationships (properties) will be discussed. In order to increase the readability of this document, all properties are grouped based on the defined perspectives (Asset, Business and Sector).

5.3.1 Asset Driven Properties

As discussed in 2.2, in order to model the relationship among entities RDF triple needs to be used. For each couple of entities like A and B with a specified relationship, R, the semantic triple is as follows: (A, R, B). For the rest of this section, all available relationships among entities are shown from different perspectives. Table 1 summarizes all asset-driven object relationships in the ontology.

Table 1. Object properties defined and modelled for asset-driven perspective

	Domain (Class)	Object Property (Relationship)	Range (Class)
1	Group	Groups, has_leader	individual
2	Individual	belongs, is_leaderOf has_Role	Group Position
3	Asset	has_role	Role
4	HW	has_role	Machine
5	SW	has_role, is_processing	App, SW
6	Asset	has_vulnerability	Vulnerability
7	Asset	has_weakness	Weakness
8	Human	is_relatedTo, has_accessTo	Process, SW, HW
9	HW	is_assignedTo	Process
10	HW	is_connectingTo, is_controlling	HW, SW
11	SW	is_hostedBy, is_installedOn, is_storedAt, is_accessing, is_controlling	HW
12	HW SW	is_trustedBy	Human

5.3.2 Business Driven Properties

Table 2 summarizes all object properties related to the business-driven perspective in the ontology.

Table 2. Object properties defined and modelled for the business-driven perspective

	Domain (Class)	Object Property (Relationship)	Range (Class)
1	Node	has_container	Business
2	Sequence_Flow	has_inclusiveGateway	Inclusive
3	Sequence_Flow	has_exclusiveGateway	Exclusive
4	Business	has_flowObject	Node
5	Node	has_incoming	Sequence_Flow
6	Activity	has_input	Input
7	Activity	has_output	Output
8	Node	has_outgoing	Sequence_Flow
9	Process	has_part	Activity Event Gateway
10	Node	has_sequenceFlow	Sequence_Flow
11	Sequence_Flow Message_Flow	has_source	Node
12	Sequence_Flow Message_Flow	has_target	Node
13	Activity Event Gateway	is_partOf	Process
14	Process Activity Event Gateway	is_proceededBy	Process Activity Event Gateway
15	Process Activity Event Gateway	is_succeededBy	Process Activity Event Gateway
16	Node	has_messageFlow	Message_Flow

5.3.3   Sector Driven Properties

Table 3 summarizes all object properties related to the sector-driven perspective in OntoCyrene.

Table 3. Object properties defined and modelled for the sector-driven perspective

	Domain (Class)	Object Property (Relationship)	Range (Class)
1	SCSP	has_partnershipWith	Partners
2	SCSP	has_department	Departments
3	SCSP	has_linkage	Internal
4	SCSP	has_linkage	External
5	SCSP	runs_process	Process

5.3.4 Security Related Properties

In addition to the above-mentioned relationship, a number of object properties were defined and modelled to reflect the relationship between threat, vulnerability, weakness and attack. Table 4 summarizes these properties.

Table 4. Object properties defined and modelled for security-related concepts

	Domain (Class)	Object Property (Relationship)	Range (Class)
1	Asset	has_vulnerability	Vulnerability
2	Asset	has_weakness	Weakness
3	Vulnerability	is_exploitedBy	Attack
4	Weakness	is_targetedBy	Vulnerability
5	Vulnerability	targets	Weakness

5.3.5 Data Properties

A number of data properties have been defined for OntoCyrene. Figure 6 shows these properties.

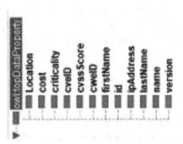

Fig. 6. OntoCyrene data properties

For asset driven perspective, the following data properties are defined: Location of the asset, asset ID, CVE ID and CWE ID related to the asset, CVSS score related to the asset, a value of criticality assigned to the asset, the cost of the asset etc. Moreover, the first name and the last name of individuals are kept through these properties. For hardware, name, id and IP address are recorded according to the defined properties. For software, ID, version and name can be stored in the ontology. From business perspective, all BPMN elements involved in the ontology may have ID and name. For sector-specific view, name, ID and location can be recorded in the ontology.

5.3.6   Connecting Points of Three Perspectives

By considering all relationships defined for the asset, business and sector perspectives, Fig. 7 depicts the connecting points of these perspectives in the ontology.

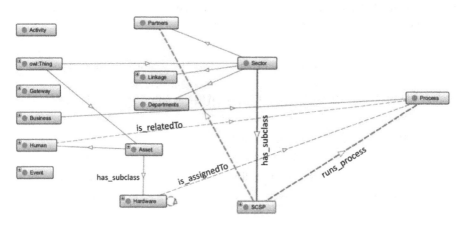

Fig. 7. Connecting points of the three perspectives

As shown in the picture, asset driven perspective has two explicit relationships with the business-driven perspective through hardware and human. In other words, by asserting i) Human "is_relatedTo" the process and ii) Hardware "is_assignedTo" the process both business and asset driven perspectives are joined to each other. Furthermore, sector view is connected to the business view via supply chain service provider (SCSP). Each process is owned and run by SCSP so by asserting the following properties sector-driven perspective is connected to the business-driven perspective: "SCSP runs_process the process".

5.4   Ontology Population

The ontology was populated using a real-world scenario in the field of vehicle transport supply chain. This scenario consists of a process called "Port Call Request".

This process was implemented using Protégé[5] software and validated by CRF[6]. Protégé is an open-source ontology editor and framework developed by Stanford University. Protégé provides an environment to build ontologies based on the simple knowledge engineering methodology. The rest of this section explains the process and the instantiation phase of this process from three different perspectives including Sector, Asset and Business.

5.4.1 Description of "PORt Call Request" Process

The "port calls" process is a request from the Shipping Line or its Ship Agent to the Port Authority and the Harbourmaster's office, requesting a berth, giving details of the call and the vessel. This process requests a berth, giving details of the call and the vessel. The Ship Agent sends the Port Authority data including the port of arrival, name of the vessel, the carrier, and previous and following ports of call. Once the port call corresponding authorisations for these requests are received the Ship Agent provides more information about passengers and crew, waste, berth requirements, expected operations (pilot, tugboats, and mooring), and other relevant data. Vehicles import/export in maritime transport is subject to local Customs' audit. Sending the request of the port call, automatically opens a Customs registry for the customs clearance of goods that must be loaded or unloaded from the vessel.

The port calls information is used by Port Authority and the Terminal Operators to manage their resources accordingly preparing equipment, personnel, etc. These communications are done using the Port Community System (PCS).

5.4.2 Ontology Population: Sector Perspective

As mentioned earlier, the populated example is in the field of the Vehicles Transport supply chain service. It concerns the vehicles import processes engaging the shipment and receipt of various types of vehicles and equipment such as trucks, vans, truck trailers, gantry cranes etc. Three aspects have been populated as sector view in the ontology for this example: SCSP (names and specs), its departments and partners.

As discussed, the name of the supply chain service provider in this example is Vehicle Transport Service. The name and ID of the SCSP were specified using the corresponding data objects in the ontology. The supply chain service provider has the following departments: Digital Transportation, Exploitation and, Port Community System. The following relationship has been used to populate the ontology with these departments: (SCSP, has_department, CRF). The main stakeholders/partners of this supply chain service provider are as follows: Port Authority, Ship Owner, Local Agent and Logistics/Transport. Figure 8 shows the populated instances for the partner class.

In order to populate the ontology, a number of relationships (Object Properties) were used. Table 5 shows them.

---

[5] Available at: https://www.protege.stanford.edu

[6] Centro Ricerche Fiat (CRF) is one of the main private research centre in Italy. Available at: https://www.crf.it/

Fig. 8. Instances for partners of the SCSP in the example

Table 5. Object properties used to implement partners of the SCSP

Instance	Relationship	Instance
SCSP	has_partnershipWith	Local_Agent, Logistics, Port_Authority, Ship_Owner

5.4.3 Ontology Population: Business Perspective

The process discussed in 5.1 was designed and implemented using BPMN. Figure 9 demonstrates this process with BPMN symbols and semantics. The diagram includes a number of activities and a parallel gateway with start/stop events to depict the procedure of the "Port Call Request". In order to implement this scheme, an encoded layout of this diagram was designed. Figure 10 shows the encoded diagram of this process.

As shown in Fig. 10, the label of all activities starts with "A". Moreover, the tags of the sequence/message flows start with "S" and the only gateway of the process is tagged using "G". Start and stop events in this process starts with "E". In order to implement this scheme, all of the encoded building blocks in Fig. 11 were populated. For activities, A1...A7 were defined and implemented as instances of the activity class. S0, S2, S3, S5, S6, S7 and S8 were implemented as instances for a sequence flow class. Moreover, S1 and S4 were populated as instances of the class "message flow".

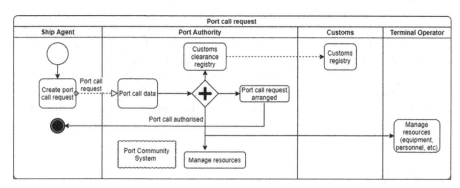

Fig. 9. BPMN diagram of "Port Call Request" process

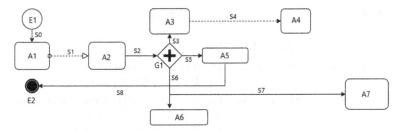

Fig. 10. Encoded BPMN diagram of "Port Call Request" process

The only gateway of this process was created as an instance of the "parallel gateway" class. All these entities were joined to the "Port Call Request" process (P1) using the following assertion: "is_partOf". As an example: (A1, is_partOf, P1). Furthermore, for all mentioned entities, another relationship was asserted in the ontology to connect them to the "Port Call" process which is: "has_part".

As an example: (P1, has_part, A1). After defining and implementing all building blocks of the scheme depicted in Fig. 3, different types of relationships among them were defined and implemented. As an example from the discussed scenario you may find all A1 corresponding relationships in the ontology: (A1, is_proceededBy, E1), (A1, is_succeededBy, A2), (A1, has_incoming, S0), (A1, has_outgoing, S1). In the same way, connecting objects were defined and asserted in the ontology (sequence and message flow). As an example, S0 corresponding relationships in terms of connecting object are as follows: (S0, has_source, E1) and (S0, has_target, A1).

5.4.4   Ontology Population: Asset Perspective.

As defined in the ontology, an asset can be human, hardware or software. According to the analysis of the "Port Call Request" process, four individuals are involved in the process including a ship agent operator, port authority operator, customs operator, and terminal operator. Furthermore, for each of these individuals, a number of resources in terms of hardware and software were assigned based on the description of the process. Table 6 lists the details of assigned hardware and software based on the description of the p1 process.

The relationships between hardware and software are asserted using the following object property: "is_installedOn". For example: (Kaspersky_av, is_installedOn, Dell_PE_R740).

5.4.5   Ontology Population: Connecting Three Perspectives

In order to connect the asset perspective to the business perspective, the following relationships were extracted and asserted in the ontology. Table 7 presents these entities and relationships:

Table 6. List of asset-driven instances and relationships implemented for P1

Instance	Relationship	Instance (HW/SW)
ship_agent_operator	has_accessTo	PCS, Office365, MS_Edge, AVG_av, Lap_Lenovo_C930, Windows_10_x64
port_authority_operator	has_accessTo	Exchange_Server, FTP_Server, SMTP_Server, SQL_Server_2019, Windows_Server_2019, PCS, HP_DL850, IIS10, Router_SLX_9640, PCS
customs_operator	has_accessTo	Office365, Windows_Server_2019, Dell_PE_R740, Kaspersky_av
terminal_operator	has_accessTo	PCS, Chrome, Office365, Lap_HP_G6, Windows_10_x64, Norton_av

Table 7. Implementing connecting points for three perspectives in the example

Instance Asset View	Relationship	Instance (Business/Sector) view
ship_agent_operator	is_relatedTo	(Business View) A1, P1, E1, E2, S0, S1
ship_agent_operator	belongs	(Sector View) Ship_Owner
port_authority_operator	is_relatedTo	(Business View) A2, A3, A5, A6, G1, S2, S3, S5, S6, S7, P1
port_authority_operator	belongs	(Sector View) Port_Authority
customs_operator	is_relatedTo	(Business View) P1, A4
customs_operator	belongs	Customs
terminal_operator	is_relatedTo	(Business View) P1, A7
terminal_operator	belongs	Port_Authority

6   Evaluation

Ontology evaluation guarantees that the designed ontology meets the application require-ment. By growing the applications of the semantic web, the need for efficient evaluating techniques has increased. In this work, we applied three evaluation methods includ-ing i) usability test, ii) evaluating by competency questions and applying iii) OntoQA approach to evaluate the ontology. In the usability test, the populated ontology was exam-ined by our partners (CRF) in order to evaluate the usability of the ontology. The next method used to evaluate the ontology is applying competency questions to see whether the ontology is competent enough to give the correct answers to the queries. Finally, a metric-based evaluation method called OntoQA will be used to examine the quality of the ontology. In the rest of this chapter, we first show the results driven by evaluating the ontology during its development. Afterwards, we present the results of designing and implementing competency questions to evaluate the ontology. Finally, the results coming from the OntoQA approach will be presented.

6.1 Evaluating the Ontology by Business Partners (CRF)

Evaluating as a part of the ontology development life cycle is proposed based on the software engineering methods [13]. In this method, evaluation and validation are within the evolution process. OntoCyrene was evaluated during development by the business partner. In doing so, the business partner (CRF) evaluated the ontology by running a number of queries against it and analysing the results. Figure 11 shows the results for one of those queries. In this example, an entity from the sector perspective (Ship_Owner) has been queried against ontology. The result indicated that the ontology is rich enough to show the model of the entities from different perspectives and their dependencies for the queried object.

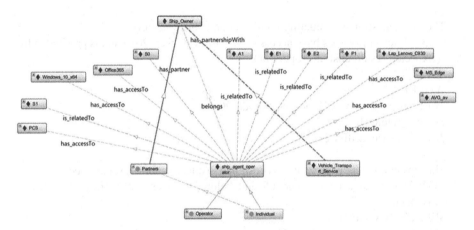

Fig. 11. Results of the executed query against Ship_Owner entity

The results of the queries confirmed that the populated scenario (Port Call Request) was modelled correctly. Furthermore, the granularity of details reflected in the results revealed that the OntoCyrene is enough rich to show the asset model and its dependencies.

6.2 Ontology Evaluation Using Competency Questions

Michel Gruniger et al. [14] proposed a method to evaluate the ontology called Competency Questions (CQ). In this method, a number of questions are designed and implemented against an ontology and the ontology should have sufficient axioms to answer those questions. In other words, a competency question expresses a question-style pattern in the natural language in order to test the ontology whether it is competent to answer the question. For OntoCyrene, we designed and implemented a number of competency questions. These questions were implemented in SPARQL. In the rest of this sub-section part of these questions are shown:

The first competency question introduced here is about the business view:

CQ1: What is the business process element which is succeeded by another element and does not have any incoming flow? (Expected result: E1).

SELECT ?x.
WHERE {
?x ex:is_succeededBy ?y.
FILTER NOT EXISTS { ?x ex:has_incoming ?z}.
}.

The next competency question was designed to evaluate both sector and business views: CQ2: What is a sector view entity which belongs to Port_Authority and is related to A6 (Activity)? (Expected result: Port_Authority_Operator).

SELECT ?x.
WHERE {
?x ex:belongs ex:Port_Authority.
?x ex:is_relatedTo ex:A6.
}.

The third question is evaluating both asset and business views:

CQ3: Which entity does have access to Windows_Server_2019 and is proceeded by A3? (Expected result: customs_operator).

SELECT ?x.
WHERE {
?x ex:has_accessTo ex:Windows_Server_2019.
?x ex:is_relatedTo ?y.
?y ex:is_proceededBy ex:A3.
}.

The next competency question was designed to query against asset and sector views:

CQ4: Who does access Office365 and belong to "Customs"? (Expected result: customs_operator).

SELECT ?x WHERE {
?x ex:has_accessTo ex:Office365.
?x ex:belongs ex:customs.
}.

The last example from the competency questions is presenting a query designed against all three views:

CQ5: What is the entity which has access to PCS and belongs to Port_Authority and is related to A5 (Activity)? (Expected result: Port_Authority_Operator).

SELECT ?x.
WHERE {
?x ex:has_accessTo ex:PCS.
?x ex:belongs ex:Port_Authority.
?x ex:is_relatedTo ex:A5.
}.

According to the results, OntoCyrene is enough competent to answer all questions.

6.3 Ontology Evaluation Using OntoQA

OntoQA [15] is an evaluation method that is based on two major groups of evaluation metrics: schema metrics and knowledge base metrics. Schema metrics show the quality and richness of ontology in knowledge representation. Knowledge base metrics evaluate the placement of instances in an ontology. In this research three of the OntoQA metrics were used to evaluate OntoCyrene namely as Inheritance Richness (IR) and Attribute Richness (AR): Inheritance Richness (IR) is defined as the average number of subclasses per class. According to Samir Tartir et al. [15] an ontology with low IR would be a deep ontology indicating that that ontology covers a specific domain in detail. On the other hand, an ontology with high IR would be a shallow ontology. Shallow ontology presents a wide range of general knowledge not in detail. Attribute Richness (AR) is defined as an indicator to show the quality of the ontology by measuring the average number of relationships (attributes) per class. It is calculated as the total number of attributes divided by the number of classes in ontology. In general, the ontology with a greater value of AR conveys more knowledge.

The calculated values of IR and AR for this ontology are 1.14 and 0.80 respectively. According to the results of the empirical studies on ontology metrics [16] the above metrics show that the ontology is rich and deep enough to represent the domain (IR and AR values greater than 0.5).

7   Conclusion

Efficient asset modelling is a challenging task in the Industrial Internet of Things environment. The scalability, heterogeneity and dynamism of such an environment increase the complexity of the modelling. In this work, we presented an ontology enhanced modelling of supply chain service. In the proposed method, three views including asset, business and sector were provided as sub-ontologies to capture all aspects of dynamism in the domain. The designed ontology (OntoCyrene) was evaluated by three methods in order to make sure that it meets the requirements. The results showed that OntoCyrene is rich enough to show the asset model and its dependencies. The evaluation also confirmed that the ontology has sufficient axioms to answer the competency questions. OntoCyrene needs to be extended from its "Certification" sub-ontology. It also needs attention in terms of designing an interface in order to be deployed in the Cyrene platform. Moreover, more research is needed to apply graph-based analysis methods to this ontology.

References

1. Annane, A., Aussenac-Gilles, N., Kamel, M.: BBO: BPMN 2.0 based ontology for business process representation. In: 20th European Conference on Knowledge Management (2019)
2. Rocha, A.P., Steels, L., van den Herik, J. (eds.): ICAART 2020. LNCS (LNAI), vol. 12613. Springer, Cham (2021). https://doi.org/10.1007/978-3-030-71158-0

3. Hinkelmann, K., Fanesi, D., Cacciagrano, D.: semantic business process representation to enhance the degree of BPM mechanization - an ontology (2015)
4. Sanfilippo, E., Borgo, S., Masolo, C.: Events and activities: is there an ontology behind BPMN? Frontiers in AI and its applications (2014)
5. Adamo, G., Borgo, S., Di Francescomarino, C., Ghidini C., Guarino, N., Sanfilippo, E.M.: Business processes and their participants: an ontological perspective. Lecture Notes in Computer Science, vol 10640 (2017)
6. Doynikova, E., Fedorchenko, A., Kotenko, I.: Ontology of metrics for cyber security assessment. In: ARES 2019: Proceedings of the 14th International Conference on Availability, Reliability and Security (2019)
7. Alfaify, Y.: Ontology development methodology, a systematic review and case study. In: International Conference on Computing and Information Technology (ICCIT), (2022)
8. Grüninger, M., Fox, M.S.: Methodology for the design and evaluation of ontologies. In: IJCIA, Montreal (1995)
9. Uschold, M., King, M.: Towards a metho dology for building ontologies. In: IJCAI (1995)
10. Fernández-López, M., Juristo, N.: Methontology: from ontological art towards ontological engineering (1997)
11. Noy, N.F., McGuinness, D.L.: Ontology development 101: a guide to creating your first ontology. Stanford University, Stanford (2000)
12. Staab, S., Studer, R., Schnurr, H.-P., Sure, Y.: Knowledge processes and ontologies. IEEE Intelligent Systems **16**(1), 26–34 (2001)
13. Gómez-Pérez, A., Rojas-Amaya, M.: Ontological reengineering for reuse. In: Proceeding of the 11th European Workshop on Knowledge Acquisition, Modeling and Management (1999)
14. Groninger, M., Fox, M.S.: The role of competency questions in enterprise engineering. In: Benchmarking—Theory and Practice (1995)
15. Tartir, S., Arpinar, I.B., Sheth, A.P.: Ontological evaluation and validation. In: Theory and Applications of Ontology: Computer Applications (2010)
16. Sicilia, M.A., Rodrígueza, D., García-Barriocanal, E., Sánchez-Alonso, S.: Empirical findings on ontology metrics. Expert Syst. Appl. **39**(8), 6706–6711 (2012)

Measuring the Adoption of TLS Encrypted Client Hello Extension and Its Forebear in the Wild

Zisis Tsiatsikas[1,2], Georgios Karopoulos[3(✉)], and Georgios Kambourakis[3]

[1] University of the Aegean, 83200 Karlovasi, Greece
tzisis@aegean.gr
[2] Atos, 14122 Athens, Greece
zisis.tsiatsikas@atos.net
[3] European Commission, Joint Research Centre (JRC), 21027 Ispra, Italy
{georgios.karopoulos,georgios.kampourakis}@ec.europa.eu, gkamb@aegean.gr

Abstract. The Transport Layer Security (TLS) protocol was introduced to solve the lack of security and privacy in the early versions of the world wide web. However, even though it has substantially evolved over the years, certain features still present privacy issues. One such feature is the Server Name Indication (SNI) extension, which allows multiple web servers to reside behind a provider hosting multiple domains with the same IP address; at the same time it allows third parties to discover the domains that end users visit. In the last few years, the Encrypted Server Name Indication (ESNI) Internet draft is being developed by the Internet Engineering Task Force (IETF); this encrypted variant of the extension was renamed to Encrypted Client Hello (ECH) in latest versions. In this paper, we measure the adoption of both these versions, given that they have substantial differences. By analyzing the top 1M domains in terms of popularity, we identify that only a small portion, less than 19%, supports the privacy-preserving ESNI extension and practically no domain supports ECH. Overall, these results demonstrate that there is still a long way to go to ensure the privacy of end users visiting TLS-protected domains which are co-located behind a common Internet-facing server.

Keywords: TLS · ECH · ESNI · Internet measurement · Network security · Privacy

1 Introduction

The evolution of the Internet gave rise to a copious amount of online services. However, although no technology has proven to be the silver bullet against the emerging cyber-security threats in these services, there is a continuous effort in alleviating the issues that come to surface. In this direction, one of the first solutions to combat security weaknesses was Secure Socket Layer (SSL), which was introduced by Netscape in 1994. In the last two decades, SSL has been

The original version of this chapter was previously published non-open access. A Correction to this chapter is available at https://doi.org/10.1007/978-3-031-25460-4_40

S. Katsikas et al. (Eds.): ESORICS 2022 Workshops, LNCS 13785, pp. 177–190, 2023.
https://doi.org/10.1007/978-3-031-25460-4_10

transformed through various upgrades, changing name and reaching the form we know today as TLS [1].

The main security properties provided by TLS are confidentiality, data integrity, and authentication in a typical client-server architecture. TLS aims to prevent eavesdroppers from inherent weaknesses in communication channels, such as Man-in-the-middle (MitM) attacks [2]. Based on the ISO reference model, it is a session layer protocol that is composed of two layers: the TLS handshake, which is used for agreeing several parameters needed for the connection establishment, and the TLS record, which is used for the actual exchange of data.

One of the TLS handshake extensions, which was introduced back in 2003, is the SNI [3]. This feature allows a client to communicate the actual domain that is being requested to a web server that hosts multiple virtual servers behind the same IP address. The procedure is as follows: the client communicates the SNI in the first TLS handshake message, known as the *ClientHello*, and this piece of data is used by the host server for forwarding the certificate of the specific virtual server that is indicated in the SNI. Unfortunately, this functionality results in a privacy leak, as the SNI is conveyed in plain text and can be easily sniffed by a malicious entity that snoops the communication channel.

Overall, in a TLS-protected communication there are three different channels that can leak private information: (Case 1) sniffing cleartext Domain Name System (DNS) queries, (Case 2) observing domains that are being visited, and (Case 3) sniffing the cleartext SNI included in the *ClientHello* message. Figure 1 offers an overview of the possible ways that an SNI-based TLS communication can divulge private information.

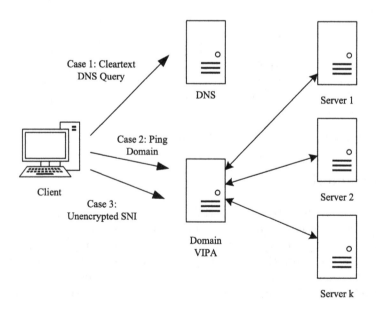

Fig. 1. Leaking channels

For (1), DNS over HTTPS (DoH) [4], DNS over TLS (DoT) [5], or DNS over QUIC (DoQ) [6], all together commonly referred to as "encrypted DNS", could be used to protect end user privacy; an overview of these protocols is provided in [7]. These protocols could also be used in conjunction with Domain Name System Security Extensions (DNSSEC) [8] to avoid DNS cache poisoning attacks. Regarding (2), since the visited server is co-located with other servers behind a provider hosting multiple domains with the same IP address, it is difficult for an attacker to distinguish which domain is actually visited. In this case, the attacker sniffs only the common IP address but is not aware of the actual domain that is being visited. As a solution to (3), the encrypted version of SNI, namely ESNI [9], was introduced a few years ago. The point of this Internet draft was to secure the information leaked in the *ClientHello* message by SNI. However, it soon became apparent that other extensions sent in cleartext in ESNI-enabled TLS handshakes, such as the Application-Layer Protocol Negotiation (ALPN), could also expose private information. The latest version of the standard, which was renamed to ECH in 2020 [10], safeguards the whole *ClientHello* message and uses a diverse approach to deliver the encryption keys compared to its predecessor.

Generally, among others, the adoption of encrypted DNS and privacy-aware TLS extensions are lately in the spotlight. For instance, according to [11], China is allegedly blocking all HTTPS/ESNI traffic, but not ECH. Similar measures are reportedly planned by Russia's Digital Development Ministry, which proposed the ban of several encryption protocols, including TLS 1.3/ESNI, DoT, DoH, and others [12]. Finally, TLS filtering and SNI-based blocking have been found to be applied in India [13,14], while DoT is widely blocked in Iran [15].

In this context, the work at hand examines the global adoption of the ESNI and ECH extensions in the top 1M sites included in the Tranco list [16]. Furthermore, we measure the availability of DoH when requesting the public keys required by ESNI and ECH and resolving the visited top 1M domain names. Last but not least, we scrutinize how ESNI and ECH operate in detail, with respect to key retrieval, key configuration in the TLS handshake phase, and the completion of HTTPS requests.

The rest of the paper is structured as follows. The next section overviews the related work. Section 3 discusses the fundamentals around TLS, ESNI, and ECH. Section 4 presents our experimental setup and measurement results, while the last section draws our conclusions.

2   Related Work

This section summarizes the works that have been presented in the literature thus far, regarding the adoption of ESNI and ECH extensions. Nearly all of these works examine the effectiveness of the ESNI and DoH/DoT standards to achieve domain name privacy.

The work in [17] provides a measurement study on the adoption of ESNI in China. The authors focus on the use of ESNI to achieve censorship circumvention. According to their study, 10.9% of the Alexa top 1 M sites support ESNI.

Moreover, based on their results, 84.5% of the websites which can be bypassed in terms of censorship are subject to IP address blocking. This indicates that even when ESNI is deployed, IP filtering cannot be avoided.

In the same direction, the authors in [18] investigate the adoption of ESNI as well as the impacts of DNS-based filtering on domain blocking. Their research is far broader in terms of geography, as it takes into account countries from diverse continents which are known to apply censorship and domain filtering. Contrariwise to the previous work, their results highlight that domain name encryption can be used to bypass censorship in more than 55% of the cases in China and more than 95% in the domains of the other examined countries, except from Iran where it was almost infeasible to circumvent any domain.

The study in [19] examines the applicability of ESNI and DoH/DoT mechanisms to lessen privacy leaks. Taking into account these mechanisms, they examine destination IP addresses to infer if multiple IP addresses are mapped to the same hostname. According to their results, 30% of the examined domains are mapped k-anonymously to more than 100 IP addresses. On the contrary, as they claim, 20% of the examined hostnames result in a one-to-one mapping, something that indicates a potential privacy leak by simply monitoring the visited hostname.

In the same direction, the authors in [20] examine the potential of inferring the server domain name by monitoring encrypted traffic relying on ESNI or DoH. After deploying a machine learning model, they state that it is possible to deduce 80% of the monitored domain names, with an F-score that exceeds 0.8.

3   Protecting the SNI in TLS Handshakes

TLS operates in the session layer of the Open Systems Interconnection (OSI) model. It makes use of both symmetric and asymmetric cryptography. The usual approach is that asymmetric cryptography is used to exchange the symmetric keys, which are then used to encrypt the traffic between the communicating parties. The different cryptographic and communication parameters are agreed between the parties during the handshake phase.

Precisely, the main purpose of a TLS handshake is to establish the following: (a) selection of the TLS version that will be used, (b) selection of the ciphers that will be used, (c) authentication of the communicating parties, and (d) generation of the keys used for confidentiality and message integrity/authenticity. The message that initiates the TLS handshake is the *ClientHello*; this is also the message where the SNI information is transmitted.

The rest of this section provides some preliminaries regarding ESNI and ECH to highlight the similarities and differences between these two major versions of encrypted SNI.

3.1   Background on ESNI

Since the ESNI is sent in the *ClientHello* message, it cannot be encrypted with the TLS keys which are negotiated later in the handshake. The solution is to use a different public key solely for ESNI. There are diverse ways to distribute the public key and metadata used for encrypting the ESNI; these include publishing it to DNS or having it preconfigured to applications, which apparently does not scale. In the rest of this section, we will present the DNS case in order to cover all the privacy issues mentioned in Sect. 1.

There are two topologies in which ESNI operates: shared and split mode. In Fig. 2a, the shared mode is depicted where the client-facing server (or ESNI service provider) and the backend server (or TLS terminator) are co-located in the same physical machine, having the same IP address. In this case, the TLS connection is terminated in this shared host who has access to the plaintext of the connection. In Fig. 2b, the split mode is presented where the client-facing server and the backend server are two different entities with different IP addresses. In the present case, the DNS records point to the client-facing server who relays the connection to the backend server; here the TLS connection is terminated in the backend server and the client-facing server does not have access to the plaintext of the connection. In the rest of the text, we will use the split mode as it is the most general case.

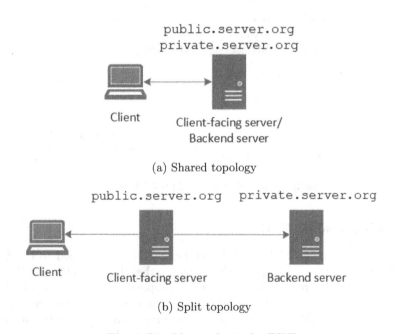

(a) Shared topology

(b) Split topology

Fig. 2. Possible topologies for ESNI

When a client wishes to establish a TLS session using ESNI, it first acquires the ESNI encryption key; this could be done through DNS and preferably using DoH/DoT/DoQ for privacy. Then, it encrypts the SNI field using this key and sends the *ClientHello* message as depicted in Fig. 3. The client-facing server decrypts the ESNI and proceeds with the handshake with the decrypted SNI information. Naturally, if the decryption is unsuccessful, the handshake process is terminated. Although it can be considered one step forward towards better privacy, the main issue with ESNI is that other sensitive fields, such as the ALPN, are not protected.

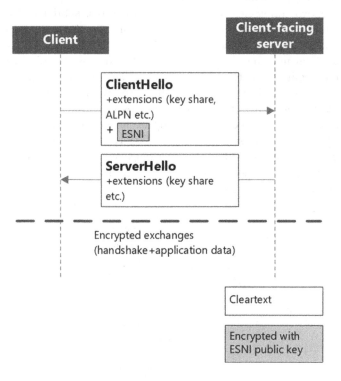

Fig. 3. Using ESNI in the TLS 1.3 handshake

3.2 Background on ECH

Similar to the case of ESNI, in ECH the key could be published to the DNS. The difference is that the type of the entry is labeled as HTTPS (TYPE 65). Thus, the point is to request from the DNS the specific type of entry for a host. The response contains an `echconfiglist` element which advertises the relevant key [21]. Figure 4 illustrates how the client-facing server can publish an ECH configuration, containing an ECH encryption public key and metadata, to a DNS server. A possible alternative to this mechanism is preconfiguring the ECH configuration to the client.

ECH is supported only in TLS v1.3 [1] and newer versions. The descriptions below are based on the latest at the time of writing Internet draft for ECH, namely v14 [10]. The main objective of ECH is to protect the entire *ClientHello* message, including all the sensitive parameters exchanged during the TLS hand-shake. One of the main differences between ESNI and ECH is that in the former

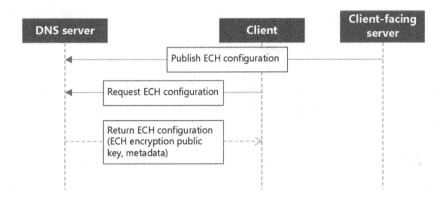

Fig. 4. Publishing an ECH public key to a DNS server

the connection is terminated if the ESNI cannot be decrypted, whereas in ECH two *ClientHello* messages are used in an attempt to complete the handshake as follows.

When a client wants to establish a TLS session with the backend server using ECH, instead of the typical *ClientHello* TLS message, it creates a *ClientHelloOuter* message with an outer SNI value pointing to the client-facing server. This message is transmitted in plaintext and contains an "encrypted_client_hello" extension, which carries a *ClientHelloInner* structure with an inner SNI value pointing to the backend server. The latter contains other sensitive data as well, such as the ALPN values; the entire *ClientHelloInner* is encrypted with the ECH public key. To initiate the TLS session, the client sends the *ClientHelloOuter* to the server. First, the decryption of the *ClientHelloInner* is tried; if it succeeds, the handshake is completed using the *ClientHelloInner* message only, otherwise it is attempted to perform a handshake with the *ClientHelloOuter*. These two processes, namely *ECH acceptance* and *ECH rejection* respectively, work as follows:

- *ECH acceptance.* The client-facing server checks some parameters of the received message, for example that the TLS version is 1.3 or above and the "encrypted_client_hello" extension is well-formed. If these checks succeed, the client-facing server forwards the *ClientHelloInner* to the backend server; if the latter is able to decrypt it, the handshake is completed between the client and the backend server with the client-facing server forwarding the respective messages. This case is depicted in Fig. 5.
- *ECH rejection.* If the backend server is unable to decrypt the *ClientHelloInner*, it notifies the client-facing server. Then, the latter completes the handshake between itself and the client with the *ClientHelloOuter*, sending the correct ECH key to the client. Finally, the client resends the *ClientHelloOuter* message using the correct key for encrypting the *ClientHelloInner*. This situation is depicted in Fig. 6.

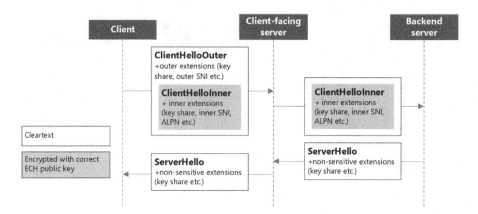

Fig. 5. The server accepts ECH

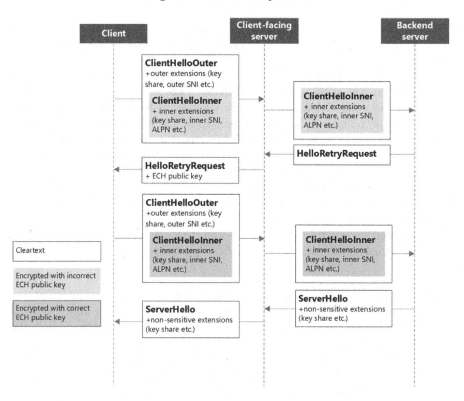

Fig. 6. ECH rejected due to incorrect ECH key

4   Measurements

We performed a large-scale measurement of the adoption of both ESNI and
ECH, based on the top 1M websites included in the Tranco list [16]. Tranco
is a combination of three well-known lists, namely Alexa, Cisco Umbrella, and
Majestic, and is already widely used by the research community. The reasons
behind selecting Tranco have to do with reliability: similar lists disagree on the
popularity of each domain, the domain rankings change significantly from day
to day, and they are open to manipulation by malicious perpetrators.

The procedure is as follows: first, we check for the existence of ESNI and
ECH key entries in DNS. If a key is found, the SNI field is encrypted using this
key; otherwise we abort the test and return back to the first step using the next
website from the list. Finally, a curl query is executed, first performing a DNS
query to retrieve the IP address of the target server and then a TLS handshake
with this same server. The main metrics we calculated during this campaign
are: (a) DoH support while querying the top 1M domain DNS records, including
ESNI/ECH keys and DNS A records, (b) ESNI support in the top 1M domains,
and (c) ECH support in the top 1M domains.

4.1   Setup

For our measurements we used a Linux Virtual Machine (VM) equipped with 4
GB of RAM and 2 CPUs, each one with a clock speed of 2.1 GHz. We developed
a bash script that retrieves ESNI/ECH public keys from DNS using the `kdig` tool
in version 2.6.5 with DoH enabled. Then, the script executes HTTPS requests
towards the websites using `curl` version 7.66.0 with DoH enabled. To parallelize
the procedure, we split the top 1M domains of the original Tranco list into 15
different files and run 15 instances of the script, each having one of these lists as
input. Figure 7 provides an overview of this procedure.

In more detail, our script executes the operations presented in the pseudocode
of Algorithm 1. After the Tranco list is split into smaller `domain_list` files, each
of these files is used as an input to an instance of the script. For each domain
in such a list, the script sends a DoH-enabled DNS request to retrieve the TXT
resource record that holds the ESNI or ECH public key for the domain (step
2). If the key exists, it is used to encrypt the SNI field (when ESNI support is
checked) or the entire *ClientHello* (when ECH support is checked); then, the
TLS handshake is initiated (steps 3–4). If the key does not exist, the script
continues without performing any request for the domain (step 6). Finally, the
results for the domain are printed in a text file for further analysis (step 8). The
data that we store are: the name of the domain, a boolean value showing if DoH
is supported for the domain (`doh_support(domain)`), a boolean value showing
that there exists a TXT record with a key in DNS (`has(public_key)`), and the
result of the curl request that shows the outcome of three operations, that is,
curl, TLS handshake and ESNI- or ECH-enabled TLS handshake (`curl_result`).

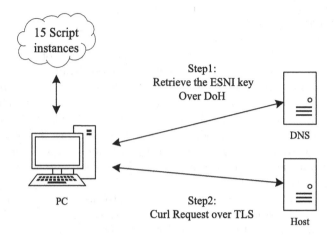

Fig. 7. Experimental setup

Algorithm 1. Query domains for ESNI and ECH support

1: **for all** domain in domain_list **do**
2:     *public_key* ← *kdig(domain)*
3:     **if** size(*public_key*) > 0 **then**
4:         *curl_result* ← *curl_tls(domain, public_key)*
5:     **else**
6:         *continue;*
7:     **end if**
8:     *print(domain, doh_support(domain), has(public_key), curl_result)*
9: **end for**

4.2 Results

We analyzed 1M domains from the Tranco top 1M list and our findings are presented in Tables 1 and 2, both as number of domains and as a percentage of domains; moreover, for easy reference, Fig. 8 graphically depicts these results. Regarding the key retrieval phase, it is perceived that only 18.2% of the domains (that is, 182,068) have an active ESNI key record stored in DNS. The key was retrieved successfully with a DoH query in all but one case, where the relevant TXT resource record retrieval was performed over plain DNS. As far as it concerns ECH, we only found one key in DNS for the "cloudflareresearch.com" domain; also in this case DoH was used for its retrieval. This last finding suggests that ECH has not been adopted yet; this is further verified by the results presented in previous work [18].

While querying the top 1M domains, we also kept data for other relevant supported standards. First, we calculated that DoH requests were completed successfully for 99.8% of the examined domains (or 998,256 domains). Regarding the curl queries, 991,323 were completed successfully and 8,677 failed; this very small number could be attributed to temporary failures of some web sites. It is

Table 1. Overall measurement results

Metric	Number of domains	% of total domains
ESNI key in DNS	182,068	18.2%
ECH key in DNS	1	–
DoH support	998,256	99.8%
Curl queries	991,323	99.1%
TLS handshake	783,416	78.3%
TLS handshake with ESNI	169,784	16.9%

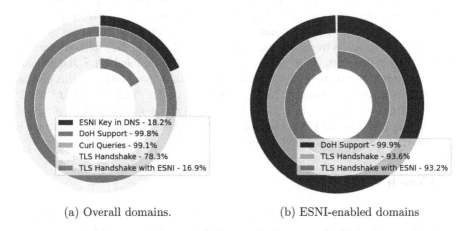

(a) Overall domains.   (b) ESNI-enabled domains

Fig. 8. ESNI/ECH and DoH support in the top 1M domains

worth mentioning that the curl queries for all the domains with ESNI key were completed successfully, but failed for the single domain with ECH key. A further observation is that, while connecting to the aforementioned domains, a TLS handshake was successful in 78.3% or 783,416 domains; this is consistent with other recent independent TLS uptake metrics [22]. This figure comprises also the 16.9% (or 169,784) of the domains that completed the handshake procedure with ESNI enabled.

Further concentrating only on the domains that support ESNI, we performed an ESNI-enabled TLS handshake to all the 182,068 domains that have an ESNI key in DNS; our findings are presented in Table 2. As stated above, only one domain did not have DoH support. Based on our measurements, in 93.6% of the domains which have been found to have an active ESNI key, the TLS handshake was successful; the handshake including the ESNI as well was successful in 93.2% of the total number of domains.

Table 2. Measurement results for domains supporting ESNI

Metric	Number of domains	% of ESNI-enabled domains
DoH support	182,067	99.9%
TLS handshake	170,450	93.6%
TLS handshake with ESNI	169,784	93.2%

Based on our findings, it can be stated that ESNI implementation in the most popular websites is ≈18%, whereas ECH implementation is practically non-existent. Regarding the retrieval of the ESNI/ECH public key, a DoH query can be performed for almost all domains (99.9%), thus, protecting end users' privacy from third-party eavesdroppers. Notably, the results in ESNI-enabled domains (Table 2) between plain TLS handshakes and ESNI-enabled TLS handshakes shows a difference of 0.4% or 666 domains. Given that these 666 domains neither are offline nor have a wrong ESNI key (in this case the TLS handshake would have failed as explained in Sect. 3.1), leads us to the conclusion that, although they have an ESNI key in DNS, the web servers of these domains are not properly configured to perform the ESNI procedure.

5   Conclusions

This paper examines the adoption of two well-known TLS extensions, namely ESNI and ECH. According to our measurements, only the ESNI extension has already been deployed, although not extensively. More precisely, we found that only 18.2% of the top 1M websites in the Tranco list have published an ESNI key in the DNS. After using these keys in the TLS handshake process, we found that these keys have been successfully used in the TLS handshake in 16.9% of the aforementioned domains.

With regards to the most recent ECH extension, we found only a single DNS record entry with a public key. Although this can be considered normal, given that the first appearance of ECH was two years ago and the specification is at the time of writing still in draft form, it shows a reluctance on the service providers' side to adopt it. On the other hand, the wide deployment of DoH provides a major milestone, as it is the main prerequisite for protecting end user privacy through ESNI/ECH.

As future work, we intent to revisit our large-scale measurements of the adoption of ESNI/ECH, as soon as the respective RFC is finalized and the standard is deployed. A further enhancement of the present work would be a more in-depth analysis of the ESNI/ECH adoption by employing the complete Tranco list that comprises 7M domain names in order to argue whether the same results are observed in less popular web sites as well. Finally, we plan to further investigate the geographic distribution of the examined domains, as well as to analyze the domains which suppress encryption mechanisms for efficient censorship.

References

1. Rescorla, E.: The Transport Layer Security (TLS) Protocol Version 1.3. RFC 8446, August 2018. https://www.rfc-editor.org/info/rfc8446
2. Kampourakis, V., Kambourakis, G., Chatzoglou, E., Zaroliagis, C.: Revisiting man-in-the-middle attacks against https. Netw. Secur. **2022**(3) (2022)
3. 3rd D.E.E.: Transport Layer Security (TLS) Extensions: Extension Definitions. RFC 6066, January 2011. https://www.rfc-editor.org/info/rfc6066
4. Hoffman, P.E., McManus, P.: DNS Queries over HTTPS (DoH). RFC 8484, October 2018. https://www.rfc-editor.org/info/rfc8484
5. Hu, Z., Zhu, L., Heidemann, J., Mankin, A., Wessels, D., Hoffman, P.E.: Specification for DNS over Transport Layer Security (TLS). RFC 7858, May 2016. https://www.rfc-editor.org/info/rfc7858
6. Huitema, C., Dickinson, S., Mankin, A.: DNS over Dedicated QUIC Connections. RFC 9250, May 2022. https://www.rfc-editor.org/info/rfc9250
7. Kambourakis, G., Karopoulos, G.: Encrypted DNS: the good, the bad and the moot. Comput. Fraud Secur. **2022**(5) (2022)
8. Rose, S., Larson, M., Massey, D., Austein, R., Arends, R.: DNS Security Introduction and Requirements. RFC 4033, March 2005. https://www.rfc-editor.org/info/rfc4033
9. Rescorla, E., Oku, K., Sullivan, N., Wood, C.A.: Encrypted Server Name Indication for TLS 1.3. Internet Engineering Task Force, Internet-Draft draft-ietf-tls-esni-03, work in Progress. https://datatracker.ietf.org/doc/html/draft-ietf-tls-esni-03
10. Rescorla, E., Oku, K., Sullivan, N., Wood, C.A.: TLS Encrypted Client Hello. Internet Engineering Task Force, Internet-Draft draft-ietf-tls-esni-14, February 2022, work in Progress. https://datatracker.ietf.org/doc/html/draft-ietf-tls-esni-14
11. ZDNet: China is now blocking all encrypted HTTPS traffic that uses TLS 1.3 and ESNI. https://www.zdnet.com/article/china-is-now-blocking-all-encrypted-https-traffic-using-tls-1-3-and-esni/. Accessed 24 Nov 2021
12. ZDNet: Russia wants to ban the use of secure protocols such as TLS 1.3, DoH, DoT, ESNI. https://www.zdnet.com/article/russia-wants-to-ban-the-use-of-secure-protocols-such-as-tls-1-3-doh-dot-esni/. Accessed 24 Nov 2021
13. Open Observatory of Network Interference: Investigating TLS blocking in India. https://ooni.org/post/2020-tls-blocking-india/. Accessed 8 July 2022
14. The Centre for Internet & Society: Reliance Jio is using SNI inspection to block websites. https://cis-india.org/internet-governance/blog/reliance-jio-is-using-sni-inspection-to-block-websites. Accessed 8 July 2022
15. Open Observatory of Network Interference: DNS over TLS blocked in Iran. https://ooni.org/post/2020-iran-dot/. Accessed 8 July 2022
16. Tranco: A research-oriented top sites ranking hardened against manipulation. https://tranco-list.eu/. Accessed 06 May 2022
17. Chai, Z., Ghafari, A., Houmansadr, A.: On the importance of encrypted-SNI (ESNI) to censorship circumvention. In: FOCI @ USENIX Security Symposium (2019)
18. Hoang, N.P., Polychronakis, M., Gill, P.: Measuring the accessibility of domain name encryption and its impact on internet filtering. CoRR, vol. abs/2202.00663 (2022). https://arxiv.org/abs/2202.00663
19. Hoang, N.P., Akhavan Niaki, A., Borisov, N., Gill, P., Polychronakis, M.: Assessing the privacy benefits of domain name encryption. In: Proceedings of the 15th ACM ASIACCS 2020, ASIA CCS 2020, pp. 290–304. Association for Computing Machinery, New York, NY, USA (2020). https://doi.org/10.1145/3320269.3384728

20. Trevisan, M., Soro, F., Mellia, M., Drago, I., Morla, R.: Does domain name encryption increase users' privacy?. SIGCOMM Comput. Commun. Rev. **50**(3), 16–22 (2020). https://doi.org/10.1145/3411740.3411743
21. Farrell, S.: A well-known URI for publishing ECHConfigList values. Internet Engineering Task Force, Internet-Draft draft-farrell-tls-wkesni-03, May 2022, work in Progress. https://datatracker.ietf.org/doc/html/draft-farrell-tls-wkesni-03. Accessed 06 June 2022
22. W3Techs: Usage statistics of Default protocol https for websites. https://w3techs.com/technologies/details/ce-httpsdefault

4th Workshop on Security, Privacy, Organizations, and Systems Engineering (SPOSE 2022)

Preface

Over recent decades, a multitude of security and privacy enhancing technologies has been developed and brought to considerable maturity. However, the design and engineering of such technologies often ignores the organizational context that respective technologies are to be applied in. A large and hierarchical organization, for example, calls for significantly different security and privacy practices and respective technologies than an agile, small startup. Similarly, whenever employees' behavior plays a significant role for the ultimate level of security and privacy provided, their individual skills, interests and incentives as well as typical behavioral patterns must be taken into account and materialized in concrete technical solutions and practices. Even though research on security- and privacy-related technologies increasingly considers questions of practical applicability in realistic scenarios, implementation decisions are still mostly technology-driven, and existing technical limitations and notions of "this is how we've always done it" hamper both innovation and application in practice.

On the other hand, a substantial body of organization-related security and privacy research already exists, incorporating aspects like decision-making and governance structures, individual interests and incentives of employees, behavioral aspects, organizational roles and procedures, organizational as well as national culture, or business models and organizational goals. However, there is still a large gap between the generation of respective insights and their actual incorporation in concrete technical mechanisms, frameworks, and systems.

This disconnection between rather technical and rather organization-related security and privacy research leaves substantial room for improving the fit between organizational practices on the one hand and the engineering of concrete technologies on the other hand. Achieving a better fit between these two sides through security and privacy technologies that soundly incorporate organizational and behavioral theories and practices promises substantial benefits for organizations and data subjects, engineers, policy makers, and society as a whole.

The aim of the 4th Workshop on Security, Privacy, Organizations, and Systems Engineering (SPOSE) therefore was to discuss, exchange, and develop ideas and questions regarding the design and engineering of technical security and privacy mechanisms with particular reference to organizational contexts. We invited researchers and practitioners working in security- and privacy-related systems engineering as well as in the field of organizational science to submit their contributions. Besides regular and short papers, we also invited practical demonstrations, intermediate reports, and mini-tutorials on respective technologies currently under development to stimulate forward-looking discussions.

The papers included on the following pages demonstrate the possible spectrum for fruitful research at the intersection of security, privacy, organizational science, and systems engineering.

Frank Ebbers and Murat Karaboga report on a user study investigating the factors contributing to the adoption of protective measures by smart speaker users. Their analysis shows that context of use, gender, attitudes toward emotion recognition, and reasons for purchase influence adoption of protective measures, but not manufacturer, model, or length of use. They argue that as shared use is quite common, manufacturers should develop security and privacy features that allow for separated usage with different settings as well as for a specific guest mode.

Abdelhadi Belfadel, Martin Boyer, Jérôme Letailleur, Yohann Petiot and Reda Yaich introduce their ongoing work on a security impact analysis framework to support security analysts and systems developers throughout the development life cycle. The proposed framework combines a higher-level, top-down risk-based analysis approach with a bottom-up MITRE-based attack modeling approach. The authors provide a process model that offers a practical structure and guidance for security assessment in an organizational context.

Stephan Wiefling, Jan Tolsdorf and Luigi Lo Iacono, in turn, report on a semi-structured interview study with data protection officers advising digital platforms – complex value-creating networks – in Germany on what they perceive as current and future challenges for the implementation of data protection requirements, how data protection can be made more effective, and whether they consider "privacy dashboards" as useful tools. From an engineering perspective, the most important finding is that the rights of data subjects are still predominantly administered and fulfilled manually, and thus in an error-prone and time-consuming manner, which urgently calls for their "digitization".

Finally, Martina Angela Sasse, Jonas Hielscher, Jennifer Friedauer and Annalina Buckmann argue that organizations' security awareness campaigns and training alone do not lead to employees' secure behavior becoming a routine. For establishing a better security preparedness, organizations need to take into account human psychology, organizational dynamics, and human motivations. They have to ensure that secure behavior is feasible, and support employees in taking the necessary steps through the security learning curve – concordance, self-efficacy, and embedding – described and explained by the authors, for secure behavior to become a routine.

Altogether, these papers, complemented by two inspiring and thought-provoking keynotes and an open-minded audience eager for discussion and constructive thinking, made the fourth edition of the workshop another success. We would thus like to thank everybody who contributed – authors, presenters, participants, reviewers, and, of course, the whole organizing team of ESORICS 2022. Special thanks goes to the Cluster of Excellence CASA – Cyber Security in the Age of Large-Scale Adversaries at Ruhr-Universität Bochum for their generous support of the workshop.

We are definitely looking forward to the next iteration of SPOSE.

October 2022

Frank Pallas
Jörg Pohle
Angela Sasse

Organization

Organizers

Frank Pallas   TU Berlin, Germany
Jörg Pohle   Humboldt Institute for Internet and
Society, Berlin, Germany
Angela Sasse   Ruhr-University Bochum, Germany

Program Committee

Zinaida Benenson   FAU Erlangen-Nürnberg, Germany
Athena Bourka   ENISA, Athens, Greece
Matthias Fassl   CISPA, Saarbrücken, Germany
Michael Friedewald   Fraunhofer ISI, Karlsruhe, Germany
Lea Gröber   CISPA, Saarbrücken, Germany
Elias Grünewald   TU Berlin, Germany
Marit Hansen   ULD, Kiel, Germany
Heleen Janssen   Cambridge University, UK
Annette Kluge   Ruhr-University Bochum, Germany
Marc Langheinrich   University of Lugano, Switzerland
Gabriele Lenzini   University of Luxembourg, Luxembourg
Peter Mayer   KIT, Karlsruhe, Germany
Sebastian Pape   Goethe University Frankfurt/Main,
Germany
Simon Parkin   TU Delft, The Netherlands
Karen Renaud   University of Strathclyde, UK
Burkhard Schäfer   Edinburgh University, UK
Andrew Simpson   University of Oxford, UK
Jatinder Singh   Cambridge University, UK
Max-R. Ulbricht   TU Berlin, Germany
Tobias Urban   if(is) and secunet, Essen, Germany
Melanie Volkamer   KIT, Karlsruhe, Germany

Influencing Factors for Users' Privacy and Security Protection Behavior in Smart Speakers: Insights from a Swiss User Study

Frank Ebbers[✉] ⓘ and Murat Karaboga ⓘ

Fraunhofer Institute for Systems and Innovation Research ISI, Breslauer Str. 48, 76139
Karlsruhe, Germany
{frank.ebbers,murat.karaboga}@isi.fraunhofer.de

Abstract. Smart speakers pose several risks to security and privacy, which users
can counter with protective measures. This paper investigates the factors contributing to the adoption of protective measures by smart speaker users. Using
survey data from Swiss participants, we first captured four different combinations
of users with (no) concerns and (no) measures. We then used six factors to examine
which of these influence protective behavior. Our findings reveal that whether or
not protective measures are taken is affected by the usage context, usage duration,
gender, opinion toward emotion recognition, and reasons for acquisition, but not
by model/manufacturer, age and education level. With our results, we want to
contribute to the ongoing discussion about influencing factors on concerns and
protective measures, using the smart speaker domain as an example.

Keywords: Smart speaker · Intelligent personal assistants · Voice assistant ·
Amazon Echo · Google Home · Apple HomePod · Privacy · Security · Protective
measures · Protective behavior · Privacy concerns · Security concerns

1 Introduction

Smart speakers (SSp) are voice-controlled hardware devices connected to the Internet.
Well-known examples are Amazon Echo or Google Home speakers. Positioned in a
user's home and equipped with artificial intelligence features and natural language processing, they are designed to support users in their daily routines. Users can play music,
set reminders, or use search engines [1]. To function as anticipated, SSp require large
amounts of personal data and various permissions to process (personal) data [2, 3]. This
poses threats to security and privacy (sec/priv) [4, 5]. In recent years, researchers have
discovered a variety of security issues that can lead to such things as eavesdropping,
remote tampering, and unauthorized access [6]. As SSp use natural language processing
and are activated via voice commands, they are in constant listening mode for recognizing "wake-up-words" [4]. The corresponding privacy concerns are diverse in nature,
given that SSp consist not only of hardware but also of software, skills, remote cloud
services and diverse default privacy settings [2, 5]. Sec/priv Concerns are exacerbated

© The Author(s) 2023
S. Katsikas et al. (Eds.): ESORICS 2022 Workshops, LNCS 13785, pp. 195–211, 2023.
https://doi.org/10.1007/978-3-031-25460-4_11

by the fact that SSp have found their way into the most private areas of users' daily lives [1, 2]. To date, little research on the sec/priv of SSp, including behavioral aspects, has been carried out [5, 7].

Prior research suggests that demographic factors, personality traits, the nature and duration of the interactions with smart speakers, the speaker models, and the individual reasons for the acquisition and utilization of smart speaker devices influence the importance users attribute to security and privacy [7]. Based on data from a user study with N = 1.000 participants from Switzerland, this paper explores in detail how these factors influence users sec/priv concerns and to what extent this leads to the adoption of protective measures (PM). In order to gain an understanding of how convenience is off-set against security and privacy [2], four combinations of factors are distinguished and examined.

The remainder of this paper is structured as follows: Sect. 2 presents theoretical findings on users' perceptions of sec/priv and the PM that are taken, which are used to generate six hypotheses to answer the research question. In Sect. 3, we present our methodology. In Sect. 4, we present the results and discuss them in Sect. 5. We conclude with an outlook on future research opportunities in Sect. 6.

2 Prior Research

2.1 Privacy and Security Threats of Smart Speaker Technology

SSp require permissions, including: access to user's phone contacts to enable interactions with them, or to access account data to make purchases [2, 3]. The type and amount of data used differs between applications and use cases. Some data are collected and compiled into profiles without the user being aware of this [4]. This can give rise to privacy concerns, as the date and time of a query, for example, allow conclusions to be drawn about the person's daily routine. In addition, account data, such as name, place of residence and payment methods are linked to interactions with the SSp. Speakers and their applications record the voice pitches not only of their owners, but also of anyone talking in the vicinity of the device at the time of recording [4]. Skills interactions may also require additional user data, such as date of birth for reminders or blood type for health apps [4]. To interact with other smart home devices, SSp exchange various types of (personal) data with other devices and servers [8]. This again allows for analyses and inferences to be made about user behavior [4], for example, about their physical health or the relationship between people in a shared household interacting with the speaker [4].

Security threats posed by SSp include unauthorized access, remote tampering or eavesdropping [6]. Mistakes in accuracy of voice verification may have comparatively benign consequences, such as a child making purchases by speaking to an Amazon Echo [9]. Other types of attacks can cause much greater damage, e.g., when attackers obtain physical access to the device. For example, it is possible to obtain personal data by inputting voice recordings [7]. Zhang et al. [10] find that hackers can emit ultrasound commands to gain complete control of the speaker without authorized users even noticing. By combining this attack with resampled audio snippets of legitimate user commands, the authors were able to fully bypass the biometric voice authentication [10].

Other attacks invoke malicious add-ons for SSp (so-called "skills"), that may operate permanently and stealthily [11]. Most SSp provide no other way to authenticate the owner than through the wake-up-word [4], and where alternatives exist, they may be poorly secured (e.g., PIN mechanisms allowing for an infinite number of re-tries [12]).

Quite frequently, a compromised SSp is a single point of failure [4] for gaining access to other smart home services, which can all be interrupted in a single strike [5, 8]. This can lead to (physical) safety-critical situations, if the speaker is connected to a smart door lock [13]. For these reasons, the sec/priv features of SSp have become an important topic in recent academic research [4, 5, 8]. Researchers are investigating technical PM [14, 15], the usability of frameworks for end users [16] and recommendations for SSp and skill providers [7].

2.2 Privacy and Security Perception and Concerns of Smart Speaker Users

Sec/priv perceptions and the concerns of end users in traditional IT systems are widely researched in computer science. For example, [17] identifies antecedents of privacy concerns as early as the early 1990s, [18] hypothesized that security concerns result from corporate actions, industry risks and individual awareness.

In the research domain of SSp, the concerns are more diverse [5] and arise from users' perceptions of not having control over the devices' various data flows [6]. [2] use data from online reviews and a customer survey and find seven different types of privacy/security concerns. These are (1) device hacking (69%), (2) personal data collection (16%), (3) constant eavesdropping (10%), (4) recording of private conversations (12%), (5) the fundamental disregard for privacy (6%), (6) data retention (curiosity about how and where information is being stored) (6%), and (7) the "creepy" behavior of devices (4%) (verbatim quote from a respondent). According to [5], security concerns can relate to different stakeholder types: co-users, service provider, authorized (law enforcement) and non-authorized (hackers) external actors. From a technical perspective, built-in cameras and microphones cause the highest user concerns [1]. In addition, users' concerns result, for example, in the rejection of online shopping via a SSp [7] or controlling smart door locks [13]. Specific features of SSp also raise concerns, in particular the always-listening mode [2, 19].

Several factors influence user concerns. These include users' demographics and personality, the nature and duration of their interactions with the speaker, and their motivation to acquire and use a speaker. These influences are discussed in more detail in the following paragraphs.

Context of Use: There are different groups of users who interact with SSp: active users who purchase and set up a speaker themselves, users who jointly purchase, set up and use a speaker, bystanders who do not actively use a speaker but are affected by a speaker set up by family members or flat mates and non-users [20, 21].

Literature allocates different levels of privacy concerns to different users, based on individual characteristics [17]. In the field of SSp "a bystander's perceived privacy can diverge from their actual privacy" [21], if they even recognize they are a bystander at all. Furthermore, it is reasonable to assume that users who actively install and use a SSp are less likely to have sec/priv concerns, because they have a sense of control over the use of the SSp [6]. Thus, we hypothesize that *users who use their speaker by themselves will use fewer PM than users who share a speaker or a bystander (H1)*.

Further research found that users of different **gender, age, and education** level perceive SSp differently [22]. Thus, older individuals would need to weigh up privacy concerns against the increased autonomy they may get from using them [1]. In general, users with higher levels of education are less concerned [23]. In [22], the authors introduce three different relationships between user groups and the speaker. They find that female users are significantly more likely to view SSp as a friend (54.0%) or pet (20.7%), in contrast to male users who are more likely to view SSp as a servant (18.3% vs 11.5% females). Such differences in relationship perceptions may explain the extent to which users perceive the need to protect themselves and/or others against threats to sec/priv. Therefore, *we assume* that *age, gender and level of education have a significant impact on PM (H2)*.

Usage Changes Over Time: Users change the way they interact with a speaker over time [5], with automation tasks in particular increasing until the 150th day of use [24]. At the same time, research indicates that users' sec/priv concerns change over time [25]. For example, in [6], users of SSp are found to develop concerns due to the increasing capabilities they associate with the technology. Other research finds that users slowly overcome their fear of using them over time [9]. Therefore, we define our *H3* as follows: *Users privacy PM change depending on the length of ownership.*

Emotion Recognition Through SSp: There is a future feature that researchers believe has great potential: Emotion recognition through both the voice and spoken content analysis [26]. Amazon has already announced plans to include these features in its Echo speakers [27]. However, privacy concerns are regarded as a major obstacle regarding the deployment of the technology [28]. To understand whether emotion recognition has an impact on privacy concerns and PM in SSp, we hypothesize that *users who are against the use of emotion recognition will tend to be more protective (H4)*.

Acquisition Reasons Influence Privacy Perception: There are different reasons, why users acquire SSp: cheap prices [29], donation [2, 9], or social influence from peers and media [9, 30]. For seniors in particular, (grand) children might set up the SSp. However, the main drivers are the perceived usefulness [9] and interest in the technology [25]. We hypothesize that there may be differences in users' perception of sec/priv concerns between these groups, which could translate into differences in PM. For example, a user study [9] finds that receiving a speaker "as a gift triggered a privacy consideration". However, to our knowledge, there is no work that investigates the relationship between acquisition reasons and PM. To investigate this further, we hypothesize that *different acquisition reasons have an impact on whether users have privacy concerns and whether they adopt PM (H5)*.

Reputation and Perception of Smart Speaker Manufacturers: Globally, Amazon, Google, Baidu, Alibaba and Apple are the market leaders in terms of SSp sold [31]. In Switzerland SSp have been late to the market and in some cases have not been launched at all. This is mainly attributed to the difficulty in understanding Swiss dialects [32]. At the time of writing, only Google and Sonos devices are officially available in Switzerland. Amazon Echo and Apple's HomePod are only available via resellers.

Technically speaking, the speakers from Amazon, Apple and Google have similar data protection functions, although they are equipped with different hardware. However, Google stores the least voice recordings [31] and Apple does not use the data to create a marketing profile, which leads different authors to consider the HomePod as the best choice in terms of privacy [31]. A survey of UK users finds that they have slightly more privacy concerns towards Amazon Echo (2.62 on Likert-5) than Google Home (2.48) [5]. These concerns in turn result in a variety of PM [9, 33]. Further, [1] found that trust depends on "established, mostly positive relationships with these companies". Thus, we assume that there are notable differences between SSp and hypothesize *that users show different PM for speakers from different manufacturers (H6).*

2.3 Protective Behavior and Measures in Smart Speaker Usage

There is a variety of research streams in SSp sec/priv protection. These include both those of technical and non-technical nature [5, 33]. However, [7] finds that SSp users mainly engage in non-technical PM. Although PM are rarely taken by end-users [5], their behaviors are still manifold. These range from reviewing and changing privacy settings [5], to using multiple profiles [9], to giving misleading information or avoiding private conversations [3, 5]. There are also more pragmatic approaches such as muting, covering, turning off, unplugging speakers or speaking quietly near them [2, 5]. At the same time, however, users report that these PM are not very convenient because they regularly interfere with the purpose of using the speaker, which may include sponta- neously giving commands without first plugging it in [9]. Therefore, deleting recordings [1, 5] is regarded to be the most prevalent PM [25]. Returning a speaker was the final resort reported by users [2].

Finally, we divided the different users into four clusters of user groups, as shown in Fig. 2. (1) Users with no concerns and no PM, (2) users with concerns and PM, (3) users without concerns but PM nevertheless. Finally, research on the Privacy Paradox in a SSp domain [5] suggests that there can be (4) users with concerns but no PM.

2.4 Research Question and Research Model

Based on the insights from the reviewed literature, our research question (RQ) is: *Do users protect themselves from the security and privacy threats posed by smart speakers, and what factors influence the PM they reported using?* We address this RQ with the research model in Fig. 1. It includes six hypotheses and considers users' statements to take sec/priv PM as a dependent variable.

3 Methodology and Survey Design

The insights from the literature review[1] in Sect. 2 served as input for the survey questions. These insights suggest that an initial understanding of the reasons for use and acquisition

---

[1] To ensure that all important keywords were included, the findings and synonyms from [4] were used. We conducted a literature review in AIS Basket of Eight publications from 2014–2022 for initial findings on SSp characteristics and privacy perceptions. Since we focus on human factors in sec/priv, we extended our repository to include publications from SOUPS, SIGSAC, SIGCHI, IEEE Security & Privacy and user studies found on statista.com.

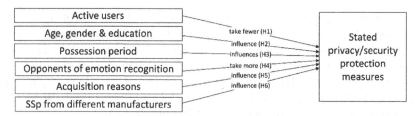

Fig. 1. Research model

is necessary, that emotion recognition is a major concern and indicated a variety of user protection behaviors and mechanisms. Accordingly, the questionnaire involved in total thirteen questions about two main topics: (1) SSp acquisition and usage and (2) related sec/priv protection aspects (see Fig. 2). Each had on average six possible answers and an open-text field. These included single and multiple choices, open-text fields and mainly Likert scales (agreement, probability, appropriateness and importance). The questionnaire in German, Italian and French can be found in an online appendix (https://doi.org/10.24406/fordatis/211). Additional demographic information included gender, age, canton of residence and education, as well as Swiss-specific characteristics such as the linguistic region. The data was analyzed using the SPSS 25 statistical software suite. The overall structure of the questionnaire is shown in Fig. 2.

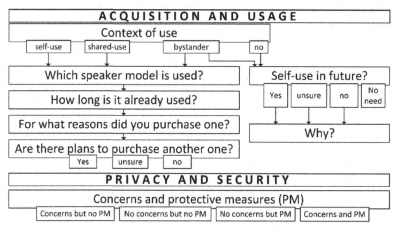

Fig. 2. General structure of the questionnaire

The questionnaire was provided in German, Italian and French. Together with a set of six experts (business informatics, political science, data analytics and surveying background, as well as a proofreader), we iteratively reviewed and adjusted the questions, scales, and grammar. In a further step, we executed a pre-test with n = 55 participants in early October 2021. After a final round of adjustments, the questionnaire was provided to the entire sample. The survey itself was carried out by IPSOS, a professional survey company that was responsible for sampling. They used acknowledged standard mechanisms and programming in order to implement the survey. IPSOS used one of their well-tested samples that ensures at recruitment stage, that participants are human and only apply once. To ensure a high quality of answers, a straightlining test was conducted to identify robotic responses and respondents who gave the same answer patterns or polar opposite statements. Furthermore, the answering speed was measured and respondents were given a notification if they were too fast (or in good time) halfway through the questionnaire. However, no entry had to be removed on the basis of the above criteria. IPSOS carried out the analysis, e.g., using Chi^2 tests for calculating significance. Data cleaning was not needed for a majority of the fields, as categories were predefined as Likert scales. Open text fields were analyzed manually (as the number was not too high) and categorized by the experts. For example, open text questions about "reasons for purchase" resulted in "curiosity", "prestige" and "increased autonomy due to walking disability". The online survey with N = 1000 representative participants in Switzerland was conducted in October 2021 (Table 1). These included German, Italian and French speaking respondents from both rural and urban areas.

Table 1. Demographics (in %, N = 1000)

Gender			Age			Linguistic region			
M	F	n/a	16 - 34	35 - 54	55 - 75	GER	FR	IT	Other
49.7	49.6	0.7	31.6	39.6	28.8	63.7	32.1	4.0	0.2

Education			Area of Residence	
Below University		University and above	Urban	Rural
70.7		29.3	77.6	22.4

4 Results

In this section, we give insight into the general usage of SSp (Table 2) and present the correlated sec/priv PM stated by the respondents. We aggregate these PM depending on different demographic characteristics (Tables 3, 4, 5, 6, 7 and 8).

4.1 Usage of Smart Speakers

SSp are present in 36.7% of all households in Switzerland. Of these, a majority possesses a Google Home (45.5%). Amazon Echo is present in 25.6% of the households, followed by Apple HomePod (20.3%), others (8.7%, mostly devices from Swisscom), and 10.4% possess more than one SSp (Table 2, significant differences in the sample structure at p < 0.01 in gray). More male (43.3% male, 30.0% female) and young respondents between 16 and 34 years old (52.8%, p < 0.01) reported having and using a SSp in their household. In general, gender, age and education level have significant influence on SSp ownership and use (p < 0.01, respectively p = 0.04 for education). Area of residence (urban or rural), on the other hand, has no significant influence.

The results show that 20.4% of users set up and use the device themselves. A shared-usage is present in 10.8% of the households, with a third person, such as flatmates or the children of elderly persons, installing the speakers in 5.5% of cases.

We find significantly younger users (16–34 years) in the category own use (30.4%) and shared use (16.1%) than users aged 35 and above. Participants with a university degree (25.6%) are more likely to use and install speakers by themselves than users without a university degree (18.2%). French-speaking users use SSp significantly less (13.4%) than Italian-speaking (30.0%) or German-speaking (23.1%) ones. A possible explanation could be found in [34], where 67% of French respondents stated that they do not see a need, and 59% have the kind of privacy concerns that prevent them from buying an SSp.

Table 2. Distribution of demographics and SSp usage with the context of use (in %)

Category / Context of use	All users	Own	Shared	Bystanders	Non
Usage	36.7	20.4	10.8	5.5	63.3
Likeliness of future usage [1]	46.6				
Gender — Female	49.6	13.1^{---}	11.5	5.4	70.0
Gender — Male	49.7	27.6^{+++}	10.3	5.4	56.7
Gender — n/a	0.7				
Age — 16 - 34	31.6	30.4^{+++}	16.1^{+++}	6.3	47.2^{--}
Age — 35 - 54	39.6	17.2	11.1	5.3	66.4
Age — 55 - 75	28.8	13.9^{--}	4.5^{---}	4.9	76.7^{+++}
Edu — Below university	70.7	18.2	11.9	5.5	64.4
Edu — University & above	29.3	25.6^{++}	8.2	5.5	60.8
Region — German	63.7	23.1	11.6	6.6	58.7
Region — French	32.1	13.4^{--}	8.4	3.7	74.5^{++}
Region — Italian	40.0	30.0	17.5	2.5	50.0
U/R — Urban	77.6	21.6	10.1	5.8	62.5
U/R — Rural	22.4	16.1	13.4	4.5	66.1
Device — Google / Nest Home	45.5	52	50.9		
Device — Amazon Echo	25.6	33.3	30.6		
Device — Apple HomePod	20.3	19.1	21.3		
Device — Other	8.7	9.8	10.2		
Device — Multiple	10.4	12.3	11.1		

[1] On a 5-Likert likeliness scale (Sum of very likely and likely)
"All users" column does not always sum up to 100% as some participants did not answer this question or use multiple speakers at the same time
over avg: +++ p<0.01; ++ p<0.05; + p<0.10 | under avg: --- p<0.01; -- p<0.05; - p<0.10;

4.2 Factors Influencing Protective Measures

Figure 2 shows three **different contexts of use** (own, shared and bystanders) as well as four combinations of user concerns and PM. For the correlation analysis, the variables "no concerns/no protection" and "concerns/no protection" were combined (CombNP). The results in Table 3 show a very low Pearson correlation (PC) of $-.045$ for own usage and CombNP. However, there is a significant ($p < 0.01$) negative correlation between own usage and "concerns/no protection" (C/NP, $-.147$). A significant correlation exists between bystanders and concerns (.148 and .149 at $p < 0.01$). There is no difference between bystanders who take PM and those who do not. A binary logistic regression shows a Cox & Snell R^2 of .023. Age serves as a control variable, as it has no significant influence (sig $= 0.430$) it can be disregarded.

Table 3. Pearson correlation for context of use and characteristics of concerns/protection

	NC/NP	NC/P	C/NP	C/P	CombNP	CombP
Own	.093	.105*	-.147**	-.078	-.045	.045
Shared	.002	-.019	.045	-.032	.040	-.040
Bystanders	-.133*	-.122*	.148**	.149**	.010	-.010

NC/NP = No concerns / no protection | NC/P = No concerns/ protection | C/NP = Concerns/ no protection | C/P = Concerns/ protection | CombNP = Combined NC/NP and C/NP | ** p<0.01 | * p<0.05

The PC analysis of **demographic factors** and concerns/protection (Table 4) shows that gender is significantly ($p < 0.01$) positively correlated to C/NP (.168) and negatively correlated to NC/NP ($-.101$). Correlating genders separately shows that females (.168, $p < 0.01$) have significantly more concerns, but take no PM. For men ($-.171, p < 0.01$), the correlation with this observation is significantly negative. Other factors show only a very low correlation.

Table 4. Pearson correlation for demographics and characteristics of concerns/protection

	NC/NP	NC/P	C/NP	C/P	CombNP	CombP
Age	-.072	-.028	.041	.077	-.028	.028
Gender	-.101	-.049	.168**	-.012	.055	-.055
Education	-.049	-.035	.020	.084	-.026	.026
Ling. region	-.012	.064	-.008	-.061	-.017	.017
Urban/rural	.041	-.095	.049	.016	.079	-.079

Correlating the **usage period** with concerns/protection, Table 5 shows that users who possessed a SSp for less than one month are significantly unconcerned and took PM to a lesser extent (.163, at p < 0.01). This PC completely reverses when a speaker is used between one and twelve months (−.162 at p < 0.01). PC values decrease sharply as the duration of use increases to over a year. This observation also holds for the combination of the two behaviors without protection (CombNP). However, this is largely explained by the PC value for NC/NP. A usage time of more than one year shows little correlation (absolute PC values < .09). However, there is a negative correlation (−.108 at p < 0.05) observed between a usage time of 1 to 3 years with regard to having concerns and taking PM (C/P). A binary logistic regression shows a Cox & Snell R^2 of 0.051, with gender and age serving as control variables. Both are not significant (0.4 and 0.68). In this regression, duration of use from one to twelve months is significant at 0.055.

Table 5. Pearson correlation table for usage period and concerns/protection

	NC/NP	NC/P	C/NP	C/P	CombNP	CombP
< 1 month	.163**	-.119*	.016	-.072	.162**	-.162**
1 – 12 months	-.162**	.127*	-.085	.145*	-.218**	.218**
1 – 3 years	-.002	.000	.088	-.108	.071	-.071
> 3 years	.062	-.059	-.003	.005	.054	-.054

Users were asked about their **reasons for acquisition** using a 5-Likert agreement scale. Spearman correlations (SC) for own usage are presented in Table 6[2]. Price significantly influences users concerns and whether or not they take PM (.204 at p < 0.01). Furthermore, price also leads users to take PM, even when there are no concerns (C/NP −.169). Persuasion appears to have a positive influence on taking PM (CombP .160 at p < 0.05). Persuaded users have fewer concerns but take PM at a significantly higher rate (.176 at p < 0.05). This observation is supported by the significant positive SC of .162 for C/NP. Logistic regression shows that the control variables gender and age are not significant (sig 0.93 and 0.80). Persuasion is significant (sig 0.02). High self-interest in using a SSp significantly leads to having concerns and taking PM (.142 at p < 0.05). Users, who purchase a speaker because friends use one show less concerns but still take PM (C/NP −.176 at p < 0.05). The expectation that the speaker will make life easier does not influence concerns or PM. The results differ greatly when it comes to shared-use. There is no significant effect on taking PM (or not). Only when the device is purchased by someone else (e.g., because the user is inexperienced) is there a significant influence on not having concerns but still taking PM (.198 at p < 0.05).

Table 7 shows SC for different **speaker models**. For the context of use "all" there is a positive correlation between "other SSp" and CombNP (.109). The only significant negative correlation is for "other SSp" and NC/P (−.117 at p < 0.05). For shared usage, there is a significant positive correlation between Google Home users and PM (.225 at p < 0.05). This follows from the significant positive correlation at NC/P (.244 at p <

---

[2] Note: The direction of the correlation (algebraic sign) in all Spearman correlation tables must be interpreted in an inverted way due to the direction of the Likert scale.

Table 6. Spearman correlation for reasons for acquisition and concerns/PM for own usage

	NC/NP	NC/P	C/NP	C/P	CombNP	CombP
Context of use: For own users						
Friends used one	-.066	-.057	.176*	-.034	.078	-.078
Makes life easier	.028	-.029	.044	-.048	.060	-.060
Cheap price	-.027	.027	.169*	-.204**	.108	-.108
Persuasion/gift	.036	-.176*	.162*	.016	.160*	-.160*
Self-interest	-.039	.059	.091	-.142*	.035	-.035
Context of use: For shared usage						
Friends used one	.130	-.094	-.111	.108	.015	-.015
Makes life easier	-.130	.105	.020	-.002	-.098	.098
Cheap price	-.108	-.021	.096	.044	-.010	.010
Persuasion/gift	.177	-.018	-.062	-.126	.102	-.102
Self-interest	-.090	.131	.047	-.125	-.039	.039
Purchased by sb.	.023	-.198*	.104	.107	.114	-.114
The direction of the correlation (algebraic sign) must be interpreted in an inverted way due to the Likert scale.						

0.05). Own usage does not show a significant correlation. However, Google correlates to C/P (.120). There is also a positive correlation between "other SSp" and CombNP (.102).

Table 7. Pearson correlation table for SSp manufacturers and concerns/protection

	NC/NP	NC/P	C/NP	C/P	CombNP	CombP
Context of use: For all users						
Amazon Echo	-.070	.089	-.036	.013	-.094	.094
Google Home	-.014	.036	-.087	.075	-.084	.084
Apple HomePod	.067	-.033	-.035	.000	.032	-.032
Other SSp	.023	-.117*	.107	.004	.109	-.109
Context of use: For shared usage						
Amazon Echo	-.009	.075	-.070	.001	-.071	.071
Google Home	-.157	.244*	-.094	-.007	-.225*	.225*
Apple HomePod	.052	-.116	.037	.043	.080	-.080
Other SSp	.072	-.168	.065	.052	.122	-.122
Context of use: For own usage						
Amazon Echo	-.106	.086	.000	.021	-.097	.097
Google Home	.059	-.071	-.081	.120	-.009	.009
Apple HomePod	.085	.028	-.110	-.030	-.008	.008
Other SSp	-.003	-.090	.133	-.023	.102	-.102

After asking for general concerns in SSp, the survey asked about their **opinion on the use of emotion recognition** in SSp. Those users who oppose its use (Table 8), are significantly more likely to have concerns and take PM (.371 at p < 0.01). Those who opposed its use and who have no concerns and do not take any PM (−.105) or take PM (−.144) are negatively correlated. However, the number of respondents to NC/P is small (61 respondents). Users having concerns but not taking PM does not give an indication whether they are opposed to it or not.

Table 8. Pearson correlation for those opposed to emotion recognition and having concerns/protection

	NC/NP	NC/P	C/NP	C/P	CombNP	CombP
Opponents	.105	.144	.029	-.371**	-.116	.116
The direction of the correlation (algebraic sign) must be interpreted in an inverted way due to the Likert scale.						

5 Discussion

While SSp offer convenience, they pose sec/priv threats which lead to concern on the part of users and to the adoption of various PM. Our results reveal that these PM vary by context of use, gender, usage duration and opinion towards emotion recognition. However, the speaker model and manufacturer is not relevant in this aspect. Further, education, linguistic region and whether users live in urban or rural areas also show no influence on the PM taken.

Users interact with a speaker in different contexts (own, shared or as bystanders). Those who actively purchase and set up a SSp show significantly less concerns and PM. However, considering PM without concerns (CombNP), own users adopt slightly less PM than the other groups. This could be due to the possibility that own users are (or at least believe they are) sufficiently informed to have no concerns and therefore do not need to take PM [2]. Bystanders are less concerned than own users and hold a similar degree to which they show and to not show PM. This could be attributed to their different familiarity with the technology and awareness that a SSp is present [1]. As own users adopt slightly less PM, we see H1 as partly confirmed.

Our results confirm that gender has significant impact on whether or not PM are taken. This is not a new observation in general sec/priv research [17]. However, our results show that sec/priv in SSp must be considered differently than in other computer systems [2, 5]. Women are significantly more concerned about sec/priv in SSp contexts than men [17]. Although age is highly significant with respect to the adoption of SSp, results show no notable influence on PM. This is interesting, as younger users tend to have less privacy concerns [23]. Furthermore, education, linguistic region and whether users live in urban or rural areas also show no influence on the PM taken. This is somewhat surprising, as particularly educated users could have shown greater awareness and thus more concerns and a need for protection [1, 23]. Thus, our results indicate differences between sec/priv research in SSp compared to other domains. Therefore, we consider H2 to be only partially confirmed.

Novice users (usage for less than one month) have less concerns and therefore take PM to a lesser extent. This effect is completely reversed after this initial period within the first year of use. Explanations for increasing concerns and PM after one year could be that users start with a playful instead of purposeful use, first familiarize themselves with the technology, learn to take PM over time [6] and perform more automation tasks (e.g., with IoT devices) over time [24]. Another explanation could be the increasing dissemination of media news about data leakages [2]. The analysis revealed a negative correlation between a usage time of 1 to 3 years and C/P. This means that participants who use a speaker between 1 and 3 years do not show a higher level of concerns or PM. This could be due to a saturation of information flows or a rising awareness within the first year of usage, which makes taking further action obsolete for these users. Since we find significant changes in the three periods of use examined, we accept H3.

Literature suggested that emotion recognition is a strong reason for privacy concerns [28]. Our results can fully support this observation in the domain of SSp, which is why we consider H4 as verified. Opponents of emotion recognition are more likely to raise concerns and take PM.

When examining the influence of different reasons for acquisition, the results show that persuasion leads own users to take PM to a greater extent, but at the same time they have less concerns. Similar results are found for own users who buy a speaker because friends are using one (see C/NP in Table 6). This can be interpreted as passive influence and supports previous findings [5]. The group of NC/P seems contradictory at first glance. However, there could be several explanations: A general cautiousness, a great sense of privacy toward guests or the fact that users with high privacy literacy are largely less concerned [35]. This group however, has no significant correlation with age, gender or residential area in our analysis. The very different situation for shared usage requires further research. At this stage of research, one possible explanation could be that there are only half as many cases of shared usage compared to own use in our data set. The low price of a speaker significantly causes users to have concerns and take PM. This confirms prior studies found in [36], as users believe audio recordings to be used as a monetization strategy. All other reasons for acquisition show substantially lower correlation values. Since the values for PM (CombP) in Table 6 are very different between the different reasons for acquisition (with some being significant and others not), we provisionally confirm H5. However, a more detailed investigation of the relationships with regard to this would certainly be useful.

The literature review found that manufacturers follow different data protection practices, although their SSp show very similar privacy settings options for PM. Whereas a survey of UK users finds Echo users to have slightly more concerns, the results of our study show little correlation between manufacturers for the sample of all users. Shared usage, however, significantly increases the amount of PM for Google Home. This could be due to the higher number of Google devices in our dataset. These observations lead us to reject H6.

Our results have implications for research and practice. They investigate factors that influence taking PM in the field of SSp and contribute to this relatively new research field. With our results, we want to contribute to the ongoing discussion about the factors which influence sec/priv concerns and PM, using the SSp domain as an example. We confirm prior findings that SSp sec/priv is not completely transferable to other computer systems.

Our results provide two insights for manufacturers. First, in regards to what factors influence the purchasing of SSp and second, what makes users concerned and take PM. As gender, age and education level influence the acquisition of SSps significantly, more targeted marketing is advisable, especially for females, as they are more concerned than males. To enhance global sales, manufactures should focus on the French population, as they use speakers less often. Furthermore, the results show that shared use is quite common, but also leads to concerns and PM. Thus, manufacturers should develop (priv/sec) features that allow for separated usage with different settings/accounts and also for a guest mode [1]. To do so, a conversation with the SSp at setup-stage could be advisable to ask specific demographics to automatically suggest pre-defined privacy settings which are then reviewed together with the user. Our results show that price is not only a reason for purchase [1], but also that a cheaper price leads users to take more PM. Because data privacy is a major concern for some users, manufacturers could focus on more privacy features as a unique selling point. On a regulatory level, it is advisable to decide on a common standard of priv/sec default settings that users can rely on. Further, a common standard for PM could also be beneficial for manufacturers, as more trust leads to fewer concerns and thus more purchases.

Finally, our work is subject to two limitations. First, there are only weak correlation values for several questions. This is due to the low number of subsamples n we had to work with for several cases, despite the representative sample of N = 1000. Second, a separate and quantitative consideration of concerns and PM, e.g., using Likert-Scales, in the survey design would have allowed for a more differentiated investigation, which could also include an analysis of specific PM. Consequently, future work could investigate additional influencing factors (e.g., trust, regulations and personality) and should distinguish between concerns and PM. All of this could be done additionally with specific PM (e.g., muting or behavioral change).

6 Conclusion

This paper has investigated which factors influence sec/priv concerns and the adoption of PM for SSp. To this end, we first evaluated the literature on the areas of sec/priv threats posed by SSp and the PM taken by users. From this analysis, we then derived six explanatory hypotheses regarding potentially relevant factors influencing the taking of PM. We then conducted a representative survey with N = 1.000 respondents in Switzerland. Our findings reveal that taking PM is affected by five of the six factors: Context of use (partially), usage duration, gender (but not age and education level), reasons for acquisition, and opinion towards emotion recognition. Different speaker models, however, have no influence. Our results indicate that taking PM and sec/priv concerns in the context of SSp are different from the predictions found in the sec/priv literature with respect to other contexts. This calls for further investigation of the relationships between PM in these contexts.

Acknowledgement. This work was partially funded by TA Swiss and the German Ministry of Education and Research.

References

1. Lau, J., Zimmerman, B., Schaub, F.: Alexa, are you listening? Proc. ACM Hum.-Comput. Interact. **2**, 1–31 (2018). https://doi.org/10.1145/3274371
2. Manikonda, L., Deotale, A., Kambhampati, S.: What's up with privacy? User preferences and privacy concerns in intelligent personal assistants. In: Furman, J., Marchant, G., Price, H., Rossi, F. (eds.) Proceedings of the 2018 AAAI/ACM Conference on AI, Ethics, and Society, pp. 229–235. ACM (2018). https://doi.org/10.1145/3278721.3278773
3. McLean, G., Osei-Frimpong, K.: Hey Alexa … examine the variables influencing the use of artificial intelligent in-home voice assistants. Comput. Hum. Behav. **99**, 28–37 (2019). https://doi.org/10.1016/j.chb.2019.05.009
4. Edu, J.S., Such, J.M., Suarez-Tangil, G.: Smart home personal assistants. ACM Comput. Surv. **53**, 1–36 (2021). https://doi.org/10.1145/3412383
5. Lutz, C., Newlands, G.: Privacy and smart speakers: a multi-dimensional approach. Inf. Soc. **37**, 147–162 (2021). https://doi.org/10.1080/01972243.2021.1897914
6. Haug, M., Rössler, P., Gewald, H.: Identification and influence of perceived risks on smart speaker use behavior. In: Gronau, N., et al. (eds.) WI2020 Zentrale Tracks, pp. 1325–1331. GITO (2020). https://doi.org/10.30844/wi_2020_l5-haug
7. Abdi, N., Zhan, X., Ramokapane, K.M., Such, J.: Privacy norms for smart home personal assistants. In: Kitamura, Y. (ed.) Proceedings of the 2021 CHI. ACM (2021)
8. Godwin, S., Glendenning, B., Gagneja, K.: Future security of smart speaker and IoT smart home devices. In: Urien, P., Piramuthu, S. (eds.) Proceedings of the 2019 MobiSecServ, pp. 1–6. IEEE (2019). https://doi.org/10.1109/MOBISECSERV.2019.8686545
9. Chalhoub, G., Flechais, I.: "Alexa, are you spying on me?": Exploring the effect of user experience on the security and privacy of smart speaker users. In: Moallem, A. (ed.) HCII 2020. LNCS, vol. 12210, pp. 305–325. Springer, Cham (2020). https://doi.org/10.1007/978-3-030-50309-3_21
10. Zhang, G., Yan, C., Ji, X., Zhang, T., Zhang, T., Xu, W.: Dolphinattack: inaudible voice commands. In: Proceedings of the 2017 ACM SIGSAC, pp. 103–117 (2017)
11. Bräunlein, F., Frerichs, L.: Smart Spies: Alexa and Google Home expose users to vishing and eavesdropping (2019)
12. Ponticello, A., Fassl, M., Krombholz, K.: Exploring authentication for security-sensitive tasks on smart home voice assistants. In: SOUPS 2021 (2021)
13. Malik, K.M., Malik, H., Baumann, R.: Towards vulnerability analysis of voice-driven interfaces and countermeasures for replay attacks. In: Second IEEE-MIPR, pp. 523–528. IEEE (2019). https://doi.org/10.1109/MIPR.2019.00106
14. Walker, P., Saxena, N.: Evaluating the effectiveness of protection jamming devices in mitigating smart speaker eavesdropping attacks using gaussian white noise. In: ACSAC, pp. 414–424 (2021). https://doi.org/10.1145/3485832.3485896
15. Vaidya, T., Sherr, M.: You talk too much: limiting privacy exposure via voice input. In: IEEE SPW, pp. 84–91. IEEE (2019). https://doi.org/10.1109/SPW.2019.00026
16. Gupta, S.D., Ghanavati, S.: Towards a heterogeneous IoT privacy architecture. In: Hung, C.-C., Cerny, T., Shin, D., Bechini, A. (eds.) Proceedings of the 35th Annual ACM SAC, pp. 770–772. ACM (2020). https://doi.org/10.1145/3341105.3374108
17. Smith, H.J., Dinev, T., Xu, H.: Information privacy research: an interdisciplinary review. MIS Q. **35**, 989 (2011). https://doi.org/10.2307/41409970

18. Goodhue, D.L., Straub, D.W.: Security concerns of system users. Inf. Manag. **20**, 13–27 (1991). https://doi.org/10.1016/0378-7206(91)90024-V
19. Mishra, A., Shukla, A.: Psychological determinants of consumer's usage, satisfaction, and word-of-mouth recommendations toward smart voice assistants. In: Sharma, S.K., Dwivedi, Y.K., Metri, B., Rana, N.P. (eds.) TDIT 2020. IAICT, vol. 617, pp. 274–283. Springer, Cham (2020). https://doi.org/10.1007/978-3-030-64849-7_24
20. Geeng, C., Roesner, F.: Who's in control? Interactions in multi-user smart homes interactions in multi-user smart homes. In: Brewster, S., et al. (eds.) Proceedings of the 2019 CHI, pp. 1–13. ACM (2019). https://doi.org/10.1145/3290605.3300498
21. Ahmad, I., Farzan, R., Kapadia, A., Lee, A.J.: Tangible privacy. Proc. ACM Hum.-Comput. Interact. **4**, 1–28 (2020). https://doi.org/10.1145/3415187
22. Wu, S., He, S., Peng, Y., Li, W., Zhou, M., Guan, D.: An empirical study on expectation of relationship between human and smart devices—With smart speaker as an example. In: 2019 IEEE Fourth DSC, pp. 555–560. IEEE (2019). https://doi.org/10.1109/DSC.2019.00090
23. Zukowski, T., Brown, I.: Examining the influence of demographic factors on internet users' information privacy concerns. In: Barnard, L. (ed.) Proceedings of the 2007 ICPS, pp. 197–204. ACM (2007). https://doi.org/10.1145/1292491.1292514
24. Bentley, F., Luvogt, C., Silverman, M., Wirasinghe, R., White, B., Lottridge, D.: Understanding the long-term use of smart speaker assistants. Proc. ACM Interact. Mob. Wearable Ubiquit. Technol. **2**, 1–24 (2018). https://doi.org/10.1145/3264901
25. Chalhoub, G., Kraemer, M.J., Nthala, N., Flechais, I.: "It did not give me an option to decline": a longitudinal analysis of the user experience of security and privacy in smart home products. In: Kitamura, Y. (ed.) Proceedings of the 2021 CHI, pp. 1–16. ACM (2021). https://doi.org/10.1145/3411764.3445691
26. MIT: How close is AI to decoding our emotions? (2020). https://www.technologyreview.com/2020/09/24/1008876/how-close-is-ai-to-decoding-our-emotions/
27. Johnson, K.: Amazon's Alexa may soon know if you're happy or sad (2019). https://ven-tur ebeat.com/2019/07/08/amazons-alexa-may-soon-know-if-youre-happy-or-sad/
28. Latif, S., Khalifa, S., Rana, R., Jurdak, R.: Poster abstract: federated learning for speech emotion recognition applications. In: Proceedings of the 19th ACM/IEEE IPSN, pp. 341–342. IEEE (2020). https://doi.org/10.1109/IPSN48710.2020.00-16
29. Ling, H.-C., Chen, H.-R., Ho, K.K., Hsiao, K.-L.: Exploring the factors affecting customers' intention to purchase a smart speaker. J. Retail. Consum. Serv. **59**, 102331 (2021). https://doi.org/10.1016/j.jretconser.2020.102331
30. Chu, L.: Why would I adopt a smart speaker?, Enschede, The Netherlands (2019)
31. Williams, A.: Smart home privacy: what Amazon, Google and Apple do with your data (2022). https://www.the-ambient.com/features/how-amazon-google-apple-use-smart-speaker-data-2765
32. Vuichard, F.: Reden statt tippen. Bilanz **4**, 21 (2020)
33. Ebbers, F.: How to protect my privacy? - classifying end-user information privacy protection behaviors. In: Friedewald, M., Önen, M., Lievens, E., Krenn, S., Fricker, S. (eds.) Privacy and Identity 2019. IAICT, vol. 576, pp. 327–342. Springer, Cham (2020). https://doi.org/10.1007/978-3-030-42504-3_21
34. Hadopi: Assistants Vocaux Et Enceintes Connectées (2019)
35. Baruh, L., Secinti, E., Cemalcilar, Z.: Online privacy concerns and privacy management: a meta-analytical review. J. Commun. **67**, 26–53 (2017). https://doi.org/10.1111/jcom.12276
36. Arnold, R., Tas, S., Hildebrandt, C., Schneider, A.: Any sirious concerns yet? – an empirical analysis of voice assistants' impact on consumer behavior and assessment of emerging policy challenges. SSRN J. (2019). https://doi.org/10.2139/ssrn.3426809

Towards a Security Impact Analysis Framework: A Risk-Based and MITRE Attack Approach

Abdelhadi Belfadel$^{(\boxtimes)}$ ⓘ, Martin Boyer, Jérôme Letailleur, Yohann Petiot, and Reda Yaich

IRT SystemX, 2 Bd Thomas Gobert, 91120 Palaiseau, France
`abdelhadi.belfadel@irt-systemx.fr`

Abstract. Cyber security assessment aims at determining the cybersecurity state of an assessed asset to check how effectively the asset fulfills specific security objectives. We are confronted with a lack of an integrated framework coupling a top-down approach such as a risk-based analysis of information systems, with a bottom-up approach such as MITRE Attack to map and understand the details of the actions taken by the attackers to evaluate a defensive coverage throughout the development life cycle. We depict in this ongoing work the description of a Security Impact Analysis Framework (SAIF) to support cyber analysts, cyber administrators, and developers in their daily tasks of security impact analysis and provide project stakeholders with sufficient security proof and defense gaps. The goal is to avoid the use of a myriad of "tool islands" to automate the security impact assessment process providing sufficient safety evidence throughout the development cycle of a project. A case study of the development of an autonomous shuttle service is used to illustrate some selected assets from the MITRE Attack approach as practical usage of this framework.

Keywords: Security impact analysis · MITRE attack · Risk-based analysis · Cybersecurity · Information systems

1 Introduction

Security flaws represent significant risks to the reliable execution of business processes and can negatively affect business value, such as reputation or profits [1]. Consequently, organizations are continually investing more resources in protecting corporate assets [2].

Cyber security assessment aims at determining the cybersecurity state of an assessed asset in order to check how effectively the asset fulfils specific security objectives [3]. It is a process of challenging assets against their cybersecurity requirements, considering the potential risks, consequences of threats, and related costs [4]. With the protective measures set up in the system, the purpose of the cybersecurity assessment is to evaluate the correct implementation and

ⓒ The Author(s), under exclusive license to Springer Nature Switzerland AG 2023
S. Katsikas et al. (Eds.): ESORICS 2022 Workshops, LNCS 13785, pp. 212–227, 2023.
https://doi.org/10.1007/978-3-031-25460-4_12

operation of controls and their adequacy and efficiency in meeting the security requirements of the system [5, 6].

In this context, the need to identify or discover analytic coverage and defense gaps during the development software or system engineering lifecycle is of high value, however, we were confronted with a lack of an integrated framework coupling a top-down approaches (risk-based analysis of information systems), with a bottom-up approach such as MITRE Attack to map and understand the details of the actions taken by the attackers to evaluate a defensive coverage to carry out these operations throughout the development life cycle. Information security standards such as ISO 27001 are stating only very abstract implementation suggestions for risk mitigation. Therefore, we aim in this work to define a comprehensive and sufficiently generic, and, thus, adaptable, framework that uses a risk-based and MITRE Attack approaches that adopts a specific process model for managing test validations and security impact assessment analysis.

2 Background and Motivation

In this section, we present first the ISO 27001, EBIOS Risk Manager (EBIOS RM) and MITRE Attack approaches. Then we give the motivation of this work.

2.1 ISO 27001

The international standard ISO 27001 outlines a model for setting up, implementing, operating, monitoring, reviewing, maintaining and improving an Information Security Management System [7]. This standard follows the Plan-Do-Check-Act (PDCA) process model, which is used to structure all information security management system processes [8]. The activities to be carried out in each phase are as follows:

1. Plan: this activity is related to risk management and information security improvement that sets policy, objectives, procedures and processes to meet outcomes consistent with overall organizational policies and objectives.
2. Do: Implement and operate the information security management system policy, processes, controls and procedures.
3. Check: Evaluate and measure process performance against the established policy, practical experience, objectives and report the results to management for consideration.
4. Act: Undertake preventive and corrective actions, based on the outcome of the management review to improve the information security management system continuously.

2.2 EBIOS RM

A well known qualitative methods to manage the risks in information systems is called EBIOS (Expression of Needs and Identification of Security Objectives)

[9]. Modular and compliant with the international standards ISO/IEC 31000, ISO/IEC 27005, ISO/IEC 27001, the EBIOS method remains the essential toolbox used by many organizations in both public and private sectors to conduct information system security risk analyses. The EBIOS method provides a common vocabulary and concepts to achieve security objectives. It can be tailored to the context of each organization and then used as a basis for developing either a complete global study of the information system, or a more detailed study of a particular system according to the five EBIOS phases as depicted by [9] in Fig. 1.

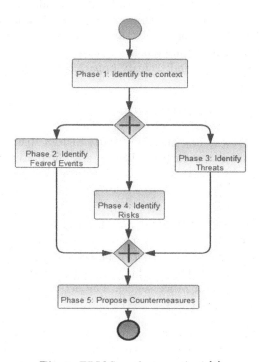

Fig. 1. EBIOS analysis method [9]

2.3   MITRE ATT&CK

The scientific community has focused on modeling patterns and techniques of cybersecurity attack from reported incidents in an attempt to anticipate adversary behavior, tactical approaches and systematic malicious actions [10,11]. In this regard, one of the most identifiable adversary models is the one proposed by MITRE ATT&CK, which tackles the who, how, and why of cyberattacking a digital infrastructure [12]. MITRE ATT&CK is a comprehensive knowledge base of adversary tactics and techniques based on real world insights into cybersecurity related threats. It has received wide acceptance from the research community and industry and has met with numerous applications such as behavioral analysis development or adversary emulation [12].

2.4 Motivation

We depict in Fig. 2 the targeted security assessment activities throughout a system engineering lifecycle in our organization. This business process cooperation viewpoint is proposed due to the lack of a hybrid framework or tools that uses a risk-based approach coupled to MITRE Attack knowledge base to carry out all activities to discover the analytic coverage and defense gaps during an engineering process (modelization, development or CI/CD phases). To achieve this goal, we aim to model and develop a framework that manages these security assessment activities with different stakeholders of a project, namely a project manager, a cyber security administrator, cyber analysts, developers and CI/CD administrators.

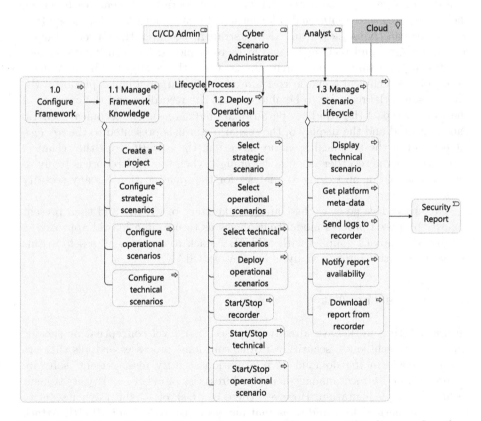

Fig. 2. Motivation - Business Process Cooperation Viewpoint. This diagram describes relationships with the targeted business processes and the Actors that perform the processes.

This targeted framework lifecycle starts with the configuration of the knowledge base by an analyst administrator (sub-process 1.1). This sub-process enables to create an instance of a project, and configure several levels of the framework's knowledge base such as the strategic level (paths of attack that a risk source could take to achieve its objective), operational level (the operating procedures likely to be used by the risk sources to carry out the strategic scenarios), technical scenarios (what compose an operational scenario), and technical attacks (refers to a technical implementation of a technical scenario). The latter is implemented as a technical attack that is reused from an existing knowledge base (such as MITRE Attack), or a technical custom attack that is a custom implementation. More details about these abstraction levels will be presented further in Sect. 4.

Once the knowledge base is set by the *analyst administrator*, a *developer* or an *analyst* can use the framework to deploy operational scenarios based on their objectives and contextual information. In this context (sub-process 1.2), an *analyst* can choose/select an existing strategic scenario, then a related operational scenario and technical scenario to be deployed for security assessment and testing in a target cloud environment. Once the related technical configuration of the technical scenario is deployed to the targeted cloud platform, the *analyst* starts the recorder to be able to start the recording and the creation of the security report (logs and key performance indicators). The technical scenario can be started and the display of the scenario status is presented to the *analyst*. At the end of the technical scenario execution, the *analyst* stops the technical scenario, and the recorder notifies the *analyst* when the final report is ready to be downloaded for an extensive analysis for the identification for any security gaps.

To achieve this goal, we first analyze the state of the art and then present a newly proposed process model that allows us to use, in a hybrid approach, a risk-based approach coupled with MITRE Attack to organize all assets in this proposed Security Impact Analysis Framework (SIAF).

3   State of the Art

Several existing work have already proposed high-level conceptual or specific frameworks, techniques, security controls, solutions, processes or tools that are already known in the domains of information security management, software engineering and project management to address risk or cyber security assessment techniques implementation. However, there is a lack of a hybrid cyber security assessment methodology and tools that merges a risk-based and MITRE Attack approaches that might be used during the development lifecycle of a system. In addition, information security standards such as ISO 27001 only provide very abstract implementation suggestions for risk assessment.

In vulnerability identification and analysis, [13] proposed an integrated risk-security assessment method based on ISO 31000 and ISO/IEC/IEEE 29119 that enables semi-automated evaluations that comprise graph-based system analysis and modelling, tests' preparation and execution.

In penetration testing category, [14] presented a risk-based approach to testing, in which the test preparation steps are driven by the results of independent risk assessments. This means focusing on the most critical system components and threats, with well-tailored testing scenarios and techniques. Authors in [15] assessed the security of 50 government agencies. The level of implementation of information security management systems and the compliance with the ISO 27001 standard and current regulations were evaluated. Based on this assessment, a number of recommendations were made to raise the level of information security in the public administration. In [16], authors proposed a generic cybersecurity management framework for the protection of business, government and society. The main objective of the authors' work is to enable managers to integrate counter-intelligence and place risk in a manageable context. [17] proposed a development methodology to implement cyber security strategies. This contribution is composed of several steps that includes requirement elicitation, security objectives, strategic moves and implementation framework repository.

In the context of check-list based evaluation, authors in [18] proposed a security assessment framework for internet banking services applied for 21 banks in Pakistan. The framework was employed by its authors to get a picture of the security of the banks analyzed and to draw guidelines for the banks, clients, and also for the State Bank of Pakistan. However, no guidance was given of other potential users of the framework. In [19], authors adopted standards and guidelines such as ISO/IEC 27001 to propose an assessment procedure that focuses on the elicitation phase of cybersecurity controls to get the set of checklist items that are most appropriate for the organizations' application domain and business context.

Some contributions [20,21] have the aim to consider attackers' capabilities, and have proposed some solutions to bridge the gap and combine top-down and bottom-up approaches. Authors in [20] illustrate how attack-defense trees fit into an existing risk analysis based on risk mitigation factors. The authors combined ISO/IEC 27002 [22] to attack-defense trees to identify the security controls that an organization needs to implement. This to reduce the likely success of the attack, and thus the overall risk. In [21], authors proposed a lightweight framework for SMEs to assess and evaluate the risks facing their organization, and to effectively allocate their limited resources. This framework is first driven by domain experts by providing attack scenarios for a specific domain, then users focus on the specification of their security practices. This information is then related to attack paths and corresponding security impacts in order to assess the total risk.

4 Security Impact Analysis Framework

To attend the objective depicted in Sect. 2.4, we propose a hybrid conceptual framework that adopts our new model based on the Know, Enter, Find and Exploit (KEFE) process model. The later uses a risk-based approach based on EBIOS RM methodology which is compliant with ISO 27001, coupled to MITRE

Attack knowledge base. This aims to support decision-making during a software or system development lifecycle for security impact assessment and enables asset reuse across projects. We describe hereafter the process model and the conceptual framework.

4.1   Know, Enter, Find, Exploit (KEFE) Process Model

This process model is designed following a hybrid approach. We perform risk-based analysis and management steps according to the five EBIOS method phases. First, we deal with context analysis. This step establishes the environment, purpose and operation and main assets of the target system. Second, we conduct the security needs analysis, by identifying feared events of the system and severity level to those events based on the harm it may induce. Third, we identify strategic scenarios and describe the threats affecting the system by studying attack methods or threats. Finally, we identify one or several operational scenarios that are aligned to the MITRE knowledge base using the Know, Enter, Find and Exploit process model which is applied to structure all the security impact assessment processes during the development, testing and CI/CD phases of an engineering process. The actions to be carried out in each phase of this process model is depicted below:

- *Know*: This phase aims to identify the vulnerabilities of the target system and gather techniques to aid in next phases of the process model. It involves information gathering (from MITRE category *Reconnaissance*) tactics that can be used during security test assessments. It also involves *Resource Development* tactics from MITRE to support targeting such as techniques stole resource that can be used to support targeting.
- *Enter*: This phase aims to gain a foot in the target system once the know phase has succeeded. It brings together techniques for stealing credentials (listed in MITRE as *Credential Access* category), gaining a foot in the target system (*Initial Access* MITRE category) or adversary-controlled code (*Execution* MITRE category).
- *Find*: This phase aims to gain knowledge about the system and observe the environment before deciding how to act. We bring several techniques to this phase from different MITRE categories as depicted in Table 1 such as *Discovery*, *Lateral Movement*, *Defense Evasion*, *Execution*, *Privilege Escalation*, *Credential Access* or *Persistence* category.
- *Exploit*: This last phase of the process model is the exploitation that aims to compromise integrity or disrupt availability by manipulating operational processes. As depicted in Table 1, several techniques might be used and are categorized in MITRE knowledge base as *Impact*, *Exfiltration* or *Command and Control* category.

An instance of the KEFE process model depicted in Table 1 combines different MITRE techniques to create an operational scenario to be implemented as

Table 1. Usage of Risk-based and MITRE ATT&CK Approaches based on the Know, Enter, Find and Exploit process model - Use case applied during the development on an autonomous vehicle system

Operational Scenarios			
Know	**Enter**	**Find**	**Exploit**
Develop Capabilities	Exploit Public-Facing	Cloud Service Discovery	Data Destruction
Gather Victim Network Infor-	Application	Exploitation of Remote Services	Data Encrypted for Impact
mation	Valid Accounts	Internal Spearphishing	Endpoint Denial of Service
Active Scanning	Deploy Container	Modify System Image	Disk Wipe
Vulnerability Scanning	Supply Chain Compro-	Software Deployment Tools	Exfiltration Over Alternative
Phishing for Information	mise	Cloud Infrastructure Discovery	Protocol
Compromise Accounts	Trusted Relationship	Command and Scripting Interpreter	Exfiltration Over C2 Channel
Compromise Infrastructure	Brute Force	Remote Services	Exfiltration Over Web Service
Obtain Capabilities	Hardware Additions	File and Directory Discovery	Resource Hijacking
Gather Victim Org Informa-	Phishing	Cloud Service Dashboard	Network Denial of Service
tion	User Execution	Modify Cloud Compute Infrastruc-	Remote Access Software
Gather Victim Identity Infor-		ture	Service Stop
mation		Exploitation for Privilege Escalation	Data Manipulation
Search Closed Sources		Pre-OS Boot	System Shutdown/Reboot
Valid Accounts		Rootkit	Account Access Removal
		Data from Information Repositories	Weaken Encryption
		Man in the Browser	Inhibit System Recovery
		Network Sniffing	

a technical scenario. The example below depicts some instances that are implemented further on as technical scenarios. A description of each level (strategic, operational, and technical scenario) is given hereafter and the hierarchy of levels are depicted in Fig. 3.

Fig. 3. KEFE model - Scenarios Hierarchisation

Strategic Scenario. High-level scenarios, called strategic scenarios. This level gathers all paths of attack that a risk source could take to achieve its objective. This is linked to the strategic scenarios identified in the risk-based methodology. However, in our context, it might be linked to a technical scenario to simulate a desired state in a target system. This scenario has the following value template that is a combination of several identified values after the realization of the risk-based method (in our context, EBIOS RM): *Source of risk/Targeted Objective/Business Values/Type of attack/method*. As an example, this value is considered as a strategic scenario instance in our framework: *Organized crime/Lucrative/Supervision of systems/Software asset*.

Operational Scenario. This represents operating procedures likely to be used by the sources of risk to carry out the strategic scenarios. In our context, all operational scenarios are linked to a strategic level, and an operational scenario should be linked to *only one* existing knowledge base at a time (in this context is MITRE knowledge base). The list of operational scenarios of a strategic one is based on the KEFE process model as mentioned in Sect. 4.1. Finally, an operational scenario is linked to *one or several* technical scenarios.

Technical Scenario. This represents two kinds of technical attacks: a technical attack or a technical custom attack. Each one of them can be implemented by one technical configuration. A *technical attack* is what composes an operational scenario. It represents a way to perform an action on a system for an attacker and is implemented following the best practice defined in an existing knowledge base (in this context MITRE). *A technical custom attack* is an action on a system that is not covered by an existing knowledge base, for instance, the creation of malware. Finally, a *technical configuration* represents the implementation of the technical or a custom attack through a containerized solution such as a docker-like configuration file.

4.2   KEFE Model Example

We depict in this section a concrete example applied in the context of the development of an autonomous shuttle service to illustrate some selected assets from the MITRE Attack approach as practical usage of the proposed KEFE model.

The operational scenario considered in this example is of an activist (or Hacktivist) attacker whose goal is to impact the availability of the service (see Fig. 4) by using the denial of the service method. To carry out this attack, there are several ways. First, in the *Know* phase, the attacker will start by developing his toolkit, he will prepare for the attack by choosing his tools or by developing them himself. Then, he will retrieve information about the target system online. The final goal of this phase is to launch a vulnerability scan. In case the attacker detects a vulnerability, he will proceed to the *Enter* phase where he will exploit the vulnerability to get inside the system. Another way to proceed would be to launch a phishing attack to gain access to a valid account. This account will allow him to implant a malicious container image. Once the container has been implemented or the flaw exploited, the attacker will now start looking for his final goal. In our case, to impact the availability as depicted in the *Find* phase. In the first scenario, he will exploit a flaw to get into the cloud system. In the second scenario, it is his container image that will perform the malicious actions. Finally, the only thing left to do is to damage the cloud VMs to make them inoperable, this is the *Exploit* phase.

This operational scenario is linked to several technical scenarios and are implemented following the best practice defined in this case on MITRE knowledge base. For instance the activity *Active scanning* of the *Know* phase is implemented according to several sub-techniques described in MITRE[1] (T1595.001 Scanning IP Blocks; T1595.002 Vulnerability Scanning and T1595.003 Wordlist

---

[1] https://attack.mitre.org/techniques/T1595/.

Scanning). Each of these sub-techniques are implemented further as a technical configuration that is a script (such as a docker configuration file) deployed in the platform under security test assessment during a CI/CD phase (see Fig. 4 for the list of selected technical tools that might be used in this example). Finally, each operational level is linked to mitigation techniques that can be used to prevent a technique or sub-technique from being successfully executed. In the given example, the *Active scanning* activity is linked to mitigation technique M1056[2].

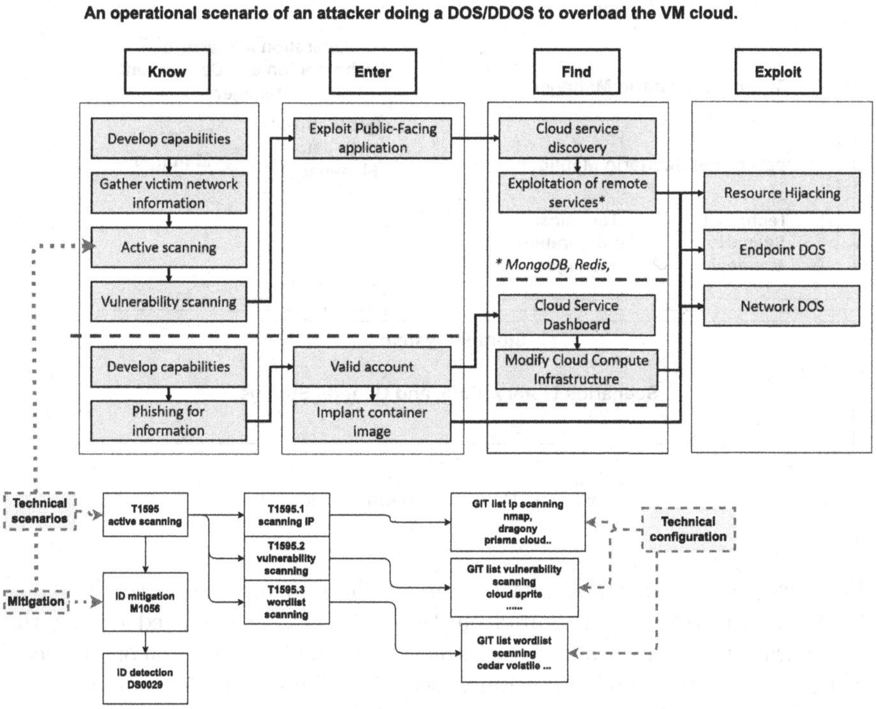

Fig. 4. KEFE model example

4.3 Conceptual Framework

The proposed SAIF framework consists of several components, which are described in this sub-section enabling the realisation of the business process depicted in Fig. 2. The connections or communications between different components will be performed through APIs or direct calls inside the same component. The technology foundations as a first and high-level analysis are described in this section, however, specific technology selections for the components are decided in later sections. As previously shown, the high-level architecture of the Framework is depicted in Fig. 5, and is composed of the following main components (from top to down):

---

[2] https://attack.mitre.org/mitigations/M1056/.

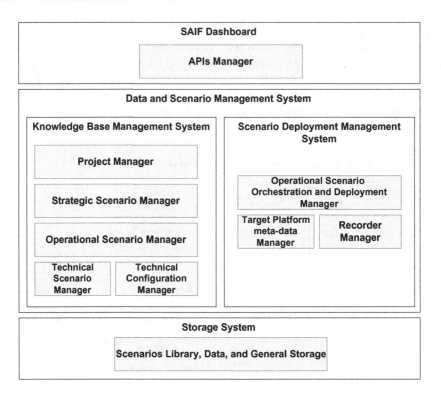

Fig. 5. Proposed framework

- Framework Dashboard: A user-friendly dashboard and interface. It allows the users to create the required entities that will be managed during the configuration and the usage of the framework such as the creation of a project, a strategic, operational, and technical scenarios. This dashboard provides also functionalities to deploy the required technical configuration to a targeted cloud platform, with a dashboard that displays the KPIs and progress of the actual running technical scenarios.
- Knowledge Base Management System (KBMS): This component will offer the required APIs to the framework's stakeholders enabling the management of the required entities (project, scenarios, technical configuration...) during the development lifecycle of a project. It is connected to the Dashboard and to the Scenario Deployment Manager that retrieves and deploys the selected scenario to a targeted cloud platform.
- Scenario Deployment Management System (SDMS): This component manages the deployment lifecycle of the selected scenarios to a cloud platform. It aims to manage the recorder that captures the logs of each deployed container, as well as the generation of a report for each deployed scenario. This component serves to retrieve KPIs from the targeted cloud platform to display in the dashboard the scenario progressions, KPIs etc.

– Data and General Storage: This component stores the data managed in the framework. This latter has different needs of data storage, e.g., scenario library, configuration files, generated log files, report or structured data. Each of them has its own requirements and constraints in terms of velocity of storage and querying. This component will offer APIs to get access to the required type of storage depending on the requirements and constraints of each component.

5   Technical Foundation

This section describes only technical insights to consider when analyzing in detail the technical requirements enabling the implementation of the targeted framework. The Cloud Computing side of the framework will be based on existing open source technology. Based on the initial design phase, the framework will follow a modern approach by combining containerization and virtualization techniques.

For the Dashboard (end user portal side) implementation, we aim to build this front-end with open source solution for creating customizable dashboards such as AngularJS[3] or VueJS[4] empowered with technologies such as Grafana[5] technology tools, that is widely used to compose observability dashboards with metrics, logs, and application data.

For the KBMS component, a python-based framework such as flask[6] might be employed to manage the configuration, retrieval and updates of the framework knowledge base. These choices are influenced by the data and general storage component that might be implemented by using document-oriented database such as MongoDB enabling the storage and querying of the data.

For the SDMS component, a job scheduler might be employed over Docker[7] /Kubernetes[8] APIs, with a solution to handle data ingestion such as Kafka[9] backbone. Regarding the infrastructure, infrastructure as a service-based solutions for IT automation to configure systems, deploy technical configurations and orchestrate operational scenarios tasks will be considered such as Ansible[10] and Terraform[11].

---

[3] https://angularjs.org/.
[4] https://vuejs.org/.
[5] https://grafana.com.
[6] https://flask.palletsprojects.com/en/2.1.x/.
[7] https://www.docker.com/.
[8] https://kubernetes.io.
[9] https://kafka.apache.org/.
[10] https://docs.ansible.com/ansible/latest/index.html.
[11] https://www.terraform.io/.

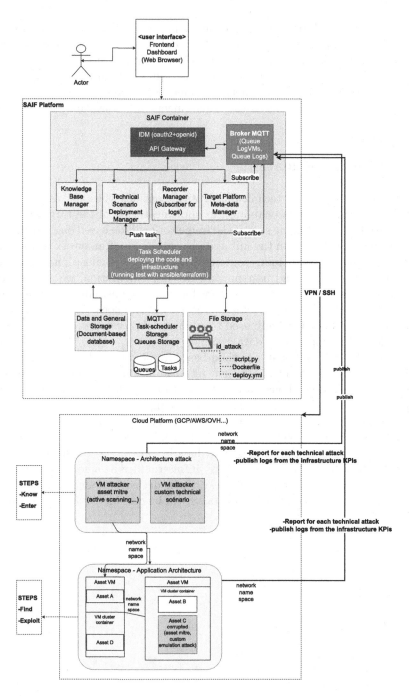

Fig. 6. SAIF Technical Architecture (Legend: Gray color refers to private components; Green color: refers to internal component with APIs for internal ones; Blue color: refers to a public accessible component with public APIs; White color: refers to a user interface component; Red color: refers to a technical attack deployed on a virtual machine or a container. (Color figure online)

Finally, the technical scenarios are containerised solution (Docker images or custom linux-based systems such as Yocto[12]), that might implement any technical tool used during a security test assessment. It should be deployed already in the target cloud environment as an image that can be invoked through the SDMS component.

6 Discussion

The Security Impact Assessment Framework is designed to assist cyber analysts, cyber administrators, and developers in their daily security impact analysis tasks. As mentioned in the opening sections, it aims to avoid the use of a myriad of "tool islands" to automate the security impact assessment process and the reuse of assets between projects by bringing together designed assessment techniques into a single repository. The goal is to provide project stakeholders with sufficient safety evidence throughout the development cycle of a project. However, there are some limitations that need to be highlighted. The proposed risk-based approach is implemented with the EBIOS framework. Thus, it requires the use of specialized skills for the determination and assessment of operating modes, in addition, it may need to use transformation models in case it is necessary to work with another approach to manage strategic and operational scenarios. With respect to the use case, the current framework implementation platform is intended to be used in a closed environment (pre-prod stage). Furthermore, the knowledge base of each project is specific and depends on the target system. Risk sources and objectives must be characterized and evaluated to select the most relevant ones, then a risk treatment solution must be identified for each risk through the design of the associated technical configuration, however, asset reuse is maximized with the possibility to reuse assets from one project to another.

7 Conclusion

Information security management is a complex and therefore time-consuming and expensive task. Organizations face changing threat landscapes and have to address them on multiple levels. Some efforts in research and industry already concentrate on increasing the automation of some aspects of information security.

We presented an ongoing work about the design of a Security Impact Assessment Framework that uses a hybrid approach aligning a risk-based and MITRE approach that adopts the Know, Enter, Find, Exploit (KEFE) model for security impact analysis. This is to assist cyber analysts, cyber administrators, and developers in their daily security impact analysis tasks and discover analytic coverage and defense gaps during the whole software or system development lifecycle. The goal is to avoid the use of a myriad of "tool islands" to automate

---

[12] https://www.yoctoproject.org/.

the security impact assessment process and provide project stakeholders with sufficient safety evidence throughout the development cycle of a project.

With our detailed perspective on the numerous components that are necessary to define a comprehensive and sufficiently generic, and, thus, adaptable, framework for security impact assessment we aim to foster a discussion on the architectural design of such a software package. While today, merely academic and very individualized solutions exist, it is likely that a more standardized and formalized framework will contribute to the practical implementation of such a security impact assessment system.

Acknowledgement. This research work has been carried out in the framework of IRT SystemX, Paris-Saclay, France, and therefore granted with public funds within the scope of the French Program "Investissements d'Avenir".

References

1. Cavusoglu, H., Mishra, B., Raghunathan, S.: The effect of internet security breach announcements on market value: capital market reactions for breached firms and internet security developers. Int. J. Electronic Commerce **9**(1), 70–104 (2004)
2. Ekelhart, A., Fenz, S., Neubauer, T.: Aurum: a framework for information security risk management. In: 2009 42nd Hawaii International Conference on System Sciences, pp. 1–10 . IEEE (2009)
3. Scarfone, K., Souppaya, M., Cody, A., Orebaugh, A.: Technical guide to information security testing and assessment. NIST Spec. Publ. **800**(115), 2–25 (2008)
4. IEC, T.: 62351-1, Power systems management and associated information exchange-data and communications security-part 1: communication network and system security-introduction to security issues (2007)
5. Chapple, M., Stewart, J.M., Gibson, D.: (ISC) 2 CISSP certified information systems security professional official study guide. John Wiley & Sons (2018)
6. Leszczyna, R.: Review of cybersecurity assessment methods: applicability perspective. Comput. Secur. **108**, 102376 (2021)
7. ISO, I.: IEC 27001 (2005) information technology, security techniques, information security management systems requirements. ISO, Geneva (2005)
8. Montesino, R., Fenz, S.: Automation possibilities in information security management. In: 2011 European Intelligence and Security Informatics Conference, pp. 259–262. IEEE (2011)
9. Abdallah, R., Yakymets, N., Lanusse, A.: Towards a model-driven based security framework. In: 2015 3rd International Conference on Model-Driven Engineering and Software Development (MODELSWARD), pp. 639–645. IEEE (2015)
10. Straub, J.: Modeling attack, defense and threat trees and the cyber kill chain, att&ck and stride frameworks as blackboard architecture networks. In: 2020 IEEE International Conference on Smart Cloud (SmartCloud), pp. 148–153. IEEE (2020)
11. Khan, M.S., Siddiqui, S., Ferens, K.: A cognitive and concurrent cyber kill chain model. In: Daimi, K. (ed.) Computer and Network Security Essentials, pp. 585–602. Springer, Cham (2018). https://doi.org/10.1007/978-3-319-58424-9_34
12. Georgiadou, A., Mouzakitis, S., Askounis, D.: Assessing mitre att&ck risk using a cyber-security culture framework. Sensors **21**(9), 3267 (2021)

13. Großmann, J., Seehusen, F.: Combining security risk assessment and security testing based on standards. In: Seehusen, F., Felderer, M., Großmann, J., Wendland, M.-F. (eds.) RISK 2015. LNCS, vol. 9488, pp. 18–33. Springer, Cham (2015). https://doi.org/10.1007/978-3-319-26416-5_2

14. Rennoch, A., Schieferdecker, I., Großmann, J.: Security testing approaches – for research, industry and standardization. In: Yuan, Y., Wu, X., Lu, Y. (eds.) ISCTCS 2013. CCIS, vol. 426, pp. 397–406. Springer, Heidelberg (2014). https://doi.org/10.1007/978-3-662-43908-1_49

15. Szczepaniuk, E.K., Szczepaniuk, H., Rokicki, T., Klepacki, B.: Information security assessment in public administration. Comput. Secur. **90**, 101709 (2020)

16. Trim, P.R., Lee, Y.-I.: A security framework for protecting business, government and society from cyber attacks. In: 2010 5th International Conference on System of Systems Engineering, pp. 1–6. IEEE (2010)

17. Atoum, I., Otoom, A., Ali, A.A.: Holistic cyber security implementation frameworks: a case study of Jordan. Int. J. Inf. Bus. Manag. **9**(1), 108 (2017)

18. Khattak, S., Jan, S., Ahmad, I., Wadud, Z., Khan, F.Q.: An effective security assessment approach for internet banking services via deep analysis of multimedia data. Multimed. Syst. **27**(4), 733–751 (2021)

19. You, Y., Cho, I., Lee, K.: An advanced approach to security measurement system. J. Supercomput. **72**(9), 3443–3454 (2016)

20. Gadyatskaya, O., Harpes, C., Mauw, S., Muller, C., Muller, S.: Bridging two worlds: reconciling practical risk assessment methodologies with theory of attack trees. In: Kordy, B., Ekstedt, M., Kim, D.S. (eds.) GraMSec 2016. LNCS, vol. 9987, pp. 80–93. Springer, Cham (2016). https://doi.org/10.1007/978-3-319-46263-9_5

21. Schmitz, C., Pape, S.: LISRA: lightweight security risk assessment for decision support in information security. Comput. Secur. **90**, 101656 (2020)

22. ISO27002, I.: IEC 27002: 2005 information technology-security techniques-code of practice for information security management (2005)

Data Protection Officers' Perspectives on Privacy Challenges in Digital Ecosystems

Stephan Wiefling[1] , Jan Tolsdorf[2]([✉]) , and Luigi Lo Iacono[2]

[1] Ruhr University Bochum, Bochum, Germany
stephan.wiefling@rub.de
[2] H-BRS University of Applied Sciences, Sankt Augustin, Germany
{jan.tolsdorf,luigi.lo_iacono}@h-brs.de

Abstract. Digital ecosystems are driving the digital transformation of business models. Meanwhile, the associated processing of personal data within these complex systems poses challenges to the protection of individual privacy. In this paper, we explore these challenges from the perspective of digital ecosystems' platform providers. To this end, we present the results of an interview study with seven data protection officers representing a total of 12 digital ecosystems in Germany. We identified current and future challenges for the implementation of data protection requirements, covering issues on legal obligations and data subject rights. Our results support stakeholders involved in the implementation of privacy protection measures in digital ecosystems, and form the foundation for future privacy-related studies tailored to the specifics of digital ecosystems.

Keywords: GDPR · Digital ecosystem · Data protection officer · Expert interviews

1 Introduction

Digital ecosystems [14] are ubiquitous, and both end users and businesses use them to exchange services and digital or analog goods: be it customer-to-customer (C2C) as with Airbnb, business-to-customer (B2C) as with Amazon Marketplace, or business-to-business (B2B) as with Google AdSense. As part of this, in many cases digital ecosystems require the processing of personal data, i.e., data relating to an identified or identifiable natural person [10] – either because individuals disclose personal data in order to participate in the digital ecosystem or because the services and goods exchanged themselves require or constitute personal data. In the process, many different actors gain access to this data. Next to platform operators and providers of services or goods, these include, e.g., providers of IT infrastructure, payment services, and logistics. The resulting complex flows of personal data and the increasing proliferation of digital ecosystems undoubtedly pose a challenge to the protection of this data, and thus to the protection of the privacy of millions, if not billions, of people worldwide. The General Data Protection

S. Katsikas et al. (Eds.): ESORICS 2022 Workshops, LNCS 13785, pp. 228–247, 2023.
https://doi.org/10.1007/978-3-031-25460-4_13

Regulation (GDPR) [10] addresses this issue by defining the responsibilities and obligations of the various actors involved in the processing of personal data and by requiring the implementation of appropriate technical and organizational measures (TOMs) to protect such data. However, there is currently a lack of insight on how digital ecosystems are mastering the challenge of putting GDPR requirements into practice.

Research Question. In this paper, we address this lack of insight from the perspective of the *service asset broker*, i.e., the entity who owns and operates a digital ecosystem's underlying digital platform. As they are at the center of digital ecosystems, insights from this stakeholder can contribute to a better understanding of the overall challenges for implementing data protection in digital ecosystems. To this end, we formulate the following research question:

RQ1: What challenges are met in practice when implementing data protection requirements in digital ecosystems from the perspective of *service asset brokers*?

Answering this research question is of high practical relevance, because practical insights and a thorough understanding of the field allow researchers and other stakeholders involved in privacy engineering and enforcement to support digital ecosystems in translating the often abstract data protection requirements into actual TOMs.

Contributions. We conducted four semi-structured interviews with seven data protection officers (DPOs) appointed by 12 digital ecosystems in Germany. On this basis, we report on the challenges that the DPOs identified in implementing data protection in digital ecosystems, who they think is responsible, and what they would like to see happen in the future to achieve more effective data protection in practice. In general, we find that DPOs demanded for action by the regulatory and supervisory bodies to increase harmonization of laws, and to provide more consistent and more accurate guidance and examples of TOMs. We further find that the implementation of data subjects' rights remains in a state of non-digitalization. In addition, DPOs considered the implementation of transparency in the processing of personal data in digital ecosystems to be a major future challenge – both for data subjects to become informed and privacy aware, and for themselves to keep track of personal data flows.

To our knowledge, our work offers the first insight into how DPOs perceive digital ecosystems putting data protection requirements into practice. We expect this focus to provide insights of high practical relevance, as DPOs guide and evaluate the privacy practices of potentially multiple digital ecosystems, making them proven experts on the data protection challenges in this subject. Our contributions support digital ecosystems and privacy engineers to implement privacy regulations more effectively. Regulators get insights into DPOs' thoughts on their privacy regulations, and the challenges they face when putting the regulations into practice. Researchers get insights from a hard-to-reach population, and directions for further research in the domain of digital ecosystems.

2   Privacy in Digital Ecosystems

Below, we provide an overview of digital ecosystems and a working definition, review relevant data protection requirements, and discuss related work.

2.1   Digital Ecosystems

The subject area of digital ecosystems is extremely heterogeneous and is essentially influenced by social, economic, computer, and natural sciences, all of which define digital ecosystems, their components, and parties differently [14]. Following recent efforts for a unified understanding, we adopt the definition that *"[a] digital ecosystem is a socio-technical system connecting multiple, typically independent providers and consumers of assets for their mutual benefit."* [14] Accordingly, a digital ecosystem is founded on the provision of at least one *ecosystem service* (e.g., software distribution) by a *service asset broker* (e.g., Google) via a digital platform (e.g., Play Store). The *ecosystem service* brokers *service assets* (e.g., apps) between *service asset providers* (e.g., app manufacturer) and *service asset consumers* (e.g., app users). Both are considered consumers of the *ecosystem service*. If required, *support providers* (e.g., PayPal) can assist *service asset brokers* in providing the *ecosystem service*. Due to the heterogeneous nature of digital ecosystems, some digital platforms cannot be clearly classified as such [14]. Additionally, the idea of digital ecosystems in practice is strongly bound to economic aspects, i.e., using advances in information and communication technology to drive business by digitalization [17].

2.2   Data Protection Requirements

The brokerage of *service assets* in digital ecosystems typically involves the processing of personal data; this is the case, e.g., when (i) personal data themselves represent *service assets* (e.g., behavioral data), (ii) personal data underlay *service assets* (e.g., user-targeted advertisements), (iii) consumers of *ecosystem services* disclose personal data to the *service asset broker* for participation, or (iv) *service asset consumers* disclose personal data to *service asset providers* in the course of the *service asset* exchange. To the extent that individuals whose personal data are processed or other actors in a digital ecosystem are located in the European Union (EU), the processing of personal data is subject to the rules of the GDPR (Art. 3)[1]. Actors who determine the purposes and means of the processing of personal data in a digital ecosystem acquire the role of a (data) controller (Art. 4). From the above definition it follows that at least *service asset brokers* (e.g., Google), but often also *service asset providers* (e.g., app manufacturer) and *support providers* (e.g., PayPal) have this role. Controllers are responsible for and must demonstrate compliance with the following fundamental principles (Art. 5): (i) *Lawfulness* denotes that personal data processing must be based on a valid legal basis prior to processing. Likely legal bases in

---

[1] Unless otherwise stated, all articles mentioned refer to the GDPR [10].

digital ecosystems include consent, the necessity of the processing for the performance of a contract, or the legitimate interests of the controller (Art. 6). (ii) *Fairness* means that personal data are not processed in a manner that is unjustifiably harmful, unlawfully discriminatory, unexpected, or deceptive to data subjects [8]. (iii) *Transparency* means that personal data processing is transparent, open, and clear to data subjects. This entails informing data subjects about the nature and scope of the processing, as well as enabling them to understand and exercise their rights (Arts. 12 - 14, 34). (iv) *Purpose limitation* means that personal data must only be obtained for specific, explicit, and legitimate purposes. The data must also not be processed in a manner incompatible with the purposes for which they were obtained. (v) *Data minimization* refers to only processing personal data that are adequate, relevant, and limited to what is necessary in relation to a purpose. (vi) *Accuracy* implies that personal data processed are accurate and up to date, and that reasonable efforts are made to delete or rectify inaccurate data in relation to a specific purpose. (vii) *Storage limitation* means that the processing of personal data does not allow the identification of data subjects for longer than is necessary for the original purpose or to comply with legal requirements. (viii) *Integrity and confidentiality* require the implementation of appropriate TOMs to ensure personal data security, including safeguards against unauthorized or unlawful processing, accidental loss, destruction, or damage. (ix) *Accountability* denotes that controllers ensure and are able to demonstrate compliance with the aforementioned principles.

To enforce these principles, the GDPR obligates controllers and entities processing personal data on the controller's behalf (i.e., processors) to implement TOMs (Art. 24) as well as to provide and implement several data subject rights. Among other things, individuals have the right to be informed about data processing and get access to their personal data (Arts. 12 - 15, 20), the rights to rectification and erasure (Arts. 16, 17), the rights to restriction and objection of processing (Arts. 18, 21), and the right to be protected against solely automated decisions with legal or similar effect (Art. 22). For infringements of the principles or the data subject rights by controllers or processors, the GDPR provides for penalties in the tens of millions of Euros or up to 4% of annual global turnover.

2.3 Related Work

Previous work on implementing the GDPR from the perspective of organizations has largely focused on identifying universal success factors, barriers, challenges, benefits, and consequences [1,21,27,28]. Specific insights on these aspects have been provided for public administrations [15], financial services industries [12], education institutions [11], and SMEs [6,25]. Few of these studies included DPOs [11,28]. In contrast, work specifically addressing digital ecosystems is thus far limited. Anwar et al. [2] conducted a review of international laws, regulations, and standards to identify and sort aspects related to (1) the protection of individuals' privacy, (2) guarantees to be made about the processing, (3) measures to be taken for the handling of information, and (4) consequences for technical implementation. Kira et al. [13] address the problem that digital ecosystems must comply with both competition policy and privacy law. They propose an integrated approach in which privacy considerations are incorporated into competition decisions to improve enforcement of both. Furthermore, some studies have touched aspects of privacy engineering when evaluating privacy issues in digital ecosystems and similar platforms. Park et al. [19] provide a conceptual model to uncover potential threats to the privacy of users of digital ecosystems due to algorithmic decisions. They argue that individuals' privacy concerns should be taken into account in the design, and that effective protection against, e.g., discrimination requires effective data minimization and processing restrictions. In addition, Van Landuyt et al. [30] describe pros and cons of using centralized versus federated approaches for both the documentation of data processing and the enforcement of data protection in digital ecosystems with inter-organizational personal data flow. Additional work remains largely focused on human factors and user studies [31]. For example, this includes studies on online social networks [5,18], mobile ecosystems [22], and sharing economies [23,29]. To the best of our knowledge, our study is the first to provide insights on the challenges of implementing data protection in digital ecosystems with the help of a very important but so far overlooked stakeholder: the DPO.

3   Methodology

We conducted a semi-structured interview study with seven DPOs representing a total of 12 digital ecosystems in Germany between December 2021 and January 2022. The following subsections provide details on the interview guideline design and study procedure, participant recruitment and background, data collection and analysis, and how we addressed ethical concerns.

3.1   Interview Guidelines Design and Study Procedure

We designed a questionnaire with an estimated interview length of 45 min, which focused on challenges in implementing data protection requirements in digital ecosystems. The interview length was chosen to accommodate the expected busy schedules of DPOs, and to obtain as much information as possible, while avoiding fatigue on the participants' side.

To ensure that our interview guidelines cover the main points of interest, we collected topics of interest using expert group discussions and literature review. The experts came from the fields of psychology, ergonomics, information security, and usable security & privacy. They were researchers, software and architecture engineers working on digital ecosystems, as well as DPOs not working for digital ecosystems. We also conducted a one-hour background interview with a digital ecosystem expert to go over the identified topic areas in greater depth. The insights gained from all these activities were used as the basis for deriving our interview guidelines. We then revised our interview guidelines by discussing them with researchers experienced in conducting interviews. Our final interview guidelines are available in Appendix A.

All interviews were conducted using remote conferencing software. Before starting the actual interview, we welcomed our participants and briefed them about the study procedure and conditions. We asked for informed consent to record the audio and video streams. We ensured anonymity and communicated our anonymization measures to the participants to counteract a social desirability bias that can occur in privacy topics [26]. Furthermore, we made it clear to the participants that there are no "right" or "wrong" answers.

The interview consisted of two parts. In the first part, we asked our study participants to give an introduction to their digital ecosystems. This served the purpose of allowing our participants to recapitulate the ecosystem and the interviewer to gain knowledge and understand the digital ecosystem. This involved questions about the actors involved, the personal data processed, the purposes for which the data are used, as well as the data flow and its depth. The second part regarded the challenges in implementing data protection requirements in digital ecosystems. We asked our participants what major challenges they have faced in the past and expect to face in the future. We also asked specifically about challenges related to the implementation of data subjects' rights and what responsibility the operator has for implementing data protection requirements in digital ecosystems. We concluded this section by asking what would be useful or helpful to make data protection more effective in the future. After that, the audio and video recording was stopped, the study participants were thanked for their time, and farewells were said. Excluding briefing and debriefing, the interviews lasted between 30 and 45 min.

3.2   Participant Recruitment, Enrollment, and Background

To recruit participants for our study, we contacted the DPOs of 24 *service asset brokers* of digital ecosystems in Germany via email. We identified these ecosystems based on Internet research using the definition in Sect. 2.1. The email included an invitation to a background discussion on data protection challenges in digital ecosystems. The email also mentioned that the contents of the conversation would be treated anonymously and stored in anonymized form.

In the end, we were able to recruit a total of seven DPOs. As is common with DPOs in Germany, six participants had a legal background. Moreover, three participants stated that they performed the function of an internal DPO, and one participant each stated that they acted as an external DPO, data protection engineer, data protection coordinator, or project manager for data protection.

3.3   Data Collection and Analysis

After the interviews were completed, we extracted the audio streams from the recordings and stored them separately. We then sent the audio recordings to an external transcription service so that the answers could be pseudonymized and coded afterwards. In the transcripts, any names of companies and persons were replaced by a generic name (e.g., "[name]" instead of "Jane Doe").

For the analysis of our interview material, we used inductive coding because the topics emerge from the content itself. In total, three coders (A, B, and C) were involved in the coding process. Coder A, the principal investigator [4], carried out the initial coding and created the code book based on the responses given in the interview material. After that, coder B also coded the full interview transcripts, using the code book created by coder A. The inter-rater agreement was 82.49% with $\kappa = 0.82$, which deemed strong consistency [16]. Coder C resolved any coding conflicts for the final analysis.

3.4 Ethical Considerations

Although our institution does not have a formal institutional review board (IRB) process, we made sure to minimize potential harm by complying with the ethics code of the German Sociological Association as well as the standards of good scientific practice of the German Research Foundation. Our study follows national and EU privacy laws, and was approved by our institution's DPO. We pseudonymized or anonymized the data after the interview. In particular, we eliminated all direct identifiers from the audio recordings before sending them to the transcription service. We further ensured that the service provider was located in Germany, complied with the GDPR, and deleted the submitted audio data after transcription and transmission to us. Any contact information was kept separate from the responses and was not linked to it.

4   Digital Ecosystems Overview

Based on the first part of our interview, this section provides an overview of the digital ecosystems covered. Overall, our study covers the perspective of four companies in Germany who act as *service asset brokers* for analog or digital goods. Two companies were market leaders (listed corporations), one company was an SME, and another company was a startup with its own newly created market segment. Depending on the company, the DPOs oversee multiple digital ecosystems simultaneously, so our results capture insights for a total of 12 digital ecosystems. The market segments include transport and travel, online social network, and online marketplaces. Three digital ecosystems focus on the B2B segment and nine on the B2C and C2C segments. In the following, we outline the stakeholders considered by digital ecosystems, the data processed within them, the purposes of the processing, and provide insights into the data flows. Detailed information on all these aspects based on our coding is available in Table 1.

Involved Stakeholders. Our participants reported a mixture of individual persons and companies that participate in the respective digital ecosystems. When asked about stakeholders' main motivations for participation, our participants cited financial benefits, added value, and workflow optimization (3/4), as well as gaining market advantage and marketing (2/4) as the primary reasons.

Data and Intended Use. Our participants explained that different types of personal data are processed in digital ecosystems. In the case of online dating, this also includes special categories of personal data (Art. 9). Identified purposes generally concern the provision and maintenance of the platform and services.

Table 1. Overview personal data processing in digital ecosystems covered.

Stakeholders	End customer (4), ecosystem operator (2), product manufacturer (2), business intelligence (1), cloud service provider (1), development partner (1), infrastructure partner (1), employees (1), online marketing (1), carriers (1)
Personal data	Name (3), address (3), email address (2), comments/messages (2), user account (2), user activities (2), payment data (2), age (1), operating system (1), consent (1), product identification number (1), pictures (1), gender (1), sexual orientation (1), VAT number (1), behavioral data (1), log data (1)
Purposes	Enabling use (4), authorization checks (2), payment processing (2), error analysis (1), fraud protection (1), traceability (1)
Recipients	Processor (3), employees (2), customer service (2), partners (2), users (1)

Note. Values in parentheses indicate the number of interviews in which we identified the topic. Baseline is four interviews.

Data Flow and Control. For the ecosystems surveyed, personal data also flows to external partners or processors (3/4), such as financial systems, cloud computing providers, insurance companies, and car workshops. Our participants explained that audits of external recipients (2/4) and the requirement to sign a data processing agreement (2/4) are used to ensure that personal data is processed for the intended purposes. To further protect personal data within the company, employees are instructed to limit data use to a specific purpose (3/4) and to follow strict instructions, particularly in customer service (1/4).

5   Data Protection Challenges

This section deals with the second part of our interview that directly addresses our research question. We translated relevant statements of our participants from German into English. We indicate the number of interviews in which we identified specific themes. These counts are intended to provide an indication and not a basis for quantitative analysis.

5.1   Implementing Legal Requirements

After our participants finished describing the digital ecosystems, we asked them what the biggest challenges were in implementing data protection requirements. Below, we report on the various challenges identified based on our analysis.

Accountability Obligations and Keeping Track. First, one participant explained the challenges arising from the controller's accountability obligation:

> "For one thing, the legal basis, ensuring the legal basis and the accountability. The purpose-related access [of the data], so that we are in a position to say: Okay, we now have no access that has no legitimate purpose [...] Then the topic of secure storage and transmission. [...] And the issue of proof of consent [...] and thus also the implementation of the right to object, which goes hand in hand with this [...]." (I1)

In this regard, some participants also found it challenging to keep track of a constantly growing digital ecosystem with many actors involved (2/4):

> "I think that the biggest challenge for an extremely fast-growing company [...] is to maintain an overview as a data protection officer and to weigh up the risks and opportunities." (I3)

To streamline proof to supervisory authorities, one DPO proposed to introduce certifications for the data protection management systems used by controllers. However, they also expressed concerns that certifications can mislead supervisory authorities into drawing wrong conclusions:

> "We have such a confusion of certifications. Everyone can come up with a certificate. We deliberately don't do it, [since controllers] [...] can pretend [...] [having] a certificate [...] that (in reality) is worth nothing" (I1)

Contractual Challenges. We further found that concluding contracts with processors can be challenging, in particular, when processors involve external partners in other legislation. In such a case, personal data processing could collide with the data protection requirements of *lawfulness* and *accountability*:

> "[...] when it comes to [data] processing, it becomes difficult, because in the context of maintenance and support activities there is always the possibility that American or Canadian [...] companies also have other American employees as subcontractors in their context." (I1)

To make it easier to conclude contracts with external partners, our participants highlighted the usefulness of standard contractual clauses provided by the EU. However, those were not seen as a one-size-fits-all solution in all use cases:

> "[A large] company like ours [...] conclude[s] a lot of contracts [with processors]. [...] This means that we are, of course, very happy that there are standard contractual clauses at the EU level [...] Beyond that, however, there are other points here and there that simply have to be agreed upon. And since other companies have the same problem, it can be a bit difficult to reach a common consensus in individual cases. Because everyone would prefer to sign a standard document that everyone knows and has agreed on. And that can be a bit exhausting." (I4)

Similarly, education about new data protection clauses can be an issue that delays contract negotiations, for instance with smaller companies (1/4):

"[...] it is sometimes the case [...] that you first have to explain them [(contractual partners)] where the new legal or regulatory challenges are. 'What does Schrems 2 actually mean, what does the conclusion of the standard contractual clauses mean?' And then to come to a reasonable result that meets the legal requirements." (I2)

Beyond that, limited personnel capacities in the legal departments responsible for data protection issues pose an additional challenge for concluding contracts (1/4):

"Due to the mass [of requests], the challenge is also often to check all measures in the desired period of time. For example, if the specific departments want to conclude contracts in a quick period of time." (I2)

Diverse Legislation. Our participants further explained that different legislation in different countries poses a challenge to operating digital ecosystems in a legally compliant manner, since it increases the required efforts (2/4):

"So I think, not only in this case, but in all cases [are] the biggest problems [...] when we have processors involved and especially when they are not located in Europe. [...] Then we have to meet extremely high requirements [...]. Then we [...] still have to send out questionnaires and evaluate them, make a risk assessment. So that, in my opinion, was the greatest challenge, at least the greatest effort." (I4)

"The legal situation in the U.S. and thus also the inadmissible, or unsatisfactory, legal situation that we have with regard to data exchange or the use of U.S. service providers [...] are the biggest pitfalls we have here. We are talking about the global economy on the one hand and data protection measures on the other." (I1)

Inferior Power to Big Tech. DPOs in our study also stated that enforcing legal requirements is difficult, even in relatively large digital ecosystems, when Big Tech companies are involved (1/4):

"Of course you often have the problem of power balance when you look at large players, such as, [...] Google, Facebook, or Amazon. Then, even if [our company] is not a small corporation, it is of course a smaller corporation compared to these large corporations. There is the particular hurdle of enforcing [...] the legal requirements on these contractual partners, who are superior in terms of power balance [...]." (I2)

Uncertainty in Interpretation of Law. New laws that impose novel and additional requirements on existing processing of personal data (e.g., cookies) often pose a challenge to DPOs in terms of their interpretation (2/4). They also criticized the lack of recommendations from the relevant supervisory authorities, making the process a huge drain on resources (1/4).

"Now [...] we all have the new TTDSG² and the cookie web tracking issue on the table, which [...] keeps us busy [...] as a large digital corporation [...]. The challenge is always the time and the legal requirements that you are [...] exposed to [...] in the legal team. And [...] you also try to catch up [with the legal requirements] as quickly as possible, and then actually implement them in practice as soon as possible." (I2)

"When a law such as the TTDSG comes into force, but there are not yet sufficient or only limited recommendations from the regulatory authorities, then [it is difficult] to conclude which legal requirements should now actually be implemented in practice." (I2)

Barriers to Transparency. DPOs expressed their concern that the obligations put forward by the GDPR essentially undermine the principle of *transparency*:

"It is precisely this balancing act [...] between the legal requirements, which of course must be implemented [...]. But also to provide users with data protection in a friendly, transparent manner and with an eye to keeping them informed, and to find a healthy balance." (I2)

"[T]he biggest problem [...] is that the GDPR intends well in principle [...] but in part has the wrong focus. [...] [W]ith all the transparency that we have to demonstrate, we are actually completely non-transparent [...]. If you look at prominent websites on the Internet and open the data privacy policies, there are usually 30, 40, 50 pages full of [...] policies. And the purpose of these is actually to make it clear to the user [...] where their data is now located and what is being collected. And [in] my opinion [...] this is actually completely non-transparent [...]." (I3)

5.2   Implementing Data Subject Rights

We explained to our participants that one of our research goals is to help digital ecosystems implement data subject rights. To this end, we asked them what major challenges digital ecosystems face in this regard. In the following, we present the different answers, grouped into themes according to our coding.

Privacy Policies. Our participants explained that setting up a company privacy policy for handling data subject rights can be challenging, because it must document necessary processes in a way comprehensible to non-legal staff who have to respond to data subject requests (3/4):

"If you look at the various departments, who, for example, handle such data subject rights in the first place and respond to inquiries. Then, of course,

---

² The Telecommunication Telemedia Data Protection Act (TTDSG) is the national adoption of the EU ePrivacy Directive in Germany. It further replaces previous regulations on data protection and secrecy for telecommunications services in Germany.

it must always comply with the legal requirements. This means that there is a need for comprehensive documentation or legal requirements that are also prepared for the relevant departments, which of course also have to be educated on a regular basis." (I2)

Requests for Erasure. Our participants expressed particular concern regarding data subjects' right to erasure (2/4). One DPO explained that requests for erasure are submitted in written form, but without a standardized format. This often leads to difficulties of interpretation in practice. Another DPO pointed out that actual erasure is difficult in practice, but too often confirmed by controllers or processors without the data actually being deleted:

"In particular, we must also pay attention to the interpretation of the wording used by the parties concerned, because when a party concerned asserts its request for deletion, 'deletion' is not always expressly mentioned, so that problems also arise here in the interpretation." (I2)

"A lot of companies have [...] many IT systems and scattered data from their respective users. And I think that many companies, simply also because of the speed that they are up against [to process deletion lawfully], have difficulties there in creating a proper deletion request." (I3)

Strict Deadlines. We further found that strict deadlines given by the law to handle data subject requests can be challenging in (complex) digital ecosystems:

"If, for example, a request under the right to access is to be processed, there is a time limit of one month [...], within which the request [...] must be answered. And depending on how the [digital] ecosystem is set up, there is the problem of time [...]." (I2)

5.3   Responsibility of Operators for the Entire Digital Ecosystem

We further asked our participants what responsibility a *service asset broker* has to ensure data protection throughout the entire ecosystem.

Data Protection Mechanisms. To protect data misuse by external partners, the ecosystems rely on contractual assurances (1/4), minimization of the amount of data stored (2/4), and a kind of social control by only working with reputable companies that would have a reputation to lose if they did not comply with data protection regulations (1/4):

"When we work with external partners, I would say they are usually larger, well-known companies. I think it's fair to say that they also have something to lose if they don't meet their data protection requirements. So [...] we make sure that the partners we work with have the right standing in the market. That's how social control works." (I4)

Data Protection as an Ongoing Process. Another responsibility mentioned to ensure data protection throughout the ecosystem was to make and see data protection as an ongoing process (1/4):

> "I don't just do data protection and then put a check mark on it, but I have to establish structures that make it possible on a continuous basis and also make it possible to have an early warning system." (I4)

Documentation of the digital ecosystem was also seen as a part to fulfill this responsibility (1/4):

> "When I launch a new application, [...] you also look again: 'Are other services integrated here? Has the topic of data protection been sufficiently addressed?' And so on. Documentation, things like that, general things. But that's also quite a lot. (laughs) You're quite busy with that." (I4)

5.4   Helpful (Future) Steps for More Effective Data Protection

To address the challenges of implementing data protection, we asked our participants what would be helpful to make data protection more effective in digital ecosystems in the future. Below, we present the themes identified by our coding.

Harmonization. Our participants greatly appreciated the harmonization of privacy laws caused by the GDPR for the implementation of legal requirements in international markets. They would therefore appreciate the regulators taking further steps in this direction, both at the international and national level (2/4):

> "It would help a lot if either the European data protection authorities were to scale down their demands a bit [...]. Or if the U.S. government, in particular, were to move a bit and keep its intelligence services under control for a while. Because that is exactly [...] why data transfer to the U.S. in particular has been made so difficult." (I1)

> "We have the problem of federalism here in Germany, so to speak. It always depends on which federal state you are located in, how strictly the data protection authorities interpret certain things. [...] [A] certain standardization would be helpful for all of us, first of all at the German level, but also with a view to the EU." (I2)

Explicit Requirements and Guidelines. Following the idea of harmonization, our participants stated that regulators and supervisory authorities should focus on consistent and clear communication of data protection requirements (2/4). In addition, DPOs sought guidance and templates to avoid problems due to different interpretations from the outset:

> "From my point of view, the legal requirements, or what is expected of us, should be communicated a bit more clearly by the regulatory authority. Because a lot of things need to be interpreted and a lot of things are actually implemented a bit differently in German law than the European legislator specifies." (I2)

"And [...] the data protection conference, as the highest national data protection body, should provide guidance, perhaps even more practical recommendations and practical examples in the form of screenshots of cookie banners, [...] [and] I could certainly imagine open online consultation hours being helpful here. Perhaps the universities could also provide support in this context." (I2)

In this regard, however, there was also a desire for supervisory bodies to have a better understanding of technology (1/4):

"We have few supervisory authorities, who are very tech-savvy. We have other supervisory authorities, who have less understanding there." (I1)

Transparency. Our participants regarded measures for improved transparency as an essential step toward more effective implementation of data protection requirements in digital ecosystems. Different aspects were addressed here. One aspect related directly to the challenge of keeping track of a growing digital ecosystem by implementing *"central transparency"*, i.e., measures that facilitate DPOs to keep track centrally of all entities and personal data flows (2/4):

"[W]e have the requirement that we must document everything. There has to be central transparency somewhere. It's not enough for someone to have thought of something good on a decentralized basis [...] [W]e also have to keep an eye on the bigger picture and have an overview." (I4)

Further aspects discussed by our participants relate to transparency and honesty about data processing towards data subjects. DPOs see a particular need to raise people's (limited) privacy awareness (3/4), believing that this would relieve data controllers from being blamed. However, DPOs also pointed out the problem that management might be concerned that transparency would reduce revenue:

"In my view, [a service asset broker is responsible for] making data protection simple and comprehensible. Especially with regard to the data subjects' rights and their exercise. 'Transparency', so to speak, and maybe also taking users by the hand a bit and showing them, 'okay, this is what we do with the data and this is what happens there. And that way, you can retain control over your data yourself', so to speak." (I2)

"If the user doesn't know what they're handing over their data for, then I think it's always a bit easy to finger-point at the provider and say 'Watch out! You were obliged to do everything right with my personal data.'. But if you had communicated transparently with them in advance, I think that would have been different." (I3)

"I believe that DPOs and customers are the ones who are easiest to deal with [...] by transparently, [...] openly and honestly explaining what is happening with the data. [...] But of course that goes hand in hand with the management perhaps not always being happy, because for platforms, personal data [...] are hard cash." (I3)

6   Discussion and Implications

Digital ecosystem providers face the challenge of meeting the various data protection requirements imposed on them as data controllers. From our interviews with DPOs we revealed various challenges for the implementation of those requirements. For discussion, we cluster them into three broader topic areas.

Action by Official Authorities. Overall, we find that several data protection challenges mentioned by DPOs implicitly or explicitly demand for action by regulators and supervisory authorities. As such, DPOs seem to consider harmonization and establishment of standard solutions as the most and direct relief to current issues of (international) personal data transfer, contract conclusion, and accountability issues in digital ecosystems. Probably due to the many different actors in digital ecosystems with different power relationships and expertise in data protection, we found repeated calls for greater clarity and specification by official bodies. In practice, businesses appear to be hesitant to come up with innovative solutions on their own in order to avoid problems with supervisory authorities. However, concrete specifications issued by authorities for the implementation of, e.g., cookie banners, as some of our participants suggested, may reduce the incentive to develop innovative and creative solutions. Instead, consolidating publications and findings to provide a summary guide to digital ecosystem developers or auditors could be a first step toward greater legal certainty. In this regard, our findings encourage future research oriented to the efforts of the European Data Protection Board to provide practical recommendations on how to assess and avoid dark patterns in interfaces that infringe GDPR requirements [9]. Solutions provided by researchers and privacy engineers may also need to be accompanied by more precise linkage to the actual legal requirements they help to address. Inspiration may be taken from the privacy pattern community to sort catalogs according to ISO 29100 [7].

Transparency Enhancements. Our findings indicate that challenges regarding transparency in digital ecosystems play a significant role. On the one hand, DPOs stated that they themselves have difficulties in maintaining an overview of data flows. At the same time, honesty and transparency toward data subjects is of particular importance. Here, DPOs considered the digital platform to have a duty to support data subjects in exercising their rights in the digital ecosystem. Our participants see a clear need for improvement in this regard, but at the same time explained that the GDPR's requirements are detrimental to comprehensible transparency. In addition, there is possible reluctance on the part of providers so as not to scare off potential customers with being "too" honest.

Digitalization Deficit in Data Protection. Our interviews showed that digitalization in digital ecosystems does not necessarily capture the implementation of data protection requirements. In particular, our participants reported error-prone and time-consuming workflows related to managing data subject rights, because they had to be handled and interpreted manually. Since the implementation of data subjects' rights is inextricably linked to the processing of personal data, it must certainly be understood as an integral business process of any digital ecosystem provider. In this regard, our finding seems surprising, because the companies do not seem to take advantage of digitalization benefits for data protection the same way they do for their core business processes (cf. Sect. 4). Our work therefore suggests that efforts are needed to truly embed data subjects' rights in digital ecosystems in a digital-native way. For example, Big Techs like Microsoft, Meta, and Google have integrated self-service tools into their products for several years to efficiently address data subject rights, especially rights related to access requests under Arts. 15 and 20. These self-service tools have come to be known as "privacy dashboards" and are seen as promising in the research community for helping both data controllers fulfill their obligations and data subjects exercise their rights more easily [3,20,24]. However, when we specifically asked our participants about their experience with such tools, they stated that they were largely unfamiliar with these types of privacy-related self-services. Nevertheless, they expressed a general interest in such tools to achieve a more efficient implementation of data subjects' rights in the future (4/4):

"Of course, if you wanted to use something like this, you would have to make sure that you don't bypass the legally mandated right to access in Article 15 of the General Data Protection Regulation. If this is within the legal limits and within the legal permissibility, then I would definitely be very open to it, especially in terms of user transparency." (I2)

In conclusion, our findings suggest that potential (off-the-shelf) solutions to strengthen data subjects' rights may be successful if they are easy to integrate for ecosystem operators and legal compatibility is made clear.

Limitations. Our results are certainly not representative of all digital ecosystems in Germany. Furthermore, recruitment bias and self-report bias are possible, as not all companies responded to our invitation and our respondents only disclosed the information they wanted to reveal. Nevertheless, our findings provide an initial overview of data protection challenges for digital ecosystems in Germany, which can serve as a basis for further studies.

7 Conclusion

Digital ecosystems are drivers of digital transformation. It is therefore important that data protection challenges are addressed in these complex systems. To better understand these challenges, we conducted interviews with seven DPOs responsible for a total of 12 digital ecosystems in Germany. Our results indicate that DPOs are aware of the *service asset brokers'* responsibility in digital ecosystems for data protection. Key challenges are accountability obligations and collaborations with processors, especially non-EU based processors. The implementation of data subject rights remains in a state of low digitalization. To strengthen data protection, DPOs expect clear, unambiguous instructions and implementation examples from official bodies. At the same time, they see transparency as a key challenge, both to maintain an overview themselves and to demonstrate transparency and openness to their users. Our findings suggest that more concrete recommendations for solutions with legal categorization and solutions for privacy self-service tools could be helpful here.

Acknowledgments. We thank Marian Hönscheid and Benedikt Malchow for helping us code the interviews. This research was supported by the project D'accord funded by the German Federal Ministry of Education and Research (grant number: 16KIS1508).

A   Appendix – Semi-structured Interview

We conducted the semi-structured interview using the main questions below. The interviews were held in German. To ease understanding, we translated the interview questions from German to English in this paper. We also included optional questions. We asked these questions only when we still had sufficient time to ask them, and when study participants had not implicitly answered these questions in the previous ones.

A.1   Introduction

- Please briefly introduce yourself, including your function in the company.
- Please briefly introduce the digital ecosystem for which you are here today.
- Please briefly describe your areas of responsibility in this digital ecosystem.

A.2   Detailed Description of the Ecosystem

- Stakeholder
    - Who is involved in the digital ecosystem and with what motivation?
    - Which actors and participants are involved?
- Data and purpose of use
    - What common personal data are processed in the digital ecosystem and for what purposes are they processed?
    - *Optional: Are there any particularly sensitive personal data that you work with?*
- Data flow
    - Who gets access to the personal data? So who are the recipients of the personal data?
    - *Optional: Where/how does which personal data flow to whom for which purpose?*
    - *Optional: To what extent does the broker influence data flows? Also on those of providers?*

- Data flow depth
  - Do you know what the recipients process the personal data for?
  - If external recipients: Do you know what external recipients process the personal data for?
  - How do you ensure that recipients use the data only for the intended purposes?

A.3   Privacy Challenges

- Based on your comments and descriptions: In your opinion, what are the biggest challenges and problems in implementing the legal requirements for data protection?
  - What have been the biggest challenges in the past?
  - What do you think will be challenges to deal with in the future?
- With our research, we want to strengthen the rights of data subjects and support digital ecosystems in their implementation. When you think about data subjects' rights, what challenges do you face in implementing them in particular?
- In your view, what responsibility does the provider of the digital ecosystem have to ensure data protection throughout the ecosystem and for all participants/actors?
  - How do you assess the responsibility for the various players in the digital Ecosystem for data protection?
  - *Optional: How is data protection ensured, e.g. at the recipients' side?*
- What do you think would be useful or helpful to make data protection in digital ecosystems more effective in the future?

A.4   Privacy Dashboards

- Do the terms "privacy cockpits" or "privacy dashboards" mean anything to you?
- Do you already use such tools or do you plan to use them in the future?

References

1. Almeida, J., da Cunha, P.R., Pereira, A.D.: GDPR-compliant data processing: practical considerations. In: Proceedings of the 18th European, Mediterranean, and Middle Eastern Conference (EMCIS), pp. 505–514 (2021)
2. Anwar, M.J., Gill, A.Q., Beydoun, G.: A review of information privacy laws and standards for secure digital ecosystems. In: Proceedings of the 29th Australasian Conference on Information Systems (ACIS), pp. 1–12 (2018)
3. Bier, C., Kühne, K., Beyerer, J.: PrivacyInsight: the next generation privacy dashboard. In: Proceedings of the 4th Annual Privacy Forum, pp. 135–152 (2016)
4. Campbell, J.L., Quincy, C.D., Osserman, J., Pedersen, O.K.: Coding in-depth semistructured interviews. Sociol. Methods Res. **42**, 294–320 (2013)

5. Chen, Z.T., Cheung, M.: Privacy perception and protection on Chinese social media. Ethics Inf. Technol. **20**(4), 279–289 (2018)
6. da Conceição Freitas, M., da Silva, M.M.: GDPR compliance in SMEs: there is much to be done. J. Inf. Syst. Eng. Manag. **3**(4), 30 (2018)
7. Drozd, O.: Privacy Pattern Catalogue: a tool for integrating privacy principles of ISO/IEC 29100 into the software development process. In: Proceedings of the 10th IFIP International Summer School on Privacy and Identity Management, pp. 129–140 (2016)
8. EDPB: Guidelines 4/2019 on article 25 data protection by design and by default, version 2.0 (2020)
9. EDPB: Guidelines 3/2022 on dark patterns in social media platform interfaces: how to recognise and avoid them, version 1.0 (2022)
10. European Union: GDPR, Regulation (EU) 2016/679 (2016)
11. Fernandes, J., Machado, C., Amaral, L.: Identifying critical success factors for the general data protection regulation implementation in higher education institutions. Digital Policy, Regul. Gov. **24**(4), 355–379 (2022)
12. Holler, M., van Giffen, B., Benzell, S., Ehrat, M.: The general data protection regulation in financial services industries: how do companies approach the implementation of the gdpr and what can we learn from their approaches? In: Proceedings of the 82th Jahrestagung des Verbands der Hochschullehrer für Betriebswirtschaft (VHB), pp. 1–11 (2020)
13. Kira, B., Sinha, V., Srinivasan, S.: Regulating digital ecosystems. Industr. Corp. Change **30**(5), 1337–1360 (2021)
14. Koch, M., Krohmer, D., Naab, M., Rost, D., Trapp, M.: A matter of definition: criteria for digital ecosystems. Digital Business **2**(2), 100027 (2022)
15. Lisiak-Felicka, D., Szmit, M.: GDPR implementation in public administrationin Poland - 1.5 year after: an empirical analysis. J. Econ. Manag. **43**, 1–21 (2021)
16. McHugh, M.L.: Interrater reliability: the kappa statistic. Biochemia Medica **22**(3), 276–282 (2012)
17. Nachira, F., Nicolai, A., Dini, P.: Digital business ecosystems. European Commission (2007)
18. Namara, M., Sloan, H., Knijnenburg, B.P.: The effectiveness of adaptation methods in improving user engagement and privacy protection on social network sites. In: Proceedings on Privacy Enhancing Technologies, vol. 2022, iss. 1, pp. 629–648 (2022)
19. Park, Y.J., Chung, J.E., Shin, D.H.: The structuration of digital ecosystem, privacy, and big data intelligence. Am. Behav. Sci. **62**(10), 1319–1337 (2018)
20. Popescu, A., et al.: Increasing transparency and privacy for online social network users – USEMP value model, scoring framework and legal. In: Proceedings of the 4th Annual Privacy Forum (APF), pp. 38–59 (2016)
21. Poritskiy, N., Oliveira, F., Almeida, F.: The benefits and challenges of general data protection regulation for the information technology sector. Digital Policy, Regul. Gov. **21**(5), 510–524 (2019)
22. Qiu, Y., Gopal, A., Hann, I.H.: Logic pluralism in mobile platform ecosystems. Inf. Syst. Res. **28**(2), 225–249 (2017)
23. Ranzini, G., Etter, M., Lutz, C., Vermeulen, I.: Privacy in the sharing economy. Tech. rep., Ps2Share (2017)
24. Raschke, P., Küpper, A., Drozd, O., Kirrane, S.: Designing a GDPR-compliant and usable privacy dashboard. In: Proceedings of the 12th Annual IFIP Summer School on Privacy and Identity Management, pp. 221–236 (2017)

25. Sirur, S., Nurse, J.R., Webb, H.: Are We There Yet? Understanding the challenges faced in complying with the general data protection regulation (GDPR). In: Proceedings of the 2nd International Workshop on Multimedia Privacy and Security (MPS), pp. 88–95 (2018)

26. Spiekermann, S., Grossklags, J., Berendt, B.: E-privacy in 2nd generation e-commerce: privacy preferences versus actual behavior. In: Proceedings of the 3rd ACM Conference on Electronic Commerce (EC), pp. 38–47 (2001)

27. Teixeira, G.A., da Silva, M.M., Pereira, R.: The critical success factors of GDPR implementation: a systematic literature review. Digital Policy, Regul. Gov. **21**(4), 402–418 (2019)

28. Teixeira, G.A., da Silva, M.M., Pereira, R.: The critical success factors of GDPR implementation: a delphi study. In: Proceedings of the 29th International Conference on Information Systems Development (ISD), pp. 1–12 (2021)

29. Teubner, T., Flath, C.: Privacy in the sharing economy. J. Assoc. Inf. Syst. **20**(3), 213–242 (2019)

30. Van Landuyt, D., Sion, L., Dewitte, P., Joosen, W.: The bigger picture. In: Proceedings of the 2nd Workshop on Security, Privacy, Organizations, and Systems Engineering (SPOSE), pp. 283–293 (2020)

31. Yun, H., Lee, G., Kim, D.J.: A chronological review of empirical research on personal information privacy concerns. Inf. Manag. **56**(4), 570–601 (2019)

Rebooting IT Security Awareness – How Organisations Can Encourage and Sustain Secure Behaviours

M. Angela Sasse$^{(\boxtimes)}$, Jonas Hielscher, Jennifer Friedauer,
and Annalina Buckmann

Human Centred Security, Ruhr University Bochum, Bochum, Germany
`Martina.Sasse@ruhr-uni-bochum.de`

Abstract. Most organisations are using online security awareness train-ing and simulated phishing attacks to encourage their employees to behave securely. Buying off-the-shelf training packages and making it mandatory for all employees to complete them is easy, and satisfies most regulatory and audit requirements, but does not lead to secure behaviour becoming a routine. In this paper, we identify the additional steps employees must go through to develop secure routines, and the blockers that stop a new behaviour from becoming a routine. Our key message is: security awareness as we know it is only the first step; organ-isations who want employees have to do more to smooth the path: they have to ensure that secure behaviour is feasible, and support their staff through the stages of the *Security Behaviour Curve* – concordance, self-efficacy, and embedding – for secure behaviour to become a routine. We provide examples of those organisational activities, and specific recom-mendations to different organisational stakeholders.

Keywords: Security learning curve · Security awareness · Security training · IT-security for IT professionals · Organisational security · Human factors in IT security

1 Introduction

The vast majority of organisations in advanced economies buy some form of secu-rity awareness or security training for their employees. But despite the ubiquitous use commercial products, of there are doubts whether these are effective. In 2015, the UK Research Institute for Sociotechnical Cyber Security (RISCS) published a report that identified a fundamental problem with existing products: they raise awareness of IT security risks, and explain what employees should do and not do to be secure - but they do not support the adoption of those behaviours in everyday practice [9]. The authors proposed a 6-step process necessary for a secure behaviour to become an embedded routine, and identified a number of measures through which organisations could to support the transition to the secure behaviour at each stage.

S. Katsikas et al. (Eds.): ESORICS 2022 Workshops, LNCS 13785, pp. 248–265, 2023.
https://doi.org/10.1007/978-3-031-25460-4_14

To date, this report had little to no effect in practice – the global business of security awareness/training has grown into an even bigger, multi-billion $ a year industry. Yet, security researchers and practitioners find that employees are not following secure behaviours [2,3,18]. And yet, security and organisational decision-makers keep buying those awareness and training products, compel busy employees to spend time and attention on working through them every year, and somehow expect a different result – bringing to mind Einstein's definition of insanity.

In this paper we present a framework for breaking this cycle by supporting the adoption of secure routines. Beyond explaining security risks telling employees the do's and don'ts of IT security, organisations need to stop the execution of existing insecure behaviours, and embed new secure ones. This requires changes to artifacts and processes that employees deal with in their working environment. Over the past decade, behavioural scientists have been pointing out how environment can help or hinder important behavioural change - most notably. Michie et al.'s Behaviour Change Wheel [23]. Thaler and Sunstein's [30] famous nudge theory showed how policy makes can create choice architectures that encourage behaviour changes that ultimately benefit the individual. Both of these approaches have been enthusiastically seized on by security researchers - see [31] for an overview. Chater and Lowenstein [11], reviewing a broad range of nudge-based interventions come to the sobering conclusion that they have led rarely been successful - because they focused exclusively on trying to persuade individuals to change, while making little to no adjustments to system around them. That is also the case in IT security - an ENISA meta-review [12] of studies trying to link human characteristic or motivational factors to "good" security found no systematic link (except self-efficacy, see Sect. 2.)

In this paper, we bring insights from behaviour change literature together with specific literature on human behaviour in security ([7,19,27,31]), and spell out what organisations need to foster secure behaviours among their employees:

1. **Conduct a feasibility check: The most basic pre-condition is: never ask employees for a security behaviour unless you have checked it is actually possible to do in their work environment.** Employees can only adopt security behaviours that are feasible are in the context of their everyday work tasks. This may sound obvious, but most commercial products deliver general-purpose advice that has never been checked for relevance to, or feasibility in, the organisation. Some packages contain outdated recommendations that - for instance, they recommend long and complex passwords, and regularly changing them, when advice by relevant national authorities (e.g. NCSC) changed over 5 years ago [24]. Simply buying a generic security awareness package or simulated phishing product, just to tick a box saying *"yes, we provide security training"* is a clear sign an organisation did not really engage with security issues and how they might affect their business.

2. **Create secure routines:** Humans are efficient because everyday behaviours are embedded in **routines or habits**. About 80–90% of behaviour at work and in daily life is carried out in this mode. Kahnemann [17] labeled this *fast thinking*, as opposed to the *slow thinking* process we apply to novel and

infrequent tasks. In the latter mode, we apply our full attention to the task, but are considerably less efficient. Switching to the slow mode can occasionally may be viable, but telling employees to switch to the slow lane and ponder security implications of everything they do is not viable in busy production environments.

3. **Protect productivity:** Humans at work are focused on their *primary production tasks* – the security tasks employees have to carry out are *enabling* or *secondary tasks.* Any time spent on secondary tasks comes at the **expense of productivity** – and that includes security awareness, education and training measures. In almost any organisation, there is a limit to how much productivity can be sacrificed for security. Thus IT security measures need to be designed to be efficient in terms of time and attention, and with the participation of employees.

4. **Respect and engage employees:** Traditionally, employees have been cast in a passive compliance role when it comes to security; studies over the past decade have shown that **employee participation and agency** lead to better security behaviour and more effective protection.

Once an organisation has security made feasible, it may still find employees follow a number of insecure routines that need to be decommissioned and/or replaced by new, secure ones [13].

2   Enabling the Acquisition of Secure Behaviours

The *Awareness Maturity Curve* (Fig. 1) was originally developed by Beyer, Dörlemann and colleagues at HP Enterprise [9]. A notional rather than an operational concept, it illustrates that most organisations only provide resources on for motivating and informing employees about IT security behaviours, and then stop - and identifies the additional stages that would be required to embed new secure behaviours. The RISCS White Paper *Awareness is only the first step* [15] presented a further steps that need to be completed to embed *secure behaviour,* and pointed out that organisations did not consider or support these.

In a similar vein, Renaud et al. [28] argue that *usability is not enough,* and present a comprehensible model (Fig. 2) of requirements for the adoption of secure technology (in this case, E2EE).

In 2021 Hielscher et al. [16] presented the first version of the *Security Learning Curve* (Fig. 3) which incorporates recent scientific advances on individual learning and learning in organisations. We argue that those insights provide the "missing links" that organisations need to support to enable the adoption of secure behaviours among their employees. The bad news is that those steps require significantly more effort from organisations than what they do at the moment: buy standard materials from external vendors, deploy in fire-and-forget mode to satisfy regulatory or audit requirements (yes, our employees have been giving "awareness training"), then complain that employees are still not following the rules. The good news is that it is possible to embed secure behaviours and reduce the likelihood of breaches and the resulting cost. Most organisations

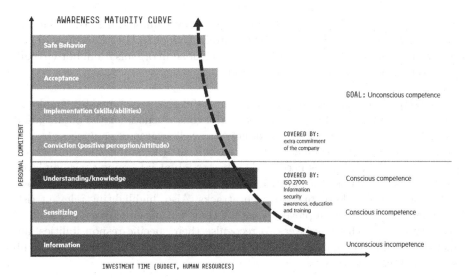

Figure 1: Hewlett Packard Enterprise Awareness Maturity Curve

Fig. 1. The original Awareness Maturity Curve, presented in 2015 [9].

already practice a similar approach to safety since the late 80s, and organisational leaders often quote the phrase *"If you think safety is important, try an accident."* The same goes for IT security: *If you think supporting the embedding of secure routines is expensive, try a security breach.*

The Security Learning Curve consists of 9 stages people pass through to embed a new secure behaviour. Only 4 are covered by present mainstream awareness products – but that does not mean they are effective as mostly in form of standard materials that reflect requirements or recommendations of government agencies (e.g. Cyber Security Essentials in the UK, NIST recommendations in the US) or regulatory bodies (e.g. PCI-DSS for payment processors). Sometimes the awareness materials have been adapted to the risks relevant to the organisation, and/or the language it uses in other communications with employees. Fewer organisations then target the material according to the risks associated to the job role. Only a vanishingly small number of organisations bother to take stock of what individual employees already know and do when it comes to cyber security, and adapt their materials accordingly - thus wasting employees' time and goodwill on repeating what they already know. In this paper, however, we focus on the remaining steps, which are currently not supported. Before examining those steps in detail, it is worth pointing out that whilst the steps mirror a path to embedding behaviour, they do not always have to be completed in this order, but overlap or run in parallel.

As pointed out in Sect. 1, feasibility of the secure behaviour is a necessary pre-condition for its adoption. In the original *Awareness Maturity Curve*, this was mentioned in the text, but not represented in the curve itself - which in hindsight was a mistake. Research has shown that when employees don't follow security policies, it is mostly because either they cannot do it [1], or because doing so would noticeably reduce their productivity [7], [19]. Parkin et al. [25] outlined an approach for tracking security workload in organisation, but virtually none keep track of their employees workload.[1]

Sensitising. This is *security awareness* in its classic sense: making employees aware of threats, and the risks and potential consequences for the organisation. Whilst many security awareness products - as well awareness campaigns by governments or law enforcement -explain specific attackers and specific forms of attack, most organisations need to do a better job at informing their employees about the specific risks the company faces, the consequences, and how employee behaviour can enable or prevent such attacks. Also, highlighting relevant risks to different groups of employees - rather than tell all employees about all IT security risks - helps employees to recognise their specific responsibilities, and motivate them to embark on the (always effortful process) of giving up a deeply embedded insecure routine.

Fig. 2. Renaud et al. [28] argue that *usability is not enough* and present a model that shows additionally required steps.

Information. Once awareness of the risk has been raised, organisations need to specify the secure behaviour employees must follow to avoid/manage the risk *after*.

Understanding. There can also be benefits providing some background knowledge beyond the secure behaviour - for instance, explaining connections between risks. Systematically building up an understanding of threats and risks beyond

---

[1] Note that in the *Awareness Maturity Curve Information* comes before *Sensitising*. In the SLC we change the order as sensitising is a necessary pre-condition for rendering people amenable to change - and that is almost always by providing information about threats and consequences.

specific secure routines helps to build a broader understanding, and can enable employees to respond to novel, "not-yet trained for" risks.

Traditional approaches to security awareness, education and training stop here – they expect that once employees have understood the risks and know what to do to avoid them, they will change behaviour. But we know from research in behaviour change that good intentions are not enough. For a new behaviour to "stick", it has to be repeated over a period of roughly 28 days to become routine. The following 5 steps are elements that need to be in place to complete the *Security Learning Curve*:

Agree to changing behaviour: Concordance. There is a difference between employees agreeing that a secure behaviour is a "probably good idea", and actively making an effort to adopt it. Secure behaviour is currently mandated by security experts, and employees are expected to *"just do it."*. But change requires effort, people have many demands on time, and - if the behaviour has been mandated without consultation - many possible excuses for not even trying. The problem is illustrated by one of the classic lightbulb jokes *Question: "How many psychiatrists does it take to change a lightbulb?" Answer: "Only one – but the lightbulb really has to want to change."*[2]

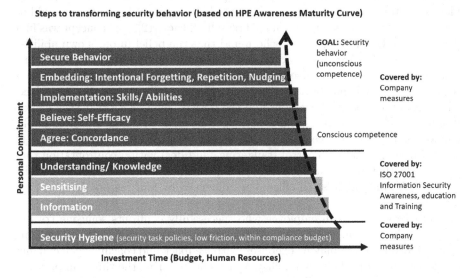

Fig. 3. The new *Security Learning Curve*, presented in 2021 by Hielscher et al. [16] that we extensively discuss in this paper.

The psychiatrist-lightbulb joke neatly conveys the central tenet of successful behaviour change: it requires positive intention and commitment from the

---

[2] In some organisations and under some circumstances it is possible to impose behaviours, but it is expensive because it requires constant monitoring and willingness to impose sanctions – such as firing employees who do not comply.

individual to make the change. In the medical sector, the approach has been adopted not only in mental health, but medicine taking [21]: *"Concordance is a new approach to the prescribing and taking of medicines. It is an agreement reached after negotiation between a patient and a healthcare professional that respects the beliefs and wishes of the patient in determining whether, when, and how medicines are to be taken."*

Applying the concept to IT security means that there needs to be a stage for employees to explicitly commit adopting the new behaviour. Most employees want to protect their organisations from harm, but they may have questions about the feasibility and effectiveness of the behaviour in the context of their own work-related goals and activities – so their needs to be an opportunity for clarification and negotiation. This means security behaviours cannot be mandated by experts without consultation. Ashenden and Lawrence [4] demonstrated the benefits of security experts explaining and negotiating the secure behaviours they want with employees, and the participatory security design case studies by Lizzie Coles-Kemp and her collaborators have shown [14] such engagement not only helps to get people "on-side", but can lead to security solutions that are more effective and less costly than ones experts had devised themselves.

Believe Behaviour is Possible: Self-efficacy. In a meta-review of studies trying to identify factors that influence cyber security behaviours, only one factor could be consistently linked to security behaviours: self-efficacy [12]. The concept was first described by Bandura et al. [5], who found that the belief in one's own abilities to do something successfully and is positively related to the implementation of a change in behaviour. Conversely, if employees have no confidence in their ability to perform a new behaviour, they are more likely not to try it in the first place. The execution of a new behaviour and the positive experience that they can do it should therefore be an essential part of IT security training. If, for example, employees have experienced in a role play that they can stop someone trying to sneak through an access control (tailgating) and deal with a confrontation that may result, they will be more willing to implement this behaviour in their daily work [6]. An individual's self-efficacy is influenced by four factors [5]:

Mastery Experience. An employee who successfully confronts someone tries to tailgate behind them is an example of positive mastery experience. Practising that behaviour in role-playing exercises, with feedback and coaching, can enhance employees' belief in their own ability. When encountering the threat in practice, they can refer back to similar scenario and recall how they acted. Direct experiences can have both positive and negative effects on self-efficacy expectations. Employees only have positive direct experiences if the action is their own and they consciously make their own decisions in this action. The belief in one's own abilities is thus strengthened by the fact that employees – since they act independently – get the feeling of having control over the situation. In the case of negative direct experiences, the feeling of loss of control and failure arises and employees begin to doubt their abilities. It is therefore important that in the case of negative direct experiences, the other three factors are taken into account so that employees are not left alone with the negative experience.

Vicarious Experience. Vicarious experience means that when employees see, for example, a video of another person mastering a situation, they assess their own abilities similarly. One of the ways employees gain vicarious experience is through everyday encounters. In this context, team members and supervisors function as social role models and, in best case, as positive examples for their own actions. Depending on the degree of self-efficacy already present, it is more likely that views and behaviours gained through vicarious experience will be internalised. Another component that can play a role in vicarious experience is the trust relationship between the employee and the observed person. For example, if a very trusted colleague is observed making a mistake and is sanctioned, this can have a negative impact on the employee's self-efficacy expectation and thus on their future behaviour. Video material and working with personas are also approaches which let employees gain vicarious experiences.

Verbal Persuasion. Verbal persuasion can happen, for example, through feedback processes. If an employee receives positive feedback when completing tasks they will become convinced that they have or can develop the skills needed to complete the task successfully. Whether an employee can be convinced to trust in their own abilities also depends on the hierarchical relationship, but also the relationship of trust, between those who communicate. A hierarchical relationship alone is not enough to convince employees that they are up to the task.

Emotional and Physiological States. Companies should not trigger fear in their employees, but give them the feeling that they can contribute to IT security themselves. But how do conditions arise that inhibit behaviour, such as the fear of behaving incorrectly? Often it is physical reactions (such as stress, tension, heart palpitations) that are triggered by external input, such as instructions, tasks or spontaneous changes. The employee's brain may interpret these physical reactions in such a way that a reaction that is expressed in actual behaviour does not occur. Employees may avoid secure behaviour because they interpret a physical reaction as a warning signal. It is therefore important not to punish employees who are unsure what to do, or panic and make mistakes. Moreover, it is crucial to identify these warning signals and behaviour-inhibiting conditions in time so that insecurity cannot take hold. In practice, however, the opposite is usually observed: fear appeals are widely used in security awareness materials to in the mistaken belief that they motivate employees. But e-mails warning about the latest threats and the consequences of 'misconduct', without taking into account that employees also need to get the feeling that they can successfully protect themselves, can backfire. Direct and indirect threats of sanctions are also common, e.g. by sending individuals or teams to follow-up training or talks with superiors for poor performance in phishing simulations.

Applying the Four Factors to IT Security Behaviours. This approach shows that it is not factors internal to employees, but the context and the situational circumstances they experience that influence whether they try to adopt new secure behaviours. In the tailgating example, avoidance behaviour can have various causes that lead to employees unconsciously deciding against secure behaviour, and not intervening when they see an attack. Low self-efficacy expectations can often be traced back to negative direct experiences or experienced negative consequences through vicarious experiences. Negative feedback or one's own physical reactions to an attack situation can also be the reason.

In an organisational context these four factors are often closely linked: negative direct experiences can cause physical reactions, which in turn can cause negative feedback from the environment (directly from superiors or colleagues, indirectly via communication by e-mail from security staff or customers) - thus reinforcing avoidance behaviour. For a good implementation of IT security measures, it is necessary to strengthen self-efficacy not just in training, but the everyday work environment, by providing positive feedback when they apply the new behaviour, and support and re-assurance if they encounter difficulties (Fig. 4).

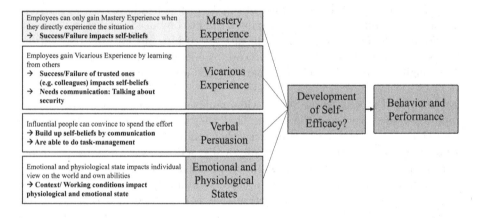

Fig. 4. Four factors influence self-efficacy.

Implementation. Once concordance and self-efficacy have been established, the next step is to embed the behaviour in the context of everyday activities. Key to achieving embedding is that a new secure behaviour cannot be embedded while the "old", insecure behaviour keeps being triggered. Established behaviour are deeply embedding in long-term memory, and triggered by cues, and then executed automatically. Every time this happens, the old behaviour is reinforced and embedded more deeply, making the embedding of the new behaviour impossible. Existing security awareness approaches implicitly suggest that once employees have received information about a secure behaviour, they just have to be motivated enough to change. This is not so: the organisation has to identify and remove the triggers of the "old behaviour from the tools, processes and environment".

Embedding. The new secure behaviour has to be repeated many times to become embedded. With every repetition, we move forward on the path to it becoming automatic, but every time the old, insecure behaviour is carried out, we go 3 steps back. Companies need to take active steps to decommission old behaviours, and remove the cues or triggers for them – a technique called Intentional Forgetting that has been successfully applied in the introduction of new safety procedures. In IT security, the need to *"take out the trash"* – removing obsolete rules and terminology, changing user interface design and processes as well as policies – is currently not understood.

Organisations can use tools to implement intentional forgetting and replace "old" insecure employee behaviours with new secure ones. First and foremost, the cues that trigger insecure behaviour – sensory, routine-related, and space and time-related stimuli – must be identified and removed. Hielscher et al. [16] provide examples of how to enable new secure behaviours by changing names for information objects and processes or re-designing desktop environments (e.g. a changed screen background/logon screen in the home office – a visual cue that is then linked to the need to connect to a VPN). Newly recruited employees can be trained in the secure behaviours, and be briefed to become "agents for change" who remind and support existing employees in their teams with the new behaviour. In organisations that have security champions [8], these can become forgetting agents who identify and eliminate triggers. The example of password managers shows that adoption becomes much easier if other applications and habits are changed at the same time. Therefore, it is recommended to combine the introduction of password managers with other changes in order to establish a link between the use of the password manager and other new cues. Nudges have been used in security to induce security behaviour security, with mixed results [31]. The SLC suggests that nudges will be ineffective if those behaviours are too effortful, or without concordance and self-efficacy being established. Nudging employees towards secure behaviours has been tried in IT security, but has neither long-term success nor is it ethically justifiable [29]. But at the embedding stage, nudges can help to remind employees that they have committed to adopt a new secure routine, and why.

Secure Behaviour. Secure behaviour becomes routine. This is the stage at which the organisation can consider using rewards for those who have managed the transition, and consider sanctions for those who won't. Organisations use psychological contracts to set expectations for employee behaviour in many areas – for instance, that bullying or harassment are unacceptable. Secure behaviours should also be seen as part of organisational citizenship. Embedding the steps of the SLC in an organisational change management process [20] helps to stage the adoption of secure routines and avoid conflicts with other organisational goals. However, due to the constantly changing threat landscape, more than routinely carried out behaviour is needed. Employees need *competence* to deal with unforeseen situations, in which routines are not sufficient, in a secure manner. We expand on this in the following.

3   Beyond Secure Routines: Building Competence for "Security Heroes"

Getting employees to develop secure habits it essential for making security efficient. Telling employees to "take 5" in the name of security every time they carry out a frequent task, such as opening an email, is unrealistic. 80–90% of human behaviour is carried out automatically, and demanding that employees stop this to take conscious cognitive decisions all the time ignores that individual and organisational productivity is built on routine.

Further, we cannot prepare employees for all possible risks – attackers innovate constantly and find new attack vectors. As soon as we have "trained" employees about an attack in an awareness campaign, attackers will have developed another way. As Janet Napolitano famously said, "Show me a 50-foot wall, and I'll show you a 51-foot ladder" (Janet Napolitano).

The true question here is: how can we prepare employees to recognise when a situation is novel or different, when they should switch from the "automatic" mode, examine the situation, and take a conscious decision? The awareness and training we provide to our employees must enable them to develop increasing maturity when it comes to security:

1. **Situational awareness:** Attackers often trigger highly learnt behaviours from employees by making a request look normal. Situational awareness can help employees to cope in new situations, and the decision not to follow established routines – if they feel secure enough to do so.
2. **Training for the things you don't normally do:** In situations of stress and uncertainty, we revert to highly learnt behaviours – this is where "training kicks in". That means that secure behaviours that we don't use all the time but need in emergencies – for instance disconnecting machines – need to be rehearsed. Link to business continuity.
3. **Agency and Active participation** in the development of security measures so they fit into the everyday work tasks and people feel included, strengthening their sense of belonging and shared responsibility.
4. **Strengthening qualities beyond security**, such as social skills, trust and cooperation, so that people feel secure to address errors, irregularities, or insecurities and know where to turn to.

Creating a work environment built on trust and cooperation, supporting employees in developing secure routines, and empowering them to confidently handle unexpected events is essential to make organisations resilient in a constantly changing threat landscape. Doing so will enable employees to become "Security Heroes" [26] in an organisation, instead of unsuccessfully trying to train them to become security xpert "mini-me"s.

However, the process does not stop here.

4   The Need for Evaluation and Continuous Improvement

Most organisations deploy IT security awareness and training in *"fire and forget"* mode - being able to tick the box "yes, we provide security awareness/training" is the only goal. An Information Security Forum (ISF) report in 2014 found that less than half of all member companies that provided security awareness or training did evaluate whether it was effective. Organisations that do evaluation use quantitative measures that are easy to collect. In a more recent survey by Proofpoint 65% of respondents used completion of training as a measure of programme effectiveness, and 55% said they conducted a post-training poll or test.[3] Very few organisations check whether employees actually understood what the correct behaviour was, or whether they adopted it.

Evaluating how effective your awareness and training is, and identifying and improving the elements that are not, should be part and parcel of offering it - after all, security awareness and training that is not effective just wastes employees' time and reduces the organisation's productivity. Second, not collecting and acting on feedback from employees creates the impression among employees that security can't be that important – because if it was, the organisation would want to know.

4.1   "Well - I Wouldn't Start from Here"

If we ask general work-based training specialist what they think of current security awareness materials, they most likely quote the Irishmen asked for directions: *"Well - I wouldn't start from here"* – "here" being putting all employees through the same programme, irrespective of what they already know, or what risk and routines are relevant in their daily work activities.

The correct place knowledge quizzes on IT security is not *after* the training, but *before* employees are given any training at all. Evaluation needs a baseline measurement: find out what your employees already know about security, what they don't know - and then deliver targeted training. An added benefit of such a stock-taking exercise is that employees should be motivated to take securion topics they have been shown they don't know.

4.2   What is Success?

Having first evaluated the current state of security knowledge of employees and adapted the campaign accordingly, we need to ask: what is success? Is it that employees are able to answer questions in a test, however "gamified" and fun, what organisations want?

Only if we have clearly defined the desired outcome, can we develop metrics to measure whether the campaign was successful. As we have argued, it is neither enough to raise awareness nor to develop secure routines among employees, but we need to foster cooperation and resilience in regard to IT security and possible attacks in a continuous process that is never finished. To evaluate this,

---

[3] Information Security Forum (2014) From Promoting Awareness to Embedding Behavior. https://www.prlog.org/12319007-information-security-forum-embedding-positive-information-security-behaviors-in-employees-is-key.html.

an iterative mixed-methods approach is necessary – to evaluate the effectiveness of campaigns and measures in organisations, and to improve said measures perpetually within organisations as well as products by providers.

Simultaneously, the correct implementation of the measures should be evaluated.

In 2019, ENISA [12] proposed a PDCA-style framework[4] (Fig. 5) for designing interventions for human aspects of security that illustrates this process:

Fig. 5. ENISA's [12] PDCA-Framework for designing interventions for human aspects of cyber security.

4.3   How to Evaluate Security Awareness

Previously we discussed that employees should develop routines. Evaluation and continuous improvement of security awareness material and secure routines is important to support the behaviour change and the development of routines and secure behaviour. Implemented solutions to raise employees' security awareness need to be evaluated to see whether there are vulnerabilities in the implementation process or whether there is another solution that might fit more in the given context. Evaluation has the goal to make visible if awareness material or training is effective and if it fits working procedures or if it creates friction.

5   Conclusions and Recommendations

Security awareness and training today is a multi-billion $ industry that promises to fix "weak" employees and turn them into a "human firewall" through online security awareness courses, simulated phishing attacks, nudges and gamification. Employees may or may not learn something from these - we don't know because

---

[4] The Plan-Do-Check-Act Cycle, is an iterative design and management method used in business for the control and continual improvement of processes and products, and is suggested in the ISO 27000 family of standards as a way of monitoring and improving security interventions. It is also known as the *Deming Cycle* after the management scientist W. Edwards Deming, the father to Total Quality Management.

organisations do not conduct meaningful evaluation studies. But research on security behaviour in organisations has consistently shown that the secure behaviour organisations proscribe to their employees is rarely adopted in practice.

The current approach to security awareness and training stops with trying to motivate employees to be secure, and providing them with information in secure behaviour. The evidence from behavioural science, from Fogg [10] to Thaler and Sunstein [30] is very clear: to successfully adopt a new behaviour, it must (a) be easy enough to do perform, and (b) people have to want to change, and (c) the behaviour must be repeated many times until it becomes embedded and automatic. Single interventions - motivating employees with threat stories, or "nudging" them with constant reminders to "be secure" - do not lead to adoption of secure behaviours, nor do they engage employees in security and encourage them to step up and become security heroes when the organisation faces new threats.

IT security, including security awareness, is seen by most decision-makers as a technical problem that can be delegated to IT and security professionals. These experts, in turn, mostly have purely technical backgrounds - and not knowing any better, they try mandate secure behaviours and expect employees to do as they are told. With the introduction of the SLC, we propose rethinking this approach - you can engineer behaviour in organisations to a large extent, but it requires work changing the processes and technology to support the target behaviour. In the following, we summarise key takeaways for different stakeholders in organisations:

5.1   Board Members

1. *"Having a security awareness programme"* is a start, and may in some cases suffice to satisfy external compliance requirements. But to protect your organisation effectively, employees need to **practice secure behaviours**, not just know about them.
2. Buying a standard security awareness package may seem a cost-effective solution. But un-targeted standard packages are not effective in changing behaviours. At worst, they burn staff time and goodwill and create a negative attitude to security. Invest in measures that provide relevant, targeted knowledge and acquisition of secure routines.
3. Most organisations have existing expertise on how to encourage and support correct behaviours: boards should encourage joined-up thinking and collaboration to bring those resources to **building secure routines**.
4. Beware of simple indicators and easy metrics: quantitative indicators such as *training completion rates and percentages of staff (not) clicking on phishing emails* may seem like objective indicators of preparedness and progress. But they are not reliable indicators of whether staff practice secure behaviours on a day-to-day basis, or whether the organisation is secure. Boards need to encourage CISOs to **develop meaningful metrics** linked to key risks, and work on continuous improvement.

5.2 For Executives

1. *Security awareness* cannot fix impossible, time-consuming and cumbersome security measures. Executives need to help CISOs to **create low-friction solutions and integrate security into business processes**.
2. You need to **encourage staff to participate in security**: to ask questions when they don't understand security rules or reasons why they are needed, report errors or rules they cannot follow, and suggest solutions.
3. Executives need to **lead by example** on secure behaviours, and embed the topic in the discourse throughout. Many companies have workplace safety as a standing items in their team meetings, information security needs to be there, too.
4. Executives need to identify and **bring together different skills and capabilities** in the organisation to foster secure behaviour – e.g. corporate communications to devise unambiguous, consistent and positive messaging, human resources to incentivise secure behaviours via organisational citizenship contracts, assessment, and remuneration.

5.3 CISOs

1. *Security awareness* is not a fix for impossible, time-consuming and cumbersome security measures. You need to work with executives and employees to **find low-friction solutions**.
2. When it comes to security awareness, more is not better - less but relevant is. Don't try to turn employees into "mini-me" versions of yourself – focus on **routines they should follow** to do their job securely, and help them acquire those.
3. Changing behaviours is a serious undertaking that requires **long-term planning and resources**. You need support from executives and other organisational functions to transform insecure behaviours into secure routines.
4. To be productive and creative, **staff need to feel secure, connected, and believe in their future** in the organisation. This is why awareness methods that involve attacking staff and sowing distrust are counter-productive.

5.4 Security Specialists

1. You need to **be approachable and helpful**: employees should come to you when cannot follow a security behaviour, or when they have made mistakes.
2. Use **respectful language** – stop using phrases such as *weakest link*, and stop blaming users [22]. Refrain from using overly technical vocabulary and try to find a common language with other employees. Only then can they truly understand – and also pass on information to their colleagues.

5.5   Security Awareness Specialists

1. Your are not a megaphone for blasting out whatever security specialists want to tell employees. Your job is to act as a broker who helps to **identify which groups need what awareness and training, and how best to deliver it** – in the context of non-production demands that employees face.
2. **Constant evaluation** - what works, and what does not - is important. To do that, you need to identify meaningful metrics on whether secure behaviours are being followed, and whether staff are engaging with security - and low-effort ways of collecting those measurements.

Acknowledgements. We would like to thank the anonymous reviewers for their helpful suggestions for improving the our exposition of the SLC, and Prof. Simon Parkin (TU Delft) and Ceri Goncalves Jones (Lego Group) for their comments and suggestions on several earlier drafts. The work was supported by the PhD School "SecHuman - Security for Humans in Cyberspace" by the federal state of NRW, Germany and (partly) also by the Deutsche Forschungsgemeinschaft (DFG, German Research Foundation) under Germany's Excellence Strategy - EXC 2092 CASA - 390781972.

References

1. Adams, A., Sasse, M.A.: Users are not the enemy. Commun. ACM **42**(12), 40–46 (1999). https://doi.org/10.1145/322796.322806
2. Alshaikh, M.: Developing cybersecurity culture to influence employee behavior: a practice perspective. Comput. Secur. **98**(November 2020) (2020)
3. Alshaikh, M., Naseer, H., Ahmad, A., Maynard, S.B.: Toward sustainable behaviour change: an approach for cyber security education training and awareness. In: Proceedings of the 27th European Conference on Information Systems (ECIS). ECIS, Stockholm & Uppsala, Sweden (2019)
4. Ashenden, D., Lawrence, D.: Security dialogues: building better relationships between security and business. IEEE Secur. Privacy **14**(3), 82–87 (2016). https://doi.org/10.1109/MSP.2016.57
5. Bandura, A., Adams, N.E.: Analysis of self-efficacy theory of behavioral change. Cogn. Ther. Res. **1**(4), 287–310 (1977)
6. Beautement, A., Becker, I., Parkin, S., Krol, K., Sasse, A.: Productive security: a scalable methodology for analysing employee security behaviours. In: Proceedings of SOUPS 2016, Twelfth Symposium on Usable Privacy and Security, pp. 253–270. USENIX Association, Berkeley (2016). https://www.usenix.org/system/files/conference/soups2016/soups2016-paper-beautement.pdf
7. Beautement, A., Sasse, M.A., Wonham, M.: The compliance budget: managing security behaviour in organisations. In: Proceedings of the 2008 New Security Paradigms Workshop, pp. 47–58 (2008)
8. Becker, I., Parkin, S., Sasse, M.A.: Finding security champions in blends of organisational culture. In: Acar, Y., Fahl, S. (eds.) Proceedings 2nd European Workshop on Usable Security. Internet Society, Reston (2017). https://doi.org/10.14722/eurousec.2017.23007
9. Beyer, M., et al.: HP enterprise - awareness is only the first step: a framework for progressive engagement of staff in cyber security (2015). https://www.riscs.org.uk/wp-content/uploads/2015/12/Awareness-is-Only-the-First-Step.pdf

10. Fogg, B.J.: Tiny Habits: The Small Changes that Change Everything. Houghton Mifflin Harcourt (2019)
11. Chater, N., Loewenstein, G.: The i-Frame and the s-Frame: how focusing on individual-level solutions has led behavioral public policy astray (2022). https://ssrn.com/abstract=4046264
12. ENISA-European Union Agency for Network and Information Security: Cybersecurity Culture Guidelines: Behavioural Aspects of Cybersecurity (2019). https://www.enisa.europa.eu/publications/cybersecurity-culture-guidelines-behavioural-aspects-of-cybersecurity
13. Heath, C., Heath, D.: Switch: How to Change Things When Change is Hard, 1st. edn. Broadway Books, New York (2010)
14. Heath, C.P., Hall, P.A., Coles-Kemp, L.: Holding on to dissensus: participatory interactions in security design. Strateg. Des. Res. J. **11**(2), 65–78 (2018)
15. Hewlett Packard: Awareness is only the first step: new white paper from RISCs, HPE and NCSC urges organisations to engage employees in order to improve cyber security
16. Hielscher, J., Kluge, A., Menges, U., Sasse, M.A.: "Taking out the Trash": why security behavior change requires intentional forgetting. In: New Security Paradigms Workshop, pp. 108–122. ACM, New York (2021). https://doi.org/10.1145/3498891.3498902
17. Kahneman, D.: Thinking, Fast and Slow. Macmillan, New York (2011)
18. KasperskyDaily: The Human Factor in IT Security: How Employees are Making Businesses Vulnerable from Within (2017). https://www.kaspersky.com/blog/the-human-factor-in-it-security/
19. Kirlappos, I., Parkin, S., Sasse, M.A.: "shadow security" as a tool for the learning organization. ACM SIGCAS Comput. Soc. **45**(1), 29–37 (2015)
20. Kotter, J.P.: Leading Change: Wie Sie Ihr Unternehmen in acht Schritten erfolgreich verändern. Verlag Franz Vahlen, München (2011)
21. Marinker, M., et al.: From compliance to concordance: achieving shared goals in medicine taking. Royal Pharmaceutical Society, in partnership with Merck Sharp & Dohme (1997)
22. Menges, U., Hielscher, J., Buckmann, A., Kluge, A., Sasse, M.A., Verret, I.: Why IT security needs therapy. In: Computer Security. ESORICS 2021 International Workshops (2022). https://doi.org/10.1007/978-3-030-95484-0
23. Michie, S., van Stralen, M., West, R.: The behaviour change wheel: a new method for characterising and designing behaviour change interventions. Implement. Sci. **6**(42) (2011)
24. National Cyber Security Center: Password administration for system owners. https://www.ncsc.gov.uk/collection/passwords/updating-your-approach
25. Parkin, S., van Moorsel, A., Inglesant, P., Sasse, M.A.: A stealth approach to usable security: helping it security managers to identify workable security solutions. In: Proceedings of the 2010 New Security Paradigms Workshop. NSPW 2010, pp. 33–50. Association for Computing Machinery, New York (2010). https://doi.org/10.1145/1900546.1900553
26. Pfleeger, S.L., Sasse, M.A., Furnham, A.: From weakest link to security hero: transforming staff security behavior. J. Homel. Secur. Emerg. Manag. **11**(4), 489–510 (2014)
27. Reeder, R.W., Ion, I., Consolvo, S.: 152 simple steps to stay safe online: security advice for non-tech-savvy users, vol. 15, pp. 55–64. IEE (2017)

28. Renaud, K., Volkamer, M., Renkema-Padmos, A.: Why doesn't Jane protect her privacy? In: De Cristofaro, E., Murdoch, S.J. (eds.) PETS 2014. LNCS, vol. 8555, pp. 244–262. Springer, Cham (2014). https://doi.org/10.1007/978-3-319-08506-7_13

29. Renaud, K., Zimmermann, V.: Ethical guidelines for nudging in information security & privacy. Int. J. Hum. Comput. Stud. **120**, 22–35 (2018). https://doi.org/10.1016/j.ijhcs.2018.05.011

30. Thaler, R.H., Sunstein, C.R.: Nudge. The Final Edition, [Revised edition, 2021] edn. Penguin Books, Yale University Press (2021)

31. Zimmermann, V., Renaud, K.: The nudge puzzle: matching nudge interventions to cybersecurity decisions. ACM Trans. Comput.-Hum. Interact. **28**(1), 7:1–7:45 (2021). https://doi.org/10.1145/3429888

3rd Cyber-Physical Security for Critical Infrastructures Protection (CPS4CIP 2022)

Preface

CPS4CIP 2022 is a forum for researchers and practitioners working on cyber-physical security for critical infrastructures protection that supports finance, energy, health, air transport, communication, gas, and water. The secure operation of critical infrastructures is essential to the security of nations and, in an increasingly interconnected world, of unions of states sharing their infrastructures to develop their economies, and to public health and safety. Security incidents in critical infrastructures can directly lead to a violation of users' safety and privacy, physical damage, interference in the political and social life of citizens, significant economic impact on individuals and companies, and threats to human life while decreasing trust in institutions and questioning their social value. Because of the increasing interconnection between the digital and physical worlds, these infrastructures and services are more critical, sophisticated, and interdependent than ever before. The increased complexity makes each infrastructure increasingly vulnerable to attacks, as confirmed by the steady rise of cyber-security incidents, such as phishing or ransomware, and cyber-physical incidents, such as physical violation of devices or facilities in conjunction with malicious cyber activities. To make the situation even worse, interdependency may give rise to a domino effect with catastrophic consequences on multiple infrastructures.

To address these challenges, the workshop aimed to bring together security researchers and practitioners from the various verticals of critical infrastructures (such as the financial, energy, health, air transport, communication, gas, and water domains) and rethink cyber-physical security in the light of the latest technological developments (e.g., Cloud Computing, Blockchain, Big Data, AI, Internet-of-Things) by developing novel and effective approaches to increase the resilience of critical infrastructures and the related ecosystems of services.

The workshop attracted the attention of the critical infrastructures protection research communities and stimulated new insights and advances with particular attention to the integrated cyber and physical aspects of security in critical infrastructures. The 3rd International Workshop on Cyber-Physical Security for Critical Infrastructures Protection (CPS4CIP 2022) was held online. The workshop was organized in conjunction with the 27th European Symposium on Research in Computer Security (ESORICS 2022), Copenhagen, Denmark, September 26–30, 2022. The format of the workshop included two keynotes and technical presentations. The workshop was attended by around 28 people on average.

The workshop received 20 submissions, of which one was withdrawn and 19 were sent for reviews, from authors in 7 distinct countries. After a thorough peer-review process, 10 papers were selected for presentation at the workshop. The review process focused on the quality of the papers, their scientific novelty, and their applicability to the protection of critical financial infrastructure and services, and the acceptance rate was 53%. The accepted articles represent an interesting mix of techniques for resilience, cyber-physical threats, risk assessment and emergency response, secure communications, honeypot management, reverse engineering, hardware tracing, cyber-physical systems security, standards, and ICS Datasets.

The workshop was supported by projects of the ECSCI (European Cluster for Securing Critical Infrastructures) cluster (https://www.finsec-project.eu/ecsci), mainly FIN-SEC (www.finsec-project.eu), ANASTACIA (www.anastacia-h2020.eu/), CyberSANE (https://www.cybersane-project.eu/), CyberSEAS (https://cyberseas.eu/), DEFENDER (https://defender-project.eu/), EnergyShield (https://energy-shield.eu/), ENSURESEC (http://www.ensuresec.eu/), EU-HYBNET (https://euhybnet.eu/), FeatureCloud (https://featurecloud.eu/), IMPETUS (https://www.impetus-project.eu/), InfraStress (www.infrastress.eu/), PHOENIX (https://phoenix-h2020.eu/), PRAETORIAN (https://praetorian-h2020.eu/), PRECINCT (https://www.precinct.info/), RESISTO (www.resistoproject.eu/), SAFECARE (www.safecare-project.eu/), SATIE (http://satie-h2020.eu), SAFETY4RAILS (https://safety4rails.eu/), SealedGRID (https://www.sgrid.eu/), SecureGas (www.securegas-project.eu/), SmartResilience (http://www.smartresilience.eu-vri.eu/), SOTER (https://soterproject.eu/), SPHINX (sphinxproject.eu/), and STOP-IT (stop-it-project.eu/), and 7SHIELD (https://www.7shield.eu). The workshop was also supported by two national projects, NORCICS (https://www.ntnu.edu/norcics) and RESTABILISE4.0 (http://www.restabilise4-0.it/). The organizers would like to thank these projects for supporting the CPS4CIP 2022 workshop.

Finally, the organizers of the CPS4CIP 2022 workshop would like to thank the CPS4CIP 2022 Program Committee, whose members made the workshop possible with their rigorous and timely review process. We would also like to thank the DTU Technical University of Denmark for hosting the workshop and the ESORICS 2022 workshop chairs for valuable help and support.

September 2022

Habtamu Abie
Silvio Ranise
Luca Verderame
Enrico Cambiaso
Rita Ugarelli
Isabel Praça

Organization

General Chairs

Habtamu Abie — Norwegian Computing Center, Norway

Silvio Ranise — University of Trento and Fondazione Bruno Kessler (FBK), Italy

Program Committee Chairs

Luca Verderame — University of Genoa, Italy

Enrico Cambiaso — National Research Council (CNR), Italy

Rita Ugarelli — SINTEF, Norway

Isabel Praça — GECAD/ISEP, Portugal

Program Committee

Dieter Gollmann — Hamburg University of Technology, Germany

Sokratis Katsikas — Norwegian University of Science and Technology, Norway

Fabio Martinelli — IIT-CNR, Italy

Einar Arthur Snekkenes — Norwegian University of Science and Technology, Norway

Omri Soceanu — IBM Research, Israel

Stamatis Karnouskos — SAP Research, Germany

Reijo Savola — VTT Technical Research Centre of Finland, Finland

Alessandro Armando — University of Genoa, Italy

Federica Battisti — University of Padua, Italy

Alessio Merlo — University of Genoa, Italy

Cristina Alcaraz — University of Malaga, Spain

Giovanni Livraga — University of Milan, Italy

Gustavo Gonzalez-Granadillo — Atos Spain, Spain

Shouhuai Xu — University of Texas at San Antonio, USA

Christos Xenakis — University of Piraeus, Greece

Mauro Conti — University of Padua, Italy

Denis Čaleta — Institute for Corporate Security Studies, Slovenia

Dušan Gabrielčič — Institute Jožef Stefan, Slovenia

Nikolaus Wirtz — RWTH Aachen University, Germany

Towards Reverse Engineering
of Industrial Physical Processes

Mariano Ceccato[✉], Youssef Driouich, Ruggero Lanotte, Marco Lucchese,
and Massimo Merro

Università dell'Insubria, Como, Italy
massimo.merro@univr.it

Abstract. The growing connectivity of Industrial Control Systems
(ICSs) in the era of Industry 4.0 has triggered a dramatic increase in
the number of *cyber-physical attacks*, i.e., security breaches in cyberspace
that adversely alter the physical processes (see, e.g., the Stuxnet worm).
   The main challenge attackers face in the development of cyber-
physical attacks is obtaining an adequate level of process comprehension. Process comprehension is defined as "the understanding of system
characteristics and components responsible for the safe delivery of service" (Green et al. 2017). While there exist a number of tools (Nmap,
PLCScan, Xprobe, etc.) one can use to develop a level of process comprehension through the targeting of controllers alone, they are limited
by functionality, scope, and detectability. Thus, to support the execution
of realistic cyber-physical attack scenario with adequate level of physical
process comprehension, we propose a black-box dynamic analysis reverse
engineering tool to derive from scans of memory registers of exposed controllers an approximated model of the controlled physical process. Such
an approximated model is developed by inferring statistical properties,
business processes and, in particular, system invariants whose knowledge
might be crucial to build up stealthy (i.e., undetectable) attacks. We test
the proposed methodology on a non-trivial case study, taken from the
context of industrial water treatment systems.

Keywords: Industrial process · Reverse engineering · Business
process · Invariants

1 Introduction

Industrial Control Systems (ICSs) are physical and engineered systems whose
operations are monitored, coordinated, controlled, and integrated by a computing and communication core [21,30]. They represent the backbone of *Critical
Infrastructures* for safety-critical applications such as electric power distribution,
nuclear power production, and water supply.

Research partially supported by the project "Dipartimenti di Eccellenza 2018–2022",
funded by the Italian Ministry of Universities and Research (MUR).

As industrial organizations are increasingly connecting their operational (OT) network with the corporate network to improve business and operational efficiency, ICSs are more and more exposed to sophisticated cyber attacks. Indeed, in the last years, several *cyber-physical attacks* [13,20,23] have targeted ICSs to take control of national critical infrastructures. Some notorious examples are: (i) the *STUXnet* worm, which reprogrammed Siemens PLCs of nuclear centrifuges in the nuclear facility of Natanz in Iran [10]; (ii) the *CRASHOVERRIDE* attack on the Ukrainian power grid, otherwise known as Industroyer [31]; (iii) the recent attack to a water treatment plant of Oldsmar, Florida, where hackers boosted the level of sodium hydroxide to 100 times higher than normal [3].

Due to the increasing number of reported cyber-physical attacks, much research work has been done to develop *intrusion detection mechanisms* (IDS) to improve the resilience of ICSs to such attacks. Standard intrusion detection techniques for ICSs rely on state estimations for detecting process anomalies (see, for instance, [14,18,32]). An anomaly is observed if the residual error exceeds a predefined threshold. However, since there exist various sources of noise in industrial processes, a fixed threshold between normal and abnormal sensor measurements is normally hard to find.

A more efficient approach is the *invariant rule-based method* [5,6]. Invariant rule-based methods make use of physical conditions that are known a-priori and that must hold for all ICS states. Any observed physical process values that break these rules are classified as anomalies. Typically, these invariant rules are defined by system engineers during the design of an ICS. However, this manual process is not only costly but also error-prone [7]. Thus, new frameworks have been recently designed to systematically generate invariant rules from information contained within ICS operational data logs [11]. Here, it is important to notice a couple of important points: i) the invariants are generated under strict control of system engineers by relying on the full knowledge of the system (sensors, actuator, communication network, etc.); ii) the invariants implemented and checked by the IDS are chosen by system engineers between a (possibly quite) large set of invariants to focus the detection on significant anomalies which are considered potential signals of malicious activities. Invariant-based IDSs can be found in recent versions of *Secure Water Treatment system* (SWaT) [25] at the center of a series of annual cyber-physical defense exercises, referred to as Critical Infrastructure Security Showdowns (CISS) [12].

In this paper, we take a different perspective: the attacker's perspective. As argued in depth by Green et al. [16,17], in order to support the execution of realistic cyber-physical attack scenarios the attacker requires an adequate level of *physical process comprehension*, including: operational field (e.g., water distribution rather than power generation), controllers (e.g., PLC, RTU, etc.) and their network topology, relevant measurements in the plant (e.g., pressure, temperature, etc.), exposed physical devices, such as sensors and actuators which may be targeted by attackers' manipulations, etc. Last but not least, in order to bypass invariant-based IDSs, it would be important for the attacker to have an approximated knowledge of the physical invariants of the system.

In this respect, we propose a prototype reverse engineering tool based on a black-box dynamic analysis to derive an approximated model of the controlled physical process from scans of memory registers of the associated controllers. Such an approximated model is derived by adapting well-known reverse engineering techniques to infer statistical properties, business processes, and state invariants from data logs capturing the state of controller registers at discrete time steps, during a period of normal operation of the target ICS. In order to show strengths and limitations of our analysis we apply our methodology to a non-trivial case study, inspired by Lanotte et al. [22], and consisting of a network of three PLCs to control (a simplified version of) the iTrust *Secure Water Treatment system* (SWaT) [25].

Outline. In Sect. 2, we provide an overview of PLCs and the Modbus communication protocol. In Sect. 3, we describe our black-box dynamic analysis for water-tank systems. In Sect. 4, we define a non-trivial running example. In Sect. 5, we apply our black-box analysis to the running example of Sect. 4. Section 6 draws general guidelines to apply our methodology to reverse engineer other industrial processes, and discuss related and future work.

2   Background

We give some background on *Programmable Logic Controllers* (PLCs), used to control industrial processes, and *Modbus*, a widely diffused ICS network protocol.

Programmable Logic Controllers. They are defined by the IEC 61131 standard [4] as "a digitally operating electronic system, designed for use in an industrial environment". The standard also states that a PLC has a *programmable memory* for the internal storage of user-oriented programs and a *temporary memory* to store the program's data during execution. PLCs have a simple ad-hoc architecture based on a central processing module (CPU) and further modules supporting physical inputs and outputs. The CPU executes the operating system of the PLC and runs a logic program defined by the user, called *user program*. Additionally the CPU is responsible for the communication with additional devices and manages the *process image*, i.e., a set of memory registers where all inputs (sensor measurements) and outputs (actuator commands) are copied. The user program operates on the process image rather than on the physical inputs and outputs, and runs in *scan cycles*. Each scan cycle consists of three phases: (i) reading inputs from the process image; (ii) execution of the controller code to compute how the physical process should evolve; (iii) writing outputs in the process image to govern the physical process as desired. The process image is refreshed by the CPU at the beginning and the end of each cycle, in particular, current physical inputs are copied in the process image and outputs are copied to the physical outputs, respectively.

The Modbus Protocol. Modbus [26] is the first and most used internal point-to-point communication protocol between PLCs, and between PLCs and HMI interfaces. Modbus TCP basically embeds a Modbus frame into a TCP frame [26]. TCP/IP masters and slaves listen and receive Modbus data via port 502. Modbus communications are of two types: (a) query/response (communications between a master and a slave), or (b) broadcast (a master sends a command to all the slaves). A Modbus transaction comprises a single query or response frame, or a single broadcast frame. A Modbus frame message contains the address of the intended receiver, the command the receiver must execute and the data needed to execute the command.

Modbus maps the temporary memory of a PLC program to four different kinds of registers: (i) *discrete output coils*; (ii) *discrete input contacts*; (iii) *analog input registers*; (iv) *analog output holding registers*; the latter registers are also used as *general memory registers* of different sizes (16–32–64 bits). The commands used to manipulate these registers are called *function codes* and they can be found within a Modbus frame. The function codes allow for *reading* coils (FC01), discrete inputs (FC02), multiple holding registers (FC03), input registers (FC04), and for *writing* single coils (FC05), single holding registers (FC06), multiple coils (FC15), multiple holding registers (FC16). Last but not least, the Modbus protocol does not have security features, meaning that an attacker could forge, drop or modify Modbus frames without being noticed.

3   A Black-Box Dynamic Analysis for Water Tank Systems

The *first objective* of our black-box analysis is to associate memory registers of the target PLCs to relevant ICS concepts, such as *measurements, actuator commands, (absolute) setpoints* (i.e., the range of measurements of physical variables), *ICS network communications*, etc. In particular, in our scans we focus on: (1) *discrete input contacts* and *analog input registers*, as they may possibly hold current *measurements* of physical variables; (2) *discrete output coils* and *analog output holding registers*, as they may possibly hold *actuator commands*; (3) *analog output holding registers*, when containing constant data such absolute setpoints; (4) *analog output holding registers*, when containing mutable data such as *Modbus-based messages* between two PLCs or one PLC and the associated HMI. For this purpose, in Sect. 3.1 we develop an ad-hoc scanning tool whose output is then used as input for a *graph analysis*, the first step of our black-box analysis.

The *second objective* of our analysis is to put in relation the runtime evolutions of these ICS concepts. At this regards, we go through a *business process analysis* enhanced with a *system-invariant analysis* (resp. Sects. 3.2 and 3.3).

3.1   A Scanning Tool for Graph Analysis of PLC Registers

Our scanning tool returns a dataset of the values associated to the registers of the target PLC, in a given time interval. Our approach was to leverage on the

IP Protocol Scan offered by the Nmap python module [24], to identify the target PLC within a range of IP addresses. Notice that we do not limit ourselves to the scanning of the standard Modbus TCP port 502, as in many ICSs the protocol Modbus runs on different ports (security through obscurity). Once both the IP address of the PLC and the Modbus port are discovered, the capture of registers values will start. We rely on the Ray module [27] to parallelize and distribute the readings of the values of the registers. Our tool reads and saves the values of all PLC registers in a given time frame with a desired time granularity. The data collected in our scans include the following (see, for instance, Listing 1.1): (1) IP addresses of the scanned PLCs, (2) port used by the Modbus protocol, (3) timestamps of the scan, (4) values saved in each PLC register.

Listing 1.1. Registers capture

```
"127.0.0.1/8502/2022-05-03 12_10_00.591": {
"DiscreteInputRegisters": {"%IX0.0": "0"},
"InputRegisters": {"%IW0": "53"},
"HoldingOutputRegisters": {"%QW0": "0"},
"MemoryRegisters": {"%MW0": "40","%MW1": "80"},
"Coils": {"%QX0.0": "0"}}
```

Our tool offers also the possibility to sniff Modbus network traffic via a MITM attack on the supervisory control network. Raw data collected during this phase are reported below (see, for instance, Listing 1.2): (1) timestamp of the involved Modbus commands, (2) (IP) addresses of communication source and destination PLCs, (3) Modbus function code, e.g., `read coil` or `write single coil`, (4) reference numbers, denoting the registers affected by the command, (5) argument of the function code, e.g., the value to write in a coil, (6) other fields: source/destination port, message length, request frame, etc.

Listing 1.2. Network captures

```
1   Time,Source,Destination,Protocol,Length,Function Code,
        ↪ Destination Port,Source Port,Data,Frame length on the
        ↪ wire,Bit Value,Request Frame,Reference Number,Info
2   2022-05-03 11:43:58.158,IP_PLC1,IP_PLC2,Modbus/TCP,76,Read
        ↪ Coils,46106,502,,76,TRUE,25,,"Response: Trans: 62;
        ↪ Unit: 1, Func: 1: Read Coils"
```

Then, our tool will make a mild *graph analysis*, based on R [2], to interpret data gathered from PLCs scans to possibly uncover patterns and trends. In particular, we first identify registers holding mutable values: this will give us an idea on which registers may contain measurements and/or actuator commands. Then, we use run charts to visualize the runtime evolution of PLC registers: this will allow to identify (relative) setpoints (bounding measurements) and information about the evolution of measurements and/or actuations (e.g., cyclic behaviors).

3.2 Business Process Analysis

The business process analysis is supported by the diagrams computed by DISCO [1], a commercial tool for process mining. Starting from a (set of) event log(s) consisting of the sequences of activities taken by a system, process mining is capable of reconstructing the business process that shows how the process was actually performed. The recovered business process is represented as a directed graph (similar to a UML Activity Diagram), whose nodes represent the activities in the process and edges represent the successor relations between activities.

Data available from PLC memory scanning and Modbus commands captured from the network represent the execution trace of an industrial control system. Business process mining can be run on these data to extract structured knowledge, and build a set of graphical representations that should support human understanding of the underlying industrial process.

In fact, *Modbus commands* capture quite naturally the intuition of a new activity that has just started. In particular, Modbus *write* commands are triggered from some change in the control system (e.g., a command to turn on an actuator that was off), whereas *read* commands are not particularly interesting to us because they are not triggered from changes in the system.

As regards *memory scans*, notice that they provide an instantaneous representations of the PLC memory. Thus, in order to capture new activities we compare the values of registers in two consecutive time instants (depending on the chosen time granularity). For instance, when a *boolean* variable changes value, an auxiliary activity is started with the transition from the old to the new value, whereas when a *numeric* variable changes, an internal flag keeps track of the change direction, which can be either *ascending* or *descending*. Only when the trend changes, e.g., from *ascending* to *descending*, another auxiliary activity is started, with the observed trend change.

The business process computed in this way is a valuable support for the analyst to obtain the overall picture of the OT network of the target ICS. In particular, it allows us to conjecture whether changes in the state of some actuators correspond to a specific trend of the evolution of measurements (such as increasing or decreasing evolution), and vice versa, whether monotone behaviors of the measurements correspond to specific changes in the state of the actuators. Furthermore, the business process allows us to possibly set a causality between Modbus communications and changes in the state of the physical process.

3.3 Invariant Analysis

For the invariant analysis we rely on Daikon [9], a framework allowing the dynamic detection of *linear invariants*, based on a *machine learning* technique that can be applied to arbitrary data. Daikon's invariant detection runs a program (or takes an execution run as input), observes the values that the program computes, and then reports properties holding in the observed executions.

Thus, we feed Daikon with our timestamped dataset of PLC memory scans enriched with a partial bounded history of registers, and informations derived from the previous phases, such as stable states, relative setpoints (in the absence of absolute ones), and slopes of the measured data.

In the following, we give a few examples of what kind of invariants we can derive from our enriched datasets associated to memory registers of single PLCs.

- Check whether some measurement is actually bounded by some (absolute and/or relative) setpoint (both the measurements and the setpoints have been possibly identified in the previous phases);
- Check whether state changes of actuators occur when measurements approach identified setpoints, and vice versa check if when measurements approach setpoints some actuator regularly changes its state;
- Check whether state invariants of some actuators correspond to a specific trend of the evolution of measurements (such as increasing or decreasing evolution), and vice versa, check whether monotone behaviors of the measurements correspond to specific state invariants of certain actuators.

Such invariants would allow the analyst to derive a more precise causality relation between sensor measurements and actuator commands.

Our invariant analysis could be used to derive more complex invariants involving more PLCs at the same time. In general, actuations occurring in one PLC might be related to changes of the measurements of subsystems governed by other PLCs. Furthermore, by looking at more PLCs at the same time, we could find potential communication messages derived from invariants on the states of specific memory registers of communicating PLCs. Of course, as expected, and as pointed out in [7], when considering two or more physical devices at the same time we may easily have a combinatorial explosion of the associated invariants. For this reason, Daikon is able to detect invariants over at most three variables.

4   Running Example

In this section, we describe a running example, implemented by Lanotte et al. [22], consisting of a network of three PLCs to control (a simplified version of) the iTrust *Secure Water Treatment system* (SWaT) [25]. SWaT represents a scaled down version of a real-world industrial water treatment plant. The system consists of six stages, each of which deals with a different treatment, including: chemical dosing, filtration, dechlorination, and reverse osmosis. For simplicity, in our use case, depicted in Fig. 1, we consider only three stages.

In the first stage, raw water is pumped in a 80 gallons tank T-201, via a pump P-101. A *valve* MV-301 connects tank T-201 with a *filtration unit* that releases the treated water in a second tank T-202 (with a capacity of 20 gallons). Here, we assume that the flow of the incoming water in T-201 is greater than the outgoing flow passing through the (motor) valve MV-301. The water in T-202 flows into a *reverse osmosis unit* to reduce inorganic impurities. In the last stage, the water coming from the reverse osmosis unit is either distributed as clean water, if required standards are met, or stored in a backwash tank T-203 and then pumped back, via a pump P-103, to the filtration unit. Here, we assume

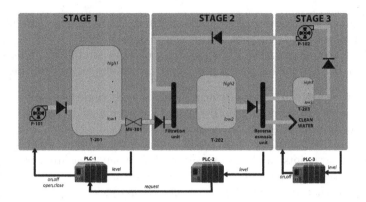

Fig. 1. A simplified industrial water treatment system.

that tank T-202 is large enough to receive the whole content of tank T-203 at any moment (the capacity of T-203 is 1 gallon).

Each tank is controlled by a dedicated PLC. In the following, we give the descriptions of the user programs of the PLCs associated to each tank.

Let us start with the user program of PLC1 managing the tank T-201. Intuitively, when the pump P-101 is off, the level of water in T-201 drops until it reaches its *low setpoint* (hard coded in the memory register) *low*1; when this happens the pump is turned on and it remains so until the tank is refilled, reaching its *high setpoint* (hard-coded in the memory register) *high*1. Thus, for instance, if the pump is off then PLC1 checks the water level of the tank T-201, distinguishing between three possible states. If T-201 reaches its low setpoint *low*1 then the pump is turned on and the valve is closed. Otherwise, if the tank T-201 is at some intermediate level between the low and the high setpoint then PLC1 listens for requests arriving from PLC2 to open/close the valve. Precisely, if PLC1 gets an open request then it opens the valve, letting the water flow from T-201 to T-202, otherwise, if it gets a close request then it closes the valve; in both cases the pump remains off. If the level of the tank T-201 reaches its high setpoint *high*1 then the requests of water coming from PLC2 are served as before, but the pump is eventually turned off.

PLC2 checks for the water level of tank T-202 and behaves accordingly. If the level reaches the low setpoint (hard-coded in the memory register) *low*2 then PLC2 sends a request to PLC1, via a proper Modbus channel to open the valve MV-301 that lets the water flow from T-201 to T-202, and then returns. The channel transmission is implemented by copying a boolean value stored in a memory register of PLC2 into a corresponding register of PLC1. Otherwise, if the level of tank T-202 reaches the high setpoint *high*2 then PLC2 asks PLC1 to close the valve, via the same channel, and then returns. Finally, if the tank T-202 is at some intermediate level between *low*2 and *high*2 then the valve remains open (respectively, closed) when the tank is refilling (respectively, emptying).

Finally, PLC3 checks for the water level of the backwash tank T-203 and behaves accordingly. If the level reaches the low setpoint $low3$ then PLC3 turns off a pump P-103, and then returns. Otherwise, if the level of T-203 reaches the high setpoint $high3$ then the pump P-103 is turned on until the whole content of T-203 is pumped back into the filtration unit of T-202.

5   A Methodology to Extrapolate Process Comprehension

The black-box analysis of Sect. 3 is now applied on the SWaT system presented in Sect. 4, as a concrete case study.

Our methodology supports a top-down understanding process, in which the attacker starts from the big picture of the industrial process, where all the collected data and trends are available at once, and they are computed in an automated way. Based on the analysis results at the higher level of details, the attention gradually moves to a lower and lower level of detail, by specifying where to focus and what part of the system to isolate for further analysis and comprehension. Of course, automated inference can in principle report an overwhelming number of system properties and invariants, and it could be hard to dig into them to identify the most informative ones according to the system under scrutiny. In this respect, a *business process analysis* will be helpful as it allows us to highlight relevant trends and to conjecture interesting properties. Subsequently, an *invariant analysis* will allow us to refine such partial knowledge to confirm or disprove trends and conjectures derived in the business process analysis.

5.1   Data Collection and Graph Analysis

The data collection process has been conducted for six hours, getting one data point per second, as the entire cycle of the system takes around 30 min. Each data point consists of 168 attributes (55 registers plus 1 auxiliary slope attribute for each PLC, explained later).

As IP addresses of PLCs are hard to read, we automatically replace them by abstract names which are arbitrarily computed by concatenating the prefix PLC to a progressive unique integer (e.g., PLC1 and PLC2).

The analysis starts by detecting the type of data contained in registers and whether they are (significant) constant or mutable data.

Property 1.   The registers PLC1_MemoryRegisters_MW0, PLC1_MemoryRegisters_MW1, PLC2_MemoryRegisters_MW0, PLC2_MemoryRegisters_MW1, PLC3_MemoryRegisters_MW0 and PLC3_MemoryRegisters_MW1 contain constant integer values (40, 80, 10, 20, 0 and 10, respectively).

Property 2.   PLC1_Coils_QX00, PLC1_Coils_QX01, PLC1_Coils_QX02, PLC2_Coils_QX00, PLC3_Coils_QX00 and PLC3_Coils_QX01 contain mutable Boolean values.

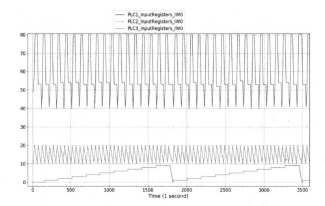

Fig. 2. Sample of the execution traces of the `InputRegisters_IW0` of the three PLCs.

Property 3. The PLC registers `PLC1_InputRegisters_IW0`, `PLC2_InputRegisters_IW0` and `PLC3_InputRegisters_IW0` contain mutable integer values.

Here, the input registers mentioned in Property 3 represent an interesting aspect to investigate further, as they might contain measurements related to the industrial process. Figure 2 shows a trace of their evolution collected during the capture by means of our tool. We can speculate that the trends of these registers are linked to a recurrent cyclic behavior, typical of tank systems.

Conjecture 1. Input registers `PLC1_InputRegisters_IW0`, `PLC2_InputRegisters_IW0` and `PLC3_InputRegisters_IW0` contain measurement values.

Moreover, from Fig. 2 we can identify the range of values for the input registers of the three PLCs.

Conjecture 2 (Relative setpoints).

- The relative setpoints of `PLC1_InputRegisters_IW0` are 40 and 80.
- The relative setpoints of `PLC2_InputRegisters_IW0` are 10 and 20.
- The relative setpoints of `PLC3_InputRegisters_IW0` are 0 and 9.

5.2   Business Process Analysis

We move on to the business process analysis to highlight relevant system behaviors.

Figure 3(a) is automatically computed by business process mining, using data about PLC2 states and Modbus commands. Here, all messages originate from PLC2, and they are all directed to PLC1; the communicated messages are then written in the coils `PLC1_Coils_QX02`.

Property 4. PLC2 sends messages to PLC1 which are recorded in `PLC1_Coils_QX02`.

We also observe that `PLC2_InputRegister_IW0` contains descending values for most of the time (33 s). Then, `PLC2_Coils_QX00` switches to **true** and shortly after (either 1 or 0 s, depending on the path) the input register inverts the trend and starts an ascending trend, that lasts for 13 s. After this interval of time, the coils return to **false** and shortly afterwards (2 s), the input register starts a descending trend.

Conjecture 3. `PLC2_Coils_QX00` determines the trend in tank T-202.

In Fig. 3(a), we can also notice that shortly after a command from PLC2 is sent to PLC1 (to set `PLC1_Coils_QX02` to **false**, but PLC1 is not show in this diagram), `PLC2_InputRegister_IW0` inverts the trend that starts descending. Conversely, shortly after `PLC1_Coils_QX02` moves to true, the input register starts an ascending trend.

We can now analyze the states of PLC1 in Fig. 4. In the bottom-left part of the diagram, we observe that when `PLC1_Coils_QX00` switches to true, an ascending trend in `PLC1_InputRegister_IW0` is started. On the other hand, when `PLC1_Coils_QX00` switches to false, after a while the trend becomes descending.

Conjecture 4. When `PLC1_Coils_QX00` changes its state from false to true, it activates an ascending trend in tank T-201.

In Fig. 3(b), a cyclic behavior is observed on PLC3, and involves two coils. When `PLC3_InputRegister_IW0` starts an ascending trend, `PLC3_Coils_QX02` is immediately set to **false**. Then, after quite a long time (27 min), `PLC3_Coils_QX00` is set to **true**, and shortly after (4 s) the trend in the input register switches to descending for 32 s. Then, almost at the same time `PLC3_Coils_QX00` switches to **false** and coils `PLC3_Coils_QX02` switches to **true**. Then, the trends in the input register are reverted again to restart the cycle.

Conjecture 5. Coils `PLC3_Coils_QX00` activates a decreasing trend in tank T-203, whereas coils `PLC3_Coils_QX02` activates an increasing trend.

5.3 Process Invariants Analysis

In this section, we confirm and refine the results obtained in the previous steps of the analysis looking for system invariants using the Daikon framework.

Setpoints. First of all, we confirm Conjecture 2 on *relative setpoints* of the water levels: six specific memory registers contain constant values coinciding with the lower and the upper relative setpoints of the three tanks. Actually, these memory registers contain the *absolute setpoints*:

```
PLC1_InputRegisters_IW0 >= PLC1_MemoryRegisters_MW0 == 40.0
PLC1_InputRegisters_IW0 <= PLC1_MemoryRegisters_MW1 == 80.0
PLC2_InputRegisters_IW0 >= PLC2_MemoryRegisters_MW0 == 10.0
PLC2_InputRegisters_IW0 <= PLC2_MemoryRegisters_MW1 == 20.0
PLC3_InputRegisters_IW0 >= PLC3_MemoryRegisters_MW0 == 10.0
PLC3_InputRegisters_IW0 <= PLC3_MemoryRegisters_MW1 == 0.0
```

Property 5. The `MemoryRegisters_MW0` and `MemoryRegisters_MW1`, associated to each PLC, contain, respectively, the lower and the upper absolute setpoints.

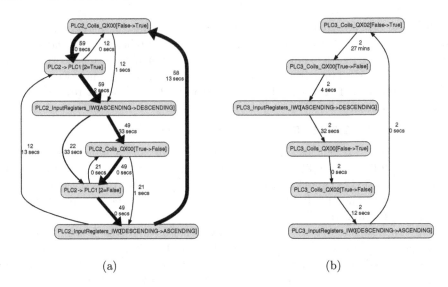

(a)   (b)

Fig. 3. (a) states in PLC2 and Modbus commands, (b) states in PLC3.

Communication Channels. We are in position to validate and refine Property refproperty:bp:channel, stating the presence of a communication channel from PLC2 to PLC1. More precisely, from `PLC1_Coils_QX01` == `PLC1_Coils_QX02` == `PLC2_Coils_QX00` we derive:

Property 6. There is a *communication channel* from PLC2 to PLC1: what it is written in `PLC2_Coils_QX00` is then copied in both registers `PLC1_Coils_QX02` and `PLC1_Coils_QX01`.

Actuator Changes and Levels' Evolution. We use Daikon to investigate the relations between the coils and the measurements.

Let us check what happens when the state of `PLC1_Coils_QX01` changes. In this case, nothing relevant arises from the analysis of PLC3. However, we get significant information from PLC1 and PLC2. As regards PLC2, when the coils `PLC1_Coils_QX01` changes from true to false, the measurements of tank T-202 reach the upper absolute setpoint as the level of water was increasing:

`PLC2_InputRegisters_IW0` == `PLC2_MemoryRegisters_MW2` == 20.0 &&   `PLC2_slope` > 0 .

Moreover, when `PLC1_Coils_QX01` moves from false to true, the measurements of T-202 reach the lower absolute setpoint as the water level was decreasing:

`PLC2_InputRegisters_IW0` == `PLC2_MemoryRegisters_MW1` == 10.0 && `PLC2_slope` < 0 .

Now, let us check what happens when `PLC1_Coils_QX01` remains unchanged for a significant amount of time (say 6 s). In this case, when the coils remains true, the level of water in T-202 increases, as `PLC2_slope` > 0.[1] Whereas

---

[1] The slope is an auxiliary attribute indicating the trend of the measurement.

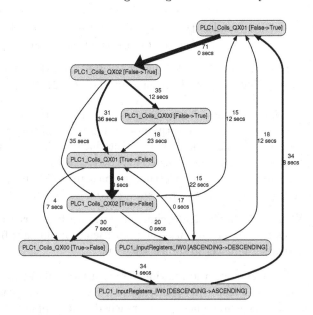

Fig. 4. Business process with states in PLC1 and Modbus commands.

when `PLC1_Coils_QX01` remains false the level of the tank is not increasing, as `PLC2_slope <= 0`. As `PLC2_Coils_QX00` is the only used coils in PLC2, from the equalities `PLC1_Coils_QX01 == PLC1_Coils_QX02 == PLC2_Coils_QX00` we can reformulate Conjecture 3 as follows:

Property 7. The level in T-202 increases iff `PLC1_Coils_QX01 == true`. The level in T-202 is non-increasing iff `PLC1_Coils_QX01 == false`.

However, `PLC1_Coils_QX01` is controlled by PLC1, and by Conjecture 4 we believe that `PLC1_Coils_QX00` determines increasing trends in tank T-201. Thus, let us check what happens when `PLC1_Coils_QX00` and `PLC1_Coils_QX01` are both false, i.e., no incoming water in both tanks T-201 and T-202. In this case, the invariant analysis says that the level in tank T-201 is stable: `PLC1_slope == 0`. On the other hand, when `PLC1_Coils_QX00` is false and `PLC1_Coils_QX01` is true the level in T-201 is decreasing while the level in T-202 is increasing: `PLC1_slope < 0` and `PLC2_slope > 0`. Recall the following invariant: `PLC1_Coils_QX01 == PLC1_Coils_QX02`. Now, we have full knowledge about all coils of PLC1 to refine Conjecture 4 on the trend of the level of water in T-201:

Property 8. The level of water in T-201 increases if and only if `PLC1_Coils_QX00 == true`. The level of water in T-201 decreases if and only if `PLC1_Coils_QX00 == false` and `PLC1_Coils_QX01 == true`.

Let us check what happens when `PLC3_Coils_QX00` remains unchanged for a significant amount of time (say 5 s). In this case, when the coils remains true, the level of water in T-203 decreases, as `PLC3_slope < 0`. Whereas, when

PLC3_Coils_QX00 remains false the level of the tank is not decreasing, as PLC3_slope >= 0. Thus, we are able to confirm the first part of Conjecture 5.

Property 9. The level of water in T-203 decreases iff PLC3_Coils_QX00 == true. The level of water in T-203 is non-decreasing iff PLC3_Coils_QX00 == false.

Actuator Changes and Setpoints. Now, we try to investigate the relation between the coils PLC1_Coils_QX00 and the setpoints in T-201. In particular, when the coils changes from true to false, the measurements have reached the upper absolute setpoint: PLC1_InputRegisters_IW0 == PLC1_MemoryRegisters_MW1 == 80.0. Conversely, when PLC1_Coils_QX00 changes from false to true, the measurements have reached the lower setpoint: PLC1_InputRegisters_IW0 == PLC1_MemoryRegisters_MW0 == 40.0. Formally,

Property 10. When PLC1_Coils_QX00 changes its state from true to false, the tank T-201 reaches the upper absolute set point; when it changes from false to true, the tank reaches the lower absolute set point.

Now, we try to investigate the relation between the coils PLC3_Coils_QX00 and the setpoints in T-203. In particular, when the coils changes from false to true, the measurements have reached the upper absolute setpoint: PLC3_InputRegisters_IW0 == PLC3_MemoryRegisters_MW1 == 10.0. Conversely, when PLC3_Coils_QX00 changes from true to false, the measurements have reached the lower setpoint: PLC3_InputRegisters_IW0 == PLC3_MemoryRegisters_MW0 == 0.0. Formally,

Property 11. When PLC3_Coils_QX00 changes its state from false to true, the tank T-203 reaches the upper absolute set point; when it changes from true to false, the tank reaches the lower absolute set point.

5.4 Discussion

At the end of our black-box analysis, we derived a quite significant comprehension on the industrial process of our case study in Sect. 4. Summarizing, we were able to get the following information:

- which registers contain measurements of the physical process (e.g., the water level) and their operative working ranges (setpoints);
- which registers contain actuator commands (e.g., pumps and valves)
- which conditions trigger changes in actuators (e.g., specific water levels trigger pumps and valves) and vice versa the causal relation between the state of actuators and the governed physical process;
- how PLCs communicate, and how such communications affect the underlying physical process.

On the other hand, there a number of information on the physics that we are not able to derive, such as: (i) sources and sinks of water in the system; (ii) the existence of pipelines between tanks; (iii) which actuators handle incoming or outcomming flows, for instance in Property 8 we cannot derive that PLC1_Coils_QX00 is actually associated to a pump governing the incoming flow in tank T-201.

6   Conclusions, Related and Future Work

From our black-box analysis in the previous section, we can draw *general guidelines* to apply our methodology to reverse engineer other industrial processes.

- *Two phases methodology:* Reverse engineering of an industrial process purely based on register scans and network captures requires first to acquire a general idea of the system. This consists in elaborating conjectures on how the industrial process works and how it is controlled. The subsequent, more formal, analysis is meant to provide support for these conjectures and build factual knowledge on the control system.
- *Correct estimation of sampling frequency:* The attacker should have enough information to understand if she is tackling a *slow* physical process, such as a water-tank system, or a *faster* process, involving, for instance, rotor engines. In fact, the most appropriate frequency to read PLCs register depends on the intrinsic speed of the process, as a too slow sampling rate might miss important events (e.g., the maximum level of water before it starts decreasing) while a too high sampling rate might confuse measurement error and actual trends (e.g., spurious trend inversions). If this information is not available, initial scans should be visualized (such as Fig. 2) to tune sampling rate.
- *Working conditions:* The attacker should start by identifying the nominal working conditions, consisting of the operative ranges of the observed measurements. In fact, the typical responsibility of a control system is to keep the physical system within safe and secure working conditions.
- *Trigger conditions:* These are conditions on the state of physical variables triggering a reaction of the controller via actuator commands to drive the physical system to a desired operational state. Identifying these trigger conditions is the subsequent goal of the attacker.
- *Causal relation between actuator commands and physical evolution:* Once actuator commands are sent by the controller, some changes should be observed in the physical process. Understanding this causal relation would allow the attacker to explain the reaction time of the physical process.
- *Physical meaning for pieces of evidence:* When the analysis is able to deliver a large number of process invariants, the attacker should be able to understand which invariants are relevant in invariant-based IDSs of the target system.

Related Work. Attackers often aim at attacking programs to alter their execution flow, for instance to subvert the outcome of a license check. Studies with professional hackers and practitioners [8] revealed that the actual attack commonly requires a preliminary investigation on the target program. Either static analysis (e.g., decompiling) and dynamic analysis (e.g., debugging) typically support a malicious reverse engineering activity, aiming at understanding the behavior of the target program, to locate interesting assets and to plan an attack strategy.

In the context of industrial control systems, Keliris and Maniatakos [19] proposed a methodology to automate the reverse engineering process of *PLC binaries*. They develop a framework whose modules are instantiated for reversing binaries compiled with CODESYS, a widely used compiler for PLCs.

Identification of hybrid dynamical systems, i.e., the automatization of the mechanistic modeling of hybrid dynamical systems from observed data, has seen a number of results spanning over two decades [29]. More recently, Yuan et al. [34] proposed a general framework for discovering cyber-physical systems directly from data. The framework involves the identification of physical systems together with their dynamics, as well as the inference of transition logics. More precisely, the proposed framework tries to understand the underlying mechanism of cyber-physical systems as well as make predictions concerning their state trajectories based on the discovered models.

Feng et al. [11] have recently designed a framework to systematically generate invariant rules from information contained within ICS operational data logs [11]. Such invariants are then selected by system engineers to generate invariant-based IDSs. Experimental results by the same authors [7,11] show that under the same false positive rate, invariant-based IDS ability to detect anomalies outperforms the residual error-based detection model by a clear margin.

Few works have addressed the need for process comprehension from an attacker's perspective; a critical precondition when seeking to achieve operational impact beyond simple denial-of-service [15,17,33].

Winnicki et al. [33] proposed an alternative approach to discover the dynamic behaviour of a cyber-physical system with *probing*. They slightly perturb the system and observe how the controls react to take the system back to the nominal status. The challenge for the attacker is to alter the system enough to make observable changes, but changes should be small enough to not be revealed as anomalies by potential intrusion detection systems.

Green et al. [17] provided two practical examples based on a Man-In-The-Middle scenario, demonstrating the types of information an attacker would need obtain, collate, and comprehend, in order to begin targeted ICS process manipulation and detection avoidance. The paper provides a step-by-step example of ICS reconnaissance, required for the successful establishment of process comprehension, and execution of network-based and host-based MITM attacks.

More recently, Green et al. [16] proposed the concept of Process Comprehension at a Distance, a novel methodological and automatable approach to the system-agnostic identification of PLC library functions, leading to the targeted exfiltration of operational data, manipulation of control-logic behavior, and establishment of covert command and control channels through unused memory.

Future Work. Our preliminary results pave the way towards novel opportunity of research, meant to deepen the knowledge on how automated reverse engineering might support and facilitate attackers in conducting campaigns against ICSs.

First of all, we are interested in quantifying the gap between the invariants that dynamic analysis can infer (attacker perspective) and the full list of those invariants that can be written by an analyst with the complete knowledge of the industrial system [5,6,11] (defender perspective). This gap might effectively estimate the distance between an invariant-based intrusion detection system and an attacker, to measure the competitive advantage of the defender (if any) and, consequently, the detection potential of an IDS.

Our automatically inferred invariants can be used to understand an ICS and support manual attack to it. However, a second line of research might consist in using these invariants also to (maybe partially) automate an attack that is capable of compromising an industrial process (e.g., to delay the water cleaning process) in a way that does not violate invariants (e.g., with a nominal level decreasing rate), with the final objective to be hard to detect by a defender.

Last but not least, as Daikon [9] detects only linear relations over at most three variables, we plan to investigate other tools, such as DIG [28], to detect nonlinear equalities and inequalities of arbitrary degrees, defined over program variables.

Acknowledgements. We thank the anonymous reviewers for valuable comments.

References

1. Fluxicon disco. https://fluxicon.com/disco/
2. R project for statistical computing (1993). https://www.r-project.org/
3. A Hacker Tried to Poison a Florida City's Water Supply (2021). https://www.wired.com/story/oldsmar-florida-water-utility-hack/. Accessed 14 May 2022
4. 3, I.S.I.: Programmable Controllers - Part 3: Programming Languages, 2nd edn. International Electrotechnical Commission (2003)
5. Adepu, S., Mathur, A.: Using process invariants to detect cyber attacks on a water treatment system. In: Hoepman, J.-H., Katzenbeisser, S. (eds.) SEC 2016. IAICT, vol. 471, pp. 91–104. Springer, Cham (2016). https://doi.org/10.1007/978-3-319-33630-5_7
6. Adepu, S., Mathur, A.: From design to invariants: detecting attacks on cyber physical systems. In: QRS-C, pp. 533–540. IEEE (2017)
7. Adepu, S., Mathur, A.: Distributed attack detection in a water treatment plant: method and case study. IEEE Trans. Depend. Secur. Comput. **18**(1), 86–99 (2021)
8. Ceccato, M., et al.: Understanding the behaviour of hackers while performing attack tasks in a professional setting and in a public challenge. Empir. Softw. Eng. **24**(1), 240–286 (2019)
9. Ernst, M.D., et al.: The Daikon system for dynamic detection of likely invariants. Sci. Comput. Program. **69**(1–3), 35–45 (2007)
10. Falliere, N., Murchu, L., Chien, E.: W32.Stuxnet Dossier (2011)
11. Feng, C., Palleti, V.R., Mathur, A., Chana, D.: A systematic framework to generate invariants for anomaly detection in industrial control systems. In: NDSS. The Internet Society (2019)
12. Furtado, F., Shrivastava, S., Mathur, A., Goh, N.: The design of cyber-physical exercises (CPXs). In: CyCon. IEEE (2022)
13. Giraldo, J., et al.: A survey of physics-based attack detection in cyber-physical systems. ACM Comput. Surv. **51**(4), 76:1–76:36 (2018)
14. Goh, J., Adepu, S., Tan, M., Lee, Z.S.: Anomaly detection in cyber physical systems using recurrent neural networks. In: HASE, pp. 140–145. IEEE Computer Society (2017)
15. Gollmann, D., Gurikov, P., Isakov, A., Krotofil, M., Larsen, J., Winnicki, A.: Cyber-physical systems security: experimental analysis of a vinyl acetate monomer plant. In: CCPS@ASIACCS, pp. 1–12. ACM (2015)

16. Green, B., Derbyshire, R., Krotofil, M., Knowles, W., Prince, D., Suri, N.: PCaaD: towards automated determination and exploitation of industrial systems. Comput. Secur. **110**, 102424 (2021)
17. Green, B., Krotofil, M., Abbasi, A.: On the significance of process comprehension for conducting targeted ICS attacks. In: CPS-SPC@CCS, pp. 57–67. ACM (2017)
18. Hadziosmanovic, D., Sommer, R., Zambon, E., Hartel, P.H.: Through the eye of the PLC: semantic security monitoring for industrial processes. In: ACSAC, pp. 126–135. ACM (2014)
19. Keliris, A., Maniatakos, M.: ICSREF: a framework for automated reverse engineering of industrial control systems binaries. In: NDSS. The Internet Society (2019)
20. Krotofil, M., Gollmann, D.: Industrial control systems security: what is happening? In: INDIN, pp. 670–675. IEEE (2013)
21. Lanotte, R., Merro, M.: A calculus of cyber-physical systems. In: Drewes, F., Martín-Vide, C., Truthe, B. (eds.) LATA 2017. LNCS, vol. 10168, pp. 115–127. Springer, Cham (2017). https://doi.org/10.1007/978-3-319-53733-7_8
22. Lanotte, R., Merro, M., Munteanu, A.: Industrial control systems security via runtime enforcement. ACM TOPS **26**(1), 4:1–4:41 (2023). https://doi.org/10.1145/3546579
23. Lanotte, R., Merro, M., Munteanu, A., Viganò, L.: A formal approach to physics-based attacks in cyber-physical systems. ACM TOPS **23**(1), 3:1–3:41 (2020)
24. Lyon, G.: Nmap (1997). https://nmap.org/
25. Mathur, A.P., Tippenhauer, N.O.: SWaT: a water treatment testbed for research and training on ICS security. In: CySWater@CPSWeek, pp. 31–36. IEEE Computer Society (2016)
26. Modbus, I.: Modbus application protocol specification v1. 1a. North Grafton, Massachusetts (2004). (www.modbus.org/specs.php)
27. Moritz, P., et al.: Ray: a distributed framework for emerging AI applications. In: USENIX, pp. 561–577. USENIX Association (2018)
28. Nguyen, T., Kapur, D., Weimer, W., Forrest, S.: DIG: a dynamic invariant generator for polynomial and array invariants. ACM Trans. Softw. Eng. Methodol. **23**(4), 30:1–30:30 (2014)
29. Paoletti, S., Juloski, A.L., Ferrari-Trecate, G., Vidal, R.: Identification of hybrid systems: a tutorial. Eur. J. Control. **13**(2–3), 242–260 (2007)
30. Rajkumar, R., Lee, I., Sha, L., Stankovic, J.A.: Cyber-physical systems: the next computing revolution. In: DAC, pp. 731–736. ACM (2010)
31. Slowik, J.: Anatomy of an attack: detecting and defeating CRASHOVERRIDE. VB2018, October, pp. 1–23 (2018)
32. Urbina, D.I., et al.: Limiting the impact of stealthy attacks on industrial control systems. In: CCS, pp. 1092–1105. ACM (2016)
33. Winnicki, A., Krotofil, M., Gollmann, D.: Cyber-physical system discovery: reverse engineering physical processes. In: CPSS@ASIACCS, pp. 3–14. ACM (2017)
34. Yuan, Y., et al.: Data driven discovery of cyber physical systems. Nat. Commun. **10**(1), 4894 (2019)

Solutions for Protecting the Space Ground Segments: From Risk Assessment to Emergency Response

Ilias Gkotsis[1](✉) ⓘ, Leonidas Perlepes[1] ⓘ, Aggelos Aggelis[1] ⓘ,
Katerina Valouma[1] ⓘ, Antonis Kostaridis[1] ⓘ, Eftichia Georgiou[2] ⓘ,
Nikolaos Lalazisis[2] ⓘ, and Vasiliki Mantzana[2] ⓘ

[1] Satways Ltd., 15 Meg. Konstantinou str., 14122 Neo Irakleio, Greece
{i.gkotsis,l.perlepes,a.aggelis,k.valouma,
a.kostaridis}@satways.net
[2] Center for Security Studies (KEMEA), P. Kanellopoulou 4, 10177 Athens, Greece
{e.georgiou,n.lalazisis}@kemea-research.gr,
mantzana.vasiliki@gmail.com

Abstract. Space sector is considered to be one of those which are essential to maintain vital economic and social functions. Critical Infrastructures or Critical Entities that belong to these sectors are exposed to a wide range of natural and man-made threats, including natural hazards, terrorist attacks, insider threats, or sabotage, but also to cyber-attacks, which are emerging especially with the use of information related systems, as in the space domain. More specifically, a physical attack on a space ground segment could make the distribution of satellite data problematic, while a cyber-attack attack on its data storage, access and exchange could affect not only the reliability of space data, but also their FAIR standards. The present work will focus on the enhancement of the preparedness and response phases of crisis management, through the use of technological and operational solutions. Thus, three tools namely CIRP-RAT, ENGAGE CSIM and ERPs are presented, including their functionalities and benefits offered to the end-users. The findings and developments presented, are linked with the EU funded project 7SHIELD, which aims to provide the European Ground Segment of Space Systems, with a holistic framework for their cyber–physical protection, enabling them to confront complex cyber and physical threats, by covering all the stages of crisis management, namely pre-crisis, crisis and post-crises.

Keywords: Space Ground Segments · Security · Resilience · Risk assessment · Command and control systems · Emergency response

1 Introduction

The EC 114/2008 directive defines Critical Infrastructure (CI) as the assets, systems, and networks located in the Member States which are essential to maintain the vital economic and social functions such as health, food, transport, energy, information systems, financial services, etc. [1]. By the time of this paper (28 June 2022), the European Parliament and the Council of the EU have reached a political agreement on the Directive for

S. Katsikas et al. (Eds.): ESORICS 2022 Workshops, LNCS 13785, pp. 291–307, 2023.
https://doi.org/10.1007/978-3-031-25460-4_16

the resilience of Critical Entities (CE) [2], which repeals the existing framework for the protection of European CIs and introduces wider obligations across sectors, including that of space. Independent to their definition, CIs or CEs are exposed to various physical threats (i.e. man-made, technological accidents, natural disasters, etc.) and cyber-attacks, which are emerging especially with the increasing use of Information Systems. In the European new security landscape, ground segments increasingly appear as potential "new targets" for "new threats", especially the hybrid ones. A cyber-physical attack on their premises, installations, communication networks etc. would cause a debilitating impact on the public safety and security of European citizens and affect also interconnected CIs. For example, a physical attack on a space ground segment could make the distribution of satellite data problematic, while a cyber-attack on its data storage, access and exchange could affect not only the reliability of space data, but also their FAIR standards: findability, accessibility, interoperability and reusability.

This paper was primarily imposed by the ever-increasing need to support the Space Ground Segments (SGS) managing in a more effective and efficient way the crisis occurring from physical and cyber-physical threats. The present work focuses on the enhancement of the preparedness and response phases of crisis management, to confront such threats (with a focus on the physical threat domain) by providing technological and operational solutions. The findings and developments that are presented, are linked with the 7SHIELD project [3], within the framework of which this research was conducted, which aims to provide the European Ground Segment of Space Systems with a holistic framework for their cyber–physical protection, covering all the stages of crisis management, namely pre-crisis, crisis and post-crisis. In meeting this aim, initially, a background analysis is conducted, focusing on the CIs crisis management process and the best practices on security solutions. Following this, the 7SHIELD project and reference architecture, as a solution to address the security and resilience needs of EU SGS, is presented. In the respect of 7SHIELD, a series of state-of-the-art technological solutions have been used, such as sensors technology, IoT, semantic reasoning, high-level analytics, decision support systems, crisis management and situational awareness focusing on the protection of ground segments of space systems. In this paper, we will focus on three specific components supporting the prevention and response phases of the crisis management process, providing the functionalities and benefits offered to the CIs operators. This paper concludes with the advancements accompanying the adoption of such solutions and the next steps for their implementation, validation and evaluation within 7SHIELD.

2 Background Analysis

In order to ensure the resilience and business continuity of a CI, the following areas of security should be considered: (a) Physical security, which mainly consists of systems for protection management, regime measures and physical surveillance of an infrastructure; (b) Information security, that deals with the provision of protection to information managed within databases and other systems, and processing data through application equipment; (c) Administrative security, ensuring the protection of documents (paper and electronic) during their creation, receipt, processing, sending, storage, etc.; (d) Personnel security, focusing on the minimization of the impact of human error, potential theft, fraud, or misuse of the organization's information resources; (e) Crisis management and planning, dealing with the optimization of the process of dealing with an emergency/situation in the system, while maintaining the basic functions of the selected area and their recovery [4]. Even though several measures are taken by the CI operators, no one can completely eliminate the respective threats and minimize the attacks targeting these infrastructures. To manage such attacks, specific management process (area (e) above), supported by several security tools and solutions that cover the areas (a) to (d) above. Nonetheless, one of the main problems that still occurs, is that of lack of integrity and of a holistic approach covering horizontal the crisis management phases. In these lines, the crisis management process, as followed by a CI (such as a SGS) before, when and after an event occurs, as well as technical solutions and means that support these safety and security processes, are described.

2.1 Critical Infrastructures Crisis Management Process

The management of a crisis does not start when the crisis occurs. The planning and coordination for response to any type of incident must be performed well in advance of an actual event. Crisis management has been defined as "the developed capability of an organization to prepare for, anticipate, respond to and recover from crises" [5]. The full cycle of crisis management consists of four phases: Preparedness, Response, Recovery, and Mitigation, as described below [6]:

(a) **Preparedness:** The aim of this phase is to prepare CIs and develop general capabilities that will enable them to deliver an appropriate response in any crisis. It is a continuous cycle of planning, organizing, training, equipping, exercising, evaluating, and taking corrective actions that internal and external stakeholders should follow closely to ensure readiness. To improve the efficiency of the CI the appropriate tools (e.g. contacts, hardware and software tools, training material/tools and exercises, etc.) must be in place.

(b) **Response:** Response begins as soon as an event is detected by an internal or external stakeholder in a manual or automated way (e.g. monitoring networks and early-warning systems, public authorities, citizens, etc.). Depending on the type of the incident (cyber and/or physical), the relevant information gets collected. Then, the crisis gets assessed, the situation is evaluated, and the relative response plan(s) are identified and activated. Emergency response is the planning and activity associated with detecting, containing, and dealing with the immediate impact of an event (i.e., putting out the fire in a fire event or shutting down the network in a cyber event). Based on the activated plans, response processes are executed and coordinated. These steps could be repeated, until processes and assets return to business as usual or to an accepted status (demobilization) and the crisis is terminated and communicated.

(c) **Recovery:** When a crisis occurs, CIs must be able to carry on with their tasks in the midst of the crisis while simultaneously planning for how they will recover from the damage caused. Steps to return to normal operations and limit damage to organization and stakeholders continue after the crisis. CIs should decide the recovery actions to be taken (based on recovery plans), by cooperating closely with internal and external stakeholders. Thereafter, evidence from the incident should be collected and analysed and an evidence report should be created. As the crisis serves as a major learning opportunity, stakeholders should review the overall process, plans, procedures, tools etc., and identify areas for improvement. Following the evaluation, lessons learnt should be identified and recommendations/revisions should be made.

(d) **Mitigation:** Mitigation refers to the process of reducing or eliminating future loss of life and property and injuries resulting from hazards through short and long-term activities. Mitigation strategies may range in scope and size.

Within these phases, several internal and external stakeholders are involved, having different needs, trying to cooperate, respond and recover from the crisis.

2.2 Best Practices and Solutions for the Crisis Management Process in CIs

In the past decade, the security landscape has dramatically changed with the introduction of several new security technologies to deter, detect, and react to more disparate attacks. CIs are constantly introducing new technologies and upgrading existing ones to ensure the security of their most valuable assets such as people, infrastructure, and property [4, 7, 8]. Common systems or measures that are used to protect (preparedness phase) and sometimes detect (triggering point of response phase) a physical threat, include among others the following: (a) Perimeter protection (e.g. fences, walls etc.), (b) Guards, (c) Building management, (d) Intrusion detection and access control, (e) Video surveillance (including video analytics), (f) Audio surveillance, (g) Chemical, Biological, Radiological, Nuclear, explosives (CBRNe) sensors, (h) Physical Security Information Management (PSIM) systems, (i) Fire detection and alarm system, (j) UAV and Counter-UAV systems, and (k) LIDAR and Radar systems with innovative detection algorithms. Further to those systems, there are also respective ones aiming to protect the CI against Information leakage/loss, prevent unauthorized access, and secure all communication in and out of the facilities. Typical systems include the following: (a) Data Protection, (b) Network Monitoring, (c) Intrusion Detection and Response Systems, (d) Endpoint Monitoring, (e) Digital Authentication and Access Control, (f) Software Development based on privacy by design techniques, (g) IoT Sensors, (h) Artificial Intelligence techniques, (i) Event recording and audit systems, and (j) Secure remote access.

Many of the above solutions consist of or are based on sensors, which are further combined with algorithms, techniques, and systems, offering advanced integrated solutions to support all phases of crisis management (as described in Sect. 2.1), applied both physical and cyber security domains. Such solutions include risk and impact assessment tools, tools for Cascading effects from physical and cyber-attacks, threat intelligence modelling and analysis tools, combined physical and cyber threat detection and early warning systems, security information management systems, decision support mechanisms, holistic emergency response and service continuity mechanisms, etc. In the following paragraphs, we will focus on and further analyse risk assessment tools that are used during preparedness phase, as well as security information management systems, which can be used in all phases of crisis management.

Risk Assessment Tools. Following the aforementioned solutions, risk and impact assessment tools and methodologies are considered crucial for the protection of CIs, as they are necessary for the calculation and understanding of the overall risk of the assets, infrastructures or systems, leading to important decisions for its mitigation. Several methodologies have been developed for CI risk assessment. Among them, a common approach is dominant consisting of some main elements: Identification and classification of threats, identification of vulnerabilities and evaluation of impact [9]. This well-established approach for evaluating risk is considered the pillar of most risk assessment methodologies. Similarly, several ways to estimate the vulnerability of each asset of the space ground segment, have been developed, starting from vulnerability indexes, mainly available for assets built following specific standards (i.e. Eurocode 8 for structures), up to using simulations or experimentation. Risk assessment, as the overall process of risk identification, risk analysis and risk evaluation, is applied dependent not only on the context of the risk management process but also on the methods and techniques used to carry out the risk assessment [10]. Novel research should aim at recognizing threat scenarios as early as possible, providing superior awareness and decision support, in order to take some security measures during preparedness phase, or sometimes quickly activate response-and-recovery strategies [11].

Physical Security Information Management Systems. CIs physical security requires the development of innovative approaches for identification, detection and mitigation of threats, vulnerabilities and risks [12]. The cyber-physical and human-in-the-loop nature of CIs protection require a set of multidisciplinary activities to be performed in order to adopt appropriate and effective protection mechanisms. As such, effective information integration and management is essential to overcome technological limitations, synthesizing data from multiple alerting systems and physical sensors [13]. PSIM provides a platform able to connect security devices or systems and advanced processing capabilities of the device information, translating data into intelligence. PSIM integrates diverse systems into a common information model in order to provide a complete Situation Assessment and Management, to effectively manage any security-related event or emergency in real-time and across CIs. PSIM system shall include functionalities such as: a) gathering of data and information from the field; b) analysis and interpretation of received data, events and alarms; c) confirmation about the authenticity of the alarms; d) resolution of critical situations and possible emergencies in real-time; e) reporting of all the tracked information [14].

Based on the above analysis, reports on security management, and the daily challenges faced by the CIs, as well as knowledge gained through the 7SHIELD project, it has been identified that even though the crisis management process is well analyzed in literature, there is a need for CIs to better understand the process, as well as to identify the involved stakeholders, their roles and responsibilities. Moreover, it has been reported that among CIs there should be a uniformity in the implementation of solutions that can support and enhance the crisis management processes, from preparedness to mitigation, as described above. It is essential for CIs not only to enhance risk perception for their facilities and be well prepared based on their specific vulnerabilities, but also to effectively and efficiently manage and share information (incident detection, evolution, resource allocation etc.), in different layers: within the CI, between the CI and its response partners, as well as among interconnected CIs.

3 7SHIELD Project and Reference Architecture

To meet the aforementioned needs, 7SHIELD aims at providing a holistic framework that enables the confrontation of complex threats by covering all four phases of crisis management. In meeting this aim, 7SHIELD integrates a series of state-of-the-art technological achievements from multidisciplinary fields, namely of the era of sensors technology, IoT, semantic reasoning, high-level analytics, decision support systems, crisis management and situational awareness focusing on the protection of critical infrastructures, such as ground segments of space systems. Thus, 7SHIELD logical architecture (a simplified view is presented in Fig. 1) has been defined with the aim to be modular and scalable at the maximum possible level.

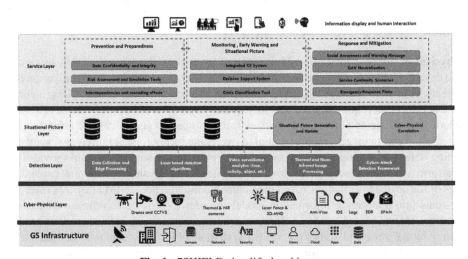

Fig. 1. 7SHIELD simplified architecture

In more detail, the **Cyber-Physical Layer** contains all the data sources/sensors providing raw data to be collected by the 7SHIELD system to protect the Satellite Ground Segment CIs. The **Detection Layer** contains cyber and physical detection software tools able to detect and notify useful information and relevant events, often (but not always) as a sort of abnormal behaviour, which then will be used by the (early) warning modules to identify a complex cyber-physical attack. The **Situational Picture Layer** contains cyber-physical correlation modules able to process, correlate and analyse the real time cyber and physical events received as input from the respective detectors in order to identify potential attacks. Finally, the **Service Layer** contains all the services used by the experts to prevent, manage and mitigate the threats associated with cyber-physical attacks in the Satellite Ground Segment domain, covering the stages of crisis management, namely pre-crisis, crisis and post-crisis.

In a nutshell, based on the above layers, the early warning mechanism estimates the level of risk before the occurrence of a cyber or physical attack. During an attack, the detection and response is effective and efficient, considering budgetary constraints. A mitigation plan is designed and automatically updated to offer a quick recovery after an intentional attack or a system failure. Security and resilience of private installations of space ground segments are also supported by business continuity scenarios, building on top of an innovative orchestration of novel monitoring and forecasting technologies. In the following section, some of these advanced solutions for the protection of Space Ground Segments developed within the 7SHIELD project will be presented, namely the CIRP-RAT tool, the ENGAGE-CSIM and the ERP module. All these components are considered part of the Service Layer enhancing the situational picture with additional information coming from the prevention and preparedness activities. All the services to support responders and decision makers during the emergency are provided in this layer.

4   Advanced 7SHIELD Solutions for Space Ground Segments

4.1   CIRP-RAT Tool

Several methodologies and handbooks for risk assessment do exist (some focusing in the security domain), some of which have been considered for the development of CIRP-RAT, such as: RAMCAP initially used for specific critical infrastructures [15]; EBIOS mainly used in France and for IT systems [16]; ISO 31000 which is used internationally applying to various sectors further to security [10], the Quick Risk Estimation Tool of UNISDR used to advise on the risks and hazards to human and physical assets [17]; Protective Measures Index and Vulnerability Index: Indicators of Critical Infrastructure Protection and Vulnerability by Argonne National Lab., used to compare the level of protection of critical infrastructure and to guide the prioritization of limited resources for improving protection and lowering vulnerability [18]; Risk Management at ESA, describing the risk management as contributed by ESA in the standard ECSS-M-00-03 [19], Risk Management in ESA's Scientific Directorate: A Case Study, presenting a practical example of the implementation of Risk Management within ESA's Science Directorate [20]; Risk Analysis and Security Countermeasure Selection, Second Edition, a handbook on risk assessment procedure and the selection of appropriate countermeasure solutions [21]. As indicated in the above methodologies, the risk is related mainly to the following three variables:

$$\text{Risk} = \text{Threat} \times \text{Vulnerability} \times \text{Consequence} \tag{1}$$

More specifically, CIRP-RAT tool considers the following parameters: i) Threat identification and scenarios definition; ii) Asset identification and characterization; iii) Existing security measures identification; iv) Impact identification; v) Impact analysis; vi) Threat, Vulnerability and Consequence analysis, vii) Risk estimation and prioritization, viii) Risk evaluation & mitigation.

The CIRP-RAT is a web-based tool, based on the CIRP platform (initially designed within EU-CIRCLE project [22] for the assessment of climate change related natural hazards), offering through a user-friendly interface the capability to conduct several what-if scenarios (assessments), in order to calculate the risk. The main components of the tool and their interconnections, in order to calculate and assess the risk are depicted in the following diagram (see Fig. 2) which distinguishes five main packages, threat, assets, measures, impact and risk, as described below in more detail.

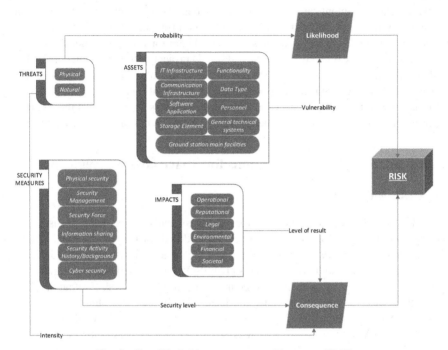

Fig. 2. Simplified risk assessment architecture of RAT

From a technical point of view, the core component of the CIRP-RAT is a web service, which manages several repositories that host information related to the CI parameters, the potential threats/hazards, available security measures, etc. This information is combined in order to set the various what-if scenarios that are related to each CI. The CIRP-RAT manages and executes these what-if scenarios in order to estimate the related impact and the risk level. The management of this information and of the scenarios is available to the users through a user-friendly Graphical User Interface. Additionally, this information is available to third-party applications/users either through a REST Web API or through its integration with any message broker (e.g. KAFKA). Using the UI that is provided by the CIRP-RAT, users can design and execute various what-if scenarios. Thus, the CIRP-RAT will calculate the risk indexes of the infrastructure on specific threats. The execution of the calculations and the access to the various data that are required are supported by the CIRP-RAT web service. Each user in order to use the CIRP-RAT functionalities has to be authenticated. After logging in to the platform, users are able to define the infrastructure characteristic and set the parameters (e.g. threats, assets, measures and impacts) of the several threat scenarios that would like to investigate (see Fig. 3).

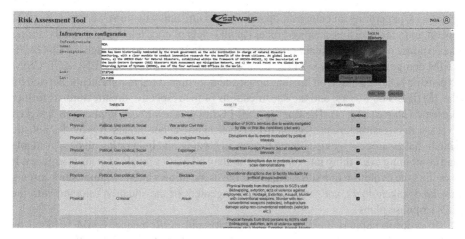

Fig. 3. CIRP-RAT configuration page

After completing all steps of the risk assessment (threat identification, assets vulnerabilities, security measures in place and impact analysis), risk-related results are generated and depicted through graphical representations (see Fig. 4). Repeating the steps for more scenarios is expected to finally produce a concrete risk assessment report, including several diagrams and prioritizing the risks, based on a risk index.

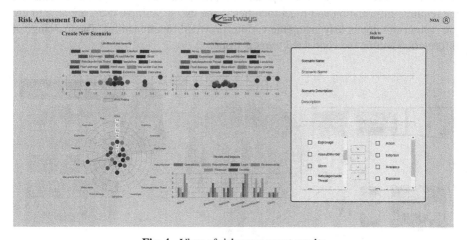

Fig. 4. View of risk assessment results

4.2 ENGAGE CSIM Solution

As mentioned in Sect. 3, in the context of 7SHIELD project, the security operation centers will host a platform that integrates all physical and cyber security sensors, raw and fused data (through correlators), and decision support tools, through standardised interfaces, generating an enhanced operational picture and situation awareness, to assist operators in the decision-making process at all levels of coordination, especially during the response phase. These functionalities are provided to the users through the ENGAGE CSIM component (expansion of the legacy ENGAGE PSIM system). ENGAGE CSIM expansion has been based on the functional and non-functional requirements, derived by the 7SHIELD end-users, and the specifications of the respective architecture, as further presented above (Sect. 3). The Engage CSIM Edition, is a software application designed to assist in infrastructure protection from physical and cyber threats. It provides holistic situational awareness by visualizing threats, analyzing and integrating all data available and combining everything into one picture among all parties involved in an emergency. It monitors the evolution of a situation, alerts the users, allows intercommunication among involved stakeholders, and supports the management of the situation (aligned with the CI's response plans).

In order to support the required modularity and performance, CSIM is based on technologies like the OSGi (Open Services Gateway Initiative) and the J2EE specifications. The CSIM high-level architecture is presented in Fig. 5. It follows the client-server principle. The server side hosts all the services required for the analysis, storing and management of the information. In more details, the server-side environment is composed by: a) The Database Servers that store the data; b) The Messaging Servers that manage the instant updates of the information to the clients, c) The GIS Servers that manage the spatial data; d) The Connection Services that manage the interfaces with external application and services, e) The overall information flow is managed by the Application Servers. The client-side is composed of a graphical user interface that provides all the required information and functionalities to the users. Multiple users are able to use the system simultaneously, using the various provided functionalities. The exchange of information among the connected users is instant.

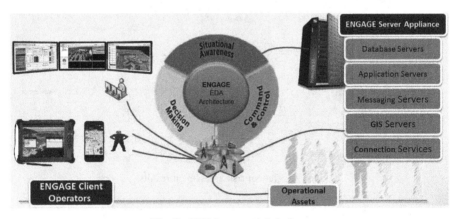

Fig. 5. CSIM conceptual design.

The component is based on a multi-user and multi-role principle. The access to the functionalities and operational information by the users is specified by the role each user has in the system. The role of each user is defined according to his responsibilities, capabilities, and hierarchy inside the organisation or among organisations. The functionalities provided to users through an advanced and intuitive graphical user interface are presented in Fig. 6.

Fig. 6. The ENGAGE PSIM graphical user interface

In a nutshell, the Engage CSIM Edition provides the following functionalities:

- The information coming from multiple and diverse sources is combined and depicted in the users friendly UI, improving the situational awareness of the users and enabling effective management of the response activities. Information from physical and detection tools, event correlators, crisis assessment tools and social media analysis tools are collected and combined for this purpose.
- Taking into consideration the list of attacks that have been detected and the status of the response activities, an overall estimation of the CI status is depicted to the users, informing them about the status of the CI, the overall severity of the attacks, the hazard types etc.
- During a crisis, commanders would like to communicate with the FRs on the field. The ENGAGE PSIM enables this communication by providing to the users the status of the FRs (e.g. their position and vital signs), and by collaborating with them and assigning to them commands/missions.
- During the response phase, users have to take a number of decisions and execute a number of response actions. The ENGAGE PSIM supports this process by incorporating the Emergency Response Plan of the CIs. These plans guide the actions of the commanders, by mentioning which action should be executed in each phase of the crisis (mission assignments, communication of the situation to external agencies, internal actions etc.).
- The person in charge can manage all resources (human and non-human) through multiple communication methods and a holistic visualization.

Important information and infrastructure can now be protected since threats and disasters are easier to deal with.

4.3 ERP Module

A key part of preparing for an emergency is developing an Emergency Response Plan (ERP). Although ERPs cannot cover all potential disruptive events or specifics of an event, the act itself of developing an ERP offers the organization a framework that facilitates a more systematic response to any emergency that may appear. The specific ERP format applied by an organization depends on the nature of the organization and its internal policies. For SGSs that are exposed to a variety of threats and hazards (physical and cyber) an all-hazards approach is the best possible course of action, thus incorporating cyber-physical emergency planning. This approach provides for ERPs of a binary nature, namely a more strategic document, on the one hand, that contains sections that are applicable to multiple emergency situations and creates the mechanism upon which the organization lies to handle an emergency (i.e., emergency Response Team structure and roster, contact lists, communication channels, logistical and decision support processes etc.), and on the other hand, detailed emergency response checklists of operational nature, that are applicable for specific types of emergency events (or combination of events in the case of cyber-physical emergencies). The all-hazards approach provides the basis for the ERPs, since planning requirements are broadly the same whether an incident is physical or cyber, and then drill down to threat-specific operational ERP playbooks describing detailed response steps.

Within the context of the 7SHIELD project, a model ERP was developed comprising both a strategic and an operational part (Table 1) and which set the basis for further fine-tuning and alignment with the SGS end-users' input that describes the best courses of response action according to the specificities of their respective organizations. In this sense, ISO 22320-2008, ASIS GDL BC 01 2005, FEMA Comprehensive Preparedness Guide (CPG)101, NIST 800-61, NFPA 1600 Standard amongst other regulations and guidelines, were consulted to identify the strategies applied, for effective response planning during a disruptive event and for the effective containment of its impacts on a SGS's assets, property, and people as well as its offered services. The common scope of these standards is to offer a combination of resources and procedures, including facilities, equipment, personnel, communications, and organizational structures that are brought together for certain managerial functions to take place regardless of the people available or involved in the emergency response, thus ensuring that a specific and sufficiently documented process is always in place for implementation. Thus, ERPs should establish an ongoing process of observation and information gathering, constant situation assessment, communication and dissemination activities, decision making and decision implementation, as well as feedback gathering leading to continuous improvement. Emergency Response Planning is therefore depicted as a cyclical process, enriched with the concept of a spiral of continuously evolving manner that aims at safeguarding the business functions of the organization. Moreover, this process defines roles and responsibilities for all members of the emergency management team within the organization, assigns responsibilities and sets lines of authority to oversee and coordinate actions, to describe the mitigation measures and to identify the available resources. Overall, the components that need to be present in any effective ERP should, in general terms, include the following: a) Emergency recognition; b) Notification; c) Situation Assessment; d) Crisis declaration; e) Plan execution; f) Communications; g) Resources management; h) Revision, Maintenance & Exercise.

Table 1. The components of the 7SHIELD ERPs

Part of ERPs	Components of the ERPs
Strategic: The strategic part of the plans describes the general emergency management policy objectives and offer general guidance by establishing the long-term policy priorities and responsibilities	1. **Introduction, scope** and **purpose** of the ERP
	2. The **concept of operations** of the SGS
	3. The **operational organization** of the SGS & **assignment of responsibilities** related to emergency management activities
	4. **Direction control** and **coordination** identifying the members of the Emergency Response Team and the persons/roles that have operational control over response assets
	5. Emergency **information collection, analysis,** and **dissemination**
	6. **Communications** & **coordination** procedures during the ER
	7. **Administration, logistics** and **general support policies and services** for all types of emergencies
	8. ERP **revision, maintenance,** and **training** process
Operational: This part is a detailed organizational process which defines and describes the roles and responsibilities, the tasks, and actions to be performed by the various emergency management stakeholders during response	9. **Threat/Emergency specific** functional **playbooks** which focus on critical operational functions and who is responsible for carrying them out, or they contain unique and regulatory response details that apply to a specific threat, in the form of standard operating procedures. These playbooks describe policies, processes, roles, and responsibilities that SGS's persons/roles and departments carry out during any pre-identified emergency and until it is resolved

Within the 7SHIELD project a series of questionnaires was distributed to SGS operators, in order to comprehend the special requirements of SGS end-users, as well as the particular conditions of the project's scenarios. The questions aimed to highlight the existing emergency response practices, organizational structures, established procedural mechanism of roles/responsibilities and; to identify organizational specific best practices for the creation of the ERPs' Threat/Emergency specific functional playbooks, indicating specific emergency response actions and the relevant SGS's stakeholders responsible for executing them. During 7SHIELD pilot demonstrations these playbooks were integrated into the ENGAGE CSIM platform in the form of lists with consecutive procedural steps which the 7SHIELD platform operators were expected to follow during an emergency. Details about the list of actions, the type of personnel that should execute these and the communications (internal or external agencies) that have to be implemented are available to users through ENGAGE CSIM, the GUI of which performs also the ERP visualization, accompanied by several functionalities.

The ERP visualization module was facilitated via different view screens. The main ERP screen was presenting the ERP steps in a structured hierarchical way, leading the operator from the successful completion of one procedural step to the other, also incorporating functional buttons and checkboxes to mark the completed steps and help the operator navigate or execute communication tasks at specific points. Also, an on-demand view screen was also made available to the operator presenting the ERP playbooks (pictured as flowcharts), to offer an easy way for the operator to visualize the ERP in a user-friendly manner. Finally, reporting functionalities were also embedded, so that a complete report with ERP action taken is available and documented (Fig. 7).

In this way, a critical part in the People-Process-Technology (PPT) framework was further developed and an existing gap in the functional integration of response plans and procedures into IC3S platforms was ameliorated, by making available a course of response actions to the operator, thus, minimizing reaction time, and response lag due to lack of effective communication, coordination, and uniformity of responses.

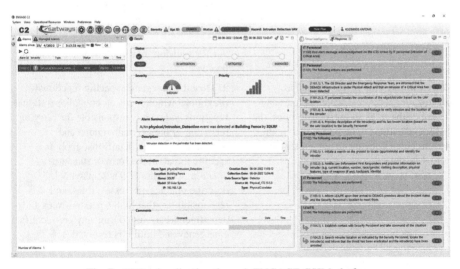

Fig. 7. ERPs visualization through ENGAGE CSIM platform

5   Conclusions and Future Work

This paper presents a set of tools that have been developed or adapted in the framework of the 7SHIELD project, which aims to support a SGS CI operator through the preparedness and response phase of crisis management, considering and addressing the needs of the specific domain. In meeting this aim, initially a background analysis of the security operating environment of such CIs has been pro-vided, describing the crisis management phases, best practices on technological solutions used and the needs of the end-users. Based on that the 7SHIELD approach has been briefly presented, focusing then on three specific tools, namely: CIRP-RAT which aims to cover the needs of the pre-crisis phase by offering risk assessment capabilities to the user; ENGAGE CSIM which is an integrated command, control and coordination system with a friendly GUI providing the user with monitoring and detection functionalities at the pre-crisis phase, but also with real-time information, incident management and situational awareness capabilities during the crisis phase; and ERP module, integrated into the CSIM, providing the response collaborative steps in a structured hierarchical way, tailor-made for the specific SGS and incident.

These tools and 7SHIELD are deployed and tested across the SGS CIs of the project in Finland, Greece, Spain, Italy, and Belgium. This prolonged piloting and demonstration process will serve as means to test and refine the deployed approach, including the effectiveness of the innovative technologies, and the robustness of the 7SHIELD platform and its modules, to ensure the interoperability of 7SHIELD across all ground segments and finally, to standardise the processes. A total of 19 use case scenarios have been designed (e.g. unauthorised entrance, UAV threat, firewall attach, spoofing, DDOS, equipment theft, fire, jamming, MITM, Ransomware, etc.), and have been prioritised, taking into consideration the probability of these cyber and physical attacks and the damage caused, the severity of cascading effects, the general security protocols applying to SGS, the analysis of vulnerabilities by internal and external security experts, and recommendations by First Responders.

As an example, during one of the above scenarios, a CI operator with the help of the tools presented, will be able to initially conduct a risk assessment (CIRP-RAT) for the threats of interest and evaluate the impact that e.g. enhancing the security measures of the infrastructure, would have on the overall risk. On top of that, with ENGAGE CSIM the user will be able to detect and manage the incident, coordinating internal and external stakeholders, implementing emergency response plans, provided with situational awareness and monitoring the crisis until it's over.

Based on the early outcomes of the validation phase of the project and the expected results, using such tools will enhance the resilience of SGS CIs by offering a deep understanding of emerging risks, existing vulnerabilities, lack of measures in place, and potential impacts on the facilities or the services. On top of that, they offer a common operational picture and enhanced situational awareness, combined with more systematic response to any emergency that may appear. In this way, it is ensured that adequate, reliable and always available services are offered by SGS, without, for example, causing debilitating impact on public safety and security of European citizens or affecting other interdependent critical infrastructures.

Acknowledgements. The work presented in this paper has been conducted in the framework of the 7SHIELD project, which has received funding from the European Union's H2020 research and innovation programme under grant agreement no. 883284 respectively. This output reflects the views only of the author(s), and the European Union cannot be held responsible for any use which may be made of the information contained therein.

References

1. Council of the EU: Council Directive 2008/114/EC of 8 December 2008 on the identification and designation of European critical infrastructures and the assessment of the need to improve their protection. EUR-Lex. https://eur-lex.europa.eu/legal-content/en/ALL/?uri=CELEX:320 08L0114

2. Union, Council of the European: Proposal for a DIRECTIVE OF THE EUROPEAN PARLIAMENT AND OF THE COUNCIL on the resilience of critical entities. EUR-Lex. https://eur-lex.europa.eu/legal-content/EN/TXT/?uri=CELEX%3A52020PC0829

3. 7SHIELD project. 7SHIELD project (GA No 883284). 7SHIELD project (2022). https://www.7shield.eu/project/. Accessed 10 June 2022

4. Hromada, M., Rehak, D., Walker, N.: Electricity infrastructure technical security: Practical application and best practices of risk assessment. In: Rehak, D., et al., (eds.) Safety and Security Issues in Technical Infrastructures, pp. 1–30. IGI Global, Hershey (2020). https://doi.org/10.4018/978-1-7998-3059-7.ch001

5. British Standard Institute (BSI): BS11200: Crisis Management – guidance and good practice. BSI (2014)

6. Mantzana, V., Georgiou, E., Gazi, A., Gkotsis, I., Chasiotis, I., Eftychidis, G.: Towards a global CIs' cyber-physical security management and joint coordination approach. In: Abie, H., et al. (eds.) CPS4CIP 2020. LNCS, vol. 12618, pp. 155–170. Springer, Cham (2021). https://doi.org/10.1007/978-3-030-69781-5_11

7. Mariš, L., Loveček, T., Zeegers, M.: Security of infrastructure systems: infrastructure security assessment. In: Rehak, D., et al. (eds.) Safety and Security Issues in Technical Infrastructures, pp. 353–382. IGI Global, Hershey (2020). https://doi.org/10.4018/978-1-7998-3059-7.ch013

8. Mantzana, V., Darra, E., Gkotsis, I.: Cyber-physical security in healthcare. In: Rehak, D., et al. (eds.) Safety and Security Issues in Technical Infrastructures, pp. 63–87. IGI Global, Hershey (2020). https://doi.org/10.4018/978-1-7998-3059-7.ch003

9. Giannopoulos, G., Filippini, R., Schimmer, M.: Risk assessment methodologies for Critical Infrastructure Protection. Part I: a state of the art. JRC (2012)

10. ISO: Risk management—Risk assessment techniques. IEC 31010:2019 (2019)

11. Giannopoulos, G., Dorneanu, B., Jonkeren, O.: Risk assessment methodology for critical infrastructure protection. https://publications.jrc.ec.europa.eu/repository/bitstream/JRC 78292/lbna25745enn.pdf. Accessed 05 June 2013

12. Fausto, A., et al.: Toward the integration of cyber and physical security monitoring systems for critical infrastructures. Sensors (Basel) **21**, 6970 (2021)

13. Kovacich, G.L., Halibozek, E.P.: The Manager's Handbook for Corporate Security: Establishing and Managing a Successful Assets Protection Program. Butterworth-Heinemann, Oxford (2003)

14. ENTELEC: ENTELEC. What is a PSIM software platform?, 14 October 2021. https://www.entelec.eu/what-is-a-psim-software-platform. Accessed 10 June 2022

15. ASME: All-Hazards Risk and Resilience: Prioritizing Critical Infrastructures Using the RAMCAP PlusSM Approach. ASME Press, New York (2009)

16. LA MÉTHODE EBIOS RISK MANAGER. https://www.ssi.gouv.fr/administration/manage
    ment-du-risque/la-methode-ebios-risk-manager/
17. Quick Risk Estimation Tool. ttps://www.unisdr.org/campaign/resilientcities/toolkit/article/
    quick-risk-estimation-qre.html
18. Petit, F.D., et al.: National Technical Reports Library. Protective Measures Index and
    Vulnerability Index. July 2013 [Online]
19. Preyssl, C., Atkins, R., Deak, T.: Risk management at ESA. ESA Bull. **97**, 64–68 (1999)
20. Schroeter, J.: Risk management in ESA's scientific directorate: a case study. ESA Bull. **107**,
    64–71 (2001)
21. Norman, T.L.: Risk Analysis and Security Countermeasure Selection. Second Edition
22. EU-CIRCLE (2018) [Online]. https://www.eu-circle.eu/

Modelling and Simulation of Railway Networks for Resilience Analysis

Kushal Srivastava[1]([✉]), Corinna Köpke[1], Johannes Walter[1], Katja Faist[1],
John Marschalk Berry[2], Claudio Porretti[3], and Alexander Stolz[1,4]

[1] Fraunhofer Institute for High-Speed Dynamics, Ernst-Mach-Institut,
EMI, Am Klingelberg 1, 79588 Efringen-Kirchen, Germany
kushal.srivastava@emi.fraunhofer.de,
alexander.stolz@mail.inatech.uni-freiburg.de
[2] Rete Ferroviaria Italiana S.p.A, Piazza della Croce Rossa, 1, 00161 Rome, Italy
j.berry@rfi.it
[3] Leonardo S.p.A, Piazza Monte Grappa n.4, 00195 Rome, Italy
claudio.porretti@leonardo.com
[4] Albert-Ludwigs-Universität Freiburg, Emmy-Noether-Straße 2,
79110 Freiburg im Breisgau, Germany
https://www.emi.fraunhofer.de, https://www.rfi.it/,
https://www.leonardo.com/en/home, https://uni-freiburg.de/

Abstract. The work focuses on the impact of disruptions on a railway transportation network. The modeling of the transportation network with the help of graph theory is presented and criticality/vulnerability assessment and impact propagation in these networks is studied. Furthermore, the work emulates defined mitigation measures in the modelled network and quantifies the resilience of the network. The results are produced from an agent-based simulation tool called CaESAR (Cascading Effects Simulation in Areas for increasing Resilience) that uses network graphs in cooperation with their behavioral characteristics. The tool is under integration with a broader framework (S4RIS platform) designed under the EU H2020 project SAFETY4RAILS aimed at integrating multiple solutions to be made available to operators and first responders for better responses in case of threats and disruptions.

Keywords: Resilience indicators · Critical infrastructure · Impact propagation · Transport networks · Graph theory

1 Introduction

Critical Infrastructures (CI) play a key role in the daily functioning of society and thus are key to overall economy of a country. Furthermore, as they grow, CI get more complex and consequently more sensitive regarding disruptive events and interdependencies. Due to this criticality, CIs have been studied for quite some time interms of risks involved and their resilience. In the project Safety4Rails, resilience has been defined as "the ability to repel, prepare for, take into account,

S. Katsikas et al. (Eds.): ESORICS 2022 Workshops, LNCS 13785, pp. 308–320, 2023.
https://doi.org/10.1007/978-3-031-25460-4_17

absorb, recover from and adapt ever more successfully to actual or potential adverse events" [3,15]. The resilience cycle as followed in the project consists of different but overlapping and intertwined phases namely, identification, protection, detection, response and, recovery [3]. Several resilience studies in the transportation area use topological models [4]. In [1], an undirected graph is used to model the transportation network. The resilience of every node is computed as the weighted average number of reliable independent paths with all other city nodes in the network (betweenness centrality). The overall resilience is then a weighted sum of all node resilience. [2] examines the interdependent rail networks in rush hours. The work emphasizes that topological shapes of the network play a key role in the dynamics of the cascades and concludes that in complex networks, cascade effects are more responsible for poor performance than failures themselves.

With an increase in digitization of transportation networks (similar to other forms of CIs), there is potential for cyber attacks that can maximize disruptions and cause delays in recovery. One example is the jamming of CCTV monitoring cameras to block visibility, occupancy, and other forms of on-ground information to operators and first responders. This can lead to delays in time-critical decisions or mismanagement of resources that can prove to be bottlenecks for trivial rescue operations. These are challenges that are assessed in this paper using the CaESAR tool. The paper is further divided into four sections. Section 2 presents the modelling technique. It briefly discusses aspects of graph theory for criticality assessment and impact propagation. Section 3 discusses the problem definition in the form of a use case. Section 4 presents the results and corresponding visualizations. Finally, Sect. 5 provides a summary and brief outlook of the work.

2   Modelling of the Network

This section describes the data and methodology used to build the network model for SAFETY4RAILS project including the models for resilience quantification, criticality assessment, impact propagation as well as a description of the use case. The SAFETY4RAILS project includes four Simulation Exercises. The networks for the Rome exercise in SAFETY4RAILS were generated from open source data available at OpenMobilityData [16]. This data is based on The General Transit Feed Specification (GTFS) (GTFS Static Overview — Static Transit — Google Developers) [17], which is a common format for public transport networks, including schedules and geographic information. This data is used to generate a representation of the public transport network consisting of nodes and edges. Two important files from the GTFS data namely, *Stops.txt* and *Trips.txt* are used. The nodes are generated according to the *Stops.txt*, which describes stops and their geographic locations as well as some further information, like the location type. Since the GTFS data contain several stops with the same name, they are consolidated to one node, where the geo-location is the average of the geo-locations of all stops with the same name. Each node contains information regarding the transportation types serving it, i.e. by which lines it is served.

Nodes are connected based on trips described in *Trips.txt*. A trip contains a series of stops, where the vehicle travels along a route at a specific time. The stops located on the corresponding trip are then connected according to it. Added edges are unique, i.e. they represent the opportunity to travel from one station to another one. Figures 1a and b are snippets from the network visualization generated by CaESAR. Figure 1a represents the modelled network using open source data. This modelling consists of the bus (yellow), tram(turquoise), metro (red), and train (blue) stations. The visualizations generated in CaESAR are interactive, and it is possible to hover over the graph nodes and get more information including the name of nodes, their degree, and geo-location (as shown in Fig. 1b).

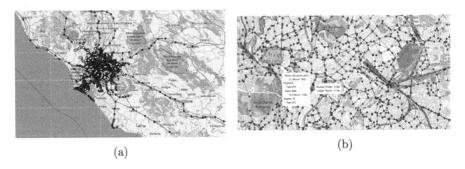

(a)   (b)

Fig. 1. The figure is a snippet of CaESAR GUI and shows the modelled network in the exercise. a) The Rome testbed as modelled using open source data available at OpenMobilityData. b) Zoomed-in version of the testbed to show the interactive dialog box and the connections. (Color figure online)

The modelling uses bi-directional graph to better represent the flow of traffic throughout the network. The implementation uses multiple python modules including Networkx [22], GeoPandas [24], Shapely [23], Bokeh [25] and NumPy [21]. The threats are modelled as objects with attributes including time of attack, list of nodes to attack and time for repair. The nodes in-turn have attributes including name, geo-location, capacity and repair times. The repair times are used in the recovery strategy of the nodes after impact. The nodes are recovered after their individual repair time has elapsed after damage.

2.1   Numerical Simulation Using CaESAR

CaESAR is a python and C++ based tool that can perform offline and online analyses of impacts on networks. The offline analysis is a stochastic analysis of the network with single-point/multi-point failures to identify worst performing combinations, while online analysis here is performing analysis of specific threats/failures in the network in real-time, based on data from a suitable integrated platform. CaESAR has been used to analyse cascading effects in different types of infrastructures such as water, electricity, and mobile phone grids. In the project RESISTO [19], CaESAR has been used to model and understand telecommunication grids [12], in SATIE [18], [20] for understanding airport networks and now is being utilized in SAFETY4RAILS for analysis of railway networks [3]. It uses network, and threats modelled as described above along with probabilities for failures, delays, and repair times with certain variance to quantify and analyze resilience of the networks. To understand cascades in the networks, it is also capable of employing different propagation algorithms. As a result of this analysis, CaESAR delivers visualizations of the propagation of impact in the network highlighting damage and recovery, resilience curves for the network and time series of states of the components in the network.

2.2   Resilience Quantification

Resilience of the network is considered as the quantified performance of the system, which is the percentage of active nodes. The state of the nodes can be considered as binary or varying between $[0, 1]$. For a network with N nodes, let s_i represent the state of the ith node, then performance θ at any time-step (t) can be defined as average of all states of nodes in the network:

$$\theta = \frac{1}{N} \sum_{i=1}^{N} s_i \tag{1}$$

While this is a basic form of performance quantification, some key performance indicators can be derived from the resulting graphs. This includes:

1. The maximum rate of performance degradation, $d(theta)/dt$. An alternate to this is the time taken to reach minimum performance.
2. Total downtime.
3. Total time for recovery.
4. Minimum performance.
5. Maximum state of recovery.

These indicators have been applied on the railway simulation grid and the results have been explained in Sect. 4

2.3   Criticality Assessment

The assessment of the criticality of nodes in the network is based on properties from graph theory. These properties have also been widely used by researchers when quantifying vulnerabilities in different applications of graph networks. An example is a work by Artemis P. and Eusebi C. [8], wherein authors have used graph properties to derive connectivity and activity density of transportation nodes over time. Another example is [10], wherein authors use the degree of each node to measure their criticality. This work focuses on the identification of critical nodes from the perspective of threats and potential disruptions and applies these metrics (degree and betweenness centrality) to achieve it. In the integrated platform of S4R, in the case of detection of an event, the gathered list of critical components is communicated to the operators, which helps in informed decision making. The two metrics "degree of nodes" and "betweenness centrality" which are briefly explained as follows:

Degree of Nodes: The degree of nodes is defined as the number of connections or edges the node has to other nodes.

Betweenness Centrality (BC): The betweenness centrality defines how much a given node is in-between others [14]. It is measured with the number of shortest paths between any two nodes in the graph, which passes through the considered node, for which the BC is being computed [14]. A target node will have a higher BC if it appears in many shortest paths. These nodes would correspond to central intersections from a topological perspective [6]. These nodes would be expected to have higher traffic than those with low BC values. With N as the total number of nodes in the graph, the BC is often normalized by a factor of $N(N - 1)$. Mathematically the BC of a node v_k is defined as [6]:

$$BC(v_k) = \sum_{v_i \neq v_k \neq v_j} \frac{\sigma_{v_i v_j}(v_k)}{\sigma_{v_i v_j}} \qquad (2)$$

where $\sigma_{v_i v_j}$ is the total number of shortest paths from node v_i to node v_j, and $\sigma_{v_i v_j}(v_k)$ is the number of those paths that cross v_k [6]. In order to demonstrate the effectiveness of these assessments, in addition to the use case, the result section also discusses the impact of failures in these nodes with the help of resilience curves.

2.4   Impact Propagation

To compute the resilience with respect to disruptive events, CaESAR uses impact propagation to estimate the consequences on the network. In the current study, connectivity of stations/nodes is used. Implicitly, failure in a station/track would first reflect in the immediately connected station and from there propagate into the network. With this as a motivation, a propagation algorithm is designed to reflect this behaviour. A custom delay is added before propagation to the next station. Since transportation networks (individual or different networks modelled as dependent) are fully connected, meaning there is no island/disconnected node, if run long enough the simulation will show an impact on every node of the network. In terms of impact propagation, impact does not necessarily mean physical damage. In this context, the impact can for example represent the number of passengers reaching their destinations. Figure 2 represents the stages of a connectivity based impact propagation in a directed graph. p_i represents the probability of propagation to the corresponding connected node. To ensure flexibility, the delay is parameterized and represented here as m.

At time-step $t = T$, impacted node is *1*, at $t = T + m$, impacted nodes are *1, 2, 3*, and after $t = T + 2m$ time-steps, impact propagates to the next stage of connected nodes *1, 2, 3, 4, 5, 6*. The recovery of nodes is independent of each other and depends on their repair times. With connectivity based propagation, this needs to be further tuned in coordination with ground staff and expert knowledge to introduce limits based on the type of impact, type of components, etc.

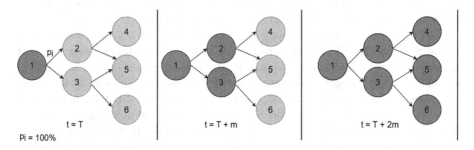

Fig. 2. Demonstration of connectivity based impact propagation in the network with 100% propagation probability and m time steps between cascade to next stages.

3 Use Case

The simulation exercise is performed in collaboration with multiple tools, integrated through an event streaming platform called Kafka. In the current work, specifically two other tools are involved namely, Ganimede and CuriX (Cure Infrastructure in XaaS). Curix is a real-time monitoring tool for technical devices (e.g. IoT, IT), which employs statistical and machine learning methods to learn normal system behaviors and hence, detect abnormal behaviors [13]. Ganimede is a tool for large scale analytics of live videos, which employs generic artificial vision algorithms based on neural networks and performs among others, object detection, classification, and density estimation [18]. The exercise considers a hypothetical scenario where there is a physical attack at the Rome Termini station coordinated with a cyber attack (DoS, Denial of Service) on the vulnerable CCTV system installed at the stations. With this information together, a threat is designed for the simulator. The analysis is performed in two phases of the resilience cycle (see Sect. 1), the prevention phase and the response phase. In the prevention phase, offline analysis is performed using aspects of graph theory and what-if analysis. Vulnerable nodes are computed based on their degree of connectivity and BC. These nodes are then plugged in the simulator as impact soure to evaluate the impact on the overall resilience of the network.

In the response phase, online analysis is performed, where in CaESAR depends on the state information from other detectors in the system to simulate impact. The obtained failures in the systems/components are mapped to threats in the network and simulated. Further analysis is performed based on the resilience curves and impact propagation visualizations. The scenario is based on the open-source network generated for Rome, where there is a co-ordinated disruption of a railway station with very high degree of connectivity using a physical attack and blocking access to key surveillance components using DOS attack. Furthermore, the time of disruption is chosen to be inline with the rush-hour to maximize impact. The physical attack is identified using Ganimede tool which focuses on detection of objects and people in each frame and their movement, while the cyber attack is detected using the platform CuriX. The simulation is setup with organized attacks at simulation time-step 5. The mitigation measures are mentioned in Table 1 and discussed further in the results section.

The tools were integrated using a Kafka platform with a Distributed Messaging System (DMS) [13]. Information is populated in DMS using different channels referred to as topics. Tools can subscribe to these topics in forms of consumer groups and get a constant feed of the messages being sent to the topic. The format of the message is pre-defined. In this exercise, JSON format is used. With the help of some specific fields like data source, event category, asset ID and event description, the receivers can program scripts to automatically filter information of use and post-process them for suitable analysis and visualization.

For this exercise, to present mitigation measures, four different scenarios are considered as follows:

1. **No measure**: Impact propagates throughout the network.
2. **Placement of security guards**: Reduction in the extent of impact and repair time.
3. **Design and implementation of suitable evacuation routes**: Reduction in the extent of impact and repair time.
4. **Re-routing of rail traffic**: Reduced repair time for the impacted station and five directly connected stations

As the mitigation measures primarily modify the state (understood as individual performance) of every node and its repair time in simulation, the extent of the impact is modelled by reducing or enhancing these parameters by a certain percentage. This information along with consequent minimum performance for the above-mentioned scenarios is listed in Table 1. This is further explained in Sect. 4.

Table 1. Table of scenarios, with and without mitigation measures employed in the exercise along with the KPIs.

Scenario	Reduction in performance of nodes (impact)	Reduction of repair time	Minimum Performance
1	0%	0%	40.98
2	50%	10%	53.74
3	75%	50%	82.21
4	0%	15%	59.04

4   Results

To respect the confidentiality of the exercise, the result of the assessment is presented using anonymized stations. In the offline analysis, five different stations from the network are selected with decreasing BC and degrees (refer to Table 2). The threats are designed accordingly and plugged into the simulator. The repair time of the nodes in the network is considered to be dependent on the degree of the node and is defined as $20+5*D_n$, where D_n is the degree of the corresponding node. The propagation delay is considered to be 2 time steps between stages of the graph. Here, 20 is an assumed base value. With a minimum degree of 2, the lowest repair time of such a node in the network will be 30 time steps. As this is a theoretical study and repair times are sensitive information, the overall recovery has been presented in an abstract manner using time-steps. Specific information from the end-users can be used to scale the overall recovery to reflect reality. In reference to Fig. 3, here the time delay between cascades is $m = 2$. Another critical assumption used in the study is that the time taken to recover a node is independent of the extent of impact (state of the node). The state information is used only to quantize the resilience with respect to a threat.

Table 2. Table of nodes considered with their properties, and measured KPIs for the system derived from the resilience curves

Station	Degree	BC	Maximum gradient	Time of outage (timesteps)	Minimum performance	Time to minimum performance
Station 1	12	0.2975	40.98	208	71.28%	63
Station 2	10	0.2531	53.74	218	71.869%	63
Station 3	14	0.0190	82.21	232	72.35%	81
Station 4	4	0.0037	59.04	284	76.20%	121
Station 5	2	0.0	59.04	294	77.82%	175

Table 2 gives the criticality analysis of the network, with both the attributes (degree and BC) and derived KPIs. As seen in Fig. 4a, for nodes with higher BC, there is an early decline in the performance. As these are highly connected nodes, impact quickly propagates in all directions of the network. Due to this, large number of nodes are impacted very quickly and so performance rapidly drops. For nodes with lower values of degree and BC, due to a lower connectivity, the impact spreads to smaller number of nodes in the beginning before reaching more dense sections of the network. This is reflected with lower gradient at the start and higher time to maximum impact (that is minimum performance). This gives more time to operators and first responders to organize suitable mitigation measures to curtail the impact. The maximum value of gradient alone does not reflect the right criticality, as it does not depend on the start of impact rather the overall impact propagation in network. Hence, even if an impact starts in a secluded node with low BC, when run long enough it reaches the center of the network. From this point, the network has same impact with cascade as it would if the damage originated in one of the dense nodes. Another key aspect is the time to minimum performance, for nodes with low BC, the performance impact is low in the beginning until the cascades. This promotes mitigation measures in respect to isolations, where such sections can be removed from the overall network to limit the damage. In terms of minimum performance, the higher the connectivity of the nodes, the lower the minimum performance is. As impact propagation uses connectivity, by the time the recovery in the network begins, higher number of nodes (that is all connected nodes) are damaged as compared to impacts originating from lower connectivity nodes.

In the online analysis, different detector tools generate events. CaESAR polls for these messages and triggers on suitable messages. In the result, an event of physical attack (explosion) at one of the central stations is considered and analyzed. The repair and propagation times are as mentioned in Table 1. Three mitigation measures are considered as defined in Table 1. Figure 4b presents the resilience curves for the scenario with and without mitigation measures. As expected, the case of no mitigation measure has the worst performance. In absence of any mitigation measures, crowd formation is expected and disruptions in multiple lines, as the station impacted is highly connected. Due to a high BC value, the impacted station lies along the route to large section of stations, disruptions are visible in multiple lines. This is represented in the form of a cascade using connectivity. Figure 3 demonstrates this cascade for two different selection of stations. Station 1 (left) and station 2(right) represents two stations placed centrally and remotely. The cascade is demonstrated using with snapshots of the state of the network at different stages (timesteps) in the simulation. The initial stage is at $t = 10$, and the final at $t = 210$. The color coding in the impact propagation gif is programmed with red representing completely failed nodes and then a spectrum to blue representing the extent of recovery. Once the node completely recovers, its color is overridden to green to distinguish undamaged nodes in the network.

Employing guards at the stations can facilitate organized and faster evacuation. This is modelled with lower recovery time, which presents as a lower drop in performance of the network when compared to no mitigation. Similarly, for rerouting traffic, it is represented by a reduction in repair times. The final consideration is the presence of planned evacuation routes. With the help of event inspectors on the ground and cooperation with law enforcement agencies (LEA),

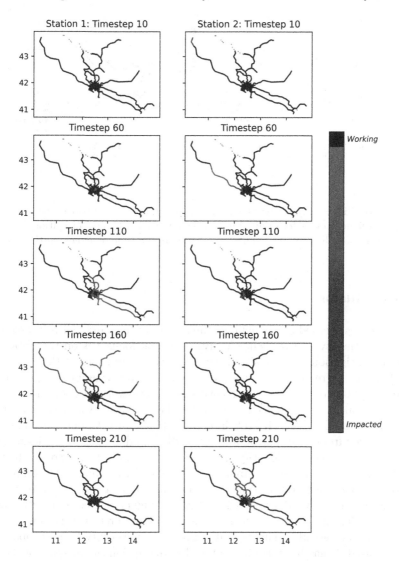

Fig. 3. Demonstration of connectivity based impact propagation in the network with 100% propagation probability and 2 time steps between cascade to next stages.

a larger portion of crowds can be evacuated with minimum damage. This is supposed to provide LEA and first responders with sufficient opportunity to clear the scene and resume operations. With faster control over the system, certain sections of the stations can still be operational, hence the state of the impacted stations is not reduced to zero. The state can be further tweaked based on the severity of impact to better quantify the performance.

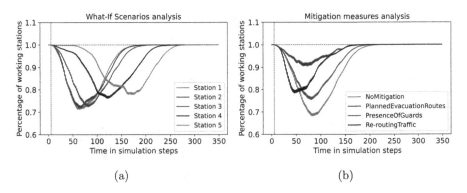

Fig. 4. a) Resilience of the network with five cases of impacted stations with decreasing BC. b) Resilience curves for original use case along with different mitigation measures. The vertical black line (at timestep = 5) represents the time of attack on the network.

5   Conclusion

This work has focused on modelling transportation networks with interconnections for criticality and resilience analysis. Special focus was on the implementation of mitigation measures and rating them to understand their effectiveness. With an increase in dependency on IoT, network components play a critical role in both operations and recovery of the network, hence, an organized cyber-physical attack has been considered. The analysis was performed using CaESAR in the SAFETY4RAILS integrated platform with detection messages being received from other partners using DMS. Two different properties of graph theory have been used to identify critical components in the network, which are then further utilized to create threats and simulated to estimate the resilience of networks. With the quantification of the area under the curve, it can be verified that the impact is more severe with nodes of higher degree and betweenness centrality. This finding is also in line with other research in this direction. To understand the cascading effects of its impacts, connectivity-based propagation has been used. It has been demonstrated that disruptions in any part of the network will have impact on the whole network unless repairs are fast. The severity of the impact of these disruptions is also dependent on the topological location of the nodes. This finding is also in line with the criticality analysis. In terms of mitigation measures, three different approaches have been examined, with the placement of security guards to handle the crowd, planned evacuation routes and, redirection of rail traffic. After discussions with end-users, the measures were translated to a simulation environment and it has been demonstrated that the correctly implemented evacuation routes will be very effective. In the future, with more cooperation from end-users and suitable partners, further mitigation measures can be studied to generate a comprehensive survey.

Acknowledgements. This project has received funding from the European Union's Horizon 2020 research and innovation programme under grant agreement No 883532. The information appearing in this paper has been prepared in good faith and represents the views of the authoring organizations. Neither the Research Executive Agency, nor the European Commission are responsible for any use that may be made of the information it contains. For more information on the project see: https:// safety4rails.eu/.

References

1. Ip, W. H., Wang, D.: Resilience evaluation approach of transportation networks. In: International Joint Conference on Computational Sciences and Optimization, 2009, pp. 618–622. https://doi.org/10.1109/CSO.2009.294
2. Alessio, P., et al.: Resilience or robustness: identifying topological vulnerabilities in rail networks. R. Soc. open sci. **6**(2), 181301 (2019). https://doi.org/10.1098/rsos.181301
3. Castanier, B., et al.: A risk and resilience assessment approach for railway networks (2021). https://doi.org/10.3850/978-981-18-2016-8_402-cd
4. Bešinović, N.: Resilience in railway transport systems: a literature review and research agenda. Transport Rev. **40**(4), 457-478 (2020)
5. Ip, W.H., Wang, D.: Resilience and friability of transportation networks: evaluation, analysis and optimization. IEEE Syst. J. **5**(2), 189–198 (2011). https://doi.org/10.1109/JSYST.2010.2096670
6. Furno, A., El Faouzi, N.-E., Sharma, R., Cammarota, V., Zimeo, E.: A graph-based framework for real-time vulnerability assessment of road networks. In: IEEE International Conference on Smart Computing (SMARTCOMP), pp. 234–241 (2018). https://doi.org/10.1109/SMARTCOMP.2018.00096
7. Pavlopoulos, G.A., Secrier, M., Moschopoulos, C.N., et al.: Using graph theory to analyze biological networks. BioData Min. **4**, 10 (2011). https://doi.org/10.1186/1756-0381-4-10
8. Psaltoglou, A., Calle, E.: Enhanced connectivity index - a new measure for identifying critical points in urban public transportation networks. Int. J. Crit. Infrastruct. Prot. **21**, 22–32 (2018). https://doi.org/10.1016/j.ijcip.2018.02.003
9. Köpke, C., Srivastava, K., Miller, N., Branchini, E.: Resilience quantification for critical infrastructure: exemplified for airport operations. In: et al. Computer Security. ESORICS 2021 International Workshops. ESORICS 2021. Lecture Notes in Computer Science(), vol. 13106. Springer, Cham (2022). https://doi.org/10.1007/978-3-030-95484-0_26
10. Bigdeli, A., et al.: Comparison of network criticality, algebraic connectivity, and other graph metrics. In: Proceedings of the 1st Annual Workshop on Simplifying Complex Network for Practitioners (2009)
11. Köpke, C., et al.: Impact propagation in airport systems. Cyber-Physical Security for Critical Infrastructures Protection, pp. 191–206. Guildford, UK, 18 September 2020. https://doi.org/10.1007/978-3-030-69781-5_13
12. Fehling-Kaschek, M., et al.: Risk and resilience assessment and improvement in the telecommunication industry, pp. 247–254 (2020). https://doi.org/10.3850/978-981-14-8593-0_3995-cd

13. Crabbe, S., et al.: SAFETY4RAILS Information System platform demonstration at Madrid Metro simulation exercise. In: Leva, M.C., Patelli, E., Podofillini, L., Wilson, S. (eds.) Proceedings of the 32nd European Safety and Reliability Conference, Copyright 2022 by ESREL2022 Organizers. Published by Research Publishing, Singapore ISBN: 981-973-0000-00-0. https://doi.org/10.3850/981-973-0000-00-0_esrel2022-paper

14. Layton, R., Watters, P.: Automating open source intelligence: algorithms for OSINT (2015)

15. Scharte, B., Hiller, D., Leismann, T., Thoma, K.: Automating open source intelligence. In: Resilien Tech. Resilience by design: a strategy for the technology issues of the future (acatech STUDY), Munich: Herbert Utz Verlag (2014)

16. OpenMobilityData. https://transitfeeds.com/p/roma-servizi-per-la-mobilita/542/latest. Accessed 28 June 2022

17. Google Transit APIs. https://developers.google.com/transit/gtfs. Accessed 28 June 2022

18. SAFETY4RAILS. https://safety4rails.eu/

19. Resisto. https://www.resistoproject.eu/

20. Satie. https://satie-h2020.eu/

21. Numpy. https://numpy.org/

22. Networkx. https://networkx.org/

23. Shapely. https://shapely.readthedocs.io/en/stable/manual.html

24. GeoPandas. https://geopandas.org/en/stable/

25. Bokeh. http://docs.bokeh.org/en/latest/

HoneyChart: Automated Honeypot Management over Kubernetes

George Kokolakis[1]([⊠]), Grigoris Ntousakis[2,3], Irodotos Karatsoris[2],
Spiros Antonatos[3], Manos Athanatos[3,4], and Sotiris Ioannidis[2,4]

[1] Georgia Institute of Technology, Atlanta, USA
gkokolakis6@gatech.edu
[2] Technical University of Crete (TUC), Kounoupidiana, Greece
{gntousakis,ikaratsoris,sioannidis}@tuc.gr
[3] Telecommunication Systems Research Institute (TSI), Chania, Greece
{gntousakis,santonatos,mathanatos}@tsi.gr
[4] The Foundation for Research and Technology - Hellas (FORTH), Heraklion, Greece
{athanat,sotiris}@ics.forth.gr

Abstract. Honeypots have been proven to be a useful tool in the arsenal of defense solutions against cyber-attacks. Over time, various honeypot solutions have been proposed to lure attackers that target both conventional networks and Industrial Control Systems. However, the current approaches do not make the deployment and usability of honeypots more attractive to defenders. In this paper we propose HONEYCHART, a framework for honeypot deployment that leverages on Helm Charts for Kubernetes to create honeypot templates from existing virtualized environments and deploy the appropriate honeypots based on the desired services. HONEYCHART allows the fast and automated deployment of containerized honeypots, allowing the defenders to focus on what really matters: the analysis of attacks, IoCs and imminent threats.

1 Introduction

A formal definition of a honeypot is a trap set to detect, deflect or in some manner counteract attempts at unauthorized use of information systems. Practically, honeypots are systems set up to lure attackers. Honeypots are non-production systems, which means machines that do not belong to any user or run publicly available services. Instead, in most cases, they passively wait for attackers to contact them. By default, all traffic destined to honeypots is malicious or unauthorized as it should not exist in the first place. Honeypots can also assume other forms, like files, database records, or e-mails.

The original goal of honeypots was to detect worms. As worms cannot afford to acquire the knowledge whether their next victim is a honeypot or not, they blindly try to attack the whole IP address space. Based on that behavior, honeypots are able to catch instances of worms by running decoy services, analyze them, and pass all the gathered information to signature generation systems and behavior analysis modules. However, as the attack landscape has changed and

© The Author(s), under exclusive license to Springer Nature Switzerland AG 2023
S. Katsikas et al. (Eds.): ESORICS 2022 Workshops, LNCS 13785, pp. 321–328, 2023.
https://doi.org/10.1007/978-3-031-25460-4_18

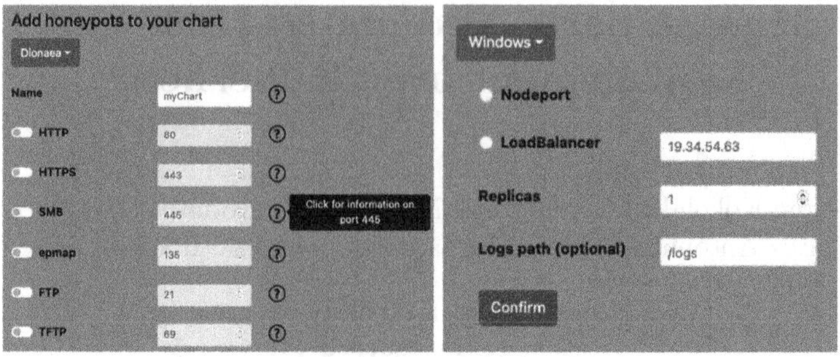

(a) Adding honeypot to chart.   (b) Using pre-configured interfaces.

Fig. 1. HONEYCHART web interface.

the existence of automated worms has become rare, the use of honeypots has also evolved. Honeypots are now used to detect worm-able attacks, like Blue-Keep [11] or provide useful insights for protecting Industrial Control Systems (ICS) and their SCADA components.

While a number of honeypot solutions have been proposed, they also suffer from a major drawback when it comes to their deployability. They all come as standalone scripts or set of software components that need to be manually deployed and monitored. Most of the current honeypot developments has not caught up with the recent advances in virtualization and container orchestration, which are now become more prevalent for production workloads and even 5G core networks [13].

In this paper we try to close the gap by proposing HONEYCHART, a framework for honeypot deployment that leverages Kubernetes to create honeypot templates from existing virtualized environments and deploy the appropriate honeypots based on the desired services. HONEYCHART comes with a set of tools to map services running inside a Kubernetes cluster into their corresponding honeypot services and propose to the security administrators a meaningful template ready for deployment. In a next step, HONEYCHART allows the fast and automated deployment of containerized honeypots. HONEYCHART has been open-sourced and is available for download from GitHub: github.com/parasecurity/honeychart.

2   Background

In this section of the paper we are going to present background information about Honeypots (Sect. 2.1), Kubernetes (Sect. 2.2), and Helm Charts (Sect. 2.3).

2.1   Honeypots

The main classification criterion of a honeypot is its level of interactivity with the attackers. Honeypots can either do simple service emulation (low-interaction), more advanced emulation (medium-interaction) or run real services (high-interaction). Low-interaction honeypots emulate IT services that are usually requested by attackers. They do not provide an actual OS, only a limited subset of the functionality attackers would expect from a server [21]. Several low-interaction honeypots have been implemented, like honeyd [23], Honeytrap [6], LaBrea [9], and Dionaea [3]. A high-interaction honeypot is a complete system, which contains a fully functional OS and all the services that it could provide. High-interaction honeypots are used to capture the maximum amount of information concerning new and old ways of attacking. Minos [17] is a microarchitecture that implements Biba's low water-mark integrity policy [15] on individual words of data. Argos [22] is a containment environment for worms and manual system compromises. It is actually an extended version of the Qemu emulator that tracks whether data coming from the network is used as jump targets, function addresses or instructions by performing dynamic taint analysis [20]. Medium-interaction honeypots attempt to mix the benefits of both low and high-interaction honeypots. They are more advanced than low-interaction honeypots, but they are not as advanced as high-interaction honeypots. The Nepenthes platform [14] and Multipot [12] honeypots fall into this category.

Honeypots have also been used for protecting SCADA networks. Conpot [1] is a low-interaction server-side ICS honeypot and supports a variety of SmartGrid use cases. Conpot supports protocols such as Modbus TCP, HTTP, IEC104, FTP, TFTP, S7Comm, BACnet, and SNMP, and it, like other honeypots, can keep track of attacks. CryPLH [16] is a high-interaction honeypot that emulates a Siemens S7-300 PLC, with HTTP/ HTTPS, S7comm, and SNMP services running on a Linux host modified to accept connections on specific ports. SHaPe [18] (Scada HoneyPot) is a low-interaction honeypot that can be used on substation automation systems. S7commTrace [24] is a honeypot based on the S7 protocol. This protocol is running on PLCs of Siemens S7-300, 400, 1200 and 1500 series. HoneyPLC [19] is a high-interaction, malware-collecting honeypot for ICS. It simulates TCP/IP, HTTP, SNMP and S7comm protocols.

2.2 Kubernetes

Kubernetes [8], at its basic level, is a system for running and coordinating containerized applications across a cluster of machines. It is a platform designed to completely manage the life cycle of containerized applications and services using methods that provide predictability, scalability, and high availability. A Kubernetes system consists of a master node and any number of worker nodes. Kubernetes deploys applications to the cluster of worker nodes after the developer submits a list of applications to the master.

2.3 Helm Charts

Helm [5], is a package manager for Kubernetes. Helm is an open-source project that was originally developed by Deis Labs and is now maintained by Cloud Native Computing Foundation (CNCF). Helm was created with the intention of giving users a better way to manage all of the Kubernetes YAML (description) files that they create on Kubernetes projects. Deis Labs developed Helm Charts as a means of resolving the description file management problem. Each chart is a collection of one or more Kubernetes manifests while a chart can also have child and dependent charts. When we run the install command for the top-level chart, Helm installs the entire project's dependency tree. The Kubernetes project's goal is to manage your containers, but it cannot use template files. Helm gives us the ability to create template files and add to them variables and functions. These files are truly generic and can be used across large teams or organizations to deploy scalable applications where their parameters can be changed at any time.

3   Implementation

In this section of the paper we are going to present the implementation details of HONEYCHART. To ease the deployment process of honeypots we have developed a tool for generating Helm Charts of containerized honeypots for deployment in a Kubernetes cluster. The charts we create can contain descriptions and deployment parameters for a single or multiple Honeypots. We support multiple honeypot types, including low-interaction and high-interaction honeypots. We create the honeypot charts via the HONEYCHART web interface (Fig. 1. We developed the front-end of HONEYCHART using HTML, CSS, and JavaScript. We developed the back-end of HONEYCHART using Node.js.

We provide to the user of HONEYCHART two main options. The user can either create custom honeypots (Sect. 3.3) or create honeypots based on pre-built templates, derived from real world scenarios, exposing specific interfaces (Sect. 3.2). The pre-built interfaces allow the user to select pre-built honeypot Helm Charts that can simulate different protocols, e.g. the PLC communication protocols or the Microsoft Windows protocols. With the custom honeypots creation option we allow the user to create custom Helm Charts configuring the supported honeypots on the platform, based on his requirements. All this functionality is supported by our web interface.

3.1   Custom Honeypots

On the Custom Honeypots page, the user fist chooses which honeypot is going to use. At the moment, there are three available honeypot images on HONEYCHART. These are Dionaea [3], Conpot [1], and Cowrie [2]. After selecting the honeypot image, the user can then enable or disable the available protocols supported by the honeypot.

In addition to the selection of the honeypot image, we are able to provide to the user multiple other configuration options. For example, the user can select which Kubernetes ServiceType they prefer for their deployment. Kubernetes ServiceType is used when a developer wants to expose an application to an IP address that is outside of the cluster. The available choices of ServiceType are Nodeport or LoadBalancer. If the user selects Nodeport, they do not need

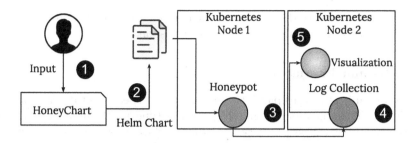

Fig. 2. Overview of HoneyChart usage.

to fill the IP address field. If they select the `LoadBalancer` option, then they must fill the IP address field using the `IPv4` format (`IBM`, `IPv4` and `IPv6` address formats).

Another configuration option available is the number of replicas and the file path for the honeypots' logs. In the replicas section the user can specify how many replicas of the Helm Chart they need. The allowed range of values is from one to 100. This information can be seen by hovering over the question mark next to the replicas text field. Logs' path allows the user to specify in which directory the honeypot logs will be extracted.

After filling the form and pressing the `Add` button the application performs a series of validations to make sure that the user's options are correct. If there is an error, the application will notify the user with a warning. Otherwise, the user has the option to add more honeypots to the chart, or finish the process by pressing the `Create` button. If they choose to add more honeypots to the chart, they just have to follow the previous steps again. Otherwise, the user downloads the charts to their computer and they can now deploy it on their Kubernetes cluster. With the options that HoneyChart provides, the user can combine services from different honeypots to build certain profiles.

After the user clicks the `Create` button the Helm Chart generation begins. The data structure gets converted to a `JSON` string on the front-end and with a `POST` request the program sends the `JSON` string to the back-end.

When the server receives the `JSON` string, it validates the name of the Helm Chart for security purposes. Afterwards the program initializes the `generic_values`, `generic_deployment`, and `generic_service` data structures. The process continues with specifying the logs path for both the container and the worker node. Depending on the selection of honeypots made by the user, the program fills out values, services and deployment data to the corresponding data structures. Then we create three YAML files, `values.yaml`, `deployment.yaml`, and `service.yaml` using the three data structures.

Now that we have all the needed information, HoneyChart creates a chart directory with all of the necessary files and directories. Then, HoneyChart moves the `values.yaml` file to the chart's root directory and the `deployment.yaml` and the `service.yaml` to the templates directory. When the chart directory is ready the server creates a zip file from the directory and then the server sends the zip file to the client as a response.

3.2   Pre-built Interfaces

At the pre-built interfaces page the user can select specific setups from a drop-down menu. Then the user can choose the service type, set the number of replicas, and the honeypot log path. Every available interface is created in the form of a JSON file. The file contains the name of the chart, the names of the honeypots that will be used, a default logs path, the services, the container ports, the protocol type for every service that is going to be used and a string that contains a description of the honeypot's services. After the user has selected the pre-built interface, the service type, the number of replicas and the log path they must click confirm to move to the next step of the process.

Pre-built Interfaces page follows the same principles as the Custom Honeypots page. First, the program initializes the data structure. Afterwards, it checks the ServiceType. If the LoadBalancer is selected then it validates the IP address. The program then fills the ServiceType and the IP address, when applicable, to the data structure. Next, it validates the replica number and registers the number to the data structure. Finally, it fills the logs path in the data structure.

When the data structure is ready then the chart information gets displayed on the page. With the information panel the user can review their choices and then they can click Create to finish the chart creation. The chart creation process is the same as the custom build option.

3.3   Automated Port Mapping

Another tool that comes bundled with HONEYCHART, is a template suggestion script that creates a Helm Chart based on services running in the Kubernetes cluster. This python script identifies the ports and protocols of each running service in the cluster and initiates a post request to HONEYCHART containing that information. Subsequently, HONEYCHART processes the request by mapping the corresponding ports and protocols that were identified with the corresponding services that the three honeypots offer and produces a Helm Chart which is sent back to the cluster.

4   Deployment

In this section of the paper we are going to present an in-depth example of a chart generation using HONEYCHART and a deployment using the generated Helm Charts.

We are going to use HONEYCHART to generate a Helm Chart for a Conpot honeypot deployment. Conpot honeypot is a low-interaction server-side

ICS/SCADA honeypot. The `ServiceType` in our example is `LoadBalancer` and we are deploying a single replica of the honeypot.

After the creation of the `Conpot` honeypot chart the user can download it in a `zip` format and the user can deploy it on their Kubernetes cluster. The file is downloaded in `zip` format. After extraction, the chart can be deployed using the following installation command. In our example the name of the chart is `conpot-chart`.

```
1  helm install conpot-chart conpot-chart
```

After running the above command with `kubelet` on the worker node it will instruct Docker to download and run the `Conpot` container image from the Dockerhub registry. To check if the pod is running we run the following command.

```
1  kubectl get pods
```

When the pod is ready we can run `kubectl` get services to display additional information about the running pods, such as `ServiceType`, `Cluster-IP`, `External-IP`, exposed ports, and the amount of time the pod is running.

```
1  kubectl get services
```

Now that we know that the pod is running properly on the Kubernetes cluster, we can scan the external IP using the `nmap` scanning tool. The `nmap` tool is an open-source Linux command-line tool for scanning IP addresses and ports in a network.

After the honeypots deployment, we harvest their `JSON` logs using filebeat [4]. Filebeat send the logs to logstash [10], where an extra processing occurs in order to get stored in an efficient format to Elastic search. Finally, visualize the logs using kibana [7].

5 Conclusion

We use honeypots to detect, deflect or counteract unauthorized access to information systems. While a large number of honeypots have been proposed and created, the deployment process of honeypots has not been improved in recent years. In this work, we proposed HONEYCHART, a framework for honeypot deployment that eases their deployment process. To ease the deployment process of honeypots we leverage the use of Helm Charts and Kubernetes. We create Helm Charts though a web-interface with a set of predefined or custom options. Then we use helm to deploy them on the desired Kubernetes cluster. We demonstrated the use of HONEYCHART on an extensive example. HONEYCHART source code is available to download from github.com/parasecurity/honeychart.

Acknowledgments. This work was partly supported by DARPA contract no. HR001120C0155. This work has also received funding from JCOP project (GA No INEA/CEF/ICT/A2020/2373266) and from European Union's Horizon 2020 program COLLABS (No 871518).

References

1. Conpot ICS/SCADA Honeypot. http://conpot.org/
2. Cowrie. https://github.com/cowrie/cowrie
3. Dionaea. https://github.com/DinoTools/dionaea
4. Filebeat. https://www.elastic.co/beats/filebeat
5. Helm. https://helm.sh//
6. Honeytrap. https://www.honeynet.org/projects/active/honeytrap//
7. Kibana. https://www.elastic.co/kibana/
8. Kubernetes. http://kubernetes.io
9. Labrea. http://labrea.sourceforge.net/labrea-info.html
10. Logstash. https://www.elastic.co/logstash/
11. Microsoft operating systems bluekeep vulnerability. https://www.cisa.gov/uscert/ncas/alerts/AA19-168A
12. Multipot. https://inc0x0.com/2019/05/multipot-web-application-honeypot-with-built-in-analysis-tools/
13. Why kubernetes over bare metal infrastructure is optimal for cloud native applications. https://www.ericsson.com/en/blog/2022/5/kubernetes-over-bare-metal-cloud-infrastructure-why-its-important-and-what-you-need-to-know
14. Baecher, P., Koetter, M., Holz, T., Dornseif, M., Freiling, F.: The nepenthes platform: an efficient approach to collect malware, pp. 165–184 (2006)
15. Biba, K.: Integrity considerations for secure computer systems. MITRE Technical report TR-3153 (1977)
16. Buza, D., Juhász, F., Miru, G., Félegyházi, M., Holczer, T.: Cryplh: protecting smart energy systems from targeted attacks with a plc honeypot. In: SmartGridSec (2014)
17. Crandall, J., Chong, F., Wu, S.: Minos: architectural support for protecting control data. Trans. Archit. Code Optim. (TACO) 3(4), 359–389 (2006)
18. Koltys, K., Gajewski, R.R.: Shape: a honeypot for electric power substation. J. Telecommun. Inf. Technol. (2015)
19. López-Morales, E., Rubio-Medrano, C., Doupé, A., Shoshitaishvili, Y., Wang, R., Bao, T., Ahn, G.J.: HoneyPLC: a next-generation honeypot for industrial control systems, pp. 279–291. Association for Computing Machinery, New York (2020)
20. Newsome, J., Dong, D.: Dynamic taint analysis for automatic detection, analysis, and signature generation of exploits on commodity software. In: Proceedings of the 12th ISOC Symposium on Network and Distributed System Security (SNDSS), pp. 221–237 (2005)
21. Peter, E., Schiller, T.: A practical guide to honeypots. https://www.cse.wustl.edu/~jain/cse571-09/ftp/honey/index.html
22. Portokalidis, G., Slowinska, A., Bos, H.: Argos: an emulator for fingerprinting zero-day attacks. In: Proceedings of ACM SIGOPS Eurosys 2006 (2006)
23. Provos, N.: A virtual honeypot framework. In: Proceedings of the 13th USENIX Security Symposium, pp. 1–14 (2004)
24. Xiao, F., Chen, E., Xu, Q.: S7commTrace: a high interactive honeypot for industrial control system based on S7 protocol. In: Qing, S., Mitchell, C., Chen, L., Liu, D. (eds.) ICICS 2017. LNCS, vol. 10631, pp. 412–423. Springer, Cham (2018). https://doi.org/10.1007/978-3-319-89500-0_36

ComSEC: Secure Communications for Baggage Handling Systems

Filipe Apolinário[1]([✉])(iD), João Guiomar[1], Éric Hervé[2], Sven Hrastnik[3],
Nelson Escravana[1], Miguel L. Pardal[4](iD), and Miguel Correia[4](iD)

[1] INOV, Lisbon, Portugal
{filipe.apolinario,nelson.escravana}@inov.pt
[2] Alstef Group, Brest, France
eric.herve@alstefgroup.com
[3] Zagreb Airport, Zagreb, Croatia
[4] INESC-ID, IST, ULisboa, Lisbon, Portugal
{miguel.pardal,miguel.p.correia}@tecnico.ulisboa.pt

Abstract. Throughout the years, the number of network attacks targeting industrial control systems (ICS) has increased. A notable example targeting airport infrastructures is false data injection attacks, where attackers try to impersonate parts of the ICS system using spoofing techniques, sending unauthorized commands to hinder the quality of service. This article presents ComSEC, a bump-in-the-wire technology for detecting attacks against integrity and replays. The article also describes the development and deployment on the simulation platform of two ComSEC prototypes for monitoring airport baggage handling systems (BHSs): 1) a virtualized version crafted for monitoring virtual machines; 2) a physical hardware version crafted for monitoring airport physical hardware systems. ComSEC was evaluated on a digital twin BHS, available on the SATIE simulation platform (https://satie-h2020.eu/) and integrated with the Zagreb airport BHS.

Keywords: Integrity verification · Critical infrastructures · Airport security

1 Introduction

Airport infrastructures [6,16], as other industrial infrastructures, are comprised of two main classes of assets: physical assets and technological assets. The realm of *airport physical assets* (such as control towers, hangars, terminals, and baggage conveyors) supports the core business of these transportation infrastructures and provides a wide type of services (air traffic control, ground control, baggage and passenger boarding, etc.) to end users who rely on the activities of these organizations (e.g., passengers, airline companies) [20]. On the other hand, the *technological assets* that comprise airport infrastructure monitoring and control of physical assets provide airport personnel with technological tools

© The Author(s), under exclusive license to Springer Nature Switzerland AG 2023
S. Katsikas et al. (Eds.): ESORICS 2022 Workshops, LNCS 13785, pp. 329–345, 2023.
https://doi.org/10.1007/978-3-031-25460-4_19

to manage and supervise the work performed on the physical assets of the airport and automate the scheduling of the tasks required to provide airport services.

Figure 1 shows that, similarly to other industries (transportation, energy supply and distribution, manufacturing, etc.), airports are cyber-physical infrastructures, typically organized as *industrial control system* (ICS) architectures [18] where physical assets connect to technological assets using different network protocols (e.g., Profinet, MODBUS, DNP3).

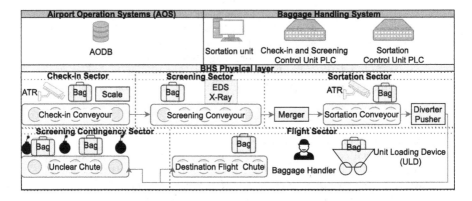

Fig. 1. Example of an airport baggage handling system (BHS) architecture.

Although industrial control systems are often *air gapped* with very strict access control policies, these cyber-physical environments have been subjected to successful cyber-attacks that were able to bypass ICS security mechanisms and issue unauthorized commands to ICS critical systems, resulting in physical equipment and safety failures. A notable example of a cyber-physical attack, Stuxnet, was able to infiltrate and shutdown an Iranian uranium enrichment plant through the Supervisory control and data acquisition (SCADA) system. From there, Stuxnet gained access to the programmable logic controllers (PLCs) that controlled the plant centrifuges. Stuxnet exploited unpatched Windows vulnerabilities and sabotaged centrifuges by making them spin up to 40% faster than normal velocity, while falsely reporting normal velocity to supervisory servers, resulting in permanent equipment damage without being noticed by operators. Another notable example of a cyber-attack on ICS systems is the 2016 Shamoon attack that, among others, targeted Saudi Arabia's General Authority of Civil Aviation (GACA). This attack was carried out using a worm malware that started by obtaining administrator access to a remote computer at the aviation center, destroyed the data on the computer and proliferated to other devices on the network. The Shamoon attack was able "to destroy critical data and hinder operations to a halt for several days". Another example is the 2019 Kemuri attack targeting a water treatment facility, where attackers were able to access from the internet the ICS system of this facility, obtained remote access to the

PLCs and performed malicious operations to alter the chemical dosage used in the water treatment procedure, putting at risk the whole treatment procedure.

In a broader sense, a high number of *attacks on cyber-physical environments* can often be classified as attacks on data integrity, often through *false data injection attacks*. In these attacks, attackers impersonate parts of the ICS system using spoofing techniques to send unauthorized commands to critical systems in order to hinder the quality of service. Common attacks often include injection of privileged operations to change a control unit state (e.g., shutdown operations or tampering state variables), or issuing operations to change the properties of the physical systems the unit is connected to (e.g., stopping baggage handling systems conveyors or shutting down explosive detection systems). Other common attacks often include, sending false messages to a SCADA or HMI system on the behalf of control units, in order to gain a false impression of the system current state for the infrastructure administrator to trigger the wrong contingency measures. Common examples of SCADA attacks include falsifying control unit readings to circumvent malicious activity detection, or falsifying readings for administrators to perform countermeasures that can hinder the quality of service (such as, shutting down control unit equipment, changing physical properties, like stopping or slowing down conveyors, etc.).

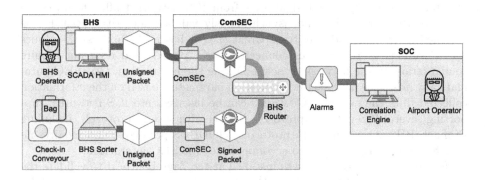

Fig. 2. Deployment of ComSEC on a BHS sending alarms to a SOC.

Protection against false data injection attacks is often difficult in ICS systems, since on one hand they are typically constructed with specific network protocols for each domain (e.g., airport systems use specific network protocols for the aviation domain, such as IATA message types or INFOPAX, while energy sectors use iec61850 network protocol suite) that typically do not include cyber security measures to assure the message integrity protection required to protect against these attacks; and on the other hand most systems are developed for long lifespan and any efforts to add additional network protection to those systems often require development costs to equip these legacy systems with the necessary cryptography means for integrity assurance. Several *security mechanisms* protect against false data injection attacks exist and can be divided into two categories, secure *tunnelling approaches* [3,4,13,14] that create a secure channel capable of providing security assurances on all data packets shared between ICS devices and *bump-in-the-wire approaches* which are cryptographic units placed between ICS devices and the local network, to update security guarantees of network protocols. However, current approaches to improving security often *introduce latency* in communication due to encryption and decryption operations, which can compromise the quality of services of time critical ICS operations.

This article describes COMSEC, a mechanism aimed at providing *integrity* and *authentication* assurances to all IP network communications. As illustrated in Fig. 2, COMSEC was developed as a bump-in-the-wire, that inspects network traffic exchanged between an ICS device and the network and digitally signs outgoing traffic. Incoming traffic is inspected and validated according to other COMSEC signatures. COMSEC is equipped with an alerting system that sends in real-time events to other intrusion detection and Security Information and Event Management (SIEM) systems, whenever integrity and authentication incidents are detected. COMSEC reduces network latency often imposed by bump-in-the-wire technology, by proposing an innovative mechanism based on Linux Netfilter kernel modules[1] that inspects outgoing traffic exchanged between ICS devices and sends the network packet digital signatures on a separate packet asynchronously through the ICS network. COMSEC has correlation capabilities to filter out network packet signatures from ICS network traffic, forward the traffic to the ICS device and asynchronously validate integrity. COMSEC is designed to be plug-and-play transparent (i.e., it has no IP address; it mimics the IP address of ICS devices connected to COMSEC) and does not require configuration on the network or hosts. During the installation, COMSEC automatically infers the necessary configuration parameters based on the information collected from the network. COMSEC can be inserted into ICS networks, supporting several ICS network protocols (tested with several protocols, including Profinet, BHS-specific network protocols, MODBUS protocols) and requires no modifications to ICS devices to accommodate COMSEC interaction.

For evaluation, COMSEC was installed at the Zagreb airport to validate the integrity of BHS communications. During this installation, we simulated false data injection attacks that were detected by COMSEC with 100% accuracy, and a low false positive rate (3%). We also integrated COMSEC with a SIEM developed in the H2020 SATIE project, named Correlation Engine, which received the COMSEC integrity alerts and correlated with other alerts coming from a detection system that monitored BHS processes, named Business Process Intrusion Detection System (BP-IDS) [12]. Thanks to COMSEC and the Correlation Engine, it was possible to detect the false data injection attack (based on COMSEC alerts), and also identify the consequences of the attack to the physical processes of the BHS (based on BP-IDS alerts). Thus showing that the mixture of different cyber and physical detection sensors can be instrumental for an holistic and complete view of the cyber-physical attack surface.

---

[1] https://www.netfilter.org/.

2   Related Work

Approaches to increase the security of unprotected industrial control system network communications have been studied over the years. These approaches can be divided into two main categories: secure tunneling approaches for creating secure links between ICS components; and bump-in-the-wire approaches that use network taps to intercept network traffic between devices and ICS network, and upgrade the network packet security assurances.

Secure tunneling approaches [3,4,13,14] allow upgrading network protocol security using secure shell tunnels (SSH) or IPSec virtual private networks (VPN). For example [3] uses SSH to secure machine manufacturing messages (MMS) exchanged between a SCADA server and ICS control units. In this case, each ICS control unit has an SSH server application, and SCADA server establishes an SSH tunnel where MMS messages are sent to a local port of the SCADA server and redirected via SSH tunnel to control unit machine. Although this approach raises confidentiality, integrity, and authentication, the approach also imposes several maintenance difficulties. First, it requires changing software applications to use the SSH tunnels instead of directly connecting to control unit devices (which can be often difficult to manage since each network protocol will have a different local port). Second, firewalling cannot be done at the network level, as all network communications are done through SSH tunnels. Thus, firewalling needs to be done at the host level to forbid network traffic sent over the SSH tunnels. Another way to perform secure tunneling while reducing the amount of configuration needed on each ICS host is to use IPSec [13,14]. In this approach, each ICS device establishes a secure channel to other devices using IPSec transport mode. In IPSec transport mode, each device establishes a secure connection to another machine where all network protocols exchanged are upgraded with two possible modes: (1) authentication headers, where the IPSec application alters outgoing packets and appends an authentication header to ensure integrity of all data present in the internet protocol (IP); (2) encapsulating security payload (ESP), where IPSec application alters outgoing traffic and replaces IP data with an encapsulation payload that contains the original packet cyphered and digitally signed. Although this approach solves confidentiality, integrity and authentication and requires less configuration than SSH tunnels (requires setting up one IPSec connection for each ICS device the machine communicates, instead of one SSH tunnel for each network protocol and host the machine communications) the approach continues to require installing IPSec software and demands from ICS devices a high level of computation requirements to ensure cryptographic properties (this can be a particular difficulty in ICS since most control unit devices do not have the computational requirements to install and run IPSec), several maintenance difficulties can also arise in ESP, namely requires firewalling cannot be done at network level since all network communications are done via IPSec, it requires firewalling at host level to forbid network traffic sent over the IPSec tunnel (which can be difficult to perform given the control units computational requirements). Aside from the aforementioned problems, tunneling approaches also introduce latency in the communication due to encryption and decryption operations, which can compromise the quality of services of time-critical ICS operations.

To reduce the amount of configuration and computational requirements on the ICS control unit devices, recent articles studied the introduction of *bump-in-the-wire devices* placed between the ICS devices and the local network. These devices are often viewed as proxies or network bridges that intercept network communications between devices, and upgrade the communications. Bump-in-the-wires improve security by *offloading computational requirements* from ICS devices. An approach [17] is to create a bump-in-the-wire to authenticate transport communication between SCADA and autonomous vehicle control units, in order to create a secure channel for the legacy machine manufacturing protocol (MMS). Another approach [19] is to design a bump-in-the-wire methodology to cypher data and provide authentication in communications. Another possible approach [9] is constructing a bump-in-the-wire to convert legacy network protocols (like the unsecure power grid network protocol IEC 61850-90-5) into the upgraded and more secure version of this protocol (IEEE C37.118.2) which provides confidentiality and integrity assurances, and can also convert it back to IEC 61850-90-5 at the receiving ICS device for backward compatibility on legacy systems. Another bump-in-the-wire approach [11] created a stealth bump-in-the-wire network bridge firewall based on Netfilter ebtables that is hidden from attackers by not having an IP address. Another approach [10] customizes bump-in-the-wire firewall to inspect MODBUS network packets and offers features for ICS administrators to create custom rules to inspect proprietary network protocols. Bump-in-the-wires [7] were also created as a bridge based on ebtables that intercepts network packets and appends authentication with message authentication codes and freshness parameters to all outgoing traffic exchanged by ICS devices for validating freshness of communication exchanged between entities. A lightweight bump-in-the-wire [5] was also proposed using hash-chaining based on a key sharing protocol exchanged between ICS devices to protect against integrity and replay attacks in a multi-hop environment. Another bump-in-the-wire [8] validated coherence between the MODBUS messages received by the control units and the physical signals issued by the control unit. Although the various approaches address integrity and replay attacks, current approaches to improve security are often *focused on particular network protocols* or need to be configured with information about hosts on the network and therefore cannot be adapted to dynamic environments where new hosts are introduced into the network.

3   ComSEC

ComSEC is a bump-in-the-wire technology to ensure integrity in ICS communication networks. It is designed to be physically connected between a device and a network router/switch, to digitally sign all network traffic sent by the device, and to validate network traffic before it reaches the device. ComSEC is able to detect and block the effects of man-in-the-middle attacks (such as false message injection and message tampering). It supports any network protocol that works over IP (e.g., TCP, UDP, MODBUS, Profinet, etc.). COMSEC notification engine sends security alerts in real time to Correlation Engine. As seen in Fig. 3, COMSEC is organized into a three-layer architecture:

1. *Physical layer* – provides the bump-in-the-wire and alert exportation. It contains two ethernet interfaces configured in bridge mode, one connected to the device and one connected to the router. These interfaces provide the bump-in-the-wire feature. The layer also has an alarm interface to export alerts to other systems.
2. *Netfilter layer* – provides a way to intercept the communications coming from and to the device. This is made using two COMSEC Kernel modules (COMSEC KMod): (1) Netfilter Outbound Module that intercepts packets sent from the device COMSEC is protecting; and Netfilter Inbound Module that intercepts network packets before they are received by the machine COMSEC is protecting.

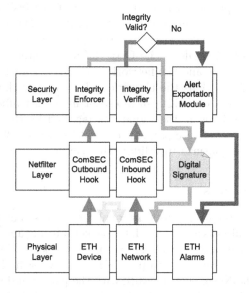

Fig. 3. Internal software architecture diagram of one COMSEC. (Color figure online)

3. *Security layer* – handles the security of the communication. It has three Linux user space modules: (1) Integrity Enforcer (IE) that signs network packets coming from the device (intercepted by Outbound Module); (2) Integrity Verifier (IV) that verifies integrity of the communication reaching the device (received by the Inbound Module); (3) Alert Exportation Module, issues alarm notifications to monitoring systems when IV identifies integrity problems.

As also seen in Fig. 3, COMSEC functioning is organized into four main workflows. First is the signing incoming packets (represented by the blue lines in the figure). Here the Ethernet (ETH) Device interface receives packets and forwards them to IE module, using the Outbound module installed in the Netfilter. The second is forwarding COMSEC signatures into the network (represented by the green lines in the figure). Here the IE module sends the signatures to the ETH Network interface. The third is validating integrity of the received network traffic (purple lines in the figure). Here the ETH Network interface receives packets and signatures and forwards them to IV module, using the Inbound module installed in the Netfilter. Forth is publishing alerts when integrity is compromised (Red lines). Here the IV notifies the alert exportation module, which sends alerts using a dedicated ETH Alarms interface.

3.1 Bridged Interfaces

To be physically installed between a device and a network router/switch, COM-SEC operates at layer 2, as a virtual bridge, with two interfaces with no IP addresses (it is transparent to layer3). This way, COMSEC is as a bump-in-the-wire between one computer and the network. For validating the integrity on communications between two devices (e.g., two servers, Server1 and Server2), two COMSECs need to be installed. The COMSECs will intercept network traffic sent between the machine and the network (COMSEC 1 for Server1 and COM-SEC 2 for Server2) and signs the network traffic to allow the other COMSEC to validate. Also, each COMSEC will intercept network traffic received by the machine and validate it using the signatures received by the other COMSECs in the network (i.e., to validate packets received from Server2, COMSEC 1 will use the COMSEC 2 signatures to validate the packet).

3.2 Netfilter Modules

COMSEC uses Netfilter to capture and analyze packets that pass through the network bridge. Netfilter is a framework for packet filtering and mangling. As can be seen in Fig. 4, each protocol defines a series of hooks, at various points (five for IPv4) in a packet's traversal of a protocol stack. At each of these points, the protocol will call the Netfilter framework with the packet and the hook number:

PRE: NF_IP_PRE_ROUTING hook, called for packets that come in after simple sanity checks, and before any routing code.

IN: NF_IP_LOCAL_IN hook, Netfilter framework is called again, after routing, if the packet was destined for a local process, and before being passed to the intended process.

FWD: NF_IP_FORWARD hook, called after routing if the packet was destined to another interface instead.

POST: NF_IP_POST_ROUTING hook, Netfilter framework is called again before being put on the network interface again.

OUT: NF_IP_LOCAL_OUT hook, called for packets that are created locally.

Kernel modules can register to listen to the different hooks for each protocol, specifying the priority of the function within the hook. When that Netfilter hook is called, each module registered at that point is called in the order of priority, being free to manipulate the packet. The module can then tell Netfilter to: **NF_DROP**: Discard the packet.

NF_ACCEPT: Continue traversal as normal.

NF_STOLEN: Forget the packet.

NF_Queue: Delegate the decision on packets to a user space software.

NF_REPEAT: Call the current hook again.

The COMSEC Netfilter kernel module (COMSEC KMod) registers to listen to the IPv4 protocol (PF_INET) on the $PRE - ROUTING$ hook with the highest possible priority. The hook used is $NF\_IP\_PRE\_ROUTING$.

When COMSEC KMod is called, first it needs to identify whether it is an inbound or outbound packet. Inbound packets are packets in which the destination is the device to which COMSEC is connected, and outbound packets are those that come from that same device, that is, outbound packets are those in which the device is the source of the packets. COMSEC performs different actions depending on the packet destinations, inbound packets are signed by COMSEC, using a user space module named Integrity Enforcer, while outbound packets are validated by COMSEC using a user space module named Integrity Verifier. In order to identify the traffic flow, that is, the inbound and outbound packets, and decide the destination of the packets, to the Integrity Enforcer or to the Integrity Verifier respectively, it is necessary to set in the COMSEC configuration which of the COMSEC bridged interfaces is connected to the device and which is connected to the network router/switch. Therefore, if a packet received on the COMSEC network bridge comes from the interface connected to the device, this packet is outbound traffic and will be sent to the Integrity Enforcer. Otherwise, if the packet comes from the interface connected to the network router/switch, this packet is inbound traffic and will be sent to the Integrity Verifier. Sending a packet to user space applications, Integrity Enforcer or Integrity Verifier, means sending the packet to the corresponding Netfilter queue (NF_Queue) target, by the COMSEC KMod. Netfilter queue (NF_Queue) allows user space modules to subscribe to Netfilter kernel events, and this way offer an interface between kernel and user space models. When a packet reaches an NF_Queue target it is placed in the queue depending on whether it should be handled by the Integrity

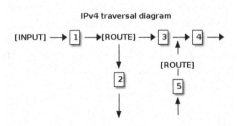

Fig. 4. COMSEC's Netfilter hooks for inspecting communications.

Enforcer or Integrity Verifier. The packet queue is a chained list with each element being the packet and metadata. The packets in the queue are then handled by the user space software asynchronously.

3.3   Integrity Enforcer

The Integrity Enforcer (IE) is a user space daemon that subscribes to a given Netfilter queue. When an outbound packet is enqueued, the Integrity Enforcer is notified by the kernel using an nfnetlink formatted message causing the execution of the Integrity Enforcer handler, a callback function that is subscribing Netfilter queue events. For each packet received by the Integrity Enforcer handler, the handler signs the packet and sends it in a raw UDP packet. This raw UDP packet functions as a control packet and is injected into the network through the interface connected to the network router/switch. The control packet will be used by the Integrity Verifier of the other ComSECs present in the network, to validate the integrity of inbound network traffic. The decision was made for ComSEC to send packet signatures over UDP raw packets instead of TCP, to facilitate its deployment in critical infrastructures without the need to keep track of the connections to other ComSEC on the network, and also not to be exposed to other devices on the network. ComSEC devices do not have IP addresses, nor have any sockets exposed to the monitored network, they function as a stealth network bridge that injects the packet signatures on behalf of the monitored devices (i.e., raw packet containing the signature has the same source and destination address of the original packet). This design makes it harder for attackers to identify the ComSEC module, but requires ComSEC signatures to be sent over sessionless communication channels (i.e., UDP) in order to be aligned with its stealth design. This makes ComSEC possibly susceptible to verification errors, due to possible control packet loss in the network. If we consider an estimated bit error rate (BER) in the network and recall that ComSEC sends a control packet for each network packet in the network, the probability of ComSEC to have verification errors is given by the following formula: $P(Error) = \dfrac{BER \times \sum\limits_{i=0}^{n} |controlPacket_i|}{\sum\limits_{i=0}^{n} |controlPacket_i| \sum |packet_i|}$

As can be seen in this formula, since control packets have almost the same size (size of the hash and metadata does not vary significantly), the probability for ComSEC to display errors depends on the BER and on the size of the packet. Given that BER in lossy networks (e.g., wireless) is typically estimated to be 10^{-5} the error rate would be negligible on the ComSEC integrity detection results giving 1 alarm every 10^5 packets. Also, since control packets are very small compared to the packet size, the probability for a bit error would be smaller than 1 out of 10^5 packets.

3.4   Control Packets

ComSEC control packets contain the necessary information for integrity validation. Control packets are sent as UDP control packets, in which the headers contain the following information required for network routing: Identification: ID of the IP header used for all control packets (defined in configuration for debugging purposes); Source and Destination Address: Same as in the packet that originated the control packet; Source and Destination Port: Control packet source and destination port (defined in configuration).

Control packet payloads are used as signatures, for integrity verification and contain the following information:

- Validations fields: Prefix: Used to differentiate control packets from other packets. It is a fixed string (e.g., "COMSEC _PACKET") that is introduced in the configuration. ComSEC ID: ComSEC identification number. Since multiple COMSECs are deployed on the same network, this ID allows the identification of the COMSEC responsible to issue each control packet. This COMSEC is defined in configuration and should be different from other COMSECs installed on the network. NFQUEUE Packet Hash: Cryptographic hash-based message authentication code (HMAC) used to evaluate the integrity of the packet that originated the control packet. The data used to calculate covers the packet IP header, transport header and data. This HMAC uses a pre-shared key present on the COMSEC file system that is shared between all COMSECs during installation. Control Packet MAC: Control packet hash-based message authentication code (HMAC). It can be used to validate the control packet (the data used to calculate is Prefix, COMSEC ID, Timestamp Nonce and Packet Hash).
- Freshness fields: Timestamp: UNIX timestamp of the creation of the control packet. Nonce: Number that can be used just once in a communication.

3.5 Integrity Verifier

Like the Integrity Enforcer, the Integrity Verifier (IV) is a user space daemon that subscribes to a given Netfilter queue. When an inbound packet is enqueued, the Integrity Verifier is notified with an nfnetlink formatted message causing the execution of a callback function (the Integrity Verifier handler). The Integrity Verifier handler will perform a set of validations in order to assess the integrity of each inbound packet. The main objective of the Integrity Verifier is to receive a network packet and the corresponding control packet from the Netfilter queue and validate integrity. Since both packets are received separately from the queue, Integrity Verifier uses a temporary knowledge database, to store information about packet or control packet until it has received both packets and has the necessary information to decide. Since COMSEC may experience data loss or intentional packet drops, at the moment the Integrity Verifier receives the first packet (network or control packet), a timer is set in the database to limit the time frame for the Integrity Verifier to decide. If this timer is reached, COMSEC raises the alert that the packet has been tampered and integrity cannot be assured.

3.6   Alert Exportation Module

COMSEC Alert Exportation Module implements alarmistic functions with automatic export of alerts. Thus, with this module, it becomes possible to configure COMSEC to send alerts to a SOC and have quick access to the incidents reported.

4   Implementation

To demonstrate COMSEC a prototype was created. COMSEC is built as a network bridge appliance that intercepts network communication packets exchanged between a host and a network switch/router. COMSEC acts as a validator component that intercepts all network traffic and validates the integrity of each network packet. Whenever integrity validation fails to be verified for a given network packet, COMSEC generates integrity alerts.

As depicted in Fig. 5, in essence, COMSEC is designed as an appliance running software composed of kernel modules and application modules.

The kernel module, installed on the Netfilter of the COMSEC appliance, intercepts communications between the monitored BHS device and network. The kernel module consists of two components: COMSEC Outbound Module that intercepts network packets sent by the BHS device to the network; and the COMSEC Inbound Module that intercepts network packets received from the network to the BHS device.

The application modules that receive the packets, inspect the network packets intercepted by the kernel modules, and perform the necessary operations to ensure the integrity of the communication. The two modules are: COMSEC Integrity Enforcer that generates message authentication codes (MACs) of all network packets sent by the BHS machine to the BHS network and forwards

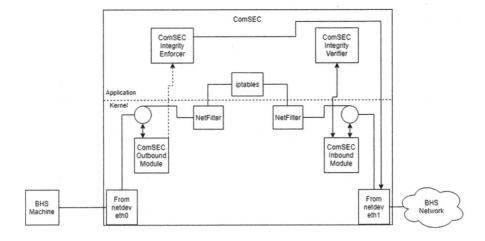

Fig. 5. COMSEC architecture installed between one BHS machine and network.

them to the BHS network to allow other COMSECs to validate integrity; and the COMSEC Integrity Verifier that compares network packets with the MACs produced by other COMSEC present in the BHS network and detects integrity attacks (e.g., unauthorized command execution, denial of service, man-in-the-middle and replay attacks).

The COMSEC prototype functions as a network bridge, allowing all traffic to and from the monitored device to pass transparently through the COMSEC network bridge. Each COMSEC will also have an isolated connection to the SATIE Correlation Engine to send alerts to the Correlation Engine.

5   Evaluation

COMSEC was integrated with a BHS. Specifically, the evaluation focused on three airport systems represented in the simulation platform: the flight information management system (FIMS), airport operation database (AODB1) and the BHS manufactured by Alstef. Under this setting, the experiments conducted to evaluate COMSEC monitored the Airbus simulation platform of the BHS operating continuously for 24 h. This simulation included a virtualized airport database that provided to the BHS sortation unit identifiers of fictitious bags and the corresponding fictitious flights assigned to physical locations of the BHS. The simulation also included, real physical equipment namely explosive detection systems (EDSs), automatic tag readers (ATRs) and conveyors. The equipment was managed by real control units connected to the BHS sortation unit in the simulation platform. The simulation used for this experiment, represented a high-fidelity with real BHS available on airports by using Emulate3D, a testing platform commonly used by BHS service providers to test their systems on contractual operating conditions before they are installed on airports. During the tests FIMS sent flight information messages. AODB issued bag check-in operations, and received messages about the bags sortation and screening decisions made by the BHS. The network traffic (24 h) used for monitoring the BHS, included a total of 1956 bags monitored and a total of 18.736.351 monitored packets. During two hours, the simulation platform was used to force the BHS to two abnormal situations. The first one, *screening anomaly*, had a duration of 22 min where the EDS screening results of 42 bags were changed by the simulation platform to route unclear bags to flight instead of the contingency chute (7 unclear bags), and clear bags to the contingency chute (33 clear bags). The second abnormal situation, "sortation anomaly", the simulation platform overwrote the BHS sortation messages to falsely route bags to different destinations. The abnormal situation had a duration of 30 min when wrong sortation orders were given for 36 bags, where bags assigned to "flight 1" were routed to "flight 2" (20) and vice-versa (16).

Table 1. CoMSEC integrity detection results for the 18736351 packets evaluated.

Type	Alerts	TN	TP	FN	FP	Accuracy	FPR
Integrity	220	18736131	213	0	7	100.0%	3.2%
Uniqueness	14656	18721695	14527	0	129	100.0%	0.88%
Both	14876	18721475	14740	0	136	100.0%	0.91%

Table 1 shows the detection results for CoMSEC to identify integrity anomalies and replays. CoMSEC monitored 18.736.351 packets and raised a total of 14747 alerts. Of the alerts raised, 220 were related to integrity problems, while 14527 were related to retransmission of network packets (uniqueness). The number of true positives (TP) is the number of attack packets that CoMSEC detected correctly. True negatives (TN) are packets correctly verified by CoMSEC as legitimate. False positives (FP) are packets wrongly judged to be an attack. False negatives (FN) are packets that were able to evade ComSEC detection. The metrics used were accuracy as $\frac{(TP+TN)}{(TP+TN+FN+FP)}$ and false positive rate (FPR) as $\frac{FP}{(TP+FP)}$.

During the evaluation, CoMSEC had 0 false negatives, showing that CoMSEC detected all anomalies and that it is a very accurate solution to assess communication integrity. This is due to the fact that CoMSEC is deterministic when assessing integrity. For each packet sent from a device CoMSEC is connected to, it will send a control packet with the signature of the packet. The non-correspondence of the signature or absence of the control packet on a receiving CoMSEC, will always generate an alert. Regarding false positives, CoMSEC shows a false positive rate of 3.2% for detecting integrity problems and 0.88% for detecting packet retransmission. Regarding integrity detection, this FPR is related to data loss during the transmission of control packets between BHS devices. The control packets are UDP packets which is a connectionless protocol. They have no guarantee of delivery, ordering, or duplicate protection. However, taking into account the reliability of current networks, a high UDP packet loss rate is unlikely (in such a case, CoMSEC may display some FPR).

CoMSEC was also integrated in the Zagreb airport and inspected the BHS network traffic. To this end, the Zagreb demonstration encompassed two stages: the installation and public demonstration.

Fig. 6. COMSEC (in blue) on the locked airport switch cabinet (orange). (Color figure online)

Two COMSEC appliances were connected on the BHS, one for each PLC. COMSEC was placed with one network interface connected to one PLC, and another network interface connected to the BHS switch, and one network interface connected to the simulation platform. During the period in which the COMSECs were deployed, they served as a bump-in-the-wire for all traffic that reached the PLCs. This deployment allowed COMSECs to completely monitor BHS activities and forward any detected integrity failures to the SOC. BHS security adminstrators used the SOC impact assessment tool called Business Impact Assessment (BIA) [15][2], to interpret ComSEC alerts and react accordingly.

During 1 month, COMSEC operated continuously, including during the normal airport operation period. Throughout the time COMSEC was active, there was no downtime or the need to intervene to do troubleshooting. This shows that COMSEC is compatible with the BHS infrastructure and capable of withstanding the normal operation conditions of the airport. A picture of the deployment can be seen in Fig. 6. The picture shows COMSEC installed on the airport cabinet. In the deployment COMSEC was strategically placed in the switch cabinet since the switch is protected by lock, showing that in an airport installation it would be very difficult to have physical access COMSEC, since it would be as difficult as accessing a network switch (which only a limited number of authorized personnel have access to).

During the Zagreb airport experiments, two staged attacks were carried out using the simulation platform: 1) Ransomware attack; 2) Change sortation messages.

The Ransomware attack starts in one of the simulation platform devices (representing the airport check-in counters computers) and automatically propagates to the simulated SCADA system through the network. This step is detected by COMSEC system which raises an alert of anomalous communication targeting

---

[2] BIA is also published as Critical infrastructure impact assessment [2].

the SCADA system. The alert is raised since the machine where the Ransomware was placed sent an unauthenticated network packet to the SCADA system.

Regarding the change of sortation messages, COMSEC detected a man-in-the-middle between BHS and PLCs; performing the change of sortation orders. This is due to COMSEC packet replay protection. This means that due to the man-in-the-middle the PLC's COMSEC will receive two network packets, the original one (sent from the PLC) and one sent by the attacker machine with the same signature, and will thus raise an alert.

6   Conclusion

This article described COMSEC, a network bridge device that validates integrity and detects replay attacks on ICS infrastructures, while imposing no significant overhead on network communications. COMSEC provides real-time alarms, as demonstrated in our evaluation. The deployment of COMSEC in a simulation platform and the Zagreb airport were also discussed in this article, showing that it can be easily deployed on current airport systems, with little configuration needed, maintenance and good detection results. From the SATIE project, it was possible to see COMSEC adds security without any additional deployment requirements, it can also be used alongside intrusion detection systems (such as BP-IDS used in the SATIE project [12,15]) to correlate alarms and identify the reasons for integrity violations. A closer look into the BP-IDS evaluation conducted on the SATIE project [1] shows COMSEC could provide an early warning packet integrity violations, which can then be correlated with a BP-IDS alarm containing the physical impact of the anomaly. The correlation of both alarms as it was done in the SATIE project provides a rich trace of the anomalous behaviour[3].

Work supported by the European Commission through contract 832969 (SATIE) and by national funds by FCT through grant UIDB/50021/2020 (INESC-ID).

References

1. Apolinário, F., Escravana, N., Hervé, E., Pardal, M.L., Correia, M.: FingerCI: generating specifications for critical infrastructures. In: Proceedings of the 37th ACM/SIGAPP Symposium on Applied Computing, SAC2022, pp. 183–186 (2022)
2. Carvalho, O., Apolinário, F., Escravana, N., Ribeiro, C.: CIIA: critical infrastructure impact assessment. In: Proceedings of the 37th ACM/SIGAPP Symposium on Applied Computing, SAC 2022, pp. 124–132, New York, NY, USA. Association for Computing Machinery (2022)
3. Chowdhury, M.M., Raddatz, H., Rossebo, J.E.: Challenges when securing manufacturing message service in legacy industrial control systems. In: Proceedings of the 2014 IEEE Emerging Technology and Factory Automation (ETFA), pp. 1–6. IEEE (2014)

---

[3] An example of correlation of both systems is available on the SATIE youtube channel: https://www.youtube.com/watch?v=z9bVvnZs6YY.

4. Dzung, D., Naedele, M., Von Hoff, T., Crevatin, M.: Security for industrial communication systems. Proc. IEEE **93**(6), 1152–1177 (2005)
5. Esiner, E., Mashima, D., Chen, B., Kalbarczyk, Z., Nicol, D.: F-Pro: a fast and flexible provenance-aware message authentication scheme for smart grid. In: 2019 IEEE International Conference on Communications, Control, and Computing Technologies for Smart Grids (SmartGridComm), pp. 1–7. IEEE (2019)
6. Falvo, M., Santi, F., Acri, R., Manzan, E.: Sustainable airports and NZEB: the real case of Rome international airport. In 2015 IEEE 15th International Conference on Environment and Electrical Engineering (EEEIC), pp. 1492–1497 (2015)
7. Genge, B., Piroska, H., Sándor, H.: PROTECT-G: protection of communications in natural gas transportation systems. In 2018 6th International Symposium on Digital Forensic and Security (ISDFS), pp. 1–5. IEEE (2018)
8. Graveto, V., Rosa, L., Cruz, T., Simões, P.: A stealth monitoring mechanism for cyber-physical systems. Int. J. Critical Infrastruct. Prot. **24**, 126–143 (2019)
9. Khan, R., Mclaughlin, K., Laverty, D., Sezer, S.: Design and implementation of security gateway for synchrophasor based real-time control and monitoring in smart grid. IEEE Access **5**, 11626–11644 (2017)
10. Li, D., Guo, H., Zhou, J., Zhou, L., Wong, J.W.: SCADAWall: a CPI-enabled firewall model for SCADA security. Comput. Secur. **80**, 134–154 (2019)
11. Likhar, P., Shankar Yadav, R.: Stealth firewall: invisible wall for network security. In: Saini, H.S., Sayal, R., Buyya, R., Aliseri, G. (eds.) Innovations in Computer Science and Engineering. LNNS, vol. 103, pp. 413–421. Springer, Singapore (2020). https://doi.org/10.1007/978-981-15-2043-3_46
12. Lima, J., Apolinário, F., Escravana, N., Ribeiro, C.: BP-IDS: using business process specification to leverage intrusion detection in critical infrastructures. In: 31st IEEE International Symposium on Software Reliability Engineering (ISSRE 2020) (2020)
13. Plesowicz, P.: A15: secure signal tunneling for SCADA and PLCs using SSH protocol. IFAC Proceed. Vol. **37**(20), 88–93 (2004)
14. Rahimi, S., Zargham, M.: Security analysis of VPN configurations in industrial control environments. In: Butts, J., Shenoi, S. (eds.) ICCIP 2011. IAICT, vol. 367, pp. 73–88. Springer, Heidelberg (2011). https://doi.org/10.1007/978-3-642-24864-1_6
15. Reuschling, F., et al.: Toolkit to enhance cyber-physical security of critical infrastructures in air transport. Cyber-Physical Threat Intelligence for Critical Infrastructures Security, pp. 254–287 (2021)
16. Sampigethaya, K., Poovendran, R.: Aviation cyber-physical systems: foundations for future aircraft and air transport. Proc. IEEE **101**(8), 1834–1855 (2013)
17. Soares, A.A., Mattos, D.M., Lopes, Y., Medeiros, D.S., Fernandes, N.C., Muchaluat-Saade, D.C.: An efficient authentication mechanism based on software-defined networks for electric vehicles. In 2019 IEEE 28th International Symposium on Industrial Electronics (ISIE), pp. 2471–2476. IEEE (2019)
18. Stouffer, K., Lightman, S., Pillitteri, V., Abrams, M., Hahn, A.: Guide to industrial control systems (ICS) security. Technical Report NIST Special Publication (SP) 800–82 Rev. 2, National Institute of Standards and Technology (2015)
19. Tsang, P.P., Smith, S.W.: YASIR: a low-latency, high-integrity security retrofit for legacy SCADA systems. In: Jajodia, S., Samarati, P., Cimato, S. (eds.) SEC 2008. ITIFIP, vol. 278, pp. 445–459. Springer, Boston, MA (2008). https://doi.org/10.1007/978-0-387-09699-5_29
20. Willemsen, B., Cadee, M.: Extending the airport boundary: connecting physical security and cybersecurity. J. Airport Manage. **12**(3), 236–247 (2018)

Methodology for Resilience Assessment for Rail Infrastructure Considering Cyber-Physical Threats

Corinna Köpke[1(✉)], Johannes Walter[1], Eros Cazzato[2], Catalin Linguraru[2], Uli Siebold[2], and Alexander Stolz[3]

[1] Fraunhofer Institute for High-Speed Dynamics, Ernst-Mach-Institut, EMI, Am Klingelberg 1, 79588 Efringen-Kirchen, Germany
`Corinna.Koepke@emi.fraunhofer.de`
[2] CuriX AG, Zugerstrasse 76B, 6340 Baar, Switzerland
`eros.cazzato@curix.ai`
[3] Albert-Ludwigs-Universität Freiburg, Emmy-Noether-Straße 2, 79110 Freiburg im Breisgau, Germany
`alexander.stolz@mail.inatech.uni-freiburg.de`

Abstract. In the EU project SAFETY4RAILS, the project partners developed a collaborative toolkit that is able to assess and eventually improve the resilience of rail and metro transportation and its infrastructure against various cyber, physical and combined cyber-physical threats. In general, to improve a property of a system such as resilience, it is necessary to assess that property first. Therefore, in this paper, we focus on the aspect of assessing the resilience by the synergistic collaboration of two tools out of this toolkit: CuriX, which is a tool for monitoring and detecting abnormal behaviour of infrastructure in the presence of threats, and CaESAR, which can asses propagation of performance losses over distributed systems that reflects its resilience. We showcase a resilience assessment for an exemplary scenario of combined cyber-physical threats which is applied to a metro system. In this assessment, the main functionalities and results of both tools as well as their combined usage will be described to demonstrate how their collaboration can contribute to an improved resilience assessment.

Keywords: Resilience · Cyber-physical threats · Detection · Impact propagation

1 Introduction

Resilience is the ability of a system to withstand certain crisis events. Typically, the life cycle of the system including crisis events is formulated in a resilience cycle that includes time before, during and after the crisis (see e.g. [7,23] and [10]). The monitoring and quantification of resilient behavior can be performed e.g. by the nine-step resilience management process [11], which is an adaptation of the

S. Katsikas et al. (Eds.): ESORICS 2022 Workshops, LNCS 13785, pp. 346–361, 2023.
https://doi.org/10.1007/978-3-031-25460-4_20

ISO 31000:2018 [12]. Especially in the cyber domain, certain resilience phases are defined, namely 'identify', 'protect', 'detect', 'respond' and 'recover' [20].

The quantification of resilience gets especially challenging when crisis events happen simultaneously and the system under consideration represents an interconnected critical infrastructure. A prominent example is a public transport network including different types of transportation modes which is the focus of this paper.

In rail operation, an increasing, number of disruptions have happened over the last years with an increasing total duration [1]. As the problem has grown in importance, the scientific output on rail infrastructure resilience has increased as well. For example, different sources for disruptions in rail operations of the New Haven Line NYC such as electricity outages and unavailability of cars and ways to increase the system's resilience by taking appropriate actions, is discussed in [6]. Most of the works focus on quantifying the resilience using different means such as data-driven, topological, simulation and optimization approaches [1]. One example for a topology based analysis is the resilience assessment of London's metro system [3]. By analyzing the graph structure of the metro grid, the authors were able to identify critical edges and unexpected dependencies in the network.

In the EU project SAFETY4RAILS, a toolkit is developed to monitor rail infrastructure before, during and after a crisis and in each resilience phase to provide decision support (see e.g. [19] and [4]). One of the tools brought to SAFETY4RAILS is CuriX (Cure Infrastructure in XaaS) [5], a software solution that follows a general approach to holistically monitor technical systems (albeit with a focus on IT infrastructure). CuriX gathers and analyses the provided key performance indicators such as time series data and log files to detect abnormal behaviour to either warn of upcoming threats or to alert current issues based on threats. Examples of this data can be performance metrics of IT infrastructure (e.g. CPU and memory usage, etc.), metric data of sensors and environment monitoring, etc. which can be pseudonymized.

Another tool brought to SAFETY4RAILS is CaESAR (Cascading Effect Simulation in Urban Areas to Assess and Increase Resilience) which is designed to predict cascades in connected infrastructure systems [10]. To this end, different simulation techniques are employed to represent the propagation of impact in infrastructure networks. The coupling of a network model and an Agent-Based Model (ABM) (see e.g. [14,16] and [15]) is here further explored. For the full list of all the tools brought into the project and the overall architecture of the toolkit, we refer to reference [21].

Given the capabilities of the two tools, we aim to showcase a resilience assessment conducted by CaESAR following a threat that impacts a certain infrastructure and is detected previously by CuriX. The combination of tools enables (i) to incorporate the detection results automatically in a resilience assessment, (ii) to estimate maximum detection times by knowing the infrastructure topology and parameters which can be considered by the detection tool and (iii) to predict large scale impacts and cascades based on detected threats. In this paper, the benefits of the tool combination is investigated in a methodological analysis based on a specific cyber-physical scenario.

We investigate a scenario in which the aim of an attack is to physically access the premises to cut the electricity supply to all the systems in a certain station, leaving it fully inoperable. This scenario is exemplified to metro and rail networks in Ankara. In this scenario, the power supply system with the connected Supervisory Control and Data Acquisition (SCADA) system, responsible for controlling the electric power and its distribution to the station, is impacted and leads to a power outage. Two variants of the power outage scenario are considered. In one variant, CuriX detects the physical access of an intruder by monitoring, for instance, door sensors protecting the SCADA system and manages to warn the system manager ahead of the potential power outage, which gives the system manager the chance to act ahead of the power outage and to therefore reduce the chance of propagating the impact. This variant considers a combined physical and cyber attack, i.e. the physical intrusion and the manipulation of the SCADA. In the other variant, the power outage happens abruptly, which CuriX manages to detect but without pre-warning. Thus, the loss of power is unavoidable and immediate. Here, the cut of power can either be introduced physically by physically attacking the infrastructure or by a cyber attack manipulating e.g. access rights and cutting the power through the SCADA system.

In the context of this scenario, we assess the impact when considering detecting and recovering capabilities for a single station in the first step and how this affects the passenger flows in surrounding stations in the second step. The structure of the paper is as follows: First, in Sect. 2 the methodology for threat detection in the station is outlined. A resilience assessment for the station is performed in Sect. 3 considering varying conditions. Further, in Sect. 4 the impact on the single station is propagated in a larger public transportation grid. Finally, in Sect. 5 the findings are summarized and an outlook is provided.

2   Threat Detection

There are various detection and monitoring system types to protect assets from cyber and physical threats. A few of them are mentioned in reference [13]:

- intrusion detection and prevention systems for the IT network;
- endpoint detection and response for end devices;
- Security Information and Event Management systems to analyse and detect attacks on the IT infrastructure by analysing collected log and event data from devices, and applications;
- and also observability tools to monitor the infrastructure from rather an operational aspect.

While many of these systems employ threshold detection and pattern matching methods to known signatures, most of these systems are also capable of employing anomaly detection methods that do not require known signatures [13]. Methods based on anomaly detection can derive insights from the behaviour of systems without the need of known signatures. In addition, these methods are applicable to heterogeneous systems and are suited for both cyber and physical threat detection such as discussed in, e.g., [2,17,18]. Anomaly detection methods can provide additional capabilities, e.g., to detect up to then unknown threats. CuriX is one of those tools aiming at the detection of known and unknown threats in a variety of infrastructures and therefore makes use of anomaly detection methods. CuriX employs statistical and machine learning-based techniques on time series data and log files to perform anomaly detection. Examples of the used techniques can be found in [8,22]. CuriX creates a model of normal system behaviour from the data, i.e. the regular behaviour of the system when used in its daily operation, and compares it to the observed behaviour. When the observed behaviour differs significantly from the created model of normal system behaviour, an anomaly is identified, i.e. abnormal behaviour. Since not every anomaly indicates a problematic state of the system which could be due to the impact of a manifested threat, CuriX provides the possibility to define customisable criteria for critical anomalies.

Given the scenario of a physical intrusion with the intention of cutting the electricity supply in the station by manipulating the SCADA system responsible for electrical power in the station, which is outlined in the introduction, we define gaining physical access to the SCADA system's room as a precondition for the intruders. Considering an intelligent access system for the room, where the access is being granted and logged based on an employee card or password entry, CuriX might be able to identify and detect any abnormal access to the SCADA system's room by monitoring the access data from the specific door. However, in the case that intruders study the behaviour such as the usual entering/leaving times to the server room and decide to act within those time frames, finding abnormal behaviour is more challenging for CuriX. Therefore, CuriX would benefit from additional data than just the entering/leaving times, for instance, by adding which persons are entering and leaving at which times.

In the first variant of this scenario, we assume that a potential intrusion to the SCADA system's room is detected by CuriX ahead of the power outage. In this variant, security personnel has the chance to take measures to prevent or system managers the chance to mitigate the impact of a power outage. CaESAR exploits this detection by conducting a resilience assessment to simulate the potential consequences of a power outage on the train and metro network. So far, we considered that CuriX is able to detect the physical intrusion as part of the kill chain, however we could also consider other parts of a possible kill chain that would lead to the same scenario outcome, for instance, cyber related events such as port scanning for reconnaissance activities or brute force attack for privilege escalation with the intention to perform a cyber attack on the SCADA system instead. In such cases, CuriX would then rather analyse the systems log files for abnormal requests in the login attempts as an example.

In the second variant of the scenario, intruders have gained physical access to the SCADA system controlling the power supply of the station without any prior detection from CuriX or any other detection system. They manipulate the SCADA system to cut the electricity supply. The consequence is the loss of availability of electrical power within the station, which could, for instance, be identified from the station's electric power consumption data or the power supply's voltage or current. We show CuriX' identification of an anomaly as a consequence of the power outage based on data motivated by reference [9] as an example in Fig. 1, which again can be used by CaESAR in its resilience assessment.

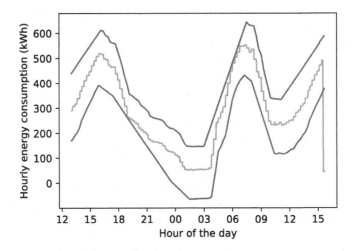

Fig. 1. The representative electric power consumption for an example station throughout the day (blue line) exhibits an abnormal drop due to the outage of the main power supply. Red lines present the upper and lower thresholds for normal behaviour. Typical amount of data to generate a model of normal system behaviour highly depend on the dynamics of the data. In the shown case, the training data covered two weeks of normal behaviour. (Color figure online)

3   Resilience Assessment

Given a threat detection for the power outage scenario from CuriX, either prior to or at the time of the power outage, CaESAR is capable of performing a resilience assessment for the impacted SCADA which controls the power supply.

3.1   Metro Station Model

Each train or metro station is composed of assets that are essential for the function it needs to fulfill. These assets can be computers, signaling, tracks, electricity supply but also employees and passengers. All these assets are interrelated and either exchange e.g. information or they impact each other in case of a failure. Based on this assumption, an asset topology model is established. As such information are sensitive, an anonymized asset network is presented in this work.

The topology model consists of assets as nodes and relations between the assets as edges, presented in Fig. 2 as lines. Nodes have certain properties such as an identifier, a name, a system they belong to and a list of nodes which they impact. This model enables the identification of critical assets based e.g. on centrality measures. Further, paths between nodes can reveal attack or damage paths and thus the network structure enables to model cascading effects in the system. The shortest path is thereby the attack path with a minimum number of assets to compromise and thus reveals potential vulnerabilities of the system. A similar approach has been presented for airport infrastructure in [16]. Once a threat is detected, the paths in the network from the entry point to vulnerable assets such as trains and passengers can be computed.

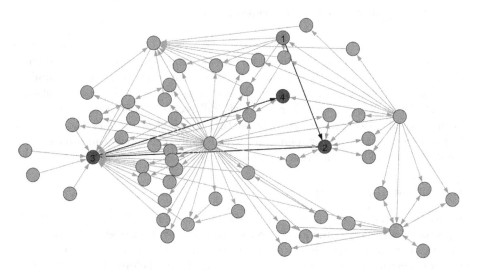

Fig. 2. Network topology for a single station. A scenario is highlighted with an initial impact on the SCADA (1), then equipment for electricity supply is manipulated (2), the functionality of the station is reduced (3) and finally the trains are impacted (4).

3.2 Simulation Specifications

The detected threat impacts a certain node in the asset network model. From there it can propagate in the network based on the edges, given the assigned propagation probability and the impact delay (see Table 1). Note, that in this resilience assessment the impact on the network is assessed in the worst case scenario when redundancy from an uninterruptible power supply is failing. The recovery of impacted nodes is controlled by restoration times, also given in Table 1. Impact delay and recovery times vary based on a normal distribution with a given standard deviation.

Table 1. Network model specifications

Parameter	Value
Iterations	1000
Time steps T	120
Time step length	1 min
Propagation probability	75%
Propagation probability after detection	25%
Mean of restoration time $mean(t_{res})$	60 min
Standard deviation of restoration time $std(t_{res})$	10 min
Mean of impact delay time	1 min
Standard deviation of impact delay time	1 min

The parameter settings are based on previous findings (see e.g. [16]) and have been updated to e.g. better represent the uncertainties by an increased number of iterations. The number of time steps is chosen to cover all resilience phases such as before, during and after the crisis/full recovery. The impact delay has been reduced based on the assumption that cyber threats, once the physical intrusion was successful, happen quite fast. Finally, the repair times have been validated by end-users in previous related projects.

3.3   Simulation Results

Based on the parameter settings and network setup along with triggering events, repeated Monte Carlo simulations are performed considering the specified uncertainties. For each simulation a performance curve is obtained which describes the performance of the network as a function of time before, during and after an incident.

The performance p ranges between 0 and 1 and at one specific time step is defined as

$$p = \frac{\sum_{n=1}^{N} p_n}{N} \tag{1}$$

with N being the total number of nodes in the network.

The area A for any performance curve $p(t)$ where t is the time is given relative to the reference area A_{ref} as

$$A_{ref} = \int_0^T p_{ref}(t)dt \tag{2}$$

$$A = \frac{100 * \int_0^T p(t)dt}{A_{ref}} \tag{3}$$

with $p_{ref} = 1$ for all t and T being the number of time steps considered. Practically, the integral is approximated by the trapezoidal rule. The estimate of A

enables to compare quantitatively different situations. In the following we compare simulations with varying detection times $t_d = \{-1, 0, 1, 2, 6, 12, 25, 50, 100\}$, restoration times $mean(t_{res}) = \{2, 6, 12, 25, 50, 100\}$ and corresponding $std(t_{res}) = \{0.3, 0.6, 1.3, 2.5, 5.0, 10.0\}$.

Dependent on when the attack/incident has been detected, and most importantly has been identified, the probability for propagation in the network is reduced (see Table 1). This reduction in propagation represents the ability to react more specifically as the threat is identified by the detection. For example, if an intruder is detected security personnel can be activated or if malware is detected IT equipment can be isolated to reduce further propagation.

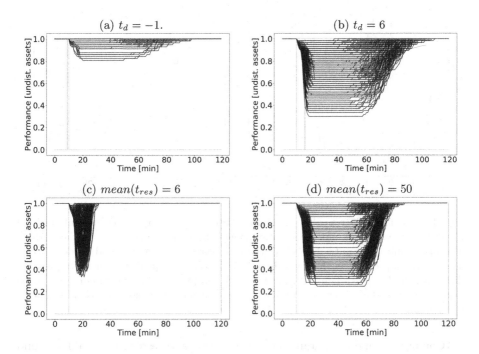

Fig. 3. Example resilience curves for 1000 repeated simulations with varying (a, b) detection time and (c, d) repair time mean and standard deviation. Performance is based on the number of undisturbed assets. Parameter settings not specifically adapted/mentioned in the headers are given in Table 1. Green dotted lines present the time of detection and red dotted lines the time of the attack.

Figure 3 presents some example simulation results for the resilience assessment of a single station. Repeated simulations lead to several resilience curves with different parameter settings. If the detection time is negative (see Fig. 3(a)) the early detection enables avoidance of the impact. However, the uncertainty in the impact propagation leads to simulation runs with minimal damage to the system even with early detection. With a detection time of $t_d = 6$ (see Fig. 3(b)) the maximum detection time is reached. With larger t_d no further increase in resilience is achieved. This is also demonstrated in Fig. 4(a).

For a mean restoration time of $mean(t_{res}) = 6$ a large impact in the system but a short duration can be observed (see Fig. 3(c)). An increasing mean restoration time leads to a larger duration of the degraded status of the assets (see Fig. 3(d)).

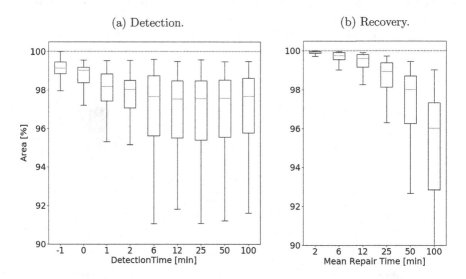

Fig. 4. Area for 1000 repeated simulations with varying (a) detection time and (b) repair time mean and standard deviation. The horizontal line in the box is the median. The upper and lower outer bounds of the box represent the upper and lower quartile. The whiskers present all data within 1.5 times the interquartile range. Outliers are discarded in this plot. The horizontal dotted line presents the maximum area to be expected when the system is not impacted. The measurement unit is performance times minute.

Comparing different parameters for detection and restoration enables to find the optimal settings to maximize the area below the curves and thus to maximize the system's resilience. The summary of these findings is given in Fig. 4. Note, that with increasing mean restoration time also the standard deviation of the restoration time is increased. This explains the larger uncertainty in cases with larger mean repair time (Fig. 4(b)).

The analysis presented in this work reveals vulnerabilities of the system and describes the behavior under varying conditions for a certain predefined threat scenario. Thus, the comparisons of different detection times are performed to prepare the system. CuriX delivers possible detection times, CaESAR derives ideal detection times and compares the impact. This combination of tools is methodological.

In a real threat situation, the simulations by CaESAR would only start once the threat is detected by CuriX. The consequent benefits are amongst others that an analysis of CaESAR is more target-oriented in terms of time and location of threats and affected assets. The exchange of information in SAFETY4RAILS is managed through a Distributed Messaging System based on a Kafka platform and json messages [4]. If a simulation is triggered by the detection, measures to e.g. reduce repair times can be simulated to support decision making. Thus, the combination of CuriX and CaESAR can be employed in different resilience phases.

4 Metro and Train Infrastructure Network

4.1 Metro Grid

In this section, the previously analyzed impact on a single station, given by its asset topology model, is now propagated and studied exemplary in the context of the train and metro network for the Ankara public transportation. The network topology is derived from publicly available sources such as metro line maps. Figure 5 presents metro and train lines for the example network with stations defined as nodes and lines defined as edges.

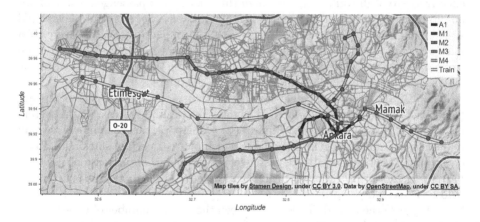

Fig. 5. Ankara metro and train map with map material from OpenStreetMap (open-streetmap.org/copyright).

4.2 Agent-based Model

On the network structure given in Fig. 5, an ABM is developed. Generally, ABM is a bottom-up modeling approach that starts by defining agents and their properties [24]. The next step in developing an ABM is the definition of internal rules [24]. Here, on each line several trains are defined which travel from node to node along the full length of the line before returning. In each timestep a certain number of passengers is generated with random start positions and target stations (see Table 2). They generate a route in the network that brings them to their

Table 2. ABM specifications

Parameter	Value
Iterations	1
Time steps	23,040
Time step length	15 seconds
New passengers per time step	appox. 2.7
New passenger per day	approx. 15,700
Impact on time step	8,000
Restore on time step	8,900
Trains per line	2
Maximum number of passengers per train	400

targets based on the shortest path in the network and switch trains if needed. If a train on a line is delayed it is assumed here that the passengers that want to go along that line wait till the train arrives.

Once a station is impacted, no train will move in or out of the station. This effectively stops all traffic going through this station and passengers will look for an alternative route. In this example, the impact on a very central node would sever many routes from each other, making the impact especially severe. If a line is cut in two parts by an incident, the trains continue to circulate on those two smaller parts. However, if both trains are in one part of the line when the incident occurs, only this specific part can be operated.

Figure 6(a) shows an incident-free period. During three days passengers are 'generated' by a simple sine-wave. At night, there are no spawns, so the system has time to flush all passengers. Figure 6(b) presents passenger numbers with an impact in the morning of the second day which blocks a certain station for about one hours. This leads to a huge passenger build-up and an increase of the total passenger amount in the peak. Still, the system manages to clear all passengers before the next day starts.

In Fig. 6(c) the (total) difference between the current number of passengers in the network and the usual number of passengers at the same time given by a base value is presented. The base values are smoothed curves for normal operation (see Fig. 6(a)). The variation from the base value is arising from the uncertainty in route generation per spawning passenger. The impact on the second day leads to a sharp increase in the passenger amount, surpassing the usual amount by a huge margin.

To enable the estimate of economic loss based on the passenger deviations during a disruptive event, the time spent per person in the system can be measured. Figure 7 shows the amount of time passengers 'waste' waiting for trains which do not arrive due to the impact or are simply filled to their capacity (which does not happen in the simulation for normal operation).

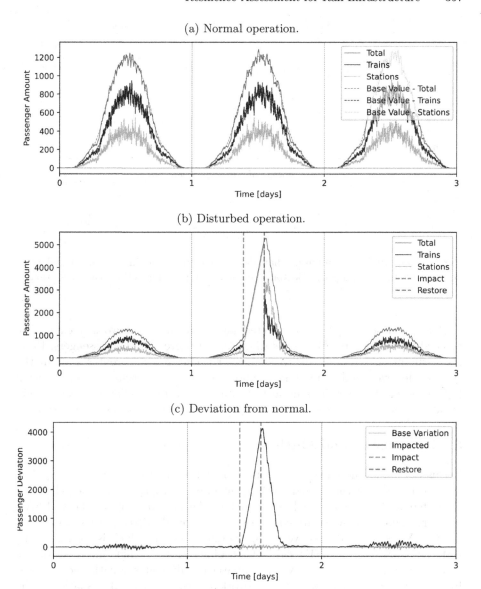

Fig. 6. Passenger numbers over three days estimated by the ABM for (a) normal operation, (b) disturbed operation and (c) the deviation between the base values of (a) and (b).

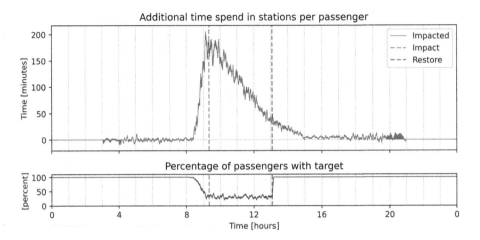

Fig. 7. Top: Additional minutes that the passengers spend in the metro and train network due to the disruption. Bottom: Percentage of passengers that reach their target.

Note, if a station is not connected any more in the network it cannot be reached by passengers. This leads to disrupted routes for the passengers. Here, the assumption is made that passengers without possible routes wait in the system. However, in disrupted metro and train systems measures would be taken to transport passengers in alternative means such as buses. Thus, the simulation results underline the need for rerouting options to recover the system faster.

5   Conclusion and Outlook

In this work, a methodology is presented to quantify network resilience for public transport infrastructure based on different impact propagation approaches and for different degrees of detail embedded in the development of the CaESAR software. The approaches are combined with anomaly detection methods from the CuriX software to improve the networks resilience, which is together with CaESAR part of the SAFETY4RAILS toolkit. First, a single metro station is modeled as an asset topology which enables to analyse attack paths along edges. Further, threat propagation in this network and the resulting degradation of the station functionality can be simulated. The simulation also enables to quantify that the earlier an attack/threat is detected, the larger are the chances to avoid further damage propagation. Furthermore, a range of ideal detection times can be quantified from the topology and the resilience assessment. In this work, it ranges between early detection with negative values, which means there is a good chance to avoid the impact altogether, and 6 min. After that time the whole system is already impacted by the attack/threat. In the latter case, recovery is another parameter to reduce the impact and thus increase the resilience. Finally, the interplay between detection and recovery governs the response of the system and both parameters contribute to the optimization of infrastructure resilience.

The second approach for impact propagation employed in this work is an ABM that operates in Ankara's metro and train network as example use-case. It enables to quantify the passenger amounts during normal and disturbed operation. Based on the additional time passengers spend in the network under disturbed conditions, the economic loss could be estimated.

Finally, the detection and single station resilience assessment can be coupled with the ABM metro and train model to estimate predictions for real-time decision support. This framework, presented in this paper for a certain example, could be employed to the assessment of infrastructure resilience in various domains.

This paper shows that the combination of the main functionalities anomaly detection, cascading effects analysis and ABM can contribute to resilience assessments of critical infrastructures. Anyway, there are aspects worth to be considered candidates for improvements: The anomaly detection described above is conducted in a univariate way without taking into account system knowledge. In future work, the system model of CaESAR could be considered within CuriX to enhance the quality (accuracy, precision) of the anomaly detection. Furthermore, the simulation results of the ABM show that time-series of passenger flow data could enrich the anomaly detection to widen the range of phenomena that could be recognized. Within the project SAFETY4RAILS, a platform is created in which several tools collaborate while in this article we exemplify the collaboration of only two tools with the additional ABM of that platform. In future articles, it is planned to report also about the collaboration of other tool-combinations.

Acknowledgement. This project has received funding from the European Union's Horizon 2020 research and innovation programme under grant agreement No 883532. The information appearing in this paper has been prepared in good faith and represents the views of the authoring organizations. Neither the Research Executive Agency, nor the European Commission are responsible for any use that may be made of the information it contains. For more information on the project see: https://safety4rails.eu/.

References

1. Bešinović, N.: Resilience in railway transport systems: a literature review and research agenda. Transp. Rev. **40**(4), 457–478 (2020)
2. Bezemskij, A., Loukas, G., Anthony, R.J., Gan, D.: Behaviour-based anomaly detection of cyber-physical attacks on a robotic vehicle. In: 2016 15th International Conference on Ubiquitous Computing and Communications and 2016 International Symposium on Cyberspace and Security (IUCC-CSS), pp. 61–68. IEEE (2016)
3. Chopra, S.S., Dillon, T., Bilec, M.M., Khanna, V.: A network-based framework for assessing infrastructure resilience: a case study of the London metro system. J. R. Soc. Interface **13**(118), 20160113 (2016)
4. Crabbe, S., et al.: Safety4rails information system platform demonstration at Madrid metro simulation exercise. In: Proceedings of ESREL2022 (2022)

5. CuriX: Cure infrastructure in XaaS - technical white paper (2021). https://www.curix.ai/wp-content/uploads/2021/09/CuriX-TechnicalWhitepaper_DE.pdf
6. Delgado, D., Aktas, C.B.: Resilience of rail infrastructure in the US Northeast corridor. Procedia Eng. **145**, 356–363 (2016)
7. Edwards, C.: Resilient nation demos (2009)
8. Fernandez, S., Schneider, C.: Neuronales netzwerk zur vorhersage von schwellwertverletzungen in zeitreihen (2021). https://web0.fhnw.ch/ht/informatik/ip6/21fs/21fs_imvs04/index.html
9. Guan, B., Liu, X., Zhang, T., Wang, X.: Hourly energy consumption characteristics of metro rail transit: Train traction versus station operation. Energy and Built Environment (2022)
10. Hiermaier, S., Hasenstein, S., Faist, K.: Resilience Engineering-how to handle the unexpected. In: 7th REA Symposium, p. 92 (2017)
11. Häring, I., et al.: Towards a generic resilience management, quantification and development process: general definitions, requirements, methods, techniques and measures, and case studies. In: Linkov, Igor, Palma-Oliveira, José Manuel. (eds.) Resilience and Risk. NSPSSCES, pp. 21–80. Springer, Dordrecht (2017). https://doi.org/10.1007/978-94-024-1123-2_2
12. Risk management - guidelines. Standard, International Organization for Standardization, Geneva, CH (2018)
13. IT Security Association Germany - TeleTrusT Task Force "State of the art": IT Security Act (Germany) and EU General Data Protection Regulation: Guidline "State of the art" Technical and organisational measures (2021). https://www.teletrust.de/en/publikationen/broschueren/state-of-the-art-in-it-security/
14. Köpke, C., et al.: Security and resilience for airport infrastructure. In: Baraldi, P., Di Maio, F., Zio, E. (eds.) Proceedings of the 30th European Safety and Reliability Conference and the 15th Probabilistic Safety Assessment and Management Conference, pp. 1191–1198. Research Publishing, Singapore (2020)
15. Köpke, C., et al.: Impact propagation in airport systems. In: Abie, H., et al. (eds.) CPS4CIP 2020. LNCS, vol. 12618, pp. 191–206. Springer, Cham (2021). https://doi.org/10.1007/978-3-030-69781-5_13
16. Köpke, C., Srivastava, K., Miller, N., Branchini, E.: Resilience quantification for critical infrastructure: Exemplified for airport operations. In: European Symposium on Research in Computer Security, pp. 451–460. Springer, Cham (2021). https://doi.org/10.1007/978-3-030-95484-0_26
17. Luo, Y., Xiao, Y., Cheng, L., Peng, G., Yao, D.: Deep learning-based anomaly detection in cyber-physical systems: progress and opportunities. ACM Comput. Surv. (CSUR) **54**(5), 1–36 (2021)
18. Marino, D.L., et al.: Cyber and physical anomaly detection in smart-grids. In: 2019 Resilience Week (RWS), vol. 1, pp. 187–193. IEEE (2019)
19. Miller, N., et al.: A risk and resilience assessment approach for railway networks. In: Proceedings of ESREL2021 (2021)
20. National Cyber Security Centre: Nis compliance guidelines for operators of essential service (oes) (2019). https://www.ncsc.gov.ie/pdfs/NIS_Compliance_Security_Guidelines_for_OES.pdf
21. SAFETY4RAILS: Deliverable d2.3: System specifications and concept architecture (2021). https://safety4rails.eu/wp-content/uploads/2022/03/S4R_RPT_D2.3_V1_6.pdf
22. Siebold, U., Ziehm, J., Häring, I.: Terror event database and analysis software. In: 4th Security Research Conference Future Security (2009)

23. Thoma, K.: Resilien-Tech: Resilience by Design: A Strategy For the Technology Issues of the Future. Herbert Utz Verlag (2014)
24. Van Dam, K.H., Nikolic, I., Lukszo, Z.: Agent-Based Modelling of Socio-Technical Systems, vol. 9. Springer, Dordrecht (2012). https://doi.org/10.1007/978-94-007-4933-7

Coverage-Guided Fuzzing of Embedded Systems Leveraging Hardware Tracing

Maximilian Beckmann[1] and Jan Steffan[2(✉)] (iD)

[1] Exploit Labs GmbH, Mergenthaler Allee 15-21, 65760 Eschborn, Germany
maximilian@exploitlabs.de
[2] Fraunhofer Institute SIT/ATHENE, 64295 Darmstadt, Germany
jan.steffan@sit.fraunhofer.de

Abstract. Fuzz testing (fuzzing) is a well-established method for identifying security weaknesses in input-data processing applications. For the analysis of conventional software, coverage-guided greybox fuzzing has proven to be particularly effective. Here, code coverage obtained through instrumentation or emulation is used to detect fuzz inputs that triggered previously unseen application behavior. These inputs are then used as seeds for subsequent mutations. However, when testing an embedded system, in particular a smaller device with monolithic firmware, software instrumentation or emulation in many cases is not feasible, either for technical reasons, owing to the unavailability of the sources and buildchain, or an unjustifiably large setup effort.

We explore the use of hardware tracing interfaces integrated into many modern *microcontroller units* (MCUs), as an alternative feedback channel for coverage-guided fuzzing which requires practically no setup effort or changes to the target system. In contrast to related work, we use the *single wire output* (SWO) interface, which is frequently available in the widely used ARM Cortex-M product line. However, this tracing mechanism suffers from severe information loss due to its limited bandwidth, obstructing the immediate distinction of application behavior. Therefore, a heuristic seed selection strategy was developed to facilitate the reliable detection of novel application behavior by leveraging hardware breakpoints and lightweight static analysis, to enable coverage-guided fuzzing from erratic traces.

Our resulting coverage-guided fuzzing framework consistently outperforms a similar blackbox setup, even under aggravated conditions.

Keywords: Coverage guided fuzzing · Embedded systems · Microcontroller

1 Introduction

During the last decade, embedded systems have not only gained tremendously in number, capabilities, and connectivity, but also in their relevance for safety and security within the physical world [13, 21]. Cyber physical systems are an integral

© The Author(s), under exclusive license to Springer Nature Switzerland AG 2023
S. Katsikas et al. (Eds.): ESORICS 2022 Workshops, LNCS 13785, pp. 362–378, 2023.
https://doi.org/10.1007/978-3-031-25460-4_21

part of safety and security-critical applications such as health care, automotive, production, and infrastructure. As part of the *Internet of things* (IoT) they have become increasingly interconnected, often using wireless interfaces that are particularly exposed to potential attacks [20]. In addition to the high exposure and security impact, rolling out security updates to embedded systems in the field in many cases is complicated, if possible at all. Therefore, it is necessary to identify security vulnerabilities in embedded systems before deployment.

1.1 Fuzz Testing Embedded Systems

Fuzz testing is one of the major methods used to identify security vulnerabilities [8,17]. A central factor for the effectiveness of a fuzzer is, how fast a good code coverage of the tested software can be achieved. In practice, not only the bare run-time of the fuzzer is relevant, but also the time a human security tester spends in order to setup and adapt the fuzzer to the system and interface under test. "Coverage-guided greybox fuzzing" promises to cut down on both the manual setup time and the run-time of the fuzzer [16,22,27]. By utilizing feedback collected at run-time, it adapts the fuzzer to the current target automatically and on-the-fly. Manual preparation and reverse-engineering effort is thereby minimized, and the fuzzer's effectiveness improves. A coverage-guided fuzzer measures the code coverage achieved for each test case, in order to detect exercised application behavior. Test cases that triggered yet unseen application functionality are selected as seeds into the corpus of input values used to generate subsequent test cases. This results in a feedback loop, leading to a rapid exploration of the software under test. As a result, coverage-guided fuzzers appear to "learn" the input structure expected by their test subjects, even without any prior information about their target.[1]

Currently, coverage-guided fuzzing is applied with great success to conventional software, running on a PC where it is relatively easy to obtain coverage information. A natural approach to use coverage-guided fuzzing to test an embedded system therefore would be to move its code from the embedded platform to a PC. This can be achieved through rehosting [1,9], i.e. cross-compiling the embedded system's source code for the host architecture. Emulation of the embedded platform [9,18,23,26] is an option if the source code is unavailable (as it is often the case in practice [25]). A major hurdle for rehosting and emulation however, are the eponymous hardware dependencies of embedded software. In fact, all hardware interactions of an application either need to be mocked up or omitted sensibly to maintain testable functionality. While emulation platforms[2] support an impressive number of embedded CPU architectures, they frequently lack out-of-the-box support for the overwhelming diversity of peripheral interfaces incorporated by modern MCU architectures, and even more so for external peripheral chips and senors found in embedded systems. This is underlined by recent research activity seeking to reduce the manual efforts involved

---

[1] A particularly vivid example is shown in https://lcamtuf.blogspot.com/2014/11/pulling-jpegs-out-of-thin-air.html.

[2] e.g. renode: https://renode.io/, QEMU: https://www.qemu.org/.

in addressing hardware dependencies. These propose to handle peripheral interaction by forwarding communication to the real device [12,14,18], automated modeling of peripheral behavior [11], or inferring expected access results from firmware inspection [6]. Nevertheless, these may not completely eliminate the involved development efforts and are frequently limited to non real-time or simple patterns of interaction. Hence, a substantial gap remains between sufficiently replicable and practically deployed hardware architectures.

1.2 Hardware Tracing as Feedback Channel

Monitoring the behavior of embedded software during run-time is desirable during regular firmware development and debugging, too [19]. To this end, most modern embedded platforms support a form of hardware instrumentation through so called "tracing interfaces". The widely used ARMv7-M architecture we chose for our study supports multiple tracing interfaces:

- The "parallel trace port" utilizes five pins as a clocked parallel interface for so called "ETM" trace transmission. This interface provides a high bandwidth and is capable of delivering a full sequence of executed instruction addresses in real time. Its use in coverage-guided fuzzing has been proposed and demonstrated previously [7,15]. In general, the applicability of such hardware tracing as coverage feedback for fuzzers is not new, and has a well-proven track record in the x86 software domain [7,10,24].
  Unfortunately, the parallel tracing interface is rarely available in finished embedded products. The required pins are usually omitted in smaller-footprint chip packages. In many remaining cases, at least some of the required pins are in use as *general purpose input/outputs* (GPIOs) by the application.
- The *single wire output* (SWO) interface is an alternative tracing interface that requires only a single pin, making it widely available and usable in many ARM Cortex-M3, -M33, -M4, and -M7 based devices [2,3]. However, its bandwidth is magnitudes lower than the parallel port. This is accounted for by the dedicated "periodic *programm counter* (PC) sampling" trace mode. Here, the PC of the monitored *central processing unit* (CPU) is sampled in a configurable clock interval, resulting in a sparse and erratic view of the traced application behavior.

If security analysts may choose the MCU package and pin layout, ETM tracing via the parallel trace port would certainly be a favorable option [15]. However, in practice testers are incapable of influencing these decisions, as we experienced throughout our activity as embedded security testers. Consequently, SWO is typically the only interface available in existing applications, especially during third-party evaluations.

1.3 Contributions

We argue, that even severely restricted hardware tracing may constitute a valuable feedback channel that enables effective coverage-guided fuzz testing. To this end, we provide the first demonstration of coverage-guided fuzz testing of embedded applications using heavily constrained tracing information. In particular, we show how coverage-guided fuzzing can be enabled to detect novel application behaviors based on the erratic information available from the SWO tracing interface of the widespread ARMv7-M architecture. Therefore, we established a mutation-based coverage-guided fuzzing algorithm by making the following three contributions:

1. First, we devised a heuristic to approximate the instruction coverage exercised by a test case based on periodic PC sampling. Beyond repeated tracing, we conduct static analysis of the target application's binary and combine this with hardware breakpoints to facilitate fast and reliable coverage estimation.
2. Based on the instruction coverage, a seed selection strategy is presented, that facilitates the heuristic to select fuzz inputs that exercise new areas of code. Seed inputs identified in this manner improve the subsequent test case generation and augment a corpus of initially provided example inputs.
3. Finally, the selection strategy was integrated with a seed scheduling and mutation strategy to obtain a full coverage-guided fuzzing algorithm. The result is then benchmarked against a similarly configured blackbox mutation-based fuzzer. Empirical evidence indicates that the coverage-guided fuzzer consistently outperforms the blackbox approach, in terms of total the vulnerabilities found and the coverage achieved over time.

Our overall goal is to demonstrate the feasibility of coverage-guided fuzz testing based on sparse and erratic feedback from constrained hardware tracing interfaces, and to encourage further research.

2 Setup for "Bare-Metal" Coverage-Guided Fuzz Testing

To conduct fuzz testing, a "test host" running the fuzzer is connected to the "target" embedded system via three interfaces as depicted in Fig. 1.

First, the test host must provide a counterpart for the peripheral interface that is to be fuzz tested. In a simple case, this may be a common feature of desktop systems, such as a Bluetooth or USB interface. Other cases may require the addition of a dedicated hardware adapter to interact with a specific target interface, such as CAN or ZigBee.

A debug probe connects the host to the *serial wire debug* (SWD) or *Joint Test Action Group* (JTAG) interface of the target MCU. This enables the fuzzer to configure the tracing interface, reset the target if required, read fault registers, or set breakpoints.

Finally, the trace data must be captured via the SWO interface of the target. We used a Segger J-Trace debug and trace probe[3] that conveniently combines the debug and trace interfaces in a single device and is capable of receiving data from the SWO interface with up to 50 MBaud. As SWO is nothing but a *universal asynchronous receiver transmitter* (UART) interface, a simple debug probe in combination with a separate fast UART adapter can also be used.

---

[3] https://www.segger.com/products/debug-probes/j-trace/.

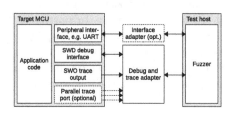

Fig. 1. Block diagram of the components involved in the execution and tracing of a test case.

Fig. 2. NRF board connected to the debug and trace probe. STM board on custom break-out board.

2.1 Evaluation of a Test Case

In the described setup, the application and tracing of a test case are as follows:

Preparation of the target. The application is set up for testing. If the MCU has not already been started, it is powered up and allowed to execute its initialization routine. Then, peripherals are set up and the control flow enters an event loop, usually performing periodic tasks or waiting for events requiring further action. At this point, the application is ready to accept input data.

Start tracing. The tracing interface is configured and enables the monitoring of the CPU's execution. From this point on, trace data is generated.

Execution of the test case. The test input is supplied to the peripheral interface and processed by the tested application. Simultaneously, it is monitored for output data. The end of a test run is determined by either *exceeding a time limit* or *receiving an expected output value*.

Stop tracing. The tracing interface is disabled to stop the generation of further trace data. All pending trace packets are collected.

Checking for faults. Finally, the status register of the CPU is checked. This way a possible crash and the causing fault are detected.

As a result, for every test run the fuzzer either receives a crash notification or a trace of the most recent execution.

2.2 Specific Challenges of Traces Obtained via Periodic PC Sampling

With the described setup we are able to receive limited coverage feedback from almost any ARM Cortex-M MCU. In this setup however, repeatedly executing the same test case may lead to different coverage views, even while always triggering the same application behavior. Therefore traces generated via periodic PC sampling can not be used directly as feedback for coverage-guided fuzzing. In this section, we discuss the effects that degrade the quality of the available feedback.

First, tracing is not perfectly aligned with the processing of a test case. Following from the tracing procedure described above, traces offer insights into the execution taking place between the "start" and "stop" tracing steps. Tracing is disabled between individual test runs, starting a moment before the application of the input data, and disabled explicitly after the processing finishes. Consequently, every trace covers portions of the execution immediately preceding and following the actual test execution. This is necessary, because the production of trace packets may not be reliably synchronized with the execution of a test case. Consequently, the described approach ensures that the entire processing of a test input is covered by a recorded trace. As a side effect though, tracing the same test input several times may result in different traces, each one covering more or less "idle" execution time at the start and end of tracing.

Furthermore, tracing covers execution unrelated to a test case. An application may implement various exception handlers, which allow for asynchronous execution of code interrupting the regular application control flow [4, pp. 513–515]. These "interrupts" may trigger independently from the processing of an input value. Likewise, concurrent threads in an embedded OS may perform operations unrelated to the current test case. In either instance, the addresses of unrelated executions can be included in the trace. Therefore, varying occurrences of concurrency introduces more variability into the tracing results.

These caveats are further aggravated by the severe information loss incurred by periodic PC sampling. The trace consists of samples of the PC on every n-th clock cycle, triggered by a countdown timer with n steps. However, the countdown is not synchronized with the test case execution. Hence, processing of an input value can begin on any countdown value from the range $[0, (n-1)]$, multiplying the number of possible outcomes by n.

Finally, the execution of instructions may require a variable number of clock cycles to finish. A common example is memory operations, either working on cached memory addresses or waiting for slower flash memory.

3   Enabling Instruction Coverage-Guided Fuzzing

A single periodic PC trace does neither allow to identify a certain control flow nor a certain differentiation of behaviors. Nevertheless, during each run of a test case, we obtain a small glimpse on the application behavior in the shape of a changing subset of the executed PCs. We therefore may still attempt to extract valuable features for seed selection, like the achieved "instruction coverage".

Instruction coverage, as the set of instructions executed by a test case, may be approximated by repeatedly tracing a test case and joining the results. Due to the nature of the periodic PC sampling though, this process is highly erratic: On the one hand, instruction addresses exercised by the seeds may be consecutively omitted during tracing. On the other hand, sporadic observation of interfering concurrent execution may lead to the reporting of additional, unrelated instruction addresses. This can lead to both false rejection of inputs actually achieving new coverage, and false-positive detection of merely-supposed new behavior.

Especially false-positives impose a serious issue for the sought improvement of test case generation. Per definition, false-positives exercise the same control flow as at least another entry from the corpus and hence feature a semantic structure deemed identical by the tested application. Assuming a fuzzer always using the same set of manipulations on seeds, fuzzing both values arguably results in a comparable probability distribution to trigger certain application behaviors.[4]

A sustained incidence of false-positive discoveries quickly results in a large corpus, where most seeds produce similar test cases. This circumstance degrades the quality of generated test cases, which ideally should result in as much diversity as possible [5]. In an extreme case, assuming "naive seed scheduling", fuzzing all seeds equally likely, this might even lead to the "starvation" of valuable seeds. Intuitively, most time would be spend mutating semantically similar seeds, instead of few ones with a larger likelihood to make further discoveries.[5]

3.1   Combating False-Positive Detection

We subsequently devise a set of heuristics which helped to reduce the residual risk of erroneous seed selection to an acceptable level.

Branch Instruction Mapping. "Branch instruction mapping" is a mechanism, reducing the number of traces needed to fully approximate the instruction coverage of a test case. To this end, the instruction addresses observed by tracing are mapped to the next succeeding branch instruction. Formally, a branch instruction is any operation that might change the PC in another way then simply incrementing it. The observation of any other type of instruction consequently implies the execution of all subsequent instructions, at least up to and including the next branch instruction.

Locating branch instructions in the raw binary of the tested application is accomplished by identifying eligible opcodes. Consequently, no disassembly or source code is required. The identified instruction addresses are then added to a sorted list referred to as the "branch instruction map". Upon tracing a certain instruction it can be mapped to the closest succeeding branch instruction, by looking up the next higher value in the branch instruction map. As a result, all instructions lying between two branch instructions are translated into the instruction address at the end of such a "block".

Intuitively, only one instruction needs to be observed to assume execution of the entire code block contained between the two next branch instructions. This allows to arrive at a consistent instruction coverage estimate with much less tracing runs required. Therefore, we safe time and are less likely to overlook genuinely achieved coverage, which might cause a false-positive detection later in the campaign.

---

[4] The exact probability distributions certainly depends from the input language implemented by the software under test and the employed fuzzing mutations, but are considered negligible for brevity here.

[5] Advanced seed scheduling is an active research topic and a promising direction for future improvements of the presented PoC.

Ignoring Samples from Interrupt Handlers. Further opportunity to eliminate unrelated observations is enabled by a configuration option of the tracing interface [4, p. 731]. The tracing logic allows enabling notifications upon entry into and exit from interrupt handlers. This allows for the identification of PC samples within a trace corresponding to interrupt handler execution. Tracing of handler code triggering independently of test cases is a major possible cause contributing to unrelated observations. Using handler entry and exit notifications to ignore the respective observations might consequently reduce the risk of false positive classifications.

However, a disadvantage is the lack of observations from handler executions actually related to a test case. In fact, a test case may deterministically trigger certain interrupt handlers. Observation from the respective handler code would be ignored, just as for every other interrupt. Accordingly, there is no coverage feedback available to guide further fuzzing towards testing the handler routine. Whether this is an acceptable blind spot needs to be decided on a per-target basis. Clearly, this is an unbearable condition when testing hardware-related code, but it might eliminate false positives when aiming for higher, application-level logic.

Triaging Observations with Breakpoints. Another option for addressing unrelated observations is an additional investigation that leverages hardware breakpoints. The ARMv7-M architecture features a limited set of PC comparators, halting the CPU when it is about to execute a specified instruction address. These hardware breakpoints can be set up programmatically via the respective configuration registers.

Accordingly, breakpoints can be used to test whether a test case covers a certain instruction address. If the test cases exercises the instruction address, processing of the test case will trigger the breakpoint and consequently halt the CPU. This condition is easily noticed by the fuzzer.

Therefore, we may use breakpoints to reliably sieve out observations of unrelated execution from traces. To this end, a hitherto unseen instruction address, reported for the most recently executed test case, is equipped with a breakpoint. Then, the test case is re-executed. The breakpoint must be hit, iff the newly observed instruction address is exercised during processing of the respective input value. Next, we re-execute all seeds once and demand that the breakpoint does not trigger on them. This allows to rule out that a certain condition unrelated to the processed input value persisted and led to the new observation. Applying this procedure to every new observation results in a reduced set of instructions which are very likely to be genuinely novel.

As a downside however, the tested application must be reset if a breakpoint was hit, to revert potential corruption caused by the inadvertent halt of the application. For applications incorporating a time-consuming initialization routine this may induce a severe time overhead. It is worth mentioning though, that observations tend to become more rare, the longer a fuzzing campaign is running [5]. Therefore, additional time spent on breakpoint triage might not only justify itself through a more pristine corpus but also becomes less of a penalty the longer a campaign is running.

3.2 A Time-Efficient Seed Selection Strategy

The presented heuristics provide a thorough approximation of the instruction coverage achieved by a test case. Another drawback that has not yet been addressed is the time required. Approximating the coverage of every test case exhaustively takes too long for coverage-guided fuzzing to remain competitive. Therefore, we switched to using the pooled "corpus coverage" for the detection of novel instruction addresses.

Formally, corpus coverage is the union of the instruction coverage of all the seeds combined. This allows us to detect the observation of completely new instruction addresses using a simple membership test on the corpus coverage. Most notably however, we may already do so with only a single trace of a test case. If any observed instruction address is not contained in the corpus coverage, we already know that there is new application behavior. In this way, we can decide how much time we want to spend on each individual fuzz input, before generating and applying a new one. Clearly, tracing a test case too few times imposes a substantial risk of overlooking present but yet unseen code and hence false rejection. As we found during our investigations though, the increase in the test-case throughput outweighs the benefit of missed observations. This holds especially true because faster test execution provides earlier chances to rectify missed discoveries sooner.

Putting all parts together, the result is the seed selection strategy as described by the pseudo-code in Fig. 3. To instantiate a full-fledged fuzzer, it must be embedded in a fuzzing loop, where in each iteration a new test case is generated by mutation and then applied to the tested application. The presented function subsequently takes the most recently executed fuzz input, the obtained trace and the currently known corpus coverage as arguments.

Seed selection then is done as follows: First, the observed instruction addresses are extracted from the trace, in line 3. If indicated by *ignore_exceptions*, the function get_observations() ignores samples from exception handler executions. Subsequently, if indicated by *use_breakpoint_triage*, observations not contained in the seed coverage yet, are verified. To this end, for every new observation verify_observation() is called in line 7 and performs breakpoint triage.

Observations withstanding the described filtering routine are almost certainly indicating novel instruction coverage. Accordingly, the causing fuzz input is traced additional times, as indicated by *trace_repetitions* and additional observations are added to the known corpus coverage. As before, the instruction addresses observed in this manner are extracted from the trace by calling get_observations(). Finally, the addresses of contiguous instructions can be inferred using branch instruction mapping, as described in Sect. 3.1. When the corresponding *use_branch_mapping* flag is set, a call to lookup_instructions() is made in line 24.

Input: *trace_repetitions, ignore_exceptions, use_breakpoint_triage,*
        use_branch_mapping

Function Select(*fuzz_input, feedback, total_coverage*) **is**
    new_coverage ← ∅;

    observations ← get_observations (*feedback, ignore_exceptions*);
    new_observations ← *observations* \ *total_coverage*;

    if *use_breakpoint_triage* **then**
        foreach *observation* ∈ *new_observations* **do**
            verified ← verify_observation (*observation*);
            if *verified* **then**
                ⌊ *new_coverage* ← *new_coverage* ∪ *observation*;
    else
        ⌊ *new_coverage* ← *new_observations*;

    if *new_coverage* ≠ ∅ **then**
        for *trace_repetitions* **do**
            crashed, feedback ← Run(*fuzz_input*);
            observations ← get_observations (*feedback, ignore_exceptions*);
            ⌊ *new_coverage* ← *new_coverage* ∪ *observations*;

    if *use_branch_mapping* **then**
        foreach *instruction* ∈ *new_coverage* **do**
            other_instructions ← lookup_instructions (*instruction*);
            ⌊ *new_coverage* ← *new_coverage* ∪ *other_instructions*;

    return *new_coverage*;

Fig. 3. Seed selection leveraging SWO-based periodic PC sampling.

4   Implementation and Evaluation

We implemented the previously devised algorithm as part of a Python-based
fuzzing framework to evaluate it under realistic conditions. The target setup
necessary to enable tracing was achieved using the pylink library[6] and a Segger
J-Trace debug probe. We also implemented decoders for the *data watchpoint and
trace* (DWT) trace protocol used to encode periodic PC sampling data which
was received over the SWO interface [4, pp. 780–796].

4.1   Target System Hardware

As test targets we selected two ARM Cortex-M4 development boards from different manufacturers (Fig. 2):

---

[6] https://github.com/square/pylink.

- A Nordic Semiconductor nRF52840 DK ("NRF") featuring an nRF52 single core MCU at 64 MHz system clock.[7] The firmware resembled a minimal bare-metal system communicating over the integrated interrupt driven UART interface.
- An ST Microelectronics NUCLEO-F429ZI ("STM") with an STM32F429ZI single-core MCU also clocked at 64 MHz.[8] This system runs a multi-threading capable mbedOS[9] *real-time operating system* (RTOS) and is representative of more complex devices. It implements a TCP/IP stack and a simple HTTP server that communicates over an Ethernet interface.

Both setups were prepared to make both their SWO interfaces and their parallel trace ports available. Accordingly, tests and benchmarks could be conducted using periodic PC sampling via SWO, whereas the full instruction trace mode could serve as a reference for the evaluation of the actually achieved coverage.

4.2   Example 1: Deeply Nested Conditional Statements

Reaching deeply nested conditions is a primary challenge in which coverage information can be beneficial during seed selection. To test this, we created a minimal example containing eight levels of nested conditions, each checking four bits of a 32 bit input value against a constant value. If all the conditionals are passed, the execution enters the inner code section and triggers a crash. This is the case exactly if the 32-bit input value is "0xdeadbeef" (in hexadecimal notation). In all other cases, the processing of the input aborts and the application returns to its initial state.

Despite its simplicity, this example closely resembles the problem faced when testing any application that processes structured input. Our example sequentially checks the input data for certain features, based on which subsequent actions are determined. More complex applications operate in the same manner, just with potentially more alternative branches for the continuation of the processing at each stage.

As a mutation strategy, we selected either one of the following two randomized editing operations with equal likelihood:

(1) the full seed is replaced with a uniform random 32-bit pattern, or
(2) an equally likely chosen byte of the seed is replaced by a uniform random 8-bit pattern.

A round-robin scheme served as a scheduling strategy to arbitrate between the seeds in the corpus, while we started with a single all zero seed 0x00000000.

In this setup, a coverage-guided fuzzer should certainly be able to produce the crash inducing input within a reasonable time. In case the feedback mechanism

---

[7] https://www.nordicsemi.com/Software-and-Tools/Development-Kits/nRF52840-DK.

[8] https://www.st.com/en/evaluation-tools/nucleo-f429zi.

[9] https://os.mbed.com/.

works reliable, the fuzzer should aggregate more and more feature complete seeds in the corpus, which each provide a one in $4 \cdot 2^8 = 2^{10}$ chance to pass the next condition with a suitable mutation from (2). Otherwise, the only option would be to hope for a very lucky outcome (one in 2^{32}) from mutation (1) or randomly added seeds eventually arriving at an almost feature complete input. Randomly added seeds however bloat the corpus and thus cause "starvation" of actually valuable seeds, as discussed in Sect. 3.

We conducted experiments using three different configurations of our proposed fuzzer, on both tested platforms:

- using only branch instruction mapping,
- additionally ignoring samples from exception handler execution
  ($ignore\_exceptions = 1$)
- additionally using breakpoint triage ($use\_breakpoint\_triage = 1$).

The tracing logic was configured to conduct periodic PC sampling in a 128 step clock cycle interval. Before addition to the corpus, seeds were traced 500 times to approximate their achieved instruction coverage, while using branch instruction mapping ($trace\_repetitions = 500, use\_branch\_mapping = 1$). Every tested setup was running until either four hours exceeded (failure) or a fuzz input resulted in a reproducible crash (success). Twenty instances of this experiment were conducted for every configuration.

The fuzzing algorithm proved itself successful on both tested platforms. For the bare-metal NRF target, success rates of 90% (no optimization), 90% (ignoring exceptions), and 85% (breakpoint triage) were achieved. On the STM platform, just the breakpoint-triage configuration maintained a 95% success rate, while there was only one successful run ignoring exceptions and none without optimizations. Investigating the individual runs, the root cause for this discrepancy appears to be the concurrent RTOS execution, which only breakpoint triage was able to eliminate reliably.

4.3   Example 2: Fuzz Testing a JSON Parser

For a more representative evaluation, we next chose "cJSON"[10] as target. In contrast to our fist example, JSON strings comprise more complex features in manifold compositions. Accordingly, there is a more diverse feature set to be explored by the fuzzer, measured in the overall instruction coverage achievable. Presumably, a well-configured coverage-guided fuzzer should reliably achieve more coverage in the same time, than a simple blackbox counterpart.

For a benchmark, we used the same NRF-board and its UART interface as before. To fuzz-test the library, a dedicated "fuzzing harness" based on the Nordic nRF5 SDK v16.0.0 was created. The resulting setup accepted strings via the UART peripheral and fed them to the cJSON parsing logic. The empty string was used as initial seed. The popular "Radamsa" mutation engine[11] was

---

[10] https://github.com/DaveGamble/cJSON.
[11] https://gitlab.com/akihe/radamsa.

used as mutation strategy. As before, the individual seeds were scheduled in a round-robin fashion.

As a baseline, we used a simple blackbox fuzzer not leveraging any execution feedback. The coverage-guided fuzzer in turn was configured to process periodic PC sampling with a sampling interval of 128 clock cycles, using branch instruction mapping, and 500 repeated tracings of seeds ($use\_branch\_mapping = 1, trace\_repetitions = 500$). We then ran experiments with each of the following optimizations:

- using only branch instruction mapping,
- additionally ignoring samples from exception handler execution
  ($ignore\_exceptions = 1$)
- additionally using breakpoint triage ($use\_breakpoint\_triage = 1$).

The blackbox and the three coverage-guided setups were each benchmarked five times, with twelve hours per run. The executed test cases were recorded including a timestamp. This allowed to obtain the accurate instruction coverage achieved over time, by replaying the series of tests subsequent to each run while tracing with ETM full trace mode. Figure 4 shows the results of the described series of benchmarks, averaged over the five runs per configuration. The x-axis refers to the time in seconds, whereas the y-axis represents the number of different instructions exercised.

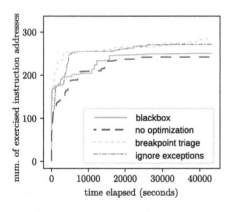

Fig. 4. Instruction coverage achieved by different configurations of the coverage-guided fuzzer per time, plotted against the results obtained from using a similar blackbox fuzzer.

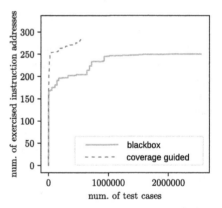

Fig. 5. Instruction coverage achieved by the coverage-guided fuzzer using breakpoint triage per number of applied test cases, plotted against the results obtained from using a similar blackbox fuzzer.

From the plots it can be seen, that two out of three coverage-guided fuzzer setups reliably outperformed the blackbox approach. Immediately after the start, all fuzzers made similar discoveries. However, while the blackbox instances slow down, the coverage-guided fuzzers continue to make substantial discoveries. The blackbox fuzzer eventually made a large fraction of the discoveries too, but ultimately staled not even half in the allotted run time. The coverage-guided instances using breakpoint triage and ignoring exceptions in turn maintained their advantage and even continued to make discoveries until the runs ended. Only the coverage-guided configuration without optimizations failed to beat the benchmark blackbox setup.

How substantial the support of proper coverage feedback is however, might best be seen in Fig. 5. The plot shows the number of test cases executed on the x-axis versus the total number of instructions observed on the y-axis. Accordingly, the coverage-guided setup achieved its superior results with roughly a quarter of the number of test cases issued by the blackbox setup. This underlines the warranted improvement in test case quality, achievable using the presented feedback mechanism.

During our experiments, we further identified two potential weaknesses within the cJSON parser:

– First, a rather simple bug was triggered by an input comprising approximately 200 opening square brackets. The result was a stack overflow caused by an unbounded recursion taking a new step for every additional bracket found in the input.
– Another, more complex bug was triggered by certain malformed strings. JSON allows the specification of 16-bit Unicode characters within strings in the form of escaped hexadecimal digits. A flaw in the corresponding parsing routine caused the parser to skip the evaluation of a character following such an escaped sequence if, for instance, the hexadecimal value was invalid. This includes parenthesis, otherwise terminating the string. Consequently, the parser continues to process the input as a string, which basically results in copying the input data into an allocated heap buffer. The string size does not match the correctly calculated buffer size, resulting in an out-of-bounds write on the heap.

The first bug was consistently found by all instances. The second bug conversely, was found by a single coverage-guided instance leveraging breakpoint triage. Although the frequency of observation of these two bugs does not enable much judgment regarding the qualities of the benchmarked algorithms, they demonstrate which results can be expected from fuzz testing. All of the found bugs were already known and fixed in the more recent upstream version of the cJSON library.

5 Conclusion

We presented a coverage-guided, mutation-based fuzzing algorithm, designed to automatically test applications running on ARMv7-M MCUs. To this end, we leverage the sparse information provided by the "periodic PC sampling" trace mode as coverage feedback. The resulting methodology can be applied to any ARM Cortex-M device, providing a SWO trace port and DWT support. At the time of writing, to our knowledge this is the first attempt to use this interface to enable coverage-guided fuzz testing of MCU based embedded systems.

Our algorithm outperforms blackbox fuzzing, which so far was the only available option if firmware needs to be fuzz tested in place on its target hardware. Accordingly, our results underline the feasibility of this new direction for the unobtrusive fuzz testing of embedded applications running on MCUs.

The described approach was implemented and evaluated under realistic conditions on two ARM Cortex-M4 platforms. Tests with a "nested conditions" example application showed that the approach is capable of reaching deeply nested conditions, consisting of small code blocks. Benchmarks conducted on the popular "cJSON" library further demonstrated its applicability to real-world, complex input structures. During both experiments, the devised fuzzer demonstrated its "learning" ability, observable in the improved quality of the generated test cases. Simultaneously, the run-time overhead introduced through tracing remains at an acceptable level, yielding a reasonable trade-off between the volume of applied inputs and their individual effectiveness. Most notably, this remains true under aggravated conditions, when the to-be-observed code sections are rather small or a highly concurrent execution environment obscures available insights.

Acknowledgments. This research work has been funded by the German Federal Ministry of Education and Research and the Hessen State Ministry for Higher Education, Research and the Arts within their joint support of the National Research Center for Applied Cybersecurity.

References

1. Amarnath, R.: Rethinking fuzzing for automotive software. In: FuzzCon Europe 2020 Automotive Edition (2020). https://www.fuzzcon.eu/event-recap-20201202
2. ARM Limited: Cortex-M3 Devices Generic User Guide (2010)
3. ARM Limited: Cortex-M4 Devices Generic User Guide (2011)
4. ARM Limited: ARMv7-M Architecture Reference Manual (2018)
5. Böhme, M., Manès, V.J.M., Cha, S.K.: Boosting fuzzer efficiency: an information theoretic perspective. In: Proceedings of the 28th ACM Joint Meeting on European Software Engineering Conference and Symposium on the Foundations of Software Engineering, ESEC/FSE 2020, pp. 678–689. ACM, New York (2020). https://doi.org/10.1145/3368089.3409748
6. Cao, C., Guan, L., Ming, J., Liu, P.: Device-agnostic firmware execution is possible: a concolic execution approach for peripheral emulation. In: Annual Computer Security Applications Conference, ACSAC 2020, pp. 746–759. ACM, New York (2020). https://doi.org/10.1145/3427228.3427280
7. Chen, Y., et al.: PTrix: Efficient Hardware-Assisted Fuzzing for COTS Binary (2019). https://arxiv.org/abs/1905.10499
8. Eceiza, M., Flores, J.L., Iturbe, M.: Fuzzing the internet of things: a review on the techniques and challenges for efficient vulnerability discovery in embedded systems.

IEEE Internet Things J. **8**, 10390–10411 (2021). https://doi.org/10.1109/JIOT. 2021.3056179

9. Fasano, A., et al.: SoK: enabling security analyses of embedded systems via rehosting. In: Proceedings of the 2021 ACM Asia Conference on Computer and Communications Security, ASIA CCS 2021, pp. 687–701. Association for Computing Machinery (2021). https://doi.org/10.1145/3433210.3453093

10. Google LLC: Honggfuzz. https://honggfuzz.dev/

11. Gustafson, E., et al.: Toward the analysis of embedded firmware through automated re-hosting. In: 22nd International Symposium on Research in Attacks, Intrusions and Defenses (RAID 2019), pp. 135–150 (2019). https://www.usenix.org/conference/raid2019/presentation/gustafson

12. Kammerstetter, M., Platzer, C., Kastner, W.: Prospect: peripheral proxying supported embedded code testing. In: Proceedings of the 9th ACM Symposium on Information, Computer and Communications Security, ASIA CCS 2014, pp. 329–340. ACM, New York (2014). https://doi.org/10.1145/2590296.2590301

13. Kocher, P., Lee, R., McGraw, G., Raghunathan, A., Ravi, S.: Security as a new dimension in embedded system design. In: Proceedings of the 41st Annual Design Automation Conference, pp. 753–760. ACM (2004). https://doi.org/10.1145/996566.996771

14. Koscher, K., Kohno, T., Molnar, D.: SURROGATES: enabling near-real-time dynamic analyses of embedded systems. In: 9th USENIX Workshop on Offensive Technologies (WOOT 2015). USENIX Association, Washington, D.C. (2015). https://www.usenix.org/conference/woot15/workshop-program/presentation/koscher

15. Li, W., Shi, J., Li, F., Lin, J., Wang, W., Guan, L.: μAFL: non-intrusive feedback-driven fuzzing for microcontroller firmware. In: Proceedings of the 44th International Conference on Software Engineering, ICSE 2022, pp. 1–12. ACM, New York (2022). https://doi.org/10.1145/3510003.3510208

16. LLVM: LibFuzzer. https://llvm.org/docs/LibFuzzer.html

17. Manes, V.J.M., et al.: The art, science, and engineering of fuzzing: a survey. IEEE Trans. Softw. Eng. **47**, 2312–2331 (2019)

18. Muench, M., Nisi, D., Francillon, A., Balzarotti, D.: Avatar^2: a multi-target orchestration platform. In: Proceedings 2018 Workshop on Binary Analysis Research. Internet Society (2018). https://doi.org/10.14722/bar.2018.23017

19. Muench, M., Stijohann, J., Kargl, F., Francillon, A., Balzarotti, D.: What you corrupt is not what you crash: challenges in fuzzing embedded devices. In: Proceedings 2018 Network and Distributed System Security Symposium, San Diego, CA. Internet Society (2018). https://doi.org/10.14722/ndss.2018.23166

20. Neshenko, N., Bou-Harb, E., Crichigno, J., Kaddoum, G., Ghani, N.: Demystifying IoT security: an exhaustive survey on IoT vulnerabilities and a first empirical look on internet-scale IoT exploitations. IEEE Commun. Surv. Tutor. **21**(3), 2702–2733 (2019). https://doi.org/10.1109/COMST.2019.2910750

21. Papp, D., Ma, Z., Buttyan, L.: Embedded systems security: threats, vulnerabilities, and attack taxonomy. In: 2015 13th Annual Conference on Privacy, Security and Trust (PST), pp. 145–152 (2015). https://doi.org/10.1109/PST.2015.7232966

22. Rawat, S., Jain, V., Kumar, A., Cojocar, L., Giuffrida, C., Bos, H.: VUzzer: application-aware evolutionary fuzzing. In: Proceedings 2017 Network and Distributed System Security Symposium. Internet Society (2017). https://doi.org/10.14722/ndss.2017.23404

23. Ruge, J., Classen, J., Gringoli, F., Hollick, M.: Frankenstein: advanced wireless fuzzing to exploit new bluetooth escalation targets. In: 29th USENIX Security Symposium 2020, pp. 19–36 (2020). https://www.usenix.org/conference/usenixsecurity20/presentation/ruge

24. Schumilo, S., Aschermann, C., Gawlik, R., Schinzel, S., Holz, T.: kAFL: hardware-assisted feedback fuzzing for OS kernels. In: 26th USENIX Security Symposium 2017, Vancouver, BC, pp. 167–182. USENIX Association (2017). https://www.usenix.org/conference/usenixsecurity17/technical-sessions/presentation/schumilo

25. Tychalas, D., Benkraouda, H., Maniatakos, M.: ICSFuzz: manipulating I/Os and repurposing binary code to enable instrumented fuzzing in ICS control applications. In: 30th USENIX Security Symposium 2021, pp. 2847–2862 (2021). https://www.usenix.org/conference/usenixsecurity21/presentation/tychalas

26. Yu, B., Wang, P., Yue, T., Tang, Y.: Poster: fuzzing IoT firmware via multi-stage message generation. In: Proceedings of the 2019 ACM SIGSAC Conference on Computer and Communications Security, pp. 2525–2527. ACM (2019). https://doi.org/10.1145/3319535.3363247

27. Zalewski, M.: American Fuzzy Lop (2013). https://lcamtuf.coredump.cx/afl/

Challenges and Pitfalls in Generating Representative ICS Datasets in Cyber Security Research

Asya Mitseva[1(✉)], Paul Thierse[2], Harald Hoffmann[2], Devran Er[3], and Andriy Panchenko[1]

[1] Brandenburg University of Technology, Cottbus, Germany
{asya.mitseva,andriy.panchenko}@b-tu.de
[2] AUCOTEAM GmbH, Berlin, Germany
{pthierse,hhoffmann}@aucoteam.de
[3] @-yet GmbH, Köln/Düsseldorf, Germany
Devran.Er@add-yet.de

Abstract. The increasing digitization and interconnection of Industrial Control Systems (ICS) to the Internet make them an attractive target for sophisticated attacks performed by experienced adversaries with high motivation and resources. As ICS incorporate decades-old devices and communication infrastructure, new generation embedded devices with computing capabilities and Ethernet-based communication protocols, the integration of proactive security protection methods is very challenging. Thus, a major line of research focuses on the development of reactive security solutions in the form of industrial intrusion detection systems (IIDS) aiming to detect anomalies in otherwise predictable "normal" ICS behavior. A crucial requirement for the assessment of the actual, real-world performance of these methods and their fair comparison is the existence of a *representative* dataset. Although the number of public ICS datasets increases gradually, it remains unclear to which extent these datasets can be considered as representative.

In this work, we identify key properties a given ICS dataset should own to be designated as representative based on typical IIDS evaluation scenarios. Our systematization of knowledge highlights that these properties are only partially represented in the existing public ICS datasets, which makes them unrepresentative, and shed light on the need for new datasets for IIDS evaluation. We further make a step into the direction of generating a representative dataset and present our ongoing work on the construction of a Hardware in the Loop tesbed of a real water distribution system. Our testbed replicates the operation of a real German medium-sized water supplier and allows for the collection of three different types of data sources, i.e., physical information, network data, and system logs. Our initial dataset contains more than 20 attacks targeting both at the distortion of the underlying physical process and at network- and system-based cyber attacks.

Keywords: Cyber physical system · Dataset · Cyber attack · Intrusion detection

S. Katsikas et al. (Eds.): ESORICS 2022 Workshops, LNCS 13785, pp. 379–397, 2023.
https://doi.org/10.1007/978-3-031-25460-4_22

1   Introduction

Industrial Control Systems (ICS) monitor and control critical infrastructures such as power grids and gas pipelines. Typically, ICS consist of two macro areas, known as Information Technology (IT) and Operational Technology (OT) [15]. While IT is composed of standard computers interconnected via traditional communication protocols, OT includes special hardware and software for monitoring and controling a given industrial facility. Overall, OT consists of *field*, *control*, and *supervisory* layers. The field layer includes different sensors and actuators, while the control layer is composed of a number of programmable logic controllers (PLCs). The sensors measure the current state of the underlying physical process, which is then reported to the PLCs. The PLCs implement a control logic used to evaluate the obtained sensor readings according to predefined or dynamically adjustable target values. Based on this evaluation, the PLCs may initiate specific commands to one or more actuators in the field layer aiming to adjust the current state of the physical process. In the supervisory layer, a Supervisory Control and Data Acquisition (SCADA) system performs a high-level visualization and control over the control and field layers and provides an overview of the current process state to the operator. While OT was mainly a standalone system in the past, nowadays it incorporates both decades-old devices and communication infrastructure, and new generation embedded devices with computing capabilities and Ethernet-based communication protocols, and is more often connected to the Internet.

While the increasing digitization and interconnection of OT to the Internet enlarges the number of possible attack surfaces against ICS [35], the integration of traditional proactive security protection methods is challenging due to the use of heterogeneous and vendor specific hardware and software with long lifetimes. Thus, a major line of research [12,13] focuses on the development of reactive security solutions in the form of industrial intrusion detection systems (IIDS) aiming to spot anomalies in otherwise predictable "normal" ICS behavior. A crucial requirement for the assessment of the actual, real-world performance of these methods and their fair comparison is the existence of a *representative* dataset. A straightforward solution would be to collect a bunch of sensor values and actuator states from a real ICS. However, ICS operators are often not willing to share such data due to confidentiality reasons and a possible disclosure of already existing system issues to the public. Moreover, the collection of data containing cyber attacks from a real ICS (i.e., executing attacks there) is even more challenging. Thus, prior works introduced different public ICS datasets (mainly collected from testbeds) that contain either physical readings such as sensor values and actuator states or network data [15]. Although the number of these datasets increased gradually in the last years, it remains unclear to which extent they can be considered as representative for the evaluation and fair comparison of different IIDS.

In this work, we identify key properties a given ICS dataset should own to be designated as representative based on typical IIDS evaluation scenarios. Our systematization of knowledge highlights that these properties are only partially represented in existing ICS datasets, which makes them unrepresentative, and shed light on the need for new datasets for ICS security research. Our goal is to motivate the community to carefully consider the generation of representative ICS datasets and to initiate a critical discussion in this direction. We further make a step into the direction of generating a representative dataset and present our ongoing work on the construction of a Hardware in the Loop (HiL) tesbed of a real water distribution system. Our testbed takes real customer requirements as an input to replicate the operation of a real German medium-sized water supplier and allows for the collection of three different types of data sources, i.e., physical readings, network data, and system logs. Our testbed and the surrounding framework allows for the generation of more than 20 attacks targeting both the distortion of the underlying physical process and network- and system-based cyber attacks. On a long term, we plan to extend and improve our testbed.

2   Key Properties of a Representative ICS Dataset

A plethora of IIDS [12,13] is suggested in literature, often designed for domain-particular ICS and evaluated on specific adversarial models. Based on our extensive survey of these works and known real-world ICS incidents, we propose a systematized set of desired properties a given ICS dataset should own to be designated as representative. Our systematization of knowledge allows for unbiased comparison of existing ICS datasets and serves as a guideline for the generation of new *representative* ICS datasets. In particular, our suggested categorization covers five main dimensions: adversarial actions, complexity and heterogeneity, extensibility and accessibility of the testbed, duration, and special requirements for IIDS evaluation.

Adversarial Actions. Based on prior knowledge about adversarial tactics and methods used in known real-world ICS incidents [21,35], we create a typical roadmap of adversarial actions, necessary to successfully attack ICS, that consists of four main steps (see Fig. 1). First, the adversary needs to gather knowledge about the target ICS environment, e.g., number of used devices and the interconnection between them, discover services accessible from outside via the Internet and, if the attacker has physical access, also on site. Next, the attacker needs to get access to the target ICS environment by using the collected information as well as further knowledge about known software vulnerabilities and other methods for compromising software and hardware. Once the attacker can communicate with and control one or more systems in the ICS, he can distribute malicious commands to these systems and manipulate physical readings to modify the underlying physical process. The impact of the attack depends on the number of compromised devices, their role in the ICS, and the layer they are located on. Overall, the impact of ICS attacks varies from a partial loss of productivity and revenue to a complete loss of availability. While in the first step the attacker mainly relies on passive methods to gain knowledge about the target ICS and in the last step the damages are almost irreversible, the use of IIDS is particularly beneficial in the second and third steps as the negative adversarial impact on ICS can be reduced if the attacks are discovered on time.

In response, a representative dataset for ICS security research should contain (*i*) a *number of cyber attacks* that cover different adversarial tactics and methods used in both the second and third steps in Fig. 1 (the first step is often passive and, hence, undetectable). We call these two categories of attacks (*ii*) *getting-access attacks* and (*iii*) *command & control (C&C) attacks*, respectively. The selection of these attacks should be carefully performed based on realistic adversarial models and capabilities. On the one hand, the chosen attacks should leave adversarial traces in different data sources, i.e., in collected (*iv*) *physical readings*, (*v*) *network traffic*, and (*vi*) *system logs*. Next, the variety of covered cyber attacks should be also defined based on the (*vii*) *location of the attacker*, i.e., on which layer in the OT the attacker can access and manipulate devices or any relevant data such as sensor readings and actuator states. The clear definition of the location of the adversary is particularly important when collecting an ICS dataset as it also determines the data source that should be used for anomaly detection. A representative ICS dataset should further contain a subset of C&C attacks that represent an attacker who tries to conceal tampering with physical readings needed to disturb the operation of a given industrial facility either by sending old legitimate measurements to SCADA, known as (*viii*) *replay attacks*, or by modifying minimally target physical readings, called (*ix*) *stealthy attacks*. On the other hand, each of the covered attack types should be executed under (*x*) *different adversarial capabilities*. Similar to [5], we consider the following types of adversarial capabilities: *unconstrained attacker* who can access and manipulate any data arbitrarily, *partially constrained attacker* who can access any data arbitrarily but can manipulate only a subset of sensor readings, actuator states or other important information, and *fully constrained attacker* who can access and manipulate only a specific subset of OT related data.

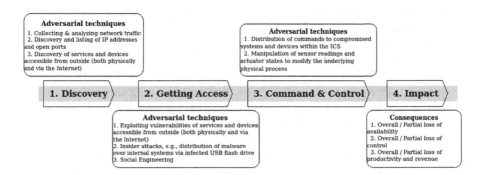

Fig. 1. An overview of a typical adversarial roadmap.

Complexity and Heterogeneity. The representativeness of an ICS dataset depends not only on the type and location of covered cyber attacks, but also on how realistic this dataset reflects (*i*) the *real complexity* of the underlying physical process as well as (*ii*) the *heterogeneity* of communication protocols typically observed in real ICS [30] and the diversity of possible data sources for data collection. The *complexity* of a replicated physical process can be quantitatively measured via (*i*) the number of linearly independent physical readings from sensors and actuators covered by the dataset and (*ii*) the number of sub-processes needed to reproduce the overall physical process.

The *heterogeneity* of the dataset defines (*i*) the presence of different communication protocols covered in the collected network traffic and (*ii*) the presence of different data sources in that dataset, i.e., physical readings, network data collected at different layers, and system logs. On the one hand, the latter property is particularly important for the fair comparison of IIDS relying on different data sources to detect anomalies in ICS. On the other hand, it also determines implicitly the set of different attack categories that can be potentially detected by IIDS.

Extensibility and Accessibility of Testbed. The underlying setup used to generate a representative ICS dataset should enable an easy extension of that dataset. Major changes of physical processes in real ICS, the integration of new technologies and protocols, and new adversarial trends should be caught up fast. Otherwise, outdated datasets can significantly slow down the overall progress in IIDS research, which is currently anyway sluggish due to the focus on IIDS highly tailored to specific domains and protocols making their comparison and the subsequent improvements extremely difficult. A representative ICS dataset should be freely accessible to the broad research community.

Duration of Recorded Data. Industrial facilities may regularly change their behavior at specific time periods. The duration of data recorded under normal system behavior should be adapted to these changes such that they are covered by the dataset. Moreover, it should include enough data to train the targeted IIDS classifier. Otherwise, an incomplete dataset may cause underfeeding of IIDS and artificially worsen its detection rate.

Special Requirements for IIDS Evaluation. To be appropriate for IIDS evaluation, a representative ICS dataset should contain (*i*) *accurate labels* of samples under attack. Moreover, to encourage further research in the evaluation of the real-world IIDS performance, the dataset should be structured in such a way that it enables the (*ii*) *use of attacks for training* if necessary. In particular, we recommend that a representative ICS dataset consists of three separate sets of data covering no attacks, several types of attacks represented by multiple samples, and another group of attacks not covered by the previous set, respectively. Such dataset would enable the analysis of the generalization capabilities of existing IIDS within and across different attack categories, which is currently only limited considered by the community [27].

3   Limitations of Existing ICS Datasets

Table 1 summarizes the key properties covered by existing ICS datasets that are briefly discussed in this section. One of the most popular ICS datasets is WAter DIstribution (WADI) [6]. It contains measurements for 123 sensors and actuators that are collected from three physical sub-processes of a water distribution testbed. Overall, WADI consists of two parts: a regular system operation recorded 14 days and 15 C&C attacks against the underlying physical process executed within two days. BATADAL [16,17] is another popular ICS dataset that is generated synthetically through a simulation of a real-world, medium-sized water distribution system located in the USA. It consists of measurements from 43 sensors and actuators and contains data for one year of normal operation and 14 C&C attacks performed within 10 months that are only partially labeled. Further datasets are provided by Morris et al. [18,20]. The first three datasets, called *power system datasets*, contain 128 physical readings from a small physical power generation testbed and comprise approximately 28 C&C attacks. Although these datasets contain different types of labels[1] that can support the evaluation of IIDS, they do not provide any information about the duration of the recorded data. The last dataset by Morris et al., called *energy management system data*, contains a large log of system information about SCADA events, device types, and other related data that was collected from a real energy management system in the USA for 30 days. However, this dataset does not contain any attacks. Shin et al. [10] collected the HAI 1.0 dataset that contains measurements from 59 sensors and actuators from a HiL-based power generation testbed [9]. This dataset comprises normal system behavior recorded within 10 days and 38 C&C attacks against the underlying physical process conducted within 5.5 days. Similar to our work, the attacks in the HAI dataset include both single attacks, in which the adversary manipulates a single physical reading only, multiple attacks tampering several physical readings in parallel, and stealthy attacks. In 2021 and 2022, two new versions of the HAI dataset [2,11] were released, in which the number of observed sensors and actuators, the variety of normal system behaviors, and the number of attacks are further extended.

Contrary to the datasets above that contain a list of reported sensor values and actuator states, other researchers focus on collecting network data from ICS. Lemay and Fernandez [28] generate a dataset of Modbus network packets that are collected through a simulation of a power grid control system. The dataset is gathered for approximately 6.30 h, whereas 6 h represent normal system operation and 12 network-based C&C attacks are executed within 30 min. The chosen attacks cover multiple easy-to-detect network attacks and side-channel attacks, in which the least significant bit of a Modbus packet is used to carry informa-

---

[1] The first dataset contains two labels indicating attack and no attack. The second dataset contains three labels indicating attack, no attack, or normal failure. The third dataset includes additionally a separate label for each attack.

tion. Morris et al. [20] publish *gas pipeline datasets*[2] that contain both network traffic from a normal system operation and 35 network-based attacks. 32 of the executed attacks are C&C and 3 of them are active reconnaissance attacks[3], in which the adversary is trying to gather information about the target ICS. While the authors provide a labeling for each separate packet, the duration of the recorded data, including the time span of the executed attacks, is not specified. Frazão et al. [23] record network data from another very simplified testbed simulating a single liquid pump only. The dataset contains network traffic of a normal system operation gathered for approximately 7.30 h and four different types of simple network flooding attacks. From each type of attack, 11 to 15 variations are executed, whereas each variation lasts from one to 30 min. Contrary to the gas pipeline datasets, this dataset does not contain any labeling of the attacks. Electra [1,4] is collected from an electric traction station and consists of two dataset versions: the first one comprises Modbus network traffic and the second one— S7comm network data. Both datasets last for about 12 h and contain six types of attacks such as false data injection, replay attacks, and reconnaissance attacks, whereas the authors do not clarify the duration of the attacks covered by these datasets[4]. Rodofile et al. [38] release further datasets of S7Comm and DNP3 network traffic. The first dataset, called *QUT_S7Comm* [37], consists of network communication with S7Comm and comprises 9 h of data and 64 attacks from 13 different network typologies. The second dataset, called *QUT_DNP3* [36], contains GOOSE and DNP3 network traffic for 40 days, whereas 24 h from them represent a normal system behavior, and approximately 161 attacks. Each of the attacks in both datasets lasts for from a few seconds to five minutes. PowerDuck [43] is collected from a testbed replicating a substation in high and extra high voltage power grids. It consists of GOOSE network packets collected for approximately 3.5 h, whereas around one hour and five minutes represent a normal system behavior. In total, the dataset contains 16 C&C network-based attacks varying from simple network flooding attacks to replay attacks.

Ndonda and Sadre [32] collected network traffic from a Heating, Ventilation, and Air Conditioning System (HVAC) that comprises seven days of normal system operation. Although this dataset contains several ICS protocols, it does not cover any attacks. CyberCity [24] contains heterogeneous network data from a simulation of an entire city comprising a power plant, a water distribution system, a bank, a hospital, and other generally available facilities in a small town. 4SICS [29] and S4x15 [33] consist of network packets from different ICS protocols such as S7Comm, Modbus, and DNP3. Although the latter three datasets cover multiple ICS protocols, which makes them attractive for IIDS research,

---

[2] We omit the discussion of another group of gas pipeline and water storage tank datasets by Morris et al. as these datasets contain unintended patterns and, thus, are broken [20].

[3] In our work, we categorize these attacks as getting-access attacks.

[4] During the preparation of this work, the website [1], which the dataset is published on, was not reachable, which hindered the investigation of this dataset.

they do not provide any labeling of the attacks, the execution of some attacks was uncontrolled, and they are not well documented.

Only a few public ICS datasets contain more than one data source. The most popular ICS dataset, called Secure Water Treatment (SWaT) [14,25], is recorded from a fully operational scaled-down physical water treatment testbed and comprises five different data collections. The first version of SWaT is the largest one and contains measurements from 51 sensors and actuators for 11 days. Similar to WADI, this dataset consists of two parts: the first seven days represent a normal system behavior and the subsequent four days contain 36 C&C attacks against the underlying physical process. The second version of the SWaT dataset includes physical measurements and network data for a normal system operation only (i.e., no attacks are recorded) that are collected within 136 h. In 2019, two new versions were further published. The first version comprises recordings of a normal system operation for four hours and six different C&C attacks executed within one hour. The second version contains process and network data for three hours, during which two malware attacks are launched. The last version of SWaT comprises four runs, whereas the duration of each one is two or four hours, and does not contain any attacks. EPIC [19] contains both physical data and network traffic for eight different operational scenarios (each 30 min long) collected from a physical Electric Power and Intelligent Control (EPIC) testbed. Nevertheless, the authors of EPIC recorded attacks only on network level that were executed from different teams within a three-day Hackathon event. QUT_S7 [7] is another dataset that includes network traffic from the communication protocol S7Comm and device logs. The dataset comprises normal system behavior and 21 C&C attacks that mainly conduct data injection and flooding.

Takeaways. None of the public ICS datasets cover both categories of attacks, namely getting-access attacks and C&C attacks. Thus, they do not replicate a complete roadmap of active adversarial actions in ICS. As a result, the limited number of cyber attacks for different adversarial capabilities or locations provided in the datasets restricts implicitly the possible scenarios for IIDS analysis. Several datasets contain network-based attacks that are simple and not particular for ICS environments. The collected network traffic do not always contain sufficient labeling of the attacks, which makes the use of such datasets difficult for IIDS evaluation. Although the majority of research on IIDS focuses on the detection of sophisticated stealthy attacks, almost no dataset contains such attacks. Only a few datasets cover a very constrained number of stealthy attacks, which makes the IIDS comparison almost impossible and the IIDS developers are forced to create synthetically own variations of existing datasets, whose representativeness is often questionable. It is surprising that datasets without any attacks or datasets without labeled attacks are generated, which make them practically not applicable for ICS security research.

The majority of ICS datasets contain only a single source of data for IIDS analysis. They provide either a set of physical measurements that are already parsed and aggregated or a bunch of network packets exchanged often by using proprietary protocols. This hampers significantly the analysis and the fair comparison of different IIDS types relying on different data sources for anomaly detection. On the other hand, the existence of multiple data sources in datasets is particularly important to identify which type of data source or a combination of several data sources is the most efficient one for accurate and fast anomaly detection. Several datasets are collected from very simplified testbeds or simulations containing a few devices only. They cannot replicate realistically a sophisticated physical process and interconnection between many devices, typically observed in real ICS, and, thus, oversimplify the anomaly detection for IIDS. Many datasets provide only a few hours of recorded data, which often does not cover all regular changes of a normal ICS system behavior. Almost no dataset provides a set of attacks that can be used for training IIDS, which hinders the analysis of the IIDS generalization capabilities.

4   Building Testbed for Generating Representative ICS Datasets

This section presents our ongoing work on the construction of a HiL tesbed of a real water distribution system. While designing and building our testbed, we aim to address the following key properties that are often overlooked in exiting ICS datasets:

1. *Execution of both getting-access and C&C attacks:* We replicate a complete roadmap of active adversarial actions in ICS by emitating an attacker who first tries to compromize a service located in the supervisory layer and, then, uses the compromised service to manipulate sensor values and to send bogus commands to actuators regulating the underlying physical process. Through his actions, the attacker leaves adversarial traces in multiple types of data sources collected by our testbed.
2. *Execution of stealthy attacks and nontrivial network-based attacks:* We generate two types of stealthy attacks, where the attacker can either manipulate any physical measurement or tamper with a subset of data readings only. In addition, we simulate network-based attacks, in which we either insert piece of malicious code imitating malware distribution or, e.g., generate network packets with malformed payload.
3. *Multiple data sources and enough data for IIDS evaluation:* We enable the collection of three different types of data sources, i.e., physical measurements, network data, and system logs from the supervisory layer.
4. *Complexity of the underlying physical process:* Our testbed replicates real water treatment and water supply processes that are typically carried out by a medium-sized German water suppler.

Overall, our testbed combines simulation tools to reproduce the underlying physical processes of a water plant with a physical PLC and an authentic SCADA system needed to monitor and control the operation of the simulated water plant. In the following, we introduce technical details about the current stage of development and future refinements of the testbed and discuss the datasets that can be collected from our testbed.

4.1 Technical Details About Our Testbed

Overview of the Underlying Physical Processes. Our testbed replicates real water treatment and water supply processes that are typically carried out by a medium-sized water supplier. We divide these processes into three groups: (*i*) extraction of water from multiple water sources, (*ii*) water filtration, and (*iii*) water distribution to customers. Figure 2 shows an overview of the simulated processes and devices regulating them.

First, we reproduce the extraction of raw water via water pumps (WPs) from seven wells. A separate WP is assigned to each of the wells and its flow rate is regularly measured and reported. The extracted raw water is then stored in water tanks. Next, the collected water is transported to the filter system, in which it is treated with different chemicals and is reabsorbed. To this end, we assign a filter to each of the water tanks storing raw water and measure the flow rate by which these filters forward clean water. Finally, the purified water is transported to another water tank, from which it is distributed to the customers. The water flow rate to the tank and the amount of water in the tank are regularly measured and reported. For the supply of water to customers, six clean water pumps (CWPs) are available to pump purified water from the tank and to distribute it to the customers. However, not all of these pumps are typically in use in practice. Instead, the water supplier aims to keep only a predefined number of pumps running within a specific pressure interval. If the amount of customer needs increases, additional CWPs are started and the pressure interval of all pumps is increased. For each of the CWPs, we measure periodically their current flow rate and pressure.

To achieve an authentic simulation of our water plant, we use data time series of real customer profiles about the quantity of purified water to be delivered that are provided by a real medium-sized water supplier. This information is presented in the form of water flow rate and pressure and is used as an input to launch the simulation of the water plant.

Design and Technical Realization. Figure 3 illustrates the architecture of our testbed. It consists of real physical devices, an emulator for network communication, and simulation tools to replicate real water treatment and water supply processes. In particular, we use a physical PLC Siemens S7-400 [39] that is connected to a physical computer running Siemens WinCC service [41] and acting as a SCADA system. The proprietary ICS protocol S7Comm [3] by Siemens is further used for communication between the PLC and the WinCC service. Both PLCs Siemens S7-400 and the Siemens WinCC services are widely used in German ICS. Beside WinCC service, in the supervisory layer we maintain an active directory service managing the permissions and access of users to the ICS resources as well as a virtual domain controller to simulate a typical scenario of a restricted access to ICS resources by user authentication. The latter is needed to allow for the execution of getting-access attacks against ICS. All physical processes of the water plant are simulated through WinMod, Matlab, and Simulink. In addition, this simulation is connected to our physical PLC and, thus, we ensure an interaction between our physical devices and the simulated

Table 1. An overview of existing ICS datasets and key properties that they cover. Notion: ■ has property, ◪ partially has property, □ does not have property, ∅ information not provided.

Properties	WADI [6]	BATADAL [17,16]	Power system datasets [20,18]	Energy management system data [20]	HAI 1.0 [10]	HAI 21.03 [11]	HAI 22.04 [2]	Lemay and Fernández [28]	Gas pipeline datasets [20]	Frazão et al. [23]	Electra Modbus [4]	Electra S7comm [4]	QUT_S7Comm [37]	QUT_DNP3 [36]	PowerDuck [43]	HVAC dataset [32]	CyberCity [24]	4SICS [29]	S4x15 [33]	SWaT 2015 [14,25]	SWaT 2017 [25]	SWaT-1 2019 [25]	SWaT-2 2019 [25]	SWaT 2020 [25]	EPIC [19]	QUT_S7 [7]
Adversarial actions																										
Total number of cyber attacks	15	14	28	0	38	50	58	12	35	71	6	6	64	161	16	0	∅	∅	∅	36	0	6	2	0	∅	21
Adversarial traces in physical readings																										
Adversarial traces in network traffic																										
Adversarial traces in system logs																										
Getting-access attacks																										
C&C attacks																										
Replay attacks / Stealthy attacks																										
Location of the attacker:																										
Field layer																	∅	∅	∅						∅	
Control layer																	∅	∅	∅						∅	
Supervisory layer																	∅	∅	∅						∅	
Adversarial capacity:																										
Unconstrained attacker																	∅	∅	∅							
Partially constrained attacker																	∅	∅	∅							
Fully constrained attacker																	∅	∅	∅							
Complexity																										
Number of measured sensors & actuators	123	43	128	∅	59	78	86	5	∅	∅	∅	∅	∅	∅	∅	58	∅	∅	∅	51	51	51	51	51	∅	∅
Number of sub-processes	3	∅	∅	∅	4	4	4	1	1	1	∅	∅	3	∅	1	∅	∅	∅	∅	6	6	6	6	6	4	1
Heterogeneity																										
Data sources:																										
Physical readings																										
Network traffic																										
System logs																										
Different communication protocols																										
Extensibility and accessibility of testbed																										
Duration	∅	∅	∅	∅			∅	∅	∅	∅	∅	∅	∅	∅	∅	∅	∅	∅	∅							
Special requirements																										
Labeling																										
Attacks for training																										

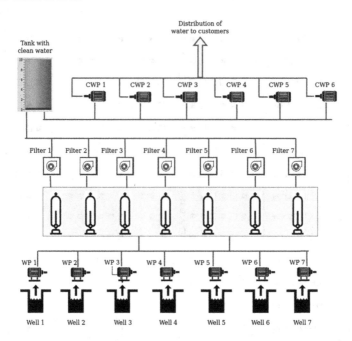

Fig. 2. An overview of the physical processes in our simulated water plant.

water plant. As PLC Siemens S7-400 can communicate with lower-level devices in the ICS hierarchy such as sensors and actuators only via the serial ICS protocol ProfiBus [34], we use a ProfiBus emulator, known as SIMBAProfiBus [40], that emulates ProfiBus fragments between our physical PLC and the simulated water plant. Thus, it enables the transaction of measurements sent from the devices in the water plantas well as actuator commands distributed by the PLC and the SCADA system.

Future Work. As next steps, we first plan to extend the physical processes simulated in our testbed. In particular, we will refine the water filtration process by inserting additional filtration steps such as chlorine dosing. The filters will be further equipped with supplemental sensors indicating the amount of collected dross over time and with special outlets needed to rinse the filters in regular time intervals. As a result, the number of collected physical measurements will be also extended. Moremore, in long term we plan to replace the ProfiBus emulator with a ProfiNet emulator and, thus, enable the collection of network traffic not only between the supervisory and control layers but also between the control and field layers. Finally, we envision to connect further PLCs to our SCADA system that will control water treatment and water supply processes in other geographical regions of our simulated water supplier.

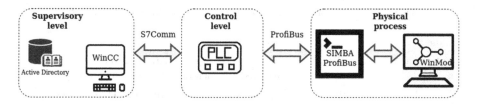

Fig. 3. Technical realization of our testbed.

4.2 Generation of ICS Datasets from Our Testbed

To launch a preliminary generation of an ICS dataset and to test the operation of our testbed, we use real customer profiles about the amount of water to be delivered presented in the form of water flow rate and pressure for 11 days in February 2022 that are provided by a medium-sized water suplier. Our testbed enables the collection of three different types of data sources, namely physical measurements from the underlying water plant simulated in our testbed, sniffing of network traffic between the supervisory and control layers, and system logs gathered from the WinCC service representing our SCADA system. As shown in Table 2, our testbed provides a list of measurements for 35 different sensors and actuators in the simulated water plant that are recorded every second. Our initial test of the testbed lasted for 11 days in total. In the first seven days, we replicated a normal ICS operation, i.e., without launching any attacks. During the remaining four days, we tested the execution of more than 20 getting-access and C&C attacks and a combination of both attack categories aiming to replicate a complete roadmap of active adversarial actions in ICS. The approximate duration of these attacks is from four to 45 min. In the following, we provide more details about our attacks.

Execution of Getting-Access Attacks. We assume that the attacker has already gathered knowledge about our simulated ICS and can access the supervisory layer of our ICS, e.g., due to wrong configuration of the firewall located between OT and IT or even completely missing firewall (a security gap often observed in practice). Next, the attacker aims to compromise the SCADA system, i.e., our WinCC service, and, thus, gain control over the underlying water plant. To this end, we prearrange different configurations, in which our WinCC service is vulnerable to one or more known software flaws or several social engineering attacks are executed against the users accessing the ICS resources. Then, our simulated attacker relies on PowerShell [31] to execute different commands and malicious pieces of code aiming to identify the pre-configured vulnerabilities and, thus, he compromises the WinCC service. The process of compromising the WinCC service leaves adversarial traces in the system logs and in the network traffic (e.g., use of unexpected protocols due to the malicious activities in the network) exchanged in the ICS that are captured by our testbed. The simulated adversarial actions are documented such that we can create correct labels for each of the collected data types.

Table 2. List of physical measurements collected from our testbed.

Name	Description
Water flow rate of a WP [m³/h]	Flow rate to pump water from a well (measured for each of the seven water pumps)
Water flow rate of a filter [m³/h]	Flow rate by which a clean water is forwarded (measured for each of the seven filters)
Water flow rate of customers [m³/h]	Current flow rate required by customers
Pressure of customers [bar]	Current water pressure required by customers
Water flow rate of the plant [m³/h]	Current flow rate provided by the plant
Pressure of the plant [bar]	Current water pressure provided by the plant
Flow rate of a CWP [m³/h]	Flow rate to pump clean water to customers (measured for each of the six clear water pumps)
Rotation speed of a CWP [Hz]	Current rotation speed of a given CWP (measured for each of the six clear water pumps)
Target pressure of each CWP [bar]	Current target pressure defined for each CWP
Level of clean water tank [bar]	Current level of water in the clean water tank
Measurement parameter Q_1 [m³/h]	Indicates when an additional CWP is launched
Measurement parameter Q_2 [m³/h]	Indicates when two additional CWPs are launched
Measurement parameter Q_3 [m³/h]	Indicates when three additional CWPs are launched

Execution of C&C Attacks. Once the adversary gained access to the WinCC service, he can tamper one or more physical measurements from the underlying water plant and send malicious commands to one or more pumps. In particular, we assume that some of attacker's intents are as follows: (*i*) tampering with the target water pressure expected by customers, (*ii*) forcing an additional CWP to be launched although this is not needed in reality, (*iii*) inserting delays when to switch on/off WPs and CWPs and, thus, generating inadequate operation time of the pumps, and (*iv*) under- and overflow of water tanks. To execute these attacks, we prepared a bunch of scripts that are launched at specific time intervals by the compromised WinCC service. Similar to the getting-access attacks above, the manipulation of physical readings leaves adversarial traces in the reported physical measurements that are regularly gathered by our testbed. Next, we perform several stealthy attacks, i.e., the adversary generates slight changes in a part of the physical readings that are difficult to be recognized but sufficient to disturb the physical process. To this end, we adopted the framework by Erba et al. [5] to be applied on authentic physical data series already collected from our testbed. Like [5], we generated two types of stealthy attacks: (i) unconstrained attacks, in which the adversary can observe and manipulate any physical measurements, and (ii) constrained attacks where the adversary tamper with a part of the readings only. All attacks are labeled manually based on their start and end time and the information about manipulated components.

Both the execution of getting-access attacks and the subsequent manipulation of physical measurements leave adversarial traces in the underlying communication infrastructure. To collect this data, we deploy an additional virtual machine in our testbed that can passively sniff and actively manipulate (if needed) network traffic exchanged between our SCADA system and the PLC. Another type of C&C attacks that are particular to ICS and can leave traces in the network traffic is the distribution of malware in legitimate network packets, forwarding of malformed packets, as well as blocking of single packets. To execute these attacks, we create an adversarial framework that processes single authentic network packets and supports the following options: (i) inserts piece of malicious code imitating malware, (ii) generates malformed network packets by shuffling the original payload, and (iii) removing single packets imitating packet blocking. The exchange of malformed packets or a partial blocking of network packets between the SCADA system and the PLC may directly disturb the underlying physical process. Finally, we can also execute simple network attacks such as port scanning, Denial of Service (DoS), replay, and man-in-the-middle attacks directly in our testbed using existing network tools. All attacks are labeled manually and packetwise based on the start and end time of the attacks and log information about each of the attacks.

5   Related Work

Analysis of Existing ICS Datasets. A bunch of surveys reviewed different aspects of ICS security research. Suaboot et al. [13] presented a broad overview of different machine learning techniques used for IIDS. Pliatsios et al. [35] published a comprehensive survey of typical ICS communication protocols and known real-world ICS incidents. Choi et al. [22] systematized 11 popular ICS datasets based only on a limited set of attacks executed at the different layers of ICS. Recently, Conti et al. [15] reviewed existing ICS datasets and testbeds and discussed popular IIDS that were evaluated with these datasets. Turrin et al. [42] analyzed the statistical distribution of sensor values between both sets of data representing normal system operation and recordings with attacks, respectively, of the three popular datasets SWaT, WADI, and BATADAL. Other studies [8,26] analyzed the statistical distribution of sensor values among the different versions of a single dataset. Contrary to our work, none of these works elaborates an extensive list of key properties an ICS dataset should own to be designated as representative for ICS security research—one of our main contributions. Moreover, these works either cover outdated list of existing public ICS datasets or only present a broad description of these datasets.

Existing Testbeds. A crucial requirement for the generation of an ICS dataset is the existence of a testbed. Therefore, several works focused on the construction of ICS testbeds in the last years. For instance, Shin et al. [9] presented the HAI testbed that interconnects three independent ICSs that are coordinated by the HiL paradigm. Goh et al. [14] built the SWaT testbed replicating six different processes of a water treatment plant. Adepu et al. [19] introduced the EPIC testbed that comprises four different stages of a real-world power system: power generation, transmission, micro-grid, and smart home. We refer the reader to [15] for further information about exiting testbeds and a detailed description of their operation. Nevertheless, none of these testbeds is publicly available, making it impossible to extend the dataset in an easy way. This requires the construction of an own testbed, in which the key properties identified in Sect. 2 can be taken into account.

6   Discussion and Conclusion

The existence of representative ICS datasets is particularly important for a real-world IIDS evaluation. In the past, an increasing number of ICS datasets were publicly released. However, none of them was critically reviewed with respect to its representativeness. In this work, we identified an extensive list of key properties a given ICS dataset should own to be appropriate for IIDS evaluation. Our categorization covers not only requirements about conducted cyber attacks but also complexity, heterogeneity, duration of the collected dataset as well as special requirements for IIDS evaluation. Through our revision of the properties of existing ICS datasets, we identified several pitfalls and gaps in these datasets, which makes them unrepresentative, and shed light on the need for new datasets for IIDS evaluation. In response, we presented our ongoing work on building a HiL testbed of a real water distribution system that aims to address several key properties that are often overlooked in prior ICS datasets. In particular, our testbed allows for execution of both getting-access and C&C attacks as well as enables the collection of three different types of data sources. Still, our testbed has several limitations to be addressed in the future. As it considers a water treatment plant only, it should be explored whether one needs further ICS scenarios for representativeness. Our testbed provides a limited number of different ICS protocols and addresses only a subset of our key properties (e.g., no different positioning of the attacker, no different layers for collection of network traffic, attack coverage according to the ICS MITRE ATT&CK matrix).

In the future, a great benefit would be an online accessibility of testbeds. This would allow for the community members to extend and influence the future dataset collection. Moreover, it is still open research question whether tools for attack mounting on existing benign traces—as done by other researchers—is an acceptable way to go for as it produces possibly statistically dispersed data that can be detected as such (dataset manipulation vs. attack detection). Finally, we plan to validate our preliminary dataset by using state-of-the-art IIDS methods that have already achieved high detection rates with prior public ICS datasets.

Acknowledgments. This work has been funded by the German Federal Ministry of Education and Research (BMBF) under the project KISS_KI Simple & Scalable and the EU and state Brandenburg EFRE StaF project INSPIRE.

References

1. Electra dataset: Anomaly detection ICS dataset. https://perception.inf.um.es/ICS-datasets/
2. HAI (HIL-based Augmented ICS) Security Dataset. https://github.com/icsdataset/hai
3. Siemens communications overview. https://snap7.sourceforge.net/siemens_comm.html
4. Gómez, Á.L.P., et al.: On the generation of anomaly detection datasets in industrial control systems. IEEE Access **7** (2019)
5. Erba, A., et al.: Constrained concealment attacks against reconstruction-based anomaly detectors in industrial control systems. In: Annual Computer Security Applications Conference, ACSAC. ACM (2020)
6. Ahmed, C.M., et al.: WADI: a water distribution testbed for research in the design of secure cyber physical systems. In: 3rd International Workshop on Cyber-Physical Systems for Smart Water Networks, CySWATER. ACM (2017)
7. Myers, D., et al.: Anomaly detection for industrial control systems using process mining. Comput. Secur. **78** (2018)
8. Zizzo, G., et al.: Adversarial attacks on time-series intrusion detection for industrial control systems. In: 19th International Conference on Trust, Security and Privacy in Computing and Communications, TrustCom. IEEE (2020)
9. Shin, H.K., et al.: Implementation of programmable CPS testbed for anomaly detection. In: 12th Workshop on Cyber Security Experimentation and Test, CSET. USENIX Association (2019)
10. Shin, H.K., et al.: HAI 1.0: HIL-based augmented ICS security dataset. In: 13th Workshop on Cyber Security Experimentation and Test, CSET. USENIX Association (2020)
11. Shin, H.K., et al.: Two ICS security datasets and anomaly detection contest on the HIL-based augmented ICS testbed. In: 14th Workshop on Cyber Security Experimentation and Test., CSET. ACM (2021)
12. Giraldo, J., et al.: A survey of physics-based attack detection in cyber-physical systems. ACM Comput. Surv. **51**(4) (2018)
13. Suaboot, J., et al.: A taxonomy of supervised learning for IDSs in SCADA environments. ACM Comput. Surv. **53**(2) (2020)
14. Goh, J., Adepu, S., Junejo, K.N., Mathur, A.: A dataset to support research in the design of secure water treatment systems. In: Havarneanu, G., Setola, R., Nassopoulos, H., Wolthusen, S. (eds.) CRITIS 2016. LNCS, vol. 10242, pp. 88–99. Springer, Cham (2017). https://doi.org/10.1007/978-3-319-71368-7_8
15. Conti, M., et al.: A survey on industrial control system testbeds and datasets for security research. IEEE Commun. Surv. Tutor. **23**(4) (2021)
16. Taormina, R., et al.: Battle of the attack detection algorithms: disclosing cyber attacks on water distribution networks. J. Water Resour. Plan. Manag. **144**(8) (2018)

17. Taormina, R., et al.: A toolbox for assessing the impacts of cyber-physical attacks on water distribution systems. Environ. Model. Softw. **112** (2019)
18. Pan, S., et al.: Developing a hybrid intrusion detection system using data mining for power systems. IEEE Trans. Smart Grid **6**(6) (2015)
19. Adepu, S., Kandasamy, N.K., Mathur, A.: EPIC: an electric power testbed for research and training in cyber physical systems security. In: Katsikas, S.K., et al. (eds.) SECPRE/CyberICPS 2018. LNCS, vol. 11387, pp. 37–52. Springer, Cham (2019). https://doi.org/10.1007/978-3-030-12786-2_3
20. Adhikari, U., et al.: Industrial Control System (ICS) Cyber Attack Datasets (2022). https://sites.google.com/a/uah.edu/tommy-morris-uah/ics-data-sets
21. ATT&CK, M.: ICS Matrix. https://attack.mitre.org/matrices/ics/
22. Choi, S., Yun, J.-H., Kim, S.-K.: A comparison of ICS datasets for security research based on attack paths. In: Luiijf, E., Žutautaitė, I., Hämmerli, B.M. (eds.) CRITIS 2018. LNCS, vol. 11260, pp. 154–166. Springer, Cham (2019). https://doi.org/10.1007/978-3-030-05849-4_12
23. Frazão, I., Abreu, P.H., Cruz, T., Araújo, H., Simões, P.: Denial of service attacks: detecting the frailties of machine learning algorithms in the classification process. In: Luiijf, E., Žutautaitė, I., Hämmerli, B.M. (eds.) CRITIS 2018. LNCS, vol. 11260, pp. 230–235. Springer, Cham (2019). https://doi.org/10.1007/978-3-030-05849-4_19
24. Hink, R.C.B., Goseva-Popstojanova, K.: Characterization of cyberattacks aimed at integrated industrial control and enterprise systems: a case study. In: 17th International Symposium on High Assurance Systems Engineering, HASE. IEEE (2016)
25. iTrust: Secure Water Treatment (SWaT) Testbed (2022). https://itrust.sutd.edu.sg/testbeds/secure-water-treatment-swat/
26. Kravchik, M., Shabtai, A.: Efficient Cyber Attacks Detection in Industrial Control Systems Using Lightweight Neural Networks and PCA (2019)
27. Kus, D., et al.: A false sense of security? Revisiting the state of machine learning-based industrial intrusion detection. In: 8th Workshop on Cyber-Physical System Security, CPSS. ACM (2022)
28. Lemay, A., Fernandez, J.M.: Providing SCADA network data sets for intrusion detection research. In: 9th Workshop on Cyber Security Experimentation and Test, CSET. USENIX Association (2016)
29. Lounge, G.: Capture files from 4SICS Geek Lounge. https://www.netresec.com/?page=PCAP4SICS
30. Mehner, S., Schuster, F., Hohlfeld, O.: Lights on power plant control networks. In: Hohlfeld, O., Moura, G., Pelsser, C. (eds.) PAM 2022. LNCS, vol. 13210, pp. 470–484. Springer, Cham (2022). https://doi.org/10.1007/978-3-030-98785-5_21
31. Microsoft: PowerShell Documentation. https://docs.microsoft.com/en-us/powershell/
32. Ndonda, G.K., Sadre, R.: A Public Network Trace of a Control and Automation System. https://arxiv.org/pdf/1908.02118.pdf
33. Peterson, D., Wightman, R.: S4x15 ICS Village PCAP Files. https://www.netresec.com/?page=DigitalBond_S4
34. (PI), P.P.I.: Profibus
35. Pliatsios, D., et al.: A survey on SCADA systems: secure protocols, incidents, threats and tactics. IEEE Commun. Surv. Tutor. **22**(3) (2020)
36. Rodofile, N.R.: DNP3 Cyber-attack datasets. https://github.com/qut-infosec/2017QUT_DNP3
37. Rodofile, N.R.: SCADA network attack datasets and process logs. https://github.com/qut-infosec/2017QUT_S7comm

38. Rodofile, N.R.: Generating attacks and labelling attack datasets for industrial control intrusion detection systems. Ph.D. thesis, Queensland University of Technology (2013)
39. Siemens: S7-400 Automation System, CPU Specifications (2009). https://cache.industry.siemens.com/dl/files/550/23904550/att_98310/v1/CPU_data_en_en-US.pdf?download=true
40. Siemens: SIMULATIONUnit Manual (2022). https://cache.industry.siemens.com/dl/files/344/109475344/att_926827/v1/HelpEN.pdf
41. Siemens: Software for the visualization of the future (2022). https://new.siemens.com/global/en/products/automation/simatic-hmi/wincc-unified/software.html
42. Turrin, F., et al.: A statistical analysis framework for ICS process datasets. In: Joint Workshop on CPS&IoT Security and Privacy. ACM (2020)
43. Zemanek, S., et al.: PowerDuck: a GOOSE data set of cyberattacks in substations. In: 15th Workshop on Cyber Security Experimentation and Test, CSET. ACM (2022)

Securing Cyber-Physical Spaces with Hybrid Analytics: Vision and Reference Architecture

Daniel De Pascale[1]([✉]), Mirella Sangiovanni[1], Giuseppe Cascavilla[2], Damian A. Tamburri[2], and Willem-Jan Van Den Heuvel[1]

[1] Jheronimus Academy of Data Science, Tilburg University, Tilburg, The Netherlands
`d.de.pascale@tue.nl`
[2] Jheronimus Academy of Data Science, TU/e - Eindhoven University of Technology, Eindhoven, The Netherlands

Abstract. Considering the massive increase in the number of crimes in the last decade, as well as the outlook toward smarter cities and more sustainable urban living, the emerging *cyber-physical space* (CPS) obtained by the interaction of such physical spaces with the *cyber* elements around them (e.g., think of Internet-of-Things devices or hyperconnected mobility), plays a key role in the protection of urban social living, e.g., social events or daily routines. For example, the hyperconnectedness of a CPS to many networks can lead to potential vulnerability. This vision paper aims to outline a vision and reference architecture where CPS protection is center-stage and where CPS models as well as so-called hybrid analytics work jointly to help the Law Enforcement Agents (LEAs), e.g., in event monitoring and early detection of criticalities. As a part of validating said reference architecture, we implement a case study in the scope of VISOR, a Dutch government project aimed at improving CPS protection using hybrid analytics. We conduct a field experiment in the Paaspop social event and festival grounds to test and select the most appropriate device configuration. There we experiment with a CPS protection pipeline featuring several components reflected in the reference architecture, e.g., the KGen middleware, a prototype tool to anonymize structured big data using genetic algorithms, and SENSEI, a framework for dark web marketplace analytics. We conclude that hybrid analytics offer a considerable ground for more sustainable CPS.

Keywords: Cyber physical space (CPS) · Internet of Thing (IoT) · Law Enforcement Agents (LEA) · Genetic algorithm (GA)

1 Introduction

Cyber-physical systems (CPS) integrate physical processes with computational engineered systems [12,14] to solve a real-world problem. An example of CPS is

S. Katsikas et al. (Eds.): ESORICS 2022 Workshops, LNCS 13785, pp. 398–408, 2023.
https://doi.org/10.1007/978-3-031-25460-4_23

self-driving cars, where the physical part (the vehicle) meets the cyber part (the self-driving software) to solve the self-driving engineering problem.

Being center-stage in supporting smarter urban living, CPS' is increasingly becoming one of the main targets of all sorts of attacks. For example, cyberattacks are often discovered in many societal scenarios (e.g., value transactions, money exchange, post and stamp services). Similarly, CPS does not stand isolated from their operational context—a physical space with sensors that intercommunicate with the CPS itself—rather they are contiguous with such context and therefore are at risk from multiple engagements in such context.

For example, in 2016, a significant distributed denial of service (DDOS) attack interrupted many Internet services in the USA and Europe [17], causing delays in civil transport, as well as economic and financial meltdowns. Garroppo et al. in [8] investigated how to identify social events by analyzing anomalies in cellular traffic data. Similarly, Yuan et al. [23] did anomaly behavior detection in a crowd scene. They propose the analysis of anomaly motion behavior between individuals investigating the optical histogram flow between frames.

To address these kinds of safety issues, several works act under the physical domain [16] (i.e., analysis of anomaly behavior patterns through IoT devices). Other works use social and dark web analysis, providing models helping Law Enforcement Agents (LEAs) to analyze marketplaces and forums trending on the dark web, extracting useful insight for future investigations [10].

In this work, we present a proposed framework to introduce a reference architecture providing an alternative approach where physical space protection models—e.g., knowledge graphs [11] obtained on the physical spaces' components and connectors—work jointly with dark web analytics to improve the detection and response against critical actions. Starting from the models executed with IoT devices data (e.g., drug trading between persons), the idea is to use social and dark web analytics to improve these models in detecting, among others, meta-data describing the drugs or creating a more appropriate response through insights extracted from the Internet or other open-source intelligence databases.

The paper is organized as follows: in Sect. 2 we discuss the vision of our approach, explaining the architecture outlined in Sect. 1. Section 3 describes the data sources used as a baseline for the proposed architecture analytics. In Sect. 4 the data received from the previous step are anonymized before the analysis. Section 5 illustrates two approaches for countering illegal trafficking activities. Section 6 is the core of this paper and its vision. It explains the general idea behind the "hybrid analytic" concept and describes the case study we aim to set up. Lastly, Sects. 7 and 8 discuss, respectively, about the limitation, discussion and conclusion of this work.

2   Cyber-Physical Space Protection: A Hybrid Analytics Approach

One of the main strengths of a cyber-physical system (CPS) is the ability to monitor and control a physical environment—such as a social event, or a public

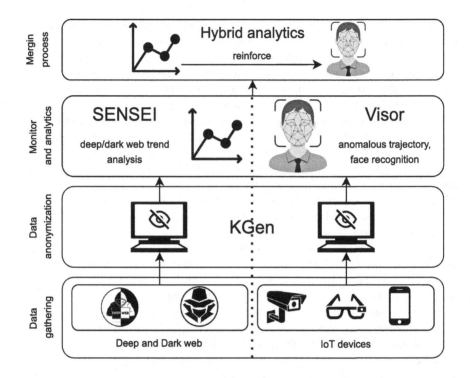

Fig. 1. Architecture of a CPS monitoring using both social event monitoring and deep/dark web analysis. It is divided into four layers: data gathering (1), data anonymization (2), monitor and analytics (3), merging process (4).

space [13]—using and interconnecting multiple sensor networks and data sources. In this type of CPS scenario, the design of models to predict fraudulent behavior plays a key role. However, the accuracy of CPS models needs to be continuously improved by using analytics that predicts critical events, e.g., terrorist attacks in a public space. Several methods protect CPS for the specific context in the state-of-the-art. For example, Nagarajan et al. [16] developed an alternative approach for anomaly detection in the CPS domain. The author proposed a deep learning technique, namely Convolutional Neural Network with Kalman Filter based Gaussian-Mixture Model, to identify anomalous behavior in the CPS context. Another CPS scenario has been provided by Du et al. [6]. Their work addresses the detection of pickpocket suspects in a large-scale public context. Studies in the literature focus on identifying anomalies in passengers' movement patterns [3]. The novelty of the work proposed in [3] is the usage of public transit records to recognize pickpocket actions.

This paper focuses on integrating information extracted from public spaces using analysis performed on the deep and dark web while blending this information with available models of the phenomenon under support, for example, the protection of the CPS and sustainable urban living within the spaces around it.

Our work provides a reference architecture to reinforce physical space protection through IoT devices augmented with deep and dark web analytics. For example, in a social event scenario, the recognition of drugs can be significantly improved if a dark web markets analysis results in massive trading of a specific drug in that area or country. This way, an analytic service model can be learned on that specific drug to improve its accuracy and deployed at the edge of the CPS. The following section generalizes this simplistic approach and outlines a reference architecture.

2.1 Reference Architecture

Figure 1 represents the multi-layer architecture offered in this work, with four different self-contained layers built on top of each other according to a layered software architecture style [2]. Each layer has a specific purpose following the typical data-intensive computing services architecture [1], from data gathering to a hybrid analytics service layer. More specifically, the hybrid analytics architecture encompasses the following four layers:

1. **Data gathering layer:** the first layer is in charge of downloading raw data from the web and social events. It includes IoT devices like smart glasses, smartphones, CCTV, and drones. Along with other devices, they collect real-time data to monitor and analyze social event scenarios. Data gathered include images, video, Global Positioning System (GPS), metadata, and sound signal, depending on the device. All the data are saved into a cloud or local storage and then passed to the next layer for the anonymization step.
2. **Data anonymization layer:** after gathering the raw data, they must be anonymized, ensuring the usability of the data. While data completely anonymized is useless, data partially anonymized can contribute to the analytics and preserve the anonymity. The data to anonymize must be structured. If data is unstructured (e.g., image, video), they bypass the anonymization layer to be directly analyzed in the monitor and analytic layer. Otherwise, all the structured data are anonymized before the following analysis. For example, item location distribution and price of a dark marketplace product must be anonymized using generalization rules [20]. Prices can be anonymized using range values criteria. Contrarily, the location anonymization process follows the generalization hierarchy criteria. For each anonymization layer, the level of abstraction is higher (e.g., Roma -> Lazio -> Italy -> Europe). The product anonymized is used in the monitoring and analytic layer (layer 3).
3. **Monitor and analytic layer:** this step of the architecture performs monitoring and analysis processes. The cyber and the physical part are analyzed separately with different results. Examples of analysis performed are 1) trend analysis for the dark web drugs monitoring, 2) anomalous trajectory and pickpocket detection for the social event monitoring. For example, coming back to the anonymized product of layer 2, using the item location, we can accomplish a trend analysis of the number of drugs in a specific country.

4. **Merging process layer:** at the end of the architecture, the analysis is joined together to check if there is an improvement in the results compared to the disjoint analysis. The main core of the hybrid analytic layer is to use the results of the dark web analysis to reinforce and improve the analysis of physical space protection models. For example, suppose the analytic on the dark web provides a massive usage of amphetamine in the Netherlands. In that case, we can set up a machine learning model trained with amphetamine to improve the accuracy of the detection process.

A more detailed description of each layer is available in the following sections.

3 Data Collection

In the first layer of the architecture in Fig. 1, the data are gathered for future analysis. The macro area sources involved in this project are twofold: a) cyber sources, with pages crawled from the deep and dark web and b) physical sources, with data gathered through IoT devices during social events.

3.1 Cyber Sources: Deep and Dark Web Pages

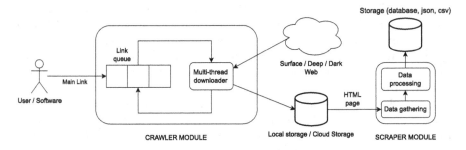

Fig. 2. Architecture of a multi-thread crawler. It represents the main workflow of the crawler, showing the iteration over a link queue list to download every web page found, and its integration with the scraper module, in charge to extract insights from the crawled web pages.

We implemented a crawler to download web pages automatically from the deep and dark web. The main goal is a solid dataset to analyze further and prevent crimes. Figure 2 shows a general architecture of the crawler. After feeding the crawler with a dark web onion link to crawl, it then downloads all the web pages, extracts information from them, and finds a new link to analyze. At first, the link queue contains only the main link. From the main link analysis, the tool extracts all the website links, puts them in the link queue, and iterates this process for each link extracted. To maximize the numbers of pages crawled, the main link might be the home page of a deep or dark website (e.g., onion links of a dark web marketplace found in the Hidden Wiki [22]). This process runs until all the links have been analyzed or the user stops the tool. Lastly, the pages downloaded and the information scraped are saved online (cloud-based solution) or locally.

3.2 Physical Sources: IoT Devices

IoT devices can be used to gather information from social events. For example, smart glasses and smartphones ease data gathering in a dynamic context. They allow the detection of entities with a low-range field of view (fov). On the other hand, drones have a high range of fov and can record video far from the action, keeping the camera focused on a specific area. In addition, CCTVs do not have any battery limitations, and the advantage is to focus on hotspot areas.

The data gathered are anonymized and stored in an encrypted hard drive to preserve their privacy, following the GDPR [21].

4   Data Anonymization

The main purpose of this architecture layer is, from one side, to anonymize the data crawled and gathered in the previous layer while keeping the main characteristics of the dataset unchanged and still useful for analysis and extraction of criminal behavior.

4.1   KGen: A Data Anonymization Tool for Structured Data

We developed KGen to ensure the right level of anonymization. KGen is a tool for data anonymization based on the k-anonymity property. As part of the project with the Dutch Tax Authority, our goal was to create a tool that could anonymize a big dataset in a reasonable time.

The main challenge is to provide a dataset anonymized while keeping the main properties of the data useful for future analysis. Moreover, it is crucial to ensure the k-anonymity property itself.

Several algorithms address the k-anonymity problem providing an optimal solution [7,15,18–20], but none among them handle big datasets. To account for the trade-off mentioned above, KGen develops an approach based on the Genetic Algorithm [9], providing a pseudo-optimal solution in a reasonable time for practical usage. In the KGen context, a solution represents a different level of generalization of each attribute to anonymize. For example, if an attribute to anonymize is a date with the format YYYY-MM-DD, there are at most two anonymization levels. In the first level, the day is obfuscated (YYYY-MM); in the second level, only the year is visible (YYYY). The scope of KGen is to minimize the level of generalization of each attribute while ensuring the k-anonymity principle.

The workflow of the approach is shown in Fig. 3. The tool generates a set of solutions containing random levels of anonymization of each attribute, starting from the dataset and a configuration file with the dataset's metadata. The

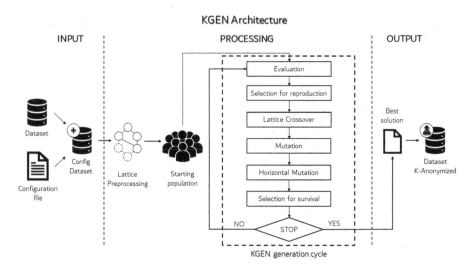

Fig. 3. KGEN Pipeline. It is divided into three steps (separated by dotted vertical lines), input, processing, and output; the KGEN-GA architecture is described in the processing step.

metadata config file has two dataset attribute information: 1) a boolean value used to determine whether a variable can be anonymized or not, and 2) the attribute type (e.g., numeric, string, data). Iterating multiple times, the genetic algorithm reaches the best pseudo-optimal solution that, in the end, is applied to the starting dataset to generate the anonymized version.

The main advantage of a genetic algorithm approach is the application of an anonymity tool even when a dataset contains lots of attributes to anonymize in a reasonable time. Nonetheless, its main disadvantage resides in the solution quality, expressed as the distance between a genetic algorithm solution and the best solution generated by a heuristic approach.

5   Data Analytics and Monitoring

After the data anonymization is performed in the previous step, the data is used for analysis and monitoring purposes. However, cyber data are different from physical data due to the data origin and the sources. Consequently, the process provides two methods: 1) analysis of cyber data crawled for the deep and dark web, and 2) analysis of data extracted from IoT devices placed in physical space. As a part of the architecture, we implement a case study to analyze the behavior of anomalous trajectories in a social event scenario, namely VISOR [4] and SENSEI [5], a web-based platform for dark web analytics.

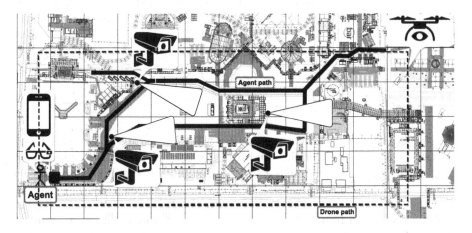

Fig. 4. Planimetry of survelliance scenario in physical event: (1) The dashed trajectory line is the path monitored by the drone, (2) the solid line has been followed by security staff, wearing smartglass and smartphone, (3) the circles, instead, are the cctv camera.

5.1 Monitor and Analytics of a Physical Environment

VISOR is a project born in collaboration with the Noord-Brabants Dutch Police and municipality stakeholders. Its primary purpose is to provide a platform for monitoring anomalous behavior in a social event (e.g., moshpit detection in a crowded concert). We led a case study focused on monitoring the social event Paaspop. The planimetry, shown in Fig. 4, represents a video surveillance scenario covered by the CCTV and the patrol done by agents and drones. In this scenario, three agents patrol the solid line in the planimetry, starting from the same point. The drone follows the dashed line, making a patrol of the event, covering the entire place. The three CCTV, represented by black circles, monitor a specific area, indicated by white cones. During the patrol, the information is sent in real-time and processed to detect illicit content (e.g., drug trading, moshpit). If the analysis recognizes an illegal event, agents on the field receive an alert notification with coordinates and images of such event.

The first study led in the VISOR project is an experience report done during the Paaspop event [4]. The next step is to experiment with the data gathered to evaluate different approaches helpful in recognizing and predicting illicit events.

5.2 Dark Web Analytics

The primary purpose of SENSEI is to build an investigation platform to help Law Enforcement Agencies (LEAs) analyze big data coming from the Dark Web. The framework provides a collection of tools for big data analysis to extract valuable insights for cybercrime investigations. The framework's features include but are not limited to trend analysis of specific temporal snapshots, network analysis of vendors, and comparison of trends between different countries to evaluate the movement of illicit goods across the world. Moreover, the platform allows narrowing the field, acting on a specific time range to provide more specific information.

6   Hybrid Analytic Services

The last layer of the architecture, namely Merging Process is the core of our research. Unlike layer 3 (Monitor and Analytic), the Hybrid Analytic layer is in charge of merging the two analyses to provide more fine-grained and detailed insights useful for an investigation.

The idea is to set up a case study with the Dutch Police to address the challenges inherited from hybrid analytics. Starting from a survey, we want to gather information regarding possible scenarios and data to build a prototype tool to help them in the monitoring process. For example, considering our study and analytics collected from the dark web marketplace accomplished by the SENSEI framework, a scenario could detect illegal trades in a Dutch Social event using the drug trend extracted from the dark web analysis as a baseline of a machine learner training process. The result of this experimentation allows us to estimate the effectiveness of our approach. For example, suppose the dark marketplace analytics show massive cocaine trades in the Netherlands, and the models used by the police show the same result. In that case, our web analytics is a good predictor for monitoring in the field. Hence, our analysis can be integrated into the real-time monitoring process to reinforce the analysis, lowering the effort of their models.

7   Limitation and Threat to Validity

This section outlines the major limitation we perceive in our work for each tool and case study.

The main limitation of KGen is the inability to anonymize unstructured data. It means that most data extracted by IoT devices, like video and images, can not be anonymized. Hence, following the GDPR principle, we need to integrate KGen with other anonymization tools if we are dealing with sensible data.

VISOR presents a threat in the monitoring process of the Paaspop event. Indeed, no specific illicit event happened during our gathering process. Hence, we could not have tested the notification alert of an illicit event on the field. A way to overcome this limitation is to lead a case study in a controlled environment where we set all the scenarios in advance.

Moreover, the crawler presents some limitations. For example, if a website is closed, obscured, or accessible through new captcha generation, the crawler can not download the website.

8   Discussion and Conclusion

In this vision paper, we introduce the architecture to facilitate the monitoring and analysis of CPS. Our architecture lays the foundation for further research using physical space protection models and social, deep, and dark web analysis. We have illustrated a preliminary study of the projects involved in this research work, passing from the KGen anonymization prototype tool to Visor and SENSEI projects.

The proposed architecture eases the monitoring and detection process in complex, critical, and dynamic scenarios. To validate our architecture, we set up a case study, namely VISOR, to monitor urban social living using hybrid analytics. We set up an experience report in the Paaspop event to validate the best IoT devices. We use SENSEI framework analytics to gather insights from the dark web and integrate them into the detection process. Then, we combine the KGen anonymization tool with the data extracted from web pages and IoT devices. Machine models could improve their efficiency in monitoring and detecting illicit goods by using information extracted from the dark web.

We conclude that the CPS might benefit from a hybrid analytic approach to improve the security level in a cyber-physical scenario.

8.1   Future Work

The following work of this project is to implement a case study with the Dutch police to evaluate the hybrid analytic approach in a different real scenario. The scope of this study is to find the best techniques for cyber-threat intelligence analysis to provide the best accuracy in a hybrid analytics context.

References

1. Casale, G., Li, C.: Enhancing big data application design with the DICE framework. In: Mann, Z.Á., Stolz, V. (eds.) ESOCC 2017. CCIS, vol. 824, pp. 164–168. Springer, Cham (2018). https://doi.org/10.1007/978-3-319-79090-9_13
2. Cervantes, H., Kazman, R.: Designing Software Architectures: A Practical Approach. Addison-Wesley Professional, Boston (2016)
3. Da Silva, T.L.C., de Macêdo, J.A., Casanova, M.A.: Discovering frequent mobility patterns on moving object data. In: Proceedings of the Third ACM SIGSPATIAL International Workshop on Mobile Geographic Information Systems, pp. 60–67 (2014)
4. De Pascale, D., Cascavilla, G., Sangiovanni, M., Tamburri, D.A., van den Heuvel, W.J.: Internet-of-things architectures for secure cyber-physical spaces: the visor experience report. arXiv preprint arXiv:2204.01531 (2022)
5. De Pascale, D., Cascavilla, G., Tamburri, D.A., Van Den Heuvel, W.J.: Sensei: scraper for enhanced analysis to evaluate illicit trends. SSRN 3976047 (2022)
6. Du, B., Liu, C., Zhou, W., Hou, Z., Xiong, H.: Detecting pickpocket suspects from large-scale public transit records. IEEE Trans. Knowl. Data Eng. **31**(3), 465–478 (2018)

7. El Emam, K., et al.: A globally optimal k-anonymity method for the de-identification of health data. J. Am. Med. Inform. Assoc. **16**(5), 670–682 (2009)

8. Garroppo, R.G., Niccolini, S.: Anomaly detection mechanisms to find social events using cellular traffic data. Comput. Commun. **116**, 240–252 (2018)

9. Goldberg, D.E., Holland, J.H.: Genetic algorithms and machine learning. Mach. Learn. **3**(2), 95–99 (1988)

10. Hayes, D.R., Cappa, F., Cardon, J.: A framework for more effective dark web marketplace investigations. Information **9**(8), 186 (2018)

11. Hogan, A., et al.: Knowledge graphs (2020)

12. Lee, E.A.: Cyber physical systems: design challenges. In: 2008 11th IEEE International Symposium on Object and Component-Oriented Real-Time Distributed Computing (ISORC), pp. 363–369. IEEE (2008)

13. Lee, E.A.: CPS foundations. In: Design Automation Conference, pp. 737–742. IEEE (2010)

14. Lee, E.A.: The past, present and future of cyber-physical systems: a focus on models. Sensors **15**(3), 4837–4869 (2015)

15. LeFevre, K., DeWitt, D.J., Ramakrishnan, R.: Incognito: efficient full-domain k-anonymity. In: Proceedings of the 2005 ACM SIGMOD International Conference on Management of Data, pp. 49–60. ACM (2005)

16. Nagarajan, S.M., Deverajan, G.G., Bashir, A.K., Mahapatra, R.P., Al-Numay, M.S.: IADF-CPS: intelligent anomaly detection framework towards cyber physical systems. Comput. Commun. (2022)

17. Perrone, G., Vecchio, M., Pecori, R., Giaffreda, R., et al.: The day after Mirai: a survey on MQTT security solutions after the largest cyber-attack carried out through an army of IoT devices. In: IoTBDS, pp. 246–253 (2017)

18. Samarati, P.: Protecting respondents identities in microdata release. IEEE Trans. Knowl. Data Eng. **13**(6), 1010–1027 (2001)

19. Sweeney, L.: Guaranteeing anonymity when sharing medical data, the Datafly system. In: Proceedings of the AMIA Annual Fall Symposium, p. 51. American Medical Informatics Association (1997)

20. Sweeney, L.: Achieving k-anonymity privacy protection using generalization and suppression. Internat. J. Uncertain. Fuzziness Knowl.-Based Syst. **10**(05), 571–588 (2002)

21. Voigt, P., von dem Bussche, A.: The EU General Data Protection Regulation (GDPR). A Practical Guide, 1st edn. Springer, Cham (2017). https://doi.org/10.1007/978-3-319-57959-7

22. Wikipedia: The Hidden Wiki (2022). https://en.wikipedia.org/wiki/The_Hidden_Wiki

23. Yuan, Y., Fang, J., Wang, Q.: Online anomaly detection in crowd scenes via structure analysis. IEEE Trans. Cybern. **45**(3), 548–561 (2014)

A Precision Cybersecurity Workflow for Cyber-physical Systems: The IoT Healthcare Use Case

Francesco Spegni[1(✉)], Antonio Sabatelli[1], Alessio Merlo[2], Lucia Pepa[1],
Luca Spalazzi[1], and Luca Verderame[2]

[1] Università Politecnica delle Marche, Ancona, Italy
{f.spegni,l.pepa,l.spalazzi}@univpm.it, a.sabatelli@pm.univpm.it
[2] University of Genoa, Genoa, Italy
{alessio.merlo,luca.verderame}@unige.it

Abstract. The IoT paradigm revolves around a tight interaction between the IT side (i.e., the thing and the software therein) and the human counterpart. From a security standpoint, both these aspects should be taken into consideration when building up reliable and effective security solutions. We argue that traditional static approaches to securing IoT fail to deal with such a complexity, as they do not take into account the dynamic nature of human beings that keep evolving while interacting with IoT device. To overcome this limitation, in this paper we put forward the idea of *precision cybersecurity* that complements the traditional security model by allowing for the definition of mechanisms and security policies which can be dynamically tailored around individuals. To this aim, we provide the first modeling of a precision cybersecurity workflow (PCW), and we implement it in a tool. Then, we apply it to a both security and safety critical IoT deployment, namely an IoT Medical-Healthcare real scenario, to prove the viability of the proposal.

Keywords: Healthcare · IoT · MQTT monitor · Precision cybersecurity

1 Introduction

Internet of Things (IoT) can be considered as the extension of the world of computing, especially the Internet, to the domain of physical objects, which thus acquire their own digital identity in order to interact both with other objects on the network and with users, creating a true cyber-physical system. Given its pervasive nature and the ability to create an ecosystem where objects and people coexist, cybersecurity issues are particularly critical. This is true especially for IoT applied to healthcare [19], the scenario we considered in this work. As a matter of fact, ENISA inserts healthcare scenarios among the critical infrastruc-

© The Author(s), under exclusive license to Springer Nature Switzerland AG 2023
S. Katsikas et al. (Eds.): ESORICS 2022 Workshops, LNCS 13785, pp. 409–426, 2023.
https://doi.org/10.1007/978-3-031-25460-4_24

tures[1]. Traditional approaches to IoT security focus on redundancy, monitoring, protection, and recovery mechanisms [4] tailored around relevant threat models [17,18]. This approach is certainly valid, but flaws in not taking into account the characteristics of *individuals*, i.e. those subjects who are essential components in a cyber-physical scenario. Just to give an example taken from the use case of this work, a given vital signal acquired by a sensor for a given individual can be considered anomalous and the same value can be perfectly normal for another one. Take the resting heart rate: for a healthy and athletic subject, it is quite normal to have it below 60 bpm, while for an elderly or diseased person this could point out an abnormal condition. This means that in this case a monitor should be customized for each individual.

Therefore, in this work, we propose a novel perspective, complementary to the traditional one, called *precision cybersecurity*. In our view, precision cybersecurity means that *security policies and mechanisms should be dynamically tailored around individuals to be protected besides to the threats to which those individuals are exposed*. In detail, our contribution is three-fold:

– We defined a *precision cybersecurity workflow* (PCW) to tackle security-critical scenarios where the IT ecosystem also affects the safety of the individual;
– We applied the methodology to an IoT Medical-Healthcare scenario where an MQTT-based telemonitoring and telerehabilitation system supports individuals with neurodegenerative disorders during their daily living;
– We proposed a prototype implementation of the PCW in the IoT scenario to demonstrate the applicability and efficacy of the methodology to mitigate cybersecurity threats.

The paper is structured as follows. The IoT Medical Healthcare scenario, its security issues, and the related mitigation techniques are depicted in Sect. 2. Section 3 introduces the precision cybersecurity workflow whereas Sect. 4 presents a first application to the proposed use case. A comparison with the related work is discussed in Sect. 5. Section 6 draws some conclusions.

2   The Use Case: IoT Medical Healthcare Scenario

The use case we adopted in this paper consists of remotely monitoring people with neurodegenerative disorders during their daily living and administering telerehabilitation therapies. Each patient wears a smartwatch in order to acquire its physiological signals (e.g., heart rate, temperature) and inertial data (e.g., acceleration) during its daily activities and during the night. Furthermore, the patient must carry out rehabilitation sessions every day, accessing videos via a web app and trying to reproduce the proposed exercises. During these sessions, the patient is also monitored via the inertial sensors of the smartphone [29,30],

---

[1] https://www.enisa.europa.eu/topics/critical-information-infrastructures-and-services/health/.

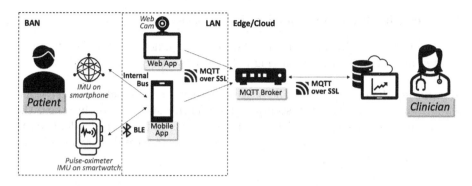

Fig. 1. Block diagram of the healthcare system.

which must be worn on the right or left side of the hip, and by a webcam. In this way, one can monitor how the various rehabilitation exercises are performed and detect any falls. Clinicians can access both raw data and some performance indexes extracted from raw data. Furthermore, the system can produce alerts when some critical conditions occur, e.g. a fall is detected or the heart rate is too high.

The overall architecture of the system is depicted in Fig. 1. Currently, on the patient side, the Body Area Network (BAN) consists of an Inertial Measurement Unit (IMU) on board the smartwatch (worn on the wrist) and an IMU on board the smartphone (worn on the hip). They all are connected to a mobile application running on the smartphone: smartwatch sensors through Bluetooth Low Energy (BLE), while the smartphone IMU relies on the internal bus. The mobile application manages data acquisition from the BAN, pre-process such data and is connected to a *Message Queue Telemetry Transport* (MQTT) [27] broker. MQTT is a lightweight messaging protocol that adopts the publish-subscribe pattern: messages sent by publishing clients to volatile messaging queues-called topics-are received and (possibly) routed by a broker to topics-subscribed clients. Topics, specified as UTF8-type strings, are hierarchically organized into levels (using the forward slash) and are used by the broker to filter and organize incoming messages. On the patient side, the architecture also provides a webcam connected to a web application running on a tablet/PC, where the images are processed for patient fall detection. The web application is also used to deliver videos proposing rehabilitation exercises and mark the exercise start and end time. The web application is also connected to the MQTT broker. The MQTT broker is connected to a cloud application, through which clinicians can monitor patient data and on the basis of such data eventually adapt the patient rehabilitation therapy.

2.1 Security Issues in Telemedicine Ecosystem

The IoT telemonitoring and telerehabilitation system described in Sect. 2 can be affected by several attacks impacting both security and privacy, as follows:

Man in the Middle (MITM). The usage of insecure or misconfigured [27] communications could affect the security of the entire system. For instance, the use of unprotected MQTT or BLE communications in the scenario depicted in Fig. 1 could allow attackers to mount MITM attacks to eavesdrop or modify the exchanged information.

Identity Spoofing. The ability of an attacker to impersonate a legit sensor, an MQTT client, or even a broker could affect the reliability and the security of the entire ecosystem [16]. For instance, if an attacker can impersonate an IMU connected to the mobile app or an MQTT client of the telerehabilitation scenario, she can inject fake sensor data, publish unauthorized messages, and subscribe to restricted MQTT topics. This attack can cause leakage of confidential information, harm the integrity of data, and even triggers a malicious alert to the clinician.

Node Tampering. If an attacker is able to compromise any of the nodes, she may use it to inject erroneous data onto the IoT system [16]. For instance, the attacker can exploit a vulnerability in the mobile app of the patient to inject or even block the data collected from the IMUs. As for the Identity spoofing attack, this attack can compromise the integrity and reliability of the exchanged data, thus, providing unreliable data to the clinicians.

Denial of Service (DoS). An attacker can mount a DoS attack in the healthcare system by: *i)* publishing many heavy messages on different topics to saturate the broker resources (CPU, Storage, Memory, and Network) [35,36], or *ii)* sending one or more heavy messages to the broker periodically to target resource-constrained clients connected to the broker that will use their resources to keep attempting the receiving of heavy messages "amplification attack" [26]).

2.2 Mitigation Techniques and Current Limitations

The IoT medical healthcare scenario of Fig. 1 can adopt several mitigation techniques to cope with some of the attacks described in Sect. 2.1. On the one hand, MITM attacks and DoS attacks can be mitigated by enforcing state-of-the-art security mechanisms. For example, the MQTT nodes and the cloud appliances can use TLS/SSL protocols, certificate verification, and mutual authentication protocols [14] to prevent MITM attacks. Also, the healthcare system may introduce several mechanisms to mitigate DoS attacks. For instance, [9] proposed a mitigation approach for DoS attacks based on QoS features of MQTT and authentication algorithms available on the protocol, and [31] presented Intrusion Detection System based on a threshold packet discarding policy to topics defined on the MQTT broker. On the other hand, however, mitigation techniques for identity spoofing and node tampering attacks present several challenges. In the first case, existing countermeasures include cryptography-based schemes or physical layer-based mechanisms that require ad-hoc solutions challenging to implement on resource-constrained IoT devices or commercial appliances [37]. In the second case, solutions for preventing node tampering attacks are strictly related to the underlying technology and environment. For instance, several solutions exists for IoT sensors [28], MQTT clients [27], or mobile applications [25]. However, adopting such techniques requires the modifications of all the nodes of the telerehabilitation system, which can be unfeasible in terms of cost and applicability (e.g., black-box components). Also, all the solutions mentioned above are individual-agnostic, i.e., they are not customized on the specificity of the patients, thereby limiting their efficacy. Finally, the healthcare system is still susceptible to specific vulnerabilities. Notable examples include the vulnerability CVE-2017-7650[2], which allowed bypassing ACLs of Mosquitto clients, and CVE-2019-11063[3], which allows an attacker in the same local area network to control IoT devices through the companion mobile app.

3 Methodology

Let us introduce a workflow for ensuring the cybersecurity of cyber-physical systems. The idea behind it stems from the observation that people are more and more surrounded by technological devices sensing and reacting to their everyday activities (smart appliances, voice assistants, cloud services, smart medical devices, ...). This evolving trend motivates the development of a methodology that:

- identifies the group of individuals to be protected;
- is capable of identifying, preventing, and reacting to very specific cyberthreats;
- is simple enough to be managed by a single person or a small group of people;
- is dynamic and ready to be adjusted whenever a change in the socio-technical context changes significantly.

Characteristics that would justify a precision cybersecurity approach may be the fact that *very small groups of people* should be protected, against *very specific threat models*, or the fact that the individuals use *very specific configurations of IoT devices*, used for *very different purposes*. For instance, the same heartbeat or acceleration sensors may be used either for tracking personal fitness activity or for monitoring a person's health status, raising alarms and contacting emergency services in case of anomalies. In these two different scenarios, the same threat (e.g. a hacker tampering with a personal device) may cause very different damages to the attacked person, thus a precision cybersecurity methodology would help addressing the two contexts differently, aiding the individual

---

[2] https://cve.mitre.org/cgi-bin/cvename.cgi?name=CVE-2017-7650.
[3] https://cve.mitre.org/cgi-bin/cvename.cgi?name=CVE-2019-11063.

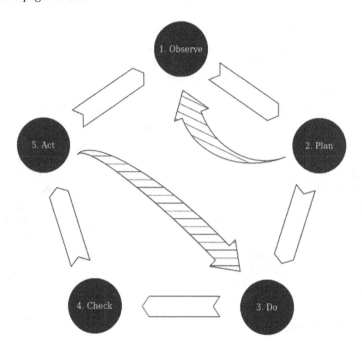

Fig. 2. The proposed methodology for a precision cybersecurity

or the system administrator to design an effective and tailored cyber-security solution for the given context.

The proposed methodology is a customization of the iterative Shewhart-Deming workflow, also called Observe-Plan-Do-Check-Act (OPDCA) cycle that is already being adopted in some cybersecurity standards (e.g., the ISO/IEC 27000 family [13]). The original OPDCA cycle can be seen in Fig. 2, by considering only the straight arrows. The proposed customization of the OPDCA cycle introduces the bended and dashed arrows in the same figure. This has the effect of splitting the original cycle into two mutually dependent sub-cycles, viz. the Observe-Plan cycle on one side and the Do-Check-Act cycle on the other side.

The former cycle is human-centric, meaning that human actors are expected to run several *sporadic activities*. The latter cycle, on the contrary, is machine-centric, implying that software services and automated actors can run frequent and complex *real-time activities* aiming at ensuring the desired cyber safety and security requirements. The two cycles are mutually dependent because by observing and planning, human operators can configure the machine in order to operate, check the results, and react accordingly; on the other side, the data collected by the machine while doing, checking, and reacting, would inspire the human operators to do new, more precise, observations and re-plan the software services and tools. Since the Observe-Plan cycle involves human operators, its tasks require *manual* and *creative* activities, the latter being in general slower to execute, in the order of days or weeks, and are thus triggered less frequently. The

Do-Check-Act cycle, on the contrary, should involve activities that are faster to execute, in the order of milliseconds or seconds, and can thus be executed in real-time. Such activities may involve recognizing known and potentially novel attack techniques as they happen and then reacting to the just identified threats.

In Fig. 3 we provide a more detailed view of how the Observe-Plan and Do-Check-Act stages can be exploded into more detailed steps in the proposed workflow for precision cybersecurity. The precision cybersecurity workflow starts by *observing* the ICT context, aiming at recognizing:

– a set of *variables* characterizing the technological phenomenons that are relevant from a cybersecurity viewpoint;
– a set of *correlations* that are expected to be observed in *"normal circumstances"* among such variables along the system execution.

Next, the aim of the *planning* stage should be:

– defining a *ruleset* that instructs the tool-chain about how to *destructure* the observed stream of events and extract from it the most updated values for each of the variables recognized at the observation stage;
– defining functions to compute higher-level variables starting from lower-level variables;
– defining *constraints* to be satisfied by relevant lower-level and/or higher-level variables; such constraints are used later to distinguish between a *secure* and an *insecure* system execution.

Note that when we talk about lower-level variables, we mean, for instance, raw variable data that are extracted from available sensors, the latter being either physical hardware sensors or virtual software sensors. On the other side, by talking of higher-level variables, we mean indices or KPIs, or even derived measures that are functionally dependent on lower-level raw data variables. The outcome of the Observe-Plan stages is a set of configuration files for the tools of the tool-chain that is supposed to execute the following *Do-Check-Act* stages.

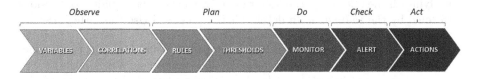

Fig. 3. A workflow for precision cybersecurity

In the proposed workflow (Fig. 3), the *Do* stage should be implemented as a continuous, stateful and real-time *monitoring* activity, where the technological context around the individual is constantly under scrutiny, by collecting real-time or almost-real-time data. The *Check* stage applies the rules of the ruleset in order to map the collected data onto higher- as well as lower-level variables.

Asynchronous rules are evaluated and applied when new values are assigned to variables while *synchronous rules* are activated at periodic intervals. Whenever a rule modifies the value of some variables the updated values are compared against the thresholds defined in the previous *Plan* stage. Whenever a check returns a positive value w.r.t. the identified thresholds, the *Do* stage takes place by triggering some configured action. The latter can, for instance, be either sending a notification to someone responsible for the overall process, or activating firewall rules (e.g. banning a set of IP addresses, or even temporarily or permanently deactivating user accounts), or maybe shutting down the attacked devices. The methodology does not limit the set of possible actions triggered at this stage, the latter depending on the toolset used to implement the methodology itself.

4   Prototype and Experimental Results

The current section will describe how each phase of the proposed methodology has been implemented using our experimental prototype. As anticipated in Sect. 2, the use case considered in this work refers to a telemonitoring and telerehabilitation system for people suffering from neurodegenerative disorders. For these patients, the prevention of accidental falls or a timely intervention after a fall are crucial to ensure a positive outcome of the rehabilitation therapy. In the context of a telerehabilitation system, this important task is demanded to the cyber-physical system developed to manage the monitoring and rehabilitation functions from the patient's home (as depicted in Fig. 1). On the one hand, the system must ensure that an alert is timely sent to clinicians and caregivers when real falls are detected; on the other hand, the system should prevent false positives alerts generated by wrong sensor readings due to Identity Spoofing or Node Tampering.

4.1   Observe Phase - Determining the Variables and Correlations

As said in the previous chapter, the first step in the methodology consists of identifying all the relevant variables for monitoring the telerehabilitation sessions performed by the *individual*. In detail, for the proposed Use Case, they are:

- *smartwatch acceleration*: lower-level variable, measured in G (gravitational units) or in m/s^2; the range of normal values is individual-dependent;
- *smartphone acceleration*: lower-level variable, measured in G or in m/s^2; the range of normal values is individual-dependent;
- output of image processing technique applied to the webcam video signal to detect possible falls: higher-level variable of Boolean type (0: normal condition; 1: fall condition).

For what concerns the correlations between variables, they can be mainly derived from previous research works studying the acceleration pattern during a fall [15,21]. Figure 4 shows a typical pattern of acceleration magnitude (A), which is expressed as:

$$A = \sqrt{a_x^2 + a_y^2 + a_z^2} \tag{1}$$

where a_x, a_y and a_z are the values read by the accelerometer in the xyz plane. The observed pattern is characterized by three phases:

- **Free fall phase:** this is the moment in which the acceleration decreases due to the falling of the person towards the ground.
- **Impact phase:** it represents the moment in which the subject touches the ground, with a sudden increase of the acceleration
- **Post impact-phase:** The instant after the impact, in which the subject lies still and the acceleration remains constant.

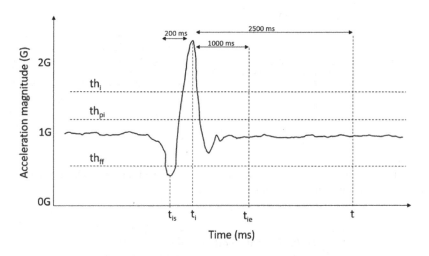

Fig. 4. Typical acceleration pattern during a fall event

According to the literature, the entire fall period lasts no longer than 2700 ms [15]. With respect to the pattern depicted in Fig. 4, t_{is} (impact start) is the time when the free fall starts, t_i is the exact moment in which the subject touches the ground, while t_{ie} (impact end) delimits the end of the fall event. Thresholds th_{is}, th_{pi} and th_{ie} are described in the next section. This pattern should be found both in smartwatch and smartphone IMUs in order to detect a real fall event. At the same time, correlation with the webcam variable cannot be established given the different nature (higher-level variable) and the domain (boolean type).

4.2 Plan Phase - Establishing Thresholds and Rules

The planning stage must define the ruleset that the MQTT monitor will use to detect anomalies. In the considered use case, a set of timed automata are introduced to show how security issues are detected and differentiated from actual

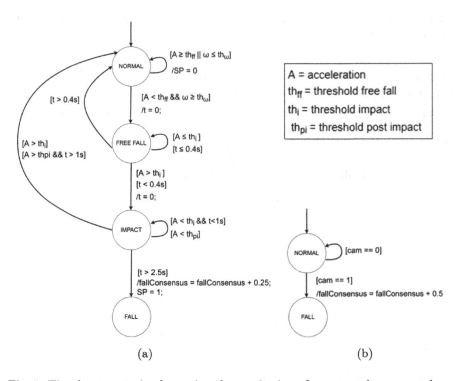

Fig. 5. Timed automata implementing the monitoring of smartwatch or smartphone variables (a) and of webcam output (b).

$$fallCons = 0 \Rightarrow allow; fallCons := 0$$
$$fallCons < 0.75 \Rightarrow suppress; fallCons := 0$$
$$fallCons \geq 0.75 \Rightarrow allow; fallCons := 0$$

Fig. 6. Ruleset for an MQTT firewall

$$fallCons = 0 \Rightarrow allow; fallCons := 0$$
$$fallCons < 0.5 \;\&\&\; SW.fall \Rightarrow alert(\text{``smartwatch tampered''}); allow; fallCons := 0$$
$$fallCons < 0.5 \;\&\&\; SP.fall \Rightarrow alert(\text{``smartphone tampered''}); allow; fallCons := 0$$
$$fallCons = 0.5 \Rightarrow alert(\text{``sensors disagree''}); allow; fallCons := 0$$
$$fallCons > 0.5 \;\&\&\; !SP.fall \Rightarrow alert(\text{``smartphone tampered''}); allow; fallCons := 0$$
$$fallCons > 0.5 \;\&\&\; !SW.fall \Rightarrow alert(\text{``smartwatch tampered''}); allow; fallCons := 0$$
$$fallCons = 1 \Rightarrow allow; fallCons := 0$$

Fig. 7. Ruleset for an MQTT intrusion detection system

important anomalous events such as an accidental fall. There are 3 automata that work in parallel: one for each sensor node (smartphone, smartwatch, and webcam).

In detail, the rules adopted for monitoring the smartphone variables are described in Fig. 5a. The automaton remains in the normal state until the acceleration magnitude A (Eq. 1) goes below a free fall threshold (th_{ff}). This event triggers the transition to the free fall state and the initialization of a timer t. Once in the free fall state, the automaton starts waiting for a possible impact, that is detected as the acceleration magnitude overcomes an impact threshold (th_i). The impact must happen within 0.4 s from the free fall detection [21], otherwise the automaton returns to the normal state. When an impact is detected, the timer is restarted to 0. Once in the impact state, if the data comes from a real fall event, the acceleration magnitude must always remain under the impact threshold and furthermore it must decrease under a post-impact value (th_{pi}) by 1 s (impact end). After 1 s from the impact, the acceleration must always be under th_{pi} in order to ascertain the post-impact phase of a fall. Finally, if the timer reaches 2.5 s and all these conditions have not been violated, a fall event is detected: the automaton switches to the fall state, a fall consensus variable is increased by a 0.25 factor and a boolean variable (SP) is set to true in order to keep memory of the sensor that detected a fall. According to the literature [15, 21], threshold values may be universal or customized on the *individual*. The rules and the states adopted for monitoring the smartwatch data are equivalent to the smartphone ones. It differs only for the boolean variable, that is named SW in this case, and the thresholds value that may be different. The webcam sends aggregated data (higher-level variable), hence the timed automaton is simpler, as shown in Fig. 5b. The webcam monitor remains in the normal state until the output of the video processing algorithm detects a fall (cam = 1). This event triggers the transition to the fall state, and the global variable of fall consensus is increased by 0.5.

Finally, a chain of rules checks the global variable $fallCons$ and the Boolean variables of the sensor nodes in order to discern a real fall from fake data, and, in case, to identify the sensor node that was attacked (see Fig. 6 and 7). The rationale behind these rules is as follows: "the more sensors agree on a normal or fall state, the more trustable this state is". Each sensor contributes to this "agreement" (i.e. $fallCons$) with a weight, the sum of sensors weight is 1, and a $fallCons$ strictly grater than 0.5 is needed to detect a fall event. Weights distribution and $fallCons$ threshold are assigned to ensure that at least two sensors should agree, but they must be "independent": a consensus between smartwatch and smartphone is not enough since a malicious attack to the smartphone may compromise data in transit from the smartwatch too. For this reason, a consensus about fall of 0.5 does not allow to detect the tampered device, whereas, in all other cases, the Boolean variable in disagreement allows it, see Fig. 6 and 7.

4.3   Do-Check-Act Cycle - A MQTT Monitor

The Do-Check-Act stages consist of the implementation of a tool that gathers messages published by clients (Do), checks the rules (Check), and in case performs some actions (Act). Therefore, in order to experiment the scenario described in Sect. 2, we settled up the testbed that is depicted in Fig. 8. Such a testbed can simulate a scenario in which a patient performs his rehabilitation therapy. For that reason, this testbed allows us to experiment with several scenarios:

1. Normal scenario: none of the clients has been tampered.
2. Scenario with a security issue: the system is targeted by an identity spoofing or node tampering attack, so that incoherent/malicious data are published. Some of the attack scenarios that are possible to test are the following:
   (a) Over threshold attack: the malicious attacker is able to intercept the MQTT packets containing the acceleration data and modify them bringing the values over/under the fall thresholds described in the previous section. The tampered device will consequently notify a fall.
   (b) Suppress attack: as the attacker can alter the data for generating a wrong fall event, he can also do the opposite to suppress a fall. The tampered device won't consequently identify a fall even if a righteous fall event has happened.
   (c) Random attack: the malicious client sends random data which can or cannot depict a fall event. It is a complete aleatory event, and data are likely to be inconsistent with respect to the data sent by the other honest clients.
   (d) External attack: if the attacker knows the broker infrastructure, such as the broker address, the port and the topic through which messages are passed, he doesn't need to strike on an existing client, but he could use a new client through which could send malicious data.

According to Fig. 8, the implemented testbed consists of the following components:

- Three MQTT clients for publishing patient data: a client embedded in a sensor (smartwatch) attached to the patient which records wrist's acceleration, a mobile app installed on the patient's smartphone for recording waist acceleration, and a client on a tablet with a camera which processes the recorded images in order to detect the fall.
- The MQTT monitor proposed in this work can act as an intermediate filter or a detection system depending on which of the ruleset is chosen (two of them are described in Fig. 6 and 7). It takes as inputs the data coming from the three clients and applies the rules for determining which of the devices (if any) is corrupted and what actions have to be taken.
- A MQTT broker (HiveMQ broker) which acts as an intermediate player that takes the messages published from the three clients and potentially forwards them to the subscribing ones.

– A subscribing client (usually the physician's mobile phone/tablet/computer) which receives the messages coming from the publishing clients and, by applying the fall model described in the previous section, aggregates the data in order to determine whether a fall happened, and in case of a positive answer notifies the physician.

Such components have been developed using Java and the MQTT library Fusesource[4]. For our experiments, we used the public MQTT broker provided by HiveMQ[5]. They both are open source and compliant with the protocol MQTT 3.1.

Each client has been implemented so that can it be configured to act either as an honest client or as a tampered client in order to simulate the various attack scenarios described above. When a client is configured as a tampered one, it publishes randomly generated data that are compliant with the given attacker models. At this point, if the MQTT monitor is disabled, the attack is successful, i.e. fake data is published without being blocked and without publishing alerts. Otherwise, when the monitor is activated, fake data is blocked or alarms are generated depending on which chain of rules has been applied (see Fig. 6 or Fig. 7).

The current implementation, together with the tested scenarios, is currently hosted on GitLab[6].

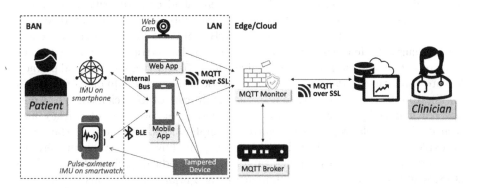

Fig. 8. Scenario with a monitor. Tablets, smartphones and smartwatches could be hacked and tampered in such a way to send inconsistent data.

5   Related Work

In this work we presented an approach to cybersecurity management that we call *precision cybersecurity*. Several cybersecurity frameworks and methodologies

---

[4] https://github.com/fusesource/mqtt-client.

[5] https://www.hivemq.com/public-mqtt-broker/.

[6] https://gitlab.com/fspegni/mqtt-stateful-firewall.

have already been developed that are based on the Deming (PDCA) cycle. The ISO 27K family of standards appeals directly to it [13] while the NIST Cybersecurity Framework [3] appears to be a customized version of the Deming cycle, when it describes the identify, protect, detect, respond, and recover functions, as well as when it explains that the framework must be applied periodically, each time identifying the current and the target security profiles. Several customizations of the Deming cycles also exist that target specific threats of restricted domains (e.g. in the smart connected toys industry [39] or in the public administration sector [34]). To the best of our knowledge, they all focus on structuring the activities executed by human actors involved in the overall process of managing the cybersecurity of an organization. Some authors have already recognized that methodologies based on the Deming cycle and focusing only on human activities are not able to address the challenges of dynamic cybersecurity [32,33], where cyber-attacks are progressive, thus evolve based on previous ones, and attackers learn how to defend against existing cyber-protection mechanisms. In our view, precision cybersecurity is a novel approach to cybersecurity since it delegates some of its activities, viz. those requiring continuous monitoring as well as precise and near-realtime evaluation, to autonomous agents, thus it is more oriented to face the challenges of dynamic cyber-security.

In this work we proposed a telerehabilitation use case, since clinicians acknowledge a great potential to telerehabilitation, and the COVID-19 pandemic has highlighted its importance. The management of cybersecurity issues are a critical requisite for its success, and should take into account the heterogeneity of devices as well as the specific characteristics of users [38]. As a consequence, cyber security in IoT-based healthcare scenarios has attracted the attention of some recent surveys. For instance, Bhuiyan et al. [5] analyzes security and privacy feature consisting of data protection, network architecture, Quality of Services (QoS), app development, and continuous monitoring of IoT telemedicine. Amaraweera and Halgamuge [1] focused on providing an overview of privacy and security issues relating to IoT healthcare applications. Chacko and Hayajneh [8] explore the role of IoT in healthcare by providing a survey on vulnerabilities, attacks, and security issues targeting IoT medical devices from 2013 to 2018, while Butpheng et al. [6] summarize the major contributions to e-Health systems from implementing robust IoT-based and cloud computing techniques.

As regards, instead, the cyber security of cyber-physical systems and IoT in general, there are numerous works focused on security, in particular on the security of the MQTT protocol. All of such approaches share a focus on possible threats. For instance, Eleman et al. [14] proposed a modified MQTT protocol for telemedicine environments that mandates security aspects such as authentication, key exchange, and confidentiality. Diro et al. [12] presented a resource-efficient end-to-end security scheme for MQTT by offloading computations and storing security parameters to fog nodes. Calabretta et al. [7] introduced MQTT-Auth, a tool to protect specific topics in MQTT. This solution is based on the AugPAKE security algorithm for guaranteeing confidentiality and onto two tokens to authenticate a topic's usage and guarantee authorization in accessing a topic, respectively. Several works introduced access control policies to manage data generated and exchanged within a single environment (e.g., [10,24]) or multiple environments (e.g. [11]). Finally, some recent works started to focus on monitoring tools, such as intrusion detection systems and firewalls. Hindy et al. [20], and Khan et al. [23] evaluated the use of Machine Learning techniques to build an intrusion detection system for MQTT-based attacks. Arseni et al. [2] proposed a reputation-based trust mechanism and application level firewall. Husnain et al. [22] presented one of the first IDSs for the MQTT protocol. Such a tool checks for IoT protocol vulnerabilities and misuse through rigorous validation of packet fields during the packet analysis phase.

All the aforementioned solutions do not take into account the specific characteristics of the users (i.e. the patients in our use case). Nevertheless, some specific application domains demand particular attention from legitimate users, request that can not be satisfied by modeling only threats, no matter how extensively and in-depth is done. Our approach is complementary to the previous ones, as the *Observe-Plan* stages allows to take into account what is relevant for the patient. Furthermore, all the solutions mentioned above share the same limitation since they require a modification of the nodes or the protocol, which may not be feasible in practice due to technical constraints (e.g., resource limitations or black-box components). Our solution, on the contrary, enables fine-grained security enforcement directly at the broker level without any impact on the connected nodes.

6   Conclusions

In this paper, we introduced the novel idea of precision cybersecurity, where security policies are dynamically adapted to the evolution of an IoT ecosystem interacting with several individuals. We discussed a first methodology (PCW) that we implemented in a tool that we applied to a real IoT-Healthcare scenario. The idea and the approach proved to be viable. A future extension of this early idea is to apply the PCW in the wild to more complex IoT scenarios.

References

1. Amaraweera, S.P., Halgamuge, M.N.: Internet of things in the healthcare sector: overview of security and privacy issues. Secur. Priv. Trust Iot Environ. 153–179 (2019)
2. Arseni, S.C., Chifor, B.C., Coca, M., Medvei, M., Bica, I., Matei, I.: RESFIT: a reputation and security monitoring platform for IoT applications. Electron. (Switz.) **10**(15), 1840 (2021)
3. Barrett, M.: Framework for improving critical infrastructure cybersecurity version 1.1 (2018). https://doi.org/10.6028/NIST.CSWP.04162018
4. Berger, C., Eichhammer, P., Reiser, H., Domaschka, J., Hauck, F., Habiger, G.: A survey on resilience in the IoT: taxonomy, classification, and discussion of resilience mechanisms. ACM Comput. Surv. **54**(7), 1–39 (2022). https://doi.org/10.1145/3462513

5. Bhuiyan, M.N., Rahman, M.M., Billah, M.M., Saha, D.: Internet of things (IoT): a review of its enabling technologies in healthcare applications, standards protocols, security and market opportunities. IEEE Internet Things J. **8**, 10474–10498 (2021)
6. Butpheng, C., Yeh, K.H., Xiong, H.: Security and privacy in IoT-cloud-based e-health systems-a comprehensive review. Symmetry **12**(7), 1191 (2020)
7. Calabretta, M., Pecori, R., Vecchio, M., Veltri, L.: MQTT-auth: a token-based solution to endow MQTT with authentication and authorization capabilities. J. Commun. Softw. Syst. **14**(4), 320–331 (2018)
8. Chacko, A., Hayajneh, T.: Security and privacy issues with IoT in healthcare. EAI Endors. Trans. Pervasive Health Technol. **4**(14) (2018)
9. Chifor, B.C., Bica, I., Patriciu, V.V.: Mitigating dos attacks in publish-subscribe IoT networks. In: 2017 9th International Conference on Electronics, Computers and Artificial Intelligence (ECAI), pp. 1–6. IEEE (2017)
10. Colombo, P., Ferrari, E.: Access control enforcement within MQTT-based internet of things ecosystems. In: Proceedings of the 23nd ACM on Symposium on Access Control Models and Technologies, pp. 223–234 (2018)
11. Colombo, P., Ferrari, E., Tümer, E.D.: Regulating data sharing across MQTT environments. J. Netw. Comput. Appl. **174**, 102907 (2021)
12. Diro, A., Reda, H., Chilamkurti, N., Mahmood, A., Zaman, N., Nam, Y.: Lightweight authenticated-encryption scheme for internet of things based on publish-subscribe communication. IEEE Access **8**, 60539–60551 (2020)
13. Disterer, G.: ISO/IEC 27000, 27001 and 27002 for information security management. J. Inf. Secur. **04**, 92–100 (2013)
14. Elemam, E., Bahaa-Eldin, A.M., Shaker, N.H., Sobh, M.A.: A secure MQTT protocol, telemedicine IoT case study. In: 2019 14th International Conference on Computer Engineering and Systems (ICCES), pp. 99–105. IEEE (2019)
15. Fáñez, M., Villar, J., de la Cal, E., González, V., Sedano, J., Khojasteh, S.: Mixing user-centered and generalized models for fall detection. Neurocomputing **452**, 473–486 (2021)
16. Firdous, S.N., Baig, Z., Valli, C., Ibrahim, A.: Modelling and evaluation of malicious attacks against the IoT MQTT protocol. In: 2017 IEEE International Conference on Internet of Things (iThings) and IEEE Green Computing and Communications (GreenCom) and IEEE Cyber, Physical and Social Computing (CPSCom) and IEEE Smart Data (SmartData), pp. 748–755 (2017)
17. Hammi, B., Zeadally, S., Khatoun, R., Nebhen, J.: Survey on smart homes: vulnerabilities, risks, and countermeasures. Comput. Secur. **117** (2022). https://www.scopus.com/inward/record.uri?eid=2-s2.0-85126601158&doi=10.1016%2fj.cose.2022.102677&partnerID=40&md5=64340c17de56a9712c366f4f4f79bba0
18. Hassija, V., Chamola, V., Saxena, V., Jain, D., Goyal, P., Sikdar, B.: A survey on IoT security: application areas, security threats, and solution architectures. IEEE Access **7**, 82721–82743 (2019)
19. Hathaliya, J.J., Tanwar, S.: An exhaustive survey on security and privacy issues in healthcare 4.0. Comput. Commun. **153**, 311–335 (2020)
20. Hindy, H., Bayne, E., Bures, M., Atkinson, R., Tachtatzis, C., Bellekens, X.: Machine learning based IoT intrusion detection system: an MQTT case study (MQTT-IoT-IDS2020 dataset). In: Ghita, B., Shiaeles, S. (eds.) INC 2020. LNNS, vol. 180, pp. 73–84. Springer, Cham (2021). https://doi.org/10.1007/978-3-030-64758-2_6

21. Hsieh, S.L., Chen, C.C., Wu, S.H., Yue, T.W.: A wrist -worn fall detection system using accelerometers and gyroscopes. In: Proceedings of the 11th IEEE International Conference on Networking, Sensing and Control, pp. 518–523 (2014). https://doi.org/10.1109/ICNSC.2014.6819680

22. Husnain, M., et al.: Preventing MQTT vulnerabilities using IoT-enabled intrusion detection system. Sensors 22(2) (2022). https://www.scopus.com/inward/record.uri?eid=2-s2.0-85122801941&doi=10.3390%2fs22020567&partnerID=40&md5=543e08cd987bcb6b63c906cf9cd57442

23. Khan, M.A., et al.: A deep learning-based intrusion detection system for MQTT enabled IoT. Sensors 21(21), 7016 (2021)

24. La Marra, A., Martinelli, F., Mori, P., Saracino, A.: Implementing usage control in internet of things: a smart home use case. In: 2017 IEEE Trustcom/BigDataSE/ICESS, pp. 1056–1063. IEEE (2017)

25. Merlo, A., Ruggia, A., Sciolla, L., Verderame, L.: Armand: Anti-repackaging through multi-pattern anti-tampering based on native detection. Pervasive Mob. Comput. 76, 101443 (2021)

26. Morelli, U., Vaccari, I., Ranise, S., Cambiaso, E.: DoS attacks in available MQTT implementations: investigating the impact on brokers and devices, and supported anti-DoS protections. In: The 16th International Conference on Availability, Reliability and Security, pp. 1–9 (2021)

27. Palmieri, A., Prem, P., Ranise, S., Morelli, U., Ahmad, T.: MQTTSA: a tool for automatically assisting the secure deployments of MQTT brokers. In: 2019 IEEE World Congress on Services (SERVICES), vol. 2642–939X, pp. 47–53 (2019). https://doi.org/10.1109/SERVICES.2019.00023

28. Pathak, A.K., Saguna, S., Mitra, K., Åhlund, C.: Anomaly detection using machine learning to discover sensor tampering in IoT systems. In: ICC 2021-IEEE International Conference on Communications, pp. 1–6. IEEE (2021)

29. Pepa, L., Capecci, M., Andrenelli, E., Ciabattoni, L., Spalazzi, L., Ceravolo, M.: A fuzzy logic system for the home assessment of freezing of gait in subjects with parkinsons disease. Expert Syst. Appl. 147, 113197 (2020)

30. Pepa, L., Capecci, M., Verdini, F., Ceravolo, M., Spalazzi, L.: An architecture to manage motor disorders in Parkinson's disease. In: IEEE World Forum on Internet of Things, WF-IoT 2015 - Proceedings, pp. 615–620. Institute of Electrical and Electronics Engineers Inc. (2015)

31. Potrino, G., De Rango, F., Santamaria, A.F.: Modeling and evaluation of a new IoT security system for mitigating dos attacks to the MQTT broker. In: 2019 IEEE Wireless Communications and Networking Conference (WCNC), pp. 1–6. IEEE (2019)

32. Rasouli, M., Miehling, E., Teneketzis, D.: A supervisory control approach to dynamic cyber-security. In: Poovendran, R., Saad, W. (eds.) GameSec 2014. LNCS, vol. 8840, pp. 99–117. Springer, Cham (2014). https://doi.org/10.1007/978-3-319-12601-2_6

33. Riesco, R., Villagrá, V.A.: Leveraging cyber threat intelligence for a dynamic risk framework. Int. J. Inf. Secur. 18(6), 715–739 (2019). https://doi.org/10.1007/s10207-019-00433-2

34. Szczepaniuk, E.K., Szczepaniuk, H., Rokicki, T., Klepacki, B.: Information security assessment in public administration. Comput. Secur. 90, 101709 (2020)

35. Vaccari, I., Aiello, M., Cambiaso, E.: SlowITe, a novel denial of service attack affecting MQTT. Sensors 20(10), 2932 (2020)

36. Vaccari, I., Aiello, M., Cambiaso, E.: SlowTT: A slow denial of service against IoT networks. Information 11(9), 452 (2020)

37. Wang, N., Jiao, L., Wang, P., Dabaghchian, M., Zeng, K.: Efficient identity spoofing attack detection for IoT in mm-wave and massive MIMO 5G communication. In: 2018 IEEE Global Communications Conference (GLOBECOM), pp. 1–6. IEEE (2018)

38. Watzlaf, V., Zhou, L., Dealmeida, D., Hartman, L.: A systematic review of research studies examining telehealth privacy and security practices used by healthcare providers. Int. J. Telerehabil. **9**(2), 39–59 (2017)

39. Yankson, B.: Continuous improvement process (CIP)-based privacy-preserving framework for smart connected toys. Int. J. Inf. Secur. **20**(6), 849–869 (2021)

2nd International Workshop on Cyber Defence Technologies and Secure Communications at the Network Edge (CDT & SECOMANE 2022)

Preface

The progressive digitalization of the public and private sectors emphasizes the reliance on network and information systems for everyday life. Their pervasive interconnectedness is expanding the attack surface for malicious cyber activities. It is of particular interest to analyse which cyber defence technologies could lead to an information advantage, enabled in part by network-centric architectures and enhanced data fusion approaches. The instrumentalization of this advantage must consider a resilient communications infrastructure at the network edge. This edge is the last physical or logical boundary where all the external network integrations and interfaces happen. According to the EU's Cybersecurity Strategy for the Digital Decade, in the coming years it will be critical that the Member States increase their ability to prevent and respond to cyber threats, and this highlights the need to boost the development of state-of-the-art cyber defence capabilities through different EU policies and instruments. Opportunities for potential collaborative cyber defence research and development actions are identified under the European Defence Fund (EDF); this demands cooperation between partners through a cross-sectorial and multi-stakeholder community. On the other hand, to achieve the EU's digital strategic autonomy and thus digital sovereignty has become a priority, and this requires an overarching vision of the information and communications technology landscape and identifying the necessary research priorities on related topics, where cyber defence stands out and demands joint multi-sectorial efforts. These urgent actions together with the emergence of innovative concepts in the field of secure communications, notably at the network edge, evidences the necessary coordination and synchronization to identify areas of common interest and dual-use endeavors. In this context, the workshop aims to facilitate cross-sectorial and dual-use related discussions between the civil and military research communities.

To this end, the 2nd International Workshop on Cyber Defence Technologies and Secure Communications at the Network Edge (CDT & SECOMANE) aimed to provide a forum where both communities exchanged information for mutual benefit. Hence, under the auspices of the 27th European Symposium on Research in Computer Security (ESORICS), workshop participants contributed with dual-use related discussions on cyber defence and secure communications. The result is a collection of high-quality scientific contributions of leading-edge researchers from academia and industry, showing the latest research results in the selected targeted fields. This volume contains revised versions of the selected papers that were presented at the 2nd CDT & SECOMANE.

October 2022

Jorge Maestre Vidal
Salvador Llopis Sanchez
Marco Antonio Sotelo Monge
Gregorio Martínez Perez
Marta García Cid

Organization

General Chairs

Jorge Maestre Vidal	Indra, Spain
Salvador Llopis Sánchez	Universitat Politecnica de Valencia, Spain
Marco Sotelo Monge	Indra, Spain
Gregorio Martínez Perez	University of Murcia, Spain
Marta García Cid	Indra, Spain

Program Committee Chairs

Gregorio Martínez-Perez	University of Murcia, Spain
Gerardo Ramis	Indra, Digital Labs, Spain
Leonardo Valdivieso	Escuela Politécnica Nacional, Ecuador
Marco Manso	PARTICLE, Portugal
Joaquin Garcia-Alfaro	Institut Mines-Telecom, France
Victor Villagrá	Universidad Politécnica de Madrid, Spain
Giovanni Comande	Scuola Superiore Sant'Anna, Italy
Sergio Martínez	Universidad Internacional de la Rioja, Spain
Alberto Huertas Celdran	Waterford Institute of Technology, Ireland
Rumen Daton Medenou	Indra, Digital Labs, Spain
Lorena Barona	Escuela Politécnica Nacional, Ecuador
Harald Schmidt	Fraunhofer FKIE, Germany

A Revisitation of Clausewitz's Thinking from the Cyber Situational Awareness Perspective

Pedro Ramón y Cajal Ramo⬭, Claudia Castillo Arias⬭,
Jorge Carlos Manzanares Martínez⬭, and Jorge Maestre Vidal⁽⊠⁾⬭

Indra Sistemas S.A., Av. de Bruselas 35, 28108 Madrid, Spain
jmaestre@indra.es

Abstract. This paper has as main purpose to revisit some of the foundations of Western military thinking, and its evolution derived from the increasingly attenuated need on making use of cyberspace as domain for resolving state-level conflicts through the use of force. This will be done on the basis of the work of the Prussian military theorist Carl von Clausewitz, and focalized in their implications when developing and operating cyber situational awareness capabilities. Rather than remaining a mere retrospective the paper will analyze the present and possible projection of some of the key concepts in geostrategic, operational planning and international law directed from the following dimensions: 1) the nature of cyber conflicts as part of war; 2) the digitalization of the society; 3) the friction forces on cyberspace operations; 4) the centers of gravity in cyberspace; and 5) decisive conditions and culminating points on cyberspace operations.

Keywords: Clausewitz · Cyber defence · Cyber situational · Politics · Strategy · Military thinking

1 Introduction

As cyberspace operations gain prominence in today's conflicts, new concepts such as cyber weapons, cyber warfare and cyber self-defence are emerging, giving rise to reflection on the extent to which cyber aggression could trigger escalation [1]. According to Carl von Clausewitz's *"principle of reciprocal action"* [2], the action-reaction dynamic leads to the progressive use of force, which raises more than reasonable doubts as to whether the patterns and thinking between state-level conflicts applicable to kinetic actions is proportionally applicable to cyber acts with a focus on the decisions made before and during the war. Since the capability of acquiring and adequate cyber situational awareness depends on the analysis and reflection of factors beyond the technical realm, such as operational, strategic, political, etc., to develop a comprehensive and projectable understanding about what is happening remains subject to the resolution of

S. Katsikas et al. (Eds.): ESORICS 2022 Workshops, LNCS 13785, pp. 431–448, 2023.
https://doi.org/10.1007/978-3-031-25460-4_25

these divergences and ambiguities of the dynamics in which physical and digital ecosystems coexist [56].

In order to guide their understanding, and thus to imbue the development of new cyber defence capabilities with such notions, this paper has as main purpose to revisit some of the foundations of Western military thinking, and its evolution derived from the increasingly attenuated need on making use of cyberspace as domain for resolving state-level conflicts through the use of force. This will be done on the basis of Clausewitz's thought, and by following in the wake of the authors under his influence.

Before continuing, it is important to point out that Clausewitz was a notable Prussian general mostly known as military theorist, who in his work *On War* [2] (published posthumously by his wife Marie von Brüh in 1832) presented some of the theories and principles about war, society, the state, morality and will that influence modern military and geostrategic thinking. At this point the reader may quite legitimately ask: *what does an old Prussian general from the 19th century have to do with understanding current and future military operations in cyberspace?*. There is not one but several answers to this question of which it is possible to highlight three of them. First that 1) nowadays *On War* is the most important single work ever written on the theory of warfare and of strategy, which attracted a wide variety of intellectuals (from military strategists, historians, political scientists, business thinkers, etc.) over the last few centuries, and up to the present day. This is due to its realism (in the direct sense, not to be confused with philosophical realism), and that Clausewitz built his concepts from the pure human and social essence, the latter marked by premises that have been shown to be continuous regarding technological advances. On the other hand, 2) Clausewitz's *opera magna* is presented in all current military doctrine, where concepts such as "centers of gravity" or the "culminating points of victory" serve as a reference for understanding modern conflicts, and thus a constant for the current development of cyberspace operations. Last but not least, 3) Clausewitz is one of the first authors to be studied in academia, on the basis of whose thinking it is possible for students and/or experts in the multidisciplinary areas that converge in cyber defence but who do not focus their work directly on this field, to address the challenges that state-level actuations on cyberspace entail. Rather than remaining a mere retrospective, beyond this Introduction (Sect. 1), the paper will analyze the present and possible projection of some of the key concepts in geostrategic, operational planning and international law with a focus on the following dimensions:

- The relationship between politics and military objectives in cyberwarfare (Sect. 2).
- The digitalization of the society and war (Sect. 3)
- The friction forces on cyberspace operations (Sect. 4).
- Centers of Gravity and cyberspace (Sect. 5).
- Cyber Decisive Conditions and Culminating Points on cyberspace operations (Sect. 6).

Finally conclusions will be drawn together with some tentative tentatively lines to continue the analysis started here (Sect. 7).

2   Political and Military Objectives in Cyberwarfare

The classic phrase attributed to Clausewitz *"War is the continuation of politics by other means"* [2] reflects war as an instrument and extension of political objectives. Therefore, its guiding nature will condition military actions and determine their acceptability seeking that the negative impact at the national level is minimized, since the purpose of the war lies in the subsequent peace. This concept of acceptability is what various political objectives are nourished by to justify military actions. The question is: *Who judges the acceptability of using an instrument like war to achieve political goals?*. The answer depends on two factors:

1. Who has, understands, and projects the information in time to assess and weigh the proportionality, justification of the actions and their expected results.
2. Power of influence over political actions.

That is why information has always been part of the political strategies that seek the justification and acceptability of military actions allowing to modulate their support and need. In this way, the control of information by governments in societies becomes a crucial element that relates political objectives to military activities. The control of information in terms of its accessibility (transparency), its understanding (explainability), timeliness (immediacy) and impact (projection), becomes the factor that builds a story about the acceptability of the consequences of a war to achieve the various political objectives. That is why cyberspace [26] in the cyberpersona layer allows maneuvering in societies to create the threshold of acceptability and in turn where adversaries can influence to create the context and justification for conflict resolution [28] by military means.

It is in this context that hegemons [45], great superpowers, take advantage of their geopolitical areas of influence by using cyberspace to control and influence the information that justifies political actions and, by extension, military actions in accordance with the threshold of acceptability. As will be seen later, the superiority or control of cyberspace is impossible on the part of governments, even more so with new private actors who are no longer mere chess pawns but geopolitical actors in themselves. Hegemons are positioned in cyberspace through two types of strategies: control of the infrastructures on which information "flows"; the specialization of manoeuvres across the spectrum of cyberspace in favor of their interests. In this way, government and private geopolitical objectives already consider cyberspace as another substrate on which to instrumentalize military actions, their acceptability, and the combination of all of them.

The state-level interactions and raise of cyber hegemons were modeled and analytically discussed in [46], which lead to deduce that hegemons of global world order emerged in cyberspace as they do in the other traditional domains.

They could be modeled through wealth and power determining the outcome of attack or cooperation amongst pairwise interacting states. However, and in contrary to traditional understanding, cyber hegemons are not exceptional states but merely occupy the tail of a continuous distribution of power and lifetimes, always channeling economic, political, diplomatic, information etc. superiority. After all, in cyberspace, wealth can buy zero-day exploits, educate and train better experts, develop advanced cyber capabilities [51], make grow a greater industry, have technological autonomy or call for more and better social commitment in defence. They enhance the ability to perform statecraft within the environment of cyberspace to create preferential outcomes, sometimes making use of the above towards political and strategical goals [47]; the latter usually referred to as cyber power. But cyberspace, as a more power-diffuse domain, is unlikely to support the kind of hegemonic behaviour in the other domains [48]. For example, the difficulty of acquiring power as wealth increases and the amount of cooperation between states difficult hegemonies to be sustained [46]. On the other hand, the cyberspace entails a multi-stakeholder reality unique in international peace and security, where governments cannot decide on all aspects of the cybersecurity and cyber defence, as responsibility and ownership for this domain is share with non-state actors [49]. Hegemons may have the wealth, but cyber power is shared as never seen before in other domains. On these premises, achieving policy objectives in cyber conflicts requires not only the availability of the necessary effectors (technology, personnel, procedures, etc.), but also a multi-sectoral consensus, which is all the more reason demands the convergence of public and private interests.

3   Digital Societies and War

The human fascination with violence and warfare is a complex reality that has been analysed over the centuries. Numerous intellectuals (Hobbes, Kant, Marx, Weber, among others) and academics have attempted to offer a detailed sociological analysis of the human relationship with war, as it has been decisive for the evolution of modern society. Many even consider it the key to transformation [3]. The apparently contradictory mechanisms of force and violence in society are crystallised when studied on the basis of certain sociological principles. It is necessary to analyse the social, given its complex nature, to understand the relationship between war and violence [4]. In his theoretical development, Clausewitz insisted that war is a conflict of interests, goals, means and movements that is in tension, with a clear relationship to the Nation State [2]. These elements are constantly under the development of strategies and manoeuvres that involve an advance on the enemy to the point of gravity to overcome him in power. Since Clausewitz locates war as a continuum of violence, at this point a reader may ask, *how can we conceive of violence in a digital world?*. As pointed by [5], the dictionary definition of violence is pre-digital, often understood as a behaviour involving physical force intended to hurt, damage, or kill someone or something. Current schools of thought that accept extending this definition to the digital age, claim that violence is related to the activities that might threaten the survival of a state over time, or as remarked by the same author, *"cyber violence conducted by states is instrumental and constitutive of both physical and non-physical acts. These acts in combination facilitate state goals, specifically the potential to win wars or achieve related policy objectives"*.

Concerning how a society may morally justify cyberwar, it is possible to reflex on the moral and legal implications of using force, given that actors such as the State possess legitimacy, through the power-political instruments of law and custom, to exercise their political will over others in a legitimate basis. This idea is encapsulated by the philosopher Thrasymachus: *"Power is the supreme right, and the dispute over the essence of right is decided by the arbitration of war"* [6]. International law establishes diplomatic standards and obligations contained in international laws that cannot be ignored, even if they are relegated to a secondary role when we are faced with a bellicose conflict. It is remarkable that *"the transverse nature means that cyber defence covers a perspective that includes the public and private sector, that is, society as a whole"* [1]. This fact, together with the difficulty of applying concepts such as attribution, perspective analysis or damage measurement, makes regulation and enforcement of laws/conventions in cyberspace very complicated, currently full of gaps thus delimiting a porous lawfare-friendly area. Regarding cyber situational awareness, to reason and project on the legitimate and proportionality of cyber actuations poses a challenging area of study full of questions to be answered.

Furthermore, statements such as Durkheim's [7] are today partly outdated since industrial development and the modernization of society have not resulted in the progressive abolition of organized violence and coercion. Nor has the emergence of supra-national institutions and international organisations led to the end of armed conflicts, beyond the development of a network of solidarity that in many contexts extends the primary understanding of patriotism beyond borders. Thus, in his work Suicide (1952) he exposes how armed conflicts generate greater political, social, and moral cohesion in societies, together with a feeling of belonging to the community. In other words, the individual stops thinking about themselves in favour of the group against the common enemy [4]. The development and the need to study and understand the consequences, dimensions and social complexities involved in the war-phenomenon after the Treaty of Versailles (1919) resulted in the emergence of polemology[1] (Bouthoul, 1942) with interpretative questions and theoretical academic proposals on the subject, based on a complex theoretical framework. In *Sur les fonctions présumées et la périodicité des guerres* (1939) [8], among numerous other interesting publications, Bouthoul proposed a correlation between population numbers and the periodicity of wars, suggesting that when the population fluctuates and rises, conflicts develop, forming what is understood by the war cycle. He even states that war is the central

---

[1] This concept, meaning the study of war, was first introduced by Gaston Bouthoul, a French-Tunisian Doctor in Law, Politics and Social Sciences. Bouthoul later founded the *Institut Français de Polémologie*, one of the few research institutes focused on the social phenomenon of war.

pillar of all civilisations. Polemology is based on the study of economic, psychological and demographic-social dimensions to analyse the war-phenomenon [9]. But the rapid digitisation of society is leading to a coexistence with this classical thought with an alternative (but complementarily) scenario, in which technologies such as 5G, Artificial Intelligence, Cloud Computing, etc. [52,53,55] as well as the rise of the digital societies, will settle a parallel direction where the civilian context became relevant, sometimes even decisive, for cyberwar development. An example of inherited social cohesion are the (civilian) hacktivist groups involved in actions for supporting the states involved in the recent conflict between Russia and Ukraine [10]. It is important to bear this in mind when identifying, defining and developing novel cyber defence capabilities; not only originated from military background but raised from cooperation with industrial, civilian, and ally states.

According to L. Quiróz, on the economic dimensions, Bouthoul argues the necessity of a solid resource base to sustain or deepen the war effort as required. He also discusses the presumed correlation between economic development and the need for territorial expansion, and the correspondence of this with the cyclical crisis of capitalism, which would accelerate the development of armed conflicts. This idea has been put forward and defended mainly by Marxist theory. The demographic conditioning factor is a crucial explanation, since both the number of inhabitants and the fluctuations that occur over the course of time correspond to the appearance and formation of elements for the emergence of conflicts. Accordingly, can be concluded that war is always related to its demographic reference. However, there are indirect factors that link demography to development, expansion and welfare, with new technologies and digitalisation being of particular relevance. At this point, new triggers such as the homogeneous distribution of rare earths (on which semiconductors, circuits, batteries, etc. relies on) among state actors may give rise future hotspots of conflict [11].

There is also an element that direct data cannot capture, but which can be verified by other analyses: the psychological problems that arise as a result of the war [12]. As discussed in [13] depending on who the attackers and the victims are, the psychological effects of cyber threats may even rival those of traditional terrorism, ranging from emotional trauma potentially leading to depression up to acute stress disorders (ASD). The study reveals that for example, victims of cyber attacks in online virtual worlds may present intrusive memories and emotional numbing. While this marks some preliminary points of reflection, there is as yet no precedent for how cyberwar might affect an individual's cognitive state, much less from a social approach (perception of risk, culture of fear, etc.).

Finally, in relation to Clausewitz's proposal, and considering Bouthoul's approaches, the question remains as to the current theoretical applications that can be applied to the various domains in which the war-phenomenon operates, with cyberspace being crucial among them. Cyberspace, now not only as a mean but also as an ultimate goal, represents a new domain in which actors operate not only in times of declared armed conflict, but also in what is also known as the grey zone. This new domain has meant a broadening of the battlefield with never-before-seen implications. As a result, questions such as cyberattacks on critical infrastructures, the control of information, the psychological and political control of target societies and concepts such as information warfare and the use of social engineering... have implied a transformation of the paradigm in the analysis of warfare, as it involves factors that modify the dynamics known to date. Hybrid warfare does not understand traditional approaches. Nonetheless, the theoretical foundations provided by these theorists can be a starting point for the development of these issues.

4   Friction Forces on Cyberspace

Clausewitzian thinking points to the notion that *"War is the realm of uncertainty; three quarters of the factors on which action in war is based are wrapped in a fog of greater or lesser uncertainty"* [2]. The concept of friction is the cause of the difference between planning 'war on paper' and 'war in reality', nowadays both fog of war and friction typically understood as belonging to the same concept [14]. Some authors call this concept a warfare variant of Murphy's Law [15], usually represented by the quote attributed to the German field marshal, known as Moltke the Elder *"no plan survives contact with the enemy"*. Clausewitz himself suggested seven major forces of friction: 1) Insufficient knowledge of the enemy; 2) rumors (information obtained by remote observation or spies); 3) uncertainty about one's own forces and their position; 4) uncertainties coming from allied troops tend to exaggerate their own difficulties; 5) differences between expectation and reality; 6) the fact that the army itself is not as powerful in reality as it was on paper; and 7) difficulties on keeping the army supplied. These make the war closer to a calculation of probabilities, to randomness, or to what Clausewitz refers to as a 'card game'. But despite if frictions, Clausewitz echoed of the mostly intellectual ability of *"even in the darkest hours, retains some glimmerings of the inner light which leads to truth"*, which he referred to as *coup d'oeil* [16], nowadays linked to the capability of acquiring a proper situational awareness and develop common strategical, operational and tactical pictures.

   It is remarkable that historically, fog of war has been considered differently on separated branches of military thinking, some of them emphasizing to counter the forces of friction by a joint understanding of the situation (e.g. NATO information-centric warfare, network-centric warfare, multi-domain mosaic warfare, etc. [17]) while others put major efforts on embracing it by fast adapting to wrong premises (e.g. Russian and German doctrines in WWII, where high grade officials positioned themselves on the front lines). This divergence is also present in current military thinking for cyber operations, although there appears to be a reverse drift of kinetic operational environments due to the state's ability to influence private actors. For example, the US Joint Doctrine for Cyberspace Operations states that *"Permanent global cyberspace superiority is not possible due to the complexity of cyberspace. Even local superiority may be impractical due to the way IT is implemented; the fact US and other national governments do not directly control large, privately owned portions of cyberspace; the broad array of state and non-state actors; the low cost of entry; and the rapid and unpredictable proliferation of technology* [57]. *Therefore, commanders should be prepared to conduct operations under degraded conditions in cyberspace"* [18]. In the opposite side, state-level actors like Chine or Russia tend to rely on domestic proxies to confront opponents over which they exercise a great deal of control but leaving space enough in the shake of deniability.

4.1 Cyber Frictions

For many authors one of the major forces of friction in cyberspace is a continuous Knightian uncertainty [19], which constitutes the no quantifiable conditions within which decisions often needs to be made, and hence a major challenge in acquiring cyber situational awareness. This impacts on threat analysis, risk assessment, cyber Course of Action (CoA) planning, etc. As concluded in [20] many of the attributes of conventional conflict that facilitate the creation and framing of probabilities for risk are difficult to discern in cyberspace, which often lead to cognitive biases. For example, differentiating the values of offensive and defensive capabilities is a very difficult task, usually leading to assume that offense is dominant [21]; that is to say, the defender tends to assume the worst while the attacker assumes a more favorable position, this being reflected in paradigms like the Zero trust security model frequent in the civilian sector and transferred to the military sector [22].

Another frictional force commonly mentioned by experts is the assumption of operating on 'good information', and that it should be enough to peel back the fog of war and prevent unexpected disruptions. Rational thinking, commonly exploited at operational research, assumes that decision-making is a cost-benefit dispute where actors will act on the basis of maximizing their benefit (e.g. game theory, Nash equilibrium [23]). In practice (i.e. the contact with the enemy), it is well known that key aspects of building decision models often fail due to human factors, the latter widely exploited in cybersecurity. On the other hand, technology is advancing so fast that it is often very difficult to incorporate it into the decision making process. The raise of Adversarial Artificial Intelligence (AI), data forgering/poisoning, counterintelligence, etc, [24], channeled by the digital realm, invite skepticism as to how the cost-benefit tradeoff, or even adversarial thinking, has been weighed when facing the same problem from the opposite intentions. The GEN. Nakasone, Commander of US Cyber Command stated in March 2018 that: *"our adversaries have not seen our response in sufficient detail to change their behavior"* [25], evidencing a flaw when practicing cyber deterrence. Experts like [20] are even critical of the current capacity to learn lessons on cyber operations, pointing out that *"judgment errors are understood in cyberspace frequently diverges from the way in which they are understood in conventional domains of interaction"*, where they can be delimited and measured in a more tangible way.

For [16], despites that forces in friction might be revealed by technical (e.g. bad network connections), operational (e.g. unexpected collateral effects) or human (e.g. programming mistakes made by humans), *"what makes friction especially interesting in cyberspace is the constantly changing structure of and the complexity of cyberspace"*. This aspect is highlighted in the Ally Doctrine [26], where cyberspace operations are characterized by asymmetric effects, anonymity, time and speeds; and when surprise entails a major principle of operation. Based on this, and since time, distance and speeds are closely related with risk analysis, the acquisition of cyber situational awareness is subject to these frictional forces to a greater extent than kinetic battle domains, to which as indicated in [20], objects and events appears to be substantially more difficult based on the technical and temporal realities of cyberspace. Additionally, in [27] it was indicated that in cyberspace many effects occur as second- or third-order consequences of actions, which are often difficult to directly connect to an initial action. The latter is often in the emerging thinking concerning hybrid warfare, in particular that focused on combining multi-domain non-linear actions that mix armed actions with non-conventional forces [28]. At this point, the reader can appreciate what a challenge it is to establish a relationship between what happens in cyberspace and the other lines of actuation (land, sea, air, etc.), mission tasks and objectives. This is probably the greater challenge in developing a platform for assisting human beings on acquiring mission-centric cyber situational awareness, seconded by the need to present all this information in a clear and understandable way to the human receptor [29].

4.2   Leveraging the Cyber Fog of War

As a final reflection on this section, it is important to mention how the state of the art approaches to counteract the friction elements described above. Inspired by Clausewitz, in [30] was emphasized that *"when we speak of destroying the enemy's forces we must emphasize controlling uncertainty with proactive cyber defense that nothing obliges us to limit this idea to physical forces: the moral element must also be considered"*, obviously positioned from a defensive posture. It should be noted that the current state of the art barely explores how to address uncertainty from an offensive military focus, for which lessons learned in the field of read teaming, pentesting, etc. may provide transferrable lessons [31]. Back to the defensive position, one of the most widely seconded proposals to take control of uncertainty and friction was presented in [16], which suggested both how take advantage of cyber frictions by making the enemy encounter more uncertainty and how clarify what the enemy is doing within the fog of war. Base on this we remark five approaches, which embrace most of the indications presented in the bibliography:

Dispersion. Distribution of the asset in order to avoid bottlenecks, reduce their criticality (from decisive cyber terrains up to key cyber terrain [32]). Avoid to replicate configurations in order to complicate enemy reconnaissance actions while making the viability of their modus operandi against cyber terrains more difficult. This defensive measure aims on increase the friction forces on which the adversary operates.

Dynamism. Another way to increase the friction forces on the attacker is to constantly shift, change, adapt, etc. [54]. As indicated in [33], the goal of Moving Target Defence (MTD) is to constantly move between multiple configurations in a cyber-system (such as changing the open network ports, network configuration, software, etc.) thereby increasing the uncertainty for the attacker; in effect, diminishing the advantage of reconnaissance that as discussed above, an attacker may have against traditional defense mechanism.

Deception. Military Deception (MILDEC) is defined by the US JP 3-13-4 [34] as the art of deterring hostile actions, increasing the success of friendly defensive actions, or improving the success of any potential friendly offensive action. The deception target is the adversary decision maker who will is intended to be influenced in terms of causing ambiguity, waste of combat power, reveal strengths, make it evidence future intentions, discourage decision-making (e.g. dissuasion by punishment) etc. Cyber tools like decoys, honeypots, etc. have proven to be very useful when clarifying the fog of war by revealing the attacker's Tactics, Techniques, and Procedures (TTPs), while contributing to create friction force on how it perceives the operational area.

Initiative and Offensive Spirit. As in the case of kinetic environments, commanders must preserve their initiative in terms of recognizing and seizing cyber opportunities. In this domain, the initiative is particularly close to the offensive spirit, since it is widely assumed that cyber attackers are often in a more favorable position than defenders. An attacker facing a defender with high initiative and offensive spirit will face more operational friction, and must consider the offensive thinking of the defender in any decision making. However, maintaining this offensive spirit is not easy, as almost all thinking inherited from cybersecurity tends to focus on risk assessment in the systems themselves.

Cognitive Dominance. As stated in [26], the cyberspace can be described in terms of three interrelated layers: physical network, logical network, and cyberpersona; which must be inseparably understood, and where optimizing cognitive, physical, social abilities entail decisive advantage over a situation or adversary. Given that in cyberspace physical strength plays a practically irrelevant role compared to intellectual strength, the latter, closely linked to the cognitive spectrum, will be very relevant. The ability to analyze the effect of what happens in cyberspace on other domains (land, sea, air, space) and in different dimensions (social, political, economic, diplomatic, etc.) will therefore be essential, in this way reducing friction. However, it is important to note that cyber commands, like every military staff will be subject to combat and operational stress, which, as discussed in [35] will impair their ability to acquire situational awareness.

5   Centers of Gravity and Cyberspace

The term Center of Gravity (CoG) or *Schwerpunkt*, was introduced by Clausewitz and usually is associate with this Prussian military theorist [2]. However, despite that Clausewitz did more than forty mentions throughout its work, its meaning has been constantly debated until today. The Prussian stated that as in nature, *"the fighting forces of each belligerent have a certain unity and therefore some cohesion. Where there is cohesion, the analogy of the center of gravity can be applied. Thus, these forces will possess certain centers of gravity, which, by their movement and direction, govern the rest; and those centers of gravity will be found wherever the forces are most concentrated"*. When linked to the operational art, Clausewitz stated that *"a major battle in a theater of operations is a collision between two centers of gravity; the more forces that can be concentrated in a center of gravity, the more certain and massive the effect"*. Hence *"it is the point against which all our energies should be directed"*. Beyond these explanations, he did not propose methods for either the identification or the assessment of CoGs, although modern actors would.

An example of this concept adoption is in the Ally doctrine AJP-5, which considers the CoG as the primary source of power that provides an actor its strength, freedom of action, or will to fight [36]. Accordingly, CoGs are identified as entities, which have critical capabilities, requirements for their performance, and vulnerabilities that may jeopardize the fulfillment of such requirements. The Allies pay particular attention of CoGs representing moral strengths at political-strategic level and CoGs representing physical strengths. Based on the above, it is remarkable that some experts concluded that information technologies have the potential of became the CoG of everyday human activity [37], also differentiating gravitational effects between (and from) its different layers: cyber-persona, logical and physical [38]. This is reinforced by the fact that the cyberspace became the backbone of the digital era, being essential for civilian socio-economic development (commerce, communications, research and development, etc.) and military applications (network-centric warfare, Federated Mission Networks (FMN), etc.). But as indicated in [39] ambiguities abound. Under the assumption of CoGs as *"characteristics, capabilities, or locations from which a military force derives its freedom of action, physical strength, or will to fight"*, for some authors the CoG may include a military force, alliance, etc. which contrast with its definition, on which it may be possible to assert that military force cannot be centers of gravity. This ambiguity is particularly relevant in the context of cyberdefence operations, where concepts like strength or moral are very difficult to link to the physical plane, and therefore to tangible entities matching the doctrinal GoC definitions.

Consequently, the proper acquisition of situational awareness has consolidated as a needed "mind state" for identifying and assessing CoGs. In cyberspace operations, when they represent a moral strength, they are probably associated with the cyber-persona layer, which is the closest to the cognitive and social dimensions in which the moral relies on. The Ally AJP-5 depicts five critical capabilities linked that an actor's moral strategic CoG mostly must posses: 1) determination (and/or alteration) of policy and strategy; 2) command of resources and means required to achieve the strategic objectives; and 3) inspiration, and emanation of moral cohesion and will to fight. Information Operations, PsyOps, etc. channelled by cyber vectors are expected to impact on their critical requirements when exploiting their critical cyber vulnerabilities. There is an extensive bibliography on cyber vulnerability exploitation for political-strategical purpose, and their connection with influence campaigns, misinformation, sensitive data exfiltration or even blackmail to decision-makers [40]. On the other hand, and in contrast with CoGs associated to moral strengths, those representing physical strengths can be found at each battle level (technical, tactical, operational, strategical, and political). They are linked to the physical sublayer of the cyberspace, thus serving the logical layer as connection between cyber-personas and kinetic assets [41]. An example of physical GoC is described in the Ally FM 3-12 concerning the Russia's Application of Cyberspace Operations and Electronic Warfare during the Russo-Ukrainian War (2014) [42]. As result of a posteriori analysis, it was concluded that Russian planners identified Ukraine's CoG as their Command and Control, Communications, Computers (C4) Intelligence, Surveillance and Reconnaissance (C4ISR) systems. In order to inject strategic, operational, and tactical chaos within Ukraine's decision-makers (thus jeopardizing key Ukrainian moral and strength critical capabilities), Russia conducted cyberspace operations and electromagnetic warfare (denial of service, manipulation of digital media, etc.) on critical C4ISR nodes.

6   Decisive Conditions and Culminating Points

In order to plan a successful military operation, it is essential to study and detail some relevant aspects. Beyond the CoG as one of the most important of these, there are also others that are of great relevance already inherited from the clausewitzian thinking, as is the case of the decisive conditions, lines of operations, cyber pressure points and culminating points (An example in Fig. 1).

Cyber Decisive Conditions (DC). Derived by the Clausewitzian concept Decisive Point, which refers to winning propositions as *"central animating idea around which we must organize all our decisions and activities in order to outperform our competitors"*, the Ally doctrine describe DCs as *"a combination of circumstances, effects or a specific key event, critical factor or function that, when realised, allows commanders to gain a marked advantage over an opponent or contribute materially to achieving an objective"* [36]. DCs are determined from the factor and centre of gravity (CoG) analysis. A DC does not necessarily constitute a battle or a physical engagement. Nor is it necessary for DC to be geographically relevant. DCs are elements of lines of operation and, like objectives and effects, need to be achievable. DCs are arranged along the lines of operation (LoO) and progress in an organised manner through the different phases. In order to achieve them, certain actions and the effects commanders want them to produce must be taken into account. Effects are recognisable changes in the behaviour or physical state of a system that result from one or more actions. Based on the DCs and the previous analysis of each actor, the operations planning group determines the necessary changes in the system/system elements of a specific actor to observe influence. To date, the bibliography about cyber DCs is reduced and dispersed, where these circumstances are mostly linked to cyber

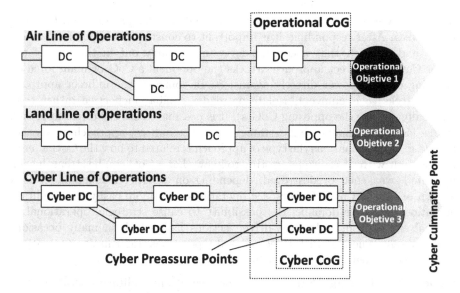

Fig. 1. Cyber lines of operation, DCs and CoGs.

decision points resulting from triggering effects on the technological assets that enable critical capabilities for the planned operations. They are usually referred to as Key Cyber Terrains (KCTs) [32], thus constituting fundamental entities to be discovered, tracked and assessed as part of the cyber situational awareness development.

Cyber Lines of Operation (LoO). The linkage between DCs to achieve an objective is referred to as LoO. Throughout any LoO it will be necessary to determine the sequence of actions, effects and DCs needed to achieve the objectives. Once the best overall approach to affect the CoG and the DCs of the key actors to be achieved have been determined, the next step in the design of operations is to determine the primary and alternative LoOs. These are used to organise operations in time, space and purpose. The determination of the LoOs will shape the development of the plan or design of the operation. There are physical and logical LoOs. A physical LoO connects a series of CDs over time, aimed at controlling geographic targets, or defeating an enemy force. They are used to connect the force to its base of operations and objectives, when positional reference to an opponent is a factor. A logical LoO, on the other hand, is used to visualise and describe the operation when an opponent's positional reference is of little relevance [36]. As indicated in [43], the Cyberspace Operations Forces accomplishes its missions within three primary LoOs: secure, operate, and defend the own information networks; defend the nation from attack in cyberspace; and provide cyberspace support as required to combatant commanders.

Cyber Pressure Points. CoGs are usually referred to as single pressure points that if pressure is applied the entire enemy system will collapse in on itself and the enemy will cease to function. But *what kind of cyber pressure points can be considered?*. After responding, it is important to consider the type of approach, direct and indirect, that a commander want to carry out in the face of the cyber CoG. The direct approach attacks the opponent's CoG or main force by applying combat power directly against it. In contrast, the indirect approach usually seeks to circumvent, isolate or render combat ineffective rather than physically destroy the opposing CoG(s). It is possible to use the direct approach at one level of command (e.g., strategic) and the indirect approach at another level (e.g., operational), as the type of approach is related to how the CoG at each level is dealt with. It is also interesting to know that a CoG can be strengthened, protected, weakened or destroyed, depending on whether a commander look at own or hostile CoGs. Cyberspace operations offer more easily than military actuations on other domains the possibility to cause strategic, operational or tactical effects from technology-driven actions [50]; which in many occasions could present synergies with Effects-Based Operations, Information Operations or even Psychological Operations [44].

Cyber Culminating Points. The objective of any military operation is to make the opponent reach its culminating point before the ally commander do. Clausewitz referred to culminating points as *"the point at which a military force is no longer able to perform its operations"*, which may be *culminating point of victory if "an attacking force, having achieved superiority over its adversary"*. In the event that the adversary does not reach this point before allies do, an operational pause may be taken. This is a temporary cessation of certain activities during the course of an operation prior to achieving the objectives to avoid culmination. It allows the force to regenerate the combat power required to proceed with the next stage of the operation (AJP-5). Culmination has both offensive and defensive applications. The attacking force reaches the culminating point when it can no longer sustain its offensive action and must shift to defence or risk counterattack and defeat. On the latter, the defending force reaches the culminating point when it can no longer mount a successful counter-offensive or defend itself and must be reinforced, disengaged, or withdrawn to avoid defeat. In analogy with the cyber DCs, the state of the art suggests that culminating points on cyber operations are linked to effects related with specific KCTs that are decisive for achieving the main mission goals, which are referred to as Decisive Cyber Terrains [32].

7   Conclusions

All of the above is of great importance for the planning of military operations, traditionally on land, sea and air, but should also serve as inspiration for the use and defence of cyberspace. Through cyberspace, and thanks to its particularities, it is possible to carry out actions that affect any strategic, operational and tactical level, as well as any battle domain. At the strategic level, for example, a commander can find a moral CoG that if properly attacked, through disinformation campaigns or disruption of communications at key moments, can provoke a change in public opinion that forces the cessation of command or the reduction of other military operations. The same can happen at the operational level, with a precise cyberattack on the command-and-control centre disrupting logistics, or at the tactical level, blocking the communications of a special forces group when it is demanding ransom. Detecting such opportunities or vulnerabilities, depending on how you look at it, allows you to pinpoint where the pressure needs to be applied. Of course, there may be multiple points of interest to attack simultaneously, and it is through cyberspace that such coordination and visualisation is also facilitated.

These elements of operational art are essential to understand and make visible/understandable for decision-makers thorough cyber situational awareness in order to lead them to achieve a design that meets the objectives and makes it possible to observe changes in the situation. It allows the establishment and ordering of means, ends and goals. And if done wisely, it also reduces the effects of friction. Still, it is virtually impossible to instantly master the challenges and opportunities presented by new technologies, but also those presented by a modern, highly interconnected society, that live monitors any military operation. The latter is vitally important to understand why many actors today choose to make use of cyberspace; most attacks will receive a media echo but will be difficult to establish a clear authorship or source of resources. Unlike a traditional kinetic military deployment, which is unlikely to go unnoticed. National objectives can be achieved in both ways, currently economic or social ones being the most desired, not territorial expansion, which necessarily requires military deployment and suffers from a very visual and violent connotation.

Acknowledgements

 This research has received funding from the European Defence Industrial Development Programme (EDIDP) under the grant agreement Number EDIDP-CSAMN-SSC-2019-022-ECYSAP (European Cyber Situational Awareness Platform).

Disclaimer. The contents reported in the paper reflect the opinions of the authors and do not necessarily reflect the opinions of the respective agencies, institutions or companies.

References

1. Ramon Y Cajal Ramo, P., Maestre Vidal, J.: Understanding the ethical and regulatory boundaries of the military actuation on the cyberspace. In: Proceedings of 16th International Conference on Availability, Reliability and Security, Vienna, Austria (2021)
2. von Clausewitz, C., Graham, J.J., Maude, F.N.: On war by Carl von Clausewitz, (translated by J.J. Graham). New & rev. ed. with introduction and notes by F.N. Maude. Kegan Paul, Trench, Trubner London (1911)

3. Semmel, B. Marxism and the Science of War. Oxford University Press, Oxford (1981). ISBN 9780198761129
4. Malesevic, S.: The Sociology of War and Violence. Cambridge University Press, Cambridge (2010). https://doi.org/10.1017/CBO9780511777752
5. Brantly, A.F.: The violence of hacking: state violence and cyberspace. Cyber Defence Rev. **2**(1), 73–92 (2017)
6. Roucek, J.S.: La sociologia de la violencia. Rev. Mexicana Opin. Publica **16**, 139–148 (2014)
7. Durkheim, É., Kerr White Health Care Collection and Simpson, G., Spaulding, J.A.: Suicide: A Study in Sociology. Free Press (1951). ISBN 9780029086605
8. Bouthoul, G.: Sur les fonctions présumées et la périodicité des guerres. Revue Sci. Econ. (Lieja) 161–174 (1939)
9. Bouthoul, G.: La guerra. Oikos-Tau (1971). ISBN 8428101779
10. Eichensehr, K.: Ukraine, cyberattacks, and the lessons for international law. Am. J. Int. Law **116**, 145–149 (2022)
11. Zhou, M.J., Huang, J.B., Chen, J.Y.: Time and frequency spillovers between political risk and the stock returns of China's rare earths. Resour. Policy **75**, 102464 (2022)
12. Llanten-Quiroz, N.F.L.: polemología como aporte metodológico para profundizar la historia de la guerra. Rev. Cientifica Gener. Jose Maria Cordova **19**(35), 705–721 (2021)
13. Bada, M. and Nurse, J.R.C. The social and psychological impact of cyberattacks. In: Emerging Cyber Threats and Cognitive Vulnerabilities, pp. 73–92 (2020)
14. Basic Aerospace Doctrine of the USAF. Air Force Manual 1-1 (1992)
15. Fairburn, N., Shelton, A., Ackroyd, F., Selfe, R.: Beyond Murphy's law: applying wider human factors behavioural science approaches in cyber-security resilience. In: Proceedings of 23rd International Conference on Human-Computer Interaction, Washington, D.C., USA, pp. 123–138 (2021)
16. Rauti, S.: Controlling uncertainty with proactive cyber defense: a Clausewitzian perspective. In: Proceedings of International Symposium on Security in Computing and Communication, Chennai, India (2019)
17. Sotelo Monge, M.A., Maestre Vidal, J.: Conceptualization and cases of study on cyber operations against the sustainability of the tactical edge. Future Gener. Comput. Syst. **125**, 869–890 (2021)
18. NATO AJP 3–13. Allied Joint Doctrine for the Deployment and Redeployment of Forces (2021)
19. Rizzo, M.J., Dold, M.: Knightian uncertainty: through a Jamesian window. Camb. J. Econ. **45**(5), 967–988 (2021)
20. Brantly, A.F.: Risk and uncertainty can be analyzed in cyberspace. J. Cybersecur. **7**(1) (2021)
21. Gartzke, E., Lindsay, J.R.: Weaving tangled webs: offense, defense, and deception in cyberspace. Secur. Stud. **24**, 316–348 (2015)
22. Buck, C., Olenberg, C., Schweizer, A., Volter, F., Eymann, T.: Never trust, always verify: a multivocal literature review on current knowledge and research gaps of zero-trust. Comput. Secur. **110**, 102436 (2021)
23. Molinero, X., Riquelme, F.: Influence decision models: From cooperative game theory to social network analysis. Comput. Sci. Rev. **39**, 100343 (2021)
24. Pauwels, E.: Hybrid CoE strategic analysis 26: how to protect biotechnology from adversarial AI attacks (2021). https://www.hybridcoe.fi/publications/cyber-biosecurity-how-to-protect-biotechnology-from-adversarial-ai-attacks/

25. Baldor, L.C.: Army officer: China, Russia Don't Fear US Cyber Retaliation (2018). https://www.washingtonpost.com/politics/army-officer-china-russia-dont-fear-us-cyber-retaliation/2018/03/01/0470ca36-1dab-11e8-98f5_ceecfa8741b6_story. html
26. NATO AJP-3.20. Allied Joint Doctrine for Cyberspace Operations (2020)
27. Lin, H.: Cyberspace and national security threats, opportunities, and power in a virtual world. In: Operational considerations in cyber attack and cyber exploitation. Georgetown University Press (2012). ISBN 9781589019195
28. Bartles, C.: Getting gerasimov right. Milit. Rev. **96**, 30–38 (2016)
29. Gunning, D., Stefik, M., Choi, J., Miller, T., Stumpf, S., Yang, J.Z.: XAI: explainable artificial intelligence. Sci. Robot. **4**, 37 (2019)
30. Thomas, R.: Cyber war will not take place. J. Strategic Stud. **35**, 5–32 (2012)
31. Yoo, J.D., et al.: Cyber attack and defense emulation agents. Appl. Sci. **10**(6), 2140 (2020)
32. Luis Martinez, A., Maestre Vidal, J., Villagrá González, V.A.: Understanding and assessment of mission-centric key cyber terrains for joint military operations. CoRR, abs/2111.07005 (2021). https://arxiv.org/abs/2111.07005
33. Sengupta, S.: A survey of moving target defenses for network security. IEEE Commun. Surv. Tutor. **22**(3), 1909–1941 (2020)
34. US JP 3–13.4. Military Deception (2012)
35. Sandoval Rodríguez-Bermejo, D., Maestre Vidal, J., Estévez Tapiador, J.: The stress as adversarial factor for cyber decision making. In: Proceedings 16th International Conference on Availability, Reliability and Security, Vienna, Austria (2021)
36. NATO AJP-5. Allied Joint Doctrine for the planning of operations (2019)
37. Gonzalez, C., Ben-Asher, N., Morrison, D.: Dynamics of decision making in cyber defense: using multi-agent cognitive modeling to understand CyberWar. In: Liu, P., Jajodia, S., Wang, C. (eds.) Theory and Models for Cyber Situation Awareness. LNCS, vol. 10030, pp. 113–127. Springer, Cham (2017). https://doi.org/10.1007/978-3-319-61152-5_5
38. Roldan, H., Reith, M.: A strategic framework for cyber attacks in the military. In: Proceedings of International Conference on Cyber Warfare and Security, Washington, USA (2018)
39. Strange, J.L., Iron, R.: Center of gravity what clausewitz really meant. US Marine Coprs Wal Coll Quantico VA (2004)
40. Starbird, K., Ahmer, A., Tom, W.: Disinformation as collaborative work: surfacing the participatory nature of strategic information operations. In: Proceedings of the ACM on Human-Computer Interaction, CSCW, vol. 3, p. 127 (2019)
41. Hakala, J., Melnychuk, J.: Russia's strategy in cyberspace. NATO CCDCOE (2021). ISBN 9789934564901
42. US FM 3-12. Cyberspace Operations and Electromagnetic Warfare (2021)
43. US JP 3–12. Cyberspace Operations (2018)
44. Orye, E., Maennel, O.M.: Recommendations for enhancing the results of cyber effects. In: Proceedings of 11th International Conference on Cyber Conflict (CyCon), Tallin, Estonia (2019)
45. Wilson, A.: La ideología que lleva al desastre: dentro de la mente geopolítica rusa (2022). https://www.elconfidencial.com/mundo/2022-05-08/ideologia-lleva-desastre-mente-geopolitica-rusa_3420170/
46. Brizhinev, D., Ryan, R., Bradbury, R.: Modelling hegemonic power transition in cyberspace. Complexity **2018**, 9306128 (2018)
47. Axelrod, R., Illiev, R.: The strategic timing of cyber exploits. In: Proceedings of American Political Science Association Annual Meeting, Chicago, IL, USA (2013)

48. Nye, J.S.: The Future of Power. Public Affairs, New York (2011)
49. Steed, D.: The Politics and Technology of Cyberspace. Routledge, London. ISBN 9781351265928
50. Sotelo Monge, M.A., Maestre Vidal, J., Martínez Pérez, G.: Detection of economic denial of sustainability (EDoS) threats in self-organizing networks. Comput. Commun. **145**, 284–308 (2019)
51. Maestre Vidal, J., Sotelo Monge, M.A.: Obfuscation of malicious behaviors for thwarting masquerade detection systems based on locality features. Sensors **20**(7), 2084 (2020)
52. Maestre Vidal, J., Sotelo Monge, M.A.: Framework for anticipatory self-protective 5G environments. In: Proceedings of 14th International Conference on Availability, Reliability and Security (ARES), Canterbury, Kent, UK (2019)
53. Maestre Vidal, J., Sotelo Monge, M.A., Villalba, L.J.G.: A novel pattern recognition system for detecting android malware by analyzing suspicious boot sequences. Knowl.-Based Syst. **150**, 198–217 (2018)
54. Maestre Vidal, J., Orozco, A.L.S., Villalba, L.J.G.: Adaptive artificial immune networks for mitigating DoS flooding attacks. Swarm Evol. Comput. **38**, 94–108 (2018)
55. Maestre Vidal, J., Sotelo Monge, M.A.: Denial of sustainability on military tactical clouds. In: Proceedings of 15th International Conference on Availability, Reliability and Security (ARES), Dublin, Ireland, pp. 1–9 (2020)
56. Sandoval Rodriguez-Bermejo, D., Daton Medenou, R., Ramis Pasqual de Riquelme, G., Maestre Vidal, J., Torelli, F., Llopis Sánchez, S.: Evaluation methodology for mission-centric cyber situational awareness capabilities. In: Proceedings of 15th International Conference on Availability, Reliability and Security (ARES), Dublin, Ireland, pp. 1–9 (2020)
57. Sotelo Monge, M.A., Maestre Vidal, J., Villalba, L.J.G.: Reasoning and knowledge acquisition framework for 5G network analytics. Sensors **17**(10), 2405 (2017)

Examining 5G Technology-Based Applications for Military Communications

Antonio Portilla-Figueras[1]([⊠]), Salvador Llopis-Sánchez[2],
Silvia Jiménez-Fernández[1], and Sancho Salcedo-Sanz[1]

[1] ISDEFE-UAH IT and IA Observatory, Department of Signal Processing
and Communications, Universidad de Alcalá, Madrid, Spain
`antonio.portilla@uah.es`
[2] Communications Department, Universitat Politécnica de Valencia, Valencia, Spain
`salllosa@masters.upv.es`

Abstract. 5G mobile communications are capturing the focus of all stakeholders in the telecommunications ecosystem. The performance in terms of throughput, latency, number of connected devices, but also their features regarding security, availability and isolation make this technology very interesting for military applications. This paper first provides an overview of the key concepts related to 5G communications, on both, technical and economical approaches and then identifies a set of applications where 5G may provide a boost up in military communications. Specifically we focus on how 5G technology may improve the performance of current communication systems on Internet of Battle Things, communications on headquarters (HQ), either large static HQ or flexible and mobile HQ, unmanned combat systems, logistics and satellite communications. We also propose, based on the Spanish 5G National Observatory classification of the key parameters recommended by the 5G Infrastructure Public Private Partnership (5G PPP), the minimum values of those parameters to implement the services proposed for military applications. Finally the paper provides some conclusions and recommendations to build military communications using this technology.

Keywords: 5G military communications · IoBT · HQ
communications · Unmaned combat system · 5G satellite
communication · Mission 5G key parameters

1 Introduction

5G mobile technology is called to be a complete revolution, not only at a technological level, but also from a social and economical perspective, as it is expected to be the predominant wireless mobile technology from 2025 on. The relevance of the whole mobile networking ecosystem could be shown by means of the following figures. In 2021, the number of mobile devices operating worldwide was 14.91 billion and it is expected to grow up to 18.22 billion by 2025 [32].

S. Katsikas et al. (Eds.): ESORICS 2022 Workshops, LNCS 13785, pp. 449–465, 2023.
https://doi.org/10.1007/978-3-031-25460-4_26

In 2021, the economy of mobile communications generated 4.500 billion $, which means a contribution to the GDP of 5% globally, and it is expected to grow up to 5.000 billion $ by 2025. The private investment reached 1080 billion $ and it generated about 12 million direct jobs and 14 million indirect jobs.

5G comes to tackle, on the one hand, the exponential growth of mobile communications traffic, and on the other, the new services' features in terms of binary rate, latency and reliability. In 2005 mobile communications traffic was below 10 Exabytes, while in 2020 it exceeded 49 Exabytes. By 2025, it is expected to reach 237 Exabytes [8].

The deployment of 5G technology started in 2017 when 3GPP signed off its first specification. From 2017 to 2019 there were a huge number of trials and pilots, as well as the first commercial 5G Non Stand Alone (NSA) deployments[1]. Since 2020 most technologically advanced countries have commercial deployments and since 2021 more than 68 mobile network operators in 38 countries are investing on 5G Stand Alone (SA) networks. By 2025, forecast from the Global System for Mobile Communication Association (GSMA) [11] estimates that 5G will be the prevailing technology in North America and comparable to LTE in Europe and Great China, see Table 1.

Table 1. Evolution of the mobile mix and mobile market penetration (MP) in %, 2020–2025

Year	2020					2025				
Region	MP	2G	3G	4G	5G	MP	2G	3G	4G	5G
G. China	83	4	2	82	12	85	0	0	52	48
Europe	86	10	20	69	1	87	1	5	59	35
North Am	84	2	10	85	3	85	1	4	45	51

Public safety, security and military fields may well benefit from this technology. In this sense NATO performed the first studies by means of the Science and Technology Organization Task Group IST-ET-096, that published the technical report "5G Technologies: A Defense Perspective" [4]. In this report five scenarios were identified:

- Scenario 1: Wireless communications between command & control (C2) center at Battalion and Brigade level.
- Scenario 2: Wireless communications between C2 center at Company and Battalion level.
- Scenario 3: Wireless communications infrastructure inside a Command Post - rapid deployable Command Post.
- Scenario 4: Fixed infrastructure - limited mobility Company-level communications.

---

[1] Stand alone is the pure native 5G technology. Non Stand Alone stands for a combined 4G-5G technology where a 5G radio access works with a 4G core network.

– Scenario 5: Full mobility Company-level communications.

In this paper we examine different potential applications of 5G for enhancing military communications, identifying the technologies that support them and determining the relation between them and the set critical parameters defined by the 5GPP to characterise the 5G verticals [23].

The rest of the paper is structured as follows: next section provides a brief description of 5G's main features and key technologies relevant for defense and military applications. Section 3 describes applications and 5G field trials. Section 4 determines key parameters defined by the 5G Infrastructure Public Private Partnership (5G PPP) that are of interest in military applications. Finally some conclusions are presented in Sect. 5.

2   Overview of Key Concepts About 5G Technology

Mario Campolargo, Director-General, DG Informatics, European Commission said about this technology "5G is not 4G+1" [5]. With this assessment it is straightforward to see that 5G is going to boost up the performance of previous mobile communications generations. The main figures of 5G and a comparison to 4G are shown in Table 2.

Table 2. Evolution of the mobile mix and mobile market penetration (MP), 2020–2025

Parameter	5G target value	Gain vs 4G (LTE)
Data rate	10 Gbps[a]	10x
Cost	2cent \$/GB	10x lower cost
Latency	<1 ms	10x lower
IoT power	10 μWh per tx	10x
Energy efficiency	2 kWh/TB	5x
Spectral efficiency	>10 bps/cell/Hz	5x
Mobility	500 Km/h	>150 Km/h
Outdoor location	Meters	10x lower
Nº connected devices	1 M/Km^2	1000x

[a] In mmWave band with maximum bandwidth may reach 20 Gbps

A large number of key techniques, technologies and facilitators are needed to provide these features, some of them related to the radio access network (RAN) and the so-called new radio (NR), and some other more specific related to the Core Network. Among the first ones are Massive Multiple Input Multiple Output (MIMO), beamforming, network densification and small cells, the use of millimeter wave communications, carrier aggregation, cloud RAN (separated radio unit (RRU) and baseband unit (BBU)), optimized Orthogonal Frequency

Division Multiple access (OFDM) and new non-orthogonal shared medium access techniques or dynamic spectrum sharing [14, 20].

The International Telecommunication Union (ITU) has defined three main scenarios for 5G mobile technology in Recommendation UIT-R M.2803 [15].

- Enhanced Mobile Broadband (eMBB).
- Ultra reliable and low latency communications (URLLC).
- Massive machine type communications (mMTC).

Relation between these three scenarios and network requirements is shown in Fig. 1, see [15]

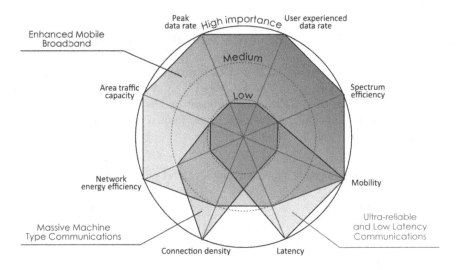

Fig. 1. Comparison of key capabilities of IMT-Advanced (LTE) (4th generation) with IMT-2020 (5th generation)

It is important to highlight that there is a tight relation between the type of scenario, parameters required and spectrum availability, as depicted in Fig. 2. Note that for some applications, a compromise between the parameters will be needed, for example, a large coverage can only be achieved in lower bands, where low bandwidths are available. Therefore, low latency or massive mobile broadband cannot be achieved. These kind of compromises are very relevant in military applications, as will be described in following Section.

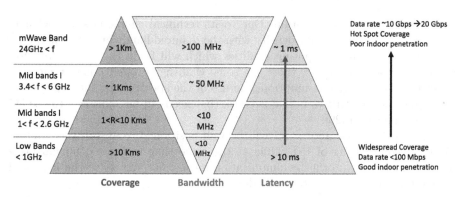

Fig. 2. Relation between coverage, bandwidth (capacity) and latency depending on the frequency band in 5G technology.

3 Applications of 5G for Military Communications

3.1 Internet of Battle Things, Wearables and 5G

The concept of command and control (C2) has evolved significantly in the last few years to include additional aspects such as command control and communications (C3), command, control, communications and computers (C4) or command, Control, communications, computers, Intelligence, Surveillance and Reconnaissance (C4ISR) among others. C4ISR is key enabler is Information and Communication Technology (ICT) on both sides: battlefield and command center, where intelligence and decision making is performed.

Considering C4ISR as the system's brain, the set of Internet of the Things (IoT) devices deployed in the battlefield are the senses. According to [18] the battlefield of the future will be composed of a large variety of interrelated smart and non smart things that will collect, cooperate, transmit and process information, forming the Internet of the Battle Things (IoBT) [31]. Among these devices we may find weapons systems, vehicles, robots and unmanned systems or human wearable sensors and devices [27].

Focusing on human's wearables, or warfighter portable devices, it is possible to categorize them into three categories. The first one are those related with soldier wellness, and are oriented to supervise soldier's healthy body condition and enhance his performance. In this category we find medical sensors, smart watches with GPS positioning, activity tracer, smart clothing, or even exo-skeleton. The second category is vision & surveillance, with devices as smart helmets or glasses and wearable cameras, which collect information regarding the soldier's environment and send it in real time to the command center, to cooperate with the rest of the platoon to complete the mission. The last one is situational awareness, with devices as augmented reality glasses, night vision googles or thermal cameras, that allow the combatant to have a better understanding and knowledge of the surroundings. Note that all the information collected by the sensing units must be transmitted, stored and processed in order to have a coherent view of the battlefield situation. Due to its technical characteristics, 5G may provide enough connectivity density with the required bandwidth. Furthermore, 5G implements edge computing facilities which will fulfill the latency requirements. On the other hand, there are some challenging open points related to cybersecurity, energy consumption, the use of the spectrum or the deployment of a dedicated network vs public network that needs to be addressed to use 5G for this application [29].

As it is described above, 5G will be well positioned to absorb the communication requirements of IoT while at the same time seek for complementarity/redundancy with other communication means. 5G may solve the increased demand of services at the tactical edge.

3.2   5G for Deployable Headquarters Communications

Deployed Headquarters for land operations are physical places where the decisions are taken by one operation commander. Considering a specific mission, there are two configurations of headquarter: Large static headquarters (LHQ), at the strategic or operational level, considering a division or army level, and light and mobile headquarter (MHQ) or command posts, deployed in the battlefield for tactical operations at a brigade or regiment level [4].

Large static headquarters are well established camps holding brick-concrete buildings and a set of logistic and communications facilities. They are not permanent infrastructures, but are expected to be used for weeks, months, or even years. An example is the NATO Rapid Deployable Corps - Spain Headquarters (HQ NRDC-ESP) that is located in Bétera, Valencia. An scheme of a LHQ is shown in Fig. 3. Mobile headquarters are characterized by flexible, easy to move infrastructures, formed by vehicles and tents that may change their location in terms of minutes. In words of General Mark A. Milley, 20th Chairman of the Joint Chiefs of Staff and former Chief of staff of the Army, "Our brigade (command post) must be able to jump within two to three minutes or they will be destroyed" [19]. A scheme of a mobile headquarter is shown in Fig. 4.

As the purpose of the LHQs differs from the MHQs, also does the communication requirements [4]. Communications inside a LHQ require fixed and stable communications to implement enhanced mobile broadband. On the other hand, global connectivity is usually guaranteed as the headquarter may be located near a public telecommunication infrastructure or is using a proper military telecommunication infrastructure with a global coverage e.g. satellite communications. Therefore inside the LHQ 5G may implement Fixed Wireless Access by means of a private network, and connect to a public 5G infrastructure specific secured service slice, by means of 5G Network Slicing (NS). Network slicing is one of the most promising 5G technologies, which allows to provide communications infrastructure as a service (IaaS) where all physical services are shared to create different and independent virtual networks with different QoS parameters and security levels for different vertical applications. The specific conditions of isolation, availability, security and performance of military communications running over public networks may be satisfied by this technology [24]. Concerning the

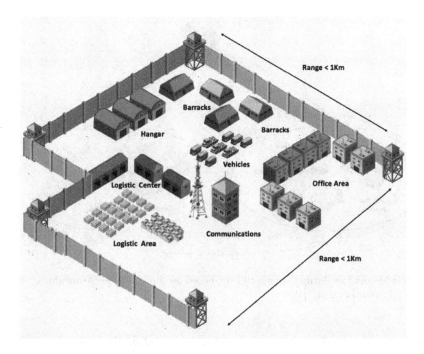

Fig. 3. Scheme of a LHQ based on NATO rapid deployable corps headquarter [21].

implementation of the 5G service, 6GHz mid bands would be a fair compromise between coverage and capacity for general purposes inside the LHQ, using 26 GHz band for specific applications on hot spots as troop training with virtual reality or autonomous logistic vehicles.

Concerning the MHQ, as they may be deployed anywhere, it is not appropriate to trust the public infrastructure for several reasons: availability, technology level and, of course, security. Therefore a proper 5G infrastructure has to be used. At this level we should divide the whole system between intra-company communications and company to MHQ communications. Intra-company communications should be provided by a mobile 5G station placed in a vehicle with some edge/fog computing capabilities. Note that latency is going to be a key driver, as strict real time information is going to be shared among the units deployed. Furthermore, the coverage range of the company should not be, in general, larger than some (few) hundred meters. Therefore mmWave band, 26 GHz, is well suited for this purpose [12]. The communication between the companies and the MHQ needs a compromise between coverage and capacity, therefore mid-bands (Sub 6GHz) should be used, in combination with beamforming techniques to reach the kilometer range required. Beamforming (either analog or digital) is a procedure that allows, given the signals of a array of transmitting antennas, to address them to a specific direction, the receiving terminal. Specifically, beamforming sends the same symbol over each transmit antenna. At the receiving end

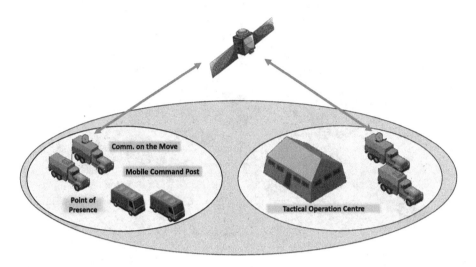

Fig. 4. Scheme of an Army Command Post based on the U.S Army Warfighting Assessment 17.1, October 2016 [19]

signals are combined using to maximize the received SNR. This gain in SNR in antenna array systems is called beamforming gain [3]. Although beamforming was already used in 4g-LTE is in 5G systems were it gets it optimum performance in combination with Massive MIMO. The use of beamforming brings many advantages as increased network capacity, better QoS or, as the objective aimed above, improved coverage range.

The Norwegian Defence Material Agency has performed a 5G pilot in the Rygga military airbase considering a fixed base station (gNB) covering the whole range of frequencies, 800 MHz, sub 6 GHz and mmWave band (64 × 64 MIMO), connected to the public network with a specific slice and complemented with a mobile 5G private network "cell on wheels". The latter consists on a fully autonomous 5G private network (the acronym of the project is FUDGE), built on a trailer, that implements edge computing capabilities for military verticals [22].

3.3   A 5G-UAV Ecosystem for Military Communications

The Unmmaned Aerial Vehicles (UAVs), also known as drones, is a clear use in military applications. Traditionally UAVs have been used for different tasks, among others, intelligence, surveillance and reconnaissance either autonomously or remotely piloted. However, as technology (and more specifically mobile technology) evolves, new applications have arisen. We can classify them into three types:

- UAV as end terminal. As described above (traditional use).
- UAVs as swarm entities oriented to Internet of the Battle Things.
- UAVs as temporary flying Base Stations (BS) in wireless communications (specifically, in 5G and beyond communications).

Being the most innovative, the use of UAVs as temporary flying 5G Base Stations, providing wireless coverage and connectivity to soldiers in the battlefield. In this sense UAVs used as 5G gNB, complement the connectivity provided by the headquarters (described in Sect. 3.2). Also, depending on the altitude and operational time, the following classification can be considered [28]:

- Low altitude platform (LAP), with short coverage and reduced operational time. This may serve as complement of the gNB deployed in a vehicle for the MHQ described in Sect. 3.2.
- High altitude platform (HAP), with large operational time (months) and large coverage. In this case, the UAV-HAP may provide connectivity to a large area, either to provide connectivity by itself or as the fixed infrastructure's complement.

Swarm UAVs are a set of light, low cost, low altitude and low range that can be operated individually or as a group. Swarm UAVs may be used for a wide range of actions [9,16]. Please note that, for coordinated actions, the provision of a reasonable level of intelligence is mandatory, usually provided by means of artificial intelligence mechanisms that agile (very short time) react to the changing environment of a battlefield. This may be implemented by multi access edge computing capabilities LAP UAVs which will implement the corresponding 5G slice, as it is proposed in [10].

Please note that merging the applications described above, a whole 5G UCS architecture for battlefield operations may be proposed in several levels.

- Layer 1 (L1): At a ground level, we may find the MHQ with a vehicle with a 5G gNB and with mobile edge computing (MEC) capabilities, due to the very short latency that some applications require. Please note that this vehicle should be connected with other command center of higher hierarchy (or even the LHQ).
- Layer 2 (L2): A Swarm IoBT UAV level in an altitude range of less than 500 m, typically a drone of Group 1 (by size and payload) as it is defined by Federal Aviation Administration's, see [13]. Their purpose is to recover multimedia information of the battlefield.
- Layer 3 (L3) A LAP 5G Connectivity level, composed by a set of LALE (Low altitude, Long Endurance) or even MAME (Medium Altitude, Medium Endurance) [7] with altitudes below 5000(LALE)-8000 (MAME) meters that provide wireless access to the swarm level and even to the shadow coverage areas provided by the 5G gNB mobile station at the ground level.

– Layer 4 (L4): An Unmanned Individual AV level, composed of a single or
  few independent aerial vehicles, typically Large UAVs, Group 5 (by size and
  payload) with different communication requirements depending on the specific
  missions. This category also involves the remotely piloted aerial vehicles.
– Layer 5 (L5): A High Altitude Plattform. With an altitude of more than
  20.000 m, the objective is, on one hand, to provide global coverage to the
  battlefield area, an, on the other hand serving as a first step in the aggregation
  network towards the command post and, finally, due to its large payload, even
  implement some fog/edge computing capabilities.

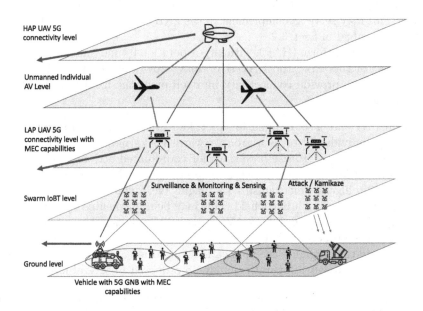

Fig. 5. Global architecture of 5G-UCS (Color figure online)

Figure 5 shows the architecture described above. Please note that lines in blue
colour represent the wireless connection between end terminals (either weare-
ables in soldiers, users, vehicles...) with the access points. The red lines represent the connectivity between the access points (5G gNB) with MEC capabilities
required for URLLC services. Finally, the green lines represent the backhaul connection to the nearest command center, either the MHQ or the LHQ, depending
on the specific service.

The use of UAVs as temporary gNB has some relevant challenges as the
energy constraints of the UAVs, the need of a tight resource and terminal allocation and study of the interference in case of a multiples UAVs, the problem
of physical security (UAVs may be taken down) and resilience and robustness of
the network against this issue and also cybersecurity. Furthermore, and from the

point of view of communications, upwards backhaul link needs special consideration. Backhaul links in the battlefield will surely be implemented by a wireless link, but the routing has an important impact in the performance of each individual service in terms of, for example, latency. Direct wireless backhaul in L1, maybe the shortest path, but it requires LOS between the MHQ and the gNB in the vehicle. In L3, we may have LOS, but the implementation of backhaul capabilities in one or some LAP UAvs may decrease the endurance of the system due to more energy consumption. In L5 we surely have LOS and the HAPs have enough energy, but note that this solution may be not valid for some URLLC services. Some studies indicate that to reach a 1 ms latency the data processing centre should not be more than 21 km away from the gNB [35][2]. All these issues, apart from frequency band allocation, have to be considered in the design of the UCS system.

3.4 Logistics and Training Applications

Out of the field of operations, 5G may enhance the performance of some relevant activities that may have some parallelism with civil applications. In this sense, Industry 4.0 is one of the early adopters of 5G technology and a promising vertical is related with Smart Logistics. 5G applications on this field are related with object tracking, autonomous ground an air vehicles operation, remote assistance for employees thought AR, monitoring and control of robots, video surveillance or ambient sensors for predictive maintenance [17,26].

There are some pilot experiences done by different armies to analyze the benefits of the application of 5G technology. For example, At Marine Corps Logistics Base Albany, the Marine Corps of the U.S. army is experimenting with 5G smart warehouse technologies for vehicular storage and maintenance [33], with a successful two day demonstration of the system in July 2021 [34]. In this pilot they are focused on very high speed and ultra-low latency for operation of autonomous vehicles for inventory management, machine learning for inventory tracking, and augmented/virtual reality applications for improved workforce efficiency.

Another successful example on civil area but with direct military application is the project 5GENESIS. The objective of the project was to evaluate the use of mobile video for Police operations in order to enhance public security. This project has been performed between the University of Málaga, the Municipality of Málaga (with the Police Department) and a commercial operator Telefónica. The Police department has played the role of final user with commercial phones to receive and transmit live video around the coverage area of the deployed 5G network [1]. Please note that in this pilot, security issues are being carried by a commercial 5G network through the corresponding slice.

Another very interesting field for the application of 5G is augmented (AR) and virtual reality (VR). AR/VR may serve for different purposes [30], from industrial production, predictive maintenance to secure and immersive troop

---

[2] This study was performed for the network of a specific Indonesian operator, but should serve as rule of dumb for range estimation.

training and even remote support for critical operations as soldier safety (remote diagnosis and surgery). Again, the U.S. army is experimenting with 5G technologies and AR/VR for tactical training at the Joint Base Lewis-McChord and the Yakima tactical training site, and also the Air Force at Tinker AFB, is using 5G for immersive education [33].

There are many other military applications of 5G that for the sake of simplicity we do not expand here. Some of them, for example, may be related with on board communications (in naval or aerial large ships) and the substitution of cable by wireless communications, with the consequent weight reduction. Out of the scope of this paper are the challenges of the application of 5G, some of them may be solved in near future (spectrum, equipment availability, evolution towards Stand Alone (SA) networks, core network funcionalities) but some others, specially cybersecurity are open points to be solved.

3.5 Enhanced Satellite Communications. A Use Case for 5G Non-terrestrial Networks (NTN)

5G non-terrestrial networks (NTN) are a new feature established in the release 17 of the Third Generation Partnership Programme (3GPP) standard of the 5G NR functions. NTN extend the 5G terrestrial connectivity that provides access to user terminals via mobile radio channels using ground base stations to potential base stations or 5G payloads in the air (e.g. HAP) already covered in Sect. 3.3. This evolving technology is being explored to demonstrate the feasibility of 5G connections using a satellite as an amplifier and a forward relay. This architecture for satellite communications represents the first attempts to integrate NTN into future 5G-beyond architectures.

Considering emerging mega constellations of satellites and the need to network future satellite capacities in space, it is worth mentioning related initiatives such as the Defence Advanced Research Projects Agency (DARPA) Space-Based Adaptive Communications Node (Space-BACN). Space-BACN aims to create a low-cost, reconfigurable optical communications terminal that adapts to most optical intersatellite link standards, translating between diverse satellite constellations. Space-BACN would create an "internet" of low-Earth orbit (LEO) satellites, enabling seamless communication between military/government and commercial/civil satellite constellations that currently are unable to interoperate. This research programme will approach an overarching satellite network whose results may inform future features of the sixth-generation mobile wireless communications (6G). It is expected that 3GPP standard release 18 will continue with the discussion about NTN and advance proposals for NTN frequency bands. Two ranges of frequencies are being discussed: FR1 (sub 6 GHz) and FR2 (beyond 10 GHz).

In the authors' views, NTN is an interesting technology that should be explored in light of the EU-space based Secure Connectivity Programme. Satellite communications provide ubiquitous coverage in areas where terrestrial networks are absent including those where military missions are deployed and in general no digital infrastructure is available. Besides, the risk that existing digital communication services could also be disrupted or be unreliable. Geostationary Earth orbit (GEO) or non-geostationary-orbit (NGSO) satellites could be equipped with payloads of 5G/UHF communications and thus offering critical secure communications and services enabling high-speed data rates and low latency regimes. 5G NTN still have a long and promising way to follow in view of enhancing satellite communications.

4   5GPP Key Parameters on Military Applications

5GPPP has defined a set of key performance indicators to characterize the technical requirements of each of the 5 verticals identified as main use cases for 5G: automotive, entertainment, energy, industry and health [2]. These indicators are:

- Binary rate (Br), with a upper bound in terms of Gbps.
- Mobility (Mb), defined as user movement speed, with a maximum value of 500 Km/h.
- Latency (Lt), with a objective minimum value of 1 ms.
- Density (Dens), maximum number of connected devices/area unit, with values as demanding as 100 devices/m^2.
- Reliability (Rl), measured as the amount of corrupted information for a fixed latency. Reliability of 99,9999 % may be required for some health related applications.
- Positioning (Pos). Some applications require errors less than 1 m.
- Coverage (Cv), area where the service must be provided with fixed requirements in terms of binary rate or latency.

The Spanish 5G National Observatory (5GNO) [23] has established the following qualitative classification of the indicators above:

- **0:** No requirements.
- **1:** Low requirements.
- **2:** Medium requirements, which may be fulfilled with current mobile technology.
- **3:** High requirements, that can not be fulfilled with current systems or they are at the edge of them.
- **4:** Very High requirements, even at the edge of the 5G technology as defined by the 5GPPP.

Following the results of the 5G pilots and trials detailed in the 5GPPP report, the 5GNO made a relation between a set of specific applications or services of different verticals and the qualitative classification of the KPI. This produced a table that is available in the report. The 5G & Beyond Observatory of the Politécnico de Milano has made an equivalent study focused on the classification of the different applications/services into the eMBB, URLLC and MMTC scenarios, see [6]. From those studies it is possible to extrapolate the requirements of the military applications of 5G described in previous sections as they are shown in Table 3. To do this, the following methodology has been applied. First we identify which civil application listed in the table of the 5GNO or in the information of the Politécnico de Milano would be the closest to the specific military application. Second, we analize the specific features of the military services in order to adapt each specific KPI. For example, *Wereable for soldier wellness* application may be identified with Health Remote Monitoring in the civil field and then may have similar KPI's. However, the number of warfighters is usually less than the number of inhabitants that may be monitored, and therefore the requirement in terms of KPI should be lowered. On the other hand the precision in the positioning of the warfighter should be more accurate, and then, this KPI should be incremented.

Please note that frequency band specified for the different applications in Table 3 may be used for both civil and military applications. This may be an issue when considering cross-border locations and the coexistence of 5G private military networks with public infrastructure. Concerning cross-border locations, the international organizations are trying to harmonise spectrum availability over large areas. For example in the EU the Radio Spectrum Group are harmonising not only the 5G priority bands, but also the bands for previous technology to guarantee service continuity [25].

Table 3. Requirements of the military applications running over 5G mobile networks.

Application	Service	Br	Mb	Lt	Dens	Rl	Ps	CV	EC	NS	F.Band	eMBB	URLLC	mMTC
IoBT	Soldier wearable	3	4	2	2	4	4	4	Yes	No	Mid Bands II	Yes		Yes
IoBT	Vision-surveillance	3	4	3	3	3	4	4	Yes	yes	Mid Bands II	Yes		Yes
LHQ Com	FWA general	3	2	2	2	4	2	2	No	No	Mid Bands I-II	Yes		
LHQ Com	FWA hot spot	3	2	2	2	3	2	2	Yes	No	mmWave	Yes		
LHQ Com	Training	4	3	4	2	4	4	2	Yes	Yes	mmWave	Yes	Yes	
MHQ Com	Internal com.	4	2	3	2	4	2	2	Yes	Yes	mmWave	Yes		
Company	Intra-company com.	3	3	3	2	4	4	3	Yes	Yes	mmWave	Yes		Yes
Company	Company-MHQ	3	4	3	2	4	3	3	No	Nos	Mid Bands II	Yes		
UAV	Swarm IoT (L2)-sensing	3	3	3	4	4	3	3	No	Yes	Mid Bands-Low Bands	Yes		Yes
UAV	Connectivity (L3)	3	3	3	3	4	3	3	Yes	Yes	Mid Bands-Low Bands	Yes		Yes
UAV	Individual mission (L4)	3	4	4	2	4	4	4	No	Yes	mmWave	Yes	Yes	
UAV	HAP (L5) bakchaul	3	4	3	2	3	3	4	Yes	No	Mid Bands I-II	Yes		
Logistics	Inventory management	3	3	4	1	4	2	2	Yes	No	Mid Bands I-II	Yes	Yes	
Logistics	AR-VR applications	4	3	4	2	4	4	2	Yes	Yes	mmWave	Yes	Yes	
Logistics	Surveillance	3	3	3	4	3	3	3	Yes	Yes	Mid Bands II	Yes		Yes
Logistics	Autonomous vehicle	2	4	4	4	4	4	4	Yes	Yes	mmWave		Yes	
SATCOM	Com. for Op. area	4	4	4	2	4	4	4	Yes	No	High Bands-	Yes		

5 Conclusions

This paper proposes potential applications of 5G mobile communications in the military field. We intended to cover a wide variety of areas, from the battlefield, going through communications intra company, mobile headquarters, large static headquarters and logistics. We also propose a five-layered architecture for an ummaned combat ecosystem based on UAV. After analyzing the set of services an applications we establish the minimum requirements they need in terms of the key parameters defined by the 5GPPP, and also a proposal of frequency bands where these services could be implemented. Although these values will depend on the specific implementation and, of course, the environmental situation, this may serve as an starting point for a potential real service deployment.

Of course there are several open points and challenges for the use of 5G in military field. Although some of them are pointed out in the paper, it is necessarary to bring them again to be considered for future work. The main one, as it could be expected, is cybersecurity. As the number of digital entrance points to the network increases, the potential risk also increases. Network slicing comes to minimise this issue, but is still a concern. Technology robustness, interworking, spectrum sharing are other issues also need consideration. Finally, backhauling, that was only outlined in previous sections, could be the bottleneck for 5G implementation. Due to the requirements in terms of binary rate, but mainly in latency, few technologies may be used. The optimum one is, of course, optical fibre, but this could be available on a LHQ but not in a MHQ or in a mobile gNB in the battlefield.

Acknowledgements. This work is supported by the *Universidad de Alcalá - ISDEFE* Chair of Research in ICT and Artificial Intelligence.

References

1. 5GPPP: 5G Public-Private-Partnership: Trials & Pilots (2021). https://bit.ly/3Mr64Ox
2. 5GPPP: 5G Public-Private-Partnership: Technology Board & 5G IA Verticals Task Force: Empowering Vertical Industries through 5G Networks - Current Status and Future Trends, 5G Public Private Partnership project (2022). https://bit.ly/35rUu5e
3. Ahmed, I., et al.: A survey on hybrid beamforming techniques in 5G: architecture and system model perspectives. IEEE Commun. Surv. Tutor. **20**(4), 3060–3097 (2018)
4. Bastos, L., G, G.C., Koprulu, A., Elzinga, G.: Potential of 5G technologies for military application. In: 2021 International Conference on Military Communication and Information Systems (ICMCIS), pp. 1–8 (2021). https://doi.org/10.1109/ICMCIS52405.2021.9486402
5. Campolargo, M.: 5G, the way forward! In: Future Mobile Summit. ETSI (2013)
6. Capone, A.: Ambiti applicativi del 5G e requisiti prestazionali minimi e target. 5G & Beyond Observatory (2022). https://bit.ly/3doK7Tb
7. Elmeseiry, N., Alshaer, N., Ismail, T.: A detailed survey and future directions of unmanned aerial vehicles (UAVs) with potential applications. Aerospace **8**, 363 (2021)
8. Ericsson: Ericsson mobility report (2021)
9. European Defence Review Online: Escribano designs a swarm system of UAVs for surveillance and recognition missions (2021). https://bit.ly/3K1xusb
10. Grasso, C., Schembra, G.: A fleet of MEC UAVs to extend a 5G network slice for video monitoring with low-latency constraints. J. Sens. Actuat. Netw. **8**(1), 3 (2019)

11. GSMA Association: The mobile economy 2022 (2022). https://www.gsma.com/mobileeconomy/

12. Harvey, J., Steer, M., Rappaport, T.: Exploiting high millimeter wave bands for military communications. IEEE Access **7**, 52350–52359 (2019)

13. Hildmann, H., Kovacs, E., Saffre, F., Isakovic, A.: Nature-inspired drone swarming for real-time aerial data-collection under dynamic operational constraints. Drones **3**(3), 71 (2019)

14. Holma, H., Toskala, A., Nakamura, T.: 5G Technology: 3GPP New Radio (2020)

15. International Telecommunication Unit: ITU-R M.2083-0: IMT Vision - Framework and overall objectives of the future development of IMT for 2020 and beyond (2015)

16. Keller, J.: The marine corps is on the hunt for a kamikaze drone swarm to back up grunts on the battlefield (2019). Task and Purpose website. https://taskandpurpose.com/military-tech/marine-corps-drone-swarms/

17. Khatib, E., Barco, R.: Optimization of 5g networks for smart logistics. Energies **14**(6), 1758 (2021)

18. Kott, A., Swami, A., West, B.: The internet of battle things. Computer **49**(12), 70–75 (2016)

19. Lombardo, C., Selby, K.: Iron brigade's combat-team pursuit of mobile command-post capabilities. Armor **128**(3), 57–61 (2017). https://bit.ly/3zWO8Hq

20. Morgado, A., Saidul, K., Mumtaz, S., Rodriguez, J.: A survey of 5G technologies: regulatory, standardization and industrial perspectives. Digit. Commun. Netw. **4**(2), 87–97 (2018)

21. NATO: NATO rapid deployable corps - Spain headquarters (2022). https://bit.ly/3zA6cW6

22. Nomeland, K.: 5G for military use. In: 2021 Joint European Conference on Networks and Communications & 6G Summit (2021)

23. Observatorio Nacional de 5G: 5G: La transformación de sectores clave (2020). https://bit.ly/3hRpSws

24. Grønsund, P., et al.: 5G service and slice implementation for a military use case. In: 2020 IEEE International Conference on Communications Workshops (ICC Workshops) (2020). https://doi.org/10.1109/ICCWorkshops49005.2020.9145236

25. Radio Spectrum Group, European Comission: Harmonising spectrum for enhanced connectivity: ready for 5G and innovation (2022). https://bit.ly/3EisDmZ

26. Rao, S., Prasad, R.: Impact of 5G technologies on industry 4.0. Wirel. Pers. Commun. **100**, 145–159 (2018)

27. Russell, S., Abdelzaher, T.: The internet of battlefield things: the next generation of command, control, communications and intelligence (C3I) decision-making. In: 2018 IEEE Military Communications Conference (MILCOM), pp. 737–742 (2018)

28. Shahzadi, R., Ali, M., Zubair, H., Naeem, M.: UAV assisted 5G and beyond wireless networks: a survey. J. Netw. Comput. Appl. **189**, 103114 (2021)

29. Sharma, Park, J., Park, H., Cho, K.: Wearable computing for defence automation: Opportunities and challenges in 5G network. IEEE Access **8**, 65993–66002 (2020)

30. Siriwardhana, Y., Porambage, P., Liyanage, M., Ylianttila, M.: A survey on mobile augmented reality with 5G mobile edge computing: architectures, applications, and technical aspects. IEEE Commun. Surv. Tutor. **23**(2), 1160–1192 (2021)

31. Suri, N., et al.: Analyzing the applicability of internet of things to the battlefield environment. In: 2016 International Conference on Military Communications and Information Systems (ICMCIS), pp. 1–8 (2016)

32. The Radicati Group: Mobile statistic report 2021–2025 (2021)

33. U.S. Department of Defense: 5G strategy implementation plan for 5G technology and applications securing 5G capabilities (2020)

34. U.S. Department of Defense: Department of defense successfully demonstrates a 5G network for smart warehouses (2021). https://bit.ly/35rUu5e
35. Yogapratama, A., Suryanegara, M.: Dealing with the latency problem to support 5G-URLLC: a strategic view in the case of an indonesian operator. In: 2020 2nd International Conference on Broadband Communications, Wireless Sensors and Powering (BCWSP), pp. 96–100 (2020)

Design of a Validation Model of the Cognitive State in Military Operations in Cyberspace

Juan León Murillo[1]([⊠])[iD], Marco Antonio Sotelo Monge[1][iD], and Víctor Villagrá[2][iD]

[1] Indra, Av. de Bruselas 35, 28108 Madrid, Spain
jmleonm@indra.es
[2] Universidad Politécnica de Madrid, Av. Complutense 30, 28040 Madrid, Spain

Abstract. This paper aims to study how the cognitive state affects decision making in the field of military operations in cyberspace. In the Spanish military doctrine, cyberspace is recognized as a field of operation and we can see how it grows in importance in the current methods of warfare that are increasingly less conventional and more oriented to the cognitive field. People follow a process by which we end up making a decision, but this can be largely affected by the situation in which we find ourselves. When we are stressed or overwhelmed, we tend to think less and act more on impulse. Decisions remain ultimately the responsibility of individuals, regardless of what an algorithm might recommend. The human brain emits waves with different frequencies that can be read to infer a certain cognitive state. A Brain-Computer Interface (BCI) allows us to establish a data transmission channel between our brain and the computer to be able to read them in real time, analyze them and determine what type of wave it is and its meaning. In this paper, we intend to study and draw conclusions about how the mental state of a person affects their decision making.

Keywords: Awareness · Biometric systems · Cyberexercise · BCI · Decision making · Cognitive state

1 Introduction

As we can see in a study by the Government of Spain on Cybercrime in the year 2020 [4] we see how internet users grow by 7% worldwide and a 5% nationally. This increase is due to several factors, in addition to the trend of development of the countries, in the last two years the Covid-19 has greatly influenced measure to the increase in remote connections. The impossibility of going to the office, the quarantines etc. They have produced an increase in the use of cloud solutions, VPN connections, virtual remote desktop services (VDI), zero-trust networks, and identity management, services and technologies for remote access, use of collaborative tools... etc. All this will generate attacks on these environments,

S. Katsikas et al. (Eds.): ESORICS 2022 Workshops, LNCS 13785, pp. 466–481, 2023.
https://doi.org/10.1007/978-3-031-25460-4_27

especially those publicly exposed, continue to grow. It is also foreseeable that attacks and vulnerabilities related to networks household and personal devices increase with the aim of accessing or spying on the company infrastructure. It is also to be expected that attacks on pharmaceutical companies, research laboratories or victims related to the sector. On the other hand, it is important to recognize that computer attacks can trigger complex situations from the cognitive point of view.

It is that the importance of being prepared that various organizations offer cybersecurity challenge platforms [5] that are intended to test professionals with the aim of demonstrating and at the same time acquiring knowledge about different cybersecurity topics and aspects. The exercises deal with a scenario in which a player faces problems in a given time and with a given score.

Decision-making is a process intrinsic to military doctrine, forming part of training at different levels, both hierarchical and environmental, the decision-making process not being the same in the different phases such as planning, conduction, critical judgement, etc. The pressure and stress to which a person is subjected during a cyber attack [23] can affect their ability to make decisions. Although it is known that there are certain causes or effectors that can increase the level of stress and consequently inhibit decision making, in this research seeks to make an assessment from the cognitive point of view from of the analysis of brain waves obtained from a BCI interface.

In this work, a series of objectives have been set:

- Be able to monitor the status of a person by reading their brain waves.
- Performing a cyber exercise in which the participant is monitored.
- Being able to check the values of the waves at certain times to try establish relationships between decisions and values.
- Send records of the data obtained to a machine in order to centralize information.

2   Theoretical Framework

2.1   Military Doctrine

In the Spanish military doctrine [1], cyberspace is recognized as an area of operation.

We understand scope of operation as the physical and non-physical spaces that condition the aptitudes and procedures of the means, forces and capacities that they must operate on them. To the traditional domains (land, sea and air) is added in the Spanish doctrine two new ones, cyberspace and cognitive, transversally, thus implying their importance since they are present in all areas.

We can observe how it grows in importance in the current methods of warfare every less conventional and more oriented to the cognitive field. Cyberspace is already consolidated as an environment of strategic, geopolitical, economic, social and individual with important implications for the security of organizations and countries. Living in a connected world, the cyber world does not knows

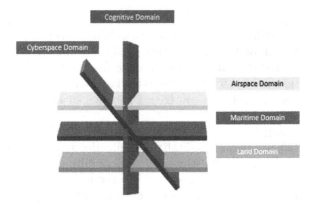

Fig. 1. Spanish doctrine

of borders, being the systems connected to the internet accessible from anywhere and currently lacks strong regulation, thus giving rise to a idyllic scenario for attackers (nations, terrorist organizations, hacktivists...) where added to the ease of access to the techniques and tools for the cybercrime constitute it as a current problem that, although it is silent, carries great danger (Fig. 1).

2.2 Cibersecurity in OTAN

The response to cyber attacks is only effective from an international perspective, where it is vital to consolidate firm collaboration agreements between States, organizations or alliances international military, private sector, industry and academia. This poses a challenge when coordinating. A scenario is generated in which people with a different language and culture must cooperate against a common goal, the cyberterrorism. While challenging the defending side, the attacking side has the advantage of going ahead and every time we observe how cybercrime grows in our environment. First of all, terrorists need their actions to be serious enough to keep a certain society in fear for a relatively long time length; and for this nothing better than an attack with damage or the possibility of serious physical damage or deadly to people. In this case, cyberspace is a field still to be explored by most influential terrorist groups, which fundamentally use the Internet as a platform for logistical support, communications, recruitment and propaganda. Secondly, terrorists need a large media apparatus that publicizes their actions as quickly and extensively as possible. In this case the terrorists do not have to make a lot of effort, the media of the countries themselves are already in charge democratic, where freedom of information is guaranteed, to perform that function and cyberspace guarantees its coverage worldwide.

Tallinn Manual. The Tallinn Manual [6] on international law applicable to cyber warfare is not a treaty, but rather it is a non-binding academic study on how the international law in cyber warfare conflicts.

Sponsored by the Cooperative CyberDefense Center of Excellence (CCD-COE, for its acronym in English) of NATO in 2009, the document was in charge of 20 experts in law international. The aim was to reach a consensus on how to interpret international law in the context of cyber wars. The manual consists of a set of more than 200 rules or guidelines, which establish how apply international law to cyber warfare. The document addresses issues such as the use of cyber mercenaries to the attack on the computer systems of units medical. In this way, it establishes when an attack can be considered a violation of the international law in cyberspace, and when and how states can respond to these.

2.3   Decision Making

People, even though the exact result of a decision is unpredictable, decision, we usually follow a marked process by which we end making a decision. There are several models that seek to reflect and divide into different stages of the process with the intention of understanding and helping in the process.

Joint Schematic Form. The following diagram schematically presents the typical decision-making process (aligned with the models of Endsley, Boyd and interaction-based theories). In the he take into account both changes in context and the impact of those changes on the mental effort endured by the individual (Fig. 2).

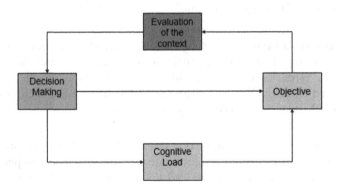

Fig. 2. Joint schematic form for decision making

2.4   Stress

Stress is recognized as a disease, being one of the most widespread today. Despite being so common, we still do not correctly know the causes that trigger it and its consequences. Effects due to its complexity. That is why it continues to be an object of study for numerous medical and psychological professionals. Although there is no full consensus on the theories, we highlight the following:

Response-Based Theories: Initiated by Seyle [10] and Cannon [11], defines stress as the state experienced by a person being exposed to a situation that exceeds the capabilities of their body. The process of coping with this situation is a mechanism called general syndrome adaptation (GSA) and consists of three phases:

– Alarm Reaction: It is the first stage and we can divide it into two sub-phases complementary:
  • Shock phase: the body seeks to defend itself against external action and adopts a defensive posture. The most characteristic symptoms of this stage are tachycardia, decreased temperature, decreased pressure blood and loss of tone.
  • Countershock phase: a complementary response to the shock phase is experienced. above with an equivalent answer, but of opposite sign, that is, hypertension, hyperglycemia, or hyperthermia.
– Resistance Stage: the body adapts to the stimulus and causes the disappearance of the symptoms generated in the previous stage.
– Exhaustion Stage: the body cannot withstand prolonged exposure to a severe stress stimulus. If we subject the organism to this prolonged exposure, we favor the reappearance of the symptoms of the first stage, causing very severe in the body if not corrected in time.

Stimulus-Based Theories: Initiated by Cox [12] defends that stress always comes from a set of stimuli external factors that alter the functioning of the organism. Stress is always something external to the person, contrary to response-based theories. We can group these stimuli external factors into eight categories used today to quantify the level of stress.

Interaction-based Theories: In this theory, the individual adopts a passive role, stress is seen as the result of particular relationships that the person maintains with his environment. Lazarus and Folkman defend in their works [13,14] that the basis of the origin of stress is cognitive evaluation, that is, due to the continuous analysis that people carry out on events and the environment. It is a complex process and is divided into three phases:

– Primary Evaluation: It is the evaluation process carried out by the person in each interaction with some type of demand, both internal and external. It is considered as the first psychological mediator of stress and gives rise to four different modalities of evaluation:

- Threat: used to anticipate possible damage.
- Damage-loss: used to overcome an accomplished damage/threat to the individual.
- Challenge: used to assess those situations in which there is at the same time a possible profit and loss.
- Benefit: used to evaluate all those circumstances whose analysis does not generates a stressful situation in the person.

– Secondary Evaluation: allows the person to value their own resources available to deal with a given situation. This assessment will depend on the personal resources that the individual has to manage the situation.
– Reevaluation: is related to all the feedback mechanisms that are they happen as the interaction between the individual and the stressful situation progresses. Thanks to this stage, the assessments made in the evaluations can be corrected. allowing a much more effective management of the resources available to a person to deal with the situation.

Procedural Model of Stress: With this model (See Fig. 3) proposed by Sandin and Ramos [15], an attempt is made to unite the different theories on the nature of the stress source. This model is structured in seven stages and seeks to organize the interaction of variables that have a direct or indirect relationship with stress.

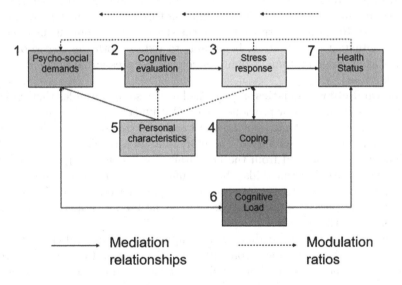

Fig. 3. Procedural model of Stress

With this model proposed by Sandin and Ramos, an attempt is made to unite the different theories on the nature of the stress source. This model is structured in seven stages and seeks to organize the interaction of variables that have a direct or indirect relationship with stress.

- **Psychosocial demands:** reference is made to the external agents that constitute the cause stress primary. These include psychosocial and environmental factors. having the environmental ones more weight than the psychosocial ones. psychosocial factors include, among other things, all situations arising from relationships intrapersonal. Among the environmental factors, or environmental stressors, we can find the natural category (cold, heat, wind, humidity, wind chill...) and artificial (noise, pollution, electromagnetic radiation...).
- **Cognitive evaluation:** it is the cognitive process that the person performs to face the different psychosocial demands that are found and all the threats that result from these claims. It is usually a process conscious and complex in which different variables are evaluated, such as the valence of the threat (positive or negative), the interdependence with other factors, predictability, that is, whether or not a threat can be expected and the level of control or what is the same the level of perception that the person has about the demand psychosocial.
- **Stress response:** measures the individual's response to a threat. They may be physiological or psychological responses, with psychological responses having greater weight in shaping the construction of the stress response. The psychological responses with special relevance are the emotional responses that, in this case, of stress, the most common are anxiety and/or depression.
- **Coping:** is defined as the set of efforts of a behavioral and/or cognitive that the individual uses to deal with the different threats caused by for psychosocial demands. Regardless of the nature of the stressor, the coping helps to change the context of the situation, being able to reduce both the degree of threat such as stress symptoms. Coping is considered a essential element to cope with stress.
- **Personal characteristics:** it is defined as the set of variables that influence transversely in the four previous stages. Within these variables we can differentiate two large groups, on the one hand, the characteristics derived from the character or personality of the individual and, on the other hand, those characteristics derived from the hereditary factors such as gender and race. People can use different skills, abilities and resources to deal with potentially stressful based on this set of variables. Depending on how an individual is able to use these resources will determine the level of impact of the agents stressors on the person.
- **Social characteristics:** they are a complement to personal characteristics. The most relevant are socioeconomic level, social support and currently social networks. The diagram shows social support, alluding to all those actions carried out in favor of an individual by third parties such as friends, family, colleagues... This support is highly conditioned by the networks due to the growth it has had in recent years and refers to the fraction of the social network that the individual actually uses to cope with problems and difficulties of life. Furthermore, in the case of social support, the effects of perceived social support are more significant than those of received social support.

– **State of health:** it depends directly on all of the above, as it is the result end of it. Health status is defined as a state of health at the psychological and physiological that a person has.

2.5 Effect of Cognitive State

We understand by survival situation that in which an individual finds himself in a generally unknown and adverse environment in which he must subsist with the resources that provides the terrain and the situation, maintaining the psychophysical conditions necessary for survive [16].

There are some basic rules in survival that mark the physical limitations for humans:

– Humans are able to survive up to three weeks without food.
– Humans are able to survive up to three days without water.
– Humans are able to survive up to three minutes without air.

To these three basic rules we can add the following:

– Humans can lose their life in three seconds in case of not making the right decision.

There are certain factors related to the psychological state that condition the way we confront the situation. Among them we find anxiety, fear, guilt, irritability, loneliness or depression, among others. Also, there are physiological conditions such as thirst, tiredness or pain.

3 Biometric Systems

In order to measure the factors that determine the state of a person we can use biometric systems. These quantify the physiological response that a person gives in different contexts (for example, when they feel stressed or overwhelmed). There are different types of biometric systems: GSR, ECG, EEG, BCI, changes in body temperature, changes in face etc. Which will be explained below. Keep in mind that each person reacts differently to situations, that is why a previous study of the individual is required for an optimal interpretation of the data obtained.

Electroencephalography: In this work we will focus on the study of brain waves through the capture of electricity produced by the brain.

Systems oriented to this approach have a good temporal resolution and a large ability to study cognitive load and emotions knowing the parts of the brain that are activated. These systems work by means of electrodes, these being sensitive to noise by the small movements, skin condition (sweating, hair). Furthermore, we must add the complexity of the brain, so it requires a lot of training and knowledge. Currently, Brain-Computer Interfaces (BCI) are booming, and that is why in this paper will study the cognitive state by means of a. It allows us to establish a channel of communication between a physical device and our brain, communicating and being able to control them through brain signals [17].

3.1 Brain Computer Interface

One of the challenges that arises when knowing the state of a person is to convert the physiological responses into data that we can manipulate. Our brain emits waves of different frequency depending on the region and the type of action we perform. [7–9]

Delta (1–4 Hz): Present during deep sleep and dominate in the brain of the children. Wide-length, rhythmic delta waves are found usually in adults with mental disorders or brain injuries In addition to being present in children with attention deficit and disorders of hyperactivity.

Theta (4–8 Hz): Occur during states of deep meditation, yoga or in academic learning processes. They are related to high levels of creativity, emotions and spontaneity of the person, but by presenting excessive amounts of this type of waves can determine that the person could be depressed, suffer from "daydreaming", may also have attention deficit disorder or feel distracted.

Alpha (8–12 Hz): Associated with states of relaxation. The absence of these types of waves can be associated with states of stress or nervousness

Beta (12–30 Hz): Recorded when the person is awake and fully active mental. When we find ourselves in situations of stress, anxiety or fear, a high amount of Beta waves is normally experienced.

4 Research Problem

The current type of war is based on a hybrid model [18] in which it seeks to alter the state cognitive function of the person in order to get him to act in a certain way. It is therefore that the need to control and know what we are facing when we meet in the face of a situation that seeks to alter our state. In this work, the problem of creating an environment that aims to change a person's status and see how it affects their decision making. For this we must obtain the necessary data through a Brain-Computer Interface [2] and, in addition, know Analyze what they mean. It is necessary to establish a connection between the machine that supports this environment with the machine where the data is collected. It is also proposed to establish a relationship between the variations of the values obtained by the headband and decisions made by the participant in the exercise, for example, checking if for high values of some type of wave, one tends to consume a track or consult the Internet. Actions such as consuming a track or using the internet are usually indicators that the user is blocked and cannot continue, this model seeks to infer their degree of stress in those moments thanks to the reading and interpretation of their brain waves.

5   Design of the Cognitive Assessment Model

For this research, a methodology has been designed in which several functionalities at the same time, giving rise to a system that monitors in real time during the perform an exercise, send records to a machine, and then assess the results (Fig. 4).

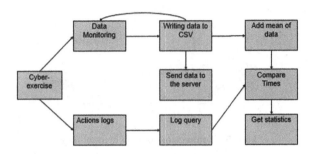

Fig. 4. Cognitive assessment model

The diagram shows the operation of the model, which starts from a realization of a cyberexercise while the participant's biometric signals are monitored. The actions that the participant takes in carrying out the test are recorded for later query. Once the exercise is finished, the record that has been kept during the performance is consulted of the exercise and is compared with the collected data, at that moment we proceed to the correlation of dates to check values at certain times. Having compared the dates, we obtain an assessment of the values at a time specific compared to the total average of that value for the entire exercise.

Headband Connection: Before getting the data, the program will search for a valid connection to the headset. For This will use the program BlueMuse [19] which allows us to have a channel established communication with the headband via Bluetooth.

Data Monitoring: To obtain data, a Python program [3] that uses the Muse SDK will be adapted. The values of some buffers will be consulted, which will be updated with the signals received from Diadem. Thanks to this program we obtain the raw values directly from the band or applying the Fourier transform for the values comprised within a period of time (epoch). These data will be displayed on the screen to facilitate verification of the correct operation at all times while they are written in a CSV type file along with a timestamp and the type of wave it is. At the end of the exercise, the mean for each wave type will be added to the CSV. With this we can compare the measurements at a given time with the total average of the exercise.

Sending Data to the Server: Thanks to RsyslogAgent [20] we can configure that everything that is written in a document sent to the machine where the exercise is performed to centralize the logs and be able to keep track of record about them. This communication will be encrypted using SSL/TLS with the certificates corresponding ones that have been generated (Fig. 5).

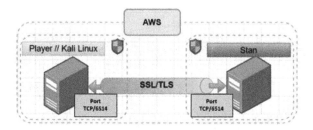

Fig. 5. Connection between machines

Actions Log and Query: During the performance of the exercise, the actions carried out by the player are recorded. through Learning Locker [21] for later consultation. Each action is registered with a specific type of verb [22]. For this work we will focus mainly on the verb "asked" which indicates having asked for help to solve the exercise. Thanks to Learning Locker we obtain a complete record of all the actions that the participant has carried out during the exercise. Once the exercise is over, we can make a query to the server so that it return the events whose verb is "asked" and we can store them together with their date for its subsequent comparison with the data obtained in the exercise.

Scenery: An Indra scanning exercise will be used, made up of a series of exercises on the use from Nmap. An exercise will be displayed in the browser in which the participant will have a remote machine accessible also from the browser. Before performing the exercise, will provide the participant with an introductory module on the use of Nmap.

Staging: This section is divided into three stages:

- Before: the participant will be provided with a document in the that you will be given information about the exercise, as well as the necessary requirements for its realization. In addition to the biometrics data processing consent document. The participant will be explained how to put on the headband.
- During: the performance of the exercise will be supervised, checking at all times that the headband is correctly positioned and connected. All help will also be offered possible to the participant, always within the limits of the exercise.

– After: A copy of the results obtained will be made for security. Then thanks the participant for their collaboration. Next, it will proceed to the evaluation of the results.

Interpretation of the Data Obtained: Once the exercise is done, we obtain the CSV filled with the measurements every second for each type of wave and, on the other hand, we will have the Learning Locker with the registered actions that we can check. We store in a list the data obtained from the headband and in a different one those obtained by querying the server. Once we have both lists, we compare the times to correlate events. When two dates coincide, we calculate the average of each type of wave to that moment and the previous ten seconds and that average is compared with the total average of the exercise for each type of wave, thus being able to assess the variation in the state of a person before resorting to asking for a hint.

6 Experiments and Results

6.1 Validation Proposal

In order to study the effect of the cognitive state on decision making, the use of a scenario is proposed in which a participant is subjected to a series of cyber-exercises or challenges in which it is intended to modify their state, for example, by performing a complex exercise itself together with different effectors. Throughout this process, the participant to observe changes in their status by means of a BCI and check the relationship that has with the different decisions that can be made in an exercise, such as ask for a hint.

For this process, Indra's CBR platform will be used, specifically an exercise on Scanning in which, to begin with, a small summary exercise will be proposed about how Nmap works.

Once the module is finished, the exercise on scanning will be carried out. For this, the participant is provided with an environment in the browser where they are proposed in order the questions, you need to answer correctly to move on to the next one. Remote access to a Kali machine is provided to the participant also via the browser in which it will perform the necessary actions to obtain the correct answer to each Question. Before starting, the participant is given a document with information on the requirements for carrying out the exercise, in addition to formally requesting consent to the collection of biometric data.

6.2 Tests and Validation

Tests have been carried out on different participant profiles, for the assessment of the state will take into account the variations obtained in the report. The brain emits Alpha type waves when it is in a state of relaxation and Beta-type when in a state of concentration, therefore, in order to determine if a person may be in a situation of stress, we can consult and Evaluate the values of these two types of wave, looking for low values of Alpha and high values of Beta. Theta type wave emission can provide us with interesting information, although it is a type of wave related to states of deep meditation or yoga, is also related to learning, so higher values of this type of wave could mean that the participant is learning something new during the exercise.

The evolution of each type of wave will be assessed in the moments before and after requesting a hint or other moments that could be a stressful situations for the participant, which will be indicated by a vertical red line.

We can obtain graphs that collect the values of each type of wave during the exercise, such as (Fig. 6):

α

Fig. 6. Alpha wave graph

β

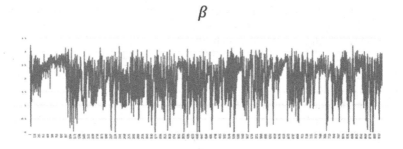

Fig. 7. Beta wave graph

These graphs can help us to deduce the state of the participant in a particular moment. That is represented in the next graph, and to clarify the different states:

- **Nervous:** low alpha values and high beta values.
- **Focused:** high alpha values and high beta values.
- **Distracted:** high alpha values and low beta values.

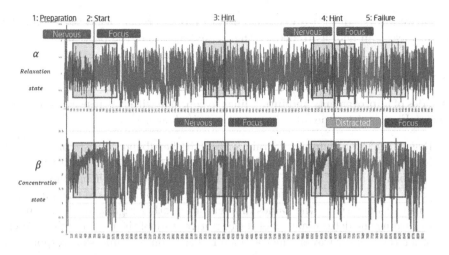

Fig. 8. Analysis of brain waves

Given these graphs we can see that in the moments before making a decision, the values obtained vary.

We can see how, in the first moment that correspond to the begging of the exercise where the player is introduced to what he is going to do. If we observe the values of the waves we can deduce that at this moment the participant was getting nervous.

In the second moment the exercise as such begins and it can be seen how the participant stopped being nervous to be focused.

In the third and fourth moment, the same pattern is repeated, the participant goes from being nervous to focused by requesting a hint.

In the fifth moment, it can be seen how, being distracted, he failed a question and returned to focusing on the exercise.

6.3   Conclusions

In this work, the current state of cybersecurity in the military field has been reviewed, in addition to give the vision that the military doctrine has on cyberspace. The importance has been stated stress and how it influences decision-making, all oriented to an environment operational. A validation model of the cognitive state has been designed in which it is intended to study if There is some relationship between certain actions and the brain waves we emit. In this particular case, a cyberexercise platform provided by Indra's Cyberrange, which proposes a challenge to a player through a series of exercises about networks. During the performance of this test, different profiles of person, all of them with some knowledge on the subject. Regarding the validation of the model, a series of graphs (See Fig. 7) have been exposed that, analyzed, They show us that at certain moments that in principle suppose more stress for us, the brain emits certain types of waves. Thanks to the graph (See Fig. 8) we can validate that when we are faced with a decision, we are more nervous or stressed, and the brain waves can help us to deduce the cognitive state of the participant.

6.4   Future Lines

A series of improvements and future lines to continue with this research is defined below. First, a list of possible improvements is shown:

- Regarding the obtaining of brain waves, the headband consists of 4 sensors from which we obtain the total value for each type of wave. With this same headband we can differentiate between the values of each hemisphere of the brain, but for more accurate measurements could be increased the number of sensors to determine the values differentiating other regions of the brain.
- Regarding the determination of the cognitive state of the person, other meters other than brain waves, such as meters based on galvanic skin response or thermal imaging.
- When doing the exercise, more verbs can be consulted than previously commented, thus being able to consult various actions and not only asking for a hint.
- As an improvement to the validation of the participant's status, it is proposed to carry out a study prior to it in different circumstances, thus being able to draw more precise.

Secondly, a series of possibilities are proposed along this line. Thanks to the fact that we have a reading of the waves together with an assessment of the variation at a given time, we can use it for diversity of ideas, for example:

- A system could be developed that, depending on the variation in a moment determined or when detecting high levels of a certain type of wave, sample one way or another the information on a screen, thus facilitating the assimilation of information and decision making by an individual.
- Following the operation of the previous point, a system could be developed that alert an individual, be it a soldier on the battlefield or the high command taking strategic decisions, if a considerable variation is detected in the values of the readings, thus being able to facilitate the knowledge of the state of oneself and helping to return to an optimal state for decision making, trying to lower the levels of stress or any state that interferes with reasoning. It can also be used as a tool to help evaluation by third parties.

Acknowledgements.

 This research has received funding from the European Defence Industrial Development Programme (EDIDP) under the grant agreement Number EDIDP-CSAMN-SSC-2019-022-ECYSAP (European Cyber Situational Awareness Platform).

References

1. Ministerio de Defensa España: Doctrina para el empleo de las FAS. Ministerio de Defensa, Madrid (2018)
2. Muse 2: Brain Sensing headband - technology enhanced meditation. https://choosemuse.com/muse-2/
3. Mutyala, A.: BCI-web-browsing: using EEG artefacts alongside focus metrics to manipulate a web browser. https://github.com/anmutechsupport/BCI-Web-Browsing
4. Ministerio del Interior Gobierno de España, Estudio sobre la cibercriminalidad en España (2020)
5. ATENEA Platform. https://www.ccn-cert.cni.es/soluciones-seguridad/atenea.html
6. NATO Cooperative Cyber Defence Centre of Excellence (CCDCOE): Tallinn Manual. https://ccdcoe.org/research/tallinn-manual/
7. Neurofeedback: Qué son las ondas cerebrales? https://www.neurofeedback.cat/que-son-las-ondas-cerebrales/
8. Ali, O.: et al.: Human emotion detection via brain waves study by using electroencephalogram (2016)
9. Koudelková, Z., et al.: Analysis of brain waves according to their frequency (2018)
10. Selye, H.: The Stress of Life. McGraw-Hill Book Co., New York (1956)
11. Cannon, W.B.: The Wisdom of the Body. Harvey's Work, New York (1932)
12. Cox, T.: Stress: A review of theories, causes and effects of stress in the light of empirical research (1978)
13. Lazarus, R.S., Folkman, S.: Stress, Appraisal, and Coping. Springer, Heidelberg (1984)
14. Lazarus, R.S.: Coping theory and research: past, present, and future. In: Fifty Years of the Research and Theory of RS Lazarus: An Analysis of Historical and Perennial Issues, pp. 366–388 (1993)
15. Belloch, A., et al.: Manual de psicopatología (2008)
16. Martinez Sánchez, J.A.: Aspectos psicológicos de la supervivencia en operaciones militares (2011)
17. Van Gerven, M., et al.: The brain-computer interface cycle. J. Neural Eng. 6, 041001 (2009)
18. Eissa, S.G.: Guerra Híbrida: una nueva forma de pensar la guerra en el siglo XXI? (2011)
19. Kowalej: Kowalej/BlueMuse: Windows 10 app to stream data from Muse EEG headsets via LSL (lab streaming layer). https://github.com/kowalej/BlueMuse
20. Rsyslog Windows Agent. https://www.rsyslog.com/windows-agent/
21. Learning Locker. https://docs.learninglocker.net/
22. Locker, L.: xAPI Appendix. https://help.csod.com/help/csod/Content/Catalog/
23. Sandoval Rodríguez-Bermejo, D., Maestre Vidal, J., Estévez Tapiador, J.M.: Framework proposal to measure the stress as adversarial factor on cyber decision making. In: Katsikas, S., et al. (eds.) ESORICS 2021. LNCS, vol. 13106, pp. 517–536. Springer, Cham (2021). https://doi.org/10.1007/978-3-030-95484-0_30

Design and Validation of a Threat Model Based on Cyber Kill Chain Applied to Human Factors

Inés Hernández San Román[1]([⊠])[iD], Marco Antonio Sotelo Monge[2][iD], and Víctor A. Villagra[1][iD]

[1] Universidad Politécnica de Madrid, Avda. Complutense 30, 28040 Madrid, Spain
ihsan@indra.es
[2] Indra, Av. de Bruselas 35, 28108 Madrid, Spain

Abstract. This document's purpose is to study the impact of the cognitive domain in cybersecurity as a field, including its implications in cyberdefense and cyberspace, a domain that has gained traction in the last years due to the growing use of new technologies in everyday life. In addition, the investigation will focus on humans' cognitive biases, how they influence decision making and how an hypothetical malicious individual could use these intrinsic vulnerabilities of the human mind in their favor to push misinformation campaigns, elaborate social engineering attacks or manipulate other people. Finally, a Cyber Kill Chain will be elaborated with the aim to illustrate the steps that the aforementioned attacker could take in order to achieve their goals successfully. The designed methodology will also be tested in a real-life scenario and will be validated by experts in the fields of cybersecurity and psychology.

Keywords: Cyber Kill Chain · Cognitive biases · Cybersecurity · Misinformation · Social engineering · Cognitive domain · Cyberspace

1 Introduction

Cybersecurity has gained increasing relevance in the last years, as it went from being of anecdotic importance to being one of the most critical requirements in software products and companies alike.

Tasks that were previously done by hand or on paper are now managed by an information system. As years go by, more and more businesses depend on a web page or social media to promote themselves, sell their products or reach out to possible clients. This dependence also implies that personal, medical or financial information of millions of people around the world are stored in these systems and, if protected incorrectly, exposed to potential threats.

In a situation like this, information security - cybersecurity - ended up playing a vital role in this scenario, since this information and its intrinsic value is of interest for vast amounts of cybercriminals who, through many methods, may try to use such data for their own benefits.

S. Katsikas et al. (Eds.): ESORICS 2022 Workshops, LNCS 13785, pp. 482–499, 2023.
https://doi.org/10.1007/978-3-031-25460-4_28

Perhaps the most known threat in cybersecurity is malware: malicious code that, once it has penetrated a machine, is able to steal information, encrypt documents or grant almost unlimited access to the system to the attacker who created it.

However, it is also notable that purely technical threats are not the only issue that modern cybersecurity has to tackle. Social engineering, for example, is a fundamental link in the chain that comprises the full scope of a possible cyberattack, and its target is not a machine, but a human being.

Therefore, we stand before a scenario in which people, with their own cognitive vulnerabilities, are a crucial factor to keep in mind not only to avoid malware dissemination, but also when considering attacks that involve misinformation, manipulation, impersonation, and so on.

With this in mind the objectives that this document intends to achieve are:

- To demonstrate that an attack that targets cognitive vulnerabilities has identifiable and definable phases
- To demonstrate that these phases can be extrapolated to a real case scenario
- To observe which cognitive biases are responsible for the success of social engineering attacks, misinformation campaigns, cognitive dominance, etcetera.

2 Background

2.1 Cognitive Biases

The study of cognitive biases and their influence in reasoning and a human being's capacity to make a decision has been a field of interest not only from the perspective of traditional psychology, but also from fields like marketing, military operations or cybersecurity. On the one hand, psychology has focused in a concept known as cognitive bias, which was proposed by Kahneman and Tversky in 1972 [1]. Cognitive biases are defined as a systematic pattern of deviation from norm or rationality in judgement [2] and are responsible for the creation of subjective realities intrinsic to an individual, and which do not correspond with objective reality. These biases also can cause the apparition of prejudice, irrational decision making or exposing the subject to manipulation.

On the other hand, the marketing field exploited these findings in order to boost sales and convince the customer to buy products he or she would not usually find useful or interesting. For example, this kind of manipulation was extensively investigated by psychologist Robert Cialdini. In his paper *Influence, the psychology of persuasion* [3], he analyzes seven principles which can persuade an individual if used correctly. And some of them are as simple as making the other person believe they are being offered a scarce good, gain his or her favor by pretending to be the kind of person this individual may feel affinity towards, among others. However, these principles are not entirely independent from the aforementioned cognitive biases, since in many cases they rely on those biases to work or an equivalence exist in one way or another. To illustrate this, a comparative table (Table 1) has been created below. On the left column are the seven principles proposed by Cialdini along with a brief description; while on the right column, the cognitive biases they are related to will be specified:

Therefore, it has been observed that most of Cialdini's principles are not foreign to psychology or to the biases present in the human mind, but rather, they are a consequence and/or a conceptualization more understandable for the general public.

In the military field, the cognitive domain has been added as one of the operational strategic domains along with the already-known domains such as air, land, maritime, space or cyberspace. This addition was carried out by well known organizations such as NATO in 2020 [16] and is considered as of high importance for future military operations [17].

Finally, in cybersecurity the exploitation of cognitive vulnerabilities has acquired a more notorious role as a result of social engineering and fraudulent campaigns, and because of their usefulness to deceive and manipulate system users to perform actions that benefit the cybercriminal and put in danger their devices or their company's. These social engineering attacks can take the form of phishing, spear-phishing or whaling, or even malware campaigns such as ransomware or scareware.

2.2   Cybersecurity in the Military Field and NATO

As mentioned in previous sections, cybersecurity is an area that is constantly growing due to the importance that new technologies are acquiring in all the different aspects of social and political reality. This includes, of course, the military sphere, terrorism and the need to protect infrastructures that are crucial for the proper functioning of society or that, if they do not function correctly, could cause the loss of human lives. They are what is known as critical infrastructures.

With that in mind, a new battlefield emerged: cyberspace. Thus, the term cyber-defense also appeared and cyberspace was integrated as a new domain for NATO in 2016 [18].

However, the disparity in existing legislation amongst different countries made it necessary to reach a consensus on how international laws should be interpreted in the event of cyberwarfare. Due to this, in 2013 the so-called "Tallinn Manual" was published in honor of the capital of Estonia, the country where the first cyberattack from one country to another took place. This manual is not a normative document, but rather, lays the foundations for the establishment of a series of proportional countermeasures in the event of a cyber attack and provides a better understanding of when an incident in cyberspace can be considered a violation of international law.

This manual was commissioned by the NATO Cooperative Cyber Defense Center of Excellence (CCDCOE) and required the collaboration of a large group of independent experts and more than three years of research into international law [19].

Table 1. Cialdini principles and cognitive biases

Cialdini principle	Related bias(es)
Principle of reciprocity: *If someone has been given a gift or done a favor, they are more likely to accept an offer or be willing to reciprocate*	–
Principle of scarcity: *A person is more likely to accept a proposal or purchase a product if they believe that it is unique and/or limited in time*	Related to the **scarcity heuristic** [4], in which it is stipulated that a person tends to give more value or importance to an element if it is scarce. In addition, this principle often seeks to take advantage of the fact that when a person is forced to make a decision in a short period of time the tendency to carry out that process in an way which is based on intuition rather than logic increases, which is associated with increased biased reasoning [5]. It is also somewhat related to the **loss aversion bias** [6], in which a person perceives a loss as more impactful than a gain, even though objectively the value is the same. In this case, the loss would be the supposed offer and/or the greater amount of money that would have to be paid for having missed the opportunity
Principle of authority: *Confidence in a person who is or appears to be an authority due to their attire or how they are presented by a third party*	Related to the **authority bias** [7,8], in which the opinion of someone who appears as an authority is given more importance or credibility, compared to people who do not have this status
Principle of unity: *It appeals to the desire to belong to a group. If the individual feels that he is part of a project, he will be involved and collaborate more effectively*	Similar to the principle of liking
Cialdini principle	Related bias(es)
Principle of consistency: *If a person has agreed to perform an activity, they are more likely to continue performing actions related to it. It can be applied incrementally*	This principle is closely related to the **escalation of commitment and irrational escalation biases** [9]. These biases explain why an individual is capable of maintaining behaviors that could be classified as irrational and that produce adverse effects for them simply because they are aligned with decisions or actions carried out previously. The initial decision may have been made rationally, but subsequent ones may be motivated solely to justify the first choice made. In the example provided by Cialdini, there are no mentions of the possibility of using this method to force the subject to make decisions that are unfavorable to them, but it could equally be applied to these cases depending on the intentions or moral code of the person who is being manipulative
Principle of liking: *It is more likely that someone will agree to a request made by an individual who is likable to them, either due to similarity, because they have been flattered by them or because they consider that they cooperate for the same goal*	This principle is related to the **in-group favoritism bias** [10], which explains how people tend to favor individuals they consider to be similar to them or belonging to the same group. In Cialdini's principle of favoritism, the goal is to find a shared characteristic or demonstrating that both subjects have a common objective. This way, it will be more likely that the person to be persuaded considers the other interlocutor as "one of their own" and will be more willing to accept their requests or agree with them. This principle can also be used to some extent to combat the **reactive devaluation bias** [11,12] and the bias known as **not invented here** [13], in which a product or idea is rejected because it comes from abroad or from someone considered as an enemy
Principle of social proof: *If an action has been done by others before, it is more likely that more people will be encouraged to do it too*	This principle is related to the **bandwagon effect** [14,15], where a person is more likely to perform an action simply because other people did too

3   State of the Art

3.1   Related Works

To prepare this document, diverse bibliography regarding biases, how they influence decision-making and how they are used from various disciplines has been consulted, as well as the appearance of the Cyber Kill Chain concept and its adaptation from the military world to computer security.

Cognitive Domain in Marketing

Marketing is perhaps one of the fields in which most research has been conducted to try to obtain economic profit by taking advantage of the biases of the human mind and behavior. For example, Robert Cialdini stands out with his two works *Influence: Science and Practice* [20] and *Influence, the psychology of persuasion* [3], where he also states how with an appropriate approach and creating an ideal scenario in the eyes of a potential client, it is possible to manipulate their behavior in a way that works in the most beneficial way for the seller.

On the other hand, authors such as Shaun B. Spencer in *The Problem of Online Manipulation* [21] delve deeper into this concept, separating it from purely traditional marketing and also linking it to the IT field, placing special emphasis on the growing activity of manipulation and exploitation of these cognitive biases in social media when suggesting content, even in real time.

Cognitive Domain and War

If the relevance of cybersecurity in the military field was previously mentioned, we have situations in which the cognitive domain has also managed to be a fundamental pillar in armed confrontations throughout history. The contribution of Yalçınkaya, Haldun et al. in the work *Good practices in counter terrorism* [22], for example, mentions how terrorist groups have taken advantage of cyberspace and cognitive domination to cause panic among the population and how systems must be protected to prevent intrusions by these groups.

On the other hand, in multiple publications of the US Army, information operations are clearly discussed, and how they can be used to manipulate both civil and military population for various purposes, including modifying beliefs, behaviors, striking fear and establishing influence.

Cyber Kill Chain Origins

Finally, it is known that the original Kill Chains had their origin in the military field, where the phases that had to be followed from the sighting of a target to its destruction were described.

This concept was adapted to computing by Lockheed Martin and its development can be seen in the document *Intelligence-Driven Computer Network Defense Reported by Analysis of Adversary Campaigns and Intrusion Kill Chains* [23]. This version had the phases of Reconnaissance, Weaponization, Delivery,

Exploitation, Installation, Command and Control (C2) and Actions on Objectives; to then define technical response modes for each of these phases and offer modes of analysis of a possible campaign, as seen in Fig. 1.

Phase	Detect	Deny	Disrupt	Degrade	Deceive	Destroy
Reconnaissance	Web analytics	Firewall ACL				
Weaponization	NIDS	NIPS				
Delivery	Vigilant user	Proxy filter	In-line AV	Queuing		
Exploitation	HIDS	Patch	DEP			
Installation	HIDS	"chroot" jail	AV			
C2	NIDS	Firewall ACL	NIPS	Tarpit	DNS redirect	
Actions on Objectives	Audit log			Quality of Service	Honeypot	

Fig. 1. Response modes matrix by Lockheed Martin

3.2   Research Problem

The cognitive state, as previously mentioned, is considered a new field of vital importance in various areas due to the ability it gives a possible actor, malicious or not, to influence the decisions and opinions of one or more individuals. That is why this research seeks to evaluate how this manipulation can be carried out, on what premises it is based on from a psychological point of view and what "vulnerabilities" inherent in the functioning of the mind are being exploited. This will be done through the study of the different existing cognitive biases and the subsequent elaboration of a Cyber Kill Chain, which is the representation of a series of steps or procedures to be followed by a potential cybercriminal to complete an attack successfully.

However, this representation until now had been based on technical elements, leaving the human factor as a mere detail in a much larger scheme focused on machines. In short, it could be said that there is no Cyber Kill Chain that evaluates the exploitation phases of cognitive vulnerabilities. That is why, in this research, it is intended to propose a Cyber Kill Chain dedicated exclusively to analyzing attacks that target human beings, as well as showing what they are based on and in what ways these vulnerabilities are currently being exploited.

4   Methodology

The proposed Cyber Kill Chain is based on those elaborated by Lockheed Martin [23] and MITRE ATT&CK [24], but adapted to the human scenario that it is intended to illustrate. To do this, the phases originally proposed by the aforementioned entities have been changed for those of reconnaissance, weaponization, distribution or delivery, expansion and persistence; which will be explained in more detail below.

4.1   Cyber Kill Chain Structure

Below, Fig. 2 portrays a schematic representation of the proposed Cyber Kill Chain, including the phases that will be described later:

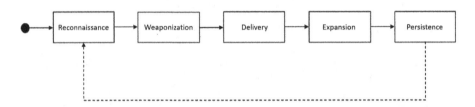

Fig. 2. Proposed methodology

4.2   Reconnaissance Phase

In this phase, the main objective is to carry out an in-depth analysis of the person or persons who you want to attack. In addition, it will be interesting to consider the following questions: Do you want to attack an individual, a group or a society as a whole? In what social, historical, cultural and/or legal context are we working? It will also be convenient to take into account factors such as age, gender and/or level of education, since these play a fundamental role in how to approach the target and give clues about the knowledge or biases that the individual may have on the subject of interest for the attack. For example, an older person is less likely to have advanced knowledge about the Internet, social media or technology when compared to a young individual between 18 and 30 years old. In the same way, someone with a lower level of education might be more likely to fall for deception or hoaxes than a person with higher education or well versed in a certain subject. In short: the more specific the objective, the more complexity and depth it requires.

4.3   Weaponization Phase

In this phase, the most optimal way to proceed is evaluated and the attack method is decided based on the information collected in the previous phase.

With a correct analysis of the victim, it will be possible to determine what biases are intended to be exploited with the attack, what type of campaign is more optimal, the attack vector to be used (social media, email, etc.) or if the specific target has some intrinsic vulnerability that has been detected in the reconnaissance phase. This last point is especially relevant in attacks on a single individual, and can be very useful when proceeding with attacks that imply familiarity with the victim (spear-phishing, whaling) or that involve some type of extortion.

4.4 Delivery Phase

In this phase the selected target or targets receive the attack. At this point there are two possible outcomes:

- Attack directed at a single individual: the success or failure of the attack is immediate, since it is possible for us to observe if they respond to it and how. If the offensive is successful, the Kill Chain ends.
- Broad-spectrum attack: in this case, we will need the attack to spread to other people to achieve the desired effect. Therefore, it will continue to the next phase. Given the nature of this type of attacks, the more targets there are, the more likely it is to succeed, since the probability of one of the links in the chain failing is greater.

4.5 Expansion Phase

The attack expands to other targets that were not necessarily part of the initial target group. The effectiveness of this phase is especially notable in attacks that make use of social media to reach the maximum number of targets, given the huge amount of people that use them nowadays. These networks are also composed by users from all kinds of backgrounds and demographics. In this way, it is possible to take advantage of the effect of biases such as the **anchoring bias** [25–27] , **confirmation bias** [28] **and/or availability cascade bias** [29] to gain an advantage over possible official versions and successfully begin to cause a distortion of the dominant narrative. Thus, the creation of alternative narratives start and those users known as "useful idiots' begin to not only believe the manipulated information provided to them, but also help spread it and defend it against possible detractors (**belief perseverance** [30]).

4.6 Persistence Phase

The attack has reached an extensive set of targets and has generated an impact on them. Therefore, it is in the attacker's interest to maintain the control they managed to establish in the previous phase. However, given that the attack has reached a very broad sector of society, it is very likely that there will be attempts by public institutions and fact checkers to dismantle the attacker's campaign. Therefore, it is proposed that this Cyber Kill Chain has the possibility to feedback itself. That is, taking into account the counterattack attempts of the institutions, the attacker can reanalyze the narrative that is trying to be sent to the population and develop a new campaign that helps not only to support the initial campaign, but also to undermine the credibility of the genuine information sources.

Thus, doubt and distrust can arise and people may adopt equidistant opinions regarding current or future information. Also, that distrust of official news could be accentuated in favor of other more palatable ones, which support the reader's pre-existing beliefs (**confirmation bias** [28]). In addition, the "useful idiots" will probably help maintain the established control and spread the new fabricated information; favoring the fact that, in the face of a dominant narrative, people have the tendency to avoid conflicts and go against the social majority, which provokes the silence of possible dissidents (**groupthink bias** [31]).

5   Case Study

Next, a case study based on a real situation will be analyzed, to later relate it to the designed Cyber Kill Chain and define its correspondence with each of its phases. More specifically, the event that will be analyzed will be the presidential elections that took place in the United States of America in 2016, where politicians Donald J. Trump and Hillary Clinton, among others, competed for the presidency of the country. The main reason for choosing this case is the international controversy that was generated as a result of the apparition of voices claiming that the electorate had been manipulated through the dissemination of what is known as "fake news".

This document is not intended to confirm or deny the existence of such actions, make attributions or relate them to the victory or defeat of the aforementioned candidates. It will simply consider it as a real scenario to show a possible use of the Cyber Kill Chain and its phases, with the aim of illustrating its usefulness in a scenario of this kind and how it fits into the proposed theoretical framework.

5.1   Experimental Background

For the preparation of this research, sources related to the use of social bots as a means to spread links to false news and their integration into the social fabric of networks have been consulted [32]. Along with statistics on the use of the Internet and social networks as a means of obtaining election news by the US adult population [33], a research indicating how much these articles were shared in relation to legitimate ones [34] and a comparative analysis of which news were shared, which political and social profile could have a higher tendency to believe false information, the possible impact of this wave of misinformation on election results, among others [35].

In these documents, we can see that approximately 62% of American adults admitted that they read news on social networks (Gottfried and Shearer 2016).

This information is especially relevant when taking into consideration that the most prevalent and profitable means of spreading misinformation are social media pages such as Facebook or Twitter, and that websites with content classified as fake news obtain up to 42% of their visits from them, as shown in Fig. 3 (Alcott and Gentzkow 2017).

In fact, it is known that the most popular fake news were shared even more than those belonging to the so-called mainstream media (Silverman 2016).

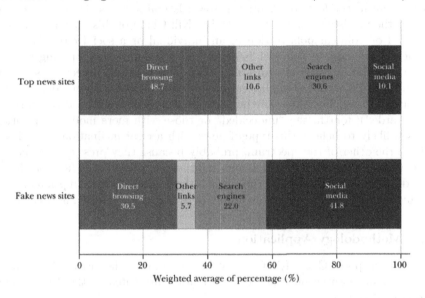

Fig. 3. Visits to fake news webpages by origin

Bessi and Ferrara (2016), specifically, analyzed this phenomenon focusing on Twitter and the bots that shared this type of content on its website, analyzing the general activity during three periods that spanned from September 16th to 24th (before the start of debates), from September 26th to October 10th (which includes the first two presidential debates and the vice presidential one on October 4th and 5th) and, finally, from October 17th to 21st (third and last presidential debate). As expected, we can see an increase in the activity of human users in the second period. However, this increase is also noticeable in the tweets produced by bots, going from 10% of the total content of the network in the first period to a total of 19% of tweets during the second one. In addition, these bots seem to integrate quite successfully into the social fabric of the network, becoming hubs for news broadcasting and being shared by both other bots and human users. Likewise, they show a prevalent tendency to emit positive tweets towards the candidate they are programmed to favor. As a consequence, these authors consider that this phenomenon could distort the perception of voters about how much genuine support one politician or another is really receiving, being related to biases already mentioned in this document such as **groupthink bias or the bandwagon effect.**

On the other hand, the research by Allcott and Gentzkov (2017) reveals the following data: first, that users were 15% more likely to give credibility to fake news if it aligned with their ideology, regardless of whether they were Democrats or Republicans (**confirmation bias**) and that this phenomenon was even more powerful for users whose social networks were ideologically segregated (echo chamber); second, that the presence of fake news could cause a decrease in users' trust in the mass media (especially among users with a republican ideology) and an increase in the level of skepticism towards real news (a detail that can be seen in the persistence phase of the Cyber Kill Chain of this document); third, the level of political polarization of an individual or a social circle is related to their willingness to believe fake news that go against the opposing political group (**confirmation bias and reactive devaluation**, especially since the definition of polarization implies negative feelings towards those considered as political enemies. Therefore, any information that is interpreted as contrary will be discarded); fourth, the "undecided" or those with more moderate positions are less likely to believe this type of news with a clear inclination towards one side or the other of the spectrum, probably because they present more neutral feelings towards each of the candidates and their supporters; and fifth, the higher the educational level, the older the age and the greater the consumption of news, the more capable users are of discerning between real and false information.

5.2 Methodology Application

Next, the proposed Cyber Kill Chain will be tested with the case study explained above, taking into account all the information presented in the *Experimental background* section.

Reconaissance Phase

In this phase, the process of studying the target would begin. In this particular case, we are facing a scenario of presidential elections in the US, so the first step will be to decide which of the two candidates one wants to favor. For the study of this scenario, it will be assumed that the attacker plans to use bots dedicated to spreading false news with the aim of favoring the Republican candidate Donald Trump and that, in addition, after noticing the rise of social media as a means to carry out discussions and political debates between users of both spectra, they will decide to use these networks to expand and give even more notoriety to the information manufactured for his interest.

Once this is done, they will study the audience they wish to address. Given that the electorate is made up of a heterogeneous group of people in terms of age, culture, gender, etc., the focus will be on their ideology. Therefore, the campaign's cornerstone will be to determine if a user leans more toward Republican or Democratic ideals.

In social media web pages such as Twitter, for example, this can be done by analyzing the keywords or hashtags used by each individual, since during the election campaign period there were specific tags that allowed us to know if a tweet intended to support (#trump2016, #trumppence16, #hillary, #imwithher) or show discontent (#nevertrump, #neverhillary) for either of the two main candidates. So once the bot detects that certain user regularly uses tags that indicate support for Trump, it will be able to start following them, interact or send them the content prepared by the attacker in the answers section, among others.

Weaponization Phase

Once the sector of the population to be targeted has been decided, the fake news that the victims are expected to receive will be carefully prepared. In this case, it is enough to take a look at the *Background* section to conclude that the best way to capture the attention of the Republican electorate is to fabricate a story that is either conveniently aligned with their ideology or that discredits the political rival towards whom they hold an emotionally negatively charged opinion.

With these data, we could cause an effect similar to the fake news page known as wtoe5news.com and the article that stated that Pope Francis had supported Donald Trump as the future president of the United States, which was shared and believed by many.

On the other hand, there were also posts with the clear intention of damaging Hillary Clinton's reputation, such as the fake news from the now defunct website denverguardian.com, which stated that an FBI agent had been found dead after leaking e-mails related to the Democratic candidate. Like the previous case, this news was widely shared on social media, especially in Republican circles. Both of them can be seen in Fig. 4.

Once the news has been created and given a striking headline that gets a possible interested reader to click and/or share it with their followers, the next phase of the Cyber Kill Chain proceeds.

Fig. 4. Fake news examples supporting Trump (left) and attacking Hillary (right) reported in a BBC and denverpost.com article respectively [36,37]

Delivery Phase

The distribution phase is where the dissemination of false news will be launched through the means mentioned in the first phase, that is, social bots.

In addition, it will be useful to check whether the attack has been successful or not, depending on the volume of Likes/Shares/Retweets obtained by the articles and the reactions observed in the target population as a whole. If it is successful and the article is palatable, credible and attractive enough for the victims, it can be said that the distribution has been successful and the news expansion phase will be triggered.

Expansion Phase

This phase is intended to achieve a massive dissemination of the fake content in a way that allows it to reach demographic groups outside of the target population. Here, the undecided or those with less marked political inclinations would be of great interest. Since although initially they showed lower disposition to believe in fabricated news or did not move through the same social circles as strongly ideological users, the availability of these news and its eventual jump to public relevance could incline some of these individuals to believe, spread and/or finally support the Republican candidate. International media and users will be of high interest here too, since despite not being a target a priori due to their inability to vote in the US elections, they do help to disseminate, give even more relevance and promote availability of the news in social media and in public conversations on the Internet (**availability cascade**).

Persistence Phase

Finally, the persistence phase is reached. In this stage, the attacker wants to maintain control over the narrative they have created, that is, they want people to keep believing in the news that they have created. Or, in any case, to create an environment in which users continue to give credibility and share the news launched in future campaigns.

Here, the point of the study by Allcott and Gentzkov comes into play, since it indicates that the presence of fake news caused a part of the electorate to begin to feel distrust towards mainstream media, an effect that was even more accentuated in the Republican electorate. This way, the target population is not only more receptive to future fake news that satisfies the need to find content that reaffirms their existing beliefs (**confirmation bias**) but will also cause them to continue consuming them in detriment of the official ones, which are perceived as inaccurate or unfair according to these same authors.

5.3 Objectives Evaluation

At the beginning of this document, three well-defined objectives were marked that had to be met once this research was completed, which consisted of identifying and observing some of the cognitive biases that allowed attacks on human beings to be carried out, demonstrating that these attacks are divisible into a certain number of differentiated phases and, finally, that these phases are usable in a real case.

After the investigation of this case study consisting of the 2016 US presidential elections and the consequent extraction of relevant information from investigations carried out by various authors, it is shown that it is possible to delimit the phases in which an attack like this can come to terms, and that these are consistent with those of the Cyber Kill Chain proposed. In addition, the biases that come into play at each moment have also been indicated, both in the background section with the findings of the papers consulted, and in each of the phases of the application of the methodology, evidencing the clear relationship that exists between these concepts. Taking this into account, it is considered that the previously indicated objectives have been successfully met.

6   Conclusion and Future Work

As a result of this research, it is verified that cognitive biases indeed have an important weight to take into account when talking about social engineering, misinformation and the cognitive domain in cyberspace. And that there are real ways and situations in which they are being systematically exploited for various purposes, such as the one that has been observed in the use case presented in this document.

Referring to the phrase "the chain always breaks at the weakest link", it is clear that the human factor is a great candidate to be that breaking point, and more and more cybercriminals, cyberterrorists and states take them into account when performing an operation that requires exploiting these vulnerabilities.

However, an individual or a society are not technical elements that can be repaired like a computer system, so the solutions to this threat should come from knowledge and awareness. Because only by knowing these biases, how they operate and how they are exploited, can a solution be offered that is truly able of mitigating the existing risks.

Looking to the future, the methodology could be improved with the inclusion of KPIs that make it possible to assess the damage and establish a comparison between the desired action and the effect achieved, as they are commonly used in the field of defence.

Also, according to what some experts have suggested in the validation questionnaire, it would be interesting to study the countermeasures for each of the phases, detailing in greater detail what actions could be carried out in each phase by the attacker to achieve the effect described in the methodology, or to further refine how it is decided whether the Cyber Kill Chain should perform the feedback stage or not.

As a detail, it would also be positive to study real scenarios in which said feedback has occurred, to see how it has been done and if it has been successful or not and why, since this aspect could not be observed in the case study taking into account the information available.

Acknowledgements.

This research has received funding from the European Defence Industrial Development Programme (EDIDP) under the grant agreement Number EDIDP-CSAMN-SSC-2019-022-ECYSAP (European Cyber Situational Awareness Platform).

7   Annex I

7.1   Model validation

In order to evaluate the proposed Cyber Kill Chain model, an expert assessment survey has been developed. In the survey, five participants belonging to the fields of both cybersecurity and psychology must answer a series of questions and, where indicated, award a score from 1 to 5 depending on how correct they consider the proposal to be. The profiles of the respondents are provided in Table 2.

Table 2. Experts' profiles

	Degree	Professional sector	Experience	Current position
Expert I	Doctorate in computer engineering	University and research	19 y	University professor and IP in cybersecurity projects
Expert II	Computer systems degree	Cybersecurity	13 y	Cybersecurity expert
Expert III	Doctorate in computer engineering	University	25 y	University professor
Expert IV	Clinic psychologist	Healthcare	39 y	Private clinic
Expert V	Biology degree	IT	24 y	Digital expert

The general objective of the questions was to ensure that the exposition of the proposal was adequate, that is, that the terms, both technical and related to human cognition, were used precisely and correctly, that the objective of the design and of each of the its phases were clear enough for the reader and that the work represented a relevant and innovative contribution to the current panorama.

In addition, special emphasis is placed on the persistence phase due to the vast differences between the ways of gaining persistence when attacking a machine and doing so when targeting a human. Likewise, this phase incorporates the detail of self-feedback, a possibility that did not exist in the original MITRE and Lockheed Marting Cyber Kill Chains that this methodology is inspired on.

Therefore, it was considered opportune to request the opinion of the experts very expressly at this stage.

The survey ends with two open questions (7 and 8) intended for the respondent to point out any detail that has not been covered by the rest of the questions and that may compromise the validity of the proposal, and to add any other suggestion that they consider appropriate to the improvement of it. Finally, after studying the answers given by the participants, it has been decided not to apply any change in the methodology for the time being. However, their contributions and suggestions will be taken into account for future lines of work in order to improve the design and make it more complete in future revisions.

7.2   Validation Results

The results obtained after analyzing the responses collected in the expert assessment survey are shown in Table 3 below. For each of the questions, the highest overall score obtained, the lowest and the average score will be indicated. In addition, in the observations section the most relevant feedback provided by the experts has been added.

Table 3. Experts' feedback

	Average score	Max	Min	Feedback
Question 1	4.2	5	3	Expert V suggests adding threat actors
Question 2	4.2	5	3	Expert II thinks that distribution phase should focus more on attack distribution and not so much on whether the attack is received or not. Expert III suggests justifying the differences between the new model and that of MITRE
Question 3	4.2	5	3	Expert I suggests creating a list of countermeasures for each phase
Question 4	4	5	2	Expert I thinks that the part where the model feedbacks itself in the last phase should be explained in more detail. Expert II suggests adding more attack techniques
Question 5	4.2	5	3	Expert III thinks that technical term are correct but that the methodology need more development
Question 6	4.4	5	3	Expert IV thinks that the terms related to human cognition are used correctly, without any contradictions or concept dispersion
Question 7				
Question 8				Expert I suggests adding an evaluation phase for the model's self-feedbacking option. As well as considering client networks

References

1. Kahneman, D., Tversky, A.: Subjective probability: a judgment of representativeness (1972)
2. Haselton, M.G., Nettle, D., Andrews, P.W.: The evolution of cognitive bias (2005)
3. Cialdini, R.: Influence, the psychology of persuasion (2001)
4. Aggarwal, P., Jun, S.Y., Huh, J.H.: Scarcity messages. J. Advert. (2011)
5. Evans & Curtis-Holmes: Rapid responding increases belief bias: evidence for the dual-process theory of reasoning (2005)
6. Kahneman, D., Tversky, A.: Prospect Theory. An Analysis of Decision Making Under Risk (1977)
7. Milgram, S.: Obedience to Authority: An Experimental View (1974)
8. Milgram, S.: Behavioral study of obedience. J. Abnormal Soc. Psychol. (1963)
9. Staw, B.M.: The escalation of commitment: an update and appraisal (1997)
10. Taylor, D.M., Doria, J.R.: Self-serving and group-serving bias in attribution (1981)
11. Ross, L., Stillinger, C.A.: Psychological barriers to conflict resolution (1988)
12. Ross, L.: Reactive Devaluation in Negotiation and Conflict Resolution (1995)
13. Piezunka, H., Dahlander, L.: Distant Search, Narrow Attention: How Crowding Alters Organizations' Filtering of Suggestions in Crowdsourcing (2014)
14. Colman, A.: Oxford Dictionary of Psychology (2003)
15. Schmitt-Beck, R.: Bandwagon Effect (2015)
16. Le Guyader, H.: Cognitive Domain: A Sixth Domain of Operations (2021)
17. du Cluzel, F.: Cognitive Warfare (2020)
18. NATO Factsheet, August 2020. https://www.nato.int/nato_static_fl2014/assets/pdf/2020/8/pdf/2008-factsheet-cyber-defence-en.pdf
19. Dra. Claudia Elizabeth Fonseca, My (Aud.) Ivonne Luz Perdomo, Lic. Miguel Arozarena Gratacos and Dr. Javier Ulises Ortiz (2014) El Manual de Tallin y la Aplicabilidad del Derecho Internacional a la Ciberguerra
20. Cialdini, R.: Influence: Science and Practice (2001)
21. Spencer, S.B.: The Problem of Online Manipulation (2020)
22. Yalçınkaya, H., et al.: Good practices in counter terrorism. Centre of Excellence Defence Against Terrorism (2021)
23. Hutchins, E.M., Clopperty, M.J., Amin, R.M.: Intelligence-Driven Computer Network Defense Informed by Analysis of Adversary Campaigns and Intrusion Kill Chains (2011)
24. MITRE ATT&CK. https://attack.mitre.org/
25. Yasseri, T., Reher, J.: Fooled by facts: quantifying anchoring bias through a large-scale experiment (2022)
26. Jost, P.J., Pünder, J., Schulze-Lohoff, I.: Fake news - does perception matter more than the truth? (2020)
27. Datta, P., Whitmore, M., Nwankpa, J.K.: A Perfect Storm: Social Media News, Psychological Biases, and AI (2021)
28. Nickerson, R.S.: Confirmation bias: a ubiquitous phenomenon in many guises (1998)
29. Kuran, T., Sunstein, C.R.: Availability Cascades and Risk Regulation (1999)
30. Anderson, C., Lepper, M.R., Ross, L.: Perseverance of Social Theories: The Role of Explanation In the Persistence of Discredited Information (1980)
31. Janis, I.: Victims of Groupthink: a psychological study of foreign-policy decisions and fiascoes (1972)

32. Bessi, A., Ferrara, E.: Social bots distort the 2016 U.S. Presidential election online discussion (2016)
33. Gottfried, J., Shearer, E.: News Use across Social Media Platforms 2016. Pew Research Center (2016)
34. Silverman, C.: This Analysis Shows how Fake Election News Stories Outperformed Real News on Facebook (2016)
35. Allcott, H., Gentzkow, M.: Social Media and Fake News in the 2016 Election (2017)
36. Wendling, M.: Solutions that can stop fake news spreading. BBC World Hacks, January 2017. https://www.bbc.com/news/blogs-trending-38769996
37. Lubbers, E.: There is no such thing as the Denver Guardian, despite that Facebook post you saw. The Denver Post, November 2016. https://www.denverpost.com/2016/11/05/there-is-no-such-thing-as-the-denver-guardian/

The Cloud Continuum for Military Deployable Networks: Challenges and Opportunities

Elisa Rojas[1]([✉])[ID], Diego Lopez-Pajares[1][ID], Joaquin Alvarez-Horcajo[1][ID], and Salvador Llopis Sánchez[2][ID]

[1] Departamento de Automática, Universidad de Alcala, Alcala de Henares, Spain
{elisa.rojas,diego.lopezp,j.alvarez}@uah.es
[2] Communications Department, Universitat Politecnica de Valencia, Valencia, Spain
salllosa@masters.upv.es

Abstract. Due to the constant demand for novel network services, including those envisioned by 5G technologies and beyond, the cloud computing paradigm has recently evolved towards distributed systems located preferably at the edge of networks. Fog, edge and even mist computing have emerged in this regard, providing multiple benefits such as low latency or bolstering security. In the specific area of military deployable networks, this so-called cloud continuum has fostered the appearance of multiple use cases, which will be analyzed in detail in this paper, together with their current and future trends in the field. This survey includes works from diverse areas, such as tactical edge, combat cloud or cyber-physical environments, for example. The main objective is to overview the main challenges and opportunities brought by these technologies, as well as future research lines, so that researchers in the field could gather and examine them with a global vision, taking into consideration the specific characteristics of military scenarios.

Keywords: Cloud continuum · Tactical edge · Combat cloud · Internet of Battlefield Things · Edge computing

1 Introduction

During the last two decades, the cloud computing paradigm (also known as on-demand computing, Internet computing or, simply, as *the cloud*) [31] has emerged and opened up a whole new range of possibilities in diverse fields, some of them even inconceivable before. This omnipresence of the cloud has been particularly fostered by the latest advances in networking and, particularly, thanks to the flourishing of technologies such as Software-Defined Networking (SDN) [41], Network Functions Virtualization (NFV) [86], and 5G and beyond [73]. Extending the cloud towards the edge of computing and network deployments, i.e. towards the users, has also benefited the appearance of multiple novel use cases and applications [55].

© The Author(s), under exclusive license to Springer Nature Switzerland AG 2023
S. Katsikas et al. (Eds.): ESORICS 2022 Workshops, LNCS 13785, pp. 500–519, 2023.
https://doi.org/10.1007/978-3-031-25460-4_29

In the specific field of military deployable networks, there is an urge for an analysis of the current needs and trends in the so-called *cloud continuum* [87], that is, when the elongation of the cloud blurs the lines between computing and networking. This situation is meaningful for the military tactical edge where there is a confluence of various communications constraints e.g. bandwidth, date rate which must be overcome to respond to an increase of information exchange requirements. Real-time information processing from heterogeneous sources is key for maintaining a shared situational awareness in support of small military units or combatants operating at a distance from the core network. These environments emphasize on the need for distributed, mobile and secure cloud applications, as well as their enabling technologies.

In this article, we review the cloud computing infrastructure in association with military communications in the battlefield using the following structure. In Sect. 2, we described the main motivation of the survey and related work. In Sect. 3, we examine keywords and trends, and describe recent use cases in relation with cloud in military deployable networks. Afterwards, in Sect. 4, we briefly provide future trends and challenges in the field. Finally, we conclude the article in Sect. 5.

2 Motivation and Related Work

In order to understand the evolution towards the cloud continuum in military deployable networks, the authors propose first to dissect the different technological enablers that make it possible.

2.1 One Cloud to Rule Them All?

Regarding traditional cloud deployments, diverse commercial on-demand cloud computing frameworks exist, such as Amazon Web Services (AWS) [1], Microsoft's Azure [3], or GoogleCloud [2]. All these three examples provide specific solutions tailored for defense. For example, Azure presents one particularly designed for the Department of Defense (DoD) of the USA. Some of the highlighted benefits of leveraging cloud computing for military frameworks include: advanced security (secured and controlled domains), novel functionalities and fastest pace of innovation, unified strategy for data collection and monitoring, and secure remote collaboration. Diverse surveys analyze the characteristics and services offered by these frameworks, agreeing on the fact that AWS seems to have the broadest customer adoption for civilian purposes [23,29]; while, for instance, the Joint Warfighting Cloud Capability Programme follows a multi-vendor strategy to acquire cloud services.

2.2 Fragmenting the Cloud into Fog, Edge and Mist

Recently, functionality deployed in cloud environments has been brought to the edge of networks, or towards end users, due to multiple benefits including lower latencies, enhanced use of network bandwidth or augmented privacy. Although literature might differ in the definitions of fog, edge or mist computing, a common aspect is that they all try to bridge the gap between the cloud and end devices [87], with a particular focus on Internet of Things (IoT) [55] due to its estimated growth in the upcoming years [5,56]. This evolution is usually addressed as the cloud or edge-to-cloud continuum [54].

Thanks to the growth of network "softwarization" and their associated open source communities and standardization bodies, and together with the support of telcos (in the need for operational costs reduction and new services), pivotal paradigms like SDN [41] and NFV [86] appeared. Both are around one decade old. The former, SDN, separates control and data plane so that the first one can be centralized into a piece of software and, as such, it provides enhanced visibility of the network and monitoring, and the appearance of novel functionalities and network services. While the latter, NFV, defines a framework to virtualize network functions so that they can be deployed in commercial off-the-shelf hardware, instead of specific appliances, hence drastically reducing costs among other advantages. These technologies have fostered the implementation of cloud computing environments and their fragmentation towards the edge or end users, hence providing a wide range of possibilities for new use cases in the cloud continuum. In fact, in the specific case of defense and to ensure appropriate levels of cybersecurity of networks and systems, deploying a full-fledged integrated NFV/SDN edge cloud platform is still considered a challenge for some scenarios, and particularly those comprising IoT devices, but also a requirement to trigger new applications [60].

Additionally, authors would like to highlight two remarkable architectural paradigms in the field of mobile networks that have fostered the cloud continuum, namely: (i) Multi-Access Edge Computing (MEC) [36], and (ii) network slicing [37]. The definition of MEC, bolstered by the European Telecommunications Standards Institute (ETSI), represents a cornerstone in 5G networks, as it offers cloud-computing capabilities and an associated service environment at the edge of the network; while network slicing facilitates the multiplexing of virtualized and independent logical networks using a common physical infrastructure, once again enabling flexible deployments of cloud environments towards the edge. They are both pillars for the application of 5G networks in military frameworks [8]. In fact, 5G is a key enabler in the field of defense, particularly in the emergence of combat cloud initiatives in support of Multi-Domain Operations (MDOs) [25,50].

3   The Cloud Continuum for Military Deployable Networks

In the specific case of cloud continuum applied in military deployable networks, this section analyzes current trends and statistics first, and later on provides a comprehensive overview of the most remarkable use cases and projects.

More specifically, we selected Google Scholar to thoroughly examine it, looking for specific keywords in relation with military cloud computing applications.

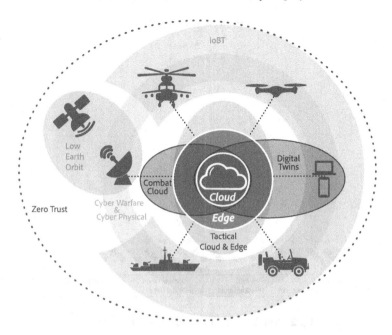

Fig. 1. Overview of the main keywords

The main purpose of it was to provide a comprehensive summary of the published works during the last two decades, with a particular focus on the last ten years, which represent the flourishing of edge environments. The main keyworks checked in relation with military frameworks were: tactical edge/cloudlet/cloud, Internet of Battlefield Things (IoBT) (including Unmanned Control System (UCS) and Unmanned Aerial Vehicles (UAVs)), combat cloud, cyber warfare, and cyber-physical battlefield. However, additional enabling tecnologies for edge cloud environments were reviewed, such as: Low Earth Orbit (LEO) and Non-Terrestrial Network (NTN), zero-trust security and digital twins, since they are currently hot topics in the field. All of these terms are graphically represented in Fig. 1, to illustrate their main relationships.

These keywords were selected after checking for initiatives applying cloud in military environments, which initially led to tactical edge and combat cloud. Afterwards, the references of those works were further examined, together with newer works that cited them as well, which provided searches about IoBT, cyber warfare, and cyber-physical battlefield. Finally, LEO and NTN, zero-trust security and digital twins were included as hot topics in the field of cloud computing and softwarized networks, as we believed they could also be applied in military deployable networks. The search for each keyword was limited to the first 200 most relevant references, and only considering publications from the most recent works up to year 2000.

The results obtained for the number of works that include these keywords is depicted in Fig. 2. This image illustrates how tactical edge/cloud is one of

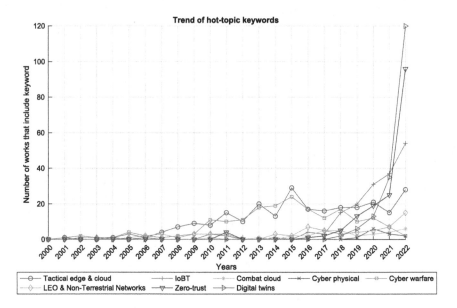

Fig. 2. Number of papers analyzed by category

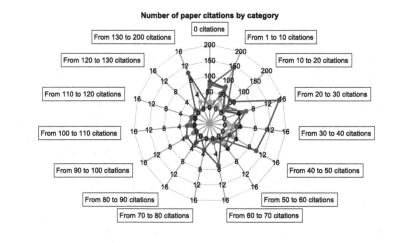

Fig. 3. Number of citations by category

the oldest trends related to cloud in military environments, but still stable in fourth position considering the number of works found in 2021 or 2022. Cyber warfare is aligned with it, but with a down trend. On the other hand, the three keywords with the highest number of works in 2021 and 2022 are digital twins, zero-trust security and IoBT, being the latter the only specific one of battlefield environments. Therefore, we could conclude that the most relevant topic in 2022 is IoBT, followed by a general growth of digital twins and zero-trust security, which might eventually boost use cases in the field of defense as well.

Additionally, Fig. 3 shows the same keywords, but instead of representing the number of works per keyword, it depicts the number of citations. Please note that the three first axes range up to 200 works, while the rest range up to 16. As it can be observed, the most cited works are the ones in relation with Cyber-Physical Systems (CPSs).

In the following subsections, we describe the most remarkable use cases and projects, classified and compared based on these keywords.

3.1 Tactical Edge

During the last decade, the use of handheld mobiles computing devices is being promoted for soldiers as it benefits in multiple types of missions. The *tactical edge* (also implemented as *tactical cloud* or *tactical cloudlet*) refers to the offloading of computation-intensive tasks (which cannot executed in mobiles devices, usually constrained in computational and battery capabilities) with the particular restrictions of military environments: hostile environments with scarce or unstable connectivity [74]. This offloading cannot be performed in traditional cloud due to the previous limitations, as cloud environments are usually located far away from the end devices. Therefore, bringing the cloud to end users or to the edge, usually in the form of cloudlets or similar environments (e.g., MEC) facilitates the actual offloading of these tasks in a close and secure way.

A sample design of tactical cloudlets is presented by Lewis *et al.* [46], which define a dialogue between cloudlet servers (e.g., hosted in military vehicles) and clients (e.g., mobile device), implemented with virtual machines. They emphasize on the need for additional security mechanisms to grant privacy during task offloading. Another example by Gao *et al.* [26] focuses on peer-to-peer offloading, instead of using a server, and analyzes how to distribute and balance the workload among mobile devices.

Regarding the use of SDN, Zacarias *et al.* [88] reflect on the use of this paradigm (together with Delay-Tolerant Networks (DTNs)) in last-mile tactical edge networking, and it considers it a key enabler for network-centric warfare, a pillar in modern military operations. They present two use cases using these technologies: (i) an intra-network partition scenario, in which an UAV collects video for reconnaissance missions, and (ii) an inter-network partition that communicates data from heterogeneous nodes. Chekired *et al.* [19] leverage distributed SDN and MEC, once again following a DTN approach, to design a Command, Control, Communications, Computers, Intelligence,

Surveillance and Reconnaissance (C4ISR) infrastructure. They also create and evaluate a Proof-of-Concept (PoC) of it.

About microservices (bolstered by NFV), one of the first architectural designs to incorporate them (instead of virtual machines), which provide lighter and more flexible implementations, is presented by Smith et al. [75]. They also envision the incorporation of SDN for the networking part, as future work, as SDN is still immature for distributed and constrained wireless deployments. Yego et al. [85] particularly focus on the implementation of a tactical edge scenario, using microservices deployed in Linux containers, comprised of heterogenous devices for emergency services and rescue operations. Tang et al. [78] consider that traditional monolithic architectures hamper collaboration, particularly in the case of data collection, in which big data could be applied. For this reason, they present a microservice-based architecture to synchronize data in a use case composed of aircraft nodes. Lim et al. [49] sketch an initial idea for microservices continuity when edge servers move founded on the MEC architecture.

Recently, several works started exploring the use of Machine Learning (ML) and Artificial Intelligence (AI) in tactical edge environments. Chin et al. [20] take as a reference the "Every Soldier is a Sensor" (ES2) concept, which leverages warfighters' proximity for boosted decision-making capabilities, to present the TAK-ML framework. This framework includes data collection, model training and model execution as part of the Tactical Assault Kit (TAK) ecosystem, and its evaluation is actually performed in a real mobile phone. Toth et al. [79] present CATE, also a prototype AI/ML framework for collaborative processing and exploitation of data at the edge. Nair et al. [57] use prediction models for task offloading in fog computing for tactical cloud. A different approach is followed by Kim et al. [39], which leverage these technologies for a federated learning environment that coordinates and balances task offloading among mobile devices.

Finally, Yang et al. [84] discuss the concept of dispersed computing for tactical edge. In this work, authors comprehensively analyze the current limitations of existing fog, edge and MEC frameworks, and argue that research needs to go beyond to design an architecture that matches the requirements of future wars. In this regard, they provide an initial architectural model and insights about it. Founded on the same ideas, but specifically based on the requirements of the DoD, Sturzinger et al. [77] present a hybrid cloud architecture.

Additionally, we would like to highlight two recent surveys in the field. Rechenberg et al. [63] consider SDN is a key enabler to foster tactical networks, but its application is still not trivial. For this reason, they analyze four research needs in the field: performance, availability, security and robustness. Sotelo Monge et al. [76] focus on cyber operations against the sustainability of the tactical edge, by surveying the concept in depth and providing cases of study for hypothesized tactical offensive/defensive scenarios. They also mention the gap in bibliography on related topics, probably due to secrecy around the tactical edge/cloud paradigm.

3.2   IoBT

In the case of IoBT (also Internet of Military Things (IoMT) or Military Internet of Things (MIoT)), the military applications are not so advanced as other IoT environments bolstered by the private sector [24]. However, Fraga-Lamas *et al.* [24] present a classification of possible scenarios for IoBT, including areas like C4ISR, fire-control systems, energy management, surveillance, collaborative and crowd sensing, smart cities, personal sensing, and logistics. Abdelzaher *et al.* [9,10] delve deeper into the particularities of IoBT in comparison to IoT and list three main challenges: (i) integration of resources (usually large scale, heterogenous and constrained), (ii) flexibility and adaptation (unifying the network as one capable of fast reaction), and (iii) learning and intelligence (usually federated). Additionally, Russell *et al.* [67] examine the implications of IoBT in Command, Control, Communications and Intelligence (C3I) (a subset of C4ISR) decision-making. They conclude IoBT drastically modifies the paradigm, from a hierarchical to a distributed planning, which implies severe changes in the military strategy. Afterwards, they also provide a decision process tailored for multi-domain operating environments [68], positively assessing the architectural benefits of IoBT.

Focusing on specific use cases deployed with UAVs and drones, and the security threats they might encompass, Bera *et al.* [15] propose a novel access control mechanism in drone-assisted battlefield surveillance, and consider incorporating blockchain in their design as future work. Golam *et al.* [28] blockchain-based secure device-to-device communication architecture, implemented with UAVs combined with MEC. Ghimire *et al.* [27] also leverage blockchain, but generalized to any type of Unmanned Vehicle (UV), and designing a scalable mechanism tailored for battlefield scenarios, which are usually constrained.

With additional emphasis on security aspects, Anwar *et al.* [13] propose game-theoretic cyber deception approach for these networks, where cyber deception is a strategy to provide false information to potential attackers to enhance protection of IoBT devices. Although their proposal is limited to two players, they consider generalizing it with the use of SDN. Kannimuthu *et al.* [34] focus on device authentication and propose a trust model based on a decision tree, to compare it with the most popular routing protocol in IoT, Routing Protocol for Low-Power and Lossy Networks (RPL). Furthermore, Zhu *et al.* [90] perform a literature review about cyberattacks and cyber defense in the field of IoBT.

Finally, also aligned with the use of ML and other prediction techniques, Kumar *et al.* [42] design a method to estimate the location of moving war-fighters when the main signal is temporarily lost. Shahid *et al.* [71] design and simulate an ML-based framework for mist computing environments, in which battlefield constrained devices (such as wearables, sensors, and micro-controllers) coexist. They simulate their framework in EdgeCloudSim, an extension of the CloudSim simulator. Alternatively, Papakostas *et al.* [62] consider IoBT present specific challenges as it is composed of multilayer networks, in which traditional IoT solutions are suboptimal. For this reason, they design a distributed algorithm for an integrated functionality of these networks, and simulate it in Matlab.

As future work, they envision the use of federated learning and its extension for scenarios with unidirectional links.

3.3 Combat Cloud

The combat cloud provides data services/applications to both manned and unmanned platforms. These platforms benefit from network cloud computing connectivity at the edge when conducting military operations, hence providing networking to weapon systems, sensors and constituting the infrastructure for advanced command and control tools [69], which is particularly relevant to aerospace environments [40,43]. For this reason, the combat cloud could be considered an enabler for IoBT and military platforms, e.g. aircrafts, naval ships, etc. working at the tactical level.

For instance, Mickel [53] analyze current trends on combat cloud in the US and Europe, with a particular focus on their impact on NATO's capability gaps. This thesis compares how the combat cloud is being developed from both perspectives, including initiatives such as the European Future Combat Air System (FCAS). Rieks et al. [64] highlights four aspects for the evolution of combat cloud: (i) new threats are emerging, (ii) information and data transfer at the edge, (iii) operational improvements and, once again, (iv) the FCAS programme. They conclude and integrative and incremental approach is required for this evolution, highlighting the importance of orchestration among clouds and even the compatibility with legacy systems.

When revising use cases in the literature, Li et al. [47] present a UAV-based combat cloud architecture with adaptative task scheduling. Nguyen et al. [58] propose an SDN-based multi-domain network for combat cloud, as they consider this type of orchestration is pivotal for combat cloud environments. Their idea leverages the Border Gateway Protocol (BGP) for the control plane as well. They use Mininet, as well as Raspberry Pi (RPi) boards with Open vSwitch (OVS), to evaluate it. Finally, a recent work by Pang et al. [61] define a semantic model to unify data treatment in combat cloud deployments and to help processing it following a "mission-oriented" approach. These three works highlight the importance of collaboration among systems and unification of heterogeneous environments and data.

3.4 Cyber-Physical Battlefield

A CPS could be defined as an evolution of sensor networks, in which cyber and physical components are effectively integrated to provide advanced services [11]. When applied to battlefield environments, In this field, few works with implemented use cases were found, which are briefly described below.

One particular use case of these systems is to emulate exercises as close as possible to reality. For instance, Visky [80] leverages CPSs for practising defending activities, with a focus on critical infrastructures. Kim et al. [38] follow a similar approach and design a platform intended for large-scale cyber exercises.

While the previous two works focus on the implementation of a CPSs for battle-fields, Zhao *et al.* [89] present a design based on ML to optimize data delivery in UAV-based CPSs. Their intention is to provide a system capable of detecting mobility of UAVs and re-routing information without the need of a GPS, to enhance privacy and security, which is particularly critical in the battlefield.

3.5 Cyber Warfare

A transversal aspect that affects any environment based on cloud is the "cyber" warfare. As the cloud is transparently located anywhere, it also implies a "delocalized" defense. Van Niekerk [59] introduces the term "information" warfare and distinguishes specific challenges in three tiers: cloud, fog, and combat resources. Additionally, Bhaiyat *et al.* [16] analyze the effects of cyber warfare on critical infrastructure, describing incidents in the US, Middle East, Africa and Ukraine.

3.6 LEO and NTNs

In the case of LEO and NTNs, few specific works were found about military implementations. This might be due to the novelty of these types of networks and also because most of military cloud deployments in non-terrestrial networks are covered already by the combat cloud concept, or as advances in 5G and beyond [30]. Additionally, LEO and NTN might be considered only a set of the so-called Space-Air-Ground Integrated Networks (SAGINs). More specifically, Shang *et al.* [72] provide a classification about SAGINs, which splits NTNs into two types: air and space, being LEO only one type of space NTN.

In this context, the work presented by Wood *et al.* [83] reviews the Commercially Augmented Space Inter-Network Operations Processing, Exploitation, and Dissemination program from the US DoD. A prototype leveraging AWS is built for rapid and scalable delivery of satellite data to tactical units.

3.7 Zero-Trust Security

Establishing trust in cloud computing environments is pivotal, particularly in military environments, which can suffer severe consequences from cyber attacks. Traditional trust mechanisms fall short in these scenarios, and the zero-trust model, whose principle is "never trust, always verify", aims to tackle this challenge [51]. Alternatively, this paradigm is also know as "perimeterless security" [35].

He *et al.* [32] survey the zero-trust architecture, providing challenges and future trends. For example, they consider access control should be segmented, granular, and dynamic (not static as in traditional frameworks). At the same time, diverse technologies should be combined to verify identities, like multifactor authentication methods. This raises an analysis of trade-offs between security and resource consumption.

Zero-trust is still a recent initiative and no specific works were found for military environments, although it will possibly be a future research topic.

3.8   Digital Twins

As a virtual mirrow image of a physical system, digital twins can help in the evolution of CPSs [33]. For this reason, there is a growing interest in the application of technology in military scenarios. Some of the advantages, as described by Mendi *et al.* [52], include: reduction of cost production, faster building and repair, enhanced prediction via the inclusion of AI/ML, high fidelity, and easy adaptability to different areas.

A preliminary study of the application of digital twins in military scenarios is presented by Li *et al.* [48]. More specifically, they describe a layered architecture and sample use cases, concluding that the major challenges in this field when applied to battlefields are: communication networks (which should be enhanced in capacity and resilience in military environments, while maintaining security), bottlenecks caused by security (as security is key, but requires time to process), immature intelligent decision-making algorithms, and fragmentation of current research efforts about digital twins. However, the trend is quite recent, so it could improve in the upcoming years. Wang *et al.* [82] first analyze the advantages of large-scale UAV in military scenarios and, afterwards, explain how these scenarios could benefit from a digital twin. To this purpose, they describe a theoretical layered digital twin framework.

3.9   Summary and Research Insights

As a summary, Table 1 outlines the previous use cases, including authors, publication years, key technologies and if they were demonstrated via a PoC. As it can be observed, most works, except for the ones related with tactical edge (which are the most numerous as well) have been published during the last three years. This is aligned with the analysis provided in Fig. 2, which depicts tactical edge and tactical cloud as one of the oldest paradigms in relation with cloud in military networks. The second topic with most works is IoBT, with a remarkable number of PoCs, while other novel hot topics like zero-trust security and digital twins are still emerging, and few use cases were found, and none with a PoC.

In the case of key technologies, we would like to highlight AI/ML and UAV as main drivers in the area. Microservices and edge/fog/mist computing approaches, together with blockchain, which generally represent distributed cloud environments, are also leveraged, as they present advantages in terms of latency and security, among others. Finally, regarding the implemented PoCs, the most common tools include Matlab and CloudSim [17] for simulation, SDN frameworks for emulation (including Mininet [44]), and RPi to test real environments.

4   Future Trends and Challenges

Cloud computing technologies embedded into a wider network infrastructure enable deployable forces to improve their mobility while maintaining an uninterrupted access to mission critical information. Cloud is a fundamental component of the global infrastructure [4] and it is key to achieve mission readiness

Table 1. Summary of use cases and research insights.

Use case	Reference	Year	Key technologies	PoC?
Tactical edge	Lewis *et al.* [46]	2014	Cloudlet server offloading	
	Gao *et al.* [26]	2014	Cloudlet peer-to-peer offloading	
	Smith *et al.* [75]	2017	Microservices	
	Zacarias *et al.* [88]	2017	SDN, DTN	
	Chekired *et al.* [19]	2019	SDN, DTN	✓ (Emulation - SDN framework)
	Yego *et al.* [85]	2020	Microservices	✓ (Emulation - Linux containers)
	Tang *et al.* [78]	2020	Microservices, big data	
	Chin *et al.* [20]	2021	ML	✓ (Real - Mobile phone)
	Toth *et al.* [79]	2021	ML, AI	
	Kim *et al.* [39]	2021	Federated learning	✓ (Simulation - Matlab)
	Yang *et al.* [84]	2021	Dispersed computing, beyond literature	
	Sturzinger *et al.* [77]	2021	Hybrid cloud, beyond literature	
	Lim *et al.* [49]	2022	Microservices, MEC	
	Nair *et al.* [57]	2022	ML server offloading	✓ (Emulation)
IoBT	Golam *et al.* [28]	2020	Blockchain, UAV	✓ (Simulation - Matlab/Python)
	Ghimire *et al.* [27]	2021	Blockchain, UV	
	Bera *et al.* [15]	2021	UAV	✓ (Real - RPi)
	Anwar *et al.* [13]	2021	Security (honeypot)	
	Kannimuthu *et al.* [34]	2021	Security (authentication), ML	
	Kumar *et al.* [42]	2021	ML	✓ (Simulation - Matlab)
	Shahid *et al.* [71]	2021	ML, mist computing	✓ (Simulation - EdgeCloudSim)
	Papakostas *et al.* [62]	2021	Distributed algorithm	✓ (Simulation - Matlab)
Combat cloud	Li *et al.* [47]	2020	Task scheduling, UAV	✓ (Simulation - CloudSim)
	Nguyen *et al.* [58]	2020	SDN, BGP	✓ (Emulation - Mininet/RPi)
	Pang *et al.* [61]	2021	Ontology/Semantic model	
Cyber-physical battlefield	Visky [80]	2019	-	✓ (Real)
	Kim [38]	2019	-	✓ (Real)
	Zhao *et al.* [89]	2019	ML, UAV	✓ (Simulation - Matlab)
Cyber warfare	-	-	-	
LEO	Wood *et al.* [83]	2021	Data offloading	✓ (Real - AWS)
Zero-trust security	-	-	-	
Digital twins	Li *et al.* [48]	2020	-	
	Wang *et al.* [82]	2021	UAV	

notably at the tactical edge. There are many tangible advantages like the increase of computing processing power or the reduction of hardware equipment to be deployed which coexist with evident disadvantages on the network infrastructure to support unprecedented levels of interconnectivity and higher data rates. Some characteristics deemed necessary towards an implementation of cloud computing technologies in the battlefield involve:

- Without preempting other configurations, Combat Cloud could facilitate the integration of military platforms into an overarching de-centralized mesh network. The type of selected architecture and requested cloud services will depend on the mission type.
- The connectivity would be 'transparent' for the end-user providing a seamless and mobile connectivity to nodes and platforms present in a theatre of military operations.
- Cross-domain synergy impacting the design of Command & Control (C2) systems. A combat cloud is key to operationalize future joint C2 systems.

– A stringent security control likely performed in collaboration with the service provider to test and assess cloud network security and incident handling. The same would apply for monitoring the cloud computing performance and establish remediation measures against failures.

The use of cloud computing in the tactical edge drives which cloud computing overarching architecture should be adopted. Tactical edge criteria are built over a 'modular edge device' which for instance shall compute capacity capable or running multiple applications in a communication degraded or disconnected environment and fully connected environment. According to [6], integrated tactical cloud solutions that extend the resources of the enterprise shall accommodate Disconnected, Intermittently Connected, Low-Bandwidth (DIL)-constrained environments.

Architectural aspects to be considered for the design of a combat cloud are:

– Capability of self-forming network (with strong identity and access control, and authentication).
– Capability of self-healing and establish redundancy including the use of AI/ML techniques to optimize performance features.
– Capability of providing a C2-automatic linking.
– Capability of providing a seamless sharing of information.
– Capability of connecting sensors and network nodes that will automatically push and pull mission-relevant and timely information.
– Capability of integrating different communication technologies like 5G and backwards interoperability.

Additionally, a comprehensive architecture would advocate for a distinction between general purpose and mission services, which may lead to a network segmentation operationalized by information exchange gateways. Some challenges to be addressed towards an implementation of a combat cloud include:

– Resilience against cyberattacks.
– Capability of operating in a contested Operational Environment.
– Capability of integrating a multitude of technologies, networks, platforms, protocols, legacy systems, etc.

In summary, there is a huge trend in the use of cloud for military environments, not only in cases like the European FCAS project [81] (as mentioned in Sect. 3.3), but also in the US and Asia. For instance, the US Navy foresees the development of naval tactical cloud computing [18], considering that military in-house developments are usually resource-constrained. The DoD is also involved in the guidance towards the application of cloud computing services for biomedical research for example [45]. Recently, the DoD also published the Cloud Native Access Point (CNAP) reference design [22], which highlights the need to evolve from legacy systems to softwarized and cloud-based ones. Finally, an alternative proposal by South Korea describes cloud as an administrative solution to integrate different military areas [21].

In the following paragraphs, we briefly sketch some future trends and challenges according to our analysis.

4.1   Merging Serverless and Resourceless Computing

With the emergence of serverless computing as an evolution of cloud [14], battlefield environments could benefit from the advantages of this paradigm, particularly at edge environments. In this regard, integrating serverless principles with constrained (or "resourceless") devices at the edge represents a significant challenge nowadays. One of the reasons is that, for example, current IoBT implementations are still relatively fragmented and platform-centred [25], which makes it difficult to integrate them into homogeneous frameworks. Another reason is the need for communication protocols in the field of constrained devices [65,84], so the limitation is even bigger when trying to incorporate softwarization or virtualization principles of cloud computing in these devices.

An interesting analysis about this challenge is provided by Yang *et al.* [84], who present guidelines for what they call "dispersed computing" for tactical edge in future works. Additionally, there is ongoing work by ETSI for an evolution of MEC in constrained devices [7], aligned as well with this need.

4.2   Federated Learning at the Edge

The use of AI/ML is clearly a must in the battlefield, as presented by the US Navy [66], for instance. More specifically, federated learning (i.e., applying this intelligent mechanisms in a distributed manner at the edge) is also a current trend, already presented in previous sections. However, improvements are still required in performance, in constrained environments as previously mentioned, or in hybrid cloud architectures [77], for instance. As a proof of the trend, the US forces recently designed an orchestrated multi-domain common operating picture based on AI [12].

4.3   Energy Management in Constrained Environments

Aligned with the previous two aspects, in constrained environments at the edge, if high computation capabilities are required to implement AI/ML, the challenge of energy management appears [70].

5   Conclusions

In this article, we have surveyed the pillar technologies and use cases related to the cloud continuum for military deployable networks. We also summarized key insights and related works as a reference. In our analysis, we have found that tactical edge and combat cloud are already well-known paradigms (supported by the US and European-funded initiatives like European Defence Fund topic on military multi-domain operations cloud), while IoBT is growing fast, and zero-trust security and digital twins seem to be quickly flourishing in the upcoming years. Finally, as future trends and challenges, we highlight the need for additional research efforts in the fields of serverless computing, federated learning, and energy management in constrained environments.

Acknowledgements. This work was partially funded by grants from Comunidad de Madrid through projects TAPIR-CM (S2018/TCS-4496) and MistLETOE-CM (CM/JIN/2021-006), and by project ONENESS (PID2020-116361RA-I00) of the Spanish Ministry of Science and Innovation.

References

1. Amazon Web Services. https://aws.amazon.com/
2. Google Cloud. https://cloud.google.com/
3. Microsoft's Azure. https://azure.microsoft.com/
4. Department of Defence, United States of America, DOD Cloud Strategy (2019)
5. 5G Alliance for Connected Industries and Automation (5GACIA) (2020). https://www.5g-acia.org/
6. The United States Army Cloud Plan 2020 (2020)
7. DGR/MEC-0036ConstrainedDevice (2022)
8. Report on the cybersecurity of Open RAN. Technical report, NIS Cooperation Group (2022)
9. Abdelzaher, T., et al.: Will distributed computing revolutionize peace? The emergence of battlefield IoT. In: 2018 IEEE 38th International Conference on Distributed Computing Systems (ICDCS), pp. 1129–1138 (2018). https://doi.org/10.1109/ICDCS.2018.00112
10. Abdelzaher, T., et al.: Toward an internet of battlefield things: a resilience perspective. Computer **51**(11), 24–36 (2018). https://doi.org/10.1109/MC.2018.2876048
11. Alguliyev, R., Imamverdiyev, Y., Sukhostat, L.: Cyber-physical systems and their security issues. Comput. Ind. **100**, 212–223 (2018). https://doi.org/10.1016/j.compind.2018.04.017
12. Andresky, N., Taliaferro, A.: Operationalizing artificial intelligence for multi-domain operations. Technical report, US Army Futures and Concepts Center Future Warfare Division (2019)
13. Anwar, A.H., Leslie, N.O., Kamhoua, C.A.: Honeypot allocation for cyber deception in internet of battlefield things systems. In: MILCOM 2021–2021 IEEE Military Communications Conference (MILCOM), pp. 1005–1010 (2021). https://doi.org/10.1109/MILCOM52596.2021.9652927
14. Baldini, I., et al.: Serverless computing: current trends and open problems. In: Chaudhary, S., Somani, G., Buyya, R. (eds.) Research Advances in Cloud Computing, pp. 1–20. Springer, Singapore (2017). https://doi.org/10.1007/978-981-10-5026-8_1
15. Bera, B., Das, A.K., Garg, S., Piran, M.J., Hossain, M.S.: Access control protocol for battlefield surveillance in drone-assisted IoT environment. IEEE Internet Things J. **9**(4), 2708–2721 (2021). https://doi.org/10.1109/JIOT.2020.3049003
16. Bhaiyat, H., Sithungu, S.: Cyberwarfare and its effects on critical infrastructure. In: International Conference on Cyber Warfare and Security, vol. 17, pp. 536–543 (2022)
17. Calheiros, R.N., Ranjan, R., Beloglazov, A., De Rose, C.A., Buyya, R.: CloudSim: a toolkit for modeling and simulation of cloud computing environments and evaluation of resource provisioning algorithms. Softw. Pract. Exp. **41**(1), 23–50 (2011)
18. Challenger, L.E.: Naval tactical cloud computing. Technical report, Gravely Naval Research Group, Naval War College Newport United States (2017)

19. Chekired, D.A., Khoukhi, L.: Distributed SDN-based C4ISR communications: a delay-tolerant network for trusted tactical cloudlets. In: 2019 International Conference on Military Communications and Information Systems (ICMCIS), pp. 1–7 (2019). https://doi.org/10.1109/ICMCIS.2019.8842820

20. Chin, P., et al.: TAK-ML: applying machine learning at the tactical edge. In: MILCOM 2021–2021 IEEE Military Communications Conference (MILCOM), pp. 108–114 (2021). https://doi.org/10.1109/MILCOM52596.2021.9652909

21. Cho, S., Hwang, S., Shin, W., Kim, N., In, H.P.: Design of military service framework for enabling migration to military SaaS cloud environment. Electronics 10(5), 572 (2021). https://doi.org/10.3390/electronics10050572

22. Department of Defense (DoD): Cloud Native Access Point (CNAP) Reference Design (RD), July 2021

23. Dutta, P., Dutta, P.: Comparative study of cloud services offered by Amazon, Microsoft & Google. Int. J. Trend Sci. Res. Dev. 3(3), 981–985 (2019)

24. Fraga-Lamas, P., Fernández-Caramés, T.M., Suárez-Albela, M., Castedo, L., González-López, M.: A review on Internet of Things for defense and public safety. Sensors 16(10), 1644 (2016). https://doi.org/10.3390/s16101644

25. Gady, F.S., Stronell, A.: Cyber Capabilities and Multi-Domain Operations in Future High-Intensity Warfare in 2030. Cyber Threats and NATO 2030: Horizon Scanning and Analysis, p. 151 (2020)

26. Gao, W.: Opportunistic peer-to-peer mobile cloud computing at the tactical edge. In: 2014 IEEE Military Communications Conference, pp. 1614–1620 (2014). https://doi.org/10.1109/MILCOM.2014.265

27. Ghimire, B., Rawat, D.B., Liu, C., Li, J.: Sharding-enabled blockchain for software-defined internet of unmanned vehicles in the battlefield. IEEE Netw. 35(1), 101–107 (2021). https://doi.org/10.1109/MNET.011.2000214

28. Golam, M., Lee, J.M., Kim, D.S.: A UAV-assisted blockchain based secure device-to-device communication in Internet of military Things. In: 2020 International Conference on Information and Communication Technology Convergence (ICTC), pp. 1896–1898 (2020). https://doi.org/10.1109/ICTC49870.2020.9289282

29. Gupta, B., Mittal, P., Mufti, T.: A review on Amazon web service (AWS), Microsoft azure & Google cloud platform (GCP) services (2021)

30. Hassan, S.S., Tun, Y.K., Saad, W., Han, Z., Hong, C.S.: Blue data computation maximization in 6G space-air-sea non-terrestrial networks. In: 2021 IEEE Global Communications Conference (GLOBECOM), pp. 1–6 (2021). https://doi.org/10.1109/GLOBECOM46510.2021.9685488

31. Hayes, B.: Cloud computing (2008)

32. He, Y., Huang, D., Chen, L., Ni, Y., Ma, X.: A survey on zero trust architecture: challenges and future trends. Wirel. Commun. Mob. Comput. 2022, 1–13 (2022)

33. Jin, A.S., et al.: Resilience of cyber-physical systems: role of AI, digital twins and edge computing. IEEE Eng. Manag. Rev. 50(2), 195–203 (2022). https://doi.org/10.1109/EMR.2022.3172649

34. Kannimuthu, P., Thangamuthu, J.: Decision tree trust (DTTrust)-based authentication mechanism to secure RPL routing protocol on internet of battlefield thing (IoBT). Int. J. Bus. Data Commun. Netw. (IJBDCN) 17(1), 1–23 (2021)

35. Karabacak, B., Whittaker, T.: Zero trust and advanced persistent threats: who will win the war? In: International Conference on Cyber Warfare and Security, vol. 17, pp. 92–101 (2022)

36. Kekki, S., et al.: MEC in 5G networks. ETSI white paper 28, 1–28 (2018)

37. Khan, L.U., Yaqoob, I., Tran, N.H., Han, Z., Hong, C.S.: Network slicing: recent advances, taxonomy, requirements, and open research challenges. IEEE Access **8**, 36009–36028 (2020). https://doi.org/10.1109/ACCESS.2020.2975072

38. Kim, J., Kim, K., Jang, M.: Cyber-physical battlefield platform for large-scale cybersecurity exercises. In: 2019 11th International Conference on Cyber Conflict (CyCon), vol. 900, pp. 1–19 (2019). https://doi.org/10.23919/CYCON.2019.8756901

39. Kim, S.: Cooperative federated learning-based task offloading scheme for tactical edge networks. IEEE Access **9**, 145739–145747 (2021). https://doi.org/10.1109/ACCESS.2021.3123313

40. Kiser, A., Hess, J., Bouhafa, E.M., Williams, S.: The combat cloud: enabling multi-domain command and control across the range of military operations. Technical report, Air Command and Staff College, Maxwell AFB, Al Maxwell AFB, United States (2017)

41. Kreutz, D., Ramos, F.M.V., Veríssimo, P.E., Rothenberg, C.E., Azodolmolky, S., Uhlig, S.: Software-defined networking: a comprehensive survey. Proc. IEEE **103**(1), 14–76 (2015). https://doi.org/10.1109/JPROC.2014.2371999

42. Kumar, S., Kumar, S., Lobiyal, D.K.: MWLP-DP: mobile war-fighters location prediction for dark phase in Internet of Battlefield Things. Trans. Emerg. Telecommun. Technol. **33**(4), e4397 (2021)

43. Laird, R.: The next phase of air power: crafting and enabling the aerospace combat cloud. Second Line of Defense (2014). Accessed 20 Nov 2014

44. Lantz, B., Heller, B., McKeown, N.: A network in a laptop: rapid prototyping for software-defined networks. In: Proceedings of the 9th ACM SIGCOMM Workshop on Hot Topics in Networks. Hotnets-IX, Association for Computing Machinery, New York (2010). https://doi.org/10.1145/1868447.1868466

45. Lebeda, F.J., Zalatoris, J.J., Scheerer, J.B.: Government cloud computing policies: potential opportunities for advancing military biomedical research. Mil. Med. **183**(11–12), e438–e447 (2018). https://doi.org/10.1093/milmed/usx114

46. Lewis, G., Echeverría, S., Simanta, S., Bradshaw, B., Root, J.: Tactical cloudlets: moving cloud computing to the edge. In: 2014 IEEE Military Communications Conference, pp. 1440–1446 (2014). https://doi.org/10.1109/MILCOM.2014.238

47. Li, B., Liang, S., Tian, L., Chen, D., Zhang, M.: An adaptive task scheduling method for networked UAV combat cloud system based on virtual machine and task migration. Math. Probl. Eng. **2020**, 1–12 (2020)

48. Li, S., Yang, Q., Xing, J., Yuan, S.: Preliminary study on the application of digital twin in military engineering and equipment. In: 2020 Chinese Automation Congress (CAC), pp. 7249–7255 (2020). https://doi.org/10.1109/CAC51589.2020.9326911

49. Lim, H., Kim, Y.: A design of network mobility management on cloud native tactical edge cloud. In: 2022 International Conference on Information Networking (ICOIN), pp. 168–170 (2022). https://doi.org/10.1109/ICOIN53446.2022.9687220

50. Machi, V.: Atos' Cyril Dujardin on European defense opportunities in 5G tech (2022)

51. Mehraj, S., Banday, M.T.: Establishing a zero trust strategy in cloud computing environment. In: 2020 International Conference on Computer Communication and Informatics (ICCCI), pp. 1–6 (2020). https://doi.org/10.1109/ICCCI48352.2020.9104214

52. Mendi, A.F., Erol, T., Dogan, D.: Digital twin in the military field. IEEE Internet Comput. **26**(5), 33–40 (2022). https://doi.org/10.1109/MIC.2021.3055153

53. Mickel, D.J.: A clouded future: on combat clouds in the US and Europe and their impact on NATO's capability gaps, August 2019. http://essay.utwente.nl/79352/

54. Milojicic, D.: The edge-to-cloud continuum. Computer **53**(11), 16–25 (2020)
55. Montero, R.S., Rojas, E., Carrillo, A.A., Llorente, I.M.: Extending the cloud to the network edge. Computer **50**(4), 91–95 (2017). https://doi.org/10.1109/MC.2017.118
56. Mourad, A., Yang, R., Lehne, P.H., de la Oliva, A.: Towards 6G: evolution of key performance indicators and technology trends. In: 2020 2nd 6G Wireless Summit (6G SUMMIT), pp. 1–5 (2020)
57. Nair, B., Bhanu, S.: Task scheduling in fog node within the tactical cloud. Defence Sci. J. **72**(1), 49–55 (2022)
58. Nguyen, H., Yego, K., Sioutis, C.: BGP based software defined networks for resilient combat cloud. In: 2020 Military Communications and Information Systems Conference (MilCIS), pp. 1–6 (2020)
59. van Niekerk, B.: Information warfare and the connected battlefield. In: DIACC - Dubai International Air Chef's Conference (2021)
60. Pan, J., Yang, Z.: Cybersecurity challenges and opportunities in the new "edge computing + IoT" world. In: Proceedings of the 2018 ACM International Workshop on Security in Software Defined Networks & Network Function Virtualization, SDN-NFV Sec 2018, pp. 29–32. Association for Computing Machinery, New York (2018). https://doi.org/10.1145/3180465.3180470
61. Pang, K., Xiong, Q.: Semantic modeling framework for mission-oriented military systems and combat cloud control. In: 2021 IEEE 7th International Conference on Control Science and Systems Engineering (ICCSSE), pp. 200–204 (2021)
62. Papakostas, D., Kasidakis, T., Fragkou, E., Katsaros, D.: Backbones for internet of battlefield things. In: 2021 16th Annual Conference on Wireless On-Demand Network Systems and Services Conference (WONS), pp. 1–8 (2021). https://doi.org/10.23919/WONS51326.2021.9415560
63. von Rechenberg, M., Rettore, P.H.L., Lopes, R.R.F., Sevenich, P.: Software-defined networking applied in tactical networks: problems, solutions and open issues. In: 2021 International Conference on Military Communication and Information Systems (ICMCIS), pp. 1–8 (2021). https://doi.org/10.1109/ICMCIS52405.2021.9486399
64. Rieks, A., Mannheim, H.: The Combat Cloud: Air C2 and Warfighting in a Multi-Domain Battlespace. Armament & Technology (2022)
65. Rojas, E., Hosseini, H., Gomez, C., Carrascal, D., Rodrigues Cotrim, J.: Outperforming RPL with scalable routing based on meaningful MAC addressing. Ad Hoc Netw. **114**, 102433 (2021). https://doi.org/10.1016/j.adhoc.2021.102433
66. Rothenhaus, K., De Soto, K., Nguyen, E., Millard, J.: Applying a DEVelopment OPerationS (DevOps) reference architecture to accelerate delivery of emerging technologies in data analytics, deep learning, and artificial intelligence to the Afloat US Navy (2018)
67. Russell, S., Abdelzaher, T.: The internet of battlefield things: the next generation of command, control, communications and intelligence (C3I) decision-making. In: MILCOM 2018–2018 IEEE Military Communications Conference (MILCOM), pp. 737–742 (2018). https://doi.org/10.1109/MILCOM.2018.8599853
68. Russell, S., Abdelzaher, T., Suri, N.: Multi-domain effects and the internet of battlefield things. In: MILCOM 2019–2019 IEEE Military Communications Conference (MILCOM), pp. 724–730 (2019). https://doi.org/10.1109/MILCOM47813.2019.9020925
69. Schanz, M.V.: The combat cloud. Air Force Magazine, July 2014

70. National Academies of Sciences, Engineering, and Medicine: Energizing Data-Driven Operations at the Tactical Edge: Challenges and Concerns. The National Academies Press, Washington, DC (2021). https://doi.org/10.17226/26183
71. Shahid, H., et al.: Machine learning-based mist computing enabled Internet of Battlefield Things. ACM Trans. Internet Technol. **21**(4), 1–26 (2021)
72. Shang, B., Yi, Y., Liu, L.: Computing over space-air-ground integrated networks: challenges and opportunities. IEEE Netw. **35**(4), 302–309 (2021)
73. da Silva, M.M., Guerreiro, J.: On the 5G and beyond. Appl. Sci. **10**(20), 7091 (2020). https://doi.org/10.3390/app10207091
74. Simanta, S., Lewis, G.A., Morris, E., Ha, K., Stayanarayanan, M.: Cloud computing at the tactical edge. Technical report, Carnegie-Mellon University, Software Engineering Institute, Pittsburgh, PA (2012)
75. Smith, W., et al.: Cloud computing in tactical environments. In: MILCOM 2017–2017 IEEE Military Communications Conference (MILCOM), pp. 882–887 (2017). https://doi.org/10.1109/MILCOM.2017.8170823
76. Sotelo Monge, M.A., Maestre Vidal, J.: Conceptualization and cases of study on cyber operations against the sustainability of the tactical edge. Future Gener. Comput. Syst. **125**, 869–890 (2021)
77. Sturzinger, E.M., Lowrance, C.J., Faber, I.J., Choi, J.J., MacCalman, A.D.: Improving the performance of AI models in tactical environments using a hybrid cloud architecture. In: Artificial Intelligence and Machine Learning for Multi-Domain Operations Applications III, vol. 11746, p. 1174607. International Society for Optics and Photonics (2021)
78. Tang, L., Hu, H., Wang, Z., Wang, J., Li, Y.: Microservice architecture design for big data in tactical cloud. In: Tian, Y., Ma, T., Khan, M.K. (eds.) ICBDS 2019. CCIS, vol. 1210, pp. 402–416. Springer, Singapore (2020). https://doi.org/10.1007/978-981-15-7530-3_31
79. Toth, S., Hughes, W.: The journey to collaborative AI at the tactical edge (CATE). In: Artificial Intelligence and Machine Learning for Multi-Domain Operations Applications III, vol. 11746, pp. 144–163. SPIE (2021)
80. Visky, M.G.: Cyber-physical battlefield for cyber exercises. In: 5th Interdisciplinary Cyber Research Conference 2019, p. 10 (2019)
81. Vogel, D.: Future Combat Air System: too big to fail; differing perceptions and high complexity jeopardise success of Strategic Armament Project (2021)
82. Wang, Y., Zhang, N., Li, H., Cao, J.: Research on digital twin framework of military large-scale UAV based on cloud computing. In: Journal of Physics: Conference Series, vol. 1738, no. 1, p. 012052, January 2021
83. Wood, P., Rossiter, D., Rose, D.: Reliability of cloud-based processing for satellite data. In: 2021 IEEE Aerospace Conference (50100), pp. 1–8 (2021)
84. Yang, H., et al.: Dispersed computing for tactical edge in future wars: vision, architecture, and challenges. Wirel. Commun. Mob. Comput. **2021**, 1–31 (2021)
85. Yego, K., Thyer, M., Jones, T., Davidson, R.: A heterogeneous tactical cloud architecture for emergency services search and rescue operations. In: 2020 Military Communications and Information Systems Conference (MilCIS), pp. 1–6 (2020)
86. Yi, B., Wang, X., Li, K., Das, S.K., Huang, M.: A comprehensive survey of Network Function Virtualization. Comput. Netw. **133**, 212–262 (2018)
87. Yousefpour, A., et al.: All one needs to know about fog computing and related edge computing paradigms: a complete survey. J. Syst. Architect. **98**, 289–330 (2019). https://doi.org/10.1016/j.sysarc.2019.02.009

88. Zacarias, I., Gaspary, L.P., Kohl, A., Fernandes, R.Q.A., Stocchero, J.M., de Freitas, E.P.: Combining software-defined and delay-tolerant approaches in last-mile tactical edge networking. IEEE Commun. Mag. **55**(10), 22–29 (2017). https://doi.org/10.1109/MCOM.2017.1700239

89. Zhao, J., Han, C., Cui, Z., Wang, R., Yang, T.: Cyber-physical battlefield perception systems based on machine learning technology for data delivery. Peer-to-Peer Netw. Appl. **12**(6), 1785–1798 (2019). https://doi.org/10.1007/s12083-019-00769-5

90. Zhu, L., Majumdar, S., Ekenna, C.: An invisible warfare with the internet of battlefield things: a literature review. Hum. Behav. Emerg. Technol. **3**(2), 255–260 (2021)

1st International Workshop on Election Infrastructure Security (EIS 2022)

Preface

Fair and secure elections are the bedrock of democracy. In today's world, voting and elections rely on a complex infrastructure comprising voter registration databases, multiple types of electronic devices (e.g., voting machines, ballot marking devices, optical scanners), protocols to securely transmit data from polling places to central processing facilities, various software applications to count, tabulate and analyze votes, and physical facilities to securely store ballots and voting equipment. People's confidence in the result of elections is heavily dependent on a nation's ability to secure such complex infrastructure and guarantee the integrity and confidentiality of the vote.

The Cybersecurity and Infrastructure Security Administration (CISA), a United States agency charged with securing the nation's cyber and physical infrastructure, has classified election infrastructure as "critical infrastructure". In fact, election infrastructure and processes are subject to attack by malicious actors just like any other critical infrastructure (e.g., energy systems, transportation systems, and financial systems). Recent events have shown how attacks against voting systems and election infrastructure, disinformation and misinformation campaigns, and claims of election fraud, whether founded or not, can affect people's confidence in the integrity of the system and alienate voters. As threats evolve and become more sophisticated, the research community is called to find novel approaches and techniques to ensure the security of voting systems and election infrastructure and the confidentiality and integrity of the vote.

The workshop on Election Infrastructure Security was established with the objective of providing researchers and practitioners in different areas of security, networking, hardware architectures, software engineering, system engineering, machine learning, and public policy with an interdisciplinary forum to present, discuss, and exchange ideas that address the challenges of current and next-generation Election Infrastructure systems. In its first edition, the workshop received a total of 10 submissions from 7 countries (Australia, Denmark, Estonia, Germany, India, Italy, USA) across four continents. Submissions were peer-reviewed by a technical program committee comprising some of the most renowned experts in election security from both industry and academia. The review process was single-blind, and each submission received between two and three reviews. Eventually, 5 papers were accepted for presentation at the workshop, which was held as a half-day virtual event on September 30, 2022. The workshop program featured opening remarks by Chris Krebs, who served as the first Director of the Cybersecurity and Infrastructure Security Agency (CISA) from 2018 to 2020, and a keynote address by Arielle Schneider, Privacy Officer at the Virginia Department of Elections.

October 2022   Massimiliano Albanese

Organization

General Chair

Karen Hoyt-Stewart   Virginia Department of Elections, USA

Program Committee Chairs

Massimiliano Albanese   George Mason University, USA
Jack Davidson   University of Virginia, USA

Steering Committee

Massimiliano Albanese   George Mason University, USA
Josh Benaloh   Microsoft Research, USA
Jack Davidson   University of Virginia, USA
Karen Hoyt-Stewart   Virginia Department of Elections, USA
Chris Krebs   Krebs Stamos Group

Steering Committee Chair

Massimiliano Albanese   George Mason University, USA

Proceedings Chair

Vincenzo Moscato   University of Naples, Italy

Publicity Chair

Giancarlo Sperlì   University of Naples, Italy

Program Committee

Josh Benaloh   Microsoft Research, USA
Matt Bernhard   VotingWorks, USA
Aleks Essex   Western University, Canada
Oksana Kulyk   IT University of Copenhagen, Denmark
Daniel P. Lopresti   Lehigh University, USA
Peter Y. A. Ryan   University of Luxembourg, Luxembourg
Carsten Schürmann   IT University of Copenhagen, Denmark
Philip B. Stark   University of California, Berkeley, USA

Vanessa Teague   Australian National University, USA
Melanie Volkamer   Karlsruhe Institute of Technology,
                                  Germany

Ballot-Polling Audits of Instant-Runoff Voting Elections with a Dirichlet-Tree Model

Floyd Everest[1] ⓘ, Michelle Blom[2] ⓘ, Philip B. Stark[3] ⓘ, Peter J. Stuckey[4] ⓘ,
Vanessa Teague[5,6] ⓘ, and Damjan Vukcevic[1,7(✉)] ⓘ

[1] School of Mathematics and Statistics, University of Melbourne, Parkville, Australia
[2] School of Computing and Information Systems, University of Melbourne,
Parkville, Australia
[3] Department of Statistics, University of California, Berkeley, CA, USA
[4] Department of Data Science and AI, Monash University, Clayton, Australia
[5] Thinking Cybersecurity Pty. Ltd., Melbourne, Australia
[6] The Australian National University, Canberra, Australia
[7] Melbourne Integrative Genomics, University of Melbourne, Parkville, Australia
damjan.vukcevic@unimelb.edu.au

Abstract. Instant-runoff voting (IRV) is used in several countries around the world. It requires voters to rank candidates in order of preference, and uses a counting algorithm that is more complex than systems such as first-past-the-post or scoring rules. An even more complex system, the single transferable vote (STV), is used when multiple candidates need to be elected. The complexity of these systems has made it difficult to audit the election outcomes. There is currently no known risk-limiting audit (RLA) method for STV, other than a full manual count of the ballots.

A new approach to auditing these systems was recently proposed, based on a Dirichlet-tree model. We present a detailed analysis of this approach for ballot-polling Bayesian audits of IRV elections. We compared several choices for the prior distribution, including some approaches using a Bayesian bootstrap (equivalent to an improper prior). Our findings include that the bootstrap-based approaches can be adapted to perform similarly to a full Bayesian model in practice, and that an overly informative prior can give counter-intuitive results. Via carefully chosen examples, we show why creating an RLA with this model is challenging, but we also suggest ways to overcome this.

As well as providing a practical and computationally feasible implementation of a Bayesian IRV audit, our work is important in laying the foundation for an RLA for STV elections.

1 Introduction

Audits of elections should provide rigorous statistical evidence in favour of the reported outcomes, or otherwise correct the result if the outcome is wrong. When the reported electoral outcome is correct, statistical audits can usually do so with less effort than a full manual count of all the ballots.

S. Katsikas et al. (Eds.): ESORICS 2022 Workshops, LNCS 13785, pp. 525–540, 2023.
https://doi.org/10.1007/978-3-031-25460-4_30

A *risk-limiting audit* (RLA) guarantees that if the reported outcome is wrong, there is a large chance that the audit will correct it; while if the reported outcome is correct, the audit does not change it [15]. The risk limit is the maximum chance that a wrong outcome will not be corrected by the audit. RLAs have been developed for a wide variety of voting systems, including plurality, multi-winner plurality, supermajority, STAR-Voting, and proportional representation schemes [2,16,17]. Indeed, any social choice function (method for determining the winner) that asks voters to select one or more candidates on their ballot paper, or to assign 'scores' to them, can be audited with existing methods [16]. However, some jurisdictions use more complex social choice functions.

Ranked-choice voting requires voters to rank candidates (or political parties parties, or other groupings of candidates) in order of preference. Some elections require a complete ranking, while others allow partial rankings. The way the votes are counted can be quite involved. A commonly used system is *instant-runoff voting* (IRV), which involves tallying the first-preference counts and then iteratively eliminating the candidate with the lowest tally and redistributing their ballots (according to the next preference on their ballots) until one candidate achieves a majority of votes. There are efficient risk-limiting methods to audit IRV contests [1,3,16].

An even more complex system, for which no risk-limiting method is known, is the *single transferable vote* (STV), designed to elect several candidates; its counting algorithm involves transferring 'surplus' votes from one candidate to others in proportion to how much that candidate's tally exceeds a 'quota'.

There are two ways in which ranked-choice voting is more complex than many other systems. First, the number of ways that a voter can fill out their ballot is very large (there are $k!$ ways to rank k candidates). This makes auditing mathematically challenging: the statistical inference required is now in a very high-dimensional parameter space. Second, the social choice functions are typically combinatorially complex, making it challenging even to calculate the 'margin' (see Sect. 2.3).

SHANGRLA [16] is a general framework for RLAs that covers a wide variety of audit types (such as ballot-polling, comparison, stratified) and voting systems (including the various systems mentioned earlier).

Some RLAs have already been developed for ranked voting: RAIRE [3] for IRV elections, and a similar recent method for 2-seat STV elections [4]. Both methods address the high dimensionality by projecting into lower dimensions. This allows them to use the SHANGRLA framework, which also comes with the benefit of automatically allowing different types of audits (ballot-polling, comparison, etc.). For most social choice functions for which there are currently SHANGRLA audits, SHANGRLA tests conditions ('assertions') that are necessary and sufficient for the outcome to be correct. In contrast, for IRV and STV, the conditions are *sufficient* not always *necessary*. In particular, the projections used in [3,4] check some but not all of the possible elimination sequences that lead to the reported winner(s) really winning. It is possible that the reported winner(s) really won, but through a different elimination sequence—in which case the audit could lead to an unnecessary full count. Several open problems thus remain, including a feasible RLA for STV elections of more than 2 seats, and an RLA for IRV when individual vote records are not available.

One strategy is to tackle the statistical inference problem directly in its natural (high-dimensional) space. Bayesian audits [12,13] are typically set up in this way, by specifying a model and prior distribution over this space. A naive application of Bayesian inference to IRV or STV will fail when there are more than a handful of candidates, because the dimension of the parameter space will be too high: the models behave poorly and the computational burden is prohibitive. An early Bayesian approach to auditing of STV [6] avoided specifying a full model, using a (Bayesian) bootstrap approach instead. This approximates a full Bayesian inference but is less computationally demanding.

We recently proposed a full Bayesian method using a Dirichlet-tree model to allow inference in high dimensions in a computationally feasible manner, and provided a proof-of-concept [8]. Here, we provide a thorough description and an extensive analysis of the approach using data from a diverse set of real elections. We do so for *ballot-polling* audits of IRV elections. Ballot-polling audits manually interpret the votes on randomly selected ballots, but do not compare those interpretations to how the voting system interpreted the same ballots. They are the simplest method to implement because they do not require much data from the voting system (but they generally require larger audit samples than *comparison audits*, which compare human interpretations of the votes to the system's record of the votes, either for individual ballots or clusters of ballots).

The Dirichlet-tree model is very flexible in how it can be set up. It also unifies many previous proposals, which turn out to be special cases of the model. We evaluate these and show that many of them work well in practice. Furthermore, we illustrate some unexpected behaviour if the model is set up in specific ways.

One important consideration in practice is whether this type of audit can be made risk-limiting. It has been shown that Bayesian audits for simpler elections can be calibrated to limit risk [10], however whether this is possible for IRV and STV is still an open problem. We use an artificial example to illustrate why this is likely to be challenging, and also point to some promising new techniques that could help solve this problem.

Our work provides a practical Bayesian IRV audit, with key insights and clear scope for how it can be generalised to STV or other ranked voting systems. It also lays the foundation for an RLA for such systems, with explicit suggestions for how the method could be adapted to limit risk.

2 Methods

2.1 Election Audits and the Dirichlet-Tree Model

We adopt and expand on our previous framework and notation [8].

Suppose there are k candidates in a given contest, and K ways for voters to vote. Across the whole contest, let p_i be the proportion of ballots that are of type i, for $i = 1, 2, \ldots, K$. The election outcome is completely determined by $\boldsymbol{p} = (p_1, p_2, \ldots, p_K)$. If we knew $\boldsymbol{p}$, we could verify the reported outcome.

An election audit involves sampling ballots from the contest and using a statistical model to infer the true outcome (e.g. by estimating $\boldsymbol{p}$), to some desired level of certainty. In a sample of ballots, let n_i be the number of observed ballots of type i. If sampling the ballots at random with replacement, the distribution of the tallies $\boldsymbol{n} = (n_1, n_2, \ldots, n_K)$ is given by a multinomial distribution.

This distribution describes the possible variation in the data. In a Bayesian audit, we combine this together with a *prior* distribution, which describes our uncertainty about the election outcome by specifying a distribution of possible values for $\boldsymbol{p}$. Given the data, this distribution gets 'updated' (using Bayes' theorem) to a *posterior* distribution: also a distribution for $\boldsymbol{p}$, but with the probability mass shifted to values that are more consistent with the data.

A distribution for $\boldsymbol{p}$ induces a distribution for the winning candidate(s). That is, for each candidate, we obtain a probability that they won the election. These are used to determine whether the data provide sufficient evidence in favour of the reported outcome.

A standard process for the audit would involve sampling some ballots, calculating the posterior probability for the reported winner(s), and comparing this to a desired threshold value (e.g. 99%). If the posterior exceeds the threshold, we terminate the audit. Otherwise, we sample more ballots and repeat the process. We stop either when we exceed the threshold, or have sampled all ballots, or possibly reached a specified sampling limit (e.g. imposed for cost reasons).

Bayesian inference is internally consistent irrespective of when we terminate the sampling, if the prior exactly reflects the analyst's beliefs. However, the chance the audit stops short of a full count when the outcome is wrong can depend on whether the prior is generative, i.e. how Nature generates votes [9].

Dirichlet and Dirichlet-Tree Priors. To start the process, we need to choose a prior distribution. When using a multinomial model for the data, a popular choice for the prior is a Dirichlet distribution. This is defined by $\boldsymbol{a} = (a_1, a_2, \ldots, a_K)$, where a_i is called the *concentration parameter*, or simply the *weight*, for ballot type i. Larger values of a_i lead to p_i being more likely to have higher values (the distribution is more 'concentrated' around that ballot type). The special case $a_1 = a_2 = \cdots = a_K = 1$ gives a uniform distribution for $\boldsymbol{p}$.

The Dirichlet distribution is a *conjugate* prior (the property that if the prior is Dirichlet, then the posterior will also be Dirichlet) and is easy to compute from the data: the posterior will have weights of the form $a_i + n_i$.

As we have previously described [8], the Dirichlet becomes unwieldy as K grows very large, and an alternative called a Dirichlet-tree was proposed [7,11]. This arranges the ballot types into a tree structure, with the branches in the tree describing choices of candidates for each place in the preference ordering. A path through the tree corresponds to a particular ordering of the candidates, and hence a ballot type. We can also accommodate partial orderings by including 'termination' branches in the tree. See Fig. 1 for an example.

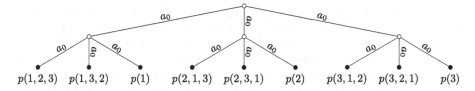

Fig. 1. Dirichlet-tree prior for IRV ballots with 3 candidates, with a weight of a_0 in each branch. For simplicity, a redundant bottom layer is not included in the tree, since ballots of the form $(1, 2, 3)$ are equivalent to $(1, 2)$.

To complete the specification, we place a Dirichlet distribution at each node in the tree, to model the conditional split of preferences locally at that node. This set of nested distributions together gives a complete distribution across all ballot types. We refer to this as a *Dirichlet-tree distribution*, with the parameters being the weights in each branch of the tree. The distribution turns out to also be conjugate and can be updated efficiently: the posterior is a Dirichlet-tree with weights of the form $a_j + n_j$ for branch j, where n_j is the number of ballots in the sample whose path through the tree traverses that branch.

Finally, we need to specify the (prior) weights for each branch. We investigated several choices for this, see Sect. 2.2.

Dirichlet Equivalence. The Dirichlet-tree generalises the Dirichlet. Specifically, any Dirichlet-tree for which the weight in each node's parent branch is equal to the sum of the weights in all of its child branches, is equivalent to a Dirichlet distribution where we remove all of the internal nodes. Figure 2 shows an example. This equivalence allows us to use a single software implementation to explore both Dirichlet and Dirichlet-tree priors.

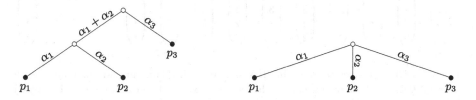

Fig. 2. Two equivalent Dirichlet-trees. The one on the right is explicitly just a Dirichlet distribution over the 3 categories.

Implementing Dirichlet-Tree Audits for IRV Elections. On a single IRV ballot, up to k candidates are ordered from highest preference to lowest. The set of possible ballot types cast in an IRV election are exactly the set of permutations on non-empty subsets of the k candidates, of which there are $f(k) = \sum_{i=1}^{k} \binom{k}{i} i!$.[1]

---

[1] https://oeis.org/A007526.

Note that $f(k)$ grows *very quickly* with k, e.g. $f(8) = 190,600$ while $f(18) = 1.7 \times 10^{16}$. To cope with this very large space, we use a Dirichlet-tree prior.

A naive approach to representing a Dirichlet-tree that assigns a non-zero probability to each possible ballot type will struggle as k gets large. In our experiments, we considered elections with k as large as 18. Representing all tree nodes explicitly would require significant memory. We can avoid this by only representing nodes that have been updated and now differ from their default prior weight. This limits the memory required to $O(kn)$ where n is the number of ballots sampled.

Our software implementation[2] allows setting a minimum and maximum depth for the tree, which is equivalent to requiring a min or max number of candidates be marked on the ballot. See Fig. 3 for an illustration. In our experiments, we always set a minimum depth of 1 (to rule out empty ballots) and sometimes also set a maximum depth (depending on the validity criteria in each contest).

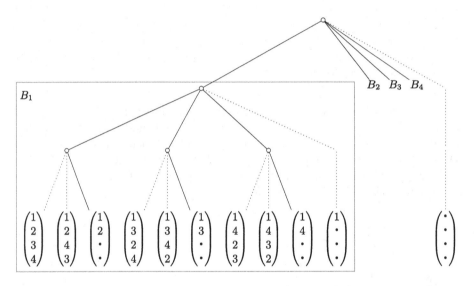

Fig. 3. A Dirichlet-tree representing IRV ballots with minimum and maximum depth set to 2 (thus, only allowing ballots that specify exactly two candidates). The dotted branches represent ballot types that have been pruned.

2.2   Choice of Prior Distribution

Dirichlet-tree with equally weighted branches (EWB). This is parameterised by a_0, the prior weight for each branch. As a default, we used $a_0 = 1$, which is equivalent to a uniform distribution on the probabilities at each node in the tree. We also explored smaller and larger values, up to $a_0 = 1000$.

---

[2] Available at: https://github.com/fleverest/elections.dtree.

Bayesian bootstrap. We can make the prior less informative by reducing the weight of each branch. In the limit where each weight is reduced to zero (equivalent to EWB with $a_0 = 0$), we obtain an improper prior. The posterior will only have positive probability ('support') on ballots that appear in the sample. This model is known as a Bayesian bootstrap [14].

Bayesian bootstrap seeded with b_0 single-preference ballots for each candidate. This prior was suggested by [6]. If there are k candidates, then we add $k \times b_0$ ballots in total to the tree. The special case $b_0 = 0$ recovers the Bayesian bootstrap. We explored values up to $b_0 = 1000$.

Bayesian bootstrap with a minimum sample size. In other words, a Bayesian bootstrap with the requirement that we need to sample at least some pre-specified number of ballots before we may stop the audit and certify the election. We set a minimum sample size of 20 when using this scheme.

Dirichlet. We used Dirichlet distributions that gave all of the maximally specified ballot types (up to the maximum depth allowed) an equal weight, a_0. In the tree-representation, these are the weights given to all lowest level branches, with the other branches' weights determined by summing them up the tree. Note that the weights in the top-level branches will vary substantially based on the structure of the tree, which depends on the number of candidates as well as the choice of minimum and maximum depth. We explored values of a_0 from 0.001 to 10.

2.3   Data

We used ballot data from elections in Australia and the USA.[3] The Australian data included 93 contests all coming from the NSW 2015 lower house election; each had 5–8 candidates and about 40k–50k ballots. The USA data included 14 contests from elections in California and Colorado; they were much more variable, having 4–18 candidates and the number of ballots ranged from 2544 (Aspen) to 312,771 (Pierce). In addition, we constructed 3 artificial 'pathological' contests that were specifically designed to be difficult to audit; each had 10 candidates and 11,000 ballots (see Sect. 3.2 for more details). The contests from California only allowed voters to mark their top 3 preferences on their ballots. We encoded this in our models by restricting the trees to have a maximum depth of 3. We did the same for the pathological contests.

Margin. To provide context for interpreting the performance of the auditing methods, we quantified how close each contest was by calculating the *margin* using `margin-irv` [5]. A positive margin is the minimum number of ballots that need to be changed in order for the reported winner to *no longer be the true winner*. A negative margin is the minimum number (expressed as a negative integer) of ballots that need to be changed in order for the reported winner to *tie with the true winner*.

---

[3] All data were sourced from: https://github.com/michelleblom/margin-irv.

2.4 Benchmarking Experiments

To demonstrate our model, and compare the proposed choices for the prior distribution, we simulated audits using the data for all of the contests described above. We used a procedure similar to earlier work [8].

Main Analyses. Our main analyses used the data faithfully, i.e. without adding any errors. For each contest, we randomly shuffled the ballots 100 times, to simulate 100 different orderings. Each simulated audit draws a sample of ballots one at a time from a given ordering. We used the same orderings (for each contest) across all of the different auditing methods (e.g. different priors) that we evaluated.

After each ballot is sampled, one at a time, we estimated the posterior probabilities (for each candidate winning) by taking the mean of 100 Monte Carlo draws from the posterior. Specifically, we took draws from the posterior predictive distribution of the ballot tallies across the whole contest (i.e. the full set of ballots), and applied the IRV social choice function to each; this gave us Monte Carlo draws from the posterior on the winning candidate.

We allowed samples of up to 1000 ballots. Figure 4 shows an example.

The possible outcomes for each audit are one of:

Certify. A desired threshold for the posterior probability is exceeded at some point during the sampling. The audit terminates at this point, and we record the sample size (number of ballots sampled). In our experiments, we used a threshold of 99%.

Do not certify. The desired threshold is not exceeded during the first 1000 ballots. (In practice, this could be a point at which the sampling is terminated and a full manual count conducted instead.)

Across the 100 orderings we can then calculate the *certification rate* (the proportion of the orderings that led to certification) and also the *mean sample size* (irrespective of certification). There is some redundancy in these measures: a low certification rate would usually lead to the mean sample size being close to 1000.

This way of measuring the mean sample size is convenient in our context, allowing easy comparison across different contests. It only measures the 'work' required in the sampling part of the audit, and not in any potential full manual count. The 'cost' of the latter could vary substantially across contests, depending on how many ballots they involve.

Ideally, we would let the simulation run beyond 1000 ballots and simply record the sample size at termination. This would have required an impractical amount of computation, given the number of experiments we ran. Our choice to limit each audit to 1000 ballots, and also to take only 100 draws from the posterior for each calculation (see above), were purely pragmatic. Nevertheless, they were sufficient to explore the general behaviour of these models.

Note that in using 100 draws, our posterior probability estimates only had a resolution of 0.01 and still have some Monte Carlo error (this is visible as low-level 'noise' in the curves in Fig. 4). If these auditing methods were to be used in a real audit, we would only do such calculations a few times and these constraints would be unnecessary. It would be straightforward and computationally feasible to use sufficiently many draws to eliminate the Monte Carlo error.

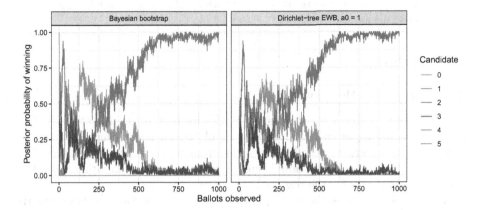

Fig. 4. Posterior probabilities from an example audit. Posterior probabilities for each candidate, vs sample size, for a simulated audit of the Lismore (NSW 2015) election, using two different priors (as labelled). The true winner is candidate 2 (green line). (Color figure online)

Generating Errors by Permuting Candidate Labels. The main analyses (described above) explore the case where there are no tabulation errors. In practice we would expect errors due to misinterpreting marks on a ballot or other sporadic mistakes, or systemic issues in how ballots are handled or interpreted.

There are many ways to model and explore the effect of such errors. For convenience, we used the following 'trick' to rapidly simulate a large number of contests where the reported outcome differed to the true outcome.

For any given contest, we can take any candidate to be the reported winner and run the audit based on that candidate. The calculations required to obtain the posterior probabilities are the same regardless, only the stopping criterion differs, and this is very fast to evaluate given a set of posterior probabilities. Thus, for a k-candidate contest, we obtain experimental results for k scenarios: one for which the reported winner is the true winner, and $k - 1$ scenarios where the reported winner is incorrect. The computational cost of the full k scenarios is essentially the same as just a single scenario.

We can interpret these scenarios in at least two different ways. First, they are equivalent to an error model where the candidate labels are switched (which is conceivable in practice, e.g. via a software error, or deliberate manipulation).

Alternatively, we can take them as an arbitrary set of examples where the reported winner is incorrect. This follows because the only information used by these Bayesian audits is the reported winner; they do not make use of any cast vote records. Thus, whether the error rate is large or small is immaterial, the same scenario could have been produced by two different contests with substantially different error rates. The only factors that will affect performance are whether the reported winner is the true winner, and how 'close' the election is. We measure the latter by calculating the margin [5].

Across all of the contests, this permutation scheme generated a large and diverse set of scenarios.

3 Results

3.1 Comparing the Priors

We generated 100 random orderings of ballots for each of the 107 contests. For each such ordering of each contest, we simulated an audit using each of the different priors, across several choices of parameter value (where applicable). Each audit was allowed to sample up to 1000 ballots, terminating once the posterior probability for the reported winner exceeded 99%.

Figure 5 summarises the performance for a large selection of these experiments. Each contest is represented by two points on each plot (one for each of the two performance measures).

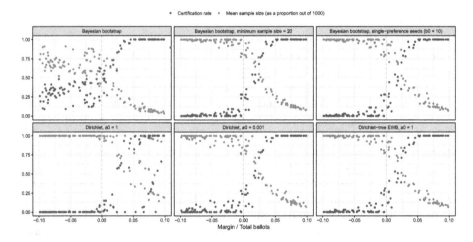

Fig. 5. Performance comparison. Certification rate (pink; y-axis) and mean sample size (blue; y-axis, as a proportion of the maximum allowed sample size) vs exact margin (x-axis; as a proportion of the total ballots) for all contests where the margin for the reported winner is between −10% and 10% of total ballots. Each panel shows the performance under a different prior, as labelled. (Color figure online)

For most methods, performance followed the expected pattern: as the margin increased, so did the certification rate, with a reduction in the sample size.

When the priors were made more informative, the models would typically respond by requiring more data before certifying, thus reducing certification rates and increasing sample sizes. However, see Sect. 3.3 for some different behaviour when using the EWB prior for some elections.

From the diverse set of contests, we can get a rough sense of what a typical value for the risk might be for real data, by looking at the (mis)certification rates for very close contests. For example, for the EWB model with $a_0 = 1$, the highest such rate is 31%. This would be considered too high in practice, and could be reduced by setting a stricter threshold on the posterior probability. (Such settings could be explored in future. In our current study design we were limited to resolution of 0.01 for the posterior probabilities, meaning that our threshold of 99% was the highest we could set).

The Bayesian bootstrap performed poorly when used in a default, naive way. This was entirely due to certifying very early in the audit, before it had enough data for its approximate posterior to stablise. The two proposed adaptations of the bootstrap both overcame this problem.

The modified bootstrap methods both performed similarly to the default EWB model ($a_0 = 1$). Any of these seem like good choices to use in practice. The bootstrap methods are faster to compute and easier to explain, so might be more suited for use in an actual audit. On the other hand, the full EWB model might be better suited for any mathematical extensions (e.g. as part of the PPR; see Sect. 4) because it has full support over the parameter space.

The Dirichlet with $a_0 = 1$ had poorer performance for many contests, and completely failed for some, most likely because it is very informative (i.e. when K is very large). How informative it is highly depends on the number of candidates. This is reflected in the large variation in performance across contests. When $a_0 = 0.001$, the performance was more reasonable across contests. However, some variation is still visible. Rather than trying to tune a good value of a_0 for each contest, we suggest simply using an EWB prior with $a_0 = 1$.

For contests with a 3-preference limit, we explored what happens if this restriction is omitted (i.e. we use a mis-specified model). Usually, this simply made the computation slower but did not change statistical performance. An exception is the Dirichlet priors, for which the total weight across the branches increased substantially when the tree structure was altered.

3.2 Pathological Examples

It is not know whether there is a way to set the threshold upset probability in Dirichlet-tree Bayesian audits to limit the risk to a pre-specified level. While in practice they perform well, we can construct artificial contests where they usually fail to find the correct winner.

Our contests had 10 candidates: A the (true) winner, B an alternate winner, and 8 supporting candidates, $C_1, C_2, \ldots, C_8$. The ballots in the contest were:

Table 1. Pathological contests. The (mis)certification rates for candidate B when it is (incorrectly) reported as the winner.

Prior	Cert. rate (%)		
	Margin: -1	-5	-50
Bayesian bootstrap	84	86	76
Bayesian bootstrap, minimum sample size $= 20$	84	86	75
Bayesian bootstrap, single-preference seeds, $b_0 = 10$	79	79	70
Dirichlet-tree EWB, $a_0 = 1$	79	79	66
Dirichlet, $a_0 = 0.001$	84	86	77
Dirichlet, $a_0 = 1$	57	54	32

- $2000 + 2m$ ballots of the form $[A]$,
- $1000 - 2m$ ballots of the form $[B]$,
- 1000 ballots of the form $[C_i, B, A]$ for each i.

In the correct count of these contests, B is eliminated first (and their ballots exhaust), then each of the supporters are eliminated (and their ballots are distributed to A since B is already eliminated) leading to A being the winner. Note that m is the margin in this contest.

If we erroneously eliminate any of the 8 supporting candidates before B, then B can never be eliminated and is declared the winner. Small errors in the count, such as would occur under random sampling, are likely to lead to at least one of the supporting candidates being eliminated.

We used $m \in \{1, 5, 50\}$ to define a set of pathological contests. Through our benchmarking experiments, we evaluated how often the contests were miscertified for candidate B by the different methods. The results are shown in Table 1.

Clearly there is a high chance of miscertifying any of these pathological elections, and it is still considerable even when the margin grows.

Note that risk-limiting auditing methods will also struggle with these pathological contests since the margins are so small. But, rather than incorrectly certifying the contest in favour of B a large proportion of the time, they would instead escalate to a full count of the ballots.

3.3 Bias Induced by Overly Informative Priors

We explored the effect of making the priors increasingly more informative (e.g. increasing a_0). The aim was mainly to help understand the behaviour of the models; very informative priors would typically be avoided in practice.

We noticed a peculiar property of the EWB model. For some elections, making the prior more informative led to shifting the posterior from favouring one candidate to strongly favouring a different candidate. See Fig. 6 for an example: the EWB model favours candidate 4 when $a_0 = 1$, but increasing this to $a_0 = 100$ shifts the support to candidate 2.

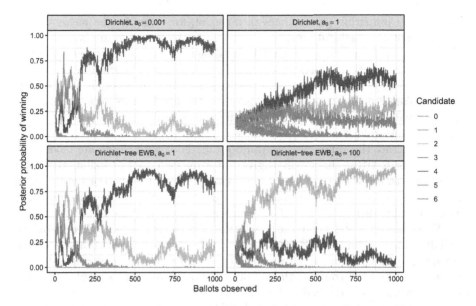

Fig. 6. Posterior probabilities with weakly and strongly informative priors.
Similar to Fig. 4, for a simulated audit of the Ballina (NSW 2015) contest, using four
different priors. The true winner is candidate 4 (blue line). The priors in the left column
are weakly informative and give similar posteriors. The priors in the right column are
strongly informative but in different ways, resulting in very different posteriors. (Color
figure online)

This was surprising because the priors were symmetric with respect to all
candidates, and because we would normally expect that making such a prior
stronger would simply dilute any 'signal' in the data. This is indeed what happens
for most elections (not displayed here) and also happens for this election if using
a Dirichlet prior.

The reason for the surprising behaviour is that the EWB prior will provide
stronger 'shrinkage' for the later preferences because the data become more
sparse as we go down the tree. If a candidate relies on preferences being
distributed to them in order to win, this can get disrupted if the shrinkage is too
strong for those preferences. We only observed this biasing effect for EWB with
large a_0, so we do not expect this to be a problem in practice, when we would
typically set $a_0 \leqslant 1$.

3.4 Comparison with Existing Methods

RAIRE (together with SHANGRLA) is an existing RLA for IRV elections, so it
is natural to ask how it compares with this new Dirichlet-tree approach.

Setting up a meaningful comparison is difficult because the methods operate
very differently. RAIRE is an RLA, guaranteeing that miscertification rates won't
exceed a given limit. The Bayesian Dirichlet-tree methods do not (yet) have this

guarantee. Comparing performance in terms of, for example, the mean sample size, will not be insightful until we can calibrate the Bayesian methods.

Another difference is that RAIRE, by design, needs to know the full set of ballots in the election in order to design its 'assertions'. It optimises its performance under the assumption that any errors are likely to be small. In contrast, the Bayesian Dirichlet-tree methods operate without using this information. This means it will likely perform worse when the error rate is indeed small, but it also makes it more robust and more widely applicable.

To illustrate this difference, we ran both methods with candidate labels permuted.[4] For RAIRE, this involved giving it a relabelled set of ballots to design its assertions, but then running the audit using the real ballots. For the Bayesian methods, it simply involved running the audit with a different reported winner, as described earlier (Sect. 2.4). The results are shown in Table 2.

This scenario is one where the tabulation incorrectly interpreted *every* ballot, a challenging case for RAIRE, because it is likely to make its assertions false even when the reported winner still won. For nearly all permutations, it responds with the need to do a full count of the ballots. The Bayesian methods only do this if the true winner gets relabelled, but not otherwise.

Whether or not this behaviour is desirable will depend on the goals of your audit. What is clear from this example, at least, is that the two methods can differ substantially. In practice, both methods could be run in tandem with the same set of data, each method providing its own benefits.

Table 2. Comparison of methods after permuting candidate labels. Contest: Aspen Mayoral election 2009 (5 candidates, 2544 ballots). The true winner was candidate 4. Methods: RAIRE/SHANGRLA, $d = 10$; Dirichlet-tree EWB, $a_0 = 1$. For each of the 120 permutations, and for each method, we show the certification rate for the reported winner and the mean sample size to audit the contest (with no sample size limit imposed). A sample size of 2544 is a full count of all ballots. Each row represents a group of permutations that gave rise to the same performance. The first permutation is the identity (no changes to the candidate labels). All other permutations involve some candidates being relabelled.

Permutations		Cert. rate (%)		Mean samp. size	
# permutations	Reported winner	RAIRE	EWB	RAIRE	EWB
1 (no change)	4	100	100	845	335
1	4	100	100	855	335
22	4	0	100	2544	335
24	1	0	1	2544	2520
72	2, 3 or 5	0	0	2544	2544

---

[4] This example is meant to be illustrative, however such a scenario is conceivable in practice as a result of a software bug or deliberate tampering.

4 Discussion

We have implemented and provided a thorough analysis of a method for ballot-polling Bayesian audits of IRV elections. The method is computationally efficient, even for elections with a large number of candidates or ballots.

The flexibility of our method allows straightforward extension to STV and other ranked voting scenarios, by changing the social choice function (to cater for different voting systems) and adapting the tree structure (to cater for any restrictions on the design of the ballots, or to improve efficiency). For example, for Australian Senate elections (which use STV), the first split in the tree could distinguish between an 'above the line' vote versus a 'below the line' vote (a detail specific to Australian Senate ballots that impacts how they are counted).

One limitation of our approach is that it is not yet known whether there is an easy way to compute or impose a risk limit. We previously mentioned some ideas to tackle this [8]. We flesh them out here in more detail:

- We could determine the maximum risk by deriving the worst-case configuration of true ballots, as was previously done for 2-candidate contests [10]. If successful, this would give either a formula or an efficient algorithm to determine a threshold for the posterior probability, given a desired risk limit.
- We could derive a prior-posterior ratio (PPR) martingale [18] using the Dirichlet-tree model. This would almost directly give a risk-limiting method, with the main challenge being to devise an efficient algorithm to determine whether the PPR threshold is achieved given a sample of ballots. While such a method would use a Dirichlet-tree model, it would not actually be a Bayesian audit: the stopping criterion is not based on a posterior threshold.

Acknowledgements. We thank Ronald Rivest for many helpful suggestions for improving the paper. This work was supported by the University of Melbourne's Research Computing Services and the Petascale Campus Initiative; and by the Australian Research Council (Discovery Project DP220101012).

References

1. Blom, M., et al.: You can do RLAs for IRV. In: Proceedings of E-VOTE ID 2020, pp. 296–310. TALTECH Press, Tallinn (2020). Preprint: arXiv:2004.00235
2. Blom, M., Stark, P.B., Stuckey, P.J., Teague, V., Vukcevic, D.: Auditing hamiltonian elections. In: Bernhard, M., et al. (eds.) FC 2021. LNCS, vol. 12676, pp. 235–250. Springer, Heidelberg (2021). https://doi.org/10.1007/978-3-662-63958-0_21. Preprint: arXiv:2102.08510
3. Blom, M., Stuckey, P.J., Teague, V.: RAIRE: risk-limiting audits for IRV elections. arXiv:1903.08804 (2019). Preliminary version appeared in Electronic Voting (E-Vote-ID 2018), vol. 11143. LNCS. Springer
4. Blom, M., Stuckey, P.J., Teague, V., Vukcevic, D.: A first approach to risk-limiting audits for single transferable vote elections. arXiv:2112.09921 (2021)

5. Blom, M., Stuckey, P.J., Teague, V.J.: Computing the margin of victory in preferential parliamentary elections. In: Krimmer, R., et al. (eds.) E-Vote-ID 2018. LNCS, vol. 11143, pp. 1–16. Springer, Cham (2018). https://doi.org/10.1007/978-3-030-00419-4_1. Preprint: arXiv:1708.00121

6. Chilingirian, B., et al.: Auditing Australian Senate ballots. arXiv:1610.00127 (2016)

7. Dennis, S.Y., III.: On the hyper-Dirichlet type 1 and hyper-Liouville distributions. Commun. Stat. Theory Methods **20**(12), 4069–4081 (1991). https://doi.org/10.1080/03610929108830757

8. Everest, F., Blom, M., Stark, P.B., Stuckey, P.J., Teague, V., Vukcevic, D.: Auditing ranked voting elections with Dirichlet-tree models: first steps. arXiv:2206.14605 (2022)

9. de Heide, R., Grünwald, P.D.: Why optional stopping can be a problem for Bayesians. Psychon. Bull. Rev. **28**(3), 795–812 (2020). https://doi.org/10.3758/s13423-020-01803-x

10. Huang, Z., Rivest, R.L., Stark, P.B., Teague, V.J., Vukcevic, D.: A unified evaluation of two-candidate ballot-polling election auditing methods. In: Krimmer, R., et al. (eds.) E-Vote-ID 2020. LNCS, vol. 12455, pp. 112–128. Springer, Cham (2020). https://doi.org/10.1007/978-3-030-60347-2_8. Preprint: arXiv:2008.08536

11. Minka, T.: The Dirichlet-tree distribution. Technical report, Justsystem Pittsburgh Research Center, July 1999. https://www.microsoft.com/en-us/research/publication/dirichlet-tree-distribution/

12. Rivest, R.L.: Bayesian tabulation audits: explained and extended. arXiv:1801.00528, January 2018

13. Rivest, R.L., Shen, E.: A Bayesian method for auditing elections. In: 2012 Electronic Voting Technology/Workshop on Trustworthy Elections (EVT/WOTE 2012) (2012)

14. Rubin, D.B.: The Bayesian bootstrap. Ann. Stat. **9**(1), 130–134 (1981). https://doi.org/10.1214/aos/1176345338

15. Stark, P.B.: Conservative statistical post-election audits. Ann. Appl. Stat. **2**(2), 550–581 (2008). https://doi.org/10.1214/08-AOAS161. Preprint arXiv:0807.4005

16. Stark, P.B.: Sets of half-average nulls generate risk-limiting audits: SHANGRLA. In: Bernhard, M., et al. (eds.) FC 2020. LNCS, vol. 12063, pp. 319–336. Springer, Cham (2020). https://doi.org/10.1007/978-3-030-54455-3_23. Preprint: arXiv:1911.10035

17. Stark, P.B., Teague, V.: Verifiable European elections: risk-limiting audits for D'Hondt and its relatives. USENIX J. Election Technol. Syst. (JETS) **3**(1), 18–39 (2014). https://www.usenix.org/jets/issues/0301/stark

18. Waudby-Smith, I., Ramdas, A.: Confidence sequences for sampling without replacement. In: Advances in Neural Information Processing Systems, vol. 33, pp. 20204–20214. Curran Associates, Inc. (2020). https://proceedings.neurips.cc/paper/2020/file/e96c7de8f6390b1e6c71556e4e0a4959-Paper.pdf. arXiv:2006.04347

Non(c)esuch Ballot-Level Comparison Risk-Limiting Audits

Philip B. Stark[(✉)]

University of California, Berkeley, CA, USA
stark@stat.berkeley.edu

Abstract. Risk-limiting audits (RLAs) guarantee a high probability of correcting incorrect reported electoral outcomes before the outcomes are certified. The most efficient are *ballot-level comparison audits* (BLCAs), which compare the voting system's interpretation of randomly selected individual ballot cards (*cast-vote records*, CVRs) from a trustworthy paper trail to a human interpretation of the same cards. BLCAs have logistical and privacy hurdles: Individual randomly selected cards must be retrieved for manual inspection; the voting system must export CVRs; and the CVRs must be linked to the corresponding physical cards, to compare the two. In practice, such links have been made by keeping cards in the order in which they are scanned or by printing serial numbers on cards as they are scanned. Both methods may compromise voter privacy. Cards selected for audit have been retrieved by manually counting into stacks or by looking for cards with particular serial numbers. The methods are time-consuming; the first is also error-prone. Connecting CVRs to cards using a unique pseudo-random number ("cryptographic nonce") printed on each card after the voter last sees it could reduce privacy risks, but retrieving the card imprinted with a particular random number may be harder than counting into a stack or finding the card with a given serial number. And what if the system does not in fact print a unique number on each ballot or does not accurately report the numbers it printed? This paper presents a method for conducting BLCAs that maintains the risk limit even if the system does not print a genuine nonce on each ballot or misreports the identifiers it used. The method also allows untrusted technology to be used to retrieve the cards selected for audit—automation that may reduce audit workload even if cards are imprinted with serial numbers rather than putative nonces. The method limits the risk rigorously, even if the imprinting or retrieval technology misbehaves. If the imprinting and retrieval systems behave properly, this protection does not increase the number of cards the RLA has to inspect to confirm or correct the outcome.

Keywords: Risk-limiting audit · Voter privacy

1 Introduction: Efficient Risk-Limiting Audits

A risk-limiting audit (RLA) is any procedure that has a known minimum chance of correcting the reported election outcome if the reported outcome is wrong, and

S. Katsikas et al. (Eds.): ESORICS 2022 Workshops, LNCS 13785, pp. 541–554, 2023.
https://doi.org/10.1007/978-3-031-25460-4_31

never changes a correct outcome. The largest chance that the audit fails to correct a wrong outcome is the *risk limit*. (The *outcome* is the political outcome—who or what won—not the exact vote tally).

RLAs require a trustworthy record of the validly cast votes, which generally entails conducting the election using hand-marked paper ballots [1,2,18] kept demonstrably secure throughout the election, canvass, and audit. Eligibility audits and compliance audits are crucial to check whether the paper trail is trustworthy [2]. There are RLA methods based on sampling individual ballots and clusters of ballots, with or without replacement, with or without stratification, with or without sampling weights, and for Bernoulli sampling [4,9,10,13,14,16,17].

There are many ways to use data from randomly selected, manually interpreted ballot cards to conduct an RLA. *Polling audits* involve manually reading votes from ballot cards, but do not require any information from the voting system other than the reported winner(s). *Comparison audits* involve comparing votes read manually from ballot cards to how the voting system interpreted the same cards. There are also *hybrid* audits, which combine polling and comparison [10].

The most efficient risk-limiting methods (those that manually examine the fewest ballot cards when reported outcomes are correct) are *ballot-level comparison audits* (BLCAs), which compare how the voting equipment interpreted individual, randomly selected ballot cards (*cast-vote records*, CVRs) to how humans interpret the same cards (*manual-vote records*, MVRs). BLCAs require the voting system to commit to CVRs before the audit starts, in such a way that individual CVRs can be matched to individual ballot cards. Constructing that matching can be challenging. Strategies used in various jurisdictions include imprinting identifiers on ballot cards after the cards have been disassociated from voters but before or while the cards are scanned, or simply trying to keep the ballot cards in the same order in which they were scanned. Counties in the State of Colorado use both of those methods.

Imprinting ballot cards or keeping track of scan order may work when ballots are scanned centrally (central-count optical scan, CCOS) or in vote centers. But when ballots are scanned in precincts (precinct-count optical scan, PCOS), imprinting serial numbers on ballots or tracking scan order may compromise the anonymity of votes: for instance, a careful observer might be able to tell that a given voter was the 17th voter to cast a ballot using a particular scanner. While it is tacitly assumed that the act of casting ballots randomizes their order, I am unaware of any study of the order in which ballot cards land in the ballot box compared to the order in which they are cast. Unless the cross section of a ballot box is at least twice the size of a ballot in at least one dimension, it seems physically implausible that ballots would be shuffled well by the act of casting. Thus, unless the cast physical ballots are mechanically shuffled before anyone has the opportunity to inspect them, it is plausible that an insider can exploit cast card order to compromise vote anonymity, whether ballots are imprinted with identifiers or not.

To take full advantage of the efficiency of BLCAs, some jurisdictions have re-scanned PCOS ballots centrally and based the audit on that rescan.[1] This entails considerable duplication of effort; moreover, it checks the second tabulation, not the official, original tabulation. Other jurisdictions[2] have piloted *hybrid* audits that use stratified sampling: ballot-level comparison in one stratum and ballot polling in another, combining the results using union-intersection tests (SUITE, [10]). CVRs from a random sample of cards tabulated using CCOS are compared to a manual reading of the votes from those cards, and an independent sample of cards tabulated using PCOS are manually interpreted but not compared to their machine interpretations. (An approach to stratified and hybrid audits that improves on SUITE was introduced by [17]; its performance was explored by [11].)

A third option is to use ballot-level comparison for CCOS and batch-level comparison for PCOS [10], i.e., a batch-level comparison audit with batches that range in size from a single ballot card to all ballot cards cast in a precinct. Only the first of these approaches yields the audit-day efficiency of ballot-level comparison audits, but at the cost of rescanning all PCOS ballots. A fourth app-roach is "lazy" ballot-level comparison audits [8], which also involve an original batch tabulation for the official election result; that tabulation does not produce CVRs linked to individual cards. The lazy audit involves a re-scan to generate CVRs linked to ballots—but only for batches from which a ballot card is selected for audit, potentially saving work if the sample size is small enough that only a fraction of batches need to be re-scanned. [8] derive such a "lazy" audit of single-winner plurality contests, and find that under some conditions (relating to the sizes of precincts, the fraction of CCOS versus PCOS votes, margins, etc.), "lazy" audits can be more efficient than "hybrid" audits [10].

If the mapping from CVRs to cards is based on the scan order, retrieving particular ballot cards for the audit involves counting into stacks of ballot cards that, in many jurisdictions, contain hundreds of cards. This manual process is time-consuming and error prone. If the mapping is based on imprinting serial numbers, retrieving individual cards is generally easier, unless the card order changes, e.g., because a batch of ballots is dropped. With the exception of [8], methods that link CVRs to cards by printing serial numbers on ballots have not contemplated whether the audit still rigorously limits the risk if something goes wrong with the imprinting, for instance, if the imprinting omits or re-uses identifiers.

This paper shows that imprinting PCOS ballot cards with unpredictable identifiers as the cards are scanned could make efficient ballot-level compari-son audits of PCOS systems possible by allowing ballot cards to be associated with their CVRs while obfuscating the link between any ballot card and the particular voter who cast that card—and without trusting the technology used

---

[1] E.g., Rhode Island https://www.brennancenter.org/sites/default/files/2019-09/Report-RI-Design-FINAL-WEB4.pdf.

[2] E.g., Michigan https://www.brennancenter.org/sites/default/files/2019-11/2019_011_RLA_Analysis_FINAL_0.pdf.

to imprint the identifiers. It also shows that untrusted technology (including untrusted auditors!) can be used to retrieve ballot cards.

The method presented here has some features in common with the method of [8], which also contemplates untrusted retrieval of cards, with the following differences:

- The method does not involve re-scanning, only an initial scan.
- The method does not require a separate "commitment" to batch subtotals, only to the CVRs.
- The proof that the method rigorously limits the risk is different and more general.
- The method works for every social choice function for which there is a known RLA method, including plurality, multi-winner plurality, supermajority, Borda count, approval voting, all scoring rules, STAR-Voting, proportional representation methods such as D'Hondt and Hamilton, and instant-runoff voting (IRV).

Nonces, IDs, and Privacy. A cryptographic *nonce*[3] (number once) is a number guaranteed to be unique (in some universe of numbers). Nonces are typically generated randomly or pseudo-randomly. If we could trust software and hardware to print a genuine nonce on each ballot card, the nonces could serve as IDs: each card would have a unique ID linking it to its CVR, but the randomness would ensure that there was no information in the ID that could compromise vote privacy.

However, such software should not be trusted. A faulty or malicious implementation—or knowledge of the seed in the pseudo-random number generator (PRNG) used to generate nonces—could compromise vote anonymity by allowing the order of casting to be recovered.[4] This paper addresses different issues: if the system cannot be trusted to imprint ballot cards with the IDs it claimed to use, can an RLA still use the reported IDs to link cards to CVRs? How? Since finding a card imprinted with a particular nonce is hard, can an RLA use untrusted technology to retrieve cards? How?

The Crux of the Matter. What if the imprinter prints the same ID on more than one ballot, misreports the IDs it printed, or fails to imprint an ID on one or more ballot cards? Could that undermine an RLA?

To see why that is a problem, consider a two-candidate plurality contest, Alice v. Bob. An attacker with control of the imprinting wants Bob to win. Suppose 3 ballot cards were cast, two showing votes for Alice and one for Bob: Alice really won. The attacker creates 3 cast vote records: the CVR with ID 17 has a vote for Alice; CVRs with the IDs 91 and 202 have a vote for Bob. According to the CVRs, Bob won. The attacker prints the number 17 on the

---

[3] See https://csrc.nist.gov/glossary/term/nonce, last visited 4 July 2022).

[4] The DVSOrder vulnerability of some Dominion systems, published in October 2022, illustrates this problem. See https://dvsorder.org/ (last visited 27 January 2023).

two cards with votes for Alice and the number 91 on the card with a vote for Bob.

Auditors select a ballot card at random, for instance using the K-cut method of [12]. They read the ID imprinted on the card. Then they look up the corresponding CVR.

That CVR will match the human reading of the ballot perfectly, no matter which ballot was selected: there is zero chance of discovering the attack. If additional ballot cards are drawn at random, there will be a nonzero probability of noticing that two ballots had been assigned the same ID, but as the number of ballots grows, the chance of detecting a duplicate in a given number of draws shrinks. Hence, sampling physical ballot cards—rather than sampling CVRs—requires verifying that the identifiers printed on the ballot cards are unique.

The uniqueness of the imprinted IDs might be checked by scanning the imprinted IDs and processing the images, but that entails trusting hardware and software to identify and report mismatches. Hence, auditing by sampling physical ballot cards requires manually inspecting every cast card to compile a list of IDs and checking that no ID was repeated.[5]

As mentioned above, checking that every card is imprinted with a unique ID can ensure that an RLA based on sampling ballot cards genuinely limits the risk, but does not ensure that the purported nonces cannot be "reverse engineered" to infer the order in which the cards were cast. That is, the check can ensure that the reported winner(s) really won, but cannot ensure the anonymity of the votes.

In the example above, non-uniqueness of imprinted IDs is not a problem if we sample CVRs and retrieve the corresponding cards, rather than sample cards and look up the corresponding CVRs, because there would be some chance that we select CVR 202 and discover that no ballot card has that ID. If we treat the "missing" card in the least favorable way for the audit (i.e., as a vote for Alice, the reported loser), the audit would still limit the risk to its nominal level. But the logistics of looking through a large pile of paper for a card imprinted with a particular identifier (pseudo-random nonce or serial number) is labor-intensive and error-prone.

Can we use technology to search for a card with the selected ID (nonce or serial), without having to trust that technology? For instance, what if the retrieval system returns a card with a different ID, or no card at all—for instance, if returning the correct card would have cast doubt on the outcome? What if more than one card is labeled with the same ID, and the retrieval system picks the card to return adversarially? This paper provides a method to use untrusted retrieval systems without compromising the risk limit.

---

[5] However, it does not require checking the list against the system's reported list of IDs: suppose that the ID on a card does not match any ID in the list of CVRs. Treating the card as if its CVR were as unfavorable as possible to every outcome (an "evil zombie" in the terminology of [3,16]), e.g., as if it showed a valid vote for every loser in a plurality contest, ensures that the audit will not stop sooner than it would have stopped if the list of IDs had been accurate.

2   Assumptions

We assume that the paper trail—the collection of ballot cards—consists of every validly cast card in the contest(s) under audit, and that those cards accurately reflect the voters' selections. As mentioned previously, this generally requires that cards were hand-marked by the voters and kept demonstrably secure, that the integrity of the paper trail was verified by a compliance audit, and that eligibility determinations have also been checked.

We assume that there is a trustworthy upper bound on the total number of validly cast cards and on the number of validly cast cards that contain each contest under audit. These might be derived from a combination of voter registration records, voter participation records (including pollbooks), and physical ballot accounting.

We consider the tabulation system, the imprinting system, and the card-retrieval system to be untrusted. How might this overall system misbehave?

1. The number of CVRs that contain the contest might not be equal to the number of cards that contain the contest.
2. The CVR list might misrepresent the votes on one or more cards.
3. The imprinting might omit or repeat one or more of the IDs in the CVR list, print one or more IDs that are not in the CVR list, or fail to imprint an ID on one or more cards.
4. The software could return a ballot card with a different ID than the ID requested, return a card with no ID, or fail to return any card whatsoever.

We must demonstrate an audit procedure that has a guaranteed minimum chance $1 - \alpha$ of proceeding to a full hand tabulation of the cards if the outcome according to the CVRs differs from the outcome according to the votes on the trustworthy collection of ballot cards. That procedure is then an RLA with risk limit α.

2.1   SHANGRLA Assorters

SHANGRLA [16] reduces RLAs to statistical tests of whether the averages of a collection of finite lists of nonnegative, bounded numbers are all greater than $1/2$. Each list results from applying an "assorter" A to the votes in a contest for each validly cast card that contains the contest (for audits that use card style data, as described in [7]) or for all validly cast cards. The number of assorters involved in auditing a contest depends on the social choice function for that contest, among other things. For instance, for a K-winner plurality contest in which there are C candidates, there are $K(C - K)$ assorters. The smallest value an assorter A can assign to any card or CVR is 0. The largest value, u, depends on the social choice function and on whether the audit is a comparison audit or polling audit, among other things [16].

Assorters can be constructed to audit every social choice function for which an RLA method is currently known, including all scoring rules (e.g., plurality,

Borda count, and approval voting), multi-winner plurality, supermajority, STAR-Voting, instant-runoff voting, and proportional representation schemes including D'Hondt [16] and Hamilton [5,6]).

Consider a single assorter, A. The value the assorter assigns to the votes on ballot card b_i is $A(b_i)$; the value it assigns to the votes in CVR c_j is $A(c_j)$. Let $\bar{A}^b$ denote the average value of the assorter applied to the ballot cards and let $\bar{A}^c$ denote the average value of the assorter applied to the list of CVRs. Define $v := 2\bar{A}^c - 1$, the *reported assorter margin*. (The averages might be over all ballot cards and CVRs, or only over the cards and CVRs that contain the contest, depending on whether card style information is used for the random selection [7,16]).

Suppose there is a 1:1 mapping between ballot cards and CVRs for a given contest, and denote the number of each N_b. An *overstatement assorter* B is an affine transformation of the original assorter applied to the votes in the CVR, minus the assorter applied to the votes on the corresponding ballot card:

$$B(b_i, c_i) := \frac{1 - (A(c_i) - A(b_i))/u}{2 - v/u},$$

where u is an upper bound on the value that the assorter assigns to any ballot card. For instance, for a plurality contest, $u = 1$. [16] shows that B also assigns a bounded nonnegative number to each ballot, and that $\bar{A}^b > 1/2$ iff $\bar{A}^c > 1/2$ and $\bar{B} > 1/2$, where $\bar{B}$ is the average value of the overstatement assorter. Note that $\bar{B}$ can be written

$$\bar{B} := \frac{1}{N_b} \sum_{i=1}^{N_b} \frac{1 - (A(c_i) - A(b_i))/u}{2 - v/u}$$

$$= \frac{1}{2 - v/u}\left[1 - \frac{1}{u}(\bar{A}^c - \bar{A}^b)\right]. \tag{1}$$

Let π be any permutation of $\{1, \ldots, N_b\}$, that is, any 1:1 mapping from $\{1, \ldots, N_b\}$ to itself. The mean of a list does not depend on its order, so

$$\bar{A}^b = \frac{1}{N_b} \sum_i A(b_i) = \frac{1}{N_b} \sum_i A(b_{\pi(i)})$$

and

$$\bar{A}^c = \frac{1}{N_b} \sum_i A(c_i) = \frac{1}{N_b} \sum_i A(c_{\pi(i)}).$$

Define

$$\bar{B}^\pi := \frac{1}{N_b} \sum_{i=1}^{N_b} B(b_{\pi(i)}, c_i).$$

It follows that

$$\bar{B}^\pi = \bar{B}. \tag{2}$$

Hence, if the number of ballots that might contain the contest equals the number of CVRs that contain the contest and π is *any* 1:1 mapping of cards to CVRs (even a mapping that does not purport to pair a given card with the CVR the voting system generated for that card), the outcome of the contest is correct if

$$\bar{B}^\pi > 1/2 \tag{3}$$

for every overstatement assorter B for that contest. We will exploit this result to construct the ballot-level comparison audit using the untrusted imprinter and untrusted card retriever.

2.2   Mismatches Between the Numbers of Cards and CVRs

Suppose the number N_b of ballot cards that might contain a particular contest is less than the number N_c of CVRs that contain the contest. Then there has been a malfunction, a procedural error (e.g., some ballots were scanned more than once or some scans or CVRs were uploaded more than once), or the integrity of the paper trail was compromised.

If the integrity of the paper trail has been confirmed by a compliance audit, ruling out the last possibility, the reported outcome can still be checked by ignoring the contest on any $N_c - N_b$ of the CVRs that contain the contest, provided it is still the case that $\bar{A}^c > 1/2$ when those CVRs are omitted. (For audits that do not use card style information, omitting the contest from CVR c_i amounts to setting $A(c_i) = 1/2$; for audits that use card style information, CVRs that do not contain the contest are simply ignored).

After this modification of the CVRs, the number of CVRs that contain the contest is equal to the number of cards that might contain the contest. Let π be *any* 1:1 mapping from those CVRs to those cards, even a mapping created by a malicious adversary. The contest outcome is correct if

$$\bar{B}^\pi > 1/2$$

for every overstatement assorter B involved in the SHANGRLA audit of the contest.

If the number N_c of CVRs that contain the contest is less than the upper bound N_b on the number of ballot cards that contain contest c, auditors can create $N_b - N_c$ "phantom" CVRs that contain the contest but no valid vote in the contest, as described in [3,16]; the corresponding value of $A(c_i) = 1/2$. These CVRs will not have IDs; if the audit selects a phantom CVR c_i, the corresponding value $A(b_i) = 0$, the value least favorable to the audit. With these phantoms, the number of CVRs that contain the contest is equal to the number of cards that might contain the contest. Let π be *any* 1:1 mapping between those CVRs and those ballot cards, even a mapping created by a malicious adversary. As before, the contest outcome is correct if

$$\bar{B}^\pi > 1/2$$

for every overstatement assorter B involved in the contest.

2.3   Limiting Risk When Imprinting and Retrieval Are Untrustworthy

We present a coupling argument that reduces the problem of conducting a ballot-level comparison RLA when the system that imprints and retrieves cards is untrusted to a standard SHANGRLA ballot-level comparison RLA.

We assume henceforth that there are just as many CVRs as ballot cards containing each contest; if not, the methods in Sect. 2.2 can be used to make them equal. If the system committed to a 1:1 mapping from CVR IDs to ballot cards before the audit began (i.e., committed to which card it would retrieve when a card with the identifier ζ of the CVR c_i was requested), a relatively simple audit procedure could provide an RLA: sampling CVR IDs, retrieving the corresponding card (if any), and comparing the CVRs to the MVRs would provide a random sample of overstatement errors, even if the mapping had been chosen maliciously, so standard ballot-level comparison RLA methods would work.

But a faulty or malicious card-retrieval system does not need to commit to the mapping from IDs to cards in advance: it can adaptively determine which card (if any) to retrieve when the auditors ask for the card with ID ζ.

We address this issue as follows. Recall that the mean of an overstatement assorter is the same for all permutations of the CVRs, as shown in Eq. 2. Thus, we first construct a canonical 1:1 mapping π from CVRs to cards. For each overstatement assorter B, $\bar{B}^{\pi} > 1/2$ iff $\bar{A} > 1/2$.

Sampling from the overstatement assorter values $\{B(b_{\pi_i}, c_i)\}_{i=1}^{N_b}$ could be used to test whether $\bar{B}^{\pi} \leq 1/2$ using any of the methods in [16,17,19]. If that hypothesis is rejected for all assorters A for all contests under audit, the audit can stop. But because the retrieval system can pick which card to retrieve *after* the card with ID ζ has been requested, there is no way to sample from $\{B(b_{\pi_i}, c_i)\}_{i=1}^{N_b}$. Auditors can always observe c_i (the auditors have the full list of CVRs), but might not be able to observe b_{π_i}. So, we define a deterministic function that couples sampling from $\{B(b_{\pi_i}, c_i)\}_{i=1}^{N_b}$ to sampling from a related population $\{L_i\}_{i=1}^{N_b}$ for which $0 \leq L_i \leq B(b_{\pi_i}, c_i)$ for all i. Because $L_i \leq B(b_{\pi_i}, c_i)$, it follows that $\bar{L} := \frac{1}{N_b} \sum_i L_i \leq \bar{B}^{\pi} = \bar{B}$. Thus if $\bar{L} > 1/2$, also $\bar{B} > 1/2$. If we can reject the hypothesis $\bar{L} \leq 1/2$, we can conclude that the original assertion $\bar{B} > 1/2$ is true.

Testing whether $\bar{L} \leq 1/2$ can be done using any of the methods in [16,17,19] or other valid statistical methods for testing whether the mean of a bounded, nonnegative population is less than a given constant. If the hypothesis $\bar{L} \leq 1/2$ is rejected for every assorter A, the audit can stop: all the original assertions have been confirmed statistically.

We now construct the canonical mapping π.

- For each CVR ID ζ:
  - Let i denote the index of the CVR with ID ζ
  - If ζ appears on exactly one ballot card, let $\pi(i)$ be the index of that card.
  - If ζ appears on more than one card, let $\pi(i)$ be the index of the card in that set that maximizes $B(b_{\pi_i}, c_i)$, with ties broken arbitrarily.

– If some ID does not appear on any card, there are leftover IDs and an equal number of leftover cards. Let π pair their indices arbitrarily.

Now π is a 1:1 mapping from CVR indices to cards, and the assertion A is true iff $\bar{B}^\pi > 1/2$.

We now construct a lower bound $L_i \leq B(b_{\pi_i}, c_i)$ that can be calculated using the CVR c_i with ID ζ and whatever card the system retrieves (or none at all) when auditors ask for the card imprinted with ID ζ. If the system returns a card with the ID ζ, then ζ was imprinted on at least one card. If it was imprinted on *exactly* one card, then the value of the overstatement assorter for that (card, CVR) pair is just $B(b_{\pi_i}, c_i)$. If ζ was imprinted on more than one card, then the value of the overstatement assorter for that (card, CVR) pair is not larger than $B(b_{\pi_i}, c_i)$, because π was constructed to maximize $B(b_j, c_i)$ across all cards $\{b_j\}$ imprinted with ID ζ. Thus, if i is the index of the CVR with ID ζ and the ID imprinted on the card b that is returned when ID ζ is requested is indeed ζ, we can take $L_i := B(b, c_i) \leq B(b_{\pi_i}, c_i)$.

If the system does not return any card when a card with ID ζ is requested, if it returns a card b with no ID imprinted on it, or if it returns a card b imprinted with an ID other than ζ, the true value of $B(b_{\pi_i}, c_i)$ is at least the value it would have if $A(b_{\pi(i)}) = 0$, i.e.,

$$B(b_{\pi_i}, c_i) \geq \frac{1 - A(c_i)/u}{2 - v/u}. \tag{4}$$

Thus, if the system fails to return a card with ID ζ when requested, we can take $L_i := \frac{1-A(c_i)/u}{2-v/u} \leq B(b_{\pi_i}, c_i)$.

Auditing using the values L_i for randomly selected IDs ζ allows us to audit the original assertions conservatively.

Note that if the imprinting and retrieval do what they are supposed to do, $L_i = B(b_{\pi_i}, c_i)$ for all i: there is no workload penalty for the protection against misbehavior. But if the system does not return a card with the ID ζ when requested, in general the audit will have to examine more ballots than it would otherwise. In general, the workload when the outcome is correct will also depend on π, but as before, if the imprinting and retrieval are correct, π is the identity: the audit compares the CVR for each card to the MVR for the same card.

3   Non(c)esuch RLAs

With these ingredients, we can now give the audit procedure.

– The voting system commits to a set of CVRs, each with an ID ζ, and commits to an ID ζ (possibly blank) on each card by printing that ID on the card. (The IDs should be pseudo-random nonces generated using an unpredictable, undisclosed seed.) We assume that the printed IDs are immutable during the audit.
– A risk limit is set for each contest under audit.

- The auditors are given a trusted upper bound on the number of cards that contain each contest under audit, a list of reported winners for each contest under audit, and the CVR list with IDs.
- Assorters and overstatement assorters are created for every contest under audit, as in SHANGRLA [16].
- The auditors check whether the assorter means for the CVRs are all greater than 1/2. If not, the reported winners did not win according to the CVRs (in the case of IRV, it is possible that a different set of sufficient assorters would all have means greater than 1/2). The audit fails and there is a full hand count.
- The auditors check whether the listed CVR identifiers $\{\zeta_i\}_{i=1}^{N_b}$ are unique. If not, the audit fails.
- The auditors next check whether the number of CVRs that contain each contest equals the number of ballot cards that contain that contest. If not, CVRs are altered or phantom CVRs are created as described in Sect. 2.2.
- The risk-measuring function for each assertion is selected, e.g., ALPHA using the truncated shrinkage estimator [17] or an estimator biased towards u [11].
- A seed for the audit's PRNG is selected, e.g., by public dice rolls.
- The measured risk for each assorter is set to 1; all assertions and all contests are marked 'unconfirmed.'
- While at least one assertion is marked 'unconfirmed':
  - Select an ID ζ at random from the CVR list. Let i denote the index of the CVR c_i with that ID.
  - If a card with ID ζ has been requested before (which could happen if the sample is drawn with replacement), use the card (if any) previously retrieved to conduct the calculation below. Otherwise, ask the system to retrieve the card with ID ζ.
  - If all validly cast cards have been retrieved, determine the correct outcome of every contest from the cards and terminate the audit. Otherwise:
    * For every contest on c_i that is under audit, for every assertion A for that contest that has not yet been confirmed, calculate the corresponding value L_i as described in Sect. 2.3. (If the system retrieved a card with ID ζ, this involves manually reading the votes from that card. If no card was retrieved or if a card with a different ID was retrieved, this only involves c_i).
    * Update the measured risk for every as-yet unconfirmed assertion using the corresponding value of L_i.
- All assertions for which the measured risk is less than or equal to the risk limit for the corresponding contest are marked 'confirmed.'
- All contests for which all assertions have been marked 'confirmed' are marked 'confirmed'.
- At any time, auditors may choose to conduct a full hand count rather than continue to sample, for instance if they judge that it would be less work. If they do, the outcome according to the hand count becomes the final outcome and the audit ends.
- End audit: all assertions have been confirmed.

This procedure can be streamlined in ways that are now conventional, for instance, by finding an initial sample size based on the reported assorter margins such that, if the accuracy of the CVRs is above some threshold, the audit can terminate without examining additional cards.

The procedure can also be modified to accommodate stratified sampling, e.g., using the methods in [10,11,17], and to use "delayed stratification" [15]. Sampling can also be targeted using card style information to reduce sample sizes [7].

4   Implementation Considerations

The seed used to generate the nonces in each precinct should include entropy that even an insider cannot know, so that the IDs (and thereby the votes) cannot be linked to the order in which ballot cards were cast.

The system should not timestamp the CVRs or digital images (or the files that contain them), or in effect the CVRs will have serial numbers—undermining the privacy protection the method is intended to provide. Since some operating systems create those timestamps automatically, there may need to be a "scrubbing" phase to remove or randomize the timestamps before the data are exported from the scanner.

As with any system that can put marks on ballots, it is crucial that the imprinter cannot create, alter, or obfuscate votes. For instance, the imprinter should only use red or green ink and should not be physically able to print near any vote target, e.g., should only be capable of printing near the left or right edge of a ballot card.

To facilitate the automated retrieval of cards with particular IDs, an OCR-friendly font should be used. Barcodes or QR codes could be used, since it is not essential to the risk-limiting property that the identifiers be human-readable (the procedure is immune to adversarial mappings), but it seems preferable to use human-readable marks.

5   Conclusion

Ballot-level comparison RLAs can use untrusted hardware and software to imprint putatively unique IDs on ballot cards as the cards are scanned and to retrieve cards that are imprinted with particular randomly selected IDs. The IDs can be pseudorandom nonces to protect the anonymity of the votes. This may be particularly useful for precinct-count optical scan (PCOS) systems because it avoids the need to re-scan ballots or to use "hybrid" audits, both of which are less efficient.

Untrusted technology can be used to retrieve ballot cards with specific IDs. This may greatly decrease the workload of BLCAs, even if the IDs are serial numbers. The non(c)esuch method can also cope with errors in the *human* retrieval of ballot cards.

The non(c)esuch method relates sampling from a population of nonnegative, bounded values of a SHANGRLA overstatement assorter B that has mean $\bar{B}$ to sampling from a related nonnegative, bounded population whose mean $\bar{L}$ is not larger than $\bar{B}$. Standard statistical tests used in RLAs [16,17,19] can be used to test the hypothesis $\bar{L} \leq 1/2$. If that hypothesis is rejected, then the hypothesis $\bar{B} \leq 1/2$ can also be rejected, allowing the audit to conclude that $\bar{B} > 1/2$. Conducting such tests for the appropriate set of SHANGRLA assertions for each contest under audit results in an RLA of those contests.

If the imprinting and retrieval systems behave properly, there is no performance penalty for protecting against their possible misbehavior: the audit sample size is the same as it would be if the imprinting and retrieval systems were trustworthy. In this sense, the method is adaptive. If the imprinting or retrieval misbehaves, in general the audit will need to examine more ballot cards than it otherwise would to confirm contest outcomes when the outcomes are still correct. Whether the imprinting and retrieval behave correctly or not, the procedure conservatively limits the risk to its nominal level.

Faulty or malicious implementations of the imprinting and retrieval, or predictability of the IDs (e.g., knowledge of the algorithm and seed for generating putative nonces) may compromise the anonymity of the votes, but cannot cause the risk to exceed the stated risk limit.

Future work will implement such a system for demonstration, using commodity hardware.

Acknowledgments. I am grateful to Marilyn Marks for helpful comments.

References

1. Appel, A., DeMillo, R., Stark, P.: Ballot-marking devices cannot assure the will of the voters. Elect. Law J.: Rules Politics Policy **19**(3), 432–450 (2020). https://doi.org/10.1089/elj.2019.0619
2. Appel, A., Stark, P.: Evidence-based elections: create a meaningful paper trail, then audit. Georgetown Law Technol. Rev. **4**(2), 523–541 (2020). https://georgetownlawtechreview.org/wp-content/uploads/2020/07/4.2-p523-541-Appel-Stark.pdf
3. Bañuelos, J., Stark, P.: Limiting risk by turning manifest phantoms into evil zombies. Technical report (2012). arXiv preprint http://arxiv.org/abs/1207.3413. Accessed 17 July 2012
4. Ottoboni, K., Bernhard, M., Halderman, J.A., Rivest, R.L., Stark, P.B.: Bernoulli ballot polling: a manifest improvement for risk-limiting audits. In: Bracciali, A., Clark, J., Pintore, F., Rønne, P.B., Sala, M. (eds.) FC 2019. LNCS, vol. 11599, pp. 226–241. Springer, Cham (2020). https://doi.org/10.1007/978-3-030-43725-1_16
5. Blom, M., et al.: Assertion-based approaches to auditing complex elections, with application to party-list proportional elections. In: Krimmer, R., et al. (eds.) E-Vote-ID 2021. LNCS, vol. 12900, pp. 47–62. Springer, Cham (2021). https://doi.org/10.1007/978-3-030-86942-7_4
6. Blom, M., Stark, P.B., Stuckey, P.J., Teague, V., Vukcevic, D.: Auditing Hamiltonian elections. In: Bernhard, M., et al. (eds.) FC 2021. LNCS, vol. 12676, pp. 235–250. Springer, Heidelberg (2021). https://doi.org/10.1007/978-3-662-63958-0_21

7. Glazer, A., Spertus, J., Stark, P.: More style, less work: card-style data decrease risk-limiting audit sample sizes. Digit. Threats Res. Pract. **2**, 1–15 (2021). https://doi.org/10.1145/3457907

8. Harrison, A., Fuller, B., Russell, A.: Lazy risk-limiting ballot comparison audits (2022). https://doi.org/10.48550/arXiv.2202.02607. https://arxiv.org/abs/2202.02607

9. Higgins, M., Rivest, R., Stark, P.: Sharper p-values for stratified post-election audits. Stat. Polit. Policy **2**(1) (2011). https://doi.org/10.2202/2151-7509.1031

10. Ottoboni, K., Stark, P.B., Lindeman, M., McBurnett, N.: Risk-limiting audits by stratified union-intersection tests of elections (SUITE). In: Krimmer, R., et al. (eds.) E-Vote-ID 2018. LNCS, vol. 11143, pp. 174–188. Springer, Cham (2018). https://doi.org/10.1007/978-3-030-00419-4_12. Preprint: arxiv.org/abs/1809.04235

11. Spertus, J.V., Stark, P.B.: Sweeter than SUITE: supermartingale stratified union-intersection tests of elections. In: Krimmer, R., Volkamer, M., Duenas-Cid, D., Rønne, P., Germann, M. (eds.) E-Vote-ID 2022. LNCS, vol. 13553, pp. 106–121. Springer, Cham (2022). https://doi.org/10.1007/978-3-031-15911-4_7

12. Sridhar, M., Rivest, R.L.: k-Cut: a simple approximately-uniform method for sampling ballots in post-election audits. In: Bracciali, A., Clark, J., Pintore, F., Rønne, P.B., Sala, M. (eds.) FC 2019. LNCS, vol. 11599, pp. 242–256. Springer, Cham (2020). https://doi.org/10.1007/978-3-030-43725-1_17

13. Stark, P.: Conservative statistical post-election audits. Ann. Appl. Stat. **2**, 550–581 (2008). http://arxiv.org/abs/0807.4005

14. Stark, P.: Risk-limiting post-election audits: P-values from common probability inequalities. IEEE Trans. Inf. Forensics Secur. **4**, 1005–1014 (2009)

15. Stark, P.: Delayed stratification for timely risk-limiting audits (2019). https://www.stat.berkeley.edu/~stark/Preprints/delayed19.pdf

16. Stark, P.B.: Sets of half-average nulls generate risk-limiting audits: SHANGRLA. In: Bernhard, M., et al. (eds.) FC 2020. LNCS, vol. 12063, pp. 319–336. Springer, Cham (2020). https://doi.org/10.1007/978-3-030-54455-3_23

17. Stark, P.: ALPHA: audit that learns from previously hand-audited ballots. Ann. Appl. Stat. (2022). Preprint: https://arxiv.org/abs/2201.02707

18. Stark, P., Xie, R.: They may look and look, yet not see: BMDs cannot be tested adequately. In: Krimmer, R., et al. (eds.) E-Vote-ID 2022. LNCS, vol. 13553, pp. 122–138. Springer, Cham (2022). https://doi.org/10.1007/978-3-031-15911-4_8

19. Waudby-Smith, I., Stark, P.B., Ramdas, A.: RiLACS: risk limiting audits via confidence sequences. In: Krimmer, R., et al. (eds.) E-Vote-ID 2021. LNCS, vol. 12900, pp. 124–139. Springer, Cham (2021). https://doi.org/10.1007/978-3-030-86942-7_9

Why Is Online Voting Still Largely a Black Box?

Michael Kirsten$^{(\boxtimes)}$, Melanie Volkamer , and Bernhard Beckert

KASTEL Security Research Labs, Karlsruhe Institute of Technology (KIT),
76131 Karlsruhe, Germany
{kirsten,melanie.volkamer,beckert}@kit.edu

Abstract. Online elections and polls are increasingly gaining ground. Since the beginning of the pandemic, many associations, companies and agencies opted for online elections at some point. Yet, most of these elections use online voting systems that are a black box for voters, even though the current state of research offers cryptographic means that would allow voters to detect potential manipulations, e.g., by methods for end-to-end (E2E) verifiability. In this paper, we report on qualitative exploratory research to determine the reasons for this situation. We evaluate responses from a panel at a national conference in Germany by specialists from official agencies, industry, and academia, whom we asked why election organizers still largely opt for systems that are not verifiable and how this could be changed. We furthermore present an exploratory study in which we asked program committee members from relevant international conferences to assess the obtained panel responses on their accuracy, relevance, and completeness. Finally, we discuss possible next steps for strengthening our findings and how to implement them to see more verifiable voting systems being used in the future.

Keywords: Online voting · Black-box systems · Panel discussion · Qualitative exploratory study

1 Introduction

Digitization in our society is on the rise and at the latest with the pandemic, the demand for remote applications over the Internet has increased significantly. A notable example are online voting and polling systems, which are increasingly gaining ground. Despite the increasing popularity and rapid dissemination, the employed systems are oftentimes opaque and apply outdated cryptographic standards. However, the state of research nowadays (and particularly in Germany – see [2]) offers cryptographic means for end-to-end (E2E) verifiability that allow to retrace individual votes through the election process in a way that both vote secrecy is ensured and voters can detect manipulations. As already the results

This work was supported by funding from the topic Engineering Secure Systems of the Helmholtz Association (HGF) and by KASTEL Security Research Labs.

S. Katsikas et al. (Eds.): ESORICS 2022 Workshops, LNCS 13785, pp. 555–567, 2023.
https://doi.org/10.1007/978-3-031-25460-4_32

from non-electronic elections are regularly getting challenged and audited publicly, we find it startling that online elections do not undergo comparable scrutiny and many election organizers still accept opaque black-box systems. Albeit the research community for electronic voting is very active, their transfer into practice appears limited as current online voting systems badly lag behind the current state of research – again, in particular, in Germany.

Our interest are the reasons for this gap and how they can be overcome, with a focus on election organizers and their considerations against or in favor of black-box voting systems. In this paper, we take the first step toward scientifically examining the reasons and explore actions to address them by using qualitative data analysis techniques. Through qualitative evaluation of a specialist panel with seven members from official agencies, industry, and academia, and a qualitative online survey with responses by 10 experts from program committees within the research community, we explore two main research questions:

1) What reasons and arguments do stakeholders and experts consider accurate or relevant for organizers to decide for using black-box online voting systems?
2) What actions do stakeholders and experts propose and consider feasible or relevant to lead organizers to use E2E-verifiable online voting systems?

Our study resulted in a list of reasons that serve as arguments for election organizers to keep using black-box online voting systems, as well as recommendations on actions to lead them towards using end-to-end verifiable systems.

2   Related Work

To the best of our knowledge, this is the first systematic research on why black-box voting systems are used. There is, however, research on the general case for online voting without specifically addressing system transparency [5]. Moreover, multiple works studied voters' subjective perceptions for online voting [1,4] and their mental models, trust and understanding of online voting and voter verification [6–8,10,11]. Besides user studies, Teague addresses the general arguments and problems regarding the current situation of e-voting systems and formulates corresponding research challenges [9].

3   Background and Overview

3.1   End-to-End Verifiability

The common security notion for voting systems of *end-to-end verifiability* (E2E-V) is concerned with providing convincing evidence as built-in functionality. Such a functionality ensures that each individual voter can themselves monitor the integrity of the election [3]. From one end to the other, this comprises that voters can independently verify (a) that their votes are correctly recorded (*cast as intended*), (b) that the representation of their vote is correctly collected in the tally (*collected as cast*), and (c) that every well-formed and collected vote is correctly included in the tally (*tallied as collected*).

E2E-V requires furthermore that it is possible to check the list for those voters who cast ballots, such that no *ballot-box stuffing* can occur, i.e., no additional votes are added to the collection (*eligibility verifiability*). The first two monitoring mechanisms are also commonly classified as *individual verifiability* since an individual voter can verify their own vote, and the third one as *universal verifiability* since the collection of votes can be verified as a whole.

More advanced security mechanisms based on E2E-verifiability also provide *accountability*, e.g., *collection accountability* denotes that, once a voter detects that their vote has not been collected as cast or intended within the vote-casting protocol, they obtain evidence that is convincing to an independent party in order to demonstrate that their vote has not been correctly collected. Yet, when aiming to provide accountability, there is a likely trade-off with the confidentiality requirement of coercion resistance, since the voter might be forced to present the obtained evidence to convince a (malicious) coercer.

3.2 Black-Box System

For this paper, we consider a black-box voting system (in short, a *black-box system*) as a system which does not provide voters with any functionality that allows them to verify that their votes are tallied as intended, cast, or collected. In such an opaque system, voters rely, in particular for election integrity, on strong trust assumptions such as: (a) They need to trust the election operating service to be trustworthy. (b) They also need to trust that neither their vote casting device nor the election server infrastructure is corrupted.

3.3 Overview

We present the panelists' responses on our two questions in Sect. 4. Further, we present and analyze the results of our survey and qualitative study with e-voting experts' considerations in Sect. 5. Finally, we provide a small discussion in Sect. 6 and conclude in Sect. 7.

4   Panel Responses from Specialists

4.1   Composition and Setup

We organized a one-hour panel discussion on the topic of "Why do election organizers decide to (only) use black-box online voting systems?" as part of the German national security conference *Sicherheit* on April 7th, 2022. The conference *Sicherheit* is steered by the special interest group *Security* (*Fachbereich Sicherheit*) within the German Informatics Society (GI – *Gesellschaft für Informatik*). The panel was composed of seven specialists from Karlsruhe Institute of Technology (KIT), Heilbronn University of Applied Sciences, IT University of Copenhagen (ITU), the Federal Office for Information Security (BSI – Bundesamt für Sicherheit in der Informationstechnik), University of Koblenz, and

POLYAS GmbH – a German commercial vendor and provider of online elections –, with a moderator from Karlsruhe Institute of Technology (KIT). Each of the panelists from academia had experience with talking to election organizers about securing elections and in particular verifiable systems.

The panel started with an introduction and some technical background by the moderator,[1] followed by short leading statements prepared by each of the panelists beforehand in response to the topic question. Thereon, after the panelists answered questions from the audience for about 30 min, the panelists were asked about their ideas regarding possible actions to get election organizers to use end-to-end verifiable online voting systems. Afterwards, again, the audience could asked questions.

In the following, we categorize, summarize, and explain both the leading statements as well as the actions proposed by the panelists.

4.2 Arguments on Current Election Organizers' Motivation

We have organized and sorted the panelists' statements on why election organizers still largely decide to use black-box online voting systems. Note that, when we use phrases such as "election organizers argue [...]", this does not mean that we interviewed election organizers, but that the panelists mentioned this from their own experience. The same holds when we talk about voters. We both provide the mentioned potential explanation and comment on it.

Transparency Dismissal. Election organizers argue that the stakes in their elections, e.g., for a university students' committee, are not as high as, e.g., for general parliamentary elections at national level, and hence they say the requirements should be allowed to be lower. For this reason, particularly verifiability mechanisms might not be needed.

With this distinction between different election scenarios, organizers dismiss arguments against opaque electronic voting systems and court decisions, that demand elections to have at least some degree of publicity or transparency. Effectively, no matter which kind or scenario of election is conducted, it is unclear how to handle complaints about suspected manipulations of the election result if the system does not provide any means of verifiability.

Voter Unawareness. Trust or distrust of voters in systems is most likely based on examinations and testimony by experts, control and inspection bodies, official agencies, certificates etc. It is less likely based on the voters' understanding of the inner workings of the voting systems. This phenomenon is similar to people who drive a car and are not interested in the inner parts of the car's engine, instead they let the car be checked on a regular basis.

---

[1] The main purpose consisted in introducing the comparison of black-box and verifiable voting systems to the audience.

As a consequence of a missing understanding of the inner workings, voters are typically unaware of specific risks concerning voting systems that may compromise the whole election and not (only) individual ballots. There is no reason for them to complain about black-box systems or to ask for alternatives.

Justification Avoidance. The development of voting systems inherently involves the need to compromise at least some degree of secrecy in favor of some integrity or vice versa. However, justifications or explanations for a particular compromise require technical understanding and potentially scare people who may feel overwhelmed and overestimate the true risks. Election organizers want to avoid this potential for more distrust and suspicion among voters, and instead opt for black-box systems or mechanisms that do usually not require any technical understanding. In order to avoid debates for mitigating the voters' suspicions, the organizers instead use (black-box) systems that – as they require little technical understanding – appear "shiny" and clean, as most voters do not ask for justifications or explanations.

Complicated Usability. The implementation of verifiability mechanisms is challenging and hard to get right, which often results in complicated mechanisms with which the voters are not familiar. Election organizers then opt for black-box solutions, in order to avoid the problems or difficulties involved with making verifiability mechanisms usable or explain their usage.

Cost-Efficiency Focus. Market economy oftentimes focuses on efficiency and saving costs instead of factors that do not directly translate to such quantitative measures, e.g., security. For example, easy-to-use software might get a higher priority than more secure software with potentially poorer usability, since the better usability avoids a costly telephone hotline. Election organizers hence do not account as much for security concerns that cannot be quantified as easily, but prioritize concerns for which there are foreseeable costs, e.g., by choosing an easy-to-use black-box system with inferior security.

Complex Decision. The choice of a suitable product is complex as there are many vendors and products with various functional and security features, and decision-makers usually lack the time, budget, capacity, and the personnel to evaluate the options and decide on a product. Election organizers have an "easier" decision with black-box solutions that are directly advertised by the vendors.

Missing Orientation. Organizers need orientation to make the right decision, e.g., regarding the decisions of other election organizers, their experiences with available systems, standards or certificates, legal requirements, and court decisions. As long as a working system is perceived as "safe enough", an organizer needs a good justification for changing the system, and the current situation mostly comprises black-box systems.

4.3　Action Proposals to Change Election Organizers' Motivation

We organized and sorted the panelists' proposed actions that they believe could lead election organizers to E2E-verifiable electronic voting systems as follows:

Active Marketing. The community and vendors should actively propose verifiable voting systems and undertake marketing measures for usable verifiable systems to actively spread the word. This creates competition among vendors and generally makes organizers aware that verifiable systems are a viable option.

Requirement Catalogs. Official agencies and institutions need to set up requirement catalogs that demand E2E-verifiability and that are practical to be demanded from election organizers. Consequently, these could turn into official recommendations, give orientation, and communicate expectations to both vendors and election organizers, e.g., by notable national agencies.

Lawmaker Awareness. The community should raise awareness among lawmakers so that they can make their assessments on the basis of the right criteria, e.g., when evaluating court cases. Once the lawmakers adopt the right criteria, there is an incentive to set similar and comparable standards that can be enforced for all publicly-employed voting systems.

Standards Enforcement. The lawmaker should set and enforce standards and regulations for secure and usable verifiable online voting systems. Clear and strict regulations should replace a vague reliance on the market and its potentially harmful dynamics, so that systems must comprise a certain level of transparency. Such levels could be the technical realization of official requirements or recommendations, and hence be incorporated by national or international standards such as the common criteria.

Trust Level Communication. In order to make an informed decision, vendors or other agencies should provide clear-cut comparisons of available systems and why or how, i.e., under which trust assumptions, they can or cannot be trusted. By this measure, election organizers are given orientation and they can align their choices with the needs, budget, and their capabilities for the election at-hand, so that they are also able to justify their decision before courts and clearly communicate the specific trust assumptions to other involved parties, e.g., interested voters, political parties, etc. As a result, election organizers gain a better orientation towards the most suitable system.

Interface Implementation. For a better usability and a more fine-grained and informed decision of election organizers, vendors should implement and offer common software interfaces and modules, e.g., one module for counting the votes, one for verifying them, etc. Such systems are more transparent and can both simplify the decision for election organizers and give them better orientation.

Voter Awareness. The community should raise awareness among voters so that they themselves pressure election organizers to use and vendors to provide end-to-end verifiable online voting systems.

5 Exploratory Study for Response Evaluation

5.1 Composition and Setup

We carried out a short qualitative exploratory online survey with 62 members of international program committees and a return of 10 completed questionnaires. We sent emails to 62 members of the program committees of the *First International Workshop on Election Infrastructure Security* (EIS 2022) as well as the tracks on *Governance of E-Voting* and *Election and Practical Experiences* at the *Seventh International Joint Conference on Electronic Voting* (E-Vote-ID 2022) between June 16 and June 23, 2022. In that email, we provided a short description and motivation of our study, the procedure of our survey, stated that participation is anonymous and can be canceled at any moment, explained the intended use of the received responses, and included a link to our anonymous survey on the platform *SoSci Survey*. This survey platform adheres to strict data privacy requirements to ensure the participants' anonymity. In the beginning of the questionnaire, every participant was given information on the study, its intended use, the information that the survey is completely anonymous and can be canceled at any moment, and then had to actively confirm their consent to participate in the study. At the end of the questionnaire, we provided our contact information to allow inquiries about the study by the participants.

Within the survey, we presented summaries of the seven leading statements and seven proposed actions by the panelists at *Sicherheit 2022*. For the arguments, we asked whether the participants consider any of them wrong or irrelevant, and for the proposed actions, whether they consider any of them infeasible or irrelevant. For both lists, we asked the participants whether they think that any relevant points are missing and, if so, which ones they think are missing.

5.2 Evaluation Methodology

After the one-week survey period, we received valid responses from ten participants, who spent on average about 13 min on our survey. We organized all responses that addressed the election organizers by the categories of the panelists' statements or into new categories where appropriate. Therein, we identified three new arguments and three new proposals for actions. From the survey responses, we could also add new aspects to two of the panelists' arguments and four of the panelists' proposed actions. In the following, we summarize the responses from the survey participants regarding their evaluations and amendments to the panelists' arguments and action proposals.

5.3   Arguments on Current Election Organizers' Motivation

Seven of the participants felt that most of the panel arguments are very much aligned with their own experiences and communication with election officials, and overall agreed with our arguments.

Accuracy or Relevance. Regarding accuracy or relevance of the arguments from the panel, four survey participants addressed the argument of voter unawareness. Two of them stated that they do not consider the voters' unawareness a current argument for election organizers to opt for black-box voting systems. They elaborated that voters are generally not the relevant group to advocate policies on specific technologies. Another two participants had the additional opinion that voters are already sufficiently aware of potential threats of election manipulations and the benefits of systems with verifiability mechanisms.

Moreover, two participants replied that the arguments of justification avoidance and focus on cost efficiency are effectively wrong arguments. They did not question their relevance for the decisions by election organizers, however. The stated reason for the inaccuracy of justification avoidance was that voters generally appreciate the fact that they are provided an option to verify the election result, or that they know that, e.g., election officials have such procedures in place, which likely compensates or eliminates potential distrust or suspicion that could arise from technical justifications or explanations. Regarding the focus on cost efficiency, they stated that favoring a black-box solution in order to save costs fails to account for potential fallout costs in case an actual election manipulation is happening or disinformation about alleged manipulations is being spread.

Further Aspects for the Arguments. Moreover, the participants also provided both new aspects to given arguments and new arguments that were not yet stated by the panelists. They had the following three further aspects to our arguments.

Transparency Dismissal. Additionally to dismissing transparency demands due to other election scenarios, participants stated a believe among some organizers that smaller jurisdictions may not have the budget, capacity or capability to offer any meaningful form of transparency or verifiability and should be excused from it. Hence, they do not find the objective of verifiability, end-to-end or not, viable or worth pursuing at all for reasons of insufficient budget or capacity.

Justification Avoidance. Other than choosing black-box systems to avoid justifications that could raise suspicions, participants added that the property of being nontransparent with no explanations is sometimes considered to be a security guarantee in itself. A potential reason might be that potential attackers can also not exploit explanations of the system for attacking or manipulating an election.

Missing Orientation. Additionally to, e.g., legal requirements that give no orientation for the decision on an online voting system, local laws oftentimes do not formulate any sensible requirements for voting systems and hence even allow virtually any technology. Therefore, more than just missing orientation, such laws do not even provide any incentive, not even for black-box systems.

Further Arguments. The participants also provided the following two new arguments that make election organizers opt for black-box systems.

Potential Misuse. Organizers of elections are interested in an orderly procedures and that elections cannot be discredited. However, the data produced by non-black-box systems with the objective of proving integrity of the vote could also potentially be misused to abusively discredit an election. Depending on the specifics of the verification mechanism, even sound verification data could be used in combination with a false pretense of having voted for a different candidate or by exchanging verification data with other voters. Election organizers might be scared on how to resolve such situations, especially when verification mechanisms do not entail accountability or conflict resolution, so that the only solution might consist in a repeated election, which election organizers generally want to avoid.

Blind Trust in Technology. Some vendors promote that technology is generally unbiased, flawless and secure, and electronic systems should be generally trusted more than human integrity. In the extreme, this favors any technological solution over any human intervention, no matter the actual trustworthiness of the employed technology. This is sometimes used to argue that any human intervention in elections should be avoided and electronic elections are generally cleaner. As a result, election organizers do not raise concerns about opaque black-box systems and the benefits of transparent systems are not even discussed.

5.4   Action Proposals to Change Election Organizers' Motivation

Six participants agreed with the proposed actions, but replied that especially the actions for raising awareness are rather unclear and challenging in their specifics.

Feasibility or Relevance. Regarding relevance of the proposed actions, nine participants agreed with the actions, but we received mixed replies on their feasibility. In the following, we provide more details on the participants' points.

Many participants generally considered raising awareness, e.g., among voters, lawmakers, etc. to be a key factor, but stated that it is generally unclear what this specifically comprises. One participant stated that voters are already sufficiently aware and appreciative of verifiable systems if these are implemented and communicated "the right way", and another participant said that awareness can easily change if experts share insights in the process, and subsequently more experts become vocal which then convinces the public, as experts generally do

not like black-box systems. Yet another participant stated that raising awareness is only likely to be effective with actually problematic results or events in
practice. One participant assessed the proposal to implement common interfaces
and modules to be on the outer limit of feasibility, mentioning that success stories for such actions are sparse, and that it might be hard or even infeasible to
agree on specific common interfaces or modules. Regarding the proposal to give
clear-cut comparisons of trust assumptions for available systems, one participant
addressed that this only works if viable alternatives exist. For no viable options,
clear-cut descriptions of trust assumptions may simply scare people with no way
to act.

Moreover, we received feedback by one participant that our question conveyed
a, not necessarily accurate, dichotomy between black-box systems and E2E-
verifiable systems. More specifically, end-to-end-verifiable systems could also be
perceived to be a version of black-box systems, since voters might also need to
trust engineers who themselves defined the verification process.

Further Aspects for the Proposed Actions. The participants provided two
new aspects for our given proposals and also four new proposals for actions that
might lead election organizers to use end-to-end verifiable online voting systems.
We describe the new aspects for the respective actions in the following.

Requirement Catalogs. Setting up requirement catalogs that demand E2E verifiability is deemed a promising measure. However, the requirements should also
be defined in an understandable way to be understood by non-engineers and are
hence easier to develop, even without a deep technical understanding.

Trust Level Communication. The comparison of systems on their trust levels
should also specifically address how they still preserve the vote secrecy and
protect against vote buying and voter intimidation. This comparison should
be on a level that is understandable to the average voter without a degree in
engineering.

Further Action Proposals. The participants also provided the following four
new proposals to lead election organizers towards using E2E-verifiable online
voting systems. In the following, the new actions are described.

Society Awareness. As much as participants assessed raising awareness to be
essential, they identified that, e.g., voters rarely advocate for policies regarding specific technologies. Therefore, they considered it to be more important to
raise awareness among the general society, media, other stakeholders, and political parties in general, i.e., not only those directly involved in lawmaking. This
action addresses the proposals for raising awareness among voters and among
lawmakers, but targets the society and media as a whole.

Cost Reduction. The development of voting systems that provide E2E-verifiability, especially with good usability, is not promoted by the market and may generally be costly. Especially as market dynamics usually prioritizes saving costs, it is sensible to reduce the development costs for such systems, for example with subsidies from official institutions, politics, or agencies.

Pilots and Demonstrations. Advertising E2E-verifiable systems can have a high impact, but also organizers or other stakeholders could get active and, e.g., do pilots and demonstrations of usable E2E-verifiable systems. This can be a first step before election organizers generally opt for such solutions. The action could be started with kiosk versions, before allowing voters to bring their own devices.

Public Auditing. Since examinations and testimony by experts typically have a great impact on the voters' trust or distrust, it might be beneficial if end-to-end-verifiable systems are publicly audited by experts. This might also lead to election organizers becoming more aware of end-to-end-verifiable systems.

6 Discussion

Our findings provide a catalog of reasons why election organizers largely opt to use opaque black-box systems for online elections and possible actions to encounter their arguments and lead them to use E2E-verifiable systems. One notable observation is that many laws on online voting systems do not provide any sensible requirements and are largely deficient. Actions to provide already a minimum of suitable requirements integrated in respective regulations and laws could already resolve arguments such as dismissing transparency requirements or avoiding justifications. Other arguments such as complicated usability or missing orientation should be encountered by actions that provide practical experiences and better comparability of available systems. Here, we received valuable proposals, e.g., to start by doing pilots and demonstrations as well as getting experts to do public audits of those systems. When such actions lead to more systems on the market, other arguments such as complex decisions and a focus on cost-efficiency could become easier to resolve. Some of the provided arguments do not specifically address voting systems, but software systems and security issues in general. Problems with software security might also become less problematic by proposed actions such as understandable requirement catalogs and raising awareness in the society and for stakeholders. For voting systems, there are actually already official recommendations, e.g., by the *Council of Europe*. However, our findings suggest that stricter requirements might be necessary. Yet, it should be noted that our survey only addressed experts. For substantiating our findings, other stakeholders such as officials, vendors, or election organizers should also be addressed specifically.

7   Conclusion

Within this paper, we addressed our hypothesis that most election organizers choose online voting systems which are a black box for voters, even though established cryptographic mechanisms allow voters to detect potential manipulations by methods for end-to-end verifiability.

7.1   Summary

We examined the conjectures why election organizers decide on using black-box voting systems and explored actions to address them by using qualitative data analysis techniques, evaluating a specialist panel with members from official agencies, industry, and academia, and a qualitative survey with experts from program committees of the research community. Our study resulted in a list of reasons that serve as arguments for election organizers to keep using black-box voting systems, as well as recommendations on actions to lead them towards using end-to-end verifiable systems. Based on our findings, we developed recommendations for organizers to improve the current situation of online voting systems.

7.2   Outlook

This paper provides a first step toward scientifically examining the current situation of online voting systems by using qualitative data analysis techniques. However, for fostering our findings, it would be interesting to conduct quantitative studies with more participants and possibly different stakeholders, e.g., by talking to election officials. Moreover, we observed mixed results on awareness and how to raise it. For this matter, it would be interesting to establish mental models to better understand the situation regarding awareness and differences across different stakeholder groups. Finally, as we also gathered a list of recommended actions, both further evaluations should be done to substantiate those proposals and experiments should be done for actually putting them into practice, maybe first with simulations and mock-ups.

Acknowledgments. The authors would like to thank the participants in the panel discussion as well as the anonymous participants in the exploratory study.

References

1. Alvarez, R.M., Levin, I., Pomares, J., Leiras, M.: Voting made safe and easy: the impact of e-voting on citizen perceptions. Polit. Sci. Res. Methods 1(1), 117–137 (2013). https://doi.org/10.1017/psrm.2013.2
2. Beckert, B., et al.: Aktuelle Entwicklungen im Kontext von Online-Wahlen und digitalen Abstimmungen. Technical report, Karlsruhe Institute of Technology (KIT) (2021). https://doi.org/10.5445/IR/1000137300

3. Bernhard, M., et al.: Public evidence from secret ballots. In: Krimmer, R., Volka-mer, M., Braun Binder, N., Kersting, N., Pereira, O., Schürmann, C. (eds.) E-Vote-ID 2017. LNCS, vol. 10615, pp. 84–109. Springer, Cham (2017). https://doi.org/10.1007/978-3-319-68687-5_6

4. Kersting, N., Baldersheim, H. (eds.): Electronic Voting and Democracy: A Comparative Analysis. Palgrave Macmillan (2004). https://doi.org/10.1057/9780230523531

5. Licht, N., Duenas-Cid, D., Krivonosova, I., Krimmer, R.: To i-vote or not to i-vote: drivers and barriers to the implementation of internet voting. In: Krimmer, R., et al. (eds.) E-Vote-ID 2021. LNCS, vol. 12900, pp. 91–105. Springer, Cham (2021). https://doi.org/10.1007/978-3-030-86942-7_7

6. Marky, K., Gerber, P., Günther, S., Khamis, M., Fries, M., Mühlhäuser, M.: Investigating state-of-the-art practices for fostering subjective trust in online vot-ing through interviews. In: 31st USENIX Security Symposium (USENIX Secu-rity 2022), Boston, MA. USENIX Association (2022). https://www.usenix.org/conference/usenixsecurity22/presentation/marky

7. Olembo, M.M., Bartsch, S., Volkamer, M.: Mental models of verifiability in voting. In: Heather, J., Schneider, S., Teague, V. (eds.) Vote-ID 2013. LNCS, vol. 7985, pp. 142–155. Springer, Heidelberg (2013). https://doi.org/10.1007/978-3-642-39185-9_9

8. Solvak, M.: Does vote verification work: usage and impact of confidence building technology in internet voting. In: Krimmer, R., et al. (eds.) E-Vote-ID 2020. LNCS, vol. 12455, pp. 213–228. Springer, Cham (2020). https://doi.org/10.1007/978-3-030-60347-2_14

9. Teague, V.: Which E-voting problems do we need to solve? In: Malkin, T., Peik-ert, C. (eds.) CRYPTO 2021. LNCS, vol. 12825, pp. 3–7. Springer, Cham (2021). https://doi.org/10.1007/978-3-030-84242-0_1

10. Zollinger, M., Distler, V., Rønne, P.B., Ryan, P.Y.A., Lallemand, C., Koenig, V.: User experience design for e-voting: how mental models align with security mech-anisms. CoRR abs/2105.14901 (2021). https://arxiv.org/abs/2105.14901

11. Zollinger, M.-L., Estaji, E., Ryan, P.Y.A., Marky, K.: "Just for the sake of trans-parency": exploring voter mental models of verifiability. In: Krimmer, R., et al. (eds.) E-Vote-ID 2021. LNCS, vol. 12900, pp. 155–170. Springer, Cham (2021). https://doi.org/10.1007/978-3-030-86942-7_11

Connecting Incident Reporting Infrastructure to Election Day Proceedings

Kamryn Parker[1], Hoda Mehrpouyan[1(✉)], Jaclyn Kettler[2], and Chad Houck[3]

[1] Computer Science Department, Boise State University, Boise, ID, USA
{kamrynparker,hodamehrpouyan}@boisestate.edu
[2] Political Science Department, Boise State University, Boise, ID, USA
jaclynkettler@boisestate.edu
[3] Idaho Deputy Secretary of State, Washington, USA
chad.houck@sos.idaho.gov

Abstract. Incidents that occur during elections are alarming if not handled properly. Currently, election incident research focuses solely on reporting incidents but not on the response that resolves the incidents. This paper attempts to understand the landscape of election incidents in Idaho in order to propose new methods to solve them. Idaho election incident resolution protocols vary from county to county so, we believe there is a sufficient need to have a framework and tool in place to unify incident reporting and resolutions in Idaho. A survey was distributed to Idaho election administrators to understand current practices and the findings indicated a clear disconnect from reporting, resolving, and general protocols for incidents on election day. The survey responses helped us design the framework for a communication tool to handle election day incidents quickly and efficiently with the intention of limiting the delay in voting.

Keywords: Election security · Incident reporting · Infrastructure

1 Introduction

Like many democratic countries, elections are a key component of American democracy. Concerns about election integrity and security have sparked large debates across the US about election laws and administration. Furthermore, claims of election fraud have contributed to reduced trust in elections [7]. Rising political tensions and low voter confidence in elections make it critical to develop processes to combat problems on election day as they arise [15].

Elections, large or small, come with the possibility of a variety of problems or obstacles. Elections may not always function as seamlessly as originally intended,

Supported by the Idaho Secretary of State Office.

S. Katsikas et al. (Eds.): ESORICS 2022 Workshops, LNCS 13785, pp. 568–584, 2023.
https://doi.org/10.1007/978-3-031-25460-4_33

making it important for election administrators to be as prepared as possible. Even when the best preparation is made, unexpected events may still occur, so responding to these incidents is just as important when planning for elections. This can be difficult since elections are administered by state and local governments in the United States [11]. As a result, the response may look different, depending on the federal or state level and the location of an election. Therefore, given the minimal state of current incident management in state elections, there is a clear need for a tool to help not only prepare and prevent, but also respond to incidents when they occur. There are currently processes in place for the response to federal incidents, but the response protocol may differ when it comes to the state level. The election day events this paper discusses will focus on the state level and be referred to as incidents where the "incident" describes some sort of issue that impacts an election day proceeding. The election protocols on which this paper is focused will be the current incident management in Idaho because of our collaboration with the Idaho Secretary of State Office. In future work, we hope to expand to other states for research purposes.

Incident reporting, specifically in the state of Idaho, is fragmented and not cohesive among counties and officials. Currently, Idaho elections are run by each county individually, meaning that these counties make their own decisions for how the elections operate outside of protocols in place that apply statewide. According to voteidaho.gov, Idaho is centralized as a paper ballot state, which means that counties do not use electronic voting systems that connect to the Internet for elections [1]. However, many of the election regulations, apart from being paper-only, are up to the county themselves to decide. For example, according to the Idaho Secretary of State's office, Camas County is a county in Idaho with roughly 1,000 residents that relies on a paper ledger-based count. Whereas Ada County, a much larger county with more than 450,000 estimated residents, uses optical scanners to count paper ballots [2]. This autonomy is helpful for counties to make decisions that make sense for their size and budgets, but this can also cause extensive diversity in other areas, such as incident reporting/response protocols, which makes voting experiences vary between voting districts [11].

Understanding how incidents are identified, tracked, and handled is vital to helping mitigate issues. It also helps states to have centralized communication between counties to effectively control and provide solutions to complex situations on election day. We ask if there is a need to have a robust incident reporting tool to guide incident reporting and response protocols in Idaho and, if so, how can this positively effect the state of Idaho and other states in the future? The goal of this paper is to show the possibility of combining incident reporting practices with established methods of incident reporting/response management systems. The researchers believe that it is urgent to have a robust incident management system for Idaho and other states in the future. The concept we propose is to ensure incidents are resolved quicker and are kept in a detailed database for future preparation. This also helps keep an audited trail of not only the acknowledgment of incidents, but also confirmation that incidents were resolved, which we suggest will help increase confidence with elections. The tool's incident information will not be readily available to the public at this time, unless an incident that occurred is called in to question, and the log can be used as clarification and reassurance for the public. The novelty of our research is to create a connection between incident communication and problem solving within elections with incident management systems from traditional Information Technology spaces. The survey we designed was motivated by the need to understand what incidents occur in Idaho and how they affect elections. The survey we develop will serve as a catalyst to fully design our prospective incident response tool.

The outline of this paper begins with the related work section, which will summarize previous research on these issues and current practices with incident response management. In Sect. 3, we will then explain our research methodology for survey design, content, and analysis of results. Next, we analyze the results of the survey on election day incidents from election administrators in the state of Idaho in the results and discussion section. From our survey, it is clear that incidents not only cause problems in Idaho but also that a centralized communication and logging system is needed to keep track of incidents as they occur and help respond to them. In the final section, we discuss what the election incidents/protocols mean for the state of Idaho and look to recommend actionable changes to the current landscape of election day incident reporting. We propose a framework for an incident reporting and response tool that counties can integrate into their election day protocol and discuss future research plans.

2   Related Works and Background

Our paper's goal is to highlight how incidents can affect an election at any scale, while also outlining a recommended framework for combating such incidents. This section will review the current work on documenting incidents occurring on Election Day. Similarly, we will highlight the common practices of typical incident management systems used in Information Technology.

2.1   Current State of Incident Reporting with Elections

Incident reporting is one way to understand and acknowledge the different risks that occur on election day. However, often when incidents have been tracked in the past, they have focused only on a specific county, not the entire state [14]. Or, it focuses on larger and much more complex issues, such as cybersecurity threats [12] that require a professional team to solve. When we study only one county and its precincts [5,14], we only see a subsection of the problems that occur on election day. These studies also focus only on reporting the incident, not on how it was resolved.

The goal of response to election incidents should be to reduce the time it takes to cast a vote for voters by mitigating any foreseeable risk or quickly resolving incidents as they occur. In recent work on this topic, incidents that occur are reported, but not resolved using the same tools. For example, a study on electronic voting machine issues in Cuyahoga County, Ohio found that nearly 90% of the precincts reported at least one incident during the 2006 primary election. Poll workers in this county were asked to report incidents using paper notes, and the findings were later recorded in a data base [13]. Common problems reported during this election included voter registration problems, voting machine issues, supply problems, and administrative problems (particularly precinct location problems). In a more recent study published in 2016, researchers documented more than sixty-six thousand (66,000) incidents in 4 different Wisconsin elections using election incident logs. These incidents were documented by poll workers who were asked to describe the incident, when it occurred, and categorize the event. The study found that the polling locations serving more voters increased the number of incidents, using direct-recording electronic voting (DRE) machines appeared to reduce the number of incidents (this could be due to potentially undetectable errors with DRE machines), and most polling locations reported few or no incidents, while few locations reported many incidents [8]. What this study and many others fail to recognize is how these incidents were handled / resolved after they were reported. Although these works (and others) are helpful in seeing the volume of incidents and their categorization, they do not include how response plays a role in election-day proceedings. A county or precinct may have its own plan of attack to solve problems, but researchers agree that having a unified command or approach will significantly help solve problems on election day [4,12]. Therefore, this paper seeks to redefine the reporting of election incidents by proposing a process for incident resolutions while also understanding the complexities of reporting incidents.

2.2 How Incidents Are Submitted

When an incident occurs, there can be many different outcomes for its recording depending on the county or state procedures. Some of these options include that the event is not documented, that the event is written down by a poll worker when instructed to [5], it is required by law in the state to document incidents, or the event is documented by a non-election official or volunteer (typically this is a voter or bystander at a precinct). The last tactic is helpful but really only needed if it is a large-scale fraudulent claim happening that is disenfranchising voters (which is a justifiably important resource to have). However, all of these outcomes lack the communication needed to resolve an incident in real time in the same unified space.

2.3 Information Technology Incident Management Systems

Incident management is a term that is used within Information Technology (IT) Operations teams to respond to unplanned events or interruptions in order to restore service to its operational state [6]. Incident management in an IT environment typically follows the protocol of identify, categorize, prioritize, and respond as the best method for operations [6].

IT management systems also commonly adopt a ticketing system in which users submit a "ticket" with their issue to the system. The ticket is then evaluated, organized, and assigned to the proper channels. Categorization is a large part of incident response because it determines how serious the problem is and then is scheduled at a priority level. For example, if a user submits an issue because one of their computer monitors is not working, that could be categorized as "minimum impact" therefore tagging the issue as "low" priority. Whereas a security breach threat could be classified as "maximum impact" and be classified as "highest priority". In terms of election infrastructure, this can be translated to various different incidents like a technology malfunction or supply shortages. Using this idea, we can see how incident response may be a critical aspect of election day proceedings. We previously considered how even election-day incident logging systems can become fractured because there is not a protocol using the same logging system to solve the incidents. So, we acknowledge this gap in election infrastructure research that we intend to fill by developing/outlining a system that tracks and provides effective response to incidents similar to Incident Management Systems we have discussed.

3   Survey Design Methodology

In order to understand the incident handling needs of a state, a survey was developed and distributed in the state of Idaho to discuss complications in previous elections. The survey is intended to provide information on the various issues that can cause delays on election day. We coordinated with the Idaho Deputy Secretary of State (SOS) to develop meaningful questions that would give us a well-rounded understanding of different incidents per county. Our survey addresses similar questions as those discussed in the related work section, but we expand on this work by focusing on how long incidents can delay voting and the current protocols counties use for incident logging. These questions will be important to answering our research question because they intentionally ask the counties to explain how they keep track of incidents, which will help us to develop a better application to manage all incidents that occur on election day. We used the November 2021 election that was held in Idaho as a point of reference for participants to use to recount events that took place on a specific election day. Since this specific election was a consolidated election that involved local offices and measures, voter turnout was lower than that of a general election. However, the researchers decided to use this time frame because it was the largest election in Idaho that occurred in 2021 when this research was conducted. In the future, we would like to expand this survey for the 2022 general election, which we will discuss more later in the paper. The survey and the following discussion focus on events that occurred on the actual day of the election. We do not ask questions about absentee voting, early voting, or after election issues, since the majority of Idahoans vote in person on Election Day [9].

The first step of our survey was to develop the participant pool and the consent process. The analysis of this study was carried out through an anonymous survey distributed to 88 election administrators in the state of Idaho, either a county clerk or an election director. From the Burden et al. 2016 article we previously referenced [8], they argue that election incident logs are more reliable since they are completed throughout the day compared to a survey. We acknowledge that this approach may be more beneficial when working with poll workers/volunteers, but since our survey contacts election administrators, we believe that there is still a benefit to understanding incident response using a survey model. Election administrators are typically the most knowledgeable on the incidents that occur in their domain/county, so, that is why we asked with them to recall various incidents that took place on election day in November 2021.

We do record the participant's election administrator role (director or county clerk) in the survey, but make the information anonymous for the analysis and results. We record this information specifically to see which officials responded the most to our survey. However, the information is disregarded and the counties are anonymized when evaluating results. The only demographic information recorded is the county they oversee, which in Idaho consists of 44 possible counties. Our participant sample was chosen because these officials should have the most knowledge of the day-of issues that can occur on election day. The participants were then emailed a link to the survey that required them to consent or not consent to their responses being used in the analysis. The participants were informed of the time it took to complete the survey and that they could stop at any time if they felt uncomfortable answering the questions. The researchers used Qualtrics XM as a service provider for the survey. The survey was live for approximately one month and the researchers reminded participants to complete the survey once during that month. The survey was closed when no more responses were submitted after a significant period of time (> 5 days). In general, the study produced 55 responses, 53 of the response results were given consent to use for analysis. Our goal was to achieve a response rate of 50%, in which we succeeded with a 60.27% response rate at the time of closing the survey.

3.1 Survey Contents

Quantitative questions[1,2] like the number of overall incidents per type and average time it took to resolve each incident type were asked to understand the volume of incidents on election day. Qualitative questions[3,4,5] like the definition of an incident, incidents that cause major delays, and how incidents are currently dealt with were asked to help uniquely identify solutions for various incidents

---

[1] On average, how much time was spent correcting a [specific incident category]?

[2] What type(s) of incident(s) did the county you oversaw encounter during the November 2021 general election. Please select all that apply.

[3] In your opinion how do you define the word "incident"? How would you define it in the context of elections?

[4] How does your county currently keep track of incidents that happen on election day?

[5] Did any of the [specific incident category] cause major delays in the voting process?

using a single system. The main contents of the survey include first asking election officers to explain in their own words what an "incident" means to them and how they would define it in the context of elections. Participants were also asked to determine the number of incidents they had encountered in each county, as well as how their county keeps track of incidents. The main portion of the survey asked participants to indicate what types of incidents their county encountered during the November 2021 election. The options to choose are listed below:

- Voter identification and/or registration error
- Voting machine error (meaning all electronic tools utilized to conduct your election, including but not limited to ballot marking devices, tabulation devices, and electronic poll books)
- Ballot handling
- Ballot or supply shortage
- Polling location issue (locked facility, incorrect location, opened late, closed early, etc.)
- Policy issue
- Administrative issue
- Public dispute or voter interference
- Other

Once items were selected, the survey asked participants to answer questions about each item. These questions included selecting the number of times this type of incident occurred, the average time spent resolving each incident occurrence, and a space to discuss in detail whether the type of incident caused significant delays in the voting process. A key part of our survey was learning the time it takes to resolve certain issues. The longer it takes to have issues resolved, the greater the potential for voter delays. Measurement of the time it can take to fix serious issues that could impact a precinct or county is important to develop response protocols.

3.2   Qualitative and Quantitative Analysis Methods

To analyze the survey results, we focused on two strategies, overall quantitative distribution and qualitative text analysis results. Since our survey was divided into qualitative and quantitative parts, it was important to analyze both equally. Quantitative reports were faster to evaluate given Qualtrics XM's built-in report building system. The Qualtrics report was custom-made to show the analysis of each quantitative response question. This method created the easiest way to quickly present the results. Using this method, we were able to aggregate values by mean or sum to show results for the whole state and not individual counties.

The qualitative results were analyzed by connecting, describing and classifying the text as described in [10]. The procedure for this analysis is to first describe the events that occurred in the study and current policies/procedures in place, then connect these descriptions through contextual meanings and influential differences, and finally classify their meaning by categorizing results that are similar for easy comparison. This process was integral to the qualitative analysis results because with it we can discover insights and similarities between counties and policies. These can then be used to create a cohesive incident response procedure with county participation in the future. We used this technique because we were able to describe the current Idaho election processes, connect these processes to the respondent responses, and then classify the responses based on common responses. These two analysis strategies helped us answer our research question to learn if there is a need for a robust incident reporting tool to guide incident reporting and response protocols in Idaho. Then, we provide an actionable framework that we believe will help Idaho in the incident response in the future.

4   Results and Discussion

An important note to make is that although we had an overall response rate of 60.27%, some questions in our survey received lower response rates. We suspect that this is most likely due to a misinterpreting of a question or the inability to recall a more specific answer we ask for. The response rates for general questions were between 49% and 58%, when more specific questions were asked, the response rate decreased. We believe that the lower rates for specific questions were due to fixed questions that did not apply to all people who answered the survey. The answers given for both the specific and general questions were still enough to be analyzed. With that being said, we will now analyze the survey report in this section.

Table 1. Incident Types of Idaho's November 2021 Election and Time Needed to Solve

Incident type	Count recorded	Average in minutes
Voter ID/registration error	14	16–30
Vote machine error	6	16–30
Ballot handling error	2	1–15
Ballot/supply shortage	8	31–60
Polling location issue	2	1–15
Policy issue	0	0
Administrative issue	3	31–60
Public dispute/interference	1	1–15
Other	14	16–30
Total	50	16–30

In section one of the survey participants were asked to select the types of incident they encountered on election day in November 2021. Table 1 shows the number of counties that observed a specific incident, not the number of incidents that occurred. The table shows the general incident categories that are presumed useful from a tool perspective and can help users better identify the incident. Respondents only recorded specific incidents if they caused major delays in the election process. We opted out of having the respondents explain each individual incident for the sake of time and response rate for our survey. The future incident tool's job will be to specifically describe each incident, not for this survey to do so.

As seen in Table 1 the most observed incidents were voter identification/registration errors or miscellaneous problems. Miscellaneous events are likely to occur, as election officials and researchers cannot always predict and/or generalize unique incidents that can occur. Furthermore, participants were instructed to indicate the average amount of time it took to resolve each type of incident they originally selected. The incidents that caused the longest waits until they were resolved were ballot/supply shortages and administrative issues.

When asked to count the number of overall incidents that occurred on election day, participants could select a value of 0 to 25 +. In our results, we observed 26 different responses to incidents on election day. Of these, County A (alias used for anonymity) reported the most incidents with 25. There were 22 responses with an incident count of less than 10 and an overall mean incident count of 4.15. What is interesting about County A's incident count is a high number, especially considering it was recorded during a consolidated election. However, this value is explained later when the participant noted that there were multiple incidents related to one specific issue. This issue was an *"incorrect coding of voters for a school trustee zone"* which caused delay for some voters.

Although this election was not a general election, these results show some important values. Voter identification and registration issues were one of the most active issues according to our results. This is similar to the study of Cuyahoga County, Ohio [5], which found that 30% of the problems reported in their county were related to voter registration problems. However, a 2009 study in Bernalilo County, New Mexico [14] found that the most common incidents were machine-related incidents (ink cartridges were empty, tampering, etc.). Machine errors made up 12% of our documented problems, but the differences in our study results and the New Mexico results may be due to differences in collections or election proceedings that caused their machines to have many problems. The study did not mention which types of machine caused the problems, which could also result in differences between those results and ours. It is important in studies like these to also include what types of machine cause errors. In our study, we strictly define a vote machine error, which includes optical scanners. However, the New Mexico study does not define whether the machines were used for counting, registration, voting, etc. so that could also explain the differences in results.

The average time estimated to resolve a specific case also yielded interesting results. Like we listed above, administrative and supply shortages caused the biggest delay for counties. However, it is important to note that the incident types with the largest count of incidents (voter ID, etc.) yielded an average resolution time between 16 and 30 min. These average wait times are not the highest recorded, but they show how significant it can be to have a delay longer than 15 min. The longer a voter waits, the longer other voters can potentially wait as well. Similarly, a supply shortage can affect the entire precinct, not just a single voter. These results show how important it can be to have a streamlined resolution process. We talk more about response later in our paper but having designated workers whose job is to resolve these issues can begin to reduce these potentially influential wait times.

4.1 Qualitative Response Results

As discussed in our methodology, we asked participants to tell us how their county tracks incidents and how they would define an incident related to elections.

Incident Description. Survey responses to define the word "incident" in the context of elections varied from response to response. The process for Idaho election days as described by Idaho's Chief Deputy Secretary of State is outlined below.

- Each county has had their state-approved election equipment logic and accuracy tested prior to election day, and has stored it in a secure manner since such testing.
- Each precinct has been issued a specific number of ballots based on voter forecasting/district
- 8 a.m. the precincts open, the first voter signs in, verifies the ballot box is empty. The ballot box is then closed and secured before the first voter can cast their ballot
- Voters continue to vote throughout the day
  - If the ballot boxes are full or counting needs to begin early, a new ballot box will replace the original box, and two election workers will begin counting the ballots in a secured room in the precinct. If electronic scanners/tabulators are used, the ballots will be secured as they are electronically scanned for tabulation
- The polls close at 8 p.m. and all voters in line by that time are given time to submit their ballot
- Precincts confirm ballot inventory counts to ballots issued
- Ballots are tabulated using either a hand count process or via electronic scanners while maintaining ballot security and inventory.

Now that the process for casting a ballot on election day has been defined, we assume that anything that happens outside of this process would be an "incident". Considering that there should be no roadblocks in this process, it should be a simple and easy task to submit a ballot. We will now look at some of the definitions submitted from our survey and analyze their interpretations compared to the process we characterized above. We provide a few responses below from our response pool that represent various responses found in the analysis.

"Situation that occurs outside the normal process/procedure"

"Situation that may cause concern of a violation of security or voting process procedures"

"An event that occurs for which further action is required to in order to proceed to complete the process"

"A News worthy issue. Something that would get you on the 10pm news"

"Any interruptions in the normal election day."

"An incident to me would be an irregularity or something requiring our attention that deviates from the normal work flow of an election."

"An occurrence or event, usually when speaking about a negative experience. In elections, this could be an interaction with the voter, equipment problems, etc."

"Anything out of the ordinary"

From these responses, we can see that there were various ways in which the participants decided to answer the question. Some respondents believed that incidents are only extreme cases of problems that could attract media attention, while others believed that an incident was anything out of the ordinary. The most frequent type of response was one that describes an incident as anything outside the normal election process. These responses are consistent with the claim we made previously, in which any situation that occurs outside of the election process is considered an incident. We propose that having an incident reporting and response protocol may help local election officials handle these incidents outside of the normal election process.

Incident Tracking Routines. Through this survey analysis, we have learned that incident tracking practices vary from county to county. We previously discussed how Idaho has a fractured approach to incident tracking, but we were not aware of those individual practices. Counties must follow the general policies and procedures for elections in Idaho, but they have their own autonomy when making procedures outside of the general rules. This includes how counties handle incident tracking and response. Again, we present response excerpts detailing how counties track incidents.

"We don't really have a policy to track incidents on election day."

"We do not have a formal process."

"Usually reported to election officials, addressed at the time and a remedy done, there is no tracking."

"Written incident report in file. The ongoing process would depend on the severity of the incident."

"Our county has an incident report folder available at every precinct to record the incident that has occurred."

"If the incident is the result of an error or omission on our part, I would document the incident and store it with election notes or election paperwork."

"They are reported to the Office and the Chief Judge is instructed to make a note. In the 2021 Election, the Chief Judge notes were not formally turned in. I have started an Election Incident Log to track these issues as they progress."

"Write it on a list."

"Going forward each chief judge, poll worker, and clerk staff will have a notebook. The type of incident, the time of incident, the name of the person(s) involved, and the remedy will be tracked. Previously, we did not keep a log."

These responses show what we already know, incident response and reporting are severed across counties. Many counties recall writing incidents on a list or taking notes of them. However, how are these stored for future use? Some counties are beginning to build an incident reporting protocol by using logs, but others still have no formal practice or don't track them at all. Other responses indicated that if they recorded incidents, they would solve them first and document the incident afterwards. Although we believe that this is a step in the right direction for incident response, we also believe that it is important to document incidents when they occur and notify appropriate personnel at the same time so that vital information is not lost when trying to recount the incident later. This can also lead to lost information, as we have discussed earlier, where information gathering can be difficult when multiple calls, emails, and texts are exchanged. This is precisely why we recommend our incident reporting and response framework so that communication can happen in the same designated space.

Counties often learn and adopt practices from each other, so we believe that having a central reporting process will help counties come together in a unified fashion to streamline the resolution process. Some respondents reflected that their county has already started an incident reporting process similar to the one we propose, as the last quote conveys. We believe that as counties start using the same framework, others will be more willing to follow suit. This framework could help counties sort out which incidents are most critical and inject resources faster into precincts or polls in need, as well as adapt their practices to better resolve incidents and prevent future ones from happening.

Incident Similarities. Finally, we looked at the similarities in incidents among the free response questions asking if any of the incidents we defined caused significant delays in the voting process. The good news is that most of the respondents said that none of these incidents caused a major delay. However, this may be different with larger elections that cause more people to vote in person. Therefore, it is important to recognize patterns in past incidents that have caused significant delays and learn from them to prevent them from happening again in the next election cycle.

We had 16 combined responses from all categories that explained a specific issue and whether it delayed or did not delay the voting process. Of these 16 responses, 8 caused a delay in the voting process. Of these eight responses, the most common problems were incorrect voter data/district information, greater than expected turnout, and precinct location location issues. Once the appropriate channels were contacted, the incident was resolved and voting could resume as normal. All of these responses indicated in some way that the voting process was *"slowed"*, *"long"*, or *"resource draining"*. Again, we believe that these responses may lead to the necessary implementation of the incident response protocol that we have built. With the right resources and structure in place, counties can work proactively to solve problems rather than reactively trying to catch up on what the incident is, how it occurred and how long a delay has been in place.

5   Framework for Election Day Incident Protocol Recommendations and Next Steps

We believe that to reduce the impact these incidents can have on election day, precincts and counties must be prepared with an action plan. Strong electoral infrastructure is an important part of election success. In turn, having effective communication lines when incidents occur will make the response and resources beneficial to all counties involved. As we have discussed throughout this paper, we can see that there is a separate approach to incident response in all counties of Idaho. The goal of this paper is again to unify incident response protocols with incident reporting to effectively assist counties and precincts in future elections. This section will describe a recommended framework and the current state of our research in this area.

To develop an effective incident reporting system, we do not intend to reinvent the wheel when it comes to the already successful systems we have seen with IT incident management. Instead, we intend to utilize these known best practices from one domain and apply them to a new domain with the modifications necessary to fit the needs of the new domain. The tool we propose will be used in the election management domain (which has not been previously done) for an advanced election ecosystem that can effectively solve incidents. Our proposed framework will follow some ideas from what we have previously learned, including the pillars of identify, categorize, prioritize, and respond. A resource that was studied for the outline of our framework was the Harvard Elections Battle Staff Playbook [3]. This playbook is geared toward election protocols for states to use as a resource. We adopted an ideology similar to that learned from this text for our own incident reporting system. This resource in combination with preexisting systems has led to this unified approach to incident management and response on election day. We have included an image of the proposed outline/process in Fig. 1 as well as a detailed explanation in the next sections.

5.1   Identification

The first pillar of the framework is **Identification** which begins at the first level of support within elections: poll workers. Poll workers are often the first to notice if an irregularity occurs in a precinct or district. Therefore, it is critical that they have access to the incident reporting tool to be able to submit incidents as they occur. It is essential that the tool is simple and easy to use, so that when an incident needs to be submitted, it is not a confusing or complicated process. The simplicity of the incident report should mean that it includes only the necessary information to know where the incident is happening, when it happened, and a description of the incident. When an event has been observed, the poll worker

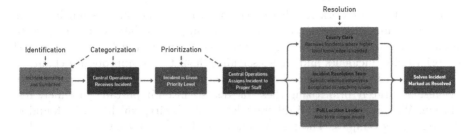

Fig. 1. A figure depicting the process of incidents being identified, classified, prioritized, assigned, and resolved using the incident reporting tool protocol we propose

would be able to quickly open up the reporting page, complete the necessary information, and submit the incident. While the incident is being processed, the poll workers will continue operations as best as possible.

If the incident has already been resolved or help beyond the precinct itself is not needed, the precinct will work together to solve the incident at the time of first acknowledgment. It is still encouraged to submit the incident for logging and review purposes after the fact and to clearly state that the incident has been resolved. Logging incidents, even if they have already been resolved, is still vital information for the state and county to obtain in order to use the information to prepare for future elections. It will also help the state keep an audit trail of all problems, so that if there are discrepancies in activities that occurred on election day, administrators can easily refer to them in the information logs.

5.2   Categorization

The second pillar of the framework is **Categorization** which can be incorporated with the identification stage and the prioritization stage. Categorization is a preference that can be chosen by each state. Considering each state has its own ideology of how incidents are handled in their state, it can be up to them what predefined categories are used for this process. Currently in Idaho, the incidents categorized that we have determined are the labels that we used in our survey we distributed. These labels were discussed at length with the Secretary of State's office to understand what problems are most persistent in Idaho elections. A state can also choose if they want to have the poll worker or submitter of the incident categorize the incident or if the receivers of the incident will categorize it. The framework we have built for Idaho includes allowing the person submitting the incident to include a predefined category for the incident, if applicable.

5.3   Prioritization

Once the incident is identified and categorized, it is now ready for the third pillar, which is **Prioritization**. In the Harvard Battle Staff Playbook, the authors describe a team of workers whose roles are to prioritize and assign incidents to election administrators, precinct supervisors, and other administrators to resolve. This team would be in a centralized location and is strictly focused on prioritizing incidents and then assigning them to the appropriate channels. Prioritization should be the second most crucial part of an incident protocol because accurately prioritizing these incidents will be important for timely resolution. We have identified 5 different levels of priority, which can be found in Table 2 with examples. The researchers chose five priority levels because elections can cause multiple variations of events with varying severity, so having more specified levels is believed to be easier for workers to prioritize.

Table 2. Incident level of prioritization

Incident priority level	Example
Level 1 - Lowest priority	More voters than projected have shown up to the polls early so there is an anticipated need for more ballots so a request is submitted before it affects voters
Level 2	There is confusion with a specific policy and clarification is needed before voting can resume
Level 3	Ballot scanning machine malfunctioning and normal trouble shooting has not solved the issue. Precinct needs to report it's results soon
Level 4	Power outage or natural disturbance causing delay in voting at a specific precinct
Level 5 - Highest priority	Active threat level compromising voters and volunteers lives in multiple precincts - alert emergency services

5.4   Response

The final pillar is **Response** which we have argued in this paper as being the most critical part of the incident protocol on election day. Response is part of this framework that we have discussed the most in terms of effective response. To be effective, communication must occur within the same channels. Through anecdotal discussions with the Idaho Secretary of State's office, it is clear that communication is fractured when incidents occur. Many times, the response is subject to "phone-tag" (repeated missed phone calls on either side), emails, or text messages that take time to parse through and decipher. Having a central location where all communication can occur is key to a successful response rate when incidents occur.

Making sure that the right people are contacted for a response is important. If it is a low-level incident, most likely a higher-level official is not needed to resolve the issue, so, having clear assignment roles is also needed for success. These assignments would occur once the prioritization of the incident has been established. When the priority level is established, the incident will be assigned to the appropriate personnel for action.

The tool we are developing enables a queue system that will take into account the number of items a specific person has in their queue to complete and assign incidents accordingly. Once the incident has been assigned, the person assigned to it can begin responding. This could include dropping off more ballots, assisting at a polling location when there is voter overload, contacting maintenance to fix a voting machine, etc. When the incident has been properly handled, the person assigned to the incident can close the ticket and mark it as "resolved". Once the incident has been resolved, the information is stored in a database for the counties to retrieve for review and preparation for the next election.

5.5 Conclusion

In this paper, we have presented an argument for the development of an election day incident reporting and response tool to mitigate voting delays in elections. We have adequately provided the results of an exploratory survey to understand the nature of incident response and reporting in the state of Idaho. The results show that incident reporting and response varies from county to county. This division in communication limits the ability of states like Idaho to handle incidents in a uniform process. This paper has provided recommendations and a framework for effective incident response management for counties, precincts, and states as a whole to communicate and solve issues on election day in one place. This is not an exhaustive illustration of all functionality in our proposed tool; however, we hope that highlighting key components will encourage other states to investigate an incident response and reporting protocol for efficient incident resolution.

In future work, we plan to present a prototype of incident logging for election administrators to test to fully develop the communication and response portion of the tool. Enough progress has been made to begin Beta testing the tool's security and functionality before deploying it to a wider audience. Future work will include a paper with a rigorous explanation of the tool once development has been completed. We anticipate being able to expand our reach to other states to learn how they communicate incident response as well. Communication has currently begun with Colorado to administer the survey to their state election leaders to compare and contrast our results with a different state. We plan to continue working closely with the Idaho Secretary of State's office to accurately monitor and solve incidents that occur within Idaho elections. We hope to make this tool easily accessible in the future so that other states may adopt its features for their own needs, helping election officials administer elections more smoothly and increasing confidence in incident response.

To view all of the responses from our survey, please email Kamryn Parker for access to our private Google drive folder.

References

1. Vote idaho. https://voteidaho.gov/elections-security-faq/
2. Voting systems by county. https://sos.idaho.gov/elections-division/voting-systems-by-county/
3. The election battle staff playbook. Defending Digital Democracy (2019). https://www.belfercenter.org/sites/default/files/2019-12/Battle%20Staff.pdf
4. Alvarez, R.M., Hall, T.E.: Building secure and transparent elections through standard operating procedures. Public Administ. Rev. 68(5), 828–838 (2008). https://doi.org/10.1111/j.1540-6210.2008.00924.x, https://onlinelibrary.wiley.com/doi/abs/10.1111/j.1540-6210.2008.00924.x
5. Alvarez, R., Atkeson, L., Hall, T.: Evaluating Elections: A Handbook of Methods and Standards. Cambridge University Press (2013). https://books.google.com/books?id=QFWHBNEEzzMC
6. Atlassian: What is incident management?. https://www.atlassian.com/itsm/incident-management
7. Berlinski, N., et al.: The effects of unsubstantiated claims of voter fraud on confidence in elections. Journal of Experim. Polit. Sci. 1–16 (2021). https://doi.org/10.1017/XPS.2021.18
8. Burden, B.C., Canon, D.T., Mayer, K.R., Moynihan, D.P., Neiheisel, J.R.: What happens at the polling place: Using administrative data to look inside elections. Public Administ. Rev. 77(3), 354–364 (2017). https://doi.org/10.1111/puar.12592, https://onlinelibrary.wiley.com/doi/abs/10.1111/puar.12592
9. Corbin, C.: Official voter turnout for idaho's may 17 primary election comes to 32.5% (2022). https://idahocapitalsun.com/2022/06/13/official-voter-turnout-for-idahos-may-17-primary-election-comes-to-32-5/
10. Dey, I.: Qualitative Data Analysis: A User Friendly Guide for Social Scientists. Taylor & Francis (2003). https://books.google.com/books?id=1OKIAgAAQBAJ
11. Beckman, F., Hannah, D., Gregory, W.: Tova: Understanding the Role of Local Election Officials: How Local Autonomy Shapes U.S. Election Administration. Ash Center Policy Briefs Series (September 2021). https://dash.harvard.edu/handle/1/37370808
12. Hall, J.L.: Towards work-practice modeling of elections and the election incident reporting system (eirs) (2005). https://josephhall.org/papers/eirs_brahms_mims.pdf
13. Kiewiet, R., Hall, T.E., Alvarez, R.M., Katz, J.N.: Fraud or failure? what incident reports reveal about election anomalies and irregularities. In: Election Fraud: Detecting and Deterring Electoral Manipulation, pp. 112–130. Brookings Institute Press (2009). https://books.google.com/books?id=HeUyo5RcI7wC
14. Odegard, D.: Behavior and error in election administration: A look at election day precinct reports (2018). https://polisci.unm.edu/common/c-sved/papers/electionbehavior.pdf
15. Pope, A.E.: Cyber-securing our elections. J. Cyber Policy 3(1), 24–38 (2018). https://doi.org/10.1080/23738871.2018.1473887

Council of Europe Guidelines on the Use of ICT in Electoral Processes

Ardita Driza Maurer[1][(✉)], Melanie Volkamer[2][iD], and Robert Krimmer[3][iD]

[1] Zurich, Switzerland
`info@electoralpractice.ch`
[2] SECUSO Research Group, Karlsruhe Institute of Technology, Karlsruhe, Germany
`melanie.volkamer@kit.edu`
[3] Institute of Political Studies, E-Voting.CC GmbH, Frutzstrasse 4,
6832 Sulz, Austria
`robert.krimmer@ut.ee`

Abstract. The paper focuses on the Guidelines on the use of ICT in electoral processes which the Council of Europe published in 2022. The paper describes the development process and the considered input. It also provides a summary of the content and explains those concepts that are new or different compared to previous or related guidelines. Finally the limitations and future improvements are discussed.

Keywords: ICT in elections · e-voting · Regulation · Security

1 Introduction

Electoral authorities may benefit from the deployment of Information and Communication Technology (ICT) to handle electoral data and processes in elections in many ways, e.g., thanks to better accessibility, more interaction, and increased transparency. However, the use of ICT also carries new challenges, arising from threats and risks to the realisation of constitutional principles like universal, equal, free and secret suffrage. Making sure that ICT-backed solutions that are used in elections comply with those principles is the ambition of a new instrument introduced by the Council of Europe on 9 February 2022: the Committee of Ministers Guidelines on the use of information and communication technology (ICT) in electoral processes in Council of Europe Member States, CM(2022)10 [2].

The Council of Europe (CoE), an international organization, is the continent's leading human rights organisation. It has the mission of safeguarding and developing democracy, human rights and rule of law. This European constitutional heritage also includes the European electoral heritage, which is reflected in the European Convention on Human Rights (ECHR), article 3 of the additional Protocol (P1-3 ECHR) on the Right to free elections. P1-3 ECHR says that the High Contracting Parties undertake to hold free elections at reasonable intervals by secret ballot, under conditions which will ensure the free expression of the opinion of the people in the choice of the legislature. The electoral principles

S. Katsikas et al. (Eds.): ESORICS 2022 Workshops, LNCS 13785, pp. 585–599, 2023.
https://doi.org/10.1007/978-3-031-25460-4_34

enshrined in P1-3 ECHR are common to CoE's 46 member States [9][1]. Individuals can seek redress before the European Court of Human Rights (ECtHR), an international Court, for violation of their rights at the national level, including of the right to free elections. The Court has extensively interpreted P1-3 ECHR. Member States are bound by the Court's final decisions.

The CoE supervises the implementation of the right to free elections not only through the judicial power of the ECtHR, but also by developing legal instruments which aim at ensuring the implementation of the rights. As far as the right to free elections and, more specifically, its application to ICT used in elections is concerned, the CoE has introduced two groups of instruments. First, CoE's advisory body on constitutional matters - the Venice Commission - has identified the principles of the European electoral heritage and explained their concrete meaning. The reference documents are the Codes of good practice in electoral matters and on referendums [3] and other interpretative declarations and studies. To be noted, the content of Article 25b ICCPR (right to free elections at the universal level) and its interpretation by the Human Rights Committee are part of the European electoral heritage. Second, the Committee of Ministers (CM) has introduced soft-law instruments about the implementation of the electoral principles to ICT-backed solutions.

This second group of soft-law instruments provides guidance on regulation of ICT in elections. It includes two types of instruments, namely on use of ICT in elections in general and on e-voting. CoE started working on e-voting at the beginning of 2000. A first recommendation, CM/Rec(2004)11 on legal, operational and technical standards for e-voting was approved in 2004. It was complemented by the Guidelines on certification and those on transparency which further developed concepts mentioned in the 2004 recommendation. The three instruments were eventually replaced by a new recommendation – the CM/Recommendation (2017)5 on standards for e-voting [8]. The new recommendation is complemented by the Guidelines on its implementation. Based on its experience with e-voting, the CoE decided to start working on a new instrument that would address all other uses of ICT in elections, to the exception of e-voting and of e-campaigning.

A dedicated working group of national experts on democracy and technology (GT-DT) was established by the European Committee on Democracy and Governance (CDDG). It was assisted by external experts, from the academia[2]. The group produced the CM/Guidelines on the use of information and communication technology (ICT) in electoral processes in Council of Europe member States that were approved by the Committee of Ministers on 9 February 2022. The CoE is the only international organisation to have issued guidance to member States on how to regulate use of ICT in elections so that it ultimately complies with the principles of free elections and any other constitutional principle applicable.

---

[1] The Council of Europe comprises 46 countries, namely all European continent countries to the exception of Belarus, and of Russia which ceased to be a member as from 16 March 2022 following its aggression of Ukraine; CM/Resolution(2022)2.

[2] The external experts were the authors of this paper.

CoE's work is based on its unique mandate to ensure the protection of the right to free elections in its member States.

This paper discusses the Guidelines on the use of ICT in electoral processes. The discussion also covers the relation between the 2022 Guidelines on ICT and the 2017 Recommendation on e-voting. The paper starts with an overview of the development process under the stewardship of the CDDG (Sect. 2) and continues with the results from the survey conducted while developing the guidelines (Sect. 3). Then it presents a summary of the guidelines and the main underlying concepts (Sect. 4). The concluding chapter discusses the relation between the Guidelines on ICT and the Recommendation on e-voting, the expected practical impact of the Guidelines and their limitations and also suggests some improvements (Sect. 5).

2   Development Process

The Committee on Democracy and Governance was in charge of the development of the guideline. Therefore, we first explain their role before we introduce the actual process.

2.1   Role of the Committee on Democracy and Governance

The European Committee on Democracy and Governance or CDDG is the CoE intergovernmental forum where representatives of the member States meet to develop European standards (recommendations, guidelines, reports), to exchange and follow up on the state of democratic governance in Europe, and to work together to strengthen democratic institutions at all levels of government [5]. The CDDG was mandated to prepare a set of requirements and safeguards to be introduced in the legislation and practices of the Council of Europe member States when using ICT in the different stages of the electoral process. The Committee of Ministers' Guidelines on the use of information and communication technology (ICT) in electoral processes in Council of Europe member States, CM(2022)10 were adopted by the Committee of Ministers on 9 February 2022 at the 1424th meeting of the Ministers' Deputies and came into force at the same date.

The CDDG's ambition and the Guidelines' aim is to ensure the integrity of the electoral process and therefore enhance citizens' trust in democracy [4][3]. The CDDG made an important step by involving, beyond its circle of national experts, also the national election management bodies (EMBs) and other election experts as well as Venice Commission - the constitutional and electoral matters' consultative body at CoE. Moreover, the CDDG involved academic experts with legal, IT and social science backgrounds (while not all experts were involved from the very beginning).

---

[3] See the CDDG webpage on Democracy and technology¿ New technologies in the electoral process at https://www.coe.int/en/web/good-governance/democracy-and-technology.

Remark: Unlike previous bodies that elaborated the two recommendations on e-voting and examined their implementation by members States during a limited number of years, the CDDG is a permanent body. This suggests that the implementation of and any follow-up work in relation to the Guidelines and to the Recommendation on e-voting will, from now on, receive continuous attention.

2.2   Process Description

The aim of the work was, that a first proposal is made by the experts and then iteratively improved and/or extended based on the expert feedback. First, a preparatory study "New technologies in the electoral cycle. Guidance from the CoE" was produced by one of the experts and presented in January 2020 to the CDDG working group [10][4]. Second, the CDDG Secretariat developed a questionnaire (see Sect. 3). By the end of 2020, the Secretariat distributed the questionnaire to countries' experts, including to national EMBs (December 2020-January 2021). Third, a summary of the answers to the questionnaire was presented to the working group on democracy and technology (GT-DT) of the CDDG on 8 February 2021. In particular, the type of technology to be addressed was discussed in this meeting.

Based on all this input, the academic experts presented a first proposal for the content of the Guidelines to the CDDG plenum on 16 Apr 2021. The draft Guidelines were discussed with the national experts, including national election experts and national EMBs. Afterwards, the feedback was considered and the guidelines were formulated by the experts. A detailed informal discussion was held with EMBs and other national electoral experts as well as Venice Commission at the GT-DT meeting of 28 May 2021 where each of the draft Guidelines was presented and discussed in detail. Decisions on how to deal with feedback were based on broad consensus.

The Guidelines were further iterated afterwards. The draft Guidelines, reflecting the May 28 discussions, were sent to member States again for consultation. This took place during July-August 2021. Seven member states provided feedback[5]. A final detailed discussion of the consolidated Guidelines was held after the consultation at the GT-DT meeting on 24 September 2021. The CDDG then approved the final document at its 29–30 November 2021 plenary meeting. Eventually, the Guidelines were approved by the Committee of Ministers (Ministers' Deputies) and became effective on 9 February 2022.

---

[4] An abridged version of this study is found in the second part (pp. 39 ff) of the publication "Digital Technologies in Elections" https://rm.coe.int/publication-digital-technologies-regulations-en/16809e803f.

[5] Austria, Estonia, Finland, Luxembourg, the Netherlands, Switzerland and the UK as well as Venice Commission.

3   Questionnaire

The following description of the factual situation in member states relies on an analysis of data gathered by the CoE secretariat through a questionnaire distributed to member States in December 2020 [6]. The answers informed the content of the Guidelines. A summary of the result is provided in the following two subsections.

3.1   Definition

To be noted, the questionnaire and the guidelines contain no positive definition of ICT-backed processes. Instead, there is a negative definition. The ICT solutions considered are all those ICT-backed solutions used in elections to the exception of e-voting and e-campaigning-related ones. E-voting is the use of electronic means to cast and/or count the vote, according to the CoE Rec(2017)5. It covers e-voting in polling stations, internet voting from an uncontrolled environment and e-counting of paper ballots. These are covered by the 2017 Recommendation. E-campaigning (including the use of social media and microtargeting techniques for opinion misformation purposes) is a quite different area, involving many players that are beyond the reach of electoral authorities (by contrast, e-voting and the ICT solutions covered by the Guidelines are planned, introduced and supervised by the electoral authority and ultimately by the State). E-campaigning is discussed in other CoE forums, namely by Venice Commission [7].

3.2   Overview

The questionnaire investigated the use of ICT solutions in elections, including their actual use and future plans, their regulation, the difficulties encountered, COVID-19 specific developments, issues related to procurement, in-house competences and resources, public scrutiny, independent verification, need for international cooperation etc. For a summary of the answers see Subsect. 3.2. The questionnaire distributed by the CoE secretariat also asked detailed questions about national regulations, including about compliance with higher-level principles, the level of detail or the regulation of aspects such as usability, confidentiality and data protection, transparency, cybersecurity, verifiability, control and accountability, cooperation with the private sector, risk strategies and contingency procedures. For a summary of the answers see Subsect. 3.3.

Detailed answers were provided by 24 member States, namely from the authorities in charge of elections[6]. The focus of the following summary is on the ICT in place and the legal requirements.

---

[6] The countries that replied were Austria, Belgium, Bosnia & Herzegovina, Croatia, Czechia, Estonia, Finland, Greece, Hungary, Latvia, Lithuania, Luxembourg, Moldova, Norway, Poland, Romania, San Marino, Serbia, Slovakia, Slovenia, Spain, Sweden, Switzerland and the United Kingdom.

3.3   Result for ICT in Place

Some 75 different types of e-documents and e-processes could be identified. ICT-backed solutions are used through all electoral processes, including planning and preparation, voting day and post-election activities. All electoral stakeholders (voters, parties, candidates, election administration staff, observers, media, translators, dispute resolution bodies, etc.) are expected to use an ICT solution at some point. Many e-solutions are web-facing. Several transmit sensitive data over the internet during the voting and the counting processes, including voter personal data on participation, or preliminary and final results. The election planning and preparation phase uses the most part of the identified e-solutions to handle the different registers for voters, observers, parties and candidates; to hire and administer staff for the different levels of election administration, to disseminate information, conduct training and public consultations, etc. In most cases, paper-print versions, namely of registers, are also distributed, as a back-up measure. Several countries have built or envisage building so-called election information or election management systems in order to centralise the administration of e-backed solutions.

Cloud-based solutions are increasingly used and so are web and mobile applications as well as of open data formats. The interaction between users and systems (possibility to submit, consult and correct information), the harmonisation of data formats, the streamlining of processes and the secure electronic exchange of documents are hot topics. While almost all countries have general governmental ICT strategies, specific strategies on use of ICT in elections are missing. In addition to a general trend towards "digital by default", there is awareness that election-related processes must remain accessible via traditional manual procedures.

The COVID-19 pandemic has challenged the organisation of elections, however CoE countries have not turned to new ICT solutions in reply to the challenge, with a few exceptions. Online processes like training of lower level commissions and of polling stations' staff or information of the public have been strengthened. Possible future disruptions are discussed, and the potential role ICT might play is considered. There is a trend towards further optimizing and increasing the flexibility of existing solutions, be they manual or e-backed ones, rather than introducing completely new solutions.

The prospects on future use of ICT in elections are mixed. In some cases, use of ICT is explicitly excluded (e.g. for voter identification, voting, counting) and countries commit to paper-based systems. ICT may only be used as a support tool (e.g. in counting the results), without legally binding results (these are only delivered by manual and paper-based processes and documents). Others foresee an increase in the use of ICT in a gradual way, by introducing, first, non-internet-connected solutions and, only later, connected ones. Yet others plan to introduce integrated election information and administration systems which include online services. Here are a few examples of e-backed solutions that some countries envisage developing: scanning of voter documents with "smart" devices, online application for alternative voting channel or alternative polling station, centralisation of access to election registers to allow voting in any electoral district, online submission of observations or of complaints, development of e-collecting platforms, of e-counting tools, and of a digital imprints regime to offer voters viewing online digital material the same transparency as to those reading printed material.

Main difficulties encountered so far include lack of digital literacy, security issues arising from short term introduction of an e-service without proper testing as well as form DDoS attacks. In a few cases, DDoS have targeted dedicated infrastructure, such as the website of the electoral commission, or have jammed the connection between a polling station and a central database. Another challenge is the large number of users from polling stations who have access to the information resources during the same, limited, time which may provoke bottlenecks. In a similar way, online services that offer electors the possibility for instance to apply to register right up to the registration deadline, may create significant pressure both on the digital infrastructure and on those administering elections if an important number of users try to access the system at the same moment. The response has been to adapt deadlines, increase capabilities, invest in the resilience and scalability of the system infrastructure e.g. by migrating to a scalable public cloud infrastructure. Respondents highlight the importance of keeping alternative solutions to ICT-backed ones (e.g. use of multiple channels for transmission of results), the importance of adequate resources for IT security, the importance of the underlying ecosystem for implementing innovative solutions in the field of elections as well as the importance of pilots and of extensive, in advance testing.

3.4   Result for National Regulatory Frameworks

The questionnaire distributed by the CoE secretariat asked detailed questions about national regulations, including about compliance with higher-level principles, the level of detail or the regulation of aspects such as usability, confidentiality and data protection, transparency, cybersecurity, verifiability, control and accountability, cooperation with the private sector, risk strategies and contingency procedures. The answers informed the content of the Guidelines.

Legal regulations of ICT-backed solutions used in elections vary a lot between countries, ranging from almost no regulation (only instructions of the election authority), to minimal regulation which indicates the objectives of the use of ICT in elections, to detailed regulation such as a specific law on the election information system. "Negative" regulations which prohibit (some) ICT in elections exist (for instance, solutions for the e-identification of voters, e-voting or e-counting are precluded in some countries). There are also regulations that impose use of some ICT in certain elections (e.g. to enable minorities to vote). If electoral procedures are regulated in several laws, the rules for use of ICT in those different procedures are found in the different regulations and may lack consistency. Other ways of regulating include referring to regulation in related fields (e.g. regulation on electronic identification, on data protection, on security of information, etc.). Here again, there is a risk of fragmentation and inconsistency. The repartition of legislative responsibilities between the local and central government and the coordination and support provided by a central agency (e.g. Digitalisation Agency), or lack of it, may increase or reduce the inconsistencies.

National regulators have the ambition of ensuring conformity with higher principles, however ways and means to achieve this vary a lot, ranging from higher legislation setting out the functionalities that an IT system should fulfil and leaving the details to the lower level regulations, to issuing internal guidelines and instructions which are reflected in contractual provisions; to considering elections as critical infrastructure and organizing their security accordingly with an important involvement of the central authorities, etc.; to requiring certification against ISO 9001 and the ISO/IEC 27000 Family of Standards attesting that information security management practices are implemented. Other approaches include referring to laws on national security or national security schemes, including, in some countries, legislation on protection against terrorism, subversion and espionage.

In many countries, especially in the eastern part of the continent, electoral rules are very precise and scrupulously describe the various stages from the pre-electoral phase to the proclamation of results; their introduction and modification is the task of the legislature. Yet, when it comes to use of ICT in elections it is less clear what should be decided by the legislator and what can be left to the lower-level regulator. The Guidelines, in particular the first one, offer guidance on this question.

Ensuring the transparency of the e-solution is an objective. Approaches include the following: a team of experts is appointed by Parliament, to monitor the use of information technology in all aspects of the organisation of elections; their reports are published; the source code of certain computer applications is made available to certain stakeholders only (e.g. political parties, national minorities organisations, etc.); some front-end components of online services (e.g. Register to Vote service) are built from components which are available in open source. However, in general, the legal framework and the operational practices do not specifically emphasize transparency of ICT solutions. Despite general transparency laws, counting or tabulation software, for instance, are hardly disclosed. They are usually covered by copyrights, business secrets, or the source code is classified to maintain system security, according to the authorities. One reason for introducing ICT solutions is to foster transparency of election data. Election information, including provisional and final results for instance, are disseminated in the form of open data suitable for machine processing and analytical purposes.

The questionnaire asked how "public control" over the election and "independent verification" of information are implemented when ICT solutions are used. Several answers point to reliance on paper documents. Another aspect is the involvement of the national CERT, or of other national bodies competent for cybersecurity (e.g. a National Institute for Cybersecurity), in controlling the ICT system used in elections and its security, by conducting cyber threat screening, risk evaluation and compliance assessment before a national elections and applying the high standards, by which the national computing centre is scrutinised, also to elections. The involvement of the mentioned bodies is seen as offering independent verification. The use of two different mediums for the same process, the transparent publication of all data in the form of open data which allows independent checks, system audits by external auditors (independent security audits), the possibility of appealing to Court, which orders a verification of the correctness of data namely by referring to paper-based process or the use of statistical methods for checking the plausibility of certain results, are mentioned as possible tools for ensuring independent verification.

4 Content of Guidelines CM(2022)10

Content wise, the main challenge in developing the guidelines was their very general nature. The guidelines are expected to cover all electoral processes (to the exception of e-voting and e-counting), from registers and registering, to signing of initiatives and referenda, to organising election administration staff and other stakeholders, election day operations, results' management and publication, dispute resolution, etc. Moreover, the guidelines should cover all sorts of ICT used, including biometric, cloud solutions, cryptographic- as well as non-cryptographic solutions, blockchain. The guidelines should not duplicate the provisions of the e-voting Recommendation.

There are in total twelve guidelines and each comes with explanations and comments.

Below we briefly provide the idea of the twelve guidelines as well as of the overarching principle of security. We also comment on the content to reflect some of the discussions related to the corresponding guideline.

4.1 G1 Principles and Requirements

The first guideline is about alignment of ICT with the principles of democratic elections and all other relevant constitutional principles. Relevant principles should be identified.

Remark: There were suggestions to list "all other principles" that apply. This is impossible to do in an international document like this guidelines. The list of applicable principles depends, among others, on the election in question and on the national (and even local) legislation. So, in addition to principles common to all countries, there are those that differ from country to country or even within the same country, depending on the election in question and on local specificities. Moreover, such principles may evolve over time. This explains why the guidelines cannot provide an exhaustive list of principles applicable to all situations.

G1 also talks about detailed legal and technical requirements for the ICT solutions to be derived from the legal principles. Those in charge with the authoritative interpretation of constitutional principles, namely the legislator, should decide on the minimum level to which principles which contradict each-other should be ensured.

Remark: No solution can reflect contradictory principles to 100%. For example: Electoral data and processes may be required for instance to respect both transparency and secrecy, which contradict each other. In such a case the aim should be to ensure a fair balance which respects the essence of all applicable principles. Defining such essence and a fair balance is a matter of legal evaluation. However, at some point it needs to be defined what is the minimum level to which each technical requirement is ensured is acceptable.

In G1, technical requirements are separated in both functional and non-functional aspects. All these aspects, as well as their development process, need to be well documented and made publicly available. Regulation should moreover introduce complaints and dispute-resolution mechanisms. With respect to security (non-functional) requirements, G1 talks about trust assumptions for the security requirements. These should be transparent and analysed as part of the risk assessment (see also G9).

Remark: This concept was not made that explicit in previous guidelines and recommendations. The Council of Europe recommendation on electronic voting does not specifically mention trust assumptions (although it recommends doing a risk assessment but without further specifying how to do so). During the discussions it was agreed that for paper-based elections as well as for any digital application including those involved in the election process, the important question to answer is, whether or not the assumptions are realistic or not. More precisely, the trust assumptions are an important input for the risk assessment, i.e. on the likelihood that a requirement will be violated. Thus, making assumptions explicit enables more informed discussions by various experts and more informed decisions by election officials. Therefore, this guideline explains the concept of (trust) assumptions and requires that they are made explicit and their realistic status is discussed. The decision about the realistic nature of assumptions is not only of a technical nature as it involves legal and political evaluations as well. Note, as this concept was not that well know, it is explained in the guidelines appendix.

4.2   G2 Usability and Accessibility

The design of ICT solutions should follow a human-centered development approach and continuous improvement by collecting users' feedback (e.g. through semi-structured interviews, focus groups, mockup feedbacking). To be noted, users can be voters, election administration staff or other. Usability criteria for wide groups of people (e.g., voters) need to be considered. ICT solutions need to be accessible to all people (see G3 what is stated if this is not the case). Legal and technical requirements for usability and accessibility, as well as their minimum fulfilment level, should be defined following guideline 1 and made transparent.

Remark: In addition to the request to define usability and accessibility requirements, the guideline states that one should take a human centered approach to make sure these requirements are met.

4.3 G3 Universally Accessible Alternative Solution

Countries are adopting "digital first" strategies prioritizing the use of e-solutions. However, when e-solutions used in elections are not universally accessible, broadly accessible alternatives need to be provided to all electoral stakeholders. Moreover, conflicts which can arise from the use of multiple channels should be considered.

4.4 G4 Integrity and Authenticity

ICT solutions should integrate authentication mechanisms to avoid unauthorized changes to ensure the integrity of the election. Integrity checks should be provided throughout all relevant phases of the election to detect unauthorized changes. ICT solutions can also be used to identify irregularities (e.g. statistical checks such as risk-limiting audits), in combination with other types of observations, informed by country specific expertise.

Remark: To the best of our knowledge, this is the first time that risk-limiting audits are mentioned in CoE guidelines.

4.5 G5 Availability and Reliability

If introduced and used, ICT solutions should be available and reliable, i.e., in line with the requirements and assumptions, even in case of system failures, user errors or attacks, and retain its functionality regardless of both hardware and software shortcomings. Alternatively, information on fallback solutions and channels should be put in place.

4.6 G6 Secrecy and Confidentiality

Information stored on the ICT should respect requirements on secrecy and confidentiality derived from the legal principles and assumptions discussed in guideline 1. Electoral law usually addresses secrecy or confidentiality of voting and participation. Other information (e.g. information found in different registers or in the protocols for transmission of results) is governed by data protection laws. In all cases, data-protection principles, like privacy by design and data minimization, are minimum requirements which need to be considered. Those electoral data that qualify as "sensitive data" require the adoption of specific measures that go beyond data protection ones. Such specific measures should be included in the relevant electoral legislation. Additionally, long-term secrecy, i.e., post quantum secrecy and confidentiality, needs to be considered as well.

Remark: Both are more prominent in these guidelines compared to others as using quantum-computers to break secrecy gets more realistic and as the General Data Protection Regulation came in 2018 into place.

Last but not least this guideline considers the trade-off between secrecy and transparency (see G7).

4.7   G7 Transparency

Transparency is a cross-cutting issue. All main decisions in relation to regulation and use of ICT in elections should be made transparent, including the assessment of minimum level of fulfilment of principles, the assessment of the realistic status of assumptions, of risks and any other step mentioned in all guidelines. All aspects of the election need to be transparent. All stakeholders should be informed about the use of ICT in the election process, its operation, its properties, and its assessment. There is a long list of transparency measures including providing access to documentation, structured data about the election process and enabling public scrutiny.

4.8   G8 Initial Evaluation

Independent experts should evaluate the ICT solutions before starting using them. They should do so in particular regarding the security, usability, and accessibility requirements while taking the trust assumptions into account for the security requirements. The evaluation approach, target, assurance level, results, and involved persons need to be defined clearly and made publicly available. Regulation should also define how to deal with changes after the initial evaluation and foresee the procedures to be followed.

Remark: After the discussion it was decided to distinguish between the evaluation in place before applying the ICT-solution the first time (G8) and a permanent evaluation once it has been introduced (which is part of G9).

4.9   G9 Risk Management

Risks of using ICT solutions should in pariculare be derived from guidelines G1 (including the trust assumptions) and G8. Risks should be continuously analysed when developing, using ICT, and preparing it for future elections. It should be decided if and how to manage these risks. The risk management approach needs to be re-considered on a regular basis and be made publicly available.

4.10   G10 Member State's Capacities

Member states need to have the necessary administrative and technical capacity and resources to assess, introduce and manage ICT solutions. Therefore, they need to have skilled labor forces and avoid outsourcing the core processes of an election to a private entity. Trained human resources, the necessary tools, and overall financial resources as well as sufficient time are important preconditions.

4.11   G11 Member State's Responsibility

Member states and involved third parties are responsible for the proper implementation and conduct of the election process. Third parties involved need to fulfil the same standards and expectations as the member States. The ultimate responsibility lies with the member State.

4.12   G12 Exceptional Circumstances

The use of ICT solutions is not a short-term remedy, rather it should be considered as a long-term plan for electoral processes. ICT may be considered as an option when dealing with exceptional events. However, authorities need to prepare in advance to a potential use of ICT under exceptional circumstances.

Remark: This guideline is motivated by the challenges EMBs faced due to the Covid-19 pandemic.

4.13   G13 Security

Security is not just one principle among others in the Guidelines. Indeed, there is no specific guideline on security in general and there was some debate on this. The guidelines consider security as being relevant to ensuring each of the principles. Therefore trust assumptions are already considered in G1. However there are also guidelines on specific security properties: G4 on Integrity and Authenticity; G5 on availability; and G6 on Secrecy and Confidentiality. Furthermore, G8 requires a security evaluation and G9 requires to justify why the underlying trust assumptions are acceptable.

5   Discussion and Future Work

5.1   Relationship Between Guidelines CM(2022)10 and Recommendation CM/Rec(2017)5

The Guidelines should not duplicate the standards of the recommendation on e-voting. But what is the relation between the two? The Guidelines are much broader in scope. As such, they are relevant also when discussing e-voting. The opposite is not necessarily true as the standards of the Rec(2017)5 are specific to e-voting process and may not apply to other ICT backed process. From this perspective, one can say that the Guidelines can be considered as a lex generalis whenever ICT is used in electoral processes, including when e-voting is used.

A grey area, where one may wonder which of the two instruments applies, is the counting process. E-counting of paper ballots falls within the scope of the 2017 Recommendation on e-voting. E-counting is considered as a form of e-voting, by the Recommendation. However, other uses of ICT during the counting process, which do not involve e-counting of paper ballots, but still are important for the outcome of the counting process, are not covered by the 2017 Recommendation of e-voting. They are thus covered by the Guidelines on ICT. Here are a few examples of such solutions: e-transmission of provisional and final results from e.g. precincts to a regional or central election administration unit; dedicated software used for automatic verification and validation of results embedding mathematical and logical checks for controlling results (the software identifies incorrect entries, arithmetical errors, etc. and alerts users about them); solutions for establishing consolidated results, usually employed by a central authority (e.g. Office of Statistics) to summarize the results, calculate the distribution of seats, publish election results and forward them for approval to the competent body; other statistical tools used for checking the plausibility of results, etc. The Guidelines on ICT apply to all these situations.

5.2 Impact

Neither the 2017 Recommendation on e-voting, nor the 2022 Guidelines on ICT in elections require a member State to introduce ICT in elections. The Council of Europe recommends countries to make sure that, if and when such solutions are used, the higher-level principles of democracy, human rights and rule of law are respected, first in the regulation and, second, during the actual use of the solution. The decision on introducing or not ICT is the prerogative of the competent national authority.

As the introduction and use of ICT solutions in the electoral processes raises complex legal questions, the aim of the Council of Europe Guidelines is to offer guidance on addressing them. The addressees are member states, namely the authorities in charge of conducting and supervising elections, be they local, regional or national. The 2022 Guidelines on ICT focus on respect of the principles of free and democratic elections which are also part of the 12 Principles of Good Governance promoted by CDDG (see Principle 1) [1].

The main contribution of the Guidelines is that they elaborate on concepts, which are "new" to the electoral field thus providing welcomed guidance to EMBs. Such concepts include notions like assumptions, minimum level of implementation of principles, risk assessment etc. Another contribution is a glossary, provided to facilitate broader understanding of the concepts explained in the Guidelines.

5.3 Limitations

One suggestion for future development stems from the perceived need for more detailed and specific instruments covering specific phases of the election process or specific technologies used. This was also underlined in the answers to the questionnaire. Encouraging dissemination and discussion, monitoring implementation, regularly exchanging experiences, discussing challenges and good practices and eventually updating the Guidelines requires a continued commitment to pursue work in this area and to build upon experiences and lessons learned. Recent experiences with biannual meetings to review implementation of Rec(2017)5 however, show that, in the absence of mid or longer term planning and resources from the CoE, these exercises may become simple formalities and bring no added value.

Ackownledgement. This work was supported by funding from the topic Engineering Secure Systems of the Helmholtz Association (HGF) and by KASTEL Security Research Labs.

References

1. 12 principles of good governance. https://www.coe.int/en/web/good-governance/12-principles (Accessed 29 August 2022)
2. 1424th meeting, 9 February 2022. https://search.coe.int/cm/pages/result_details.aspx?objectid=0900001680a575d9. (Accessed 29 August 2022)
3. Code of good practice in electoral matters. https://www.venice.coe.int/webforms/documents/?pdf=CDL-AD(2002) 023rev2-cor-e (Accessed 29 August 2022)
4. Democracy and technology. https://www.coe.int/en/web/good-governance/democracy-and-technology. (Accessed 29 August 2022)
5. European committee on democracy and governance (cddg). https://www.coe.int/en/web/good-governance/cddg. (Accessed 29 August 2022)
6. European committee on democracy and governance (cddg). https://rm.coe.int/cddg-2021-5e-replies-to-questionnaire-on-new-technologies-2787-6853-63/1680a216f1. (Accessed 29 August 2022)
7. Principles for a fundamental rights-compliant use of digital technologies in electoral processes. https://www.venice.coe.int/webforms/documents/?pdf=CDL-AD(2020) 037-e. (Accessed 29 August 2022)
8. Recommendation cm/rec(2017) 5 of the committee of ministers to member states on standards for e-voting. https://search.coe.int/cm/Pages/result_details.aspx?ObjectId=0900001680726f6f. (Accessed 29 August 2022)
9. Resolution cm/res(2022) 2 on the cessation of the membership of the russian federation to the council of europe. https://search.coe.int/cm/Pages/result_details.aspx?ObjectId=0900001680a5da51. (Accessed 29 August 2022)
10. Maurer, A.D.: Digital technologies in elections-questions, lessons learned, perspectives, p. 39 ff (2020). https://rm.coe.int/publication-digitaltechnologies-regulations-en/16809e803f

1st International Workshop on System Security Assurance (SecAssure 2022)

Preface

This part contains the accepted papers for the 1st International Workshop on System Security Assurance (SecAssure 2022). The workshop was co-located with the 27th European Symposium on Research in Computer Security (ESORICS 2022) and was held in a hybrid mode in Copenhagen on September 30, 2021.

The advancement in information and communication technology has revolutionized social and economic systems. The government, as well as commercial and non-profit organizations, rely heavily on information to conduct their business. Aside from the significant benefits of information and computing systems, their increasing connectivity, criticality, and comprehensiveness present new challenges for cybersecurity professionals. Information and services that are compromised in terms of confidentiality, integrity, availability, accountability, and authenticity can harm an organization's operations, so this information and data need to be protected. For this reason, it has become a crucial task for security researchers and practitioners to manage the security risks by mitigating the potential vulnerabilities and threats with new techniques and methodologies, thus ensuring the acceptable security assurance of an information and computing system, so the stakeholders can have greater confidence that the system works as intended or claimed. Security assurance can be defined as the confidence that a system meets its security requirements and is resilient against security vulnerabilities and failures. According to NIST, security assurance is a measure of confidence that the security features, practices, procedures, and architecture of an information system accurately mediates and enforces the security policy.

SecAssure 2022 brought together researchers from academia, and practitioners from industry and government bodies on a forum to meet and exchange ideas on recent research and future directions for security assurance. The workshop received 10 submissions. An open peer review method was used. Each submission was assigned three reviewers. The review process resulted in 5 high-quality full papers that were accepted to be presented in the workshop and included in the proceeding. The papers cover topics related to (1) security assurance methodologies, like quantitative security assurance, and (2) security assurance techniques, like techniques related to vulnerability detection and risk assessment.

September 2022

Basel Katt
Habtamu Abie
Ankur Shukla
Sandeep Pirbhulal

Organization

General Chair

Basel Katt	Norwegian University of Science and Technology, Norway
Habtamu Abie	Norwegian Computing Center, Oslo, Norway
Sandeep Pirbhulal	Norwegian Computing Center, Oslo, Norway
Ankur Shukla	Institute for Energy Technology, Norway

Program Committee Chairs

Basel Katt	Norwegian University of Science and Technology, Norway
Habtamu Abie	Norwegian Computing Center, Oslo, Norway
Sandeep Pirbhulal	Norwegian Computing Center, Oslo, Norway
Ankur Shukla	Institute for Energy Technology

Program Committee

Mauro Conti	University of Padua, Italy
Michael Felderer	University of Innsbruck, Austria
Eduardo B. Fernandez	Florida Atlantic University, USA
Arda Goknil	SINTEF, Norway
Dieter Gollmann	Hamburg University of Technology, Germany
Volker Gruhn	University of Duisburg-Essen, Germany
Martin Gilje Jaatun	University of Stavanger, Norway
Pontus Johnson	KTH Royal Institute of Technology, Sweden
Sokratis Katsikas	Norwegian University of Science and Technology, Norway
Hanno Langweg	HTWG Konstanz University of Applied Sciences, Germany
Nuno Laranjeiro	University of Coimbra, Portugal
Phu H. Nguyen	SINTEF, Norway
Ethiopia Nigussie	University of Turku, Finland

Juha Röning	University of Oulu, Finland
Rejjo Savola	University of Jyväskylä, Finland
Sebastian Schrittwieser	University of Vienna, Austria
Einar Snekkenes	Norwegian University of Science and Technology, Norway
Ketil Stølen	SINTEF, Norway
Simon Tjoa	St. Poelten University of Applied Sciences, Austria
Denis Trcek	University of Ljublana, Slovenia
Edgar Weippl	University of Vienna, Austria
Shao-Fang Wen	Norwegian University of Science and Technology, Norway
Christos Xenakis	University of Piraeus, Greece

Additional Reviewers

Gulshan Kumar
Jacky Mallett

SAEOn: An Ontological Metamodel for Quantitative Security Assurance Evaluation

Shao-Fang Wen[(⊠)] and Basel Katt

Department of Information Security and Communication Technology, Norwegian University of Science and Technology, Gjøvik, Norway
`{shao-fang.wen,basel.katt}@ntnu.no`

Abstract. Security assurance is a critical aspect in determining the trustworthiness of information and communication technology systems. Security assurance evaluation (SAE) is the process responsible for gathering assurance shreds of evidence to check if the defined security requirements are fulfilled. SAE can be generally categorized into qualitative and quantitative methods. As there is still a dearth of studies on the quantitative SAE, this paper intends to fill this gap by proposing an ontological quantitative security assurance evaluation metamodel (SAEOn). This ontology allows us to define the entities of the SAE and the assurance metrics separately and relate them to each other in a modular way. With the formal definition of SAE metamodel, the constructed knowledge content can be reused, shared, and exchanged over time. Moreover, the proposed metamodel is structured in a hierarchical fashion, by which we believe the ontology is sufficiently generic and highly customizable that can be applied in various application domains. In this paper, we present the proposed SAEOn ontology in detail, covering the aspects of design, implementation, and evaluation.

Keywords: Security assurance · Quantitative approach · Security metrics · Ontology

1 Introduction

Security assurance is a technique that helps organizations to appraise the trust and confidence that a system can be operated correctly and securely [15]. Security assurance has been seen as a critical aspect in determining the trustworthiness of Information and Communication Technology (ICT) systems. In detail, Security assurance evaluates, reports, and monitors the security posture of ICT systems to see whether the security features, practices, procedures, and architecture accurately mediate and enforce the security policy before being disseminated or delivered to the target audience [23]. Security Assurance Evaluation (SAE) is the process that is responsible for gathering "assurance" shreds of evidence to check if the defined security requirements are fulfilled [14]. SAE can be generally categorized into qualitative and quantitative methods. Qualitative methods are employed to study events or regulatory control of the system under evaluation, while quantitative SAE applies computational and mathematical techniques for deriving

© The Author(s), under exclusive license to Springer Nature Switzerland AG 2023
S. Katsikas et al. (Eds.): ESORICS 2022 Workshops, LNCS 13785, pp. 605–624, 2023.
https://doi.org/10.1007/978-3-031-25460-4_35

a set of SAE metrics (hereinafter "metrics") to express the assurance level that a system reaches [25]. According to the findings of a systematic literature review, Shukla et al. [25] concluded that a major of the SAE research has been focused on the qualitative perspective and very few efforts have been made toward developing a quantitative SAE methodology. Consequently, there are still no standards or widely accepted methods, models, taxonomy, or tools for quantitative SAE.

This paper aims to complement the research gap by proposing an ontological quantitative SAE metamodel, called SAEOn. With a metamodel, we define different types of *information* and the corresponding *relationships* allowed in SAE modeling. Ontologies, on the other hand, have been regarded as an effective approach to semantic-driven modeling and have been used in various research fields such as education, information integration, and knowledge management [21]. Ontologies and metamodels can be particularly useful in reusability, communication, and organization of knowledge [1]. The main benefit of the ontology-based metamodel is the availability of a formal, encoded description of the domain knowledge: that is, all the concepts, their attributes, and their inter-relationships will be well-defined and represented [2]. Due to the formalization, encoded knowledge can be represented and to some degree interpreted by machines and enables the formal analysis of the domain, which allows an automated or computer-aided extraction and aggregation of knowledge from different sources and possibly in different formats [8].

This research work is built on the research works on quantitative SAE by the authors in [15, 32] that add particular ontology-modeling techniques for advancing the contribution. The primary objective is to formulate an explicit SAE ontology that can extend the quantitative SAE framework with the formal definition of *assurance components* (which will be explained later) as well as assurance metrics modeling. In this paper, we present the proposed SAEOn ontology, covering the aspects of design, implementation, and evaluation. The rest of this paper is organized as follows. In Sect. 2, we provide an overview of related work. The quantitative security assurance evaluation model is introduced in Sect. 3. Section 4 explains the details of the proposed ontology-based metamodel while the ontology evaluation is described in Sect. 5. The conclusion is presented in Sect. 6.

2   Related Work

An ontology is "an explicit formal specification of a conceptualization" [8]. This is further elaborated that an ontology is a formal description of the concepts and relationships in an area of interest, simplifying and abstracting the view of the world for some purpose [29]. There is a large number of research papers related to the field of ontology-based security assurance and evaluation. Among them, we can highlight papers aimed at modeling the security assurance methodologies, security assessment techniques, as well as ontology-based security metrics management.

Raskin et al. [22] are one of the first to introduce ontological approaches to security evaluation. He implies that one of the ultimate goals is the inclusion of semantic data sources to facilitate the formal specification of the information security community know-how for the support of routine and time-efficient measures to prevent and counteract computer attacks. Analyzing the current state of the art, a major portion of ontologies directly relate to the Common Criteria (CC) methodologies [10]. With the strict, standardized, and repeatable methodology, the CC assures implementation, evaluation, and operation of a security product at a level that is commensurate with the operational environments. Yavagal et al. [33] present an ontological approach to the modeling of the CC security functional requirements, which produces a structure where the high-level requirements identified in the non-leaf nodes are decomposed into specific criteria in the leaf nodes. To conquer the time-consuming issue of CC assurance evaluation, Ekclhart et al. [3] developed a CC Ontology, focusing on modeling the security requirements documented in CC. Based on ontology, a tool is created to support the CC evaluation process in several ways, for example, document preparation, linking, and tagging.

Some research efforts have attempted to employ ontology-based techniques in security assessment or for integrating security assurance methodologies. For instance, Franco Rosa et al. [5] propose a security assessment ontology, named SecAOnto, to conceptualize the main knowledge in the domain of security assessment, aiming to support security assessment methods based on assessment criteria. The core concepts included in SecAOnto can be generally categorized into (1) system assessment, (2) information security, and (3) security assessment. Wang et al. [31] propose an ontology-based approach to analyzing and assessing the security posture of software products. It provides quantitative measurements for a software product based on an ontology built for vulnerability management, called OVM [30]. Gao et al. [6] proposed an ontology-based framework for assessing the security of network and computer systems from the attacker's perspective. The proposed taxonomy consists of five dimensions, which include attack impact, attack vector, the target of attacks, vulnerability, and defense.

In addition, some ontologies for security assessment are proposed in specific domains or contexts. For example, in the domain of the Internet of Things (IoT), Gonzalez-Gil et al. [7] proposed a context-based security evaluation ontology (IoTSecEv) to describe the different security preferences of the end-users of an IoT device, based on concerns and interests in different security elements, such as threats, vulnerabilities, security mechanisms or features. Moreover, in the context of the cloud system assessment, Koinig et al. [16] established a knowledge-based ontology (Contrology) for capturing the knowledge required to audit a cloud computing environment. Their work is based on the ontology proposed by Fenz and Andreas [4], which consists of six classes: assets, controls, security attributes, security recommendations, threats, and vulnerabilities. Lastly, Powley et al. [20] proposed an Evaluation Ontology (EO) that facilitate the modeling of evaluation processes and outcome in automobile industries, specifically for connected vehicles, it aims to integrate different types of evaluation into a single model for all activities at all levels of all organizations in an enterprise.

3 Quantitative Security Assurance Evaluation Metamodel

In this section, we present in detail the proposed quantitative SAE model, including the general model structure and the SAE metrics calculation.

3.1 General Model Structure

To achieve quantitative SAE in a meaningful way, it is essential to be able to model what it is meant and how to measure it. Figure 1 is a graphical representation of the general model structure, while Table 1 describes the symbols used in the model. As shown in Fig. 1, the proposed SAE metamodel is represented as a five-level hierarchical structure, in which each node represents a distinct *assurance component*. First, the evaluation of an assurance target (i.e., the targeted system under evaluation) is decomposed and examined through two perspectives: *Security Requirement* and *Vulnerability*. Our position is that SAE should be quantitative by distinguishing two critical perspectives of security management: the protection side and the weakness side of the assurance target. Each perspective is composed of one or more criteria, and each criterion is composed of one or several elements until reaching the lowest level. The SAE scores of assurance components are computed using a bottom-up approach, which involves the estimation of the lowest possible level of detail.

Such a hierarchical structure allows security stakeholders to view the assurance results at various levels of abstraction, meanwhile, providing more fine-grained evaluation and thus enabling root-cause analysis [9]. Moreover, hierarchical decomposition enables the reduction of complex domain problems into simple ones that are easier to manage [9, 24]. For simplicity of presentation, we use 'assurance' in short to represent the term 'security assurance' in all component names. The concepts for each component are described below.

Assurance Target: An assurance target is a product or system that is the subject under security evaluation, such as an information system, part of a system or product, or a cloud ecosystem. The evaluation serves to validate claims made about the assurance target.

Assurance Perspective. Assurance perspectives describe the interrelation or relative significance in which an assurance target is evaluated. In our approach, two perspectives on cyber security are taken into the evaluation: security requirements and vulnerabilities. The former addresses the positive side of system security while the latter considers the negative side. We argue that even if security mechanisms are properly elucidated at the requirement stage, they could result in weakness if they are inappropriately implemented or deployed. Consequently, while evaluating security assurance, security requirement improves the assurance posture, and, contrariwise, the existence of vulnerabilities lead to a reduction of the assurance level. Such concepts will be inherited by the rest of the assurance components.

Assurance Criteria. Assurance criteria are the specific properties that will be selected, tested, and measured to confirm the sufficiency of system security to be offered to users. These criteria are part of the "target" that the work is planned to achieve (or eliminate in the perspective of vulnerabilities). In our approach, assurance criteria play an especially important role in the SAE, which provide a basis for comparison among different assurance targets; a reference point against which another system can be evaluated. In Table 2, we give an exemplary criterion set for an assurance target in the domain of web applications.

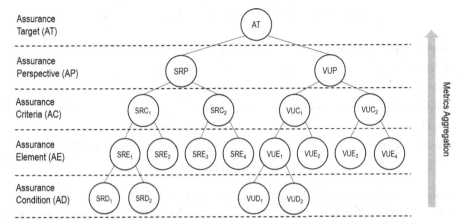

Fig. 1. Sample hierarchical structure of the security assurance evaluation

Table 1. Symbols used in the assurance evaluation

Symbol	Description
AT	Assurance target
SRP	Security requirement perspective
VUP	Vulnerability perspective
SRC	Security requirement criteria
VUC	Vulnerability criteria
SRE	Security requirement element
VUE	Vulnerability element
SRD	Security requirement condition
VUD	Vulnerability condition

Concerning security, not all security requirements should be treated equally important [15]. Likewise, the vulnerabilities in need of fixing must be prioritized based on which ones pose the most immediate danger. To reflect that, one must specify a numeric factor for each assurance criteria: *Weight* for security requirement criteria and *Risk* for vulnerability criteria. The weight factor expresses how security is emphasized in the assurance target and it must be done based on the application context. On the other hand, from the perspective of vulnerabilities, the term risk can be defined as the probability and the consequence of an unwanted incident caused by existing vulnerabilities.

Assurance Element. Assurance criteria are narrated in detail by a set of assurance elements. Like in assurance criteria, assurance elements are divided into security requirement elements and vulnerability elements. The formal represents a requirement item

Table 2. Exemplary assurance criteria in web applications

Security requirement criteria	Vulnerability criteria
Authentication	Broken Access Control
Access Control	Cryptographic Failure
Validation, Sanitization and Encoding	Injection
Error Handling	Security Misconfiguration
Data Protection	Identification and Authentication Failure

needed to be fulfilled, while the latter indicates a particular kind of vulnerability potentially existing in the assurance target. Table 3 lists the exemplary elements with the corresponding assurance criteria.

Assurance Condition. An assurance condition is specifically defined according to the organizational contexts, which include special circumstance items, such as the deployment environment, the organization's current state, and security concerns. Besides, assurance conditions can be also represented as test cases performed to check to what extent the security requirements' conditions and the vulnerabilities' conditions are true. Table 4 represents the exemplary security requirement conditions under the element of 'Password Security'. We conceive the SAE as an aggregated value of the low-level assurance conditions that is directly quantified from the respective test results, which can truly reflect the assurance level of the assurance target.

Table 3. Exemplary assurance elements (security requirement elements)

Security requirement criteria	Security requirement element
Authentication	Password Security
	Credential Storage
	Credential Recovery
	One Time Verifier
Validation, Sanitization, and Encoding	Input Validation
	Sanitization and Sandboxing
	Output Encoding
	Deserialization Prevention

Table 4. Exemplary assurance conditions (security requirement conditions)

Security requirement element	Security requirement condition
Password security	The passwords should be at least 64 characters are permitted, and passwords of more than 128 characters are denied
	Password truncation is not performed. However, consecutive multiple spaces may be replaced by a single space
	Password change functionality requires the user's current and new password

3.2 Assurance Metrics Calculation

SAE is a systematic process of assigning meaningful scores to the assurance target that indicates its security posture [18]. With the term "evaluation" we refer to the assignment of a *metric* to each component in the model. Metrics represent measurement or evaluation indexes that are given attributes to satisfy the security assurance evaluation. Our quantitative SAE approach divides the assurance metrics calculation into three sequential phases, explained as follows.

Assurance Element Evaluation Phase. The first phase of assurance evaluation is responsible for the assessment of the element of the SAE model, from the quantification of the corresponding assurance conditions. In our test-based methodology, each assurance condition is mapped to one test case to decide the fulfillment score (for security requirements) or the existence score (for vulnerabilities). A test case that shows that a security requirement (condition) is not fulfilled will be assigned a value of 0; 1 means that a test case result indicates the fulfillment of a requirement, and 0.5 indicates partial fulfillment. Similarly, the existence score for vulnerability conditions has two value options, where 0 means no vulnerability existence indicated by the test results, and 1 represents the existence of the vulnerability with the corresponding assurance condition. We define a metric *ActSRD* as a measurement to reflect the actual (calculated) score of SRE. The value of *ActSRE* is obtained by averaging the fulfillment scores of the related SRD. The following formula represents the calculation of the i-th SRE score (represented as $ActSRE_i$):

$$ActSRE_i = \frac{\sum_{j=1}^{n} ActSRD_{ij}}{n}, \forall ActSRD \in \{0, 0.5, 1\} \tag{1}$$

where,

$ActSRD_{ij}$: the fulfillment score of the j-th SRD associated with the i-th SRE

n: the number of SRD associated with the i-th SRE.

Similarly, the formula used for calculating the VUE score is defined as the average of the corresponding VUD existence score, represented below:

$$ActVUE_i = \frac{\sum_{j=1}^{n} ActVUD_{ij}}{n}, \forall ActVUD_{ij} \in \{0, 1\} \tag{2}$$

where,

$ActVUD_{ij}$: the existence score of the j-th VUD associated with the i-th VUC

n: the number of VUD associated with the i-th VUC.

Assurance Criteria Evaluation Phase. The second phase of assurance evaluation is responsible for the calculation of assurance criteria scores. Based on the previous discussion, the actual score of the i-th SRC, represented by ActSRCi, is measured based on the average value of its respective SRE and obtained by multiplying a weight factor to express the levels of importance. The scale of the weight factor ranges from 1 to 10, where 1 is assigned to SRC that are least essential, while 10 is the maximum expressing a vital requirement. The formula to calculate ActSRCi is defined as:

$$ActSRC_i = WghSRC_i \times \frac{\sum_{j=1}^{n} ActSRE_{ij}}{n}, \forall WghSRC_i \in [1, 10] \qquad (3)$$

where,

$ActSRE_{ij}$: the assurance score of the j-th SRE associated with the i-th SRE

$WghSRC_i$: the weight factor that corresponds to the i-th SRC

n: the number of SRE associated with the i-th SRC.

Likewise, the assurance metric $ActVUCi$, represented by the i-th vulnerability criteria, can be calculated using the average value of correspondent VUEs, considering the risk factor of vulnerabilities as well. In our model, the scale of the resulting risk value could range from 0 to 10, where 0 represents that the corresponding VUC is least likely to fail, while 10 is considered the maximum risk. The formula to derive the i-th $ActVUC$ is defined as:

$$ActVUC_i = RskVUC_i \times \frac{\sum_{j=1}^{n} ActVUE_j}{n}, \forall RskVUC_i \in [0, 10] \qquad (4)$$

where,

$ActVUE_{ij}$: the assurance score of the j-th VUE associated with the i-th SRC

$RskVUC_i$: the risk that corresponds to the i-th VUC

n: the number of VUE associated with the i-th VUC.

Assurance Target Evaluation Phase. The third phase of evaluation is responsible for the calculation of the overall assurance score for the assurance target. At first, we obtain a summative assurance score for each assurance perspective by accumulating the correspondent assurance elements. Table 5 presents the two metrics for the actual SRP and VUP scores respectively.

Consequently, the overall security assurance score ($ActSAS$) of the assurance target is derived from the difference between the overall security-requirement score ($ActSRP$) and vulnerability score ($ActVUP$). Thus, the formula is as follows:

$$ActSAS = ActSRP - ActVUP \qquad (7)$$

It can be noticed that the scale of $ActSAS$ is highly influenced by the number of security requirements as well as vulnerabilities included in the evaluation model (Eqs. 5, 6).

Table 5. Formulas for calculating actual scores of SRP and VUP

	Actual score of SRP		Actual score of VUP	
Metrics	$ActSRP = \sum_{i=1}^{n} ActSRC_i$ n: the number of SRC	(5)	$ActVUP = \sum_{i=1}^{n} ActVUC_i$ n: the number of VUC	(6)

This leads to a variant range of assurance scores among different assurance targets, and further, makes it difficult to interpret to take decisions among various systems. In this regard, *ActSAS* must be normalized to a common scale for a more comprehensive and understandable value, named the assurance level (*SAL*). We adopt the min-max normalization method [13], which preserves the relationships among the original data values. The formula of this generic normalization method is presented as follows:

$$v' = \frac{v - min_A}{max_A - min_A}(newmax_A - newmin_A) + newmin_A \qquad (8)$$

where,

min_A and max_A: the minimum and maximum values of an attribute

$newmin_A$ and $newmax_A$: the new minimum and maximum values after normalization

v: the old value of an attribute

v': the new value after normalization.

The convention we follow for the *SAL* is that it lies in the interval between 0 and 10, where 0 corresponds to the worst possible level of security assurance, while 1 to the excellent assurance level. Thus, the formula for metric *SAL* can be defined as:

$$SAL = \frac{ActSAS - MinSAS}{MaxSAS - MinSAS} \times (10 - 0) + 0 = \frac{ActSAS - MinSAS}{MaxSAS - MinSAS} \times 10 \qquad (9)$$

4 Ontology Design and Construction

In this section, we describe in detail the design and construction of the Security Assurance Evaluation Ontology (SAEOn) based on the proposed SAE model, providing sufficient justification for the ontological approach. An overview of the ontology design is depicted in Fig. 2. In a nutshell, SAEOn prescribes constructing a semantic model based on the metamodel of the quantitative SAE that defines classes of assurance and assurance metrics that capture the security knowledge required for security assessment and analysis. The metrics are assigned to corresponding assurance components through inference rules and reasoning engines. The inference rules serve as a bridge for the connections between assurance components and assurance metrics. The specific modules of the approach are described in the following sections.

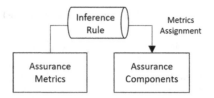

Fig. 2. Overview of the ontology design

4.1 Assurance Component Modeling

This study employs OWL (Web Ontology Language), a markup language based on W3C RDF/XML [27], as the notation for representing SAEOn and adopts Protégé [26] as the OWL editing tool of the ontology construction. The OWL is a Semantic Web language designed to represent rich and complex knowledge about things, and relations between things, while Protégé is a free, open-source, and integrated development platform that provides a suite of facilities to create and manage ontological models. Using Protégé, the security assurance model presented in the previous section is easily transposed into an ontology that can be described in an equivalent XML-based format. In SAEOn, each component of the security assurance model is represented by one OWL *Class* having the same name and role. To have a finer classification and enable inference within the ontology, a *SubClassOf* type restriction is added to the model to represent the concepts of *Security Requirement* and *Vulnerability* accordingly. Figure 3 resents the class hierarchy in the Protégé.

Relationships between the classes are represented as *Object Property* in Protégé, following camel-case syntax naming conventions [19]. The object properties refer to these properties with classes as both domains and ranges. Table 6 lists object properties in the ontology and their associated constraints, while Fig. 4 illustrates the relationships between classes after the configuration.

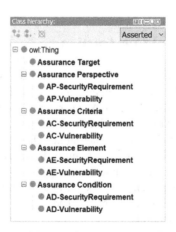

Fig. 3. Classes of the security assurance ontology in Protégé

Table 6. Objective properties of the security assurance ontology

Object property	Domain	Range
hasAssurancePerspective	Assurance Target	Assurance Perspective
hasAssuranceCriteria	Assurance Perspective	Assurance Criteria
hasAssuranceElement	Assurance Criteria	Assurance Element
hasAssuranceCondition	Assurance Element	Assurance Condition

Fig. 4. Illustration of relationships between classes

4.2 Assurance Metrics Modeling

The metric model includes a set of metrics, which is defined as a *Data Property* assertation in Protégé, with a numeric range. Figure 5 shows an example of the definition of a data property. The naming of data properties in SAEOn follows the pattern: *segment1* '-' *segment2*, where *segment1* represents the assurance component, and *segment2* is the metric. For example, *AT-SAS* and *SRP-ACT*, represent 'the security assurance score of the assurance target' and 'the actual score of SRP', respectively. To distinguish those data properties needed calculation (i.e. assurance metrics) from others, we model the list of data properties hierarchically, in which an additional node *AssuranceMetrics* (also a data property) is created to categorize the metrics that needed calculation, depicted in Fig. 5, area (a). In addition, we create three customized annotation properties: *shortName*, *rule,* and *sequence* to represent the description, calculation rules, and calculation sequences of assurance metrics respectively, also shown in Fig. 5, area (b).

In addition, to model what calculation algorisms the metrics refer to, a new annotation is created, named *rule,* which can be assigned to data properties flexibly. The content of the *rule* is a SPARQL statement used to retrieve and aggregate data from the ontology (Fig. 8 area(b)). SPARQL [28] is a W3C-recommended semantic query language, able to retrieve and manipulate data stored in RDF format. With this feature, we can easily encode calculation algorisms for assurance metrics and centralized the maintenance in the ontology.

Through data properties, we have built a set of meaningful metrics upon those introduced in Sect. 3.2. For example, the SPARQL for deriving the actual score of SRC (i.e., *ActSRC* in Eq. 3) is shown in Listing 1. For abbreviating the URI (Uniform Resource Identifier) of the SAEOn ontology, we use saeon for Prefix declaration in SPARQL.

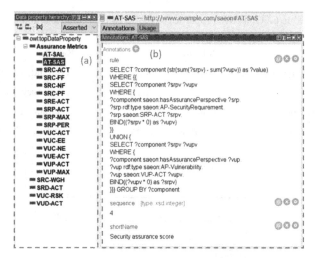

Fig. 5. Configurations of data properties in Protégé

Listing 1. The SPARQL for calculating the actual score of SRC (SRC-ACT)

```
SELECT ?component (str(AVG(?v) *AVG(?w)) as ?value)
WHERE {
    ?component rdf:type saeon:AC-SecurityRequirement.
    ?component saeon:hasAssuranceElement ?ae.
    ?ae saeon:SRE-ACT ?v.
    ?component saeon:SRC-WGH ?w.
}
GROUP BY ?component
```

Due to space limitations, only a few selected SPARQL rules are presented under this section, while others could have been excluded. Another example of metrics is *SRC-FF*, representing the 'Numbers of fully fulfilled security requirements in SRC'. The SPARQL to derive the metric is presented in Listing 2.

Listing 2. The SPARQL for calculating the numbers of fully fulfilled SRC (SRC-FF)

```
SELECT ?component (str(count(*)) AS ?value )
WHERE {
    ?at saeon:hasAssurancePerspective ?ap.
    ?ap saeon:hasAssuranceCriteria ?component.
    ?component sao:hasAssuranceElement ?ae.
    ?ae saeon:SRE-ACT ?v.
    ?component rdf:type saeon:AC-SecurityRequirement.
    FILTER(?v = 1)
}"
GROUP BY ?component
```

To assess the overall performance of the security requirement perspective, we define a metric *SRP-PER*, calculated using the ratio between the actual score and maximum score of SRP, which are derived using the summation of *SRC-ACT* (Eq. 5) and *SRC-WGH* respectively. It is noted that the possible maximum score of SRC always equals its weight value. The SPARQL for calculating *SRP-PER* is presented in Listing 3.

Listing 3. The SPARQL for calculating the performance of SRP (SRP-PER)

```
SELECT ?component (str(sum(?v) / sum(?w)) AS ?value)
WHERE  {
          ?component saeon:hasAssuranceCriteria ?ac.
          ?ac saeon:SRC-WGH ?w.
          ?ac saeon:SRC-ACT ?v.
          ?ap rdf:type saeon:AP-SecurityRequirement
}
GROUP BY ?component
```

The last example is *AT-SAS*, i.e., the security assurance score of an assurance target. The SPARQL is shown in Listing 4, in which a UNION statement is utilized to synthesize the scores of *AT-SAS, SRP-MAX,* and *VUP-MAX* from different result sets

Listing 4. The SPARQL for calculating security assurance score (AT-SAS)

```
SELECT ?component
(str((SUM(?sas)-SUM(?min)) / (SUM(?max) - SUM(?min)) * 10)AS ?value)
WHERE {{
    SELECT ?component ?sas ?min ?max
    WHERE {
        ?component saeon:AT-SAS ?sas.
        BIND((?sas * 0) AS ?min).
        BIND((?sas * 0) AS ?max).
        ?component rdf:type saeon:AssuranceTarget
    }}
UNION{
    SELECT ?component ?sas ?min ?max
    WHERE {
        ?component saeon:hasAssurancePerspective ?ap.
        ?ap rdf:type saeon:AP-SecurityRequirement.
        ?ap saeon:SRP-MAX ?max.
        BIND((?max * 0) AS ?sas).
        BIND((?max * 0) AS ?min).
    }}
UNION {
    SELECT ?component ?sas ?max ?min
    WHERE {
        ?component saeon:hasAssurancePerspective ?ap.
        ?ap rdf:type saeon:AP-Vulnerability.
        ?ap saeon:VUP-MAX ?vup.
        BIND((?vup * -1) AS ?min).
        BIND((?vup * 0) AS ?sas).
        BIND((?vup * 0) AS ?max).
}}}GROUP BY ?component
```

The next design consideration is the metrics calculation order, which should follow the three phases of the assurance evaluation (presented in Sect. 3.2). In this respect, we use a customized annotation '*sequence*' to indicate the computing sequences of metrics along the metrics aggregation process. To reduce the dependence between metrics in the same evaluation phase, meanwhile, to simplify the metrics calculation sequencing, all the metrics are directly calculated based on those in the previous phase. With this design principle, the calculation sequence can be decided simply following the evaluation phase, except for *AT-SAS* and *AT-SAL*, which are set in the (extra) fourth and fifth phases because of their interdependence. Table 7 shows the completed list of the configured data properties, representing metrics names, descriptions, and calculation sequences. With the features described above, the metrics metadata structured in the ontology is characterized as a repository of metrics with semantic descriptions and flexible metrics configuration.

4.3   Metrics Assignment Modeling

We model the metrics assignment by using SWRL (Semantic Web Rule Language) [12], and expressive OWL-based rule language is used which efficiently derives implicit facts from explicitly given ones. Based on the classes and properties that have been modeled in SAEOn, the rules of metrics assignment are expressed in SWRL. For example, the rule to assign an initial score to *AT-SAS* can be exemplified in SWRL as follows.

AssuranceTarget(?at) $\rightarrow$ *AT-SAS(?at, 0)*

This rule implies that the range value of the data property *AT-SAS* will be given '*0*' for all OWL individuals that are members of the OWL class *AssuranceTarget*. In SAEOn, we have configured 20 SWRL rules for data property inference. Due to the space limitation, Table 8 presents the partial rules used within the ontology.

Table 7.   Data properties and their annotations

Data property	Short name	Sequence
AT-SAL	Security assurance level	5
AT-SAS	Security assurance score	4
SRP-MAX	Max. score of overall security requirements	3
SRP-ACT	Actual score of overall security requirements	3
SRC-WGH	Weight factor of SRC	
SRC-ACT	Actual score of SRC	2
SRE-ACT	Actual score of SRE	1
SRD-ACT	Actual score of SRD	
VUP-MAX	Max. score of overall security vulnerabilities	3
VUP-ACT	Actual score of overall security vulnerabilities	3
VUC-RSK	Risk factor of VUC	
VUC-ACT	Actual score of VUC	2
VUE-ACT	Actual score of VUE	1
VUD-ACT	Actual score of SRD	

Table 8. Excerpt of SWRL rules used within the ontology

No	Rule
R01	AssuranceTarget(?t) → AT-SAL(?t, 0)
R02	AssuranceTarget(?t) → AT-SAS(?t, 0)
R03	AP-SecurityRequirement(?sr) → SRP-ACT(?sr, 0)
R04	AP-SecurityRequirement(?sr) → SRP-MAX(?sr, 0)
R05	AP-SecurityRequirement(?sr) → SRP-PER(?sr, 0)
R06	AC-SecurityRequirement(?sr) → SRC-ACT(?sr, 0)
R07	AC-SecurityRequirement(?sr) → SRC-WGH(?sr, 0)
R08	AE-SecurityRequirement(?sr) → SRE-ACT(?sr, 0)
R09	AD-SecurityRequirement(?sr) → SRD-ACT(?sr, 0)
R10	AP-Vulnerability(?vu) → VUP-ACT(?vu, 0)
R11	AC-Vulnerability(?vu) → VUC-ACT(?vu, 0)
R12	AC-Vulnerability(?vu) → VUC-RSK(?vu, 0)
R13	AE-Vulnerability(?vu) → VUE-ACT(?vu, 0)
R14	AD-Vulnerability(?vu) → VUD-ACT(?vu, 0)

4.4 Individuals Creation

To fill the ontology, we took an exemplary assurance target in the domain of web applications, named *System1*, which is a cloud platform for creating and maintaining virtual servers and networks. For this to work, we leveraged the Open Web Application Security Project (OWASP) as the knowledge source to model the knowledge items in the domain of web applications. Three OWASP project materials are chosen: OWASP Application Security Verification Standard (ASVA) [19], OWASP Top 10 [19] and OWASP Web Security Testing Guide (WSTG) [19]. The first material is used to construct knowledge items for security requirements, while the last two are synthesized for the vulnerability items. Once the domain knowledge is collected, we create OWL *individuals* for modeling the knowledge items. Figure 6 demonstrates the configuration of an individual under the class of *AC-SecurityRequirement*, named *System1-SRC-01*. This individual (i.e., a specific security requirement criteria) is declared with two corresponding assurance elements. We use customized annotations to provide auxiliary information about the individual, for example, *shortName* and *Resource*. Furthermore, all assurance conditions are given an initial score randomly for later metrics calculation.

To assign the metrics to the corresponding individuals, we process the inference from SWRL rules with the Drools rule engine [17]. Figure 7 shows the inferred results of data properties in different individuals (*System1* and *System1-SRC-01*).

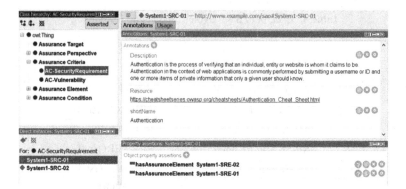

Fig. 6. Configuration of individuals in Protégé

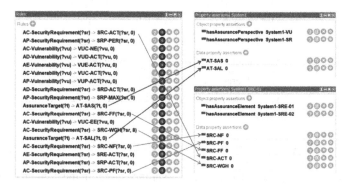

Fig. 7. SWRL Rules in Protégé and the corresponding inferences

5   Ontology Evaluation

We took a task-based evaluation approach [11] to verify the fundamental aspects of the developed ontology. This evaluation aims to assess what domain tasks have to be supported by an ontology and how the ontology can be used to accomplish certain tasks [21]. In this regard, we employed a competency question (CQ) approach, thorough answers to SPARQL queries executed as part of performing tasks. If the SPARQL queries can extract individuals as a response, it signifies that the CQs have succeeded in covering the defined objectives of the ontology. Therefore, three exemplary CQs were developed considering how the ontology fulfills the use cases.

CQ 1. List all assurance components relates to security requirements for the assurance target '*System1*' and mark the assigned score for assurance conditions.
CQ 2. List the assurance scores to provide an overview of the assurance evaluation result for the assurance target '*System1*'.
CQ 3. List the metrics to be calculated with the corresponding SPARQL for assurance components of SRC and SRE, sorting by the calculation sequence.

The corresponding SPARQL statement for each evaluated CQ and the execution result in the Protégé editor are depicted in Figs. 8, 9 and 10.

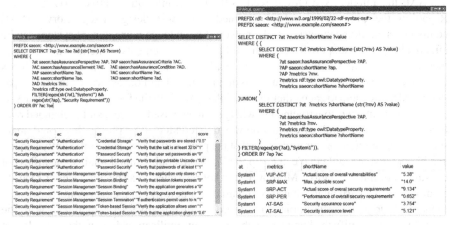

Fig. 8. The SPARQL statement and the execution result of CQ 1

Fig. 9. The SPARQL statement and the execution result of CQ 2

Fig. 10. The SPARQL statement and the execution result of CQ 3

6 Conclusion

In this paper, we have presented the design, development, and evaluation of the ontological SAE metamodel (SAEOn) as well as the underlining quantitative SAE approach. Regarding the aim of this study, we argued that a well-designed repository of SAE components, assurance metrics, and a powerful knowledge management system can be effectively used to support SAE, such as security requirements/vulnerabilities criteria, metrics selection, and assurance score calculation, amongst others. This ontology allows us to define the entities of the security assurance model and the assurance metrics separately and relate them to each other in a modular way. With the formal definition of assurance components, the constructed knowledge can be reused, shared, and exchanged over time. Although the ontology evaluation was only conducted on one application domain (i.e., the web application), it is obvious that the proposed ontology is sufficiently generic and highly customizable that can be applied in more application domains, regardless of the subject of the evaluation. Moreover, it is not restricted to a specific facet of security assurance, nor a particular security standard or framework. In a larger context, we plan to use SAEOn as a starting point for a thorough quantitative SAE approach. With the model, we can identify the knowledge objects in any application domain that are relevant to security assurance. The next step would be to model a comprehensive set of SAE metrics in the ontology that could ultimately enhance quantitative SAE. Furthermore, there is a need to develop a metrics calculation engine (software programs) using semantic web technologies to integrate SAEOn so that the automatic metrics calculation can be realized as well as the maintenance of the ontology.

Acknowledgment. This research work is financially supported by the SFI Norwegian Centre for Cybersecurity in Critical Sectors (NORCICS, NFR project number: 310105).

References

1. Atkinson, C., Kuhne, T.: Model-driven development: a metamodeling foundation. IEEE Softw. **20**(5), 36–41 (2003)
2. Berners-Lee, T., Hendler, J., Lassila, O.: The semantic web. Sci. Am. **284**(5), 28–37 (2001)
3. Ekclhart, A., Fenz, S., Goluch, G., Weippl, E.: Ontological mapping of common criteria's security assurance requirements. In: Venter, H., Eloff, M., Labuschagne, L., Eloff, J., von Solms, R. (eds.) SEC 2007. IIFIP, vol. 232, pp. 85–95. Springer, Boston, MA (2007). https://doi.org/10.1007/978-0-387-72367-9_8
4. Fenz, S., Ekelhart, A.: Formalizing information security knowledge. In: Proceedings of the 4th International Symposium on Information, Computer, and Communications Security. ACM (2009)
5. de Franco Rosa, F., Jino, M., Bonacin, R.: Towards an ontology of security assessment: a core model proposal. In: Latifi, S. (ed.) Information Technology – New Generations. AISC, vol. 738, pp. 75–80. Springer, Cham (2018). https://doi.org/10.1007/978-3-319-77028-4_12
6. Gao, J.-B., et al.: Ontology-based model of network and computer attacks for security assessment. J. Shanghai Jiaotong Univ. (Sci.) **18**(5), 554–562 (2013)
7. Gonzalez-Gil, P., Skarmeta, A.F., Martinez, J.A.: Towards an ontology for IoT context-based security evaluation. In: 2019 Global IoT Summit (GIoTS). IEEE (2019)

8. Gruber, T.R.: A translation approach to portable ontology specifications. Knowl. Acquisition **5**(2), 199–220 (1993)
9. Heitlager, I., Kuipers, T., Visser, J.: A practical model for measuring maintainability. In: 6th International Conference on the Quality of Information and Communications Technology (QUATIC 2007). IEEE (2007)
10. Herrmann, D.S.: Using the Common Criteria for IT Security Evaluation. Auerbach Publications, Boca Raton (2002)
11. Hlomani, H., Stacey, D.J.S.W.J.: Approaches, methods, metrics, measures, and subjectivity in ontology evaluation: a survey. Semant. Web J. **1**(5), 1–11 (2014)
12. Horrocks, I., et al.: SWRL: a semantic web rule language combining OWL and RuleML. W3C Member Submission **21**(79), 1–31 (2004)
13. Jayalakshmi, T., Santhakumaran, A.: Statistical normalization and back propagation for classification. Int. J. Comput. Theory Eng. **3**(1), 1793–8201 (2011)
14. Katt, B., Prasher, N.: Quantitative security assurance metrics: REST API case studies. In: Proceedings of the 12th European Conference on Software Architecture: Companion Proceedings (2018)
15. Katt, B., Prasher, N.: Quantitative security assurance. In: Exploring Security in Software Architecture and Design, pp. 15–46. IGI Global (2019)
16. Koinig, U., Tjoa, S., Ryoo, J.: Contrology-an ontology-based cloud assurance approach. In: 2015 IEEE 24th International Conference on Enabling Technologies: Infrastructure for Collaborative Enterprises. IEEE (2015)
17. O'Connor, M., et al.: Supporting rule system interoperability on the semantic web with SWRL. In: Gil, Y., Motta, E., Benjamins, V.R., Musen, M.A. (eds.) ISWC 2005. LNCS, vol. 3729, pp. 974–986. Springer, Heidelberg (2005). https://doi.org/10.1007/11574620_69
18. Ouedraogo, M., et al.: Appraisal and reporting of security assurance at operational systems level. J. Syst. Softw. **85**(1), 193–208 (2012)
19. OWASP: OWASP Web Security Testing Guide. https://owasp.org/www-project-web-security-testing-guide/. Accessed 26 Jan 2022
20. Powley, S., et al.: An evaluation ontology applied to connected vehicle security assurance. In: INCOSE International Symposium. Wiley Online Library (2019)
21. Raad, J., Cruz, C.: A survey on ontology evaluation methods. In: Proceedings of the International Conference on Knowledge Engineering and Ontology Development, part of the 7th International Joint Conference on Knowledge Discovery, Knowledge Engineering and Knowledge Management (2015)
22. Raskin, V., et al.: Ontology in information security: a useful theoretical foundation and methodological tool. In: Proceedings of the 2001 Workshop on New Security Paradigms (2001)
23. Ross, R.S.: Managing information security risk: organization, mission, and information system view (2011)
24. Saaty, T.L.: Decision making with the analytic hierarchy process. Int. J. Serv. Sci. **1**(1), 83–98 (2008)
25. Shukla, A., et al.: System security assurance: a systematic literature review. arXiv preprint arXiv:2110.01904 (2021)
26. Tudorache, T., et al.: WebProtégé: a collaborative ontology editor and knowledge acquisition tool for the web. Semant. Web **4**(1), 89–99 (2013)
27. W3C: RDF 1.1 XML Syntax. https://www.w3.org/TR/rdf-syntax-grammar/. Accessed 26 Jan 2022
28. W3C: SPARQL 1.1 Query Language. https://www.w3.org/TR/sparql11-query/. Accessed 27 Jan 2022
29. Wand, Y., Storey, V.C., Weber, R.: An ontological analysis of the relationship construct in conceptual modeling. ACM Trans. Database Syst. (TODS) **24**(4), 494–528 (1999)

30. Wang, J.A., Guo, M.: OVM: an ontology for vulnerability management. In: Proceedings of the 5th Annual Workshop on Cyber Security and Information Intelligence Research: Cyber Security and Information Intelligence Challenges and Strategies (2009)
31. Wang, J.A., et al.: Ontology-based security assessment for software products. In: Proceedings of the 5th Annual Workshop on Cyber Security and Information Intelligence Research: Cyber Security and Information Intelligence Challenges and Strategies (2009)
32. Wen, S.-F., Shukla, A., Katt, B.: Developing security assurance metrics to support quantitative security assurance evaluation. J. Cybersecur. Priv. **2**(3), 587–605 (2022)
33. Yavagal, D.S., et al.: Common criteria requirements modeling and its uses for quality of information assurance (QoIA). In: Proceedings of the 43rd Annual Southeast Regional Conference, vol. 2 (2005)

A Comparison-Based Methodology for the Security Assurance of Novel Systems

Peeter Laud[(✉)] and Jelizaveta Vakarjuk

Cybernetica AS, Tallinn, Estonia
{peeter.laud,jelizaveta.vakarjuk}@cyber.ee

Abstract. In this paper, we advocate the position that the security certification of one system should make the certification of other similar systems easier, if one can present the evidence that the second system is at least as secure as the first system. We present a development of this idea, stating the components of such comparative evidence. We stretch the idea of propagating the certification to less similar systems, if one can present a sequence of systems from the certified one to the novel one, where each system is evidenced to be at least as secure as the previous one. We apply our methodology to authentication systems, where we show that a system based on threshold cryptography is at least as secure as widely used smartcard-based systems.

1 Introduction

Our critical systems are built on top of, and their security assurances depend on smaller subsystems, whose security is of utmost importance, and where the society has chosen security certification as the methodology to ensure that these subsystems satisfy the required properties. These small systems and devices include smartcards, hardware security modules, trusted execution environments, but also certain communication devices, operating systems and application software. A lot of trust is placed on the outcomes of certification, hence this process is expensive [9] and conservative [20]. When a certified system has been updated, then the new version has to pass the certification again. A system making use of novel security technologies may have hard time passing certification at all, because these technologies may not map cleanly to the categories specified in certification procedures.

In Common Criteria (CC) certification [8], we speak of *Targets of Evaluation* (ToE); this is the well-delimited system that is expected to pass certification. A *Security Target* (ST) document is compiled for certifying a particular ToE; it gives the boundaries of ToE, and lists the security requirements that ToE is expected to fulfill. These requirements are taken from standardised lists, enumerated in CC specifications. A security target may comply with, i.e. contain one or more *Protection Profiles* (PP), which are themselves lists of security requirements. The security requirements are either *Security Functional Requirements*

S. Katsikas et al. (Eds.): ESORICS 2022 Workshops, LNCS 13785, pp. 625–644, 2023.
https://doi.org/10.1007/978-3-031-25460-4_36

(SFR), referring to the security technologies that the ToE may use in a certain manner in order to obtain certain security properties, or *Security Assurance Requirements* (SAR), which refer to the good practices used during the design, development, and operation of the ToE. In this paper, we use CC-related terms, but our proposed methodology should be applicable to other certification frameworks, too.

When a ToE evolves, then it may still fulfill the same SFRs listed in the ST of the old ToE, but it may fulfill them in novel manner. When a ToE makes use of novel technologies, it may be difficult to map the technical protections it offers to the fulfilment of SFRs in the ST. In both cases, it may be helpful to not match the new ToE directly against SFRs, but to compare the new ToE to the old one and make sure that the new one is *at least as secure*. This is the position we advocate in this paper: comparing two ToE-s—one with existing certification against a ST, and the other that we desire to get certified against a similar ST—can simplify the certification process, while preserving the assurances of the existing certification. The comparison establishes, that for any attack against the novel system, there exists an attack against the certified system that is no more difficult to perform, and with the same or worse consequences. We argue that such arguments should be accepted by certification bodies. Even if they are not directly accepted, the outcomes of the comparison should guide the vendor in changing the evidence documentation that supports the claims of ToE satisfying the ST.

Our proposal is similar to *game-based* security proofs of cryptographic primitives [1]. In cryptography, security definitions define an interactive attack game that is played between the adversary and the environment; the latter provides an interface to the adversary through which the primitive may be invoked in well-defined ways. The primitive is deemed secure if no adversary's probability of *winning* the game exceeds a certain value. A typical security proof presents a different game where the same adversary obviously has only a low probability of winning, and then argues that in the original game, the adversary's win is not much more likely.

In these security proofs, it is common to introduce *intermediate* games, such that any two neighbouring games differ only slightly from each other, simplifying the argument that the adversary's winning probability in i-th game is at most negligibly larger than in the $(i + 1)$-st game. Here the zeroth game comes from the security definition, and the final game is the one where the adversary's win is obviously unlikely. We advocate that we can do something similar for certification: the zeroth ToE is the novel one that we want to certify, the final ToE has already been certified, and we may introduce "intermediate" ToE-s that are easier to compare against the previous and next ones.

Related Work. The certification of evolving systems, the simplification of updating the evidence, and the reuse of evaluation results have been the topic of a statement from the CC Recognition Arrangement Management Committee [16]. Methods for using CC together with agile product development [18,19], and for continued certification of cyber security products [5] have been proposed. But we are aware of only a few attempts to show the security of one system by comparing it to another one, where the latter one has already been deemed secure [3]. The other example is Trusted Computer System Evaluation Criteria (TCSEC), where the system evaluation process included the Rating Maintenance Phase (RAMP). The goal of RAMP was to provide an instrument to extend evaluation of a certified system to a new version of that system by analysing changes that were introduced [10].

In the rest of this paper, we describe our proposal for comparing two systems in more detail. We will then give an example of comparing two systems, where one of them is based on well-established hardware security technologies, while the other one makes use of threshold cryptography. In order to compare them against each other, we come up with a couple of intermediate systems, and argue that each of them is at least as secure as the next one.

2 Proposed Methodology

Suppose we have a ToE T', for which we want to provide evidence that it matches a security target. We also have another system T, which we have already shown to match the same or a similar security target. We have the detailed specifications of both T and T', such that we can make a list of all potential weaknesses that an adversary may exploit in T or in T'. We may already have used these lists to create the security target [7]. For describing the processes of T and T', BPMN [11] may be a good choice, perhaps annotated further [14,17] to show the protection mechanisms in use. We create lists of weaknesses with high granularity, considering each data storage, movement, or processing step as something that the adversary may obtain information from, or tamper with the inputs and outputs of. The high granularity also means that an adversary may exploit one weakness either fully, or not exploit it at all, but there are no partial exploitations. Let W be the set of all weaknesses of T, and W' the set of all weaknesses of T'. Also, let $\mathcal{W}$ [resp. $\mathcal{W}'$] be the set of subsets of W [resp. W']. When an adversary performs an attack against T or T', then the set of weaknesses it exploits is an element of $\mathcal{W}$ or $\mathcal{W}'$.

The security target specifies the operational environment of the ToE, including the threats, organisational policies, and security assumptions. Hence not any set of weaknesses is considered exploitable against the system T. Rather, the security target specifies the set of *considered sets of weaknesses* $\mathcal{W}_C \subseteq \mathcal{W}$ that contains only such sets of weaknesses that an adversary may *attempt* to exploit according to the security target. Here the attempts by the adversary do not correspond to his success; rather, the ToE is meant to employ measures that make the adversary unsuccessful. It is natural to assume that $\mathcal{W}_C$ is downwards closed: if $\mathbf{w}_1, \mathbf{w}_2 \in \mathcal{W}$, $\mathbf{w}_1 \subseteq \mathbf{w}_2$, and $\mathbf{w}_2 \in \mathcal{W}_C$, then also $\mathbf{w}_1 \in \mathcal{W}_C$.

The security target for T' similarly specifies $\mathcal{W}'_C \subseteq \mathcal{W}'$. As T' has not been certified yet, our methodology may bring adjustments to the precise definition of $\mathcal{W}'_C$; hopefully not reducing it by too much.

To each set of weaknesses of T or T' we can attach two (abstract) quantities: the *difficulty* (for the adversary) of exploiting this set of weaknesses, and the *seriousness* of the effects of successful exploitation by the adversary. We do not define the structure of these quantities, but we require that there is a (partial) order on them. Hence we get two preorders on $\mathcal{W} \cup \mathcal{W}'$: for two sets of weaknesses $\mathbf{w}_1$ and $\mathbf{w}_2$ we write $\mathbf{w}_1 \prec_D \mathbf{w}_2$, if exploiting all weaknesses in $\mathbf{w}_1$ is no more difficult for the adversary than exploiting all weaknesses in $\mathbf{w}_2$. We also write $\mathbf{w}_1 \prec_S \mathbf{w}_2$ if the effects of exploiting $\mathbf{w}_1$ are no worse than the effects of exploiting $\mathbf{w}_2$. A natural corollary of these definitions is, that if $\mathbf{w}_1 \subseteq \mathbf{w}_2$, then also $\mathbf{w}_1 \prec_D \mathbf{w}_2$ and $\mathbf{w}_1 \prec_S \mathbf{w}_2$.

It is possible that for some $\mathbf{w}_1 \neq \mathbf{w}_2$ we have both $\mathbf{w}_1 \prec_D \mathbf{w}_2$ and $\mathbf{w}_2 \prec_D \mathbf{w}_1$ (denote this $\mathbf{w}_1 \sim_D \mathbf{w}_2$), hence $\prec_D$ is not an order, but only a preorder. The same applies to $\prec_S$. It may be difficult to describe all refinements that $\prec_D$ and $\prec_S$ have with respect to the subset inclusion. However, an imprecise description does not invalidate the outcomes of our proposed analysis.

We want to show that for each $\mathbf{w}' \in \mathcal{W}'_C$, there exists some $\mathbf{w} \in \mathcal{W}_C$, such that $\mathbf{w} \prec_D \mathbf{w}'$ and $\mathbf{w}' \prec_S \mathbf{w}$. We thus have to present a function $f : \mathcal{W}'_C \to \mathcal{W}_C$, such that $f(\mathbf{w}') \prec_D \mathbf{w}'$ and $\mathbf{w}' \prec_S f(\mathbf{w}')$ for all $\mathbf{w}' \in \mathcal{W}'_C$. We have found it easier to present not a function f, but a relation $F \subseteq \mathcal{W}' \times \mathcal{W}$, requiring that each $\mathbf{w}' \in \mathcal{W}'_C$ is related to at least one element of $\mathcal{W}_C$.

Each element of $\mathcal{W}'$ [resp. $\mathcal{W}$] is a subset of W' [resp. W]; hence it has the natural representation as a characteristic vector of type $W' \to \{0, 1\}$ [resp. $W \to \{0, 1\}$]. The entire relation F is thus represented as a boolean function $\phi : ((W' \,\dot{\cup}\, W) \to \{0, 1\}) \to \{0, 1\}$, which in turn is conveniently represented as a boolean formula. The variables of this formula are exactly the weaknesses of T and T'.

We say that two systems T and T' are *similar* if there is enough relationships $\prec_D$ and $\prec_S$ between the corresponding attack sets. If the systems T and T' are sufficiently dissimilar, then the construction of ϕ may fail, because of the lack of relationships $\prec_D$ and $\prec_S$ between attack sets $\mathbf{w} \in \mathcal{W}$ and $\mathbf{w}' \in \mathcal{W}'$. Such lack of (obvious) relationships may inform us of the security mechanisms that we need to use in T' in order to follow our methodology—the security mechanisms used by T' have to be strong enough to justify the addition of $\prec_D$- or $\prec_S$-relationships between attack sets against T and T'. These mechanisms may also be necessary for T' to match the security target. If intermediate systems have been introduced, then the requirements to use stronger security mechanisms may propagate from T through these systems all the way back to the system T'.

3   Example

In this section, we show how to use the proposed methodology to compare two authentication systems, where the user's browser establishes a secure connection with a relying party's (RP) server, and the user is authenticated during this process. In both systems, the RP server, knowing the public key of the user, generates a challenge, which has to be signed with the corresponding private key. The systems differ in how the private key is stored, and how the signature is generated.

An authentication system has to provide processes for the full lifecycle of a user's keypair: how it is generated, how a certificate is issued for it, how the RP finds the public key, how the challenges are signed, how the key is revoked. A full comparison of the two systems has to consider all of them. For concreteness, in this paper we will only focus on the authentication process itself, which includes the signing, and also some details of the storage of the private key.

The first system T has a smartcard as its centerpiece, containing the user's private key, and issuing signatures with it when activated. There exist protection profiles for such devices [12,13], and a number of cards or chips on the card have been certified to satisfy them. A typical use of a smartcard is as part of the Client Certificate Authentication (CCA) in the Transport Layer Security (TLS) protocol [15].

The second system T' uses threshold cryptography [4], sharing the private key between the user's phone and a central server. It can be used to authenticate the client end in an established TLS session. When attempting to directly certify such a system, it may be difficult to argue that the user has sufficient control over the private key—neither the phone nor the remote server alone provides such control.

3.1   Authentication with a Smartcard

When a relying party wants to make sure it is talking to a device of a user with a given public key, it will create a challenge bit-string and ask the device to sign it. If the corresponding private key is stored in a smartcard, used with a card reader, then the challenge goes from the client application to the card reader, then together with the PIN (entered by the user on the PINpad if the card reader has one, and on the keyboard otherwise) to the smartcard, which checks the PIN and creates the signature, which then moves back the same way. If there have been too many wrong entries of the PIN, then the card locks up. The whole process is displayed as a BPMN diagram in Fig. 1, split into relatively atomic pieces.

The card stores the private key, and the PIN. The user also knows the PIN. Inside the card, the PIN entered by the user is compared against the PIN that the card is storing. The environment of the card is protected, meaning that the PIN and the private key (or any details about it) cannot be read out, and the logic that it executes cannot be thwarted. The card reader is also protected, in that the PIN entered on its pad will only be sent to the card and not anywhere else.

This process, and the protection offered by it is considered a good example of two-factor authentication, showing that the user knows the PIN (knowledge factor), and the user has the card (possession factor). It is considered a good example even if the PIN entry is less isolated from the outside world, i.e. when the user enters the PIN on the computer.

Weaknesses of a System with a Smartcard. In this process, the following weaknesses can be identified. These are the elements of the set W—the possible locations where an adversary could mount an attack. As the system T is

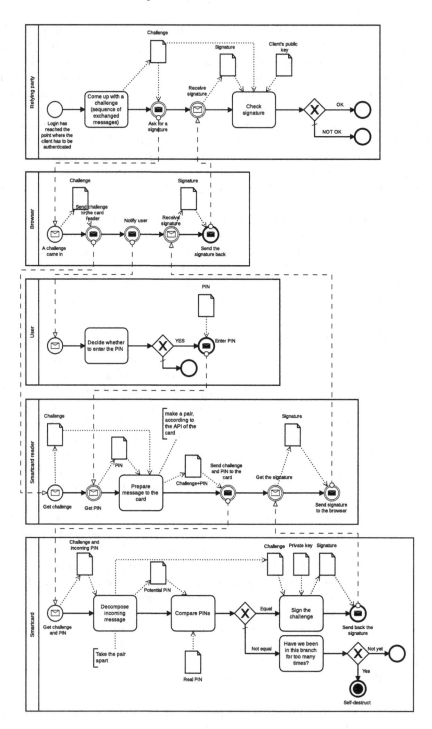

Fig. 1. The smartcard system

considered secure, none of these locations, or their combinations are actually an exploitable weakness, i.e. $\mathcal{W}_C = \mathcal{W}$.

Possible attacks against the relying party

(RP1) Affect the computation of the challenge
(RP2) Learn the challenge
(RP3) Modify the challenge while it is sent to the browser
(RP4) Change the outcome of the signature check
(RP5) Accept the log-in, even if the signature does not check

Possible attacks against the browser

(B1) Learn the challenge
(B2) Modify the challenge while it is sent to the card reader
(B3) Modify the signature while it is sent to the relying party

Possible attacks against the user

(U1) Learn the PIN from the user
(U2) Change the PIN

Possible attacks against the smartcard reader

(SCR1) Learn the PIN that the user entered
(SCR2) Change the challenge that is sent to the smartcard
(SCR3) Change the PIN that is sent to the smartcard
(SCR4) Change the signature while it is sent to the browser

Possible attacks against the smartcard

(SC1) Learn the PIN
(SC2) Interfere with the PIN comparison procedure
(SC3) Make the decision of the PIN check take the other path
(SC4) Make the decision about counts of incorrect PINs take the other path
(SC5) Learn the private key
(SC6) Change the private key
(SC7) Change the challenge that enters the computation of the signature
(SC8) Learn the signature
(SC9) Change the signature sent back to the smartcard reader

3.2   Authentication with SplitKey

In systems relying on threshold cryptography, where the private key is stored in a secret-shared manner, several storage devices with the shares of the key have to be present in order to make use of that private key. If all the storage devices offer strong properties of unclonability, tamper-resistance and similar, then we can have even stronger security properties for the authentication process, compared to using just a single device.

However, we typically want to use threshold cryptography in order to reduce the requirements on the devices storing, and on the procedures for accessing individual shares of the private key. If we still want to argue that our authentication procedure has strong security properties similar to logging in with a smartcard, then we have to involve the properties of several devices in our arguments.

In particular, the SplitKey technology [2] for signature creation shares the private key among two devices, such that one of the devices - the phone - does not offer a strong protection for its key share. Hence, in an authentication system based on SplitKey, when arguing about the possession of a private key, we have to involve the second device in our arguments. This involvement may touch the physical properties of that device, as well as technical and organisational properties controlling the access to it.

The authentication procedure is depicted in Fig. 2, in similar detail to the previous figure. Let us recall that in SplitKey, an RSA private key has been shared between the user's phone and the server, and the keyshare on the phone is encrypted with a low-entropy key (derived from the PIN that the user enters). If the adversary has obtained just the encrypted keyshare, then it cannot recognize, which PIN is the correct one. However, the server can recognize if it has received a signature share from the phone that has been created with a wrong keyshare.

When the phone has received the challenge, it asks the user to input the PIN. In order to help the user understand the context, in which the signing of the challenge is about to occur, the phone shows the user a short *control code*, derived from the challenge. The same control code is shown to the user by the relying party's website. The user is supposed to enter the PIN only if the control codes match.

Weaknesses of a SplitKey-Based System. Considering the steps in Fig. 2, we can list the following possible weaknesses.

Attacks against the relying party:

(RP1) Affect the computation of the challenge
(RP2) Learn the challenge
(RP3) Affect the computation of the control code
(RP4) Learn the control code
(RP5) Modify the challenge while it is sent to the phone
(RP6) Change the outcome of the signature check
(RP7) Accept the log-in, even if the signature does not check

Attacks against the browser

(B1) Learn the control code
(B2) Change the control code, when it is shown to the user

Attacks affecting the user

(U1) Learn the PIN from the user
(U2) Change the PIN

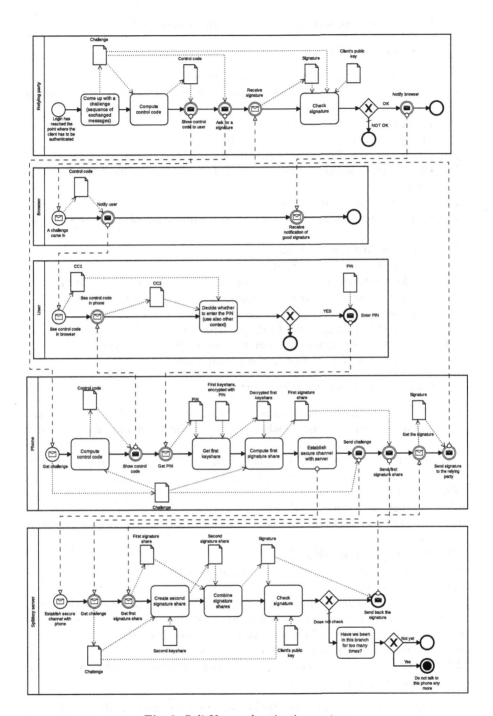

Fig. 2. SplitKey authentication system

(U3) Cause the user to incorrectly compare the control codes

Attacks against the phone

(P1) Affect the computation of the control code

(P2) Change the control code on the phone screen, where it is shown to the user

(P3) Learn the PIN that the user enters

(P4) Learn the encrypted first keyshare (encrypted with PIN)

(P5) Learn the plain first keyshare

(P6) Change the encrypted first keyshare, before it has been decrypted with the PIN

(P7) Change the plain first keyshare

(P8) Change the challenge that enters the computation of the first signature share

(P9) Learn the first signature share

(P10) Change the first signature share

(P11) Interfere with the establishment of the secure channel with the SplitKey server, thereby obtaining the capability to read and/or change messages sent over it

(P12) Change the challenge sent to the SplitKey server

(P13) Change the first signature share sent to the SplitKey server

(P14) Change the signature sent to the relying party

Attacks against the Splitkey server

(SS1) Interfere with the establishment of the secure channel with the phone, thereby obtaining the capability to read and/or change messages sent over it

(SS2) Interfere with the establishment of the secure channel with the phone, thereby confusing the server on the identity of the phone

(SS3) Learn the second keyshare

(SS4) Change the second keyshare

(SS5) Change the challenge that goes into the second signature share creation process

(SS6) Learn the second signature share

(SS7) Interfere with the signature combination process

(SS8) Learn the signature

(SS9) Change the client's public key, against which the signature is checked

(SS10) Interfere with the signature checking procedure

(SS11) Make the decision of the signature check go otherwise

(SS12) Change the signature sent back to the phone

(SS13) Make the decision about counts of unsuccessful signature creations take the other path

Among the attacks against the SplitKey system, we can identify the following relationships for $\prec_D$ and $\prec_S$. If the adversary learns both the PIN and the encrypted first keyshare, then he also has the plain first keyshare: $\{P5\} \prec_X$

{P3, P4} and {P5} $\prec_X$ {U1, P4}, where X may be both D and S. Changing a value has no greater effect than changing everything that is computed from this value. In particular, {SS4} $\prec_S$ {SS7} $\prec_S$ {SS10} $\prec_S$ {SS11, SS12} and {P6} $\prec_S$ {P7} $\prec_S$ {P12} $\prec_S$ {SS7}. The same relationships generally continue to hold when we add the same additional attacks to both sides of $\prec_X$.

We are using threshold cryptography, where the adversary learning just a single share of a secret should not yet affect the seriousness of attacks that he can perform. In particular, we would like to state that {P5} $\cup$ **w** $\prec_S$ **w** for a significant class of attack sets **w** that do not contain attacks against the second keyshare. We state this for all **w** that do not contain SS3 or SS6. Instead of the set {P5}, we can also consider other sets that imply the knowledge of the first keyshare or signature share: {P3, P4} and {P9}.

3.3   First Intermediate System

The systems T and T' are too different for the direct application of the comparison methodology we gave in Sect. 2. As we see below, we can cross this gap by proposing a couple of intermediate systems.

We change the system T' into the system T_1, where instead of computing the first signature share on the phone, we move all the computations into the Splitkey server. We let the Splitkey server store the user's private key share encrypted with the user's PIN and we send the PIN together with the challenge from the phone to the SplitKey server. The authentication process in the first intermediate system is depicted in Fig. 3.

Weaknesses of the First Intermediate System. Obviously the possible attacks against the relying party, browser, and user are the same as in the SplitKey-based system, as there have been no changes to this part of the system. Attacks against the phone and the server have changed; quite often, the change is simply in the target device.

   Attacks against the phone

(P1) Affect the computation of the control code
(P2) Change the control code on the phone screen, where it is shown to the user
(P3) Learn the PIN that the user enters
(P4) Interfere with the establishment of the secure channel with the SplitKey server, thereby obtaining the capability to read and/or change messages sent over it
(P5) Change the challenge sent to the SplitKey server
(P6) Change the signature sent to the relying party
(P7) (**new**) Change the PIN sent to the SplitKey server

   Attacks against the SplitKey server

(SS1) Interfere with the establishment of the secure channel with the phone, thereby obtaining the capability to read and/or change messages sent over it

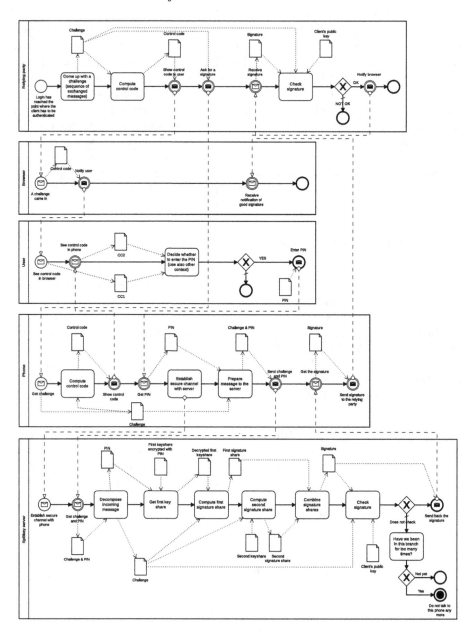

Fig. 3. The first intermediate system

(SS2) Interfere with the establishment of the secure channel with the phone, thereby confusing the server on the identity of the phone

(SS3) Learn the second keyshare

(SS4) Change the second keyshare

(SS5) Change the challenge that goes into the second signature share creation process

(SS6) Learn the second signature share

(SS7) Interfere with the signature combination process

(SS8) Learn the signature

(SS9) Change the client's public key, against which the signature is checked

(SS10) Interfere with the signature checking procedure

(SS11) Make the decision of signature check go otherwise

(SS12) Change the signature sent back to the phone

(SS13) Make the decision about counts of unsuccessful signature creations take the other path

(SS14) (**moved**) Learn the PIN received from the phone

(SS15) (**moved**) Learn the encrypted first keyshare (encrypted with PIN)

(SS16) (**moved**) Learn the plain first keyshare

(SS17) (**moved**) Change the encrypted first keyshare, before it has been decrypted with the PIN

(SS18) (**moved**) Change the plain first keyshare

(SS19) (**moved**) Change the challenge that enters the computation of the first signature share

(SS20) (**moved**) Learn the first signature share

(SS21) (**moved**) Change the first signature share

For the system T_1, we can again identify certain relationships for $\prec_D$ and $\prec_S$. All the relationships from T' are present, except that some of them have changed their numbers (and also moved their target from the phone to the server). We also assume that the different values the server computes during the signature creation process are equally difficult for an adversary to learn or change; thus $\{SS16\} \prec_D \{SS3\}$, $\{SS6\} \sim_D \{SS20\} \sim_D \{SS8\}$ and $\{SS5\} \sim_D \{SS19\}$.

We also have relationships between the weaknesses of T' and T_1. We may assume that if $\mathbf{w}$ is a set of weaknesses for both of them (i.e. the names are the same), then $T'.\mathbf{w} \sim_S T_1.\mathbf{w}$. If the targets of the weaknesses in $\mathbf{w}$ are also the same, then also $T'.\mathbf{w} \sim_D T_1.\mathbf{w}$. For example: $\{T'.P4\} \sim_S \{T_1.SS15\}$, but $\{T'.P4\} \not\sim_D \{T_1.SS15\}$.

Comparison Between T' and T_1. We can now write down the formula ϕ that matches each set of attacks against T' with a set of attacks against T_1. Denote $\mathcal{L}.K \equiv (\mathcal{L}.P3 \wedge \mathcal{L}.P4) \vee \mathcal{L}.P5$ and $\mathcal{R}.K \equiv (\mathcal{R}.SS14 \wedge \mathcal{R}.SS15) \vee \mathcal{R}.SS16$, i.e. "K" denotes the adversary's ability to learn the first keyshare. The formula ϕ is the conjunction of the following statements:

- $T'.RPi \Leftrightarrow T_1.RPi$ for $i \in \{1, \ldots, 7\}$
- $T'.Bi \Leftrightarrow T_1.Bi$ for $i \in \{1, 2\}$
- $T'.Ui \Leftrightarrow T_1.Ui$ for $i \in \{1, 2, 3\}$

- $T'.\mathrm{P}i \Leftrightarrow T_1.\mathrm{P}i$ for $i \in \{1, 2, 3\}$
- $T'.\mathrm{P}i \Leftrightarrow T_1.\mathrm{P}(i - 7)$ for $i \in \{11, 12\}$
- $T'.\mathrm{P}14 \Leftrightarrow T_1.\mathrm{P}6$
- $T'.\mathrm{SS}i \Leftrightarrow T_1.\mathrm{SS}i$ for $i \in \{1, \ldots, 13\}$
- $(T'.\mathrm{K} \text{ and } T'.\mathrm{SS3}) \Leftrightarrow (T_1.\mathrm{K} \text{ and } T_1.\mathrm{SS3})$
- $(T'.\mathrm{K} \text{ and } T'.\mathrm{SS6}) \Leftrightarrow (T_1.\mathrm{K} \text{ and } T_1.\mathrm{SS6})$
- $(T'.\mathrm{P9} \text{ and } T'.\mathrm{SS3}) \Leftrightarrow (T_1.\mathrm{SS20} \text{ and } T_1.\mathrm{SS3})$
- $(T'.\mathrm{P9} \text{ and } T'.\mathrm{SS6}) \Leftrightarrow (T_1.\mathrm{SS20} \text{ and } T_1.\mathrm{SS6})$

Sets of attacks against the relying party, browser and user have not changed, therefore the sets from the SplitKey system are equivalent to the corresponding sets in the first intermediate system. Also, certain attacks against the phone and the SplitKey server are the same in both systems as these are not connected to the changes we introduced in the first intermediate system.

Attacks involving the adversary learning one or both shares of the key and the signature are the most interesting ones. As the discussion of $\prec_S$ above shows, we can disregard attacks where the adversary learns only one of the shares, as they are no more powerful than learning no shares at all. The last four equivalences above state that if an attack set $\mathbf{w}$ against T' allows the adversary to learn a first share (of the private key, or the signature) and a second share, then we match it with an attack set $\mathbf{w}'$ against T_1 where the adversary also learns the same first share and the same second share. The seriousness of these attacks is the same—$T'.\mathbf{w} \sim_S T_1.\mathbf{w}'$, because the adversary obtains the same knowledge and interferes with the same operations. The difficulty is also the same, although the phone should be easier to attack than the Splitkey server—the set $\mathbf{w}$ contains either $T'.\mathrm{SS3}$ or $T'.\mathrm{SS6}$, hence $\mathbf{w}'$ contains either $T_1.\mathrm{SS3}$ or $T_1.\mathrm{SS6}$, but these are at least as difficult to perform as $T_1.\mathrm{SS16}$ or $T_1.\mathrm{SS20}$.

3.4   Second Intermediate System

We change the system T_1 into the system T_2, where instead of computing a combined signature from two signature shares, the Splitkey server generates a single signature using a single private key. The private key is not encrypted with the user's PIN. Instead, the server verifies the correctness of the user's PIN received together with the challenge, by comparing the PIN received from the phone with one stored on the server side. The authentication process in the second intermediate system is depicted in Fig. 4.

Weaknesses of the Second Intermediate System. Attacks against the relying party, browser, user, and phone are the same as for the first intermediate system.

Attacks against the Splitkey server

(SS1) Interfere with the establishment of the secure channel with the phone, thereby obtaining the capability to read and/or change messages sent over it

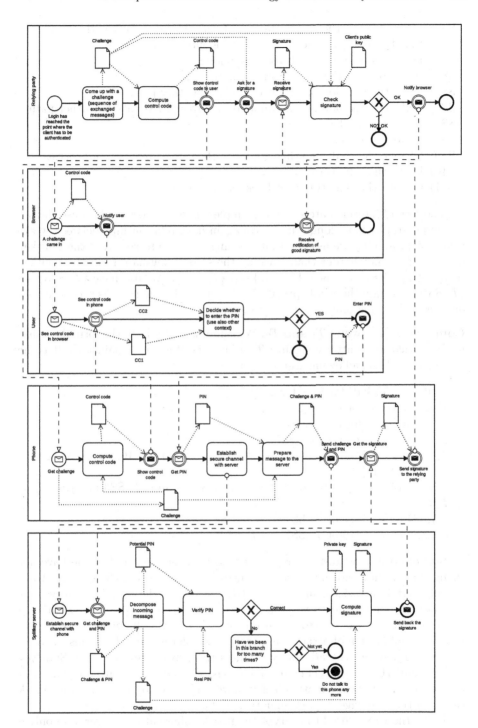

Fig. 4. The second intermediate system

(SS2) Interfere with the establishment of the secure channel with the phone, thereby confusing the server on the identity of the phone

(SS3) Learn the PIN received from the phone

(SS4) Interfere with the PIN verification process

(SS5) Make the decision of PIN check take the other path

(SS6) Make the decision about counts of incorrect PINs take the other path

(SS7) Learn private key

(SS8) Change private key

(SS9) Change the challenge that goes into the signature creation process

(SS10) Learn the signature

(SS11) Change the signature sent back to the phone

The second intermediate system is simpler than the first one because threshold cryptography is no longer used. We again have relationships between weaknesses of T_1 and T_2: we assume that learning the private key from the Splitkey server of T_2 is not harder than learning the second keyshare from the Splitkey server of T_1. We hence have $\{T_2.\text{SS7}\} \prec_D \{T_1.\text{SS3}\}$. We also have $\{T_1.\text{SS3}\} \prec_S \{T_2.\text{SS7}\}$: learning the whole private key definitely has at least as serious consequences as learning only one keyshare.

Comparison Between T_1 and T_2. We can now write down the formula ϕ that matches each set of attacks against T_1 with a set of attacks against T_2. It is the conjunction of the following statements:

- $T_1.\text{RP}i \Leftrightarrow T_2.\text{RP}i$ for $i \in \{1, \ldots, 7\}$
- $T_1.\text{B}i \Leftrightarrow T_2.\text{B}i$ for $i \in \{1, 2\}$
- $T_1.\text{U}i \Leftrightarrow T_2.\text{U}i$ for $i \in \{1, 2, 3\}$
- $T_1.\text{P}i \Leftrightarrow T_2.\text{P}i$ for $i \in \{1, \ldots, 7\}$
- $T_1.\text{SS}i \Leftrightarrow T_2.\text{SS}j$ for $(i, j) \in \{(1,1), (2,2), (14,3), (10,4), (11,5), (13,6), (8,10), (12,11)\}$
- $(((T_1.\text{SS14} \text{ and } T_1.\text{SS15}) \text{ or } T_1.\text{SS16} \text{ or } T_1.\text{SS20}) \text{ and } (T_1.\text{SS3} \text{ or } T_1.\text{SS6})) \Leftrightarrow T_2.\text{SS7}$
- $(T_1.\text{SS4} \text{ or } T_1.\text{SS17} \text{ or } T_1.\text{SS18}) \Leftrightarrow T_2.\text{SS8}$
- $(T_1.\text{SS5} \text{ or } T_1.\text{SS19} \text{ or } T_1.\text{SS7}) \Leftrightarrow T_2.\text{SS9}$

Sets of attacks against the relying party, browser, user and phone have not changed as we have not introduced changes to these parts of the system. Additionally, certain attacks against the SplitKey server are the same in both systems as these are not related to the changes we introduced in T_2. In T_2, we have a single private key that is stored on the SplitKey server. It means that we can match a combination of attacks that retrieve keyshares from T_1 against a single attack in T_2, where the adversary extracts the private key from the SplitKey server. Similarly, attacks changing challenges, keyshares, or signature shares, or interfering with the combination of signatures in T_1 are no worse than the attack changing the challenge, key, or signature in T_2.

In T_1, the PIN is used to decrypt the first keyshare at the server, and only a single PIN can make the following signature check succeed. Hence it makes sense to state that the attacks T_1.SS10 on interfering with the signature check, and T_1.SS11 on subsequently changing the control flow, are the same as the attacks T_2.SS4 and T_2.SS5 that interfere with the comparison of PINs and subsequent branching.

3.5 Comparing the Second Intermediate System and the Smartcard System

The attacks against the smartcard system T have been described in Sect. 3.1. There is still a significant difference between T_2 and T, due to the use of different hardware components, but as we see below, we can overcome this by introducing and justifying $\prec_D$-relationships among the attacks against T_2 and T.

Comparison Between T_2 and T. The formula ϕ is the conjunction of the following statements:

- T_2.RP$i \Leftrightarrow T$.RPi for $i \in \{1, 2\}$
- T_2.RP$i \Leftrightarrow T$.RP$(i-2)$ for $i \in \{5, 6, 7\}$
- T_2.U$i \Leftrightarrow T$.Ui for $i \in \{1, 2\}$
- T_2.P$i \Leftrightarrow T$.SCRj for $(i, j) \in \{(3, 1), (5, 2), (7, 3), (6, 4)\}$
- T_2.SS$i \Leftrightarrow T$.SC$(i-2)$ for $i \in \{3, \ldots, 11\}$
- T_2.P4 or T_2.SS1 $\Leftrightarrow T$.SCR1 and T.SCR2 and T.SCR3 and T.SC9

Most of the attacks against the relying party and user are the same in both systems. One difference comes from the fact that smartcard system does not have Control Codes, thus, the attacks against them in T_2 are vacuously successful in T. We matched a set of attacks against the phone in T_2 against similar attacks targeting smartcard reader in the smartcard system. We have not matched T_2.RP3, T_2.RP4, T_2.B1, T_2.B2, T_2.P1, and T_2.P2 with anything in T as all of these attacks are related to the Control Codes and the smartcard system does not have this protection mechanism employed.

The set of attacks against the SplitKey server in T_2 is almost identical to the set of attacks against the smartcard in the smartcard system, except attacks related to the communication channel. However, the SplitKey server and smartcard have different hardware, hence we need to introduce the relationships $\{T$.SC$i\} \prec_D \{T_2$.SS$(i+2)\}$ for the analysis to go through. Also, the attacks related to the communication channel in T_2 are matched with the set of attacks where the adversary learns and changes the values sent over that channel (e.g. PIN, challenge), and this again requires extra $\prec_D$-relationships. These requirements on $\prec_D$ are discussed below.

3.6 Propagation of the Security Requirements

We described which attacks are equivalent to each other in the neighbouring systems. Now, we analyse these to identify security requirements that should be in place in the SplitKey system for the above listed attacks to be equivalent to each other.

The communication channel between the phone and SplitKey server must offer the same level of protection as smartcard system offers against SCR1, SCR2, SCR3, SC9 attacks. This requirement arises when we move from the second intermediate system to the smartcard system, as attacks against the communication channel are removed at this point. However, we identified that attacks against the communication channel are equivalent to the attacks against the smartcard system that involve learning and modifying information sent to the smartcard. The requirement of protecting the communication channel propagates through T_2 and T_1 back to T'.

We introduced the relationship $\{T.\text{SC5}\} \prec_D \{T_2.\text{SS7}\}$, requiring that the Splitkey server protects the private key at least as strongly as the smartcard. The same requirement holds for T_1, except that there is no private key in T_1. We can verify that it will be sufficient to strongly protect only the second keyshare: $\{T_2.\text{SS7}\} \prec_D \{T_1.\text{SS3}\}$. The same requirement propagates to T'.

It should be as hard to interfere with the signature verification process in the SplitKey server as it is to interfere with the PIN verification in the smartcard. There are attacks targeting the PIN verification process in the smartcard system and in T_2. However, T_1 and T' have attacks against signature verification. Signature verification in the SplitKey system serves to verify whether the user correctly decrypted their part of the private key to create their signature share, meaning that the user entered the correct PIN code. In the smartcard system, the PIN is verified straightforwardly by comparing the code stored in the card with the one received from the user.

It should be as hard to interfere with the signature creation/combination process in the SplitKey server as it is in the smartcard system. In the smartcard system and in T_2, the adversary can modify the challenge that enters the computation of the signature. In T_1 and T', the adversary can modify challenges for two signature shares—on the phone side and on the server side. If the SplitKey server receives an incorrect signature share from the phone and decides not to discard it but use it further, it means that it can successfully execute attacks against the signature verification process, that were covered in the previous requirement. Therefore, in this requirement, we focus on the server side attacks, where the adversary can not only change the challenge for the second signature share but also interfere with the signature combination process.

It should be as hard to change the server's private key share that is used to create the signature in the Splitkey server as it is in the smartcard system. In the smartcard system and T_2, adversary can attempt to change the single private key that will be used to create signature. In T_1 and T', the adversary may target two shares of the private key. With the modified user's share of the private key, adversary will create a signature share that will not pass the verification procedure. If the server decides to use incorrect signature share, it means that one can execute attacks against signature verification that were covered before. Therefore, this requirement again focuses on the modifications on the server side.

It should be as hard to capture the PIN entered by the user from the phone as it is to capture the PIN from the smartcard reader. Starting from the smartcard system, where the PIN is sent to the smartcard through the smartcard reader this requirement propagates all the way back to the SplitKey system, where the user enters the PIN in the phone. It may be difficult to argue that this requirement is satisfied, if a smartcard reader with PINpad is used in T. It will be easier to argue for it, if computer's keyboard is used in T.

4   Conclusion

We have presented the case that comparison-based arguments can be useful for providing the evidence that a system satisfies certain security properties, and, in particular, that a ToE satisfies a Security Target. It remains to be determined, how scalable the proposed methodology is – how much effort this methodology will require in different practical applications for evolving and novel ToEs, and what kind of tool support will be useful. The proposed methodology also needs evaluation by certification laboratories.

In our example, we have compared authentication systems. We hope that it is possible to similarly show that a threshold cryptography based system may be a qualified electronic signature creation device (QSCD) [6], by again comparing it to systems making use of smartcards.

References

1. Bellare, M., Rogaway, P.: The security of triple encryption and a framework for code-based game-playing proofs. In: Vaudenay, S. (ed.) EUROCRYPT 2006. LNCS, vol. 4004, pp. 409–426. Springer, Heidelberg (2006). https://doi.org/10.1007/11761679_25
2. Buldas, A., Kalu, A., Laud, P., Oruaas, M.: Server-supported RSA signatures for mobile devices. In: Foley, S.N., Gollmann, D., Snekkenes, E. (eds.) ESORICS 2017. LNCS, vol. 10492, pp. 315–333. Springer, Cham (2017). https://doi.org/10.1007/978-3-319-66402-6_19
3. Buldas, A., Saarepera, M.: Electronic Signature System with Small Number of Private Keys. In: Ellison, C.M., Polk, W.T., Hastings, N.E., Smith, S.W. (eds.) NISTIR 7085: 2nd Annual PKI Research Workshop Proceedings, pp. 110–122. National Institute of Standards and Technology (NIST) (2004)
4. De Santis, A., Desmedt, Y., Frankel, Y., Yung, M.: How to share a function securely. In: Proceedings of the Twenty-Sixth Annual ACM Symposium on Theory of Computing (STOC '94). pp. 522–533. Association for Computing Machinery, New York, NY, USA (1994)
5. Dupont, S., et al.: Incremental Common Criteria Certification Processes using DevSecOps Practices. In: IEEE European Symposium on Security and Privacy Workshops, EuroS&P 2021, Vienna, Austria, September 6–10, 2021, pp. 12–23. IEEE (2021)
6. European Parliament and Council of European Union: Regulation (EU) no 910/2014 of the European Parliament and of the Council of 23 July 2014 on electronic identification and trust services for electronic transactions in the internal market and repealing Directive 1999/93/EC. OJ L 257, 28.8.2014, pp. 73–114 (2014)

7. Hernandez-Ardieta, J.L., Blanco, P., Vara, D.: A methodology to construct Common Criteria security targets through formal risk analysis. In: Proceedings of XII Spanish Meeting on Cryptology and Information Security (RECSI 2012) (2012)

8. ISO/IEC 15408–1/2/3:2005 - Information technology - Security techniques - Evaluation criteria for IT security

9. Keblawi, F., Sullivan, D.: Applying the common criteria in systems engineering. IEEE Secur. Priv. **4**(2), 50–55 (2006)

10. National Computer Security Center: Rating Maintenance Phase Program Document Version 2. Rainbow Series, NCSC-TG-013 V2 (1995). https://web.archive.org/web/20110720184904/http://iaarchive.fi/Rainbow/NCSC-TG-013%20PINK%20version%202.pdf

11. OMG: Business Process Model and Notation (BPMN). http://www.omg.org/spec/BPMN/2.0/

12. PP-Module for User Authentication Devices, Version 1.0. National Information Assurance Partnership (2019)

13. prEN 14169–1:2009: Protection profiles for Secure signature creation device - Part 2: Device with key generation. Technical Committee CEN/TC 224 (2009)

14. Pullonen, P., Matulevičius, R., Bogdanov, D.: PE-BPMN: privacy-enhanced business process model and notation. In: Carmona, J., Engels, G., Kumar, A. (eds.) BPM 2017. LNCS, vol. 10445, pp. 40–56. Springer, Cham (2017). https://doi.org/10.1007/978-3-319-65000-5_3

15. Rescorla, E.: The Transport Layer Security (TLS) Protocol Version 1.3. RFC 8446 (2018). 10.17487/RFC8446. https://www.rfc-editor.org/info/rfc8446

16. Reuse of Evaluation Results and Evidence (Oct 26th 2002), information Statement on behalf of the Common Criteria Recognition Arrangement Management Committee, Document no. 2002–08-009-002

17. Salnitri, M., Dalpiaz, F., Giorgini, P.: Designing secure business processes with SecBPMN. Softw. Syst. Model. **16**(3), 737–757 (2017)

18. Sinnhofer, A.D., Raschke, W., Steger, C., Kreiner, C.: Evaluation paradigm selection according to Common Criteria for an incremental product development. In: Tverdyshev, S. (ed.) International Workshop on MILS: Architecture and Assurance for Secure Systems, MILS@HiPEAC 2015, Amsterdam, The Netherlands, January 20, 2015. Zenodo (2015)

19. Sinnhofer, A.D., Raschke, W., Steger, C., Kreiner, C.: Patterns for Common Criteria Certification. In: Link, C., Eloranta, V. (eds.) Proceedings of the 20th European Conference on Pattern Languages of Programs, EuroPLoP 2015, Kaufbeuren, Germany, July 8–12, 2015. pp. 33:1–33:15. ACM (2015)

20. Sun, N., et al.: Defining security requirements with the common criteria: Applications, adoptions, and challenges. IEEE Access **10**, 44756–44777 (2022)

Automation of Vulnerability Information Extraction Using Transformer-Based Language Models

Fateme Hashemi Chaleshtori[(✉)] [ID] and Indrakshi Ray [ID]

Colorado State University, Fort Collins, CO 80523, USA
{fatemeh,iray}@colostate.edu

Abstract. Identifying and mitigating vulnerabilities as rapidly and extensively as possible is essential for preventing security breaches. Thus, organizations and companies often store vulnerability information, expressed in natural language, and share them with other stakeholders. Disclosure and dissemination of this information in a structured and unambiguous format in a timely manner is crucial to prevent security attacks. Many existing automated vulnerability information extraction techniques use rule-based strategies like Pattern Matching and Part-of-Speech Tagging, and Machine Learning models built on Conditional Random Fields (CRF). There are also hybrid models that integrate NLP and pattern recognition to create semi-automated systems. We propose an alternative approach using Transformer models, including BERT, XLNet, RoBERTa, and DistilBERT, which have been shown to have promising performance in many NLP downstream tasks such as for Named Entity Recognition (NER) and Co-reference Resolution in an end-to-end neural architecture. We fine-tune several language representation models similar to BERT, on a labeled dataset from vulnerability databases, for the task of NER so that we can automatically extract security-related words and terms and phrases from descriptions of the vulnerabilities. Our approach allows us to extract complex features from the data without requiring feature selection, thus eliminating the need for domain-expert knowledge. It also outperforms the CRF-based models. Additionally, it is able to detect new information from vulnerabilities whose description text patterns differ from those specified by rule-based systems.

Keywords: Cybersecurity · Vulnerability · Information extraction · Natural Language Processing · BERT · Co-reference resolution

1 Introduction

Cyberattacks have become increasingly frequent and damaging, and forestalling them is an uphill battle. Learning about the potential vulnerabilities of a system

This work was supported in part by funds from NSF under award number IIS 2027750, CNS 1822118 and from NIST, Statnett, Cyber Risk Research, AMI, ARL, and NewPush.

and attempting to block all possible ways to exploit these vulnerabilities lessen the likelihood of experiencing cyber-attacks. Initial disclosures of information about vulnerabilities, exploits, user actions, system specifications and configurations, and the attacks tend to come in the form of text sources, such as mailing lists, before being integrated into vulnerability databases. Security analysts must use this information to investigate whether their own systems are susceptible to comparable vulnerabilities. Such assessments must be conducted at the earliest to prevent security breaches.

Since vulnerability information is stored as natural language documents, security analysts must devote time to understanding this. Attempts are underway to facilitate this process by automating the extraction of vulnerability information from natural language texts [11, 21, 22, 32, 33, 41]. Information extraction is the task of searching and analyzing unstructured data to discover structured information in it [20]. Rule-based techniques such as Part-of-Speech tagging and Pattern Matching are commonly used for vulnerability information extraction [11, 33, 41]. Such techniques determine linguistic patterns for different terms based on the text's grammatical structure and look for them in the text to extract important information units. Although such models can be highly accurate in a specific target domain, the downside is that they are labor-intensive and fail to extract key information when the text is in a form that does not adhere to the patterns specified in the rules [8].

One of the most important subtasks of information extraction is Named Entity Recognition (NER). NER is the task of scanning a text to automatically identify major entities in it and classify them into predefined categories, such as location, person, and organization [16]. Vulnerability information extraction processes may benefit from NER because it can direct attention to critical cybersecurity entities in a text. However, the existing off-the-shelf NER tools [4–6, 10] do not support domain-specific entities and need further modification and training.

Multi-class classifiers like Support Vector Machine (SVM) [7, 29] and Conditional Random Field (CRF) [6, 22] are models that are frequently used for addressing the NER task. CRF is a machine learning model used for data classification and is suitable for labeling sequential data like text, where the status of neighbors, such as words surrounding a target word, can affect the predicted class for the target instance [40]. Authors in [22] used the same CRF-based architecture used by Stanford NER [6] and trained it on a manually annotated security dataset to build a domain-specific named entity tagger. Such a method necessitates feature selection which requires domain expertise.

Deep learning models such as Long Short-Term Memory (LSTM) [17, 18, 31] and pre-trained transformer-based language models like BERT [14] have been utilized to improve the task of NER. LSTM processes a sentence word by word, and its architecture causes a bias towards the latest words in a text sequence and cannot capture long dependencies [19]. Models like BERT, on the other hand, take the whole sentence as one input rather than word by word, and thus, they focus on all words equally and can better capture the connection between the words. Hence, BERT can achieve a better performance than LSTM on the task of NER [27]. Such language representation models have outperformed all previous models in common NLP tasks, such as question answering [14]. Authors in [25] leverage the BERT model for solving NER in historical and contemporary German texts.

1.1 Proposed Approach

We propose the use of Transformers-based NLP language representation models for vulnerability information extraction. We use a labeled dataset to fine-tune different Transformer-based models, to develop a domain-specific NER system. But before that, we perform Co-reference Resolution, which replaces the references to an entity with the original entity itself. Using this method, the meaningful names and entities will be returned to the text.

The dataset that we use consists of vulnerability descriptions with over 1500 security-related sentences. These sentences are split into words and tokens and tagged with eleven different labels (ten security-related and one for non-security-related tokens), resulting in more than 48K tagged entities [22].

For Co-reference Resolution, we utilized the model proposed in [24]. Their model is based on SpanBERT [23], which focuses on better representing and predicting text spans.

To build our domain-specific NER, we use different variations of language model representations that are based on Transformers [39], such as BERT [14], XLNet [43], RoBERTa [28], and DistilBERT [34]. Then, we add a classification layer on top for detecting and categorizing the named entities. The above models are all considered pre-trained language models. Utilizing pre-trained language representation models, like other deep learning models, offers the advantage of automatically detecting word-level and character-level features. Consequently, selecting a subset of features from the data to be used for model preparation is no longer necessary.

The advantage of our method is that the proposed model can be applied to any vulnerability dataset without any alteration or modification. In addition, a significant advantage of this model, over non-deep learning models, is that it eliminates the need for feature engineering and feature selection because rather than extracting features from text and deciding which ones are appropriate to give to the model as input, the raw text data is given to the model. Subsequently, security analysts can benefit from this model with no assistance from computer science specialists. Moreover, our approach performs better when compared to rule-based methodologies, where particular fixed patterns and templates need to be characterized for different vulnerability descriptions.

1.2 Our Contributions

We fine-tune several Transformer-based machine learning models for the task of NER in the cyber-security field on a labeled dataset containing more than 1500 sentences and over 48K tokens before Co-reference Resolution and more than

50K tokens after it. Ours is the first work that tests Transformer-based language representation models to address the problem of automatic vulnerability information extraction. The model that we present outperforms the CRF model on a security-related NER task. Additionally, we are the first to study the impact of Co-reference Resolution on vulnerability information extraction. We also introduce a mechanism to ensemble the results of different Transformer-based models by majority voting, and this also increases the performance.

1.3   Paper Roadmap

In the rest of the paper, we discuss the related research that has been conducted in Sect. 2; next, we describe the required background knowledge for this work in Sect. 3; then, we describe our proposed approach in detail in Sect. 4. Finally, we conclude the paper and point out some interesting future directions in Sect. 5.

2   Related Works

Some earlier works have been done to extract vulnerability information from text. Many of them have focused on a specific task. Authors in [38] investigated how to automatically extract vulnerability information useful for attack graph construction. In [33], the authors aimed to summarize the vulnerability descriptions and categorize them according to a taxonomy modeled for the industry. The authors have manually inspected 130 common vulnerabilities and concluded that there are some recurrent linguistic patterns in the descriptions that could be used for automating the process of recognizing the relevant and key information, and they are trying to detect such patterns in the text. Their approach consisted of two main steps: information extraction and vulnerability classification. The authors developed a tool named CVErizer that automatically and accurately classifies software vulnerabilities with the help of rule-based pattern recognition and also helps vulnerability assessors understand software vulnerabilities by providing summaries of their descriptions.

Jones et al. [21] proposed a bootstrapping semi-supervised NLP model, which needs limited labeled training data to extract security entities and their relationships from the text. The goal is to extract information in the form of relations having syntax ⟨ *subject entity, predicate relation, object entity* ⟩. An example of such a relation is ⟨ *software vendor, is a vendor of, software product* ⟩. They searched the text corpus for mentions of a few known seed instances, and when an instance is found, the model generates some patterns from the surrounding text automatically. This work focuses on relation extraction from text, whereas our objective is NER.

Using data from the National Vulnerability Database and other text sources, the authors in [22] proposed a model to provide a data representation of cybersecurity-related notions associated with vulnerability descriptions. The authors used the data they collected and manually annotated it to train a CRF-based classifier with the Stanford Named Entity Recognizer [6,15]. To evaluate the model, they used five-fold cross-validation. On average, they achieved a precision score of 83%, a recall score of 76%, and an F1 score of 80%. The major benefit of using machine learning models is that they automate the process of extracting important information, and they can perform well on various input data with no change. We use the dataset provided by this work, but instead of the CRF model, we are leveraging the Transformer-based language representation models to address the same problem.

Weerawardhana et al. [41] also try to extract key security-related terms from vulnerability databases. The authors presented two models for vulnerability information extraction: a machine learning module based on CRF and another module that benefits from Part-of-Speech tagging. For the machine learning module, they follow the same approach as in [22] for feature selection and training the model. The Part-of-Speech tagging model is rule-based, and the goal is to detect grammatical patterns in the text. They define a set of patterns for software names and versions, file names, modifiers, vulnerability types, etc., and then they try to find security terms that match these patterns. The latter model has outperformed the CRF-based model. The limitation of this approach is that this model may fail if a new style or pattern is introduced in a vulnerability description that does not match the predefined patterns.

Authors in [32] target security advisories that may contain threat information or vulnerabilities. To extract useful information from text, they use NLP, semi-supervised pattern identification, and matching methods. They use NLP first to split the text into sentences and then tokenize them. Subsequently, they apply their pattern identification model to that data. This work is not using NLP as a language representation tool. After extraction, they model the data based on the Structured Threat Security Expression model [9].

3   Background

Our work utilizes Transformer-based language representation models for vulnerability extraction using Co-reference Resolution and Named Entity Recognition techniques. Transformer-based models have an architecture designed for sequence-to-sequence tasks where the goal is to transform a sequence of objects into another sequence, such as the task of natural language text translation.

Transformer-Based Language Models. BERT [14] is an open-source pretrained deep learning model. BERT benefits from transformer blocks to produce vector representations for the input sentence. BERT has been trained on a huge corpus of data and optimized on two unsupervised NLP tasks that do not need labeled data, Next Sentence Prediction and Masked Language Modeling. After training, the model is ready for other tasks like NER. Although training such models for a domain-specific purpose needs a very large amount of data and is computationally expensive, researchers have shown that even fine-tuning them on smaller datasets that are more accessible can lead to improvements [37,45].

The RoBERTa model [28] is trained on a much larger dataset than BERT. Note that BERT is trained on the English Wikipedia and BookCorpus [46] of size 16G, whereas the dataset used for training RoBERTa contains CC-NEWS data (76G), OpenWebText data (38G), and Stories (31G) as well as the English Wikipedia and BookCorpus (16G). Additionally, it has been optimized for the task of Masked Language Modeling (MLM) with a Dynamic Masking Pattern instead of a Static Masking Pattern. Another difference between the BERT model and the RoBERTa model is that RoBERTa does not train for the task of Next Sentence Prediction.

XLNet [43] is another transformer-based language representation model. The XLNet model presents permutation language modeling to improve the training, in which all tokens are predicted but in random order. This assists the model with learning bidirectional connections, and consequently, it better handles dependencies and relations between words. XLNet was trained on a very large data corpus with more than 130 GB of text data which is much bigger compared with the volume of data used for training the BERT model.

The DistilBERT model [34] is a 40% smaller model compared to BERT (BERT has 110M parameters and DistilBERT has 66M parameters.) but with the same general architecture. As it is smaller, it is 60% faster and has achieved almost the same performance as BERT in the language understanding tasks.

Natural Language Processing Tasks. Two main NLP tasks that we focus on are Named Entity Recognition (NER) and Co-reference Resolution.

There is a common usage in the natural languages of pronouns to serve both as subjects and as objects of sentences. Due to this, it becomes more challenging to automatically identify key entities within natural language text. The purpose of Co-reference Resolution is to resolve multiple references to a particular entity in a text document. By detecting which entity each pronoun refers to and substituting it with the known entity, we can obtain more useful information from the text.

Many Reinforcement Learning and Deep Learning techniques [12,13,26,42, 44] have been leveraged to address this problem. Basically, potential candidates for referring entities should be determined, and then based on their features, most likely, the reference entity should be paired with the referring entity.

One of the classical sequence labeling tasks is NER, also known as Named Entity Identification or Entity Chunking. The purpose of NER is to scan an unstructured text to automatically identify major named entities in a text that usually carry important information and classify them into predefined categories [30], such as person, organization, location, time, date, currency, percentage, etc. Essentially, it is the process of transferring the task of information extraction into a classification problem. The application of NER in vulnerability information extraction is relatively well studied, but how Coreference Resolution can advance this task needs more research.

4   Our Approach

We first discuss the dataset that we use for fine-tuning the models, its arrangement, content, and the steps we take to prepare the data for transferring in the proper format, ready to be fed into our deep learning models. We then elaborate on our approach for the vulnerability information extraction task and the experiments we conducted. This includes Co-reference Resolution, which has two sub-tasks: (i) locating entities that refer to other entities and (ii) replacing the referring entities along with their associated tags with the reference entities and their tags. Afterward, we used this data to fine-tune different Transformer-based Models for the purpose of domain-specific NER. Then, we have a majority voting ensemble model that merges the result of the top three best performing models. Finally, we discuss the results and compare them to other approaches.

4.1   Data Preparation

We use a dataset of vulnerability descriptions obtained from [22]. This dataset contains vulnerability information gathered from the Common Vulnerabilities and Exposures (CVE) database [2], Microsoft Security Bulletins [3], Adobe Security Bulletins [1], as well as several security-related blog posts. There are individual files for each vulnerability description. Table 1 lists the number of files and sentences associated with each source. In this dataset, sentences are broken up into tokens (words and symbols), which are manually annotated with ten security labels by 12 Computer Science students. This dataset contains 48K tokens, out of which over 10K entities are tagged as security-related. Each token is assigned one label. Whenever the token is not security-related, it receives the 'O' label; otherwise, an appropriate security label is assigned to it. Following are the security labels:

Table 1. Number of sentences per security source.

Source	Adobe	Blogs	Microsoft	CVE	Total
#Files	50	20	50	50	**170**
#Sentences	275	437	495	299	**1506**

OPERATINGSYSTEM Tags the name of the operating systems. Examples include Ubuntu 16.0, Windows 10, and Macintosh.

CONSEQUENCES Refers to the final results of the attack. Examples include arbitrary SQL commands, device crashes, and sensitive information leaks.

SOFTWARE Refers to the name of software. Examples include System.Net, Outlook, and Visual Studio.

MODIFIER Tags the version of a software or operating system that follows the name of the software or operating system. Examples include 8.0.3 or before 2.4.1.

NETWORK Refers to network-related terms. Examples include SSL, TCP, and HTTPS.

ATTACK It marks the terms that are closely related to the attack. Examples include man-in-the-middle, brute force, and phishing.

MEANS Tags the way to attack. Examples include crafted websites, unspecified vectors, and SQL injection.

HARDWARE Hardware devices involved in the attack. Examples include CPU, processor cores, and server.

FILE Files involved in the attack. Examples include restorer.php, index.php, and EOSDataServer.exe.

OTHER Other technical terms that cannot be put in other security-related categories. Examples include webpage and administrative user rights.

O Non-security-related tokens.

The following steps are done to preprocess the dataset.

Step 1: Fix the inconsistencies between the labels. Some examples in the dataset had incomplete labels or typographical errors. For example, in some cases, *OPERATING* was used instead of *OPERATINGSYSTEM*; the two labels *OTHER* and *OTHER_TECHNICAL_TERMS* refer to the same category. Sometimes extra characters are at the end of some of the labels, such as in *SOFTWAREr*. We fixed such irregularities by partial term matching, using some of the initial characters of the labels that make them unique. We looked for the primary characters and changed the label to the right one.

Step 2: Remove the labels and concatenate the tokens to form a full text and split the text into sentences. The Transformer-based models require data in a format that has two columns, *token* and *label*. In the dataset from [22], there was no separation between sentences. We used the Python Natural Language Toolkit (NLTK) [10] to break the data into sentences instead of applying fixed rules like considering punctuation symbols only or doing it manually because the NLTK library does this job more accurately. We first remove the labels and connect the tokens to one another by inserting a space in between. Then, we employ the *tokenize.sent_tokenize* function from the NLTK library, and it returns a list of sentences. This function is insensitive to additional spaces before punctuation marks, and it can deal with those, so the concatenating spaces that appear before punctuation symbols will not cause any trouble.

Step 3: Identify the end of sentences and insert a new line. Based on the list that the *tokenize.sent_tokenize* function gives out we separate the sentences by adding one new line at the end of each sentence.

Step 4: Reinsert the labels. Once the sentences are separated, we add the labels to the corresponding tokens and transfer the data into the desired format of two columns, namely, *token* and *label*.

Step 5: Accumulate the data from different files into one file. Finally, we gather all the information from the various polished documents in the dataset into one record.

The format is now suitable to be utilized for the fine-tuning phase.

4.2 Co-reference Resolution

Co-reference Resolution can bring the major entities back to the text, originally referred to by pronouns. We utilize the model proposed in [24] to detect the co-references. Their approach is built on BERT instead of an LSTM-based encoder. This model takes a piece of text as input and detects the co-references, and marks them in the text. A sample is provided below:

– Note that while Shockwave and Flash Player are both {Adobe → *Adobe*} products, {they → *Shockwave and flash player*} are two separate things.

The model detects instances where an entity is referring to another entity and puts the referee and the reference inside curly brackets, suggesting that the referee can be replaced with the reference it found. Interestingly, we observed some redundant suggestions in which the model recommends that one word be replaced with itself, which is not adding any additional information, like the word *'Adobe'* in this example. However, it is also capable of finding meaningful connections between words.

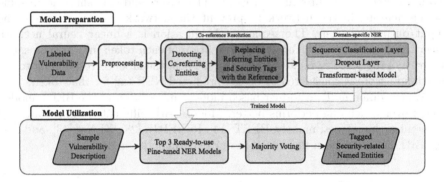

Fig. 1. Proposed approach. After preprocessing the data, we detect and replace the co-references and their assigned tags. We then use this data to prepare a domain-specific NER model.

4.3 Application of NER

Regular NER tools have a broad set of labels to search for in a given text. For example, the Stanford NER [6] supports only three labels: *Person*, *Location*, and *Organization*. NLTK NER tool [10] supports six more labels, none of which are security related. We consider a new set of security labels mentioned in Sect. 4.1 for our domain-specific NER.

We treat the NER task as a classification task. Each word will get a tag in a sentence; this implies that the relation of a word with the other words in the same sentence is captured in our model. The training data that we use has a consistent format; each token is assigned a label, and the model knows the sentence that each word belongs to in light of the fact that the sentences are separated in the dataset.

Figure 1 illustrates the overall structure of our model and the steps we take to achieve our goal. Transformer-based models for NLP are general-purpose language representation models incorporating special types of deep neural networks, known as Transformers, and are trained on a huge volume of unlabeled data to comprehend natural language text. These models take text as their input, tokenize it into words and symbols, and then produce vector representations for them. To boost the performance of these models and make them produce more meaningful representations for domain-specific words (security-related words and labels in this case), we fine-tune our network on the security-related dataset described earlier for the particular task of NER. Consequently, a *Dropout Layer* and a *Sequence Classification Layer* are added on top of the Transformer-based model. The use of dropout layers is a common practice in designing neural network architectures to prevent overfitting. This layer randomly shuts down some of the neurons in the network to prevent the network from memorizing the input/output relations. The sequence classification is a linear neural network layer that transforms the vector representation of each token into 11 scores, one for each of the security-related NER labels. Then, the label corresponding to the maximum score is considered to be the predicted NER tag for that token.

We try different Transformer-based models, in addition to the BERT model, to discover which one performs better. Models with different training data and different architectures, namely, BERT [14], RoBERTa [28], XLNet [43], and DistilBERT [34] have been fine-tuned in our experiments.

4.4   Experiments

Resolving the Co-references. Utilizing the model provided in [24], we processed the whole dataset to find the co-references. We used the version that benefits from SpanBERT-large [23]. For the input, we give the content of each text file, which describes one vulnerability at a time. Our analysis shows that, on average, one text file contains 375 tokens (using the BERT tokenizer). So, in most cases, it does not exceed the maximum number of tokens (512) that SpanBERT can accept. Referring entities and references are shown as pairs in the output. So, after the files are processed, we have new files containing co-references, and now, we need to replace them with the original entity. Afterward, we should restore the security tags assigned to each word. Table 2 shows this replacement for the example we discussed earlier.

Table 2. Replacing the referee with the reference along with the security tags.

Original data		After co-reference resolution	
Token	Tag	Token	Tag
Note	O	Note	O
that	O	that	O
while	O	while	O
Shockwave	SOFTWARE	Shockwave	SOFTWARE
and	O	and	O
Flash	SOFTWARE	Flash	SOFTWARE
Player	SOFTWARE	Player	SOFTWARE
are	O	are	O
both	O	both	O
Adobe	O	Adobe	O
products	O	products	O
,	O	,	O
they	O	**Shockwave**	**SOFTWARE**
are	O	**and**	**O**
two	O	**Flash**	**SOFTWARE**
separate	O	**Player**	**SOFTWARE**
things	O	are	O
		two	O
		separate	O
		things	O

For this goal, we prepared a Python script that iterates through a file containing both tokens and tags and searches for each token in its respective text file with the co-references detected. When searching for the token, it looks for the co-reference detection format ({Referee token(s) → Reference token(s)}), and once it finds any, it will do the replacement of both the token and the tag. After this, it will then write the updated tokens and tags to another file. However, we found some inconsistencies between the tagged files and the corresponding plain text files; for example, some words are missing in the tagged files compared to the text files. This issue is causing problems with how the code iterates through and searches for tokens, so we had to resolve it manually. Moreover, the vulnerability descriptions are not split into tokens that are assigned security tags in a deterministic manner, which also prevents our automatic approach of replacing the entities and the tags from working well.

Fine-Tuning the Transformer-Based Models with Cross-Validation.
This experiment aims to find out if the results obtained by the experiments that have been done in [22] and [41] can be improved. We use the same dataset as in [22] to fine-tune different models and to have a fair comparison of the models. Similar to [22], we apply five-fold cross-validation for fine-tuning the models. Now, we need to adjust the model configuration parameters. We tried different learning rates and various numbers of epochs to learn the best setting for each model. A specific set of hyperparameters leads to the best performance for different models even with the same general architecture. Table 3 shows the most

suitable hyperparameters for fine-tuning each model. We utilized a linear learning rate schedule, a maximum sequence length of 512, and the Adam optimizer algorithm for all models.

Table 4 presents the evaluation metrics achieved by five-fold cross-validation training. For each fold, 20% of the data is saved for validation, and the rest is utilized for training. The reported metrics are the mean of the weighted (micro) average of 5 different folds for each model. Since the data is unbalanced and the number of instances in each class is different, to drop the adverse consequence of the model's low performance in classes with fewer samples and not to overvalue the high performance of the model for classes with more samples, we report the weighted average for precision, recall, and F1 score to have a fair demonstration of the models' performance. As table 4 reveals, the XLNet-Base-Cased model has the best performance among the seven models that we tested.

Merging the Results of Different Models by Majority Voting. To further improve the performance, we stack three best-performing models considering both the F1 score and recall, which are XLNet-Base-Cased, BERT-Base-Cased, and RoBERTa-Large, and then we apply the majority voting between the output labels for each token. Figure 2 depicts this technique. For each sentence that is given to the three models as input, we gather the labels that they produce for every token. Then, in method (I), we check if at least two out of the three models agree on the label allocated to a token. In that case, the majority voting module outputs that label for that particular token. On the off chance that each of the three models predicts different labels for a token, we assume that this token is non-security-related and assign the label 'O' to it. The class-wise average performance of this model is represented in Table 9 for the five-fold cross-validation. We also tried another way of merging the results, method (II), in which whenever two models label a token as 'O', but the last one assigns a security-related tag to the token, we keep that tag instead of 'O'. In other scenarios, method (II) chooses the label in the same manner as method (I).

Impact of Co-reference Resolution Co-reference Resolution added a total of 1771 tokens to our dataset, most of which were in the files from security blog

Table 3. Best hyperparameters (learning rate (LR), number of epochs, and batch size (BS)) for each model.

Model	LR	#Epoch	BS
RoBERTa-Base	3.00e–5	10	24
RoBERTa-Large	3.00e–5	10	8
BERT-Base-Cased	7.00e–5	15	8
BERT-Large-Cased	1.00e–4	10	8
DistilBERT-Base-Cased	1.50e–4	10	8
XLNet-Base-Cased	5.00e–6	20	8

Table 4. Results (**P**recision, **R**ecall, **F1** score) of the 5-fold cross-validation experiment with original data.

Model	Metric	Fold 1	Fold 2	Fold 3	Fold 4	Fold 5	Avg.
BERT-Base-Cased	P	83.25	76.92	84.03	82.93	77.1	**80.85**
	R	82.06	81.74	82.03	85.06	78.42	81.86
	F1	82.65	79.26	83.02	83.98	77.76	81.33
BERT-Large-Cased	P	81.7	72.93	81.85	79.23	74.8	78.1
	R	81.24	82.1	83.47	81.9	78.22	81.39
	F1	81.47	77.24	82.65	80.54	76.47	80
DistilBERT-Base-Cased	P	82.61	77.01	83.9	80.97	75.89	80.08
	R	80.68	84.1	80.55	82.6	77.92	81.17
	F1	81.63	80.4	82.19	81.78	76.89	80.58
RoBERTa-Base	P	80.79	77.6	82.26	85.77	77.64	80.81
	R	71.97	71.7	70.4	56.52	56.59	65.44
	F1	76.12	74.53	75.87	68.14	65.46	72.02
RoBERTa-Large	P	83.66	72.34	82.11	83.41	77.03	79.71
	R	81.85	80.28	83.69	85.51	78.62	81.99
	F1	82.74	76.1	82.89	84.45	77.82	80.8
XLNet-Base-Cased	P	83.37	76.54	82.17	83.62	77.22	80.58
	R	82.54	86.23	84.28	86.01	81.19	**84.05**
	F1	82.95	81.09	83.21	84.8	79.16	**82.24**

Table 5. Results of the 5-fold cross-validation experiment after replacing co-references.

Model	Metric	Fold 1	Fold 2	Fold 3	Fold 4	Fold 5	Avg.
BERT-Base-Cased	P	77.12	84.93	77.88	80.38	84.39	80.94
	R	78.84	80.14	82.52	78.64	84.23	80.87
	F1	77.97	82.47	80.13	79.5	84.31	80.88
BERT-Large-Cased	P	76.31	81.46	74.61	77.92	82.31	78.52
	R	77.77	79.85	81.69	79.38	84.03	80.54
	F1	77.03	80.65	77.99	78.64	83.16	79.49
DistilBERT-Base-Cased	P	76.82	85.54	77.03	81.11	85.11	81.12
	R	77.06	78.74	81.69	79.04	82.91	79.89
	F1	76.94	82	79.29	80.06	84	80.46
RoBERTa-Base	P	73.72	82.41	85.84	84.82	82.46	81.85
	R	65.72	60.03	61.07	61.86	64.94	62.72
	F1	69.49	69.46	71.36	71.54	72.66	70.9
RoBERTa-Large	P	79.13	84.57	77.61	82.9	78.67	80.58
	R	78.93	81.5	79.55	82.69	83.58	**81.25**
	F1	79.03	83	78.57	82.8	81.05	80.89
XLNet-Base-Cased	P	85.3	82.63	83.24	80.8	82.13	**82.82**
	R	83.3	81.93	81.66	79.91	79.38	**81.25**
	F1	84.29	82.28	82.45	80.36	80.73	**82.02**

Table 6. Average results of the majority voting between the three models: XLNet-Base-Cased, RoBERTa-Large, and BERT-Base-Cased, fine-tuned by cross-validation using the original data. Method (I) is the standard majority voting approach and method (II) is prioritizing security-related tags over the tag 'O' to increase the Recall.

Model	Metric	Fold 1	Fold 2	Fold 3	Fold 4	Fold 5	Avg.
Majority Voting (I)	P	85.06	76.55	84.72	84.91	79.57	82.16
	R	81.41	81.92	83.42	85.51	79.33	82.32
	F1	83.2	79.14	84.07	85.21	79.45	82.21
Majority Voting (II)	P	78.29	68.51	75.79	77.64	68.91	73.83
	R	85.62	85.52	86.48	89.67	83.4	**86.14**
	F1	81.79	76.07	80.78	83.22	75.47	79.47

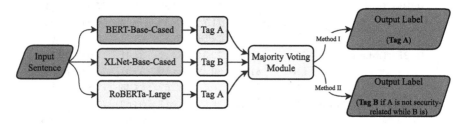

Fig. 2. Structure of the majority voting method to combine the results of three best-performing models. In method I, regardless of the predicted tags, the one that at least two models predict is chosen. In method II, in case two models output the tag 'O' but the third outputs a security-related tag, the tag 'O' is ignored despite being the majority. Aside from that, it works exactly as method I.

Table 7. Number of tokens before and after co-reference resolution (CR).

		Abode	Blogs	Microsoft	CVE	Total
Securitytags	Orig. data	2765	517	2064	5439	**10785**
	After CR	2765	547	2070	5457	**10839**
	Difference	0	30	6	18	**54**
Non-security tags	Orig. data	7847	12550	9010	8494	**37901**
	After CR	7847	14235	9042	8494	**39618**
	Difference	0	1685	32	0	**1717**

posts. This could be because the vulnerability descriptions found in companies' security bulletins or in vulnerability databases are written in a more formal structure, and the attempt is to write a less ambiguous report compared to blog posts. Table 7 presents the number of tokens before and after Co-reference Resolution for both security tagged and non-security tagged tokens.

4.5   Discussion

We select the best-performing model based on the *Recall* metric on the ground that in this context, it is more desirable to find more security terms in a vulnerability description even though this means the output will be noisy and the model will incorporate non-security-related terms in the output. It is better to discover and gather all of the key terms from a given vulnerability description than to miss some of them while the output is more precise.

According to the average result of five runs in the cross-validation training, the XLNet-Base-Cased model achieves better results compared to other models in view of recall and F1 score, and with regards to precision, it achieves a score almost identical to BERT-Base-Model.

In our attempt to add more meaningful terms and entities to vulnerability reports using co-reference resolution, we found that only 3.05% of the replaced entities were security-related (Table 7). Comparing the results presented in Tables 4 and 5 indicates that although the scores are close before and after the co-reference resolution, this approach has not improved performance overall (Table 8). It is, therefore, reasonable to believe that co-reference resolution has made the report more complex without adding much useful information.

Table 8. Comparing the average results of 5-fold cross-validation fine-tuning before and after Co-reference Resolution (CR).

Model	Metric	Orig. data	After CR	Difference
BERT-Base-Cased	P	80.85	80.94	0.09
	R	81.86	80.87	−0.99
	F1	81.33	80.88	−0.45
BERT-Large-Cased	P	78.1	78.52	0.42
	R	81.39	80.54	−0.85
	F1	80	79.49	−0.51
DistilBERT-Base-Cased	P	80.08	81.12	1.04
	R	81.17	79.89	−1.28
	F1	80.58	80.46	−0.12
RoBERTa-Base	P	80.81	81.85	1.04
	R	65.44	62.72	−2.72
	F1	72.02	70.9	−1.12
RoBERTa-Large	P	79.71	80.58	0.87
	R	81.99	81.25	−0.74
	F1	80.8	80.89	0.09
XLNet-Base-Cased	P	80.58	82.82	2.24
	R	84.05	81.24	−2.81
	F1	82.24	82.02	−0.22

Table 9. Average class-wise performance of the majority voting model (Method (II)).

Class	F1	R	P	Support
SOFTWARE	90.52	95.16	86.35	903
OPERATINGSYSTEM	94.95	97.75	92.34	305
CONSEQUENCES	73.94	85.5	65.83	288
MODIFIER	71.69	84.46	63.01	242
MEANS	61.2	72.29	54.59	214
OTHERS	46.09	48.89	44.3	137
NETWORK	38.92	37.45	42.1	26
ATTACK	41.02	43.91	43.08	24
FILES	88.05	88.18	92.32	11
HARDWARE	2.67	2.5	2.86	4
Weighted Avg.	79.47	86.14	73.83	2153
Macro Avg.	60.91	65.61	58.68	2153

The results reported in [22] show that the CRF classifier can achieve the values of 83%, 76%, and 80% for precision, recall, and F1 score, respectively, for the task of NER, adjusted for vulnerability information extraction. The XLNet-Base-Cased model, fine-tuned on the same data with a cross-validation technique, outperforms this model in terms of recall and F1 score by obtaining a score of 84.05% for recall, and 82.24% for F1 score. The improvement in the recall metric is significant. Even though the precision score is decreased by 2.42%, the recall score that the XLNet-Base-Cased model achieves is 8.05% higher than the CRF model. Figure 3 shows a sample vulnerability description that our ensemble model with the majority voting method (II) has tagged.

Fig. 3. An example vulnerability description tagged by our system (majority voting method (II)).

The method presented in the second experiment that merges the outputs of three models fine-tuned on the original data, prioritizing the security tags over the tag 'O', achieves a recall score of 86.14%. This indicates that the ensemble model with majority voting increased the average recall score by 2.09% and 10.14% compared to the XLNet-Base-Cased, and proposed CRF model by [22], respectively. Even with the consideration of the computational costs [35, 36] of our model, this is a significant improvement considering the importance of the recall metric for this task. It is easy to increase the recall of a binary classification problem by labeling all of the input samples as 1 (positive); however, in this case, we have ten different classes, so increasing the recall requires detecting the majority of tokens belonging to each class, which is extremely challenging. In this context, a recall rate of 86.14% for a ten-class NER problem is quite high, and the 10.14% improvement we have achieved over the previous model that used the same data is considerable.

Authors in [41] analyzed the performance of the CRF-based NER framework introduced in [22] compared with their machine learning model, which has the same architecture and is based on CRF as well, on the labels that are common between these two models, which are *FILE, MODIFIER, OPERATING SYSTEM, SOFTWARE*, and *CONSEQUENCES* (referred to as *IMPACT* in [41]) in spite of the fact that the data corpus used for training the models in these two works are different. Their ML model has a similar performance to the model proposed in [22]. Then, they compared their machine learning model with the Part-of-Speech (PoS) tagging approach, which emphasizes the grammatical structure of the text, both trained on the same dataset. Their results indicate that PoS tagging performs better than the machine learning approach regarding precision and F1 score. Table 10 compares the PoS tagging model with our method that ensembles best-performing models by applying majority voting on the predicted labels. In this comparison, we are only referring to the labels that both methods support. For three out of the five labels, our model obtains better scores, and the macro average of all metrics in five classes shows that our model outperforms the PoS tagging approach.

Other than the performance, another viewpoint to think about for comparing these models is that in Part-of-Speech tagging, a specialist ought to define befitting guidelines, rules, and linguistic patterns to extract information in each security category while our approach is ready to use. This implies that when the number of categories grows, new patterns and structures should be set, and furthermore, the vulnerability description text style or format is liable to change, and old patterns may not succeed in finding correct terms in an unfamiliar text.

Table 10. Comparing the performance of our approach and POS tagging approach proposed in [41].

Class	Ensemble Transformer-based Models with Majority Voting Method (II)			Part-of-Speech Tagging		
	P	R	F1	P	R	F1
FILE	88.05	88.18	92.32	72	96	81
CONSEQUENCES	73.94	85.5	65.83	94	80	86
OPERATINGSYSTEM	94.95	97.75	92.34	26	90	40
SOFTWARE	90.52	95.16	86.35	71	77	74
MODIFIER	71.69	84.46	63.01	99	97	98
Macro Average	83.83	90.21	79.97	72.4	88	75.8

Table 11. Number of samples per class in the train and test sets.

Class	#Train instances	#Test instances	Test/Train(%)
SOFTWARE	4518	903	19.99
OPERATINGSYSTEM	1527	305	19.97
CONSEQUENCES	1440	288	20
MODIFIER	1208	242	20.03
MEANS	1071	214	19.98
OTHERS	688	137	19.91
NETWORK	134	26	19.4
ATTACK	120	24	20
FILES	57	11	19.3
HARDWARE	22	4	18.18

It is also worth mentioning the differences in performance among different security classes. Based on Table 9, recall is positively correlated with support, with a Pearson correlation coefficient of 0.5917. According to Table 11, test and train sets have very similar class distributions, and it is clear that the proposed model is more accurate in classes where the model is exposed to more samples. There are also some exceptions like FILES, where we are observing a high recall score of 92.32% with relatively few samples (57) of this class in the train set. This could be because of the special format of entities tagged as FILES where there is usually a suffix like *.py* added to the end of the file name, which can help the model to detect such entities.

5   Conclusion

We propose a deep learning model to automatically extract vulnerability information from the natural language vulnerability description text. This model is a NER system that uses transformer-based language representation models and extracts security-related words and phrases from the text. After applying Co-reference Resolution and replacing all terms that refer to a specific entity with the reference entity in the dataset, we train this system on the domain-specific data, which enables it to recognize security-related entities. We also propose an ensemble model based on our three top-performing models. This ensemble model applies a majority voting mechanism to the predictions of XLNet-Base-Cased, BERT-Base-Cased, and RoBERTa-Large with a heavier weight for security-related tags over the tag 'O'. It introduced a 2.09% improvement in the recall score over the best single model. We use a real-world labeled vulnerability dataset containing more than 48K tokens for both training and evaluation of the model. Our results demonstrate 10.14% improvements in the average recall by merging the result of three of our best-performing models over the older approaches in the literature that are based on Conditional Random Fields NER systems. This is a significant improvement, considering the importance of the recall metric for this task. Besides the progress in performance, this method removes the need for feature engineering because the input data is the raw text and not some features extracted from it. Moreover, because of the nonlinear mapping between input and output that deep learning models provide, more complex features are indeed used in the training phase. Also, unlike the rule-based method such as Pattern Matching and Part-of-Speech tagging, new text styles are not a challenge for this model, and it can perform well on any vulnerability dataset.

References

1. Adobe security bulletins and advisories. https://helpx.adobe.com/security/security-bulletin.html Accessed 26 July 2021
2. Cve database. https://cve.mitre.org Accessed 26 July 2021
3. Microsoft security bulletins. https://docs.microsoft.com/en-us/security-updates/securitybulletins/securitybulletins, Accessed 26 July 2021
4. Neuroner: A named-entity recognition program based on neural networks and easy to use. http://neuroner.com Accessed 4 Aor 2022
5. spaCy entityrecognizer. https://spacy.io/api/entityrecognizer. Accessed 6 Apr 2022
6. Stanford named entity recognizer (ner). https://nlp.stanford.edu/software/CRF-NER.html Accessed 6 Apr 2022
7. AbdelRahman, S., Elarnaoty, M., Magdy, M., Fahmy, A.: Integrated machine learning techniques for arabic named entity recognition. IJCSI **7**(4), 27–36 (2010)
8. Aggarwal, C.C., Zhai, C.: Mining text data. Springer Science & Business Media (2012). https://doi.org/10.1007/978-1-4614-3223-4
9. Barnum, S.: Standardizing cyber threat intelligence information with the structured threat information expression (stix). Mitre Corporation **11**, 1–22 (2012)
10. Bird, S., Loper, E., Klein, E.: Natural Language Processing with Python. O'Reilly Media Inc., Sebastopol, CA, USA (2009). https://www.nltk.org/
11. Bridges, R.A., Jones, C.L., Iannacone, M.D., Testa, K.M., Goodall, J.R.: Automatic labeling for entity extraction in cyber security. arXiv preprint arXiv:1308.4941 (2013)
12. Clark, K., Manning, C.D.: Deep reinforcement learning for mention-ranking coreference models. arXiv preprint arXiv:1609.08667 (2016)
13. Clark, K., Manning, C.D.: Improving coreference resolution by learning entity-level distributed representations. arXiv preprint arXiv:1606.01323 (2016)
14. Devlin, J., Chang, M.W., Lee, K., Toutanova, K.: Bert: Pre-training of deep bidirectional transformers for language understanding. arXiv preprint arXiv:1810.04805 (2018)
15. Finkel, J.R., Grenager, T., Manning, C.D.: Incorporating non-local information into information extraction systems by gibbs sampling. In: Annual Meeting of the Association for Computational Linguistics. pp. 363–370 (2005)
16. Golshan, P.N., Dashti, H.R., Azizi, S., Safari, L.: A study of recent contributions on information extraction. arXiv preprint arXiv:1803.05667 (2018)
17. Gunawan, W., Suhartono, D., Purnomo, F., Ongko, A.: Named-entity recognition for indonesian language using bidirectional lstm-cnns. Procedia Comput. Sci. **135**, 425–432 (2018)

18. Hammerton, J.: Named entity recognition with long short-term memory. In: Natural Language Learning Conference at HLT-NAACL 2003, pp. 172–175 (2003)

19. Hochreiter, S., Schmidhuber, J.: Long short-term memory. Neural Comput. **9**(8), 1735–1780 (1997)

20. Jiang, J.: Information extraction from text. In: Mining text data, pp. 11–41. Springer (2012). https://doi.org/10.1007/978-1-4614-3223-4_2

21. Jones, C.L., Bridges, R.A., Huffer, K.M., Goodall, J.R.: Towards a relation extraction framework for cyber-security concepts. In: Annual Cyber and Information Security Research Conference. pp. 1–4 (2015)

22. Joshi, A., Lal, R., Finin, T., Joshi, A.: Extracting cybersecurity related linked data from text. In: 2013 IEEE International Conference on Semantic Computing, pp. 252–259. IEEE (2013)

23. Joshi, M., Chen, D., Liu, Y., Weld, D.S., Zettlemoyer, L., Levy, O.: SpanBERT: Improving pre-training by representing and predicting spans. arXiv preprint arXiv:1907.10529 (2019)

24. Joshi, M., Levy, O., Weld, D.S., Zettlemoyer, L.: BERT for coreference resolution: Baselines and analysis. In: Empirical Methods in Natural Language Processing (EMNLP) (2019)

25. Labusch, K., Kulturbesitz, P., Neudecker, C., Zellhöfer, D.: Bert for named entity recognition in contemporary and historical german. In: Conference on Natural Language Processing, Erlangen, Germany, pp. 8–11 (2019)

26. Lee, K., He, L., Lewis, M., Zettlemoyer, L.: End-to-end neural coreference resolution. arXiv preprint arXiv:1707.07045 (2017)

27. Li, J., Sun, A., Han, J., Li, C.: A survey on deep learning for named entity recognition. IEEE Trans. Knowl. Data Eng. **34**(1), 50–70 (2020)

28. Liu, Y., et al.: Roberta: A robustly optimized bert pretraining approach. arXiv preprint arXiv:1907.11692 (2019)

29. Mansouri, A., Affendey, L.S., Mamat, A.: Named entity recognition approaches. Int. J. Comput. Sci. Netw. Secur. **8**(2), 339–344 (2008)

30. Mohit, B.: Named entity recognition. In: Zitouni, I. (ed.) Natural Language Processing of Semitic Languages. TANLP, pp. 221–245. Springer, Heidelberg (2014). https://doi.org/10.1007/978-3-642-45358-8_7

31. Na, S.H., Kim, H., Min, J., Kim, K.: Improving lstm crfs using character-based compositions for korean named entity recognition. Comput. Speech Lang. **54**, 106–121 (2019)

32. Ramnani, R.R., Shivaram, K., Sengupta, S.: Semi-automated information extraction from unstructured threat advisories. In: Innovations in Software Engineering Conference, pp. 181–187 (2017)

33. Russo, E.R., Di Sorbo, A., Visaggio, C.A., Canfora, G.: Summarizing vulnerabilities' descriptions to support experts during vulnerability assessment activities. J. Syst. Softw. **156**, 84–99 (2019)

34. Sanh, V., Debut, L., Chaumond, J., Wolf, T.: Distilbert, a distilled version of bert: smaller, faster, cheaper and lighter. arXiv preprint arXiv:1910.01108 (2019)

35. Saravani, S.M.: Redundant Complexity in Deep Learning: An Efficacy Analysis of NeXtVLAD in NLP. Colorado State University Theses and Dissertations (2022). https://hdl.handle.net/10217/235603

36. Saravani, S.M., Banerjee, R., Ray, I.: An investigation into the contribution of locally aggregated descriptors to figurative language identification. In: Proceedings of the Second Workshop on Insights from Negative Results in NLP, pp. 103–109 (2021)

37. Saravani, S.M., Ray, I., Ray, I.: Automated identification of social media bots using deepfake text detection. In: Tripathy, S., Shyamasundar, R.K., Ranjan, R. (eds.) ICISS 2021. LNCS, vol. 13146, pp. 111–123. Springer, Cham (2021). https://doi.org/10.1007/978-3-030-92571-0_7

38. Schuppenies, R., Meinel, C., Cheng, F.: Automatic Extraction of Vulnerability Information for Attack Graphs. University of Potsdam, Hasso-Plattner-Institute for IT Systems Engineering (2009)

39. Vaswani, A., et al.: Attention is all you need. arXiv preprint arXiv:1706.03762 (2017)

40. Wallach, H.M.: Conditional random fields: An introduction. Technical Reports (CIS) p. 22 (2004)

41. Weerawardhana, S., Mukherjee, S., Ray, I., Howe, A.: Automated extraction of vulnerability information for home computer security. In: Cuppens, F., Garcia-Alfaro, J., Zincir Heywood, N., Fong, P.W.L. (eds.) FPS 2014. LNCS, vol. 8930, pp. 356–366. Springer, Cham (2015). https://doi.org/10.1007/978-3-319-17040-4_24

42. Wiseman, S., Rush, A.M., Shieber, S.M.: Learning global features for coreference resolution. arXiv preprint arXiv:1604.03035 (2016)

43. Yang, Z., Dai, Z., Yang, Y., Carbonell, J., Salakhutdinov, R., Le, Q.V.: Xlnet: Generalized autoregressive pretraining for language understanding. arXiv preprint arXiv:1906.08237 (2019)

44. Young, T., Hazarika, D., Poria, S., Cambria, E.: Recent trends in deep learning based natural language processing. IEEE Comput. Intell. Mag. 13(3), 55–75 (2018)

45. Zhang, R., et al.: Rapid adaptation of bert for information extraction on domain-specific business documents. arXiv preprint arXiv:2002.01861 (2020)

46. Zhu, Y., et al.: Aligning books and movies: Towards story-like visual explanations by watching movies and reading books. In: IEEE International Conference on Computer Vision, pp. 19–27 (2015)

Product Incremental Security Risk Assessment Using DevSecOps Practices

Sébastien Dupont[1]([✉]), Artsiom Yautsiukhin[2], Guillaume Ginis[1],
Giacomo Iadarola[2], Stefano Fagnano[2], Fabio Martinelli[2], Christophe Ponsard[1],
Axel Legay[3], and Philippe Massonet[1]

[1] CETIC, Charleroi, Belgium
{sebastien.dupont,guillaume.ginis,christophe.ponsard,
philippe.massonet}@cetic.be
[2] CNR, Rome, Italy
{artsiom.yautsiukhin,giacomo.iadarola,stefano.fagnano,
fabio.martinelli}@iit.cnr.it
[3] UCLouvain, Louvain-la-Neuve, Belgium
axel.legay@uclouvain.be
https://www.cetic.be, https://iit.cnr.it, https://uclouvain.be

Abstract. Security risk assessment is often a heavy manual process, making it expensive to perform. DevOps, that aims at improving software quality and speed of delivery, as well as DevSecOps that augments DevOps with the automation of security activities, provide tools and procedures to automate the risk assessment. We propose a solution to integrate risk assessment with DevSecOps activities and processes in order to make the risk assessment more continuous and automated. The solution is illustrated on a use case where the firewall of a robot vehicles is updated while risk assessment is done in an iterative manner. This approach aims at facilitating assessment (and certification such as EUCC) processes.

Keywords: Risk assessment · DevOps · DevSeCops · Certification · Incremental · Security · Cybersecurity · STRIDE · EUCC

1 Introduction

The need to deliver software with a high level of quality and velocity is a main consideration for software engineering activities. Various methods have been proposed to achieve those two targets, the DevOps methodologies in particular aim at streamlining development and operations activities using for example automation. While security is an integral part of software quality and has an impact on delivery speed, it is often overlooked in DevOps implementations. DevSecOps purpose is to focus on the integration of security activities (such as security testing, risk assessment, etc.) with development and operations activities.

Our aim is to analyze how the risk assessment and more globally the risk management can be considered through the entirety of the DevSecOps cycle,

S. Katsikas et al. (Eds.): ESORICS 2022 Workshops, LNCS 13785, pp. 666–685, 2023.
https://doi.org/10.1007/978-3-031-25460-4_38

and not only as an initial risk assessment. While we studied the link between risk assessment and DevSecOps in the European Union's Horizon 2020 SPARTA project, it was only analysed in the initial planning phase of a new cycle [1].

The well-known standard ISO27001 [2] defines risk management as the process of identifying risks, assessing risks, and taking steps to reduce risks to an acceptable level. More specifically, risk management aims at cancelling or at least minimising (mitigating) the adverse impacts and losses that a deliberate attack, a failure/error or an accidental 'environmental' threat may cause and, where possible, reduce the probability of such events.

Although today security risk assessment can be used in the software development process, the available methods [3–6] cannot be automated and heavily rely on the knowledge of the risk analyst. Moreover, the available risk assessment methods do not use measurements provided by other security tools or require tools developed specifically for supporting the risk assessment method. In other words, integration of such methods into the modern DevSecOps pipeline is questionable (if not impossible).

An important driver for our work is the new directive NIS-2 (Network and information security 2)[1] which establishes that "Member States and the EU commission will be able to oblige specific certification in certain sectors for certain products, services or processes, to prove or ensure compliance with the directive.".

Certification covers all the needs for risk assessment and management. This process is based on schemes that include, for example, all of the audits (list, duration, frequency, etc.) or even the process of collecting the list of company assets. By decree (see Cybersecurity Act[2]), it is up to ENISA (European Union Agency for Cybersecurity) to decide which certification schemes will be chosen. The first list of candidates for the EU Cybersecurity Certification (EUCC) has been updated in May 2021[3]. Those are the results of a month-long public consultation. These schemes have been fully set up, which means that they are not obligatory yet.

Three schemes are in the making: Common Criteria (products), Cloud Computing, and 5G. Before these voluntary schemes can be made obligatory, ENISA says that "there will be large consultations of stakeholders and Member States on the possible impacts, deadlines, cost, and available alternatives of these mandatory certifications".

The main contribution of this publication is our solution on how to integrate risk assessment and DevSecOps so that the risk assessment activities can be performed in a more continuous manner. To achieve this, first, we develop a risk assessment computational model which can be used for automatising the risk assessment process, minimally relies on input from an operator and is able to operate with inputs provided by other security tools. This computational model is tailored for measuring cybersecurity risks specifically for software products by

---

[1] https://eur-lex.europa.eu/legal-content/EN/TXT/?uri=COM:2020:823:FIN.

[2] https://eur-lex.europa.eu/eli/reg/2019/881/oj.

[3] https://www.enisa.europa.eu/publications/cybersecurity-certification-eucc-candidate-scheme-v1-1.1.

focusing on the key assets of a software product, considering the widely-used STRIDE[4] threats, and based on the catalogue of security practices from the ISO/IEC 15408 standard, known as Common Criteria [7]. It is implemented through a DevSecOps pipeline that integrates risk assessment using the "Self-Assessment Tool for Risk Assessment (SATRA)"[5] and the "Vacsine"[6] security orchestration and automation tool.

This paper is structured as follows. Section 2 provides background on DevSec-Ops and Risk Assessment for software security. We also outline the need and main requirements for an incremental risk assessment process for software products. Section 3 describes our risk assessment computational model and its application as a part of the incremental risk assessment process. Section 4 illustrates the benefits of the incremental risk assessment in a DevSecOps pipeline for the firewall of a robot vehicle. Finally, we discuss further research problems (Sect. 5): how our approach can operationalize certification schemes such as EUCC, and how to improve modeling of the DevSecOps process with higher level languages and exchange formats.

2 Incremental Risk Assessment and DevSecOps

2.1 DevSecOps Practices

The ever present need to improve software quality and speed of delivery has produced various practices that combine software lifecycle activities (building, testing, integration, delivery, etc.) in a continuous way. The DevOps approach integrates software development with operations activities and processes. It is related to Agile software development methods and aims at minimizing the time to add new features to software while ensuring a high level of quality. In order to break organizational "silos" of specialists, DevOps emphasizes the importance of communication between involved stakeholders : developers, system administrators, network engineers, analysts, testers, etc. This approach relies on the "CAMS" [8] (Culture, Automation, Measurement, Sharing) characteristics, and on a "shift-left" paradigm where quality considerations are taken into account as soon as possible in the software development lifecycle. While DevOps focuses on building quality and reliable software as fast as possible, it does not directly address security. DevSecOps aims at complementing DevOps with security processes and tooling to ensure continuous security assessment and improve security posture. DevSecOps augments software development in several ways. For example, the "left-shift" in applying security activities enables quicker detection, investigation and resolution of security issues, reducing their impact and cost [9,10]. Another benefit of DevSecOps is the continuous security monitoring of the target system that is facilitated by automation and ensures vulnerabilities can be detected with minimal human intervention [11,12]. DevSecOps also

---

[4] https://docs.microsoft.com/en-us/previous-versions/commerce-server/ ee823878(v=cs.20).
[5] https://satra.iit.cnr.it/.
[6] https://github.com/cetic/vacsine.

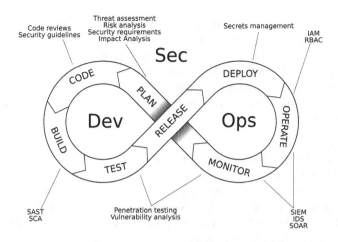

Fig. 1. DevSecOps - Security activities integrated with development and operations

helps DevOps adoption [13] by ensuring that the security aspects are covered by specialized tools and methodologies. DevSecOps activities are varied and cover the whole software lifecycle: threat modeling and risk assessment, vulnerability assessment through static code and dependency analysis (SAST, SCA) and dynamic testing (penetration, scanning, security drills, etc.). Figure 1 illustrates an example integrated DevSecOps process [1] where the security activities are aligned with the various DevOps software lifecycle phases.

The next chapters describe the need to link the DevSecOps cycle with the risk assessment and how it is possible to make it in an incremental or even in a continuous way. We will detail the requirements necessary and the current practice for incremental risk assessment.

2.2 The Need for Incremental and Continuous Risk Assessment

Incremental Risk Assessment. In the scope of this article, we use the term "security feature" to refer to development practices aimed at improving the security of the product (including project management aspects, security design and coding solutions, tests, etc.). When developing a product, developers use some of these features. The more of them are applied correctly, the more secure the final product becomes. On the other hand, each security feature requires time and effort to implement, and thus increases the cost of the final product. In other words, there is a need for a decision making approach for ensuring that the right amount of features are implemented to reach the required security level. Risk assessment is often used to serve this purpose.

Figure 1 illustrates that the DevSecOps process is iterative, which also can be seen as a version of the iterative design and management method *Plan-Do-Check-Act* that is the basis of the cyber risk management for networks and systems [14,15]. Risk management is defined as an iterative process triggering new risk assessment as required by the evolution of the environment (e.g. new threats) and the system itself. In other words, we may see DevSecOps as a risk management process for securing software products. I.e., securing a product becomes an ever going process which constantly returns to the planning step for re-evaluation of initial assumptions and adequacy of the implemented security features. This evaluation should be risk-based in order to ensure a balanced approach to security.

Continuous Risk Assessment. Although iterative risk assessment integrated in the DevSecOps process is a novelty by itself, it is possible to go further and make risk assessment truly continuous. In order to achieve this, risk should be computed after every step of the DevSecOps process. In this case, the current risk level will be available to the person responsible for the on-going step, allowing timely reaction to the identified issues.

The problem with this approach is to find a reasonable way to assess risk for the complete product at some intermediate step, i.e., before finishing the complete development cycle. Two solutions could be applied in order to cope with this issue. First, implementation of security features during the following steps of the DevSecOps process could be considered flawless. This makes the risk assessment process simpler and less dependent on the evaluation (since, ideally, all security features could be either verified by existing tools or be simply assumed). The downside of this approach is that the risk level at every step could be treated only as the best possible, and it will, most probably, degrade during the following steps.

The second approach is to use a target security level by questioning those who are responsible for securing the software product about all the planned (targeted) security features. This planning can be linked with Security Target (ST) or Protection Profile (PP) concepts used in Common Criteria [7].

After fulfillment of a step, features which relate to this step could be checked by applicable verification tools. Those security features that are to be implemented at the following steps are seen as planned and are to be verified once the corresponding step is executed. The advantage of this approach is that the target risk level is set up in the beginning and it is possible to monitor if the development at every step is good enough to ensure this level (even without finishing the further steps).

In this paper we report our results applying risk assessment for every increment of a DevSecOps cycle, i.e., *we focus on the incremental risk assessment.* This is mostly due to fact that continuous implementation requires a large number of integrated verification tools (at least one for each step). Having only one verification tool integrated with our risk assessment process allows us to report practical results for the incremental risk assessment. On the other hand, our risk assessment approach is ready to be used continuously, as we describe above.

2.3   Requirements for Flexible Incremental Risk Assessment

In general, existing risk assessment methods could be used to support a DevSec-Ops process, re-evaluating it at every iteration. On the other hand, most of such methods are not efficient, since they do not follows the "CAMS" requirements. Most of them are very time consuming, costly, and depend on the analyst. In order to integrate a risk assessment approach into the DevSecOps process, it should satisfy the requirements in the following way:

- culture - risk assessment is an integral part of the secure development process.
- automation - the assessment is performed automatically, i.e., with minimal human intervention.
- measurement - the assessment is based on the measurements, rather than on values assigned by an analyst.
- sharing - the information is automatically shared with stakeholders (developers, security experts, product owners, ...).

2.4   Current Practices of Incremental Software Risk Assessment

Software risk assessment includes analysis of different risks. Software risks include organisational (related to communication and organisational problems), technical (related to the quality problems) and environmental risks (related to environment and external development of sub-components) [16]. Cyber security risks assessment, the focus of this article, is only a part of the technical risks assessments.

The idea of applying risk assessment for securing the developing software was introduced as soon as it has been realised that exploiting its existing vulnerabilities may lead to significant losses [3]. There are a number of generic approaches to risk assessment which are not focused on cyber risks in particular [17]. Being generic, these approaches lack specific methods to identify security risks. Usually, they detect existing vulnerabilities and estimate possible losses due to cyber attacks and focus more on the computational model. On the other hand, there are also specific approaches with the focus on cyber security risk assessment.

It is possible to single out several types of such approaches, depending on initial assumptions, available information, and the state of the software development lifecycle at which the approach is applied. The major part of the approaches aim to evaluate risks for the software to be developed and to identify the countermeasures which should be implemented to counter these risks [4–6]. Usually, these approaches are based on a threat modelling technique as its core, which helps the evaluator to break the global threats into more specific ones. The most used threat modelling technique is an attack tree (e.g., Y. Zhang et al., [18]) or a very similar type of tree (e.g., D. Verdon; and G. McGraw [4] or M. Sahinogly [6]). D. Verdon; and G. McGraw [4] outline the need for risk assessment in different phases of the software development lifecycle, and underline the need for a threat modelling for computing risks (especially, during the design phase). M.

Sahinogly [6] proposed a similar technique where levels in the tree denote a vulnerability (a unit which may contain it), a threat and a possible countermeasure (one per threat).

In all these approaches, once a threat model is created, parameters (usually, denoting likelihood of an attack and its severity) are assigned to the most detailed nodes and are aggregated for acquiring the overall risk level. In some cases, intermediate/transition values must be assigned to other nodes of the graph, which are required for the aggregation [5]. We should underline that these approaches depend on the evaluator who should construct the tree and assign all values. Moreover, although most of these approaches claim to be software focused, they have no software specific concepts embedded in the core model. In other words, many of the proposed approaches are not grounded in the software development process, and can be applied for securing systems or networks as well as software.

Another set of approaches aims to evaluate COTS software products [19,20]. In other words, they aim more at selecting the most secure software or analysing the security risk level of a concrete software version after it has been released. The approach is based on identification of available vulnerabilities. Usually, these vulnerabilities are assigned with the parameters associated with their CVSS score[7]. The scores are further aggregated in order to evaluate the overall risk level of the software.

The approach to a software risk assessment proposed in our paper aims to help the developer in selecting the suitable security features and analyse security of the software product at every iteration of its lifecycle. Thus, at the moment of evaluation, the database of the relevant vulnerabilities and their CVSS scores per the product may not be available or be insufficient for analysis. Moreover, we propose a method which exploits expert knowledge to reduce the knowledge required for conducting a customised risk analysis. In short, our method does not require building a customary model and values (often of unclear nature) assigned by the analyst. Instead, we rely on the best practices proposed by a well-known and widely-used standard and leave for the analyst only to determine the core assets and their significance, leaving the rest for the computation engine. Finally, the proposed method can be used for the incremental development since it does not depend on the evaluator (neither for building the computation model, nor for setting up intermediate values). Thus, our method can re-evaluate risks on the fly, once the information about changes in security practices is sensed (by an external monitoring tool) and reported to the risk computation engine.

3   Modeling DevSecOps and Incremental Risk Assessment Processes

In this section we present the model and the process for our incremental risk assessment and describe how it could be integrated into the DevSecOps process.

---

[7] https://www.first.org/cvss/.

The model of our risk assessment is developed having in mind CAMS require-ments, in particular the ones for automatic risk assessment and usage of mea-surements. Although it is based on the generic principles for cyber security risk assessment [2], it is tailored for being applicable for assessment of risk levels of a software product (in contrast to the majority of risk assessment models which are more applicable for systems or networks).

Our process separates as much as possible the steps which are specific to the Target of Evaluation (ToE), i.e., asset identification and estimation, and those which are common for all ToEs. The latter part is standardized by using com-mon set of threats (STRIDE), set of considered controls (defined by Common Criteria), and a predefined list of asset types. Thus, for a specific ToE, an analyst is only required to provide the information about assets, and the rest of the pro-cess is performed automatically using values predefined by experts. This splitting removes the burden of defining and estimating cyber-risk-specific relations for the analyst. Furthermore, our framework is integrated in the DevSecOps pro-cess and can obtain the information about implemented controls automatically (using input from external monitoring tools), additionally reducing the burden for the analyst. In short, our framework reduces the effort, time and required cyber security knowledge for the analyst to a minimum, leaving the rest for automatic computation using a knowledge base defined by experts.

Figure 2 describes graphically our model: the part within the dashed box rep-resents the internal elements and relations, and the elements outside it denote the required input data. In short, first the core risk components (i.e., *assets*, *vulnerabilities*, and *threats*) are defined. Assets and vulnerabilities, considered as lack of specific *security features*, are received as **input**, and threats are pre-defined. Then, our **computation model** defines how to derive *expected total impact* per threat by mapping provided assets to asset types (step 1) and using the latter to compute the required impact values (step 2). Next, survival prob-abilities per threats are computed by aggregating specific security features in security controls (step 3) and estimating the probability for a threat to pass all these controls (step 4). Finally, these intermediate values are combined to compute risk.

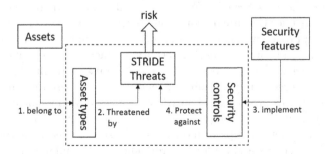

Fig. 2. Risk assessment model.

3.1   Defining Core Risk Components

Assets. The main asset types considered by our model are: (1) internal process; (2) external process; (3) user data.

The *internal process* refers to the correct functionality of the developed software. Since this functionality may depend on the internal data (e.g., some internal parameters, configuration, various attributes, etc.), this data is considered as a part of the internal process. Thus, confidentiality problems related to the internal process usually mean the loss of confidentiality of the internal data.

The *external process* refers to the context in which the developed software product is expected to be executed. An external process asset allows taking into account supply chain attacks, i.e., the attacks on the product aiming to cause impact on the external process (and its resources). For example, sensitivity of an infotainment device may be considered as low, but an access to the main bus and other modules of the car could make it a target for causing significant damage (e.g., a car incident). For clear definition of the scope of the risk analysis, we consider only those functionalities of the context which are authorised for the ToE (e.g., launching code execution or accessing data).

The *user data* is the information provided by or generated for the user (e.g., logs). This information is not essential for the process to function correctly, but is often of high importance for the user. The user data is always *processed* by the tool, i.e., contained in the tool (e.g., in dedicated memory) for a short period of time, but is also often *stored* by the tool. In the latter cases, more precautions must be taken to secure its storage (e.g., encryption, authentication, access control mechanisms, etc.). Additional precautions must be taken if this data could be *transferred* and *exported* (similarly to the internal data).

Threats. Our risk assessment approach aims at identifying the most problematic threats which are relevant for the ToE. We apply the STRIDE threats for analysis. STRIDE is a well-known and widely-accepted threat analysis approach for software products, which increases usefulness of the provided results. The STRIDE threat model includes the following six threats: *Spoofing, Tampering, Repudiation, Information Disclosure, DoS,* and *Elevation of privileges.*

Vulnerabilities/Lack of Security Features. Finally, we need to identify the vulnerabilities which let the threats compromise assets in the system. In our model, we follow an approach which assumes a vulnerability in case of lack of a security feature (which can be a management activity, a practice or a specific technique). For example, lack of a firewall does not allow the software to filter access to/from outside and increases the possibility of sending unauthorised commands to the system (elevation of privileges). The set of security development practices used in the model should be as complete as possible, covering all important security aspects. Therefore, we set up our model with the security features from the most known cyber security standard for IT products, i.e., Common Criteria [7]. Security features are grouped in *security controls* as it is defined by the standard. We consider both security *functional controls*, as those that cover available vulnerabilities and decrease the probability of a threat to occur, as well as security *assurance controls*, which indicates how well the implemented security functional requirements fulfill their purpose. In the following discussion on how our model estimates the survival probabilities for threats, we will adjust the strength of functional controls depending on the overall assurance (computed by aggregating the achieved coverage for assurance controls).

3.2   Input

Our approach requires two types of input to compute risk level for a ToE. First, our model needs a list of assets, their types and their expected impact levels related to compromising confidentiality, integrity and availability. This input is provided by the user filling in a special table. Both processes (internal and external) are unique and obligatory assets for an assessment, but there may be several sets of user data.

For a more targeted analysis, we separate those user data which can be processed, stored, transmitted and/or exported/imported. The impact levels assigned to the user data are considered the same for these sub-types. In short, internally, our list of considered assets is slightly larger than the one visible to the user ($n_{at} = 6$): (1) internal process, (2) external process, (3) processed user data, (4) stored user data, (5) transmitted user data and (6) exported/imported user data.

Thus, a user is expected to enter $n_a \in \mathbb{N} \geq 2$ items of input data. Each of these assets is mapped to at least one asset type (a user data item can be mapped to up to four asset types). This mapping can be formalised with a set of weights ($\boldsymbol{AM}$), of which each element $am_{i,j} \in \{0; 1\}$ denotes if a j-th asset is of an asset type i. Moreover, the impact values for all assets can be denoted as three sets AV^C, AV^I, and AV^A.

The second set of inputs is a list of the implementation status of all security features ($n_{sf} \in \mathbb{N}^+$) applied to secure the ToE. It can be seen as a set of Boolean values SF in which every element denotes satisfaction or failure of the corresponding security feature implementation.

The list of considered threats is predefined and is based on the STRIDE approach as it is pointed out above. For a more targeted analysis, we consider the six STRIDE threats for every asset type denoted above. Moreover, we single out the threats related to the internal data leaving the ToE: transferred or exported, since being for some time out of ToE's control, they require specific protection. At the same time we may filter out some threats from consideration, since for user data only Tampering, Information Disclosure and DoS threats and for external process only elevation of privileges are relevant; reducing the total amount of considered threats up to $n_t = 31$.

Every threat is associated with a relative frequency of occurrence/attempts: TF set. These frequencies are fixed in the current version of our tool, but can be made an input parameter without any modification of the computational model.

Table 1. Parameters of the risk assessment computational model

Definition	Variable	Domain	Size
Input parameters			
Three sets of **impact values**; one per asset	$AV^{C/I/A}$	$\mathbb{R}_{\geq 0}$	n_a
Assets to asset types **mapping**	$\boldsymbol{AM}$	$\{0;1\}$	$n_{at} \times n_a$
Security features implementation status	SF	$\{0;1\}$	n_{sf}
Internal parameters			
Threat frequencies	TF	$\mathbb{R}_{\geq 0}$	n_t
Impact degree of a threat on an asset type	$\boldsymbol{AT}$	$\mathbb{R}_{\geq 0}$	$n_t \times n_{at}$
Contributions of security features to control coverage	$\boldsymbol{SC}$	$[0;1]$	$n_c \times n_{sf}$
Contributions of assurance controls to oc	CO	$[0;1]$	$n_c{}^A$
Reduction probability of a functional control	$\boldsymbol{CR}$	$[0;1]$	$n_t \times n_{c_F}$
Portions of control coverage not affected by the oc	CP	$[0;1]$	n_{c_F}
Intermediate parameters			
Expected loss per threat	TL	$\mathbb{R}_{\geq 0}$	n_t
Survival probability of a threat	TP	$[0;1]$	n_t
Control Coverage	CC	$[0;1]$	n_c
Adjusted Control Coverage	$\overline{CC}$	$[0;1]$	n_{c_F}
Overall assurance coefficient	oc	$[0;1]$	1

Table 1 lists all parameters used by our model[8]. Note that an analyst is required to provide only the input parameters. Other parameters are contained in the knowledge base of the tool and are implemented by experts only once. Although we acknowledge the difficulty in defining values for the knowledge base, we should underline that this task is to be performed only once and is defined by experts who have very good security knowledge and (hopefully) access to large amount of historical data.

3.3 Risk Assessment Computation Model

Expected Total Impact Per Threat. As the first step, we estimate the impact for confidentiality, integrity and availability for every asset type by grouping the reported assets and their impact values according to the asset types they *belong to* (see step 1 in Fig. 2). This can be done by using the $\boldsymbol{AM}$ mapping and the estimated impact per asset provided by the user as:

$$\sum_{\forall 0 \leq i \leq n_a} am_{j,i} * av_i^C \tag{1}$$

---

[8] In this paper we use the following notation. Capital letters (e.g., TF) denote sets and lowercase letters denote single values (e.g., oc). The same lowercase letters as the set name with indexes denote specific element of this set (e.g., tf_i). Bold capital letters denote a set of variables which is more convenient to represent as a matrix (e.g., $\boldsymbol{AM}$), and their elements require two indexes (e.g., $am_{i,j}$). n always denotes size of a set.

The next step is to compute the expected loss for possible threat occurrences (see step 2 in Fig. 2). For performing this step, our model defines three sets AT_C, AT_I, and AT_A of size $n_t \times n_{at}$ which denotes the degree up to which a specific threat causes one of the three impacts for an asset type. At the end, we sum up the expected losses or the three impact types ($X = \{C, I, A\}$) and obtain the expected amount of loss per threat TL (of size n_t).

$$\forall\, k \leq n_t\,.\, tl_k = \sum_{X=\{A,I,C\}} \sum_{\forall j \leq n_{at}} at_{k,j}^X * \left(\sum_{\forall i \leq n_a} am_{j,i} * a_i^X \right)$$

Survival Probability. The next step is to compute the probability for a threat to successfully pass all security controls, i.e., a *survival probability* (i.e., a set TP of size n_t). First, we estimate how many security features belonging to the same security control are implemented, i.e., how well security controls are *covered* (see step 3 in Fig. 2). Then, we adjust some of these values taking into account the evaluated assurance coefficient. Finally, the adjusted values for coverage of security controls are used to evaluate the survival probability of the considered threats (see step 4 in Fig. 2).

All security features can be aggregated to estimate coverage of the related controls. This step is not obligatory from the formal model perspective, but makes management of internal values simpler because it significantly reduces the amount of elements: $n_{sf} < n_c$, where n_c is the total amount of controls. This operation is done using a usual weighted function. A weight denotes the degree of contribution of a security feature to the corresponding control. These weights could be seen as a set SC[9] (of size $n_c \times n_{sf}$) and the resulting coverage of controls CC could be computed as:

$$\forall m \leq n_c\,.\, cc_m = \sum_{\forall l \leq n_{sf}} sc_{m,l} * sf_l \qquad (2)$$

As said above, all security controls are split in two sets: security functional controls and security assurance controls; similar to the structure of the Common Criteria. Security functional controls help to reduce specific threats (e.g., reply attacks or attacks on authentication), and assurance controls (e.g., composition vulnerability analysis or evaluation of security objectives) ensure that security functional controls are properly implemented. Moreover, assurance controls do not target specific threats, but are relevant for reducing all of them. Therefore, the assurance controls are used to compute the *overall assurance coefficient oc*, which serves to adjust the coverage (which denotes its effectiveness) of security functional controls. By doing this, not only are we able to say that some security control are present, but also to decrease the effectiveness of this control if there is not enough evidence to ensure that this control is well planned and well implemented.

---

[9] In fact, for a control m only a few $sc_{m,l} \neq 0$, i.e., only a limited amount of security features contributes to a security control. Moreover, in most cases, for a security feature l, there is only one $sc_{m,l} \neq 0$.

Since we split all controls in two sets, so we do for $CC = CC^F \cap CC^A$, with CC^F (of size n_{c^F}) containing coverage of all security functional controls and CC^A (of size n_{c^A}) contains coverage of assurance controls. First, we compute the overall assurance coefficient (oc), using a weighted function:

$$oc = \sum_{\forall p < n_{c^A}} cc_p^A * co_p \tag{3}$$

where CO denotes the degree of contribution of an assurance control to the overall assurance. Now we may use oc coefficient to correct the coverage of functional controls.

Since not all security function controls are affected equally by the assurance controls, we also use a set CP (of size n_{c^F}) to denote the portion of a security functional control coverage which is not affected by the quality of its implementation. Now, the corrected coverage ($\overline{CC}$) of every security functional control can be computed as:

$$\forall\, q < n_{c^F} \,.\, \overline{cc}_q = cc_q^F * (cp_q + oc * (1 - cp_q)) \tag{4}$$

Every security functional control has some probability to prevent a specific threat. These probabilities are represented as a set CR (of size $n_t \times n_{c^F}$). The probability of survival for a threat (TP) is computed as a failure of all available controls to reduce it:

$$\forall\, k < n_t \,.\, tp_k = \prod_{\forall q < n_{c^F}} (1 - cr_{k,q} * \overline{cc}_q) \tag{5}$$

Risk Computation. The final step is the aggregation of the computed values for every threat. For completing this step, we only need to multiply the corresponding values for frequency (TF), survival probability (TP) and expected loss (TL). The computation of risk is performed using the classical formula for risk computation:

$$\forall k < n_t \,.\, risk_k = tf_k * tp_k * tl_k \tag{6}$$

Finally, it is possible to aggregate risks for the same types of threats from STRIDE and/or compute the overall risk value:

$$Risk = \sum_{\forall k < n_t} risk_k \tag{7}$$

3.4   Incremental Risk Assessment Process for DevSecOps Approach

A software product constantly evolves according to the DevSecOps process; once it completes the whole cycle (iteration), it returns to the beginning. The risk assessment should restart at this point as well. Moreover, similarly to the DevSecOps process, risk assessment should not start from scratch, but continue evaluating risk considering the most up to date information, i.e., become incremental.

There are two types of input in our risk assessment model: assets and security features. Our approach for risk assessment has the main focus on the identification and estimation of changes in security features, since this information can be sensed and automatically provided for update of the risk level. Changes in assets or their sensitivity, on the other hand, are more subjective and can be provided/updated by a human operator only. In other words, although our approach can consider changes in risk level due to changes in assets, this part of the analysis is still manual because of lack of the technology to automatise it.

The initial settings are the most comprehensive (similar to the initial effort for product development), and include many checks which are hard to obtain with automatic measurements (e.g., analysis of security objectives or security functional requirements). We acknowledge that the state of the art verification tools cannot cover 100% of such checks and we are constrained to gather large amount of information by directly questioning the developers. On the other hand, our approach is devised to work also with 100% of information provided by verification tools, i.e., human involvement for vulnerability evaluation step could be removed from the loop once the supporting technology is ready. The only input from a human operator required by our approach and that cannot be substituted by an automatic tool is the identification of assets and estimation of possible losses.

In short, our iterative risk assessment approach starts with questioning the analysts about available assets and planned security features. Then, during the further development steps, various verification tools could be used to confirm presence of these features and our computational model can apply these evaluations for re-computing risks.

In order to simplify the communication between verification tools and the risk computation engine, we implement a simple proxy which helps to map the results reported by the verification tools into the evidence supporting claims about implementation of security features (see Fig. 3). This tool-feature mapping proxy allows the computation engine and tools to work without modification of their usual process. Only two modifications should be made to plug in a new tools: 1) a new entry in the database of the proxy containing the mapping, and 2) an API call of the tool reporting the verification results.

The proposed model is good for the incremented risk assessment because it has little dependency on the human input and the fixed set of verified security features. Ideally, a human operator is only required to provide input about assets in the beginning. The rest, theoretically, can be detected by the tools. As it was discussed in Sect. 2.2, for continuous assessment, we also could treat all non-yet-verified values as "satisfied" and analyse how much risk is added at *every step* due to imperfect application of security practices.

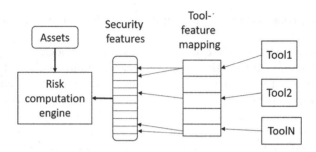

Fig. 3. Mapping the results of verification tools and security features.

3.5 Composing Incremental Risk Assessment and DevSecOps Processes

The part in charge of composing incremental risk assessment and the DevSecOps process is the orchestrator. In the DevSecOps approach, this central tool is in charge of managing the DevOps pipeline for Continuous Integration/Continuous Deployment (CI/CD) and also their security aspects. In our case, the Vacsine tool from CETIC is in charge of this aspect and will make the interface between the different operations of the pipeline and the risk assessment tool.

Figure 4 proposes a sequence diagram of the interaction between the risk assessment tool and the developer in the different phases of the DevSecOps process as they will be orchestrated. For each phase of the process, Vacsine will launch the appropriate tools that perform security checks on the software :

– Static Application Security Testing (SAST) tools in the Build phase;
– Software Component Analysis (SCA) in the Build phase;
– Dynamic Application Security Testing (DAST) tools in the Test phase;
– ...

Each of these tools is associated with security features that need to be respected. After each step, an update of the status of the security features, depending on the results of this tool, is sent to the risk assessment tool.

The tool will process the risk level according to this new status and inform the orchestrator of the result in order to decide if the next phase can be started or not.

Concerning the CAMS characteristics, the orchestrator will ensure the Automation, the Measurement of the security features coverage and the Sharing of this measurement with the risk assessment tool and the developer.

4   Illustration of Benefits of Incremental Risk Assessment in DevSecOps

4.1 Secure Firewall Update Case Study

The secure firewall example is a simple supply chain attack used in the SPARTA project to demonstrate how incremental certification could be done with DevSec-

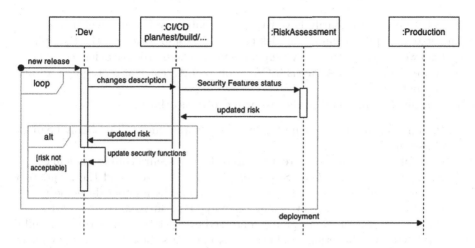

Fig. 4. Sequence diagram of the risk assessment in a CI/CD pipeline

Ops processes (see [1]). The risk assessment in the DevSecOps cycle was considered in the Plan phase as illustrated in Sect. 2.2.

In the Plan phase of the DevSecOps cycle for this case study, the risk assessment is made on autonomous vehicles taking part in a platoon. These vehicles will be called rovers and each one is protected by a firewall. All the risks identified have been treated by design and tested, and the rovers finally enter the Operate phase without any risk assessment performed after the Plan phase. Then two changes were studied :

- a change request to update the firewall (for bugs/vulnerabilities correction);
- a compromise of the package repository revealing an unsuspected flaw.

In both cases, the risk assessment is performed again in a new Plan phase and the results are influenced by the vulnerabilities corrected/discovered.

With the risk assessment approach described in this paper, it is the implementation of the security features at each step of the Dev part of the DevSecOps cycle that determines the risk. This gives a more procedural approach of the risk and gives a more precise view as those security features concern all the phases of the Dev part of the cycle. The security features equivalent to the two changes studied are :

- the use of the latest external component to build the rovers and avoid importing external vulnerabilities;
- making penetration tests to check for undiscovered/unconsidered flaws in the test phase;
- the use of secure update mechanisms (using certificates or checksum verification).

The implementation of these security features clearly conditions the risk as it was the case with the vulnerabilities in the original case study. The difference is that we don't necessarily have to assume that these features will be correctly implemented and determine the risk based on assumptions from the Plan phase. Instead we can verify that they were implemented and produce evidence for each: Software Composition Analysis (SCA) tools report, penetration tests report and release notes.

Practically, this means that the risk will evolve as follow :

- Plan phase: the risk is computed but is inaccurate and will probably be made of assumptions;
- Code phase: perform code reviews according to secure coding guidelines; example : the use of OWASP Secure Coding Practices and the mandatory reviews of pull requests before merging the code by another developer;
- Build phase: SAST and SCA analysis may be performed; example : Snyk and Sonarqube can be used to check the source code for buffer overflows, SQL injections and other possible flaws introduced in the code or in the libraries used;
- Test phase: DAST and penetration tests may be performed; example : OpenVAS and Nessus can be used to scan the software for possible vulnerabilities when it is running;
- Release phase: secure update mechanisms may be used; example : use of Secure Hash Algorithms (SHA) or certificates to verify the authenticity and integrity of the released software package;
- Operate phase: monitoring and intrusion detection systems may be used; example : IDS and monitoring tools need to be adapted to the product developed, but they can be used to detect vulnerabilities that can be exploited and were not detected in the previous phases.

After each phase, and according to the evidences retrieved, the risk can be recomputed and becomes more and more accurate. At the end of the release phase, it can condition the deployment of a new version of the software if the risk is deemed acceptable.

4.2   Implementation of Incremental Risk Assessment in a DevSecOps Process

The proposed implementation relies on CETIC Vacsine security orchestrator and CNR SATRA risk assessment service. The target system for risk assessment is a member of a platoon of robot cars running the ROS Robot Operating System. The platform for the vehicles is DonkeyCar, it combines a remote controlled car with the RaspberryPi 4 single board controller to provide a test platform for autonomous vehicles.

Vacsine orchestrates the DevSecOps process, it sends updated information at each step to the REST interface of SATRA and in return receives the updated risk. Vacsine uses the GitLab-CI engine to manage the continuous integration and deployment steps using its YAML configuration to model the workflow. An example step is to automatically provision security testing environments (sandboxes) to deploy the new version of the system and perform dynamic security testing such as vulnerability scans with OpenSCAP. Those environments are managed using the Infrastructure as Code approach of the Kubernetes container orchestration engine, which facilitates automation.

SATRA is implemented as a service and can be operated through GUI or API. The SATRA GUI is more suitable for setting up the initial parameters and displaying the results in a user-friendly manner. Operation through GUI is more suitable for the planning phase, during which the analyst plans the security features to secure the developing product. The API is required for integration with other tools, like Vacsine. It allows interacting with SATRA in a fully automatic way (including the phase for setting up a practice) if required. Moreover, the API is more suitable for an iterative process, which allows automatizing a risk assessment process and using its results. SATRA is run over a Tomcat 8 on Apache2 Web Service. The backend of SATRA is developed in Java with the Springboot 5 framework. The GUI uses JSP, HTML, Javascript and CSS. The service uses a database (MySQL), which stores the values for the risk assessment computation and the data provided by a user (via GUI or API). Finally, Python REST API's are supported with OpenAPI documentation to communicate with the main service and perform computations.

5   Conclusion and Future Work

While building software is done with increasing agility, for example by following DevOps practices to ensure quality and rapid release cycles, security is still poorly integrated and automated in the software life cycle. Risk assessment in particular still relies on manual processes with few automated steps. Where DevOps mainly focuses on development and operations activities, DevSecOps aims at also taking into account the security activities.

This paper proposed a solution to perform security risk assessment in a more continuous way by integrating it deeper into the software lifecycle. We achieved this by automating the risk assessment process using a risk assessment computational model based on STRIDE and Common Criteria so that human operator input is minimized. We illustrated this solution on a case study where the firewall of robot vehicles needs to be updated, and where the update process can only go forward to the next phase if the newly computed risk is acceptable. To validate our approach on the case study, we prototyped an incremental risk assessment within a DevSecOps process. For this purpose, we relied on and adapted the "Self-Assessment Tool for Risk Assessment (SATRA)" and the "Vacsine" security orchestration and automation tool.

We claim that the incremental security risk assessment process proposed in this paper is the best way to operationalize these certification schemes. Indeed:

- We define the inputs and threats to be taken into account to conduct an effective and accurate risk analysis. The identification also allows to impact only what is necessary. This will lead to reduced costs and increased efficiency.
- We propose a calculation model based on STRIDE. This is widely used by the community, which guarantees acceptance of the results by users. Due to

its wide use, STRIDE also makes it possible to deduce an appropriate and thoughtful response to threats. Nevertheless, SATRA tool can be used with another list of threats after defining the required relations which are required by the model.

– Our model significantly reduces the amount of information to be provided as input for risk computation, making the risk assessment as faster, simple and less subjective as possible.

– We show how our calculation model can be incorporated into an incremental risk analysis based on a clearly defined DevOps process. This approach makes it possible to isolate new needs and directly assess their impact on the development process.

We believe our approach will help make certification processes smoother and more impactful. It is generic and can easily be adapted to all the strategic areas identified by the EUCC.

Our approach uses the generic CI/CD GitLab-CI language for modeling the DevSecOps process. While very flexible, it could be augmented by the use of higher level modeling with for example the TOSCA Open Services for Lifecycle Collaboration (OSLC) specification or approaches to model continuous security such as ADOC [21].

While the mapping between the security features and tools presented here is basic, security tools can produce detailed outputs that can be used as input to subsequent tools or for security monitoring. This could be achieved by relying on (or extending) standard security information exchange formats. For example, code analysis tools can produce the results of a code analysis using SARIF (Static Analysis Results Interchange Format), OWASP SCAP/Oval/Xccdf/DS for SAST, PTES and IDMEF (Intrusion Detection Message Exchange Format) for intrusion tests and detection, MISP - Open Source Threat Intelligence Platform and Open Standards For Threat Information Sharing, etc.

Acknowledgment. This paper was supported in part by European Union's Horizon 2020 research and innovation programme under Grant Agreement No. 830892, project "Strategic programs for advanced research and technology in Europe" (SPARTA).

References

1. Dupont, S., et al.: Incremental common criteria certification processes using devsecops practices. p. 12 (2021). https://ieeexplore.ieee.org/abstract/document/9583720
2. ISO. ISO/IEC 27000 Family - Information Security Management Systems. https://www.iso.org/isoiec-27001-information-security.html (2013)
3. Boehm, B.: Software risk management: principles and practices. IEEE Softw. **8**(1), 32–41 (1991)
4. Verdon, D., McGraw, G.: Risk analysis in software design. IEEE Secur. Priv. **2**(4), 79–84 (2004)
5. Baca, D., Petersen, K.: Countermeasure graphs for software security risk assessment. J. Syst. Softw. **86**(9), 2411–2428 (2013)

6. Sahinoglu, M.: An input-output measurable design for the security meter model to quantify and manage software security risk. IEEE Trans. Instrum. Meas. **57**(6), 1251–1260 (2008)
7. ISO/IEC. Common Criteria for Information Technology Security Evaluation, version 3.1 revision 5 ed
8. Edwards, D.: What is devops. Retrieved **3**, 2014 (2010)
9. Myrbakken, H., Colomo-Palacios, R.: DevSecOps: a multivocal literature review. In: Mas, A., Mesquida, A., O'Connor, R.V., Rout, T., Dorling, A. (eds.) SPICE 2017. CCIS, vol. 770, pp. 17–29. Springer, Cham (2017). https://doi.org/10.1007/978-3-319-67383-7_2
10. Rajapakse, R.N., Zahedi, M., Babar, M.A., Shen, H.: Challenges and solutions when adopting devsecops: a systematic review. Inf. Softw. Technol. **141**, 106700 (2022)
11. Díaz, J., Pérez, J.E., Lopez-Peña, M.A., Mena, G.A., Yagüe, A.: Self-service cybersecurity monitoring as enabler for devsecops. IEEE Access **7**, 100283–100295 (2019)
12. Hsu, T.H.-C.: Hands-On Security in DevOps: Ensure Continuous Security, Deployment, and Delivery with DevSecOps. Packt Publishing Ltd, Birmingham (2018)
13. Mohan, V., Othmane, L.: Secdevops: Is it a Marketing Buzzword. Department of Computer Science, Technische Universität Darmstadt, Darmstadt (2016)
14. ISO/IEC. ISO/IEC 27005:2008 Information technology - Security techniques - Information security risk management (2008)
15. NIST. Risk management framework for information systems and organizations. a system life cycle approach for security and privacy. NIST, Tech. Rep., (2018). https://csrc.nist.gov/projects/risk-management/about-rmf on 09/05/2022
16. Sadiq, M., Rahmani, M.K.I., Ahmad, M.W., Jung, S.: Software risk assessment and evaluation process (sraep) using model based approach. In: International Conference on Networking and Information Technology **2010**, 171–177 (2010)
17. Khan, M.A., Khan, S., Sadiq, M.: Systematic review of software risk assessment and estimation models. Int. J. Eng. Adv. Technol. **1**(4) (2012)
18. Zhang, Y., Jiang, S., Cui, Y., Zhang, B., Xia, H.: A qualitative and quantitative risk assessment method in software security. In: 2010 3rd International Conference on Advanced Computer Theory and Engineering(ICACTE). vol. 1, pp. V1–534-V1-539 (2010)
19. Das, R., Sarkani, S., Mazzuchi, T.A.: Software selection based on quantitative security risk assessment. In: 2012 IEEE 14th International Symposium on High-Assurance Systems Engineering, pp. 171–172 (2012)
20. Mkpong-Ruffin, I., Umphress, D., Hamilton, J., Gilbert, J.: Quantitative software security risk assessment model. In: Proceedings of the 2007 ACM Workshop on Quality of Protection, ser. QoP 2007. New York, USA: Association for Computing Machinery, pp. 31–33 (2007)
21. Kumar, R., Goyal, R.: Modeling continuous security: a conceptual model for automated DevSecOps using open-source software over cloud (ADOC). Comput. Secu. **97**, 101967 (2020)

SLIME: State Learning in the Middle of Everything for Tool-Assisted Vulnerability Detection

Eric Lesiuta[✉][iD], Victor Bandur[iD], and Mark Lawford[iD]

McMaster University, Hamilton, ON L8S 3L8, Canada
`{lesiutej,bandurvp,lawford}@mcmaster.ca`

Abstract. Behavioural state machine models of software systems are a valuable tool for validating behaviour, but creating state machine models of existing implementations manually is highly undesirable. Fortunately, automata learning frameworks exist that completely automate the critical aspect of automata learning. However, some manual setup is usually required outside of the critical learning algorithm to create a test harness into which the system under test (SUT) and learning algorithm can function. In this paper we present a new architecture for automata learning that uses existing learning algorithms and a generic man-in-the-middle (MITM). Our architecture significantly reduces this manual setup effort. The learned state machine can be used to help uncover potential flaws in the implementation of client, server, their overall interaction and even the client-server protocol itself. These flaws can potentially be exploited by a malicious client, an impostor server, or a man-in-the-middle. Two sets of rules to automatically assist with identifying flaws in the state machine are presented, and are used to visually annotate the potential flaws in the learned model. Additionally, flaws can be detected via regression testing by comparing the learned state machine models to ones previously learned. Automatically generated and annotated state machine models of systems can be used as evidence in security, safety, and reliability assurance.

Keywords: State machine learning · LearnLib · Security · Testing

1 Introduction

Finite state machine models of systems are valuable for validating their behaviour, from manual inspection to formal verification. This is especially true for systems where security is a concern, as state machine models can help identify the existence of various paths or states in the system that an adversary could target. However, most systems lack state machine models, or even specifications adequate enough to construct a state machine model [6,17]. Creating state machine models of software manually can be very difficult, time consuming, and error prone. Even more so when lacking a specification and having to rely on

© The Author(s), under exclusive license to Springer Nature Switzerland AG 2023
S. Katsikas et al. (Eds.): ESORICS 2022 Workshops, LNCS 13785, pp. 686–704, 2023.
https://doi.org/10.1007/978-3-031-25460-4_39

source code, which may not even be available. Even if a formal model is given, there is then the problem of verifying that the implementation corresponds to the model. By trying to automatically learn a state machine directly from the implementation, we can get a model of (at least part of) the actual behaviour of the system under test (SUT). A correct behavioural state machine representation of the system can be used to help uncover logical flaws which may require a sequence of actions to trigger, such as vulnerabilities. As development of the implementation progresses, the model can be relearned and compared with previous versions to detect regressions at the model level. The learned models are also useful as documentation to assist others with understanding the system.

In this paper, we focus on active learning of client-server systems. In active learning the system being learned is subject to tailored external stimulus [1]. This is in contrast to passive learning where learning is achieved strictly from passive observation. In this paper, we present State Learning In the Middle of Everything (SLIME), a method and system which significantly simplifies part of the setup required for a client-server system to undergo active state machine learning. We discuss how the models learned with our system differ from the models learned via existing techniques, and present tool assisted analysis of our models to pinpoint possible vulnerabilities, with examples of real systems.

1.1   Background and Related Work

To learn state machine models, we use the well-known L* algorithm [2] as implemented by LearnLib, an automata learning framework [11]. Learning is achieved through querying an oracle [1] with symbols from a finite input alphabet and receiving symbols from a finite output alphabet. The oracle is a test harness for the SUT, that can be thought of as a stateless implementation of the client that translates input alphabet symbols directly into client messages to send to the SUT, and the responses into output alphabet symbols which are answers to the queries [6]. Through repeated queries, the learning algorithm iteratively creates and revises hypotheses of a state machine representation of the system, then tests these hypotheses. Testing continues until the behaviour of the learned state machine matches that of the SUT up to some predefined transition depth. The resulting state machine from learning the SUT is represented as a Mealy machine. This method has been used successfully in a number of cases [4–8,18].

Although the learning step is automatic, the initial setup, which involves manually creating a test harness, still requires considerable effort and knowledge of the system being learned. One approach to creating test harnesses automatically is doing interface analysis of the API, and having a mapper that translates the input alphabet symbols into method invocations [15]. This style of learning yields a state machine at an API level. However, an obvious or well-defined API may not always be available, so this would not be applicable for a completely black box system.

1.2 Contributions

Here we present SLIME, a system for active automata learning of client-server systems using LearnLib. It uses a new approach for creating a test harness to automate a large portion of the initial setup. SLIME learns the behaviour of both client and server together directly from both their implementations. This allows us to reveal potential flaws in the implementation of either side, or from the interaction of both, some of which could lead to security vulnerabilities. This is done by making use of a man-in-the-middle (MITM) between a client and server. The MITM is able to intercept every message the client and server send, and either "Allow", "Deny", or perform various modifications to each message before it is received by the opposite party. Note, for blackbox systems where it is impossible to disable encryption such as TLS, the appropriate keys and certificates must be provided. In this setup, instead of the input alphabet symbols representing messages a client could send, the input alphabet symbols represent the actions that the MITM can perform. Both the client and server messages are then part of the output alphabet. By observing the system response to the different actions that the MITM can perform, a state machine of the composition of the client and server with the MITM can be learned.

For the state machine learned using our system, we present two methods for automatically highlighting some of the potential flaws in the state machine of this composed system. For other unwanted behaviour that is not automatically flagged, someone with knowledge of the client-server protocol can visually inspect the state machine to assist with identifying potential issues. Flaws that arise from updates to the code can also be automatically detected by simply comparing the newly generated state machine to one from a previous version, making it useful as a tool for test-driven development. The model, or a translation of it into a suitable formalism, can be further analyzed using other appropriate automated techniques such as model checking.

2 Design of the SLIME Framework

In this section we introduce SLIME, how it makes use of a MITM as the central component of a test harness, and how the MITM facilitates manipulation of the SUT, which is a single client-server pair.

2.1 Test Harness

From the perspective of the learning algorithm, the test harness is like an oracle machine, a black box that answers queries about the behaviour of the SUT. The queries are the various actions that the MITM can perform (the input alphabet). The responses are the messages sent between the client and server (the output alphabet). The architecture of the system is shown in Fig. 1. The red arrow (1) represents communication between the learning algorithm and the test harness. The main controller translates the input alphabet symbols into actions for the

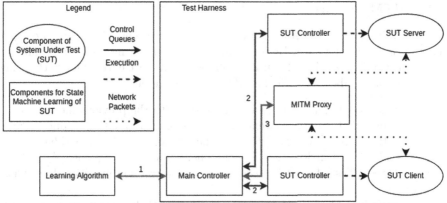

1 - Learner queries (Main Controller receives list of input alphabet symbols or sends list of output alphabet symbols)
2 - SUT Control Commands (Main Controller sends Start/Kill/Get commands or receives code trace)
3 - MITM Control Commands (Main Controller sends Get/Allow/Block/Replace commands or receives SUT message)

Fig. 1. An overview of the state machine learning architecture

MITM, and the responses back into output alphabet symbols. The green arrows
(2) represent communication between the main controller and SUT controllers,
which are responsible for restarting the SUTs between learning sessions, and for
capturing trace/code coverage data, if enabled. The blue arrow (3) represents
communication between the main controller and the MITM, where the actions
are broken down into variations of allowing, denying, or modifying the messages
exchanged between client and server.

The test harness is able to reset the SUT between learning sessions, where
each session consists of a sequence of input alphabet symbols to be delivered
to the MITM, and the sequence of output alphabet symbols obtained from
the MITM in response. The learning process consists of executing thousands
of learning sessions. The input alphabet symbols used by the learning algorithm
to query the test harness are abstract representations of the different actions
that the MITM can perform. Similarly the output alphabet symbols received by
the learning algorithm from the test harness are abstractions of the communications between client and server. They are the result of a user-defined mapper
that can map any raw message to a symbol in the finite set of output alphabet
symbols. A generic mapper was created that works for messages consisting of a
set of field-value pairs. The mapper discriminates messages based on the set of
fields, mapping each distinct set of fields to its own output alphabet symbol. The
field values themselves are ignored because they are not used in our system by
design, as well as to reduce the size of the output alphabet. Further, random field
values, as found in many systems, can introduce behavioural non-determinism
that prevents the learning algorithm from functioning. This is discussed below.

2.2   MITM Actions

The basic input actions "Allow" and "Deny" were discussed earlier, and their function is straightforward. Besides allowing or denying messages, any number of actions can be added to the input alphabet of the test harness for performing additional manipulations with the MITM. For example,

- Replay-simple: Replace the current message with the previous message
- Replay-intended: In the context of a series of manipulations, conditionally replace the current message with what the previous message would have been; this is illustrated in Fig. 4, where the client sends the sequence $A \rightarrow B \rightarrow C \rightarrow D$ regardless of what it receives, and the server simply echoes back what it receives
- Replay-similar: Replace the current message with the most recent message that maps to the same symbol as the current message
- Replace-message: Replace the message body with a constant string
- Replace-nonce: Conditionally replace a nonce with a constant value
- Blank-message: Replace the message body with an empty string

All of these actions can be applied to client requests as well as server responses. The only condition is that the effect of the action inside the system must be deterministic. For example, an action that causes a replacement in a field value with a random value chosen internally by the test harness can result in differing output alphabet symbols across learning sessions, causing the learning algorithm to fail. To avoid this, each value used would have to be represented by its own input alphabet symbol. However this comes at a high cost, because these symbols would increase the size of the input alphabet, and because the learning algorithm tries each action at every state. Consider the system represented by the NFA shown in Fig. 2, where a nonce[1] sent by the client is, in one session, echoed back by the server and, in a different session, replaced by the test harness with an internally-chosen value. Without knowledge of the replacement, the resulting learned model is non-deterministic. However, by internally tracking whether the nonce received is the same or different from the one sent, and pushing that information to the level of the alphabet, we can see that the system can instead be represented by the DFA shown in Fig. 3.

Input alphabet symbols can also represent MITM actions that are only meant to apply if a certain set of conditions are met as specified by the user. For example, replaying a previous message which maps to a specific symbol. In the case where the conditions are not met, if for example a message matching the specified mapped symbol is not found, the system is sent to a terminal state where the learning algorithm will cease searching for paths following that sequence of transitions.

---

[1] An arbitrary number meant to be used only once to ensure previous messages cannot be used in a replay attack.

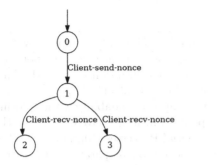

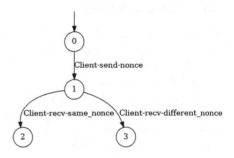

Fig. 2. An NFA for simple client which appears non-deterministic

Fig. 3. A previously non-deterministic client observed with a better choice of alphabet

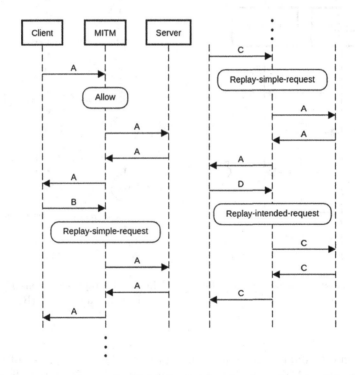

Fig. 4. A message sequence chart showing replay-simple and replay-intended. First replay-simple sends the previously allowed "A", the second replay-simple sends the previously re-sent "A", and replay-intended sends the "C" that would have been sent without interference from the MITM.

2.3   Example System

We provide an example illustrating how a simple SUT can be composed with a MITM to create a Mealy machine model. This example illustrates the notation and state machine structure, and will provide some intuition on how the final learned state machine relates to the SUT. It also illustrates how the learned Mealy machine model is condensed in order to improve readability without losing information, by combining request and response transitions into one. We use the simple terminology of Communicating Sequential Processes [10], namely "α" to refer to alphabets of state machines, and the notion of parallel composition (synchronous product) of two deterministic state machines.

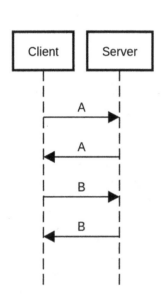

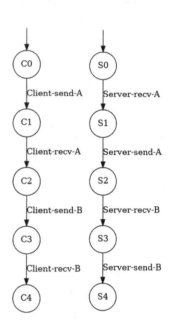

Fig. 5. A message sequence chart for the simple client and server

Fig. 6. DFA representations of the simple client (L) and server (R)

To begin, a simple communication is provided by the sequence of messages shown in Fig. 5. A deterministic finite automaton (DFA) of the client and a DFA of the server are shown in Fig. 6. The client has the alphabet $\alpha client$ = { Client-send-A, Client-recv-A, Client-send-B, Client-recv-B }. The server has the alphabet $\alpha server$ = { Server-send-A, Server-recv-A, Server-send-B, Server-recv-B }. In order to simplify the composition with a MITM (Fig. 7), we assume for now that the only actions that the MITM can perform are "Allow" and "Deny". The alphabet of the MITM is therefore $\alpha client \cup \alpha server \cup$ {*Allow*, *Deny*}. The synchronous product of the MITM, client and server is then constructed. Since the client and the server alphabets are disjoint, and

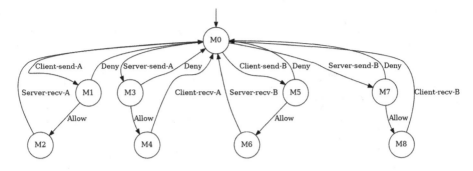

Fig. 7. A DFA for a simple MITM

the MITM alphabet is a superset of both the client and server alphabets, the order in which each is composed with the MITM does not matter. The composition of the state machines results in a DFA (Fig. 8) of the test harness where $\alpha testharness = \alpha MITM \cup \alpha client \cup \alpha server = \alpha MITM$.

This DFA can be condensed into a Mealy machine by taking the possible MITM actions (Allow or Deny) as the input and the following sent message as the output for each transition. This can be done because the DFA for the MITM was constructed to contain the full alphabet of the client and server, and because it alternates strictly between MITM actions and client/server messages. This gives us the Mealy machine shown in Fig. 9 with $\alpha input = \{Allow, Deny\}$, which is a more compact representation than the initial product DFA. The sent messages are used instead of the received messages for $\alpha output$ since they are the messages seen by the MITM, and depend on the current state and MITM action. In contrast, the received messages are only implied to happen depending on the sent message and the MITM action. In order for each transition to contain an input alphabet symbol and an output alphabet symbol, the first request sent from the client before it receives any input will not be used by the learning algorithm, and will not be included in the state machine of the test harness. It can be omitted since the test harness must be deterministic as a prerequisite for state machine learning to occur, so the first request will always be the same symbol from the output alphabet. It follows that any user interaction must be deterministic and supplied ahead of time. Systems can also be pre-seeded to run up to a specific point before starting the learning process. Therefore, different options as a result of user interaction must be learned separately as different state machine models. Next, all final states can be combined into a single "STOP" state (Fig. 10). The symbol "null" is used to indicate that no message was sent by either the client or the server, modeling a timeout in the implementation. Terminal "STOP" states where the communication has ceased are omitted from the final diagram to reduce size. Any action not shown to be taken from a given state implies the result was this termination. This Mealy representation is now closer to what the learning algorithm is able to generate.

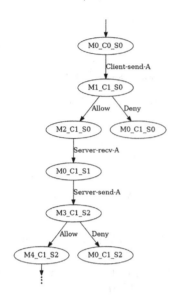

Fig. 8. Part of a DFA for the test harness

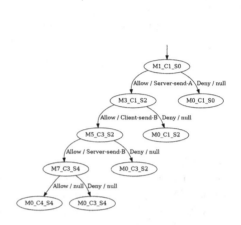

Fig. 9. A Mealy machine representation of the test harness

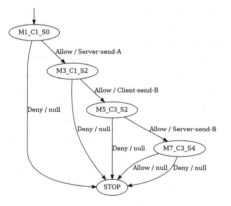

Fig. 10. Combining STOP states

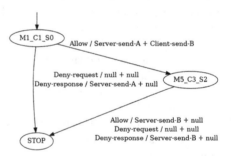

Fig. 11. A condensed Mealy machine representation the system with combined edges

In order to further condense the resulting Mealy machine for readability, input actions can be defined as applying to both the request and response, and the output symbols are concatenated. This is based on the assumption that the client will always send a single request, then wait a set amount of time to receive a single response before sending the next request. The MITM will insert "null" symbols as necessary so that the output symbols will always alternate between client and server so that they can be concatenated as pairs. Since "Allow" implies allowing both request and response, to implement "Deny" the new input alphabet will contain symbols for "Deny-request" or "Deny-response". This table shows the condensed input symbols for "Allow" and "Deny".

Symbol	Allow Request	Allow Response
Allow	Yes	Yes
Deny-request	No	N/A
Deny-response	Yes	No

Doing this, and combining edges with the same start and end state into a single edge with multiple labels gives us the Mealy machine representation shown in Fig. 11. Since the resulting output symbols from allowing the first request and first response would be the first response (from allowing the request) and the subsequent request (from allowing the response), the corresponding output symbol will now be represented as the "response + request" symbols from the original αoutput. For readability, transitions are also highlighted in an assigned colour based on the input alphabet symbol (which represents the MITM action). This is purely cosmetic and conveys no additional information.

Lastly, unlike the state machine presented in this example, where the states are named based on the corresponding states from the individual components, the states in the learned model produced by our system are named arbitrarily. This is due to the learner having no context of the underlying system and identifying states solely based on the outputs (server response and next client request) provided for a given input (MITM action).

3 Automatic State Machine Annotation for Vulnerability Detection

By learning the state machine of the interaction of a client and server with a MITM, we can automatically detect some potentially problematic patterns. We do this by looking at deviations from the happy path, which is the default route without any interference from the MITM – the input alphabet symbol on each transition along the happy path is "Allow". The goal of the first method is to identify vulnerabilities that can enable an adversary to skip part of the happy path, as would happen when an attack bypasses authentication. The goal of the second method is to identify vulnerabilities that can enable an adversary to access messages which should not be accessible outside of the happy path, without the requirement of returning to the happy path. In order to describe these methods, we will use the following definitions:

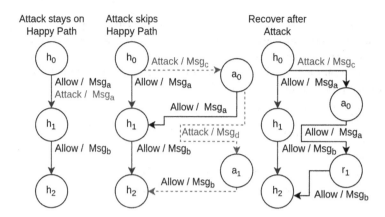

Fig. 12. Example flow patterns from three different systems which respond differently to an attack, one of the systems has flaw which is automatically highlighted with a red dashed line

- A Mealy Machine Model representation of the system is a 6-tuple $M = (Q, q_0, I, O, \delta, \lambda)$, where Q is the finite set of states, q_0 is the initial state where $q_0 \in Q$, I is the input alphabet, O is the output alphabet, $\delta : Q \times I \to Q$ is the transition function, and $\lambda : Q \times I \to O$ is the output function
- T is the set of all transitions in M where a transition $t \in T$ is a 4-tuple (q, q', i, o) where $t.q \in Q, t.q' \in Q, t.i \in I, t.o \in O$

3.1   Happy Path Bypass

The first method assumes that every step of the happy path is critical, and will highlight paths that diverge from the happy path but then return without making up for the skipped "Allow" transitions. All non-allow transitions will be referred to as attack transitions. An example of this is shown in Fig. 12, middle, where an attack skips part of the happy path. This state machine shows two possibilities, one where it only skips a single transition then returns to the happy path, but emits the skipped message, and another where it skips two transitions then returns to the happy path, but emits only one of the skipped messages. An example of it safely returning to the happy path is shown in Fig. 12, right, where the system recovers from the attack. The transitions from the bypassed segment of the happy path still take place and occur in the same order. Note that this condition does not guarantee that the system recovered correctly and is therefore a false negative. False positives can also occur if there is a special recovery message that the system uses to return to the happy path and which does not match the message from the bypassed segment. Also note that the recovery state r_1 is only there for illustration, and it is not obvious why it differs from h_1. This is due to this illustration being only an extract of the full system without every possible transition being shown. Note also that the system illustrated in Fig. 12, right, is assumed to be different from the system illustrated in Fig. 12, middle. In a real system, the recovery state may not be necessary and an allow after the attack returns directly to state h_1 like it does in Fig. 12, middle. There may be cases where a highlighted attack is harmless, or where a non-highlighted attack followed by recovery is actually still harmful. However, deciding this is non-trivial and requires a deeper understanding of the system. In the third case, where the attack transition follows the happy path without diverging to another state, the transition doesn't need to be flagged for visibility since transitions along the happy path are already clearly visible as shown where the attack stays on the happy path in Fig. 12 (left). The pseudocode for this method is given in Algorithm 1.

3.2 Anomalous Message Access

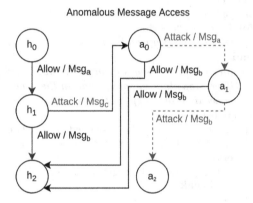

Fig. 13. Example of a flaw that can be automatically detected and highlighted with a red dashed line

The second method is called Anomalous Message Access. This method assumes that all messages that occur due to allow transitions are important, and that no attack transition should be able to trigger these messages. The purpose is to detect potential information leakage at points where an attacker may be able access it, such as confidential data outside of an authenticated session. An example of this is shown in Fig. 13 where an attack is able to access Msg_a and Msg_b. The set of transitions this method highlights is as such:

$$\{t \in T | (\exists u \in T)(\nexists v \in T)[t.i \neq \text{``Allow''} \wedge u.i = \text{``Allow''} \wedge u.o = t.o \\ \wedge v.i = \text{``Allow''} \wedge v.o = t.o \wedge v.q = t.q \wedge v.q\prime = t.q\prime]\} \tag{1}$$

Data:

- h is a list of states along the happy path without repetitions
- skipped_msgs is a temporary variable of type list for tracking the skipped output alphabet symbols along the happy path
- Path (*start, end*) is a function that returns a set of all possible non-cyclic paths from *start* $\in Q$ to *end* $\in Q$, where each path is an ordered list of $t \in T$, and no intermediate state belongs to h

Result: F is a set of flagged transitions to highlight
begin

$\quad F \longleftarrow \emptyset$

$\quad$ **for** i *from* 0 *to* Length(h) $- 2$ **do**

$\quad\quad$ **for** j *from* $i + 1$ *to* Length(h) $- 1$ **do**

$\quad\quad\quad$ *i and j form a sliding window along the happy path*

$\quad\quad\quad$ **forall** $p \in$ Path(h_i, h_j) **do**

$\quad\quad\quad\quad$ *Get output messages along the section of the happy path skipped by path p*

$\quad\quad\quad\quad$ skipped_msgs $\longleftarrow [\,]$

$\quad\quad\quad\quad$ **for** k *from* i *to* j **do**

$\quad\quad\quad\quad\quad$ skipped_msgs.*append*($\lambda(h_k,$ "*Allow*"))

$\quad\quad\quad\quad$ **end**

$\quad\quad\quad\quad$ *Remove output messages if they were accounted for by an "Allow" transition in path p, and in the same order in which they occur in the happy path*

$\quad\quad\quad\quad$ **foreach** $t \in p$ **do**

$\quad\quad\quad\quad\quad$ **if** $t.i =$ "*Allow*" $\wedge t.o =$ skipped_msgs$_0$ **then**

$\quad\quad\quad\quad\quad\quad$ skipped_msgs $\leftarrow$ skipped_msgs.*tail*()

$\quad\quad\quad\quad\quad$ **end**

$\quad\quad\quad\quad\quad$ **if** Length(skipped_msgs) $= 0$ **then**

$\quad\quad\quad\quad\quad\quad$ **break**

$\quad\quad\quad\quad\quad$ **end**

$\quad\quad\quad\quad$ **end**

$\quad\quad\quad\quad$ *If there were any output messages unaccounted for, highlight the path*

$\quad\quad\quad\quad$ **if** Length(skipped_msgs) > 0 **then**

$\quad\quad\quad\quad\quad$ **forall** $t \in p$ **do**

$\quad\quad\quad\quad\quad\quad$ $F \longleftarrow F \cup \{t\}$

$\quad\quad\quad\quad\quad$ **end**

$\quad\quad\quad\quad$ **end**

$\quad\quad\quad$ **end**

$\quad\quad$ **end**

$\quad$ **end**

end

Algorithm 1: Happy Path Shortcut

This method works by highlighting attack transitions between a pair of states that has the same output alphabet symbol as an allow transition elsewhere. However, it does not highlight the attack transition if there is also an allow transition between the same pair of states with the same output alphabet symbol. The reason for this is that the attack likely did not have an effect on the system different from doing nothing (that is, without interference from the MITM). However if such a transition follows one that was highlighted, it may still be significant. For example if the highlighted attack transition grabbed a session cookie, the following transition, whether it is an allow or an attack, could potentially be accessing confidential data. Since the learner has no context of the meaning of messages, it cannot determine with certainty how dangerous certain transitions are, in terms of what is highlighted and what is not, so it is up to a user doing a manual inspection to decide what is significant.

3.3   Other Opportunities for Automated Support

In addition to these methods for highlighting potential flaws, the source code of the SUT can be used to generate a table that maps each transition to a list of all functions that are called during that transition. When combined with the annotations presented above, this mapping can assist with locating the flaws in the source code, identifying the parts of the code responsible for a given section of the state machine, as well as measuring how much of the implementation has been exercised in creating the learned state machine model. Further, by relearning and comparing the state machines between different versions of the implementation, behavioural changes whether intended or not, can be identified.

4   Results

SLIME was used to learn Mealy machine models of both a reference implementation of Uptane, a framework for automotive over-the-air updates [12], as well as client-server interaction with a WordPress server. The results are summarized in Figs. 14 and 15. Please note that layout restrictions lead to cosmetic rearrangement of some states and transitions. In both instances, learning took between 3 and 5 h on a modern desktop computer system, with input alphabets containing 5 symbols. Moreover, state machine learning with SLIME requires significantly less development effort than existing approaches owing to the fact that our system makes use of both client and server implementations. The advantage is that the only additional implementation work required consists of building minor instrumentation to facilitate starting and stopping client and server, key handling and symbol mapping. Existing approaches require construction of a custom client in addition to similar instrumentation on the side of the server, effectively discarding an existing part of the SUT implementation.

The Uptane client was configured to repeatedly check for and apply updates if they are available. Due to size constraints, only a section of the full model is shown in full detail. The happy path is highlighted in blue. The Happy Path Bypass method was used to highlight transitions with a red dashed line that merit further inspection to insure that they do not represent a potential vulnerability allowing an attacker to bypass one or more important steps in the protocol. The paths $11 \rightarrow 15 \rightarrow 14$, $11 \rightarrow 16 \rightarrow 20 \rightarrow 18$, and $11 \rightarrow 14 \rightarrow 18$ all

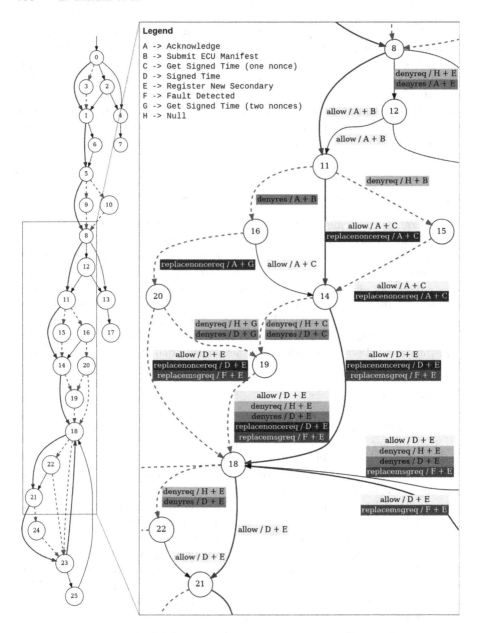

Fig. 14. A Learned mealy machine model for uptane

show cases of a nonce being replaced. The path $11 \rightarrow 14 \rightarrow 18$ also happens to be along the happy path, and the nonce replacement is shown by the "replacenoncereq" transitions which should stand out as non-"Allow" transitions along the happy path. Such a replacement in this case can be used for a partial upgrade attack, a form of attack in which the firmware version of select electronic control units (ECU) is held back [3]. The result of this attack is a mismatch of software versions between components of the system, which can open a pathway for a vulnerability [12].

The client in the WordPress example is a user with a web browser, therefore a client was created from a mechanized browser which was given a set of actions to perform. This is to demonstrate that SLIME can be used to learn useful state

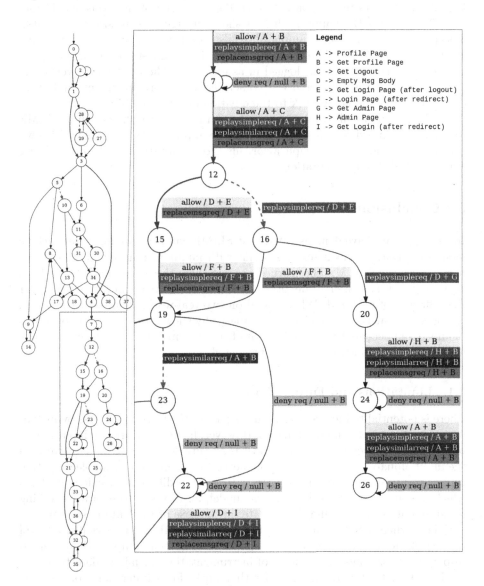

Fig. 15. A Learned mealy machine model for WordPress

machine models from arbitrary client-server systems without a specific protocol. The Anomalous Message Access method was used to identify transitions with a red dashed line. This successfully identifies a case of CVE-2012-5868 where logging out does not invalidate the session cookie, making the admin page accessible via a replay after logging out. This is seen in path $19 \rightarrow 23$, which takes place after the user logs out, where instead of letting the request "Get Profile Page" go through, a "Get Profile Page" is replayed from when the user was still logged in, and gets the response "Profile Page" instead of the expected "Empty Msg Body" along the happy path (not shown in figure do to size constraints). The path $12 \rightarrow 16$ is an example of a false positive, where instead of letting the request "Get Logout" go through, the previous request "Get Profile Page" is replayed so the user remains logged in as expected. The most recent version of WordPress tested is 5.8.2, and the vulnerability was present in this and every other major version going back to the creation of CVE-2012-5868.

Although these vulnerabilities were known in advance, the design of SLIME uses no prior knowledge of these facts, as the approach implements well-known attack types and generic graph algorithms for annotation, both of which are agnostic of SUT implementation.

5   Conclusions

In this paper we have demonstrated that SLIME can learn useful state machine models of arbitrary client-server systems with minimal setup by creating a test harness using a MITM. The learned models show the happy path taken by a client and server, as well as any other path that the system can take while under the influence of a MITM. When tested on two real-world client-server systems, the presented methods are able to automatically show a case where a nonce was modified and accepted to the detriment of the system, and a case where a replay attack was used to gain access to a protected page.

5.1   Limitations and Future Work

There is potential to include user input as part of the learning process by including user actions in the input alphabet. However, having too large an input alphabet significantly increases run time, as it is already necessary to be selective with the input alphabet actions. A possible method to maintain reasonable execution time is to pre-seed the client and server to reach a different specific state from which to start learning a state machine model, for example to separate checking for an update from installing an update, in the case of the Uptane system.

The learned models can be adapted for use by software fuzzers [9,13,14,16] to fuzz client/server messages at a specific state, then compare the observed response with the model as a form of instrumentation for failure detection.

To automatically create a mapper that works for a wider range of systems, machine learning could be used to cluster messages and map each cluster to a specific alphabet symbol. Machine learning could also potentially be used for automatically highlighting hazardous transitions, and could take knowledge of message content into account.

References

1. Aarts, F., Kuppens, H., Tretmans, J., Vaandrager, F., Verwer, S.: Improving active mealy machine learning for protocol conformance testing. Mach. Learn. **96**(1), 189–224 (2014)
2. Angluin, D.: Learning regular sets from queries and counterexamples. Inf. Comput. **75**(2), 87–106 (1987)
3. Chowdhury, T., et al.: Safe and secure automotive over-the-air updates. In: SAFE-COMP 2018: 37th International Conference on Computer Safety, Reliability, and Security, Vasteras, Sweden, September 18–21 (2018)
4. Daniel, L.A., Poll, E., de Ruiter, J.: Inferring OpenVPN state machines using protocol state fuzzing. In: 2018 IEEE European Symposium on Security and Privacy Workshops (EuroS&PW), pp. 11–19. IEEE (2018)
5. De Ruiter, J.: A tale of the openSSL state machine: a large-scale black-box analysis. In: Brumley, Billy Bob, Röning, Juha (eds.) NordSec 2016. LNCS, vol. 10014, pp. 169–184. Springer, Cham (2016). https://doi.org/10.1007/978-3-319-47560-8_11
6. De Ruiter, J., Poll, E.: Protocol state fuzzing of TLS implementations. In: USENIX Security Symposium, pp. 193–206 (2015)
7. Fiterau-Brostean, P., Jonsson, B., Merget, R., De Ruiter, J., Sagonas, K., Somorovsky, J.: Analysis of {DTLS} implementations using protocol state fuzzing. In: 29th USENIX Security Symposium (USENIX Security 20), pp. 2523–2540 (2020)
8. Fiterău-Broştean, P., Lenaerts, T., Poll, E., de Ruiter, J., Vaandrager, F., Verleg, P.: Model learning and model checking of SSH implementations. In: Proceedings of the 24th ACM SIGSOFT International SPIN Symposium on Model Checking of Software, pp. 142–151. ACM (2017)
9. Gascon, Hugo, Wressnegger, Christian, Yamaguchi, Fabian, Arp, Daniel, Rieck, Konrad: PULSAR: stateful black-box fuzzing of proprietary network protocols. In: Thuraisingham, Bhavani, Wang, XiaoFeng, Yegneswaran, Vinod (eds.) SecureComm 2015. LNICST, vol. 164, pp. 330–347. Springer, Cham (2015). https://doi.org/10.1007/978-3-319-28865-9_18
10. Hoare, C.A.R.: Communicating sequential processes. Commun. ACM **21**(8), 666–677 (1978)
11. Isberner, Malte, Howar, Falk, Steffen, Bernhard: The Open-Source LearnLib. In: Kroening, Daniel, Păsăreanu, Corina S.. (eds.) CAV 2015. LNCS, vol. 9206, pp. 487–495. Springer, Cham (2015). https://doi.org/10.1007/978-3-319-21690-4_32
12. Karthik, T., et al.: Uptane: securing software updates for automobiles. Escar Europe (2016)
13. Ma, R., Wang, D., Hu, C., Ji, W., Xue, J.: Test data generation for stateful network protocol fuzzing using a rule-based state machine. Tsinghua Sci. Technol. **21**(3), 352–360 (2016)
14. Ma, Rui, Zhu, Tianbao, Hu, Changzhen, Shan, Chun, Zhao, Xiaolin: SulleyEX: a fuzzer for stateful network protocol. In: Yan, Zheng, Molva, Refik, Mazurczyk, Wojciech, Kantola, Raimo (eds.) NSS 2017. LNCS, vol. 10394, pp. 359–372. Springer, Cham (2017). https://doi.org/10.1007/978-3-319-64701-2_26

15. Merten, Maik, Isberner, Malte, Howar, Falk, Steffen, Bernhard, Margaria, Tiziana: Automated learning setups in automata learning. In: Margaria, Tiziana, Steffen, Bernhard (eds.) ISoLA 2012. LNCS, vol. 7609, pp. 591–607. Springer, Heidelberg (2012). https://doi.org/10.1007/978-3-642-34026-0_44

16. Petrica, L., Vasilescu, L., Ion, A., Radu, O.: Ixfizz: integrated functional and fuzz testing framework based on sulley and spin. Sci. Technol. **18**(1), 54–68 (2015)

17. Raffelt, H., Steffen, B., Berg, T.: LearnLib: a library for automata learning and experimentation. In: Proceedings of the 10th International Workshop on Formal Methods for Industrial Critical Systems, pp. 62–71 (2005)

18. McMahon Stone, Chris, Chothia, Tom, de Ruiter, Joeri: Extending automated protocol state learning for the 802.11 4-way handshake. In: Lopez, Javier, Zhou, Jianying, Soriano, Miguel (eds.) ESORICS 2018. LNCS, vol. 11098, pp. 325–345. Springer, Cham (2018). https://doi.org/10.1007/978-3-319-99073-6_16

Correction to: Measuring the Adoption of TLS Encrypted Client Hello Extension and Its Forebear in the Wild

Zisis Tsiatsikas⬛, Georgios Karopoulos$^{(\boxtimes)}$⬛,
and Georgios Kambourakis⬛

Correction to:
Chapter 10 in: S. Katsikas et al. (Eds.): *Computer Security. ESORICS 2022 International Workshops*, LNCS 13785, https://doi.org/10.1007/978-3-031-25460-4_10

The chapter Measuring the Adoption of TLS Encrypted Client Hello Extension and Its Forebear in the Wild was previously published non-open access. It has now been changed to open access under a CC BY 4.0 license and the copyright holder updated to 'The Author(s)'. The book has also been updated with this change.

The updated version of this chapter can be found at
https://doi.org/10.1007/978-3-031-25460-4_10

© The Author(s) 2023
S. Katsikas et al. (Eds.): ESORICS 2022 Workshops, LNCS 13785, p. C1, 2023.
https://doi.org/10.1007/978-3-031-25460-4_40

Correction to: The Effects of the Russo-Ukrainian War on Network Infrastructures Through the Lens of BGP

Zisis Tsiatsikas⬤, Georgios Karopoulos⬤,
and Georgios Kambourakis⬤

Correction to:
Chapter 5 in: S. Katsikas et al. (Eds.): *Computer Security.*
ESORICS 2022 International Workshops, **LNCS 13785,**
https://doi.org/10.1007/978-3-031-25460-4_5

The chapter "The Effects of the Russo-Ukrainian War on Network Infrastructures Through the Lens of BGP", written by Zisis Tsiatsikas, Georgios Karopoulos, and Georgios Kambourakis, was originally published electronically on the publisher's internet portal without open access. With the author(s)' decision to opt for Open Choice the copyright of the chapter changed on on 25 January 2024 to © Authors, 2024 and the chapter is forthwith distributed under a Creative Commons Attribution 4.0 International License (http://creativecommons.org/licenses/by/4.0/).

Funded by: European Commission, Joint Research Centre.

The updated version of this chapter can be found at
https://doi.org/10.1007/978-3-031-25460-4_5

© The Author(s) 2024
S. Katsikas et al. (Eds.): ESORICS 2022 Workshops, LNCS 13785, pp. C2, 2024.
https://doi.org/10.1007/978-3-031-25460-4_41

Author Index